SAILING
BOATS
OF THE WORLD

a guide to classes

Edited by Rhonda Budd

Prentice—Hall   Englewood Cliffs, NJ

First American edition published 1974
by Prentice-Hall, Inc.

Sailing Boats of the World edited by Rhonda Budd
Copyright © 1974 by Rhonda Budd

Printed in Great Britain

Library of Congress Cataloging in Publication Data

Budd, Rhonda
  Sailing boats of the world
  Bibliography: p.
  1. Sailboats. 2. Sailing ships. I. Title.
VM351.B82   623.82'2   73-22237

ISBN 0-13-786129-X

Contents

Foreword

When I was first approached by Rhonda Budd with the request that I write a Foreword to a book she was just completing entitled *Sailing Boats of the World*, I thought "How interesting—but how comprehensive can this be". One might say that I was sceptical and rather apprehensive.

However at our first meetung my fears were soon dispelled by her obvious competence and grasp of the subject. Indeed my doubts grew into positive admiration and enthusiasm. Here was a young lady with the ability, the tenacity and the courage to get involved in many months of work and research to produce a staggering work covering well over 1,000 different classes of sailing boats from dinghies to large ocean racers and cruisers. Of course I knew she came from a family connected with sailing—her father was a well-known sail-maker in the Bosham area and indeed had himself produced a book on sail-making for the do-it-yourself enthusiast.

A first glance at the *Contents* page gives one a clue to the enormous range of the book, but on turning to the *Index* one is staggered by the hundreds of class names that many of us have never heard of, coming as they do from all over the world.

To thumb through the pages and pages of accurate line drawings and descriptions of various yacths is intriguing and instructive, and of great interest as well are the colour plates of yachts from all over the world.

I can visualise this book becoming a treasured possession on every yachtman's bookshelf for reference or discussion. It will be of great value to the prospective owner looking for his first boat who needs guidance on the type of yacht he wants and which will suit his needs. Here are all the well known and proven classes of yachts under one cover for him to choose from, saving many weeks of search and anxiety and perhaps disappointment later. The whole family can browse through these pages and become involved in the final choice.

The book is also a must for Yacht Clubs and will be appreciated by members to refer to, and perhaps settle many arguments.

It will also be an asset to reference libraries where it will be much sought after.

I commend this mine of information to budding yacht designers, who have individual tastes in their ideas of the perfect sailing boat. They will learn much and perhaps save themselves the pitfalls and glaring mistakes that many designers have made.

In short this will be a classic the world over, and I congratulate Rhonda Budd on producing such a book.

Alec Rose.

Preface

Sailing Boats of the World is conveniently arranged and indexed for easy use.

Dinghies, defined as smaller boats with no accommodation, are grouped together apart from racers and cruisers.

Those dinghies designed specifically for racing are separated from general purpose and day dinghies and sailing surfboards. There is some overlap in that many racing dinghies are used for general purposes and in that all classes of dinghies have been raced at some time, somewhere, by somebody. A particular dinghy can be traced by using the alphabetical index at the back of the book.

Within each dinghy section monohulls are listed together, followed by the multihulls.

A list of dinghies either not at present in production, older designs or those not as widely popular as the boats fully documented, are featured under the *also available* heading.

Boats with accommodations are listed in length overall order, as it is completely impossible to decide which boats are racers and which cruisers when all are marketed and used as both. In any case most builders can supply any boat in racing or cruising versions.

Boats under 20', 20', 30' and 40' plus are grouped together for easy comparison. Multihulls are again listed separately within each section.

As well as full page entries there is a list of boats under the heading *also available* that are older and less popular models. Boats currently not in production—though secondhand ones are normally available—are also listed separately. Over the years many of these will come back into production with modifications.

There is a complete alphabetical list of boats featured in the book, whether listed or documented in full. This comprises approximately 1,600 names.

An international manufacturers' index is supplied so that readers can write to local builders and suppliers for full and completely up-to-date information and prices. This list includes addresses of associations.

All information readily available has been included though for the sake of conformity it has been standardised. Although every effort has been made to ensure accuracy, specifications do change and vary, particularly when a boat is built by several builders. Some designs are built under

7

different names in different countries. These have been indicated where known, but some designs will be featured more than once. Where no plan is available either from builder or supplier, two boats have been listed to a page.

The price given for each boat must be used as a guide only. Prices increase constantly. Currency exchange rate fluctuate continually making it difficult to give accurate estimates for imported boats. The buyer must remember that the price given does not normally include all the equipment necessary to sail the boat away. A man with £10,000 to spend must look for a basic price of £7,000–£8,000.

Sailing Boats of the World is a book for all yachtsmen, whether owners or dreamers, to browse through, to note the development of design. It is a book for all yacht clubs for members to refer to and settle arguments: a book to show prospective buyers what is on the market: a book for all reference libraries where its list of boats and manufacturers will be constantly referred to.

This is the only reference work to cover all types of boats from all over the world. Apologies to any designers and builders whose boats have been missed inadvertently. The Editor would be pleased to hear from you.

Index of illustrations

Acknowledgements

To Gareth who initiated this project and contributed to its completion.

Thank you to my father for helping to obtain much of the information used in the book.

Thanks to Chris for his patience and practical help and to everyone without whose encouragement and aid this book would never have seen the light of day.

Rhonda Budd

SAILING VESSELS
an introduction

The history of boats and boatbuilding is the story of man's constant struggle against nature.

Since the beginning of recorded history man has continually succumbed to the triumphant call of the seas to come and do battle. The uncontrollable elements have always had an inevitable attraction, but as the conquest of the air proved too difficult to our predecessors, all attention was focused upon the oceans.

As they improved in performance and style, ships become increasingly important. First as a means of transport of peoples and goods. Second for the discovery of unchartered isles and the spread of cultures, ideas, skills and ways of life. And third for the less honourable purpose of domination of other nations. Today air has taken over all these functions and boats have become objects of pleasure, leisure and excitement.

But this is no reason to suppose that the numerous developments and phases of the history of the boat will suddenly stop short. Papyrus, sail, wood, steam, iron, container, hydrofoil—what next?

Modern ships have evolved from simple craft constructed thousands of years ago. The principles remain the same. Man noticed that wood floats upon water and that he could be transported in this manner if the area of wood was large enough. Quickly afterwards he learned that collections of timber made for much stabler vessels.

The Egyptians, according to recorded history, were the first ship-builders with evidence of their boats navigating the Nile as far back as 5,000 BC. However, it is believed that the Polynesians must have been constructing their own vessels many years before this date.

Egyptian boats were made from papyrus reeds and short uncontinuous strips of acacia. The boats were double-ended, decorated with figure-heads. They had no keel and were completely dependent on their great beam for stability. But this very wide, heavy beam plus short strips of acacia led to problems of longitudinal weakness. As a result a long truss was often stretched from stem to stern to give the necessary strength and support.

Propulsion was principally via oars, with often as many as twelve oarsmen employed, though a "square sail" was sometimes carried as additional power. The sail was in fact not "square" but called thus because it was set square across the centre line of the boat and was really only suitable for running before the wind.

A boat of Egyptian origins displaying all the features listed above has been dated at 1,480 BC.

The Polynesians were at this date building outrigger boats, flat-bottomed, multi-hull vessels that were light and stable. Also around the Tigris boats were being constructed out of animal skins. They were either inflated and fastened several at a time to a wooden support platform, or they were stretched over a round platform. The latter was called a guffa, and the same design is still used by native tribes of Africa and South America.

The Minoans of Crete developed a completely different kind of design. They dominated trade in the Eastern Mediterranean from a very early period until 2,000 BC in boats dug out from tree trunks. They were planked on either side and built up in that manner. The bottom of the boat was very heavy, being the remains of the trunk and this fact aided the boats stability and sea kindliness. The principle of the keel was thus developed, with the lesson learnt that low centre of gravity leads to greater stability. The Minoan ships were narrower and faster than the Egyptian vessels, with speeds of up to nine miles an hour recorded.

The Phoenicians ousted the Cretans as the dominant sea power in 2–1,500 BC with fast and light boats constructed with straight keels and high end posts. Two banks of oars were fitted on either side and bow rams placed on the front for battle purposes. Here was the first sign of gradual change from complete reliance on oars to more faith in sails.

In the northern latitudes boats seem to have developed along very similar lines as those in the Mediterranean but at a much later date. However, the Norsemen or Vikings revolutionised the general thinking behind boat construction and propulsion.

The Norsemen developed the concept of the clinker built boat. This method of construction employs the overlapping of wood planks to give greater strength and water tightness to boats. The traditional construction had been the carvel design where planks were placed edge to edge. Steering Norse-style was efficiently carried out by one or two oars placed at the stern of the ship.

These early Viking ships showed appreciation of the following basic scientific principles which are universally applicable to all boat construction:

(i)   Archimede's Principle or the principle of buoyancy
(ii)   the importance of hydrodynamic designs. Sleeker lines and pointed bows undoubtedly give faster speeds.
(iii)   the idea of the keel developed, with designers realising that the lower the centre of gravity in a boat the greater its stability.

As these boats gradually got larger and more sophisticated and longer journies were envisaged, more power became necessary. Manpower was not efficient or economic enough to suffice. Sails now came into their own.

Previously sails had been set square and were only used for catching winds from astern. However, the Vikings, being thoughtful souls, turned the sails edge on to face the oncoming wind. Thus the "fore and aft" principle of rigging was born. It was realised that the pressure of the wind causes the sail to form an aero-foil section. Air thus has to flow faster over the top of the curve than underneath it causing a partial vacuum above the curve. The vacuum, plus the high pressure under the curve, has the effect of pulling the boat along. Aeroplanes function on the same basic principle.

The fore and aft principle was also being experimented with in the Eastern Mediterranean and Indian Ocean and its arrival in the shipping world heralded "The Age of Sail".

Now that the principle had been established experiments were made with the shape of sails. The long cruises of discovery and trade gave practical experience for men to learn from their mistakes. It soon became established that the triangular sail was best for work close to the wind whilst a four sided sail was ideal for catching the maximum amounts of wind where strong following winds were encountered.

Between the 15th and 17th centuries there were vast improvements in flexibility of design and performance plus major navigational advances. Sea power became of the utmost importance with communications between Empires and their colonies maintained by sturdy vessels able to carry sailors for defence purposes and goods for trade and consumption. Ships became recognised as true fighting instruments and various combinations of hull design and rigging were developed. The ships of Sir Francis Drake and the Armada used four sided and triangular sails in many combinations to alter performance and increase manoeuvrability. Sideports were introduced about 1500 for guns to be mounted on lower decks.

As the years passed sail remained in the ascendancy with strength and reliability the pass-words of ship design, and of crew discipline. It was from the 18th Century that the Navies of all the civilised world became the disciplined and honoured forces that they are today. It was also from this time that designs were exchanged between Europe and America. The latter were now building much sleeker craft than the English had ever thought of, and they carried more sail area. *The Cutty Sark* is the prime example of the "new look". *The America* coming over from the USA in 1851 and beating the classic European designed boats competing in the first international Americas Cup, clinched the argument in favour of more experimentation.

Sailing was not now considered only a necessity but also a pleasure and the word yacht as applied to non-commercial vessels entered the English language. It originates from the Dutch word "jachtschiff" applied in the 17th Century to the fast, light, sloop rigged sailing vessels that had been developed there. The first leisure sailor in England had been Charles II but few had followed his example. The first recorded Yacht Club was founded in Ireland — the Cork Harbour Water Club — and racing up the Thames did take place in the late 1700s. But it was the 1800s that was to see the birth of numerous clubs and annual races all over the world.

In 1812 the Royal Yacht Squadron was formed at Cowes, followed in 1823 by the Royal Thames Yacht Club. In America the New York Yacht Club was formed in 1844 supported most enthusiastically by the Stevens family who were great pioneers in yacht design. 1862 saw the formation of the Royal Sydney Yacht Squadron in Australia. Later in the century the Yacht Racing Association in England and the North American Yacht Racing Union were formed to establish rules of design and conduct at sea.

Different hull shapes were experimented with to increase speed and efficiency. The long hollow bow and short full after body, a major feature of many modern yachts, was introduced in America and Europe in the 1850s. In America the new style slim entrance was to partially replace the shoal, centreboard boats previously sailed. As these had been very fast in flat waters and extremely stable they did not die out altogether. The scow also developed in Canada at this time. Alongside experiments with shape went experiments with materials—bronze, copper, steel and iron were all used in the construction of sailing yachts.

Richness in variety was thus a major feature of the day.

To reduce the necessity of individually designed boats, which were extremely costly to produce, one-design rules were introduced in the late 1800s. These laid down broad limits on size, materials and rigging and proved very successful in attracting more individuals to the sport. They also had the effect of making designers produce faster and faster boats within strict limits. The principles of boat-building now developed into a science.

Following on from one-design rules came the first International Rules for the measurement and rating of sailing yachts. The first rules were agreed upon in 1906 and 1908. The participants at the conferences of the International Yacht Racing Union had decided that it was their task to develop rules that would combine habitability with speed. This would thus encourage the speed merchants whilst catering to the man who could not leave all his luxuries behind when taking to the water. The success of the new international rules was overwhelming with hundreds of new yachts built at much lower costs.

The International Association has never looked back with many developments and innovations to the rules being introduced at periodic intervals.

The modern Bermudan rig with its high perpendicular was introduced, proving very efficient with 25-40% less sail area producing the same or greater spped than had been achieved with complicated rigs. Alongside the usual offshore cruising races that took place, ocean-going racing now came into vogue. In 1905 the sport officially started but it proved then, as at present, much more popular in America than it ever was in Europe. From these meagre beginnings great races and series have developed and hundreds of cups are awarded annually for ocean races.

So by the end of the 19th century one can identify three major types of sailing sports.

(i)   class racing   which encouraged the production of faster boats within limits

(ii) handicapping   which offered sport and amusement to out-classed racers and cruisers

(iii) cruiser racing   which helped develop the high standards of comfort and number of amenities to be found aboard the most modest sized yachts

The power of sail was now confined to the areas of sport and pleasure, for it had been ousted in commercial fields by newer developments. At the mercy of the wind, sailing yachts were considered too unreliable for urgent cargoes compared with the new steamships developed in the early 18th century. These were powered at first by mechanical extensions of the oar—paddles as in Mississippi river boats—but these were soon replaced by propeller screws which proved much more effective.

The first propeller appeared in 1893. Steam engines led to steam turbines. The internal combustion engine arrived on the scene as a commercial proposition in 1892 and the diesel motor gradually ousted steam in importance. Today modern ships are either steam turbine or diesel motor powered, with nuclear reactors becoming increasingly important as a method of propulsion.

Yachting used to be the sole perogative of rich men but no longer, for the 20th century has seen the arrival of the dinghy on a massive scale, establishing sailing as a pleasure within every man's grasp. Many different designs of small boats at very reasonable prices have appeared and these can be divided into the following different types. Designs most suited to out-and-out racing carrying 2 or 3 crew; those suitable for family racing with a larger capacity; those for general purposes which are stabler than the two above, and with more space for stowing gear. There are also single-handers for lone sailors which are developments of sailing surfboards or canoes and are designed either completely for fun or for serious class racing. Not to be forgotten are the small racing catamarans that are lighter and faster in high winds but which tend to be less effective in light airs. Multi-hulls in larger sizes, cats and trimarans, have also increased greatly in popularity for cruising.

These are especially recommended for enormous or sociable families, as up to 14 berths can be included in larger models! Note that the larger of the dinghies are normally fitted with fixed keels whilst the smaller decked ones are fitted with a centreboard.

Dinghy associations have emerged establishing one-design rules for classes. These rules have encouraged competitions of pure sailing skill instead of allowing crews to become reliant on gadgets. Races and meetings are now organised on a national scale with handicap racing organised by small clubs.

Designers this century, however, have not confined themselves solely to the improvement of boats on traditional lines and methods of propulsion. The most striking developments in recent years must be the hydrofoil and hovercroft. Both work on similar principles to the aeroplane when in motion. The hydrofoil rides over the surface of the water on stilts which terminate in ski-like foils. The drag of the hull in the water is non-existent and thus very high speeds of up to 70 knots can be achieved. The hovercraft sucks in air through a giant fan in the top of the vessel and pumps it out below a flattened hull. Flexible skirts contain the expelled air and thus the craft rides on a cushion of air on almost any surface.

The hovercraft is propelled by aero-engines and can be compared with a very low altitude vertical take-off plane.

Improvements have also been made in other areas such as container ships, oil tankers and submarines. And they are all further nails in the coffin of commercial sailing vessels. Though maybe positions will be reversed when this planet does finally run dry of natural resources.

But as the commercial element has died— except in some areas where traditional designs have remained for many centuries—so the power of sail has emerged as a major leisure industry. The magic of battling against the natural elements has returned—this time for pleasure only.

Lone sailing around the world and across oceans is the manifestation of man's wish to match himself against the elements with the sail his only method of propulsion and direction.

Every effort must be made to prevent the complete demise of larger traditional sailing vessels. There seems no likelihood at present that small boats will ever be in danger of extinction. But it would be a very great tragedy if the lofty masts and acres of canvas of former years were to give way completely to production line models. simply because of lack of enthusiasm and money available.

DINGHIES
an introduction

A dinghy is a small open boat which may have decking but will not have any cabin.

Dinghies have become very popular since the second World War with numerous new and exciting designs emerging from Europe and America. Class associations to enforce strict design and safety rules as well as encouraging development of higher standards have also grown up as boats have become officially recognised.

Successful experimentation with new materials has led to cheaper, lighter and easily maintained boats which has brought sailing within reach of suburban dwellers. Most dinghies can either be placed on top of cars or easily trailed many miles to suitable stretches of water. The growth of sailing clubs with their concurrent weekly race meetings, social activities and annual regattas has also encouraged the emergence of that strange breed of person—the dinghy sailor.

Dinghies can be grouped into five sections, each kind with different primary functions. Decide upon priorities before finally committing yourself to a purchase.

a. *racing dinghies*

Almost all kinds of dinghies are raced by someone, somewhere at some point in time but obviously those specifically designed for racing will give greatest enjoyment and produce the best results. Racing dinghies, of which the *Fireball* is a good example, are built with speed, ease of handling and seaworthiness in mind. A designer must keep uppermost in mind the following points when conceiving a new speed machine.

(i)   the need of a relatively large sail area
(ii) hull and spars must be light thus reducing displacement
(iii) shape of the hull must reduce wave-making resistance, be slim underwater and have a limited beam
(iv) only a small area of the hull must be in contact with the water, again to reduce resistance
(v)   the hull should be shaped so as to give dynamic lift for planing and have low drag

All these points are essential facets of a racing dinghy but they also tend towards instability in fresh wind. Natural stability thus has to be increased by the helmsman and his crew. Their weight must be

19

employed to its greatest advantage in keeping the boat upright at
all times. Artificial aids are allowed, though some class associations
restrict their use, to enable crews to increase effectiveness of their
counter-balancing weight. The most common aids are toe straps,
sliding seats and trapezes all allowing the crew to go as far
outboard as possible.

From the above it is obvious that racing dinghies are for
energetic, experienced and courageous sailors. They should not be
bought for youngsters, novices or for people whose only wish is to
mess about in boats.

b. *family and pram dinghies and dayboats*
Basically these boats are roomier, much stabler and less hard work
to sail than the thoroughbreds above. Many of these dinghies
however do have good racing performances as well. The *Seafly*
is a good example.

These boats carry less sail area, are beamier with a rounded bow,
are much more heavily built and have more space for storage.
Comfort in the form of seats is usually provided, and there is
generally room for four or five persons without utterly destroying
the boat's performance.

Many of these dinghies also have energetic class associations which
enforce strict rules on safety and design.

c. *cruising dinghies*
These are suitable for family outings around the harbour or to other
shores for picnics and other day outings.

These boats are stabler that the other types mentioned. The hull
is beamier and heavier with a relatively short mast and small sail area.

There is much more space aboard for stowing gear, camping
equipment and picnic hampers.

Though comparatively slow these designs are easy to sail without
much physical effort. One disadvantage is that their weight makes
them less easy to handle in and out of the water.

d. *single-handers*
Most single-handers are una-rigged—with just one sail—to make it
easier to handle.

(i)   light displacement canoes and dinghies such as
        10 sq m Canoe are designed solely for 1 person and include
        all the aids necessary to improve performance e.g. sliding seats.
        These boats tend to be very narrow and unstable but their
        performance is fantastic. They are the fastest boats among the
        monohulls.
(ii)   surfboards such as the *Minisail* and the *Sailfish*. The majority
        of these types of boats are cheap and great fun to sail. They

20

can be launched and beached anywhere. Not for long
voyages or for families for as their name suggests they are as
flat as a surfboard and not very much larger. They have a very
fast performance.

e. *catamarans*

This is the name given to those boats designed with two narrow
hulls joined by a sailing platform to give a broad beam. The idea was
developed from native outriggers sailed in the South Seas. Because
of their great beam catamarans are very stable but as each hull is very
slim they are very fast in fresh winds—much faster than monohulls in
fact. However, because of the two hulls there is a greater wetted
surface leading to frictional resistance and thus lower speeds in light
airs. The two hulls also cause great resistance when turning sharply
and thus reducing their usefulness in restricted areas.

There are more problems with car-topping and trailering of
catamarans as well, though many can be completely dismantled.

Consider well before choosing the type of dinghy you require as the
wrong choice can lead to unhappy experiences and loss of enthusiasm.

Many people get more enjoyment from making their boats
than from the actual sailing of them. A dinghy can easily be constructed
throughout the winter months for enjoyment in the summer. Kits
for many boats can be bought reasonably and in various stages of
completion. A dinghy made of wood or GRP can be bought made but
unfinished: a boat of wood can be bought completely in parts or just
the plans purchased: the hull of a GRP dinghy can be bought for
completion. Some boat-builders have sole licenses for building some
classes and it is not permitted to construct these privately. If a boat
is built at home it must be measured and inspected by the local
official of the class association before the boat can compete under
that class name.

With numerous classes of boats and numerous clubs available, a
system of handicapping has been introduced so that dinghies of
different sizes and performances can compete together. In the UK the
Portsmouth Yardstick scale of numbers has evolved. The table is built
up from average times sent in by sailing clubs throughout the year.
Generally the faster the boat the lower the number. Most of the
popular boats are handicapped at around 100.

The formula then used by sailing clubs to determine the actual
times of boats looks like this:

$$\frac{\text{Actual time in minutes} \times 100}{\text{Portsmouth yardstick number}} = \text{time for the race}$$

Handicapping is used generally in the UK and Europe for sailing clubs
are normally made up of a various assortment of boats. In America,

however, it is more likely that dinghy sailors will buy boats already popular in their State. In this way large fleets of boats are found together eliminating the need for handicapping.

The joy of sailing is now within the grasp of many thousands of people the world over because of the dinghy. Without the development and stupendous growth of this type of boat many would still be dreaming of taking to the water and experiencing the complete sense of freedom that comes with travelling the seas—be it only in a fourteen foot daysailer.

RACING DINGHIES
monohulls

AJAX 23

Design:	Oliver J. Lee, England 1967	
Supplier:	Oliver J. Lee, England	
Rating:	Portsmouth yardstick 91	
Specifications:	*Construction:*	GRP
	LOA:	7.09m/23'3
	Beam:	1.96m/6'5
Sails:	Area	20m^2/215 sq.ft.
	Spinnaker area	20.6m^2/222 sq.ft.
Rigging:	Sloop	
Price Guide:	On application	
Summary:	Over 70 boats now in circulation in the U.K.	

ALBACORE
National

Design:	Uffa Fox, England 1954 and evolved in the Portsmouth area.
Supplier:	Knight & Pink U.K. Albacore Association U.K. U.S. Albacore Association U.S.A. Annapolis Sailboat Builders U.S.A.
Rating:	Portsmouth yardstick 94

Specifications:

Construction:	GRP or wood
LOA:	4.57m/15'0
Beam:	1.55m/4'1
Draft:	0.13 m/5" cb up
Displ:	109kg/240 lbs

Fittings:	Aluminium spars. Hiking straps.
Variations:	Variations in sail plan, construction and weight available.
Sails:	Area 11.6m²/125 sq.ft. Spinnaker area 11.6m²/125 sq. ft.
Rigging:	Bermudan sloop
Price Guide:	£450–£500/$1,350–1,500us
Summary:	A popular racing dinghy world-wide. One of the fastest dinghies available without the complications of spinnaker or trapeze. Over 5,000 sail numbers have now been recorded.

ARROW

Design:	John C. Thorpe, Canada 1972
Supplier:	Arrow Information, Canada
Specifications:	*Construction:* GRP
	LOA: 3.76m/12'4
	Beam: 1.45m/4'9
	Draft: 0.1m/4" cb up
	Displ: 57kg/125 lbs
Fittings:	Aluminium spars. Hiking straps fitted. Centreboard boat.
Sails:	Area 9.3m^2/100 sq. ft. Spinnaker area 10.4m^2/112 sq.ft.
Rigging:	Una
Price Guide:	$745us
Summary:	Single-hander. Small but popular class world-wide.

ATLANTIC

Design:	W. Starling Burgess, U.S.A. 1927
Supplier:	Richard P. Edie, U.S.A. Atlantic Association U.S.A.
Specifications:	*Construction:* GRP or wood
	LOA: 9.33m/30'7
	Beam: 1.98m/6'6
	Draft: 1.44m/4'9
	Displ: 2070kg/4,559 lbs
	Ballast: 1,287kg/2,835 lbs
Fittings:	Keelboat. Spars aluminium or wood. Air tanks for flotation.
Sails:	Area 35.6m^2/383 sq.ft. Spinnaker 45.3m^2/487 sq.ft. Sail plan open.
Rigging:	Sloop
Price Guide:	$6,000
Summary:	3 crew. An American class.

BANSHEE

Design: Richard L. Reid U.S.A.

Supplier: Banshee Incorporated U.S.A.
Banshee National Association U.S.A.

Specifications: *Construction:* GRP
LOA: 3.96m/13'0
Beam: 1.49m/4'11
Draft: 0.1m/4" cb up

Fittings: Centreboard boat. Aluminium spars.

Sails: Area 8.2m^2/88 sq.ft.

Rigging: Una

Price Guide: $700us

Summary: Single-hander. Easily righted. Can be car-topped. High
performance sailing at low cost.

BARRACUDA

Design:	Chrysler U.S.A.
Supplier:	Chrysler Sailboats U.S.A. Marshall Technical Services U.K.

Specifications:

	Construction:	GRP
	LOA:	4.04m/13'3
	Beam:	1.37m/4'6
	Draft:	0.08m/3'' cb up
	Displ:	84kg/185 lbs

Fittings:	Centreboard boat. Aluminium spars.
Sails:	Area 8.8m^2/95 sq.ft. Spinnaker not official.
Rigging:	Sloop
Price Guide:	On application
Summary:	Single-handed. May be trailed.

BOSUN

Design:	Ian Proctor England
Supplier:	R. Moore and Sons (Wroxham) England Bosun Association U.K.
Est. Rating:	Portsmouth yardstick 102

Specifications:	*Construction:*	GRP
	LOA:	4.27m/14'0
	Beam:	1.68m/5'6
	Draft:	0.13m/5''
	Displ:	182kg/400 lbs

Fittings:	Mast 6.71m/22'0 high Aluminium spars.
Sails:	Area 10.70m^2/115 sq.ft.
Rigging:	Sloop
Price Guide:	£400—460
Summary:	Ideal safe dinghy for racing, cruising, family use, tuition and hire. 2/3 crew. 1,100 registered boats in circulation.

BRITISH MOTH

Design:	Sydney Cheverton, England
Supplier:	J. G. Claridge England British Moth Association England
Est. Rating:	Portsmouth Yardstick 110
Specifications:	*Construction:* Wood or GRP *LWL:* 2.65m/8'6 *LOA:* 3.02m/11'0½ *Beam:* 1.18m/4'1 *Draft:* various *Displ:* various
Fittings:	Mast of various metals 5.99m/19'8 high. Completely decked to 3' astern of bow. Side decks 10'' wide centreboard of ¾'' thick wood.
Sails:	Area 5.90m^2/64 sq.ft. (Cruising) 7.43m^2/80 sq.ft. (Racing)
Rigging:	Una
Price Guide:	On application — approximately £500
Summary:	Single-hander. Trapeze not permitted. Her performance in light winds cannot be bettered but there is no guarantee of safety in heavy weather.

CADET
International

Design:	Jack Holt U.K. 1947
Supplier:	Jack Holt U.K. International Cadet Association U.K. Western Sailcraft Limited Canada
Est, Rating:	Portsmouth yardstick 129

Specifications:

Construction:	Wood and grp or GRP
LOA:	3.22m/10'7
Beam:	1.26m/4'2
Draft:	0.17m/7" cb up
Displ:	54.43kg/120 lbs

Fittings:	Aluminium spars. Centreboard boat. Hiking straps fitted.
Sails:	Area 5.2m^2/56 sq.ft. Spinnaker area 4.6m^2/50 sq.ft.
Rigging:	Bermudan sloop
Price Guide:	£280
Summary:	2 crew. A very popular dinghy world-wide. Ideal for young people and approved by the IYRU. Over 7,000 boats in circulation.

CHALLENGE

Design:	Bill O'Brien England 1972
Supplier:	Challenge Association England
Rating:	Portsmouth yardstick 87
Specifications:	*Construction:* GRP
	LOA: 5.03m/16'6
	Beam: 1.75m/5'9
	Displ: 91kg/200 lbs
Sails:	Area 14.5m^2/156 sq.ft.
	Spinnaker area 16.7m^2/180 sq.ft.
Rigging:	Sloop
Price Guide:	Varies
Summary:	Proving popular as a handy and swift racer. Improvements and modifications being introduced all the time.

CLIPPER

Design:	Craftmakers Limited England
Supplier:	Craftmakers Limited England
Est. Rating:	Unknown
Specifications:	*Construction:* GRP
	LWL: 4.30m/14'1
	LOA: 4.52m/14.10
	Beam: 1.64m/5'4
	Draft:
	Displ: 90.72kg/200 lbs
Fittings:	Centreboard boat. Mast height 6.7m/21'0
Variations:	Outboard may be attached.
Sails:	Area 11.94m^2/125 sq.ft.
Rigging:	Sloop
Price Guide:	£350+
Summary:	A fast, stable boat with no vices. Long, shallow hull with rounded chines. 2/3 crew. Can be trailed.

CHERUB

Design:	Various, England 1954
Supplier:	Caisley-Steele England International Cherub Association N.Z.
Rating:	Portsmouth yardstick 96
Specifications:	*Construction:* Any *LWL:* 3.66m/12'0 *LOA:* 3.66m/12'0 *Beam:* 1.54m/5'0 *Draft:* 0.08m/3" *Displ:* 49.90kg/110 lbs
Fittings:	Mast 6.10m/20' long. Built in buoyancy.
Sails:	Area 10.22m^2/110 sq.ft.
Rigging:	Sloop
Price Guide:	£300–320
Summary:	Exceptionally sea-worthy. true racing dinghy. Well-balanced and responsive. Good for beginners. Sailed world-wide.

CONTENDER
International

Design:	Robert Miller England 1967
Supplier:	Rondar Boats U.K. Contender Association U.S.A.
Est. Rating:	Portsmouth yardstick 87
Specifications:	*Construction:* GRP or marine plywood *LWL:* 4.75m/15'7 *LOA:* 4.88m/16'0 *Beam:* 1.42m/4'8 *Draft:* 0.14m/4'' cb up *Displ:* 100kg/220 lbs
Fittings:	Centreboard boat. Aluminium spars. Built-in buoyancy.
Sails:	Area 11.1m^2/120 sq.ft.
Rigging:	Una
Price Guide:	£400/6,765 francs (French)
Summary:	Single-hander. A new racing dinghy selected by the IYRU for international status. A real challenge to first-class dinghy helmsmen.

DEMON

Design:	Advance Sailboat Co., U.S.A. 1963	
Supplier:	Advance Sailboat Co., U.S.A.	
	Demon Association U.S.A.	
Specifications:	*Construction:*	GRP
	LWL:	3.81m/12'6
	LOA:	4.65m/15'3
	Beam:	1.6m/5'3
	Draft:	0.17m/7'' cb up
	Displ:	125kg/275 lbs
Fittings:	Centreboard boat. Aluminium spars.	
Sails:	Area 10.8m^2/116 sq.ft.	
	Spinnaker area 12.5m^2/135 sq.ft.	
Rigging:	Sloop	
Price Guide:	$1,360us	
Summary:	2 crew. Sailed in the States only. Self rescuing. Exceptional windward performance with power and stability.	

17' DOLPHIN

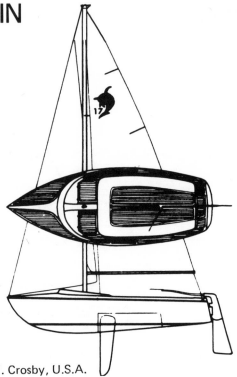

Design:	W. F. Crosby, U.S.A.
Supplier:	Peter A. Geis U.S.A. Dophin Sailboats U.S.A.
Est. Rating:	Portsmouth yardstick 103
Specifications:	*Construction:* GRP or marine plywood *LWL:* 3.20m/10'6 *LOA:* 5.18m/17'0 *Beam:* 1.74m/5'8 *Draft:* 0.61m/2'0 *Displ:* 226.8kg/500 lbs
Fittings:	Mast 7.92m/26'0 high. Centreboard boat. Aluminium spars.
Sails:	Area: 10.86m^2/137 sq.ft. Spinnaker area 21.52m^2/270 sq.ft
Rigging:	Sloop
Price Guide:	$15 for set of plans.
Summary:	A national design in the U.S.A. No specific builders in the U.K. but plans are available from Peter Geiss'. Good performance in rough seas or light airs. High aspect ratio sail plan. Trapeze used.

DRAGON

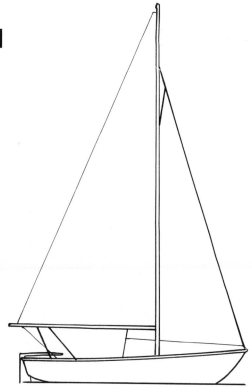

Design: Johan Anker, Holland 1928

Supplier: Borresens Bootswerft Denmark
International Dragon Association, England
American International Dragon Association, America
Kelvin Savell U.S.A.

Est. Rating: Portsmouth yardstick 89

Specifications:
Construction:	GRP or wood
LOA:	8.89m/29'2
Beam:	1.96m/6'5
Draft:	1.2m/3'11
Displ:	1,698kg/3,740 lbs
Ballast:	999kg/2,200 lbs.

Fittings: Spars — wood or aluminium.

Sails: Area 26.6m^2/286 sq.ft.
Spinnaker area 23.6m^2/254 sq.ft.

Rigging: Sloop

Price Guide: 57,000 Danish Krones/$6,500—10,000us

Summary: Popular, top-class boat worldwide. 3 crew. Plans
available.

18 FOOT SKIFF

Design:	Hugh Cook, Australia circa. 1890
Supplier:	Eighteen Foot Skiff Association England
Est. Rating:	Portsmouth yardstick 73
Specifications:	*Construction:*
	LWL:
	LOA: 5.39m/17'9
	Beam: 1.83m/6'0
	Draft: 0.49m/1'8
	Displ: 114kg/250 lbs
Sails:	Area 148.6m^2/1,600 sq.ft.
	Spinnaker area 111.5m^2/1,200 sq.ft.
Rigging:	Choice of rigs.
Price Guide:	On application.
Summary:	3 crew. Sailed mainly in Australia.

ESTUARY

Design:	Morgan Giles/Thames Structural Plastics, England
Supplier:	Thames Structural Plastics England
Rating:	Portsmouth secondary yardstick 99
Specifications:	*Construction:* GRP
	LWL: 5.10m/16'9
	LOA: 5.49m/18'0
	Beam: 1.83m/6'0
	Draft: 0.30m/11"
	Displ: 386kg/850 lbs
	Ballast: 227kg/500 lbs
Fittings:	Keelboat. Mast height 9.45m/31'0
Sails:	Area 20m^2/210 sq.ft.
	Spinnaker area 12m^2/139 sq.ft.
Rigging:	Bermudan sloop
Price Guide:	£665
Summary:	An exciting combination of dinghy with a ballasted keelboat. Raced only in the U.K.

ENTERPRISE
International

Design: Jack Holt, U.K. 1956

Supplier: Aln Boatyard U.K.
Enterprise International U.K.
Enterprise Association U.S.A.
Small Craft of Canada

Rating: Portsmouth yardstick 98

Specifications:

Construction:	Wood or grp or a mixture.
LWL:	3.810m/12'6
LOA:	4.02m/13'3
Beam:	1.6m/5'3
Draft:	0.17m/7'' cb up
Displ:	100kg/220 lbs

Fittings: Spars — wood or aluminium. Positive buoyancy.

Variations: Racing and cruising versions available.

Sails: Light blue woven fibre cloth.
Area 10.5m^2/113 sq.ft.
Spinnaker area 11.1m^2/120 sq.ft.
Racing and cruising suits available.

Rigging: Sloop. One forestay and 2 shrouds.

Price Guide: £350/$600—1,200us

Summary: 2 crew. Safe for beginners, manageable for children and yet sporty enough for the racing man. Over 16,000 boats launched. Kits available.

ETCHELLS 22

Design:	E. W. Etchells, U.S.A. 1966
Supplier:	Allan Teitge Boat Builders U.S.A.
	Etchells 22 National Association U.S.A.
	Robertsons Scotland

Specifications:

Construction:	GRP
LOA:	9.3m/30'6
Beam:	2.13m/7'0
Draft:	1.37m/4'6
Displ:	1,510kg/3,325 lbs
Ballast:	987kg/2,175 lbs

Fittings:	Keelboat. Aluminium spars. Positive flotation.
Sails:	Area 27m^2/291 sq.ft.
	Spinnaker area 37.2m^2/400 sq.ft.
Rigging:	Sloop
Price Guide:	£ on application/$6,900us
Summary:	3 crew. Trailable. Small class at present but growing in popularity.

FENNEC

Design:	Y. Mareschal, France
Supplier:	Fennec Dinghies U.K. Fennec Association U.S.A.
Specifications:	*Construction:* GRP *LOA:* 3.51m/11'6 *Beam:* 1.45m/4'9 *Draft:* 0.15m/6" cb up
Fittings:	Centreboard boat. Aluminium spars.
Sails:	Area 8.5m^2/92 sq.ft. Spinnaker not allowed.
Rigging:	Sloop
Price Guide:	£240
Summary:	2 crew. Increasing in popularity as a small, fast racing dinghy worldwide. Self rescuing.

FINN
Olympic

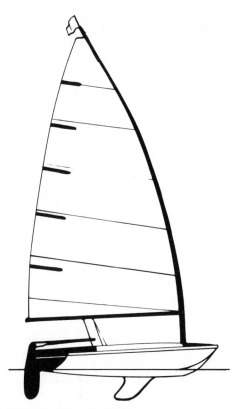

Design:	Rickard Sarby, Finland 1952
Supplier:	Comextra U.K. Nautica Corporation U.S.A. Finn International Association Holland
Rating:	Portsmouth yardstick 91

Specifications:	*Construction:*	GRP or wood
	LWL:	4.34m/14'2½
	LOA:	4.5m/14'9
	Beam:	1.47m/4'10
	Draft:	0.17m/7" cb up
	Displ:	145kg/319 lbs

Fittings:	Spars — wood, aluminium or grp. Centreboard boat. Mast 6.66m/21'11 high. Flexible mast.
Sails:	Area 10.6m^2/114 sq.ft.
Rigging:	Una
Price Guide:	£750/$1,600us
Summary:	Single-hander. Popular worldwide. New freedom on construction allowed since 1974

FIREBALL

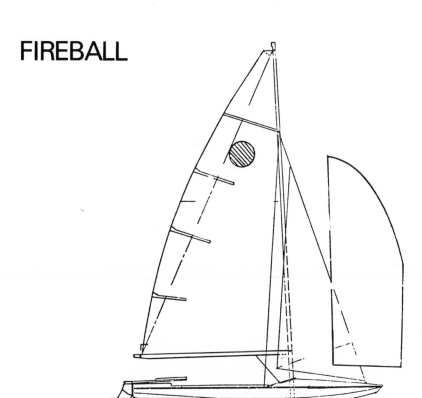

Design:	Peter Milne, England 1962
Supplier:	J. L. Gmach, U.K. Fireball International Association U.K. J. M. McClintock & Co. U.S.A.
Rating:	Portsmouth yardstick 85
Specifications:	*Construction:* Wood or grp or composite. *LOA:* 4.93m/16'2 *Beam:* 1.45m/4'9 *Draft:* 0.17m/7'' cb.up *Displ:* 79kg/175 lbs
Fittings:	Spars — aluminium or wood. Mast 6.78m/22'3 high.
Variations:	Constructional options available.
Sails:	Area 11.4m^2/123 sq.ft. Spinnaker area 11.1—13m^2/120—140 sq.ft.
Rigging:	Sloop
Price Guide:	£500/$1,600—1,800 us
Summary:	2 crew. Straps and trapeze used by crew. A one-design dinghy of exceptional performance. Plans and hulls, in various stages of completion, available.

5·5 METER
International

Design:	Open design
Supplier:	5.5 National Association U.S.A.
Specifications:	*Construction:* Wood
	LOA: 9.75m/32'approx.
	Beam: 1.98m/6'6 max.
	Draft: 1.37m/4'6
	Displ: 2,043kg/4,500 lbs max
	Ballast: Open
Fittings:	Aluminium spars.
Sails:	Area 29.3m^2/315 sq.ft.
	Combination of areas of main and jib open.
	Spinnaker 55.7–74.3m^2/600–800 sq.ft.
Rigging:	Sloop
Price Guide:	$12,000us approx.
Summary:	3crew.

505 INTERNATIONAL

Design:	John Westell, England 1954
Supplier:	Comextra U.K.
	505 International Association U.K.
Est. Rating:	Portsmouth yardstick 81
Specifications:	*Construction:* Wood or grp with plywood foredeck
	LWL: 4.42m/14'6
	LOA: 5.03m/16'6
	Beam: 1.85m/6'1
	Draft: 0.15m/6'' cb up
	Displ: 127kg/280 lbs
Fittings:	Spars — aluminium or wood. Mast 7.32m/24'0 high.
Variations:	One design boat but can be modified within set specifications.
Sails:	Area 16m^2/172 sq.ft.
	Spinnaker area 19.5m^2/210 sq.ft.
Rigging:	Bermudan sloop
Price Guide:	£700 max./$2,100us
Summary:	2 crew. Popular worldwide. A first-class racing dinghy with a very high reputation. Over 5,000 boats in circulation.

FIREFLY
National

Design:	Uffa Fox, U.K.
Supplier:	Fairey Marine U.K. Firefly Association U.S.A.
Est. Rating:	Portsmouth yardstick 100
Specifications:	*Construction:* Wood or GRP *LWL:* 3.66m/12'0 *LOA:* 3.66m/12'0 *Beam:* 1.39m/4'7 *Draft:* 0.25m/10'' cb up *Displ:* 114kg/250 lbs
Fittings:	Aluminium spars. Built in buoyancy. Mast height 6.40m/21'0.
Sails:	Area 9.3m^2/100 sq.ft.
Rigging:	Bermudan sloop
Price Guide:	£370
Summary:	2 crew. A one-design racing dinghy decked forward of the mast. A very popular club dinghy.

FLEETWIND

Design: Alan Eckford, England 1952

Supplier: Bossoms Boatyard England

Est. Rating: Portsmouth yardstick 108

Specifications:
Construction:	GRP or marine plywood
LOA:	3.70m/12'1½
Beam:	1.37m/4'6
Draft:	0.91m/3'0
Displ:	63.50kg/140 lbs

Fittings: Mast 6.1m/20'0 high. Centreboard or daggerboard boat. Built-in buoyancy.

Variations: Interior layout can be varied.

Sails: Area 8.8m^2/95 sq.ft.

Rigging: Bermudan sloop

Price Guide: £260

Summary: Designed to provide excellent performance at any wind strength. Good looking with fine lines.

FLY

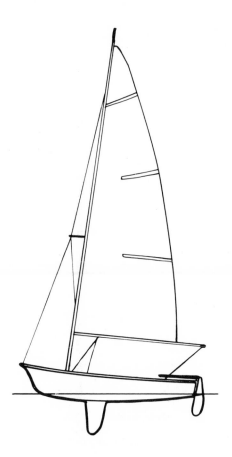

Design: R. Fillery and K. Ford

Supplier: Home built. Information from M. Rimmer England

Specifications: *Construction:* Marine plywood
LWL: 2.34m/7'8
LOA: 2.89m/9'6
Beam: 1.14m/3'9
Draft: 0.74m/2'5
Displ: 38.56kg/85 lbs

Fittings: Mast 4.57m/15'0 high

Sails: Area 372m^2/40 sq.ft.

Rigging: Una

Price Guide: Not built professionally.

Summary: Designed to teach young people single-handed racing. Good performance.

FLYING DUTCHMAN
Olympic

Design:	Uffa van Essen, Holland 1951
Supplier:	Jachtwerf van Dusseldorp, Holland Kingsfield Marine England Advance Sailboat Corporation U.S.A. Flying Dutchman International Association Holland Flying Dutchman National Association U.S.A.
Rating:	Portsmouth yardstick 78

Specifications:

Construction:	GRP or wood
LWL:	5.79m/19'0
LOA:	6.04m/19'10
Beam:	1.7m/5'7
Draft:	0.15m/6" cb up
Displ:	165kg/364 lbs

Fittings:	Aluminium spars. Centreboard boat. Mast 7.01m/23'0 high
Sails:	Area 36.2m^2/390 sq.ft. Spinnaker area 17.7m^2/190 sq.ft.
Rigging:	Sloop
Price Guide:	£1,000/$2,500us
Summary:	Sleek boat sailed worldwide. 2 crew. Trapeze used. The fastest 2-man centreboard dinghy in the world. Over 4,000 have been built.

FLYING FIFTEEN

Design:	Uffa Fox, England 1948
Supplier:	Wyche & Coppock England Flying Fifteen International Association, Scotland Flying Fifteen National Association, U.S.A.
Est. Rating:	Portsmouth yardstick 89

Specifications:

	Construction:	GRP or wood
	LOA:	6.1m/20'0
	Beam:	1.52m/5'0
	Draft:	0.76m/2'6
	Displ:	329kg/725 lbs
	Ballast:	182kg/400 lbs

Fittings:	Fixed keel. Spars aluminium or wood.
Variations:	International and national racing versions, which vary in length, are available.
Sails:	Area 14.2m^2/153 sq.ft. Spinnaker area 12.4m^2/133 sq.ft.
Rigging:	Sloop
Price Guide:	£600—£700/$2,500us
Summary:	Very popular racing dinghy especially in Great Britain. Trailable. 2 crew. Very stable.

FLYING JUNIOR

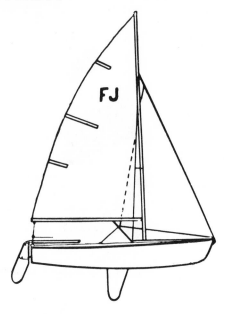

Design:	Uffa van Essen, Holland 1956
Supplier:	Jachtwert van Dusseldorp Holland Tiptree Marine & Pleasurecraft England Flying Junior International Association Holland Advance Sailboat Corporation U.S.A.
Est. Rating:	Portsmouth yardstick 98
Specifications:	*Construction:* GRP *LOA:* 4.01m/13'2 *Beam:* 1.6m/5'3 *Draft:* 0.15m/6" *Displ:* 91kg/200 lbs
Fittings:	Aluminium spars. Centreboard boat
Variations:	Custom or sports models available
Sails:	Area 9.3m²/100 sq.ft. Area 7m²/75 sq.ft.
Rigging:	Bermudan sloop
Price Guide:	$1,000–1,400us
Summary:	An extremely popular racing dinghy worldwide — about 10,000 boats built. International status granted in 1972.

FOURTEEN FOOT
International

Design: Various 1928. Redesigns 1972 and 1973

Supplier: J. G. Claridge England
14' International Association Canada
US International 14 Association U.S.A.

Est. Rating: Portsmouth yardstick 88

Specifications: *Construction:* Various
LWL: 4.27m/14'0
LOA: 4.27m/14'0
Beam: 1.42m/4'8
Draft: Unrestricted
Displ: 102.05kg/225 lbs

Fittings: Mast 6.86m/22'6 high. Spars — any material.
Centreboard boat

Sails: Area 11.61m^2/125 sq.ft.
Spinnaker area unlimited

Rigging: Bermudan sloop

Price Guide: £500/$1,800us

Summary: A high performance international development class
for 2 men. Trapeze allowed. Suitable for sea, lake or
river.

51

14` DAYBOAT
Yachting World

Design:	G. O'Brien Kennedy, England 1950
Supplier:	J. Stone & Son England
Est. Rating:	Portsmouth yardstick 108
Specifications:	*Construction:* Various
	LWL: 4.21m/13'10
	LOA: 4.27m/14'0
	Beam: 1.74m/5'7½
	Draft: 0.25m/10''
	Displ: 204.12kg/450 lbs
Fittings:	Mast 6.25m/20'6 high. Wood or aluminium spars.
Variations:	Optional built in buoyancy
Sails:	Area 12.26m^2/132 sq.ft. Spinnaker area 5.21m^2/56 sq.ft.
Rigging:	Bermudan sloop or gunter
Price Guide:	£450
Summary:	2 or 3 crew. A roomy, stable and seaworthy dinghy. Good windward performance in rough weather.

420
International

Design:	Christian Maury, France 1960
Supplier:	Jack Holt U.K. 420 International Association Germany Lanaverre S.A. Holland The Anchorage U.S.A.
Est. Rating:	Portsmouth yardstick 96
Specifications:	*Construction:* GRP *LWL:* 4.02m/13'2 *LOA:* 4.19m/13'9 *Beam:* 1.66m/5'5 *Draft:* 0.15m/6" cb up *Displ:* 98kg/216 lbs
Fittings:	Spars — wood and aluminium
Variations:	Alternative mast position which enables single-handed sailing with una rig — known as the 420 solitaire.
Sails:	Area 10.2m^2(7.9 + 2.3)/110 sq.ft. (85 + 25) Spinnaker area 8.8m^2/95 sq.ft.
Rigging:	Sloop
Price Guide:	£520/$1,200–1,500us
Summary:	2 crew. Trapeze and straps used. Versatile, easily rigged and exciting to sail. Popular worldwide.

470
Olympic and International

Design:	Andre Cornu, France 1964
Supplier:	Jack Holt U.K. 470 International Association France Mormark Systems U.S.A.
Est. Rating:	Portsmouth yardstick 86
Specificatiɔns:	*Construction:* GRP *LWL:* 4.42m/14'5½ *LOA:* 4.72m/15'6 *Beam:* 1.68m/5'6 *Draft:* 0.15m/6'' cb up *Displ:* 115kg/254 lbs
Fittings:	Aluminium spars. Mast 6.86m/22'6 high. Self-drain cockpit.
Sails:	Area 12.7m²/137 sq.ft. Spinnaker area 13m²/140 sq.ft.
Rigging:	Bermudan sloop
Price Guide:	£520/$1,700−1,800us
Summary:	Over 14,000 boats in circulation. 2 crew. Tremendous racing dinghy. Will make its debut at the 1976 Olympics.

GP 14

Design:	Jack Holt, England 1949
Supplier:	Bourne Plastics England Knight & Pink Marine U.K. GP14 International Association U.K.
Est. Rating:	Portsmouth yardstick 99
Specifications:	*Construction:* Wood, GRP or mixture *LWL:* 4.11m/13'6 *LOA:* 4.27m/14'0 *Beam:* 1.54m/5'0 *Draft:* 0.18m/7" *Displ:* 132.9kg/293 lbs
Fittings:	Wooden or aluminium spars. Mast 7.01m/23'0 high.
Sails:	Area 11.35m²/122 sq.ft. Spinnaker area 7.80m²/84 sq.ft. Reduced rig also available 4—4½ oz. material allowed.
Rigging:	Masthead sloop
Price Guide:	£360/$1,600us
Summary:	2 crew. Outside support, outriggers and inside ballast are all prohibited. A robust, maintenance free dinghy, ideal for tuition.

GRADUATE
National

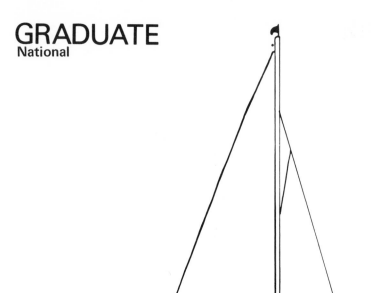

Design:	Wyche & Coppock Limited, England 1954
Supplier:	Wyche & Coppock Limited, England
Rating:	Portsmouth yardstick 103

Specifications:	*Construction:*	Marine plywood or GRP
	LWL:	3.66m/12'0
	LOA:	3.81m/12'6
	Beam:	1.44m/4'8½
	Draft:	0.20m/8''
	Displ:	83.92kg/185 lbs

Fittings:	Mast 5.79m/19'0 high
Sails:	Area 8.36m^2/90 sq.ft.
Rigging:	Bermudan sloop
Price Guide:	£275
Summary:	A hard chine dinghy of frameless construction that provides inexpensive class racing. Achieved national status in the U.K. in 1967. Sailed worldwide.

GULL

Design:	Ian Proctor, U.K. 1957
Supplier:	Lloyd Channing Assoc. England Avon Sailboats U.S.A. BAYC U.S.A.
Est. Rating:	Portsmouth yardstick 116
Specifications:	*Construction:* GRP or plywood *LOA:* 3.35m/11'0 *Beam:* 1.22m/4'0 *Draft:* 0.05m/2'' cb up *Displ:* 79kg/175 lbs
Fittings:	Aluminium spars. Centreboard boat. Built-in buoyancy.
Sails:	Area 7.1m^2/76 sq.ft.
Rigging:	Gunter or Bermudan sloop
Price Guide:	£230/$695us
Summary:	2 crew. Very popular throughout the world. Stable enough to teach youngsters and yet can be sailed in all weathers. Kits and plans available.

HARRIER

Design:	Keith Callaghan, England
Supplier:	Craftmakers U.K.
Specifications:	*Construction:* GRP
	LWL: 4.12m/13'6
	LOA: 4.27m/14'0
	Beam: 1.92m/6'3
	Draft: 0.12m/4½"
	Displ: 91kg/200 lbs
Fittings:	Mast 5.75m/19'0 high. Stayed metal mast. Built-in buoyancy.
Sails:	Area 8.5m^2/95 sq.ft.
Rigging:	Una
Price Guide:	£340
Summary:	Single hander. Strictly one design racing dinghy. Planes readily.

SEAFLY

Design:	S. J. Herbert, England 1962
Supplier:	South Devon Boat Builders England
Rating:	Portsmouth yardstick 93
Specifications:	*Construction:* GRP or marine plywood
	LWL: 4.27m/14'0
	LOA: 4.5m/14'9
	Beam: 1.75m/5'9
	Draft: 1.17m/3'10
	Displ: 127kg/280 lbs
Fittings:	Mast 6.55m/21'6 high. Built-in buoyancy.
Sails:	Area 11.2m^2/120 sq.ft. Spinnaker 12.5m^2/135 sq.ft.
Rigging:	Sloop
Price Guide:	£350±
Summary:	Deep vee form hull with chine swept to stem head makes this an exceptionally stiff boat on all points of sailing. One of the fastest, non-trapeze dinghies around.

HERON

Design:	Jack Holt, U.K. 1951
Supplier:	Bossoms Boatyard U.K. Heron International Association U.K.
Rating:	Portsmouth yardstick number 120
Specifications:	*Construction:* Wood or GRP *LWL:* 3.34m/11'0 *LOA:* 3.43m/11'3 *Beam:* 1.37m/4'6 *Draft:* 0.17m/7'' cb up *Displ:* 64kg–70kg/140 lbs wood – 155 lbs grp
Fittings:	Centreboard boat. Wooden spars. Mast 5.03m/16'6 high.
Sails:	Area 6.5m^2 (4.8 + 1.7)/70 sq.ft. (52 + 18)
Rigging:	Gunter
Price Guide:	£230/$550us
Summary:	2 crew. Vast majority sailed in the U.K. and in Australia where the boat has national status.

HORNET
National

Design:	Jack Holt, U.K. 1952
Supplier:	Roy Rigden, U.K. Hornet National Association U.K.
Rating:	Portsmouth yardstick 87
Specifications:	*Construction:* Wood or GRP *LOA:* 4.88m/16'0 *Beam:* 1.39m/4'7 *Draft:* 0.15m/6" *Displ:* 136kg/300 lbs
Fittings:	Wood or aluminium spars. Mast 6.82m/22'5 high. Built-in buoyancy.
Sails:	Area 11.2m^2/121sq.ft..– 13.23m^2/139 sq.ft. Spinnaker area 13.02m^2/140 sq.ft.
Rigging:	Bermudan sloop
Price Guide:	£550
Summary:	2 crew. Kits and plans available. Trapeze and sliding seat used. Genoa now fitted.

INTERNATIONAL 110

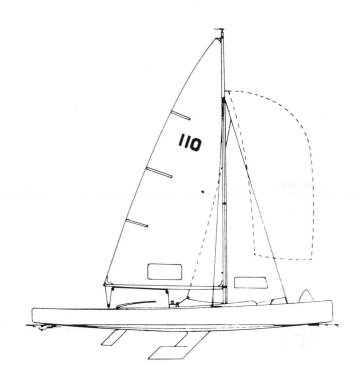

Design:	C. Raymond Hunt, U.S.A. 1939

Supplier:	International 110 Association, U.S.A.

Specifications:	*Construction:*	Wood or grp
	LOA:	7.32m/24'0
	Beam:	1.27m/4'2
	Draft:	0.84m/2'9
	Displ:	409kg/900 lbs.
	Ballast:	136kg/300 lbs

Fittings:	Aluminium spars. Positive flotation.

Sails:	Area 15.5m²/167 sq.ft. Spinnaker area 18.6m²/200 sq.ft.

Rigging:	Sloop

Price Guide:	$3,000us

Summary:	2 crew. Trapeze used. A very high performance keelboat. Easily trailed.

JET

Design:	Christian Maury, France 1967
Supplier:	Jet American Association U.S.A. Comextra England
Specifications:	*Construction:* GRP *LOA:* 4.75m/15'7 *Beam:* 1.7m/5'7 *Draft:* 0.17m/7" cb up *Displ:* 136kg/300 lbs
Fittings:	Aluminium spars. Centreboard boat.
Sails:	Area 14.8m^2(10.5 + 4.3)/159 sq.ft. (113 + 46)
Rigging:	Sloop
Price Guide:	$1,495us
Summary:	2 crew. May be trailed and car-topped. Trapeze used.

JIFFY

Design:	Ian Proctor, England
Supplier:	Armshire Reinforced Plastics England Miniscus Limited England
Specifications:	*Construction:* Moulded GRP *LOA:* 2.29m/7'6 *Beam:* 1.22m/4'0 *Draft:* 0.99m/3'3 *Displ:* 43.1kg/95 lbs
Fittings:	Mast 2.26m/7'5 high. Built-in buoyancy
Sails:	Area 3.35m^2/36 sq.ft.
Rigging:	Lateen
Price Guide:	On application
Summary:	An attractive quality built small racing dinghy. Distribution of the Jiffy is now well-spread. Widely used as tender to larger vessels. Designed initially for racing.

JAVELIN

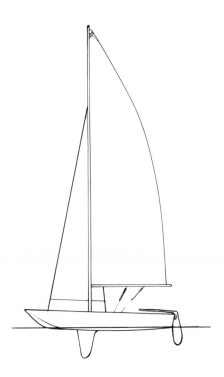

Design:	Peter Milne, England
Supplier:	Southern Service Boat Centre England
Est. Rating:	Portsmouth yardstick 81
Specifications:	*Construction:* GRP
	LOA: 5.36m/17'7
	Beam: 1.68m/5'6
	Draft: 0.23m/9"
	Displ: 136.08kg/300 lbs
Fittings:	Centreboard boat. Mast 7.24m/23'9 high. Built-in buoyancy.
Sails:	Area 13.94m^2/150 sq.ft. Spinnaker area 15.79m^2/170 sq.ft.
Rigging:	Sloop
Price Guide:	£500–£600
Summary:	A handsome, high performance dinghy that is quick to respond without being over-sensitive. Sailed mainly in the U.K.

JOLLYBOAT

Design:	Uffa Fox, U.K. 1953
Supplier:	Sailing Dynamics Inc. U.S.A. Jollyboat Owners Association England Jollyboat Association U.S.A.
Rating:	Portsmouth yardstick 82
Specifications:	*Construction:* GRP *LWL:* 5.33m/17'6 *LOA:* 5.49m/18'0 *Beam:* 1.62m/5'4 *Draft:* 0.15m/6'' cb up *Displ:* 129kg/285 lbs
Fittings:	Aluminium spars. Centreboard boat.
Sails:	Area 14.9m^2/160 sq.ft. Spinnaker area 18.6m^2/200 sq.ft.
Rigging:	Sloop
Price Guide:	On application
Summary:	2 crew. Trapeze used. Self-rescuing. Overall performance in the range of the Flying Dutchman and 505 class.

KESTREL

Design:	Ian Proctor, England
Supplier:	J. L. Gmach U.K. Kestrel Association U.S.A.
Rating:	Portsmouth yardstick 92
Specifications:	*Construction:* GRP *LWL:* 4.34m/14'3 *LOA:* 4.75m/15'7 *Beam:* 1.62m/5'4 *Draft:* 0.17m/7'' cb up *Displ:* 120kg/265 lbs
Fittings:	Aluminium spars. Centreboard boat. Mast 6.86m/22'6 high. Built-in buoyancy.
Sails:	Area 12.6m^2/136 sq.ft. Spinnaker area 15.3m^2/165 sq.ft.
Rigging:	Bermudan sloop
Price Guide:	£360
Summary:	2 crew. Ideal for the man who appreciates the qualities of a good performance dinghy and yet also needs a family boat.

LARK

Design: Michael Jackson, England 1967

Supplier: John Baker U.K.
                     Wyche & Coppock U.K.
                     Simonds Boats U.S.A.

Rating: Portsmouth yardstick 93

Specifications: *Construction:*   GRP
                     LOA: 4.06m/13'4
                     Beam: 1.68m/5'5½
                     Draft: 0.15m/6" cb up
                     Displ: 91kg/200 lbs

Fittings: Keelboat. Aluminium spars. Centreboard boat. Mast
                     6.71m/22'0 high.

Sails: Area 9.8m^2 (7 + 2.8)/105 sq.ft. (75 + 30)
                     Spinnaker area 7.4m^2/80 sq.ft.

Rigging: Sloop

Price Guide: £390/$1,345us

Summary: 2 crew. Strict one-design class but allows individuality
                     in selection of gear and sails. Buoyancy distribution
                     carefully placed to provide easy self-recovery.

LASER
International

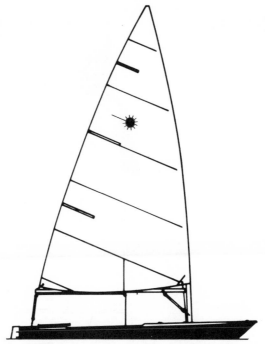

Design:	Bruce Kirby & Ian Bruce, Canada 1970
Supplier:	Performance Sailcraft Canada Laser Association Canada Performance Sailcraft (UK) England Satlspirit Holland
Rating:	Portsmouth yardstick 95

Specifications:

Construction:	GRP
LWL:	3.81m/12'6
LOA:	4.25m/13'11
Beam:	1.37m/4'6
Draft:	0.1m/4'' cb up
Displ:	57kg/125 lbs

Fittings:	Aluminium spars. Centreboard boat. Built-in buoyancy.
Sails:	Area 7.1m^2/76 sq.ft.
Rigging:	Una
Price Guide:	£250/$765us/2,370D.Fl.
Summary:	Single-hander. Majority sailed in the U.S.A. The carefully designed planing hull — plus its lightness — means the Laser jumps up in a plane long before other boats of its size. Easily righted. Can be car-topped.

LAZY E

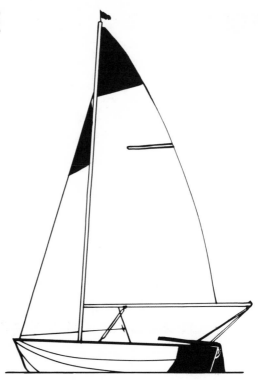

Design:	Jack Holt, England 1962
Supplier:	Jack Holt England
Est. Rating:	Portsmouth yardstick 94

Specifications:

Construction:	Marine plywood
LOA:	4.57m/15'0
Beam:	1.6m/5'3
Draft:	1.01m/3'4
Displ:	102kg/225 lbs

Fittings:	Mast 6.71m/22'0 high. Wooden spars.
Variations:	Variations in interior arrangements and cockpit fittings allowed
Sails:	Area 12.6m^2/136 sq.ft. Spinnaker area 7.5m^2/81 sq.ft.
Rigging:	Sloop
Price Guide:	On application.
Summary:	Most popular in the U.K. and Australia.

LEADER

Design:	John Mace and J.G. Pollard, England 1962
Supplier:	Trowbridge & Sons U.K.
Rating:	Portsmouth yardstick 97

Specifications:	*Construction:*	Wood and GRP
	LOA:	4.27m/14'0
	Beam:	1.66m/5'5
	Draft:	1.07m/3'6
	Displ:	111kg/245 lbs

Fittings:	Wooden spars. Centreboard boat. Mast 6.40m/ 21'0 high
Sails:	Area 10.96m^2/118 sq.ft. Spinnaker 9.29m^2/100 sq.ft.
Rigging:	Sloop
Price Guide:	£390
Summary:	2 crew. An ideal boat both for newcomers and experienced sailors who want a racing dinghy with room for the family. Kits available.

LIGHTNING
International

Design:	Sparkman & Stephens U.S.A. 1938
Supplier:	Allen Boat Co. U.S.A. International Lightning Association U.S.A.
Rating:	Provisional Portsmouth yardstick 96

Specifications:

Construction:	GRP
LOA:	5.79m/19'0
Beam:	1.98m/6'6
Draft:	0.44m/1'5
Displ:	318kg/700 lbs

Fittings:	Spars — wood or aluminium. Positive flotation.
Sails:	Area 16.5m2(11.1 + 5.4)/178 sq.ft. (120 + 58)
Rigging:	Sloop
Price Guide:	$2,750us
Summary:	3 crew. Responsive, points high and accelerates quickly in puffs.

MARK

Design:	W. Morton, England 1961
Supplier:	Mark Association, England
Rating:	Portsmouth yardstick 103

Specifications:

Construction:	Wood
LOA:	3.66m/12'0
Beam:	1.45m/4'9
Draft:	0.99m/3'3
Displ:	59kg/130 lbs

Fittings:	Spars to specification. Rudder assembly optional.
Sails:	Area 7.4m^2/80 sq.ft.
Rigging:	Una
Price Guide:	On application
Summary:	High performance single-hander. Easy to handle and rig. Class rules restrict hull shape and sail plan to close limits. Individual internal arrangements can be made.

MAYFLY

Design:	J. V. Kelley, England 1956
Supplier:	South Devon Boatbuilders England
Rating:	Portsmouth yardstick 105
Specifications:	*Construction:* Marine plywood or GRP with wood deck.
	LWL: 3.66m/12'0
	LOA: 3.89m/12'9
	Beam: 1.68m/5'6
	Draft: 0.91m/3'0
	Displ: 95kg/210 lbs
Fittings:	Mast 5.94m/19'6 high. Built-in buoyancy.
Sails:	Area $8.4m^2$/90 sq.ft. Spinnaker area $9.66m^2$/105 sq.ft.
Rigging:	Sloop
Price Guide:	£350
Summary:	Officially approved by the Royal Yachting Association for training purposes. Stable and seaworthy. Also suitable for racing and cruising.

MERLIN-ROCKET
National

Design: Various, England 1951

Supplier: Aln Boatyard England

Rating: Portsmouth yardstick 91

Specifications: *Construction:* Timber or GRP. Clinker
                     LWL: 4.27m/14'0
                     LOA: 4.27m/14'0
                     Beam: 2.11m/6'11
                     Draft: optional
                     Displ: 99kg/217 lbs

Fittings: Centreboard boat. Mast height varies.

Variations: Built-in buoyancy optional.

Sails: Area 9.8m^2 — 10.2m^2/105 — 110 sq.ft.
                     Spinnaker area 7.4m^2/80 sq.ft.

Rigging: Bermudan sloop

Price Guide: On application

Summary: Restricted class which allows latitude in hull shape, internal layout and sail plan. Over 2,500 boats registered in the U.K.

NATIONAL TWELVE

Design: Various, England 1935

Supplier: Wyche & Coppock England
                     Information from: RYA England

Rating: Portsmouth yardstick 98

Specifications: *Construction:* Various
                     LWL: 3.66m/12'0
                     LOA: 3.66m/12'0
                     Beam: 1.37m/4'6
                     Draft: 1.22m/4'0
                     Displ: 93kg/205 lbs

Fittings: Mast 6.55m/21'6' high

Variations: Optional built-in buoyancy.

Sails: Area 83.6m^2/90 sq.ft.

Rigging: Bermudan sloop

Price Guide: £400

Summary: Light, responsive and exhilerating sail. Kits available. A development class.

MIRROR

Design:	Holt & Bucknell, U.K. 1960
Supplier:	Mirror Boats U.K. International Mirror Association England U.S. Mirror Association U.S.A.
Rating:	Portsmouth yardstick 122
Specifications:	*Construction:* Wood with GRP on seams *LOA:* 3.3m/10'10 *Beam:* 1.39m/4'7 *Draft:* 0.15m/6'' cb up *Displ:* 30kg/ 65 lbs
Fittings:	Mast height 3.20m/10'6. Wooden spars. Centreboard boat. Built-in buoyancy.
Sails:	Area 6.4m^2(4.6 + 1.8)/69 sq.ft. (49 + 20) Spinnaker area 6m^2/65 sq.ft.
Rigging:	Gunter
Price Guide:	£140/$300us in kit form.
Summary:	2 crew. Must be the most successful small racing dinghy in the world — with registered numbers over 38,000. Ideal for beginners.

MIRROR 14

Design:	Peter Milne, U.K. 1970
Supplier:	Mirror Boats U.K. Mirror 14 Association England
Rating:	Portsmouth yardstick 91
Specifications:	*Construction:* Plywood with GRP on seams. *LWL:* 3.98m/13'1 *LOA:* 4.42m/14'6 *Beam:* 1.68m/5'6 *Draft:* 1.09m/3'7 *Displ:* 82kg/180 lbs
Fittings:	Spars — aluminium and wood. Centreboard boat. Mast 6.71m/22'0 high. Built-in buoyancy.
Sails:	Area 12.2m^2 (9.3 + 2.9)/131 sq.ft. (100 + 31) Spinnaker area 11.6m^2/125 sq.ft.
Rigging:	Sloop
Price Guide:	£290/$1,295us
Summary:	Kits available. 2 crew. Trapeze used. Very popular in England, Canada, America and Australia. Shaped for speed.

MOTH
International

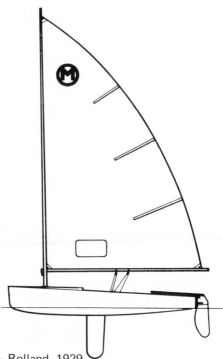

Design:	Open — Rolland, 1929
Supplier:	Wm. McCutcheon U.K. Lanaverre — France Navy Holland Moth International Association U.K. Moth National Association U.S.A.
Rating:	Portsmouth yardstick 107
Specifications:	*Construction:* Any *LWL:* 3.35m/11'0 *LOA:* 3.35m/11'0 *Beam:* 2.23m/7'4" max. *Draft:* Open *Displ:* Open
Fittings:	Spars — any material. Daggerboard. Mast 6.25m/20'6 maximum height.
Sails:	Area 7.9m^2/85 sq.ft.
Rigging:	Una
Price Guide:	£220/$800—1,200us
Summary:	Single-hander. Over 10,000 in circulation, making it the largest restricted class in the world. Sailed in 20 countries.

NATIONAL EIGHTEEN

Design:	Uffa Fox, Ian Proctor and Bob Anderson, England 1938	
Supplier:	Small Craft (Blockley) Ltd. England	
Rating:	Portsmouth yardstick 90	
Specifications:	*Construction:*	GRP, marine plywood or clinker
	LOA:	5.49m/18'0
	Beam:	1.83m/6'0
	Draft:	0.30m/1'0
	Displ:	249kg/550 lbs
Fittings:	Mast 9.15m/30' high. Built-in buoyancy.	
Sails:	Area 17.65m^2/190 sq.ft. Spinnaker area 17.65m^2/190 sq.ft.	
Rigging:	Sloop	
Price Guide:	On application	
Summary:	An economical dual-purpose craft, easy to handle in all weathers.	

OK
International

Design:	Knud Olsen, Sweden 1957	
Supplier:	Wyche & Coppock England	
Rating:	Portsmouth yardstick 98	
Specifications:	*Construction:*	Marine plywood or GRP
	LWL:	3.57m/11'9
	LOA:	4.01m/13'2
	Beam:	1.42m/4'8
	Draft:	0.18m/7"
	Displ:	72kg/159 lbs
Fittings:	Built-in buoyancy. Mast height 6.34m/20'9½.	
Sails:	Area 8.4m^2/90 sq.ft.	
Rigging:	Una	
Price Guide:	£350 $800 − 1,200us	
Summary:	Single-handed. IYRU recognised. A fast, thorough-bred boat that gives great competitive sailing. International status hoped for in 1974	

OPTIMIST PRAM
International

Design:	Clark Mills, U.S.A. 1947
Supplier:	Optimist Club U.S.A. Dobsons Yacht and Boatbuilders England
Rating:	Portsmouth yardstick 144

Specifications:	*Construction:*	Wood or grp
	LWL:	2.16m/7'1
	LOA:	2.33m/7'8
	Beam:	1.17m/3'10
	Draft:	0.15m/6" cb up
	Displ:	30kg/65 lbs

Fittings:	Centreboard boat. Wooden spars. Built-in buoyancy or bags. Mast 2.36m/7'9 high.
Sails:	Area $3.3m^2$/35 sq.ft.
Rigging:	Una
Price Guide:	£95/$250us
Summary:	Single-hander. Very popular because of low cost, stability, simplicity and good sailing qualities. Especially good for young people.

OSPREY MK 111
National

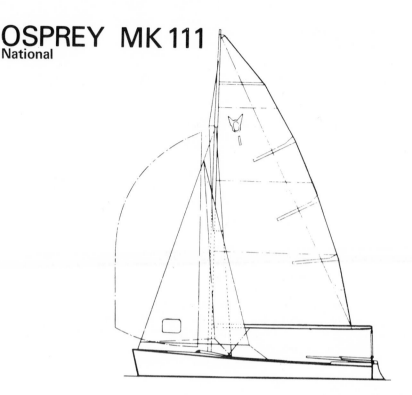

Design:	Ian Proctor, U.K. 1955/1974	
Supplier:	J. L. Gmach U.K.	
Rating:	Portsmouth yardstick 83	
Specifications:	*Construction:*	GRP or composite or marine plywood
	LWL:	5.18m/17'0
	LOA:	5.33m/17'6
	Beam:	1.78m/5'10
	Draft:	0.15m/6'' cb up
	Displ:	134kg/295 lbs
Fittings:	Centreboard boat. Aluminium spars. Built-in buoyancy.	
Sails:	Area 13.9m^2/150 sq.ft. Spinnaker area 13.9m^2/150 sq.ft.	
Rigging:	Sloop	
Price Guide:	£500	
Summary:	2 crew. Trapeze used. Largest fleets to be found in Britain and Singapore. Spinnaker chutes now allowed.	

OTTER

Design:	O'Brien Kennedy, England 1963
Supplier:	John Baker, England
Rating:	Portsmouth yardstick 112
Specifications:	*Construction:* GRP
	LOA: 3.55m/11'8
	Beam: 1.47m/4'10
	Draft: 1.07m/3'6
	Displ: 73kg/160 lbs
Fittings:	Centreboard boat. Mast 5.23m/17'2 high.
Sails:	Area 7m^2/75 sq.ft. Spinnaker area 6.5m^2/70 sq.ft.
Rigging:	Bermudan sloop
Price Guide:	£250
Summary:	2/4 crew. A racing and general purpose dinghy. One of the best dinghies of its kind. It has a very active class association.

PEGASUS

Design:	Uffa Fox, U.K. 1958
Supplier:	Pegasus World Association, England
Rating:	Portsmouth yardstick 94
Specifications:	*Construction:* Wood and GRP or GRP
	LOA: 4.42m/14'6
	Beam: 1.47m/4'10
	Draft: 0.1m/4"
	Displ: 91kg/200 lbs
Fittings:	Centreboard boat. Aluminium spars.
Sails:	Area 12.7m^2 (7.5 + 5.2)/137 sq.ft. (81 + 56) Spinnaker area 16.7m^2/180 sq.ft.
Rigging:	Sloop
Price Guide:	£ on application/$1,280us
Summary:	2 crew. Hiking straps and trapeze allowed. Self-rescuing. Can be trailed. Kits and plans available.

PACER

Design:	Jack Holt, England 1967
Supplier:	Polycell Prout England
Est. Rating:	Portsmouth yardstick 107

Specifications:	*Construction:* GRP or marine plywood in kit form
	LWL: ·3.73m/12'3
	LOA: 3.83m/12'7
	Beam: 1.47m/4'10
	Draft: 1.12m/3'8
	Displ: 59kg/130 lbs

Fittings:	Aluminium spars. Mast 5.69m/18'8 high. Built-in buoyancy.
Sails:	Area 9.8m^2/105 sq.ft. Spinnaker area 7.43m^2/80 sq.ft.
Rigging:	Sloop
Price Guide:	£250
Summary:	Has a lively performance and yet safe and stable enough for youngsters. The hull planes readily. The class is established in Australia, Canada, U.K. and Holland. Kits available.

PISCES

Design:	Julian West, England 1972
Supplier:	Glass Ships Limited England
Rating:	Portsmouth yardstick 103
Specifications:	*Construction:* GRP
	LWL: 3.76m/12'4
	LOA: 4.04m/13'3
	Beam: 1.3m/4'3
	Draft: 0.10m/4"
	Displ: 52kg/115 lbs
Fittings:	Double hulled. Non skid deck. Centreboard boat.
Sails:	Area $7m^2$/75 sq.ft.
Rigging:	Bermudan sloop
Price Guide:	£200
Summary:	A fast one-design single hander for racing and recreation. Responsive and well-balanced. Easily rigged and can be car-topped.

REDWING

Design:	Uffa Fox, England 1939
Supplier:	Redwing Association England
Rating:	Portsmouth yardstick 98
Specifications:	*Construction:* Wood
	LOA: 4.27m/14'0
	Beam: 1.52m/5'0
	Displ: 125kg/275 lbs
Fittings:	Wooden spars
Sails:	Area $11.6m^2$/125 sq.ft.
Rigging:	Sloop
Price Guide:	On application
Summary:	Sturdy, able, fast and fun to sail. Design commissioned by the Hove Sailing Club, England

PHANTOM

Design:	Brian Taylor and Paul Wright, England 1971
Supplier:	Paul Wright, England Southern Service Boat Centre, England
Rating:	Portsmouth yardstick 93

Specifications:	*Construction:*	GRP and marine plywood.
	LWL:	4.21m/13'10
	LOA:	4.42m/14.6
	Beam:	1.68m/5'6
	Draft:	0.15m/6''
	Displ:	68kg/150 lbs

Fittings:	Alloy spars. Mast height 6.10m/20'0. Built-in buoyancy.
Sails:	Area 9.8m^2/105 sq.ft
Rigging:	Una
Price Guide:	£350+
Summary:	Single-hander. Available in kit form only. A simple stitch and glass construction. Easy to handle and quick to recover from capsize.

12 sqm SHARPIE

Design:	G. Kroger, 1928
Supplier:	12 sq.m. Sharpie Association England
Rating:	Portsmouth yardstick 91
Specifications:	*Construction:*
	LOA: 5.99m/19'7½
	Beam: 1.43m/4'9
	Displ: 230kg/507 lbs
Sails:	Area 12m^2/129 sq.ft.
Price Guide:	£650
Summary:	About 100 Sharpies exist in the U.K. and Europe. Much more is being done to try and improve the racing facilities for the class.

SILVER STREAK

Design:	Paul Wright, England 1964
Supplier:	Silver Streak Association England
Rating:	Portsmouth yardstick 98
Specifications:	*Construction:* GRP
	LOA: 4.11m/13'6
	Beam: 1.8m/5'1
	Displ: 123kg/270 lbs
Fittings:	Aluminium spars
Sails:	Area 11.2m^2/120 sq.ft.
	Spinnaker area 8.4m^2/90 sq.ft.
Rigging:	Sloop
Price Guide:	On application.
Summary:	A small but active class in the U.K.

SCORPION
National

Design: Taprell Darling, England 1960

Supplier: Dobsons Boat Builders England

Rating: Portsmouth yardstick 94

Specifications: *Construction:*   GRP and wood
                     LWL: 4.14m/13'7
                     LOA: 4.27m/14'0
                     Beam: 1.47m/4'10
                     Draft: 1.07m/3'6
                     Displ: 82kg/180 lbs

Fittings: Mast 6.1m/20' high. Wooden spars. Built-in buoyancy.

Sails: Area $9.8m^2$/105 sq.ft.
                     Spinnaker area $11.15m^2$/120 sq.ft.

Rigging: Sloop

Price Guide: £400

Summary: No vices and easy to control. 3 crew. About 1,500
                     boats in circulation in the U.K.

SHOOTING STAR

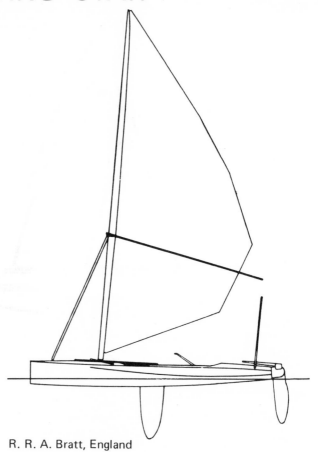

Design:	R. R. A. Bratt, England	
Supplier:	R. R. A. Bratt England	
Specifications:	*Construction:*	GRP
	LOA:	4.88m/16'0
	Beam:	1.52m/5'0
	Draft:	0.91m/3'0
	Displ:	95kg/210 lbs
Fittings:	Centreboard boat. Mast 7.01m/23'0 high.	
Sails:	Area 10.0m^2/107 sq.ft.	
Rigging:	Una	
Price Guide:	£600	
Summary:	2 crew. Powerful hull — planes easily. Quick and simple to handle rig, with a high boom.	

SIGNET

Design: Ian Proctor U.K. 1961

Supplier: S.W.A.L.E. U.K.
Signet Association U.S.A.

Est. Rating: Portsmouth yardstick 108

Specifications:

Construction:	Plywood
LWL:	3.51m/11'6
LOA:	3.79m/12'5
Beam:	1.45m/4'9
Draft:	0.13m/5" cb up
Displ:	86kg/190 lbs

Fittings: Mast 5.79m/19'0 high. Centreboard boat. Aluminium spars. Built-in buoyancy.

Sails: Area 8.2m^2 (5.9 + 2.3)/88 sq.ft. (63 + 25) Spinnaker area 8.4m^2/90 sq.ft.

Rigging: Bermudan sloop

Price Guide: £270/$1,200—1,400us

Summary: Kits and plans available. 2 crew. Popular worldwide. Suitable for beginners though essentially a racing dinghy.

SNIPE
International

Design:	William Crosby, U.S.A. 1931
Supplier:	Stone Marine U.K. Stamin Boat Co. U.S.A. Snipe Association U.S.A.
Rating:	Portsmouth yardstick 97

Specifications:

Construction:	Wood or grp
LWL:	4.19m/13'9
LOA:	4.72m/15'6
Beam:	1.52m/5'0
Draft:	0.15m/6'' cb up
Displ:	182kg/400 lbs

Fittings:	Daggerboard. Spars — wood or aluminium. Built-in buoyancy. Mast height 6.15m/20'1½
Sails:	Area 11.9m^2/128 sq.ft.
Rigging:	Bermudan sloop. High boom rig.
Price Guide:	£550/$1,650us
Summary:	Over 20,000 boats numbered. Sailed worldwide, with European and World Championships held annually.

SOLO
National

Design:	Jack Holt, U.K. 1958
Supplier:	Howell-Everson, U.K. Solo World Association U.K. Solo Canadian Association Canada
Est. Rating:	Portsmouth yardstick 102

Specifications:

Construction:	GRP wood or composite
LOA:	3.71m/12'5
Beam:	1.6m/5'3
Draft:	0.13m/5'' cb up
Displ:	68kg/150 lbs

Fittings:	Centreboard boat. Spars — aluminium or wood. Built-in buoyancy.
Sails:	Area 8.4m^2/90 sq.ft.
Rigging:	Una
Price Guide:	£370/$800us+
Summary:	Single-hander. Sailed in the U.K, Holland, Canada and Australia. Kits available. Double chined hull and fully battened sails are features of the class.

SOLING
Olympic Class

Design: Jan Linge, Denmark 1966

Supplier: Tyler Boat Co. England
International Soling Association Denmark
U. S. Soling Association U.S.A.
Abbott Boat Works Canada

Rating: Portsmouth yardstick 84

Specifications:
Construction:	GRP
LOA:	8.15m/26'9
Beam:	1.91m/6'3
Draft:	1.3m/4'3
Displ:	999kg/2,200 lbs
Ballast:	579kg/1,275 lbs

Fittings: Keelboat. Mast height $9.3m^2$/30'6. Built-in buoyancy.

Sails: Area $21.7m^2$/233 sq.ft.
Spinnaker area $33m^2$/355 sq.ft.

Rigging: Sloop

Price Guide: £ on application/$4,700us

Summary: 3 crew. An exciting sailing boat. First chosen for the Olympics in 1972

STRALE

Design:	E. Santarelli, Europe 1968
Supplier:	Northrup & Associates U.S.A. Whites (Camberley) England Larsson Trade U.S.A.

Specifications:	*Construction:*	GRP
	LWL:	4.34m/14'3
	LOA:	4.9m/16'1
	Beam:	1.58m/5'2
	Draft:	0.15m/6" cb up
	Displ:	120kg/265 lbs

Fittings:	Centreboard boat. Aluminium spars. Mast height 6.91m/22'8
Sails:	Area 13.5m^2/145 sq.ft.
Rigging:	Bermudan sloop
Price Guide:	£620
Summary:	2 crew. Trapeze used. Features a long cockpit, centre mainsheet arrangement and bendy rig — which are typical of continental modern designs.

SWORDFISH
National

Design:	Uffa Fox England 1948
Supplier:	J. W. Davis & Sons England
Rating:	Portsmouth yardstick 94

Specifications:	*Construction:*	Wood
	LOA:	4.57m/15'0
	Beam:	1.55m/5'1
	Displ:	136kg/300 lbs

Fittings:	Metal spars. Centreboard boat
Sails:	Area 12.1m^2/130 sq.ft. Spinnaker 7.4m^2/80 sq.ft.
Rigging:	Sloop
Price Guide:	On application
Summary:	Inaugurated after the second World War as a boat of quality yet stable and comfortable.

SQUIB
National

Design:	Oliver J. Lee England 1968
Supplier:	Oliver J. Lee England
Rating:	Portsmouth yardstick 91
Specifications:	*Construction:* GRP
	LOA: 5.79m/19'0
	Beam: 1.88m/6'2
	Displ: 681kg/1,500 lbs
Fittings:	Keelboat
Variations:	Outboard can be attached.
Sails:	Area 16.1m^2/173 sq.ft.
	Spinnaker 13.5m^2/145 sq.ft.
Rigging:	Sloop
Price Guide:	On application.
Summary:	3 crew. Gained national status in 1971. Can be trailed.

STAR
International

Design:	William Gardner, U.S.A. 1911
Supplier:	Buchan Boat Works U.S.A. Star National Association U.S.A.

Specifications:	*Construction:*	GRP or wood
	LOA:	6.91m/22'8
	Beam:	1.73m/5'8
	Draft:	1.01m/3'4
	Displ:	663kg/1,460 lbs
	Ballast:	409kg/900 lbs

Fittings:	Keelboat. Aluminium spars.
Sails:	Area 26.5m^2/285 sq.ft.
Rigging:	Sloop
Price Guide:	On application
Summary:	2 crew. Trailable. No hiking assists. allowed. No buoyancy added.

SUPER TIKI

Design:	George Marzin, France
Supplier:	Societé des Bois et Plastiques — France Iles of Norbury England
Rating:	Portsmouth yardstick 87
Specifications:	*Construction:* GRP
	LWL: 4.57m/15'0
	LOA: 4.88m/16'0
	Beam: 1.98m/6'6
	Draft: 1.22m/4'0
	Displ: 130kg/287 lbs
Fittings:	Built-in buoyancy.
Sails:	Area 16m^2/172 sq.ft. Spinnaker area 20.9m^2/225 sq.ft.
Rigging:	Sloop
Price Guide:	£650
Summary:	Trapeze used. 2 crew. A fast, centreboard boat with alternative interior arrangements.

SWALLOW
National

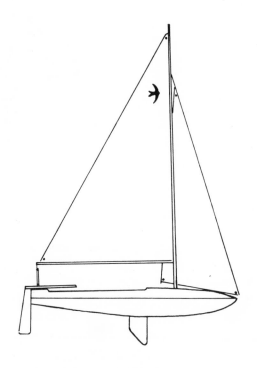

Design:	Pearson Bros. U.K. 1971	
Supplier:	Pearson Bros. Ltd. U.K.	
Specifications:	*Construction:*	GRP
	LOA:	3.66m/12'0
	Beam:	1.27m/4'2
	Draft:	0.08m/3" cb up
	Displ:	45kg/99 lbs
Fittings:	Centreboard boat. Aluminium spars. Built-in buoyancy. Pivotting centreplate.	
Sails:	Area 8.1m^2/87 sq.ft.	
Rigging:	Sloop or una	
Price Guide:	£205/$645us	
Summary:	1–2 crew. Ideal as a holiday boat.	

TANGO

Design:	Peter Milne, England 1973
Supplier:	Blue Peter Marine England
Rating:	Portsmouth yardstick 98

Specifications:	*Construction:*	Aluminium and ABS
	LWL:	4.03m/13'3
	LOA:	4.47m/14'8
	Beam:	1.67m/5'6
	Draft:	0.15m/6½''
	Displ:	108kg/240 lbs

Fittings:	Built-in buoyancy. Mast height 6.63m/21'9
Sails:	Area 11.23m²/121 sq.ft.
Rigging:	Sloop
Price Guide:	£425
Summary:	Built to strict one-design rules. Designed specifically for junior racing. Very efficient sail-plan.

10 SQUARE METRE CANOE

Design:	Open design — P. Nethercot originally.
Supplier:	Avalon Boats England International Canoe Federation Sweden American Canoe Association U.S.A.
Est. Rating:	Portsmouth yardstick 78

Specifications:

Construction:	GRP
LWL:	5.21m/17'1
LOA:	5.21m/17'1
Beam:	1.01m/3'4
Draft:	1.07m/3'6
Displ:	62kg/137 lbs

Fittings:	Centreboard boat. Spars — any material. Built-in buoyancy. Mast height 5.79m/19'0
Sails:	Area 10m^2/107.64 sq.ft. A smaller rig under development for junior racing.
Rigging:	Sloop
Price Guide:	£400/$1,400—1,600us
Summary:	The fastest single-handed sailing craft in the world. A one-design class. Sliding seat used.

TURTLE

Design:	Thames Marine, England 1970
Supplier:	Thames Marine England
Rating:	Portsmouth yardstick 118

Specifications:

Construction:	GRP
LWL:	2.64m/8'8
LOA:	3.48/11'5
Beam:	1.45m/4'9
Draft:	0.86m/2'10
Displ:	54kg/120 lbs

Fittings:	Centreboard boat. Mast 5.15m/16'10½. Self-rotating mast.
Sails:	Area 8.8m^2/95 sq.ft. (racing) 8.1m^2/87 sq.ft. (cruising) Spinnaker area 6.31m^2/68 sq.ft.
Rigging:	Sloop
Price Guide:	Price on application.
Summary:	2 crew. Planes easily and points well. Minimum maintenance.

TEMPEST
Olympic Class

Design:	Ian Proctor, England 1963
Supplier:	G. W. Parker U. K. Tempest National Association U.S.A. O'Day Corporation U.S.A.
Rating:	Portsmouth yardstick 82

Specifications:

Construction:	GRP	
LWL:	5.87m/19'3	
LOA:	6.71m/22'0	
Beam:	1.93m/6'4	
Draft:	1.09m/3'7	
Displ:	499.4kg/1,100 lbs	
Ballast:	227kg/500 lbs	

Fittings:	Retractable keelboat. Optional wood or aluminium spars. Built-in buoyancy.
Sails:	Area 23m^2/247 sq.ft. Spinnaker area 20.9m^2/225 sq.ft.
Rigging:	Sloop
Price Guide:	£1,500/$3,350us
Summary:	Very fast racing dinghy. Popular worldwide, and an Olympic class. 2 crew. Trapeze used — spinnaker chute accepted 1974.

12 METER
International

Design:	Open
Supplier:	12 Meter International Association, England
Specifications:	*Construction:* Wood or aluminium
	LOA: 19.81m/65'0
	Beam: 3.66m/12'0''
	Draft: 2.74m/9'0
	Displ: 31,780kg/70,000 lbs.
Fittings:	Optional spars.
Sails:	Area 167.2m^2/1,800 sq.ft.
Price Guide:	On application
Summary:	Crew 10—11.

VAGABOND YW

Design:	Jack Holt, England
Supplier:	Avacraft England
Rating:	Portsmouth yardstick 112
Specifications:	*Construction:* Marine plywood
	LWL: 3.35m/11'0
	LOA: 3.58m/11'9
	Beam: 1.45m/4'9
	Draft: 0.79m/2'7
	Displ: 85kg/188 lbs
Fittings:	Centreboard boat. Built-in buoyancy. Mast height 5.18m/17'0
Sails:	Area 8.1m^2/87.5 sq.ft.
Rigging:	Bermudan gunter
Price Guide:	£275
Summary:	2/4 crew. A comfortable, well designed racing dinghy, popular in Europe.

TOY

Design:	Tony Allen, England 1967
Supplier:	R. C. Marine U.K. Skene Boats Canada
Rating:	Portsmouth yardstick 91
Specifications:	*Construction:* GRP *LWL:* 3.96m/13'0 *LOA:* 4.57m/15'0 *Beam:* 1.22m/4'0 *Draft:* 0.13m/5" *Displ:* 65.8kg/145 lbs
Fittings:	Centreboard boat. Aluminium spars. Mast height 5.80m/19'0
Sails:	Area 8.36m^2/90 sq.ft.
Rigging:	Una
Price Guide:	£300
Summary:	Single-hander — use of sliding seat. Fast both up and downwind. Popular worldwide.

VULCAN

Design:	Peter Milne, England
Supplier:	South Devon Boat Builders England
Est. Rating:	Portsmouth yardstick 90
Specifications:	*Construction:* GRP
	LWL: 4.6m/15'1
	LOA: 5.08m/16'8
	Beam: 1.73m/5'8
	Draft: 1.09m/3'7
	Displ: 127kg/280 lbs
Fittings:	Retractable firm keel. Mast 6.86m/22'6 high.
Sails:	Area 13.9m^2/150 sq.ft.
	Spinnaker area 13m^2/140 sq.ft.
Rigging:	Bermudan sloop
Price Guide:	On application.
Summary:	A high performance racing boat. Rights itself extremely quickly. 2 crew.

ZENITH

Design:	Ian Proctor, England
Rating:	Portsmouth yardstick 92
Specifications:	*Construction:* Marine plywood
	LWL: 4.11m/13'6
	LOA: 4.42m/14'6
	Beam: 1.78m/5'10
	Draft: 1.24m/4'1
	Displ: 91kg/200 lbs
Fittings:	Mast 7.19m/23'7. Built-in buoyancy.
Sails:	Area 12.6m^2/136 sq.ft.
	Spinnaker area 11.6m^2/125 sq.ft.
Rigging:	Sloop
Price Guide:	On application
Summary:	High performance, one design racing dinghy. Trapeze used. Kits available.

VAURIEN
International

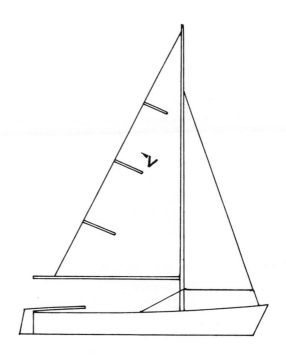

Design:	Jean-Jacques Herbulot, France
Supplier:	Annapolis Boat Rentals U.S.A.
Specifications:	*Construction:* Wood
	LOA: 4.04m/13'3
	Beam: 1.45m/4'9
	Draft: 0.08m/3"
Fittings:	Wooden spars. Centreboard boat.
Sails:	Area 8m²/86 sq.ft.
	No spinnaker allowed.
Rigging:	Sloop
Price Guide:	On application
Summary:	2 crew. Self-rescuing.

WAYFARER

Design:	Ian Proctor, U.K. 1958
Supplier:	R. Moore U.K.
	Avon Sailboats U.S.A.
	Wayfarer Association U.K.
	Wayfarer Association U.S.A.
Est. Rating:	Portsmouth yardstick 97

Specifications:

Construction:	GRP or wood
LWL:	4.52m/14'10
LOA:	4.82m/15'10
Beam:	1.85m/6'1
Draft:	0.02m/8"
Displ:	166kg/365 lbs

Fittings:	Centreboard boat. Spars — aluminium or wood. Built-in buoyancy.
Sails:	Area 11.6m^2/125 sq.ft. Spinnaker area 11.6m^2/125 sq.ft.
Rigging:	Bermudan sloop
Price Guide:	£550/$1,745us
Summary:	2/4 crew. A safe roomy family dinghy for cruising or racing. Kits available. RYA approved.

WINEGLASS

Design:	Trevor Kirby, England 1960
Supplier:	Harviglass U.K.
	Wineglass Association U.S.A.
	Wineglass Association U.K.
Rating:	Portsmouth yardstick 96
Specifications:	*Construction:* GRP
	LWL: 4.27m/14'0
	LOA: 4.57m/15'0
	Beam: 1.78m/5'10
	Draft: 0.15m/6''
	Displ: 109kg/240 lbs
Fittings:	Centreboard boat. Aluminium spars. Mast 6.86m/ 22'6. Built-in buoyancy.
Sails:	Area 11.4m^2(7.4 + 4)/123 sq.ft. (80 + 43)
Rigging:	Sloop
Price Guide:	£550/$1,395us
Summary:	2 crew. General purpose dinghy for family cruising and racing. Very stable despite her quickness.

XOD

Design:	A Westmacott, England 1909
Supplier:	R & A Hamper England
Rating:	Portsmouth yardstick 99
Specifications:	*Construction:* Carvel
	LOA: 6.31m/20'8½
	Beam: 1.78m/5'10¼
	Displ: 1,362kg/3,000 lbs
Fittings:	Keelboat
Sails:	Area 17.1m^2/184 sq.ft.
	Spinnaker area 14.9m^2/160 sq.ft.
Rigging:	Bermudan sloop
Price Guide:	On application
Summary:	Crew optional. Can be trailed. A well-established character racing dinghy.

WILDFIRE

Design:	Ian Proctor and George O'Day, England
Supplier:	J. L. Gmach, England Wildfire National Association U.S.A.
Rating:	Portsmouth yardstick 95

Specifications:

Construction:	GRP
LOA:	5.11m/16'9
Beam:	1.91m/6'3
Draft:	1.19m/3'11
Displ:	309kg/680 lbs

Fittings:	Aluminium spars. Keelboat — removeable. Mast 7.62m/25'0 high. Built-in buoyancy.
Variations:	Variations in rig and sail plan available.
Sails:	Area 15.3m^2/165 sq.ft. Spinnaker area 14.9m^2/160 sq.ft.
Rigging:	Bermudan sloop
Price Guide:	£600/$2,000us secondhand approx.
Summary:	2 crew. Built originally for the American market but successful worldwide now.

YNGLING

Design:	Jan Linge, Denmark
Supplier:	International Yngling Association Norway North American Yngling Association U.S.A.

Specifications:

Construction:	GRP
LOA:	6.38m/20'11
Beam:	1.73m/5'8
Draft:	1.07m/3'6
Displ:	599kg/1,320 lbs
Ballast:	309kg/680 lbs

Fittings:	Keelboat. Aluminium spars. Spade rudder.
Sails:	Area 13.9m^2/150 sq.ft. Spinnaker area 20.9m^2/225 sq.ft.
Rigging:	Sloop
Price Guide:	$2,800us
Summary:	3 crew. A one-design world class, with an impressive performance.

ZEF

Supplier:	Larsson Trade U.S.A. Whites (Camberley) England
Specifications:	*Construction:* GRP *LOA:* 3.68m/12'1 *Beam:* 1.55m/5'1 *Draft:* 0.74m/2'5 *Displ:* 91kg/200 lbs
Fittings:	Double hull construction. Aluminium spars. Mast height 5.08m/16'8
Variations:	Outboard may be attached.
Sails:	Area 8.9m^2/96 sq.ft.
Rigging:	Sloop
Price Guide:	£300/$800us
Summary:	Unsinkable. Especially designed for yachting schools, but as she points so well 'Zef' is a real challenge to experienced dinghy sailors.

RACING DINGHIES
multihulls

APOLLO CATARAMAN

Design:	Neil Coster, England 1969
Supplier:	Prout Marine, England Ocean Catamarans, U.S.A. Apollo Association, England
Rating:	Estimated Portsmouth yardstick 72
Specifications:	*Construction:* GRP or cold moulded wood *LOA:* 5.49m/18'0 *Beam:* 2.29m/7'6 *Draft:* 0.76m/2'6
Fittings:	Mast 7.72m/25'4 high. Centreboard boat.
Sails:	Area 13.9m^2/150 sq.ft.
Rigging:	Cat rigged
Price Guide:	£400/$1,750us
Summary:	An 'A' Class racing catamaran. Single-handed.

AQUA CAT 12

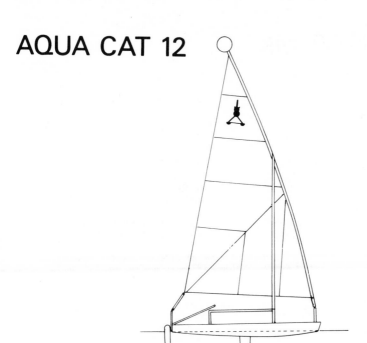

Design:	American Fiberglass Corporation, U.S.A. 1961
Supplier:	American Fiberglass Corporation U.S.A. J. Dunhill Enterprises, England
Rating:	Portsmouth yardstick 100
Specifications:	*Construction:* GRP *LOA:* 3.71m/12'2 *Beam:* 1.85m/6'1 *Draft:* 0.13m/5'' *Displ:* 75kg/165 lbs
Fittings:	Daggerboards. 2 symmetrical hulls, connected with aluminium tubes. Aluminium spars. Canvas decking.
Variations:	By removing mast and hulls the boat is easily converted into a swimming platform.
Sails:	Area 8.4m^2/90 sq.ft. (racing suit) Area 7.24m^2/78 sq.ft. (standard suit)
Rigging:	Una
Price Guide:	£295/$795us
Summary:	1 or 2 racing crew. Simple and quick to rig with an exciting performance. Over 14,000 registered boats worldwide, making it the largest catamaran class.

COUGAR Mk III

Design:	Richard E. Brown, U.S.A.
Supplier:	·Arrowglass Boat and Manufacturing Corporation, U.S.A. International Cougar Catamaran Association, U.S.A.

Specifications:

	Construction:	GRP
	LOA:	5.72m/18'9
	Beam:	2.44m/8'0
	Draft:	0.13m/5"
	Displ:	281kg/620 lbs

Fittings:	2 symmetrical hulls connected by a bridge deck. Aluminium spars. Centreboards. Positive flotation.
Sails:	Area 23.2m^2(14.9 + 8.3)/250 sq.ft. (160 + 90) No spinnaker allowed.
Rigging:	Sloop
Price Guide:	$2,175us
Summary:	2 crew.

PAPER TIGER

Design:	Ron Given, N.Z. 1969
Supplier:	High Performance Sailboat Sales, U.S.A. Paper Tiger World Association, New Zealand Paper Tiger Association, U.S.A.

Specifications:

	Construction:	Plywood or grp
	LOA:	4.27m/14'0
	Beam:	2.13m/7'0
	Draft:	0.13m/5"
	Displ:	64kg/140 lbs

Fittings:	2 symmetrical hulls connected with aluminium. Aluminium spars. Daggerboards.
Sails:	Area 9.3m^2/100 sq.ft.
Rigging:	Una
Price Guide:	$1,095us
Summary:	Single-hander. An exciting, fast catamaran.

AUSTRALIS INTERNATIONAL

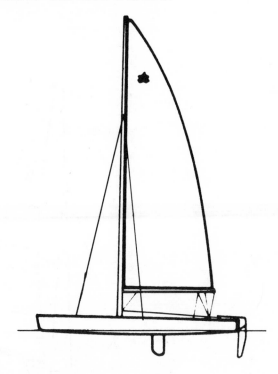

Design:	Graham Johnston, Australia 1967
Supplier:	Sail Craft, England International Australis Association, Australia Australis Association, U.S.A.
Specifications:	*Construction:* GRP or wood *LOA:* 5.49m/18'0 *Beam:* 2.29m/7'6 *Draft:* 0.15m/6" *Displ:* 107kg/235 lbs
Fittings:	Daggerboards. 2 symmetrical hulls connected by aluminium tubes. Aluminium spars.
Sails:	Area 13.9m^2/150 sq.ft. No spinnaker allowed.
Rigging:	Una
Price Guide:	£ on application/$1,650us
Summary:	Single-hander, racing catamaran. Top class. Can be trailed and car-topped.

`C´ CLASS INTERNATIONAL

Design:	Open
Supplier:	'C' Class World Association, C/o IYRU England
Specifications:	*Construction:* Open
	LOA: 7.62m/25'0 max.
	Beam: 4.27m/14'0 max.
	Draft: No limit
	Displ: Unrestricted
Fittings:	2 hulls. Spars — any material
Sails:	Area 27.9m^2/300 sq.ft. max.
Rigging:	Cat rigged
Price Guide:	On application
Summary:	2 crew. Trapeze, hiking board and straps used. One of the fastest cats around.

CONDOR ONE DESIGN

Design:	John Mazzotti, England 1970
Supplier:	Zygal Boats, England
Rating:	Portsmouth yardstick 71
Specifications:	*Construction:* GRP or wood in kit form
	LWL: 4.47m/15'8
	LOA: 5.00m/16'4
	Beam: 2.23m/7'4
	Draft: 0.15m/6''
	Displ: 95.26kg/210 lbs
Fittings:	Mast 8m/26'0 high. Built-in buoyancy.
Sails:	Area $17m^2$/183 sq.ft.
Rigging:	Cat
Price Guide:	£480
Summary:	An exceptionally dry cat that can be righted from capsize without assistance. Light to handle. Easy to dismantle. 2 crew.

HYDRA CATAMARAN

Design:	Mike West, England 1970
Supplier:	Allan Bell Catamarans, England Hydra Association, England
Rating:	Portsmouth yardstick 73
Specifications:	*Construction:* GRP or wood *LWL:* 4.88m/16'0 *LOA:* 4.93m/16'6 *Beam:* 2.29m/7'6 *Draft:* 0.78m/2'7 *Displ:* 74.8kg/165 lbs
Fittings:	Mast 7.92m/26'0 high. Mast and boom alloy. Centreboard pivoting with automatic up and down-haul. Rudder pivoting wood aerofoil blades.
Sails:	Area 19.5m^2/210 sq.ft. 5½ oz. Terylene.
Rigging:	Cat rigged
Price Guide:	£450 to £500
Summary:	2 crew. Fast, light racing cat. Can be car-topped. This is the smaller version of the successful Tornado cat.

PACIFIC CAT

Design:	Carter Pyle, U.S.A. 1959
Supplier:	Newport Boats, U.S.A. Pacific Cat Association, U.S.A.
Specifications:	*Construction:* GRP *LOA:* 5.64m/18'6 *Beam:* 2.41m/7'11 *Draft:* 0.15m/6''
Fittings:	2 symmetrical hulls connected by a bridge deck. Aluminium spars. 2 centreboards.
Sails:	Area 24.7m²(18.4 + 6.3)/266 sq. ft.(198 + 68) Spinnaker area 32.5m²/350 sq. ft.
Rigging:	Sloop
Price Guide:	$2,195us
Summary:	2 crew. High speed catamaran with rugged construction. Very popular in California. Can be trailed.

SHARK

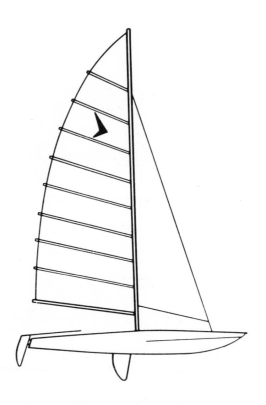

Design:	J. R. MacAlpine-Downie, U.S.A. 1963
Supplier:	Aero-Craft Boats, U.S.A.
	American Shark Association, U.S.A.

Specifications:	*Construction:*	GRP or wood and GRP
	LOA:	6.1m/20'0
	Beam:	3.05m/10'0
	Draft:	0.08m/3''
	Displ:	204kg/450 lbs

Fittings:	2 symmetrical hulls connected with a bridge deck. Centreboards. Aluminium spars.
Sails:	Area 25.3m^2(17.6 + 7.7)/273 sq.ft. (190 + 83)
Rigging:	Sloop
Price Guide:	$3,000us
Summary:	2 crew. Trapeze used.

SHEARWATER CATAMARAN

Design:	Prout Brothers, U.K. 1957
Supplier:	Allan Bell, U.K. McNichols Boat Sales, U.S.A.
Rating:	Portsmouth yardstick 75
Specifications:	*Construction:* GRP or plywood *LOA:* 5.03m/16'6 *Beam:* 2.29m/7'6 *Draft:* 0.17m/7'' *Displ:* 116kg/255 lbs
Fittings:	2 symmetrical hulls connected with aluminium. Daggerboards. Aluminium spars. Sliding seat.
Sails:	Area 21.8m^2/235 sq.ft.
Rigging:	Bermudan sloop
Price Guide:	£500/$ on application
Summary:	2 crew. Trapeze used. A fast, exhilerating and safe sail. Best performance in rough weather.

SIZZLER

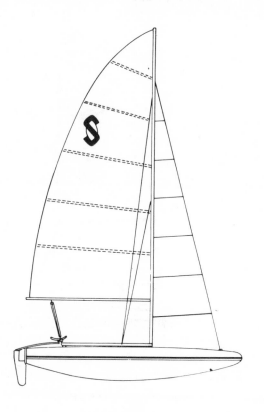

Design:	Paul F. Swenson, U.S.A. 1969
Supplier:	Great Lakes Sports Manufacturing, U.S.A.

Specifications:	*Construction:*	Aluminium
	LOA:	5m/16'5
	Beam:	2.29m/7'6
	Draft:	0.2m/8''
	Displ:	107kg/235 lbs

Fittings: 2 symmetrical hulls connected with aluminium. Aluminium spars. Mast 7.01m/23'0 high.

Sails: Area 13.9m^2 (10.2 + 3.7)/150 sq.ft. (110 + 40)

Rigging: Sloop

Price Guide: $1,675us

Summary: 1 or 2 crew. Built only in America. The first aluminium cat on the market — combines advance design with modern production techniques. Light, strong and fast.

SOL CAT

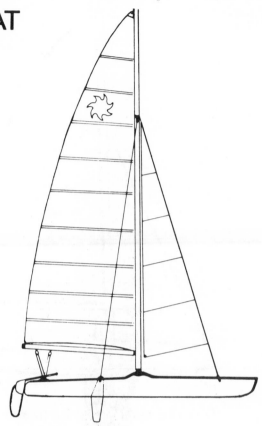

Design:	Gene Vernon, U.S.A.	
Supplier:	Sol Cat Catamarans Inc., U.S.A.	
Specifications:	*Construction:*	GRP
	LOA:	5.56m/18'3
	Beam:	2.44m/8'0
	Draft:	0.13m/5''
	Displ:	143kg/315 lbs

Fittings: Daggerboards. 2 symmetrical hulls connected with aluminium. Aluminium spars.

Sails: Area 20.4m^2 (16.2 + 4.2)/220 sq.ft. (175 + 45)

Rigging: Sloop

Price Guide: $1,795us

Summary: 2 to 4 crew. High performance catamaran. Placed first in the 1972 World's Multihull Championship Efficiency Trials.

SWIFT

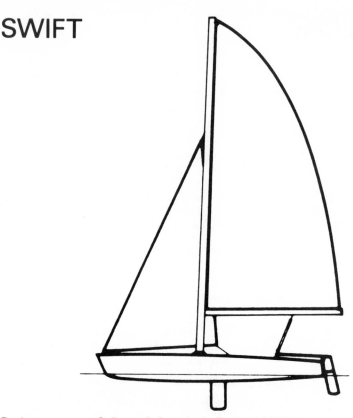

Design:	G. Prout & Sons Ltd., England 1954
Supplier:	G. Prout & Sons, England Kingsfield Marine, England
Rating:	Portsmouth yardstick 87

Specifications:

Construction:	GRP and marine plywood
LOA:	4.42m/14'6
Beam:	1.78m/5'10
Draft:	0.53m/1'9
Displ:	114kg/251 lbs

Fittings:	Mast height 6.4m/21'0. Built-in buoyancy.
Sails:	Area 13m^2/140 sq.ft.
Rigging:	Bermudan sloop
Price Guide:	£380
Summary:	2 crew. A very fast, popular catamaran worldwide. Fleets can be found in the U.K., U.S.A. Scandinavia and Thailand. Rolled decks and trampoline introduced in 1973

TORNADO
OLYMPIC CATAMARAN

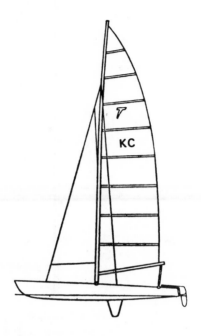

Design:	Rodney March, England 1967
Supplier:	Zygal Boats U.K. Alleman Enterprises, U.S.A. International Tornado Association, U.K.
Rating:	Portsmouth yardstick 63
Specifications:	*Construction:* Wood, wood and GRP or GRP sandwich.
	LOA: 6.09m/20'0
	Beam: 3.02m/10'0
	Draft: 0.17m/7''
	Displ: 127kg/280 lbs
Fittings:	2 symmetrical hulls connected with aluminium. Aluminium spars. 2 centreboards.
Sails:	Area 20.4m^2 (14.9 + 5.5)/220 sq.ft. (160 + 60)
Rigging:	Bermudan sloop
Price Guide:	£800/$2,600 to $3,300us
Summary:	2 crew. Trapeze used. An international class, almost 2,000 boats in circulation.

UNICORN

Design:	John Mazzotti, England 1964
Supplier:	Trowbridge & Sons, England
Rating:	Portsmouth yardstick 71
Specifications:	*Construction:* GRP or marine plywood
	LWL: 5.26m/17'3
	LOA: 5.49m/18'0
	Beam: 2.29m/7'6
	Draft: 0.76m/2'6
	Displ: 91kg/200 lbs
Fittings:	Mast 7.92m^2/26.0 high. Metal spars.
Sails:	Area 13.9m^2/150 sq.ft.
Rigging:	Cat rigged
Price Guide:	£525
Summary:	A fast one design 'A' class racing catamaran, that has won all the major racing trophies in the last 5 years.

GENERAL PURPOSE
AND DAY DINGHIES
monohulls

AERONAUT

Design:	Aero-Nautical Inc., U.S.A. 1968
Supplier:	Aero-Nautical Inc., U.S.A.

Specifications:

Construction:	GRP
LOA:	4.22m/13.10
Beam:	1.22m/4'0
Draft:	0.13m/5'' cb up
Displ:	63kg/139 lbs

Fittings:	Aluminium spars. Foam flotation.
Sails:	Area 7.0m²/75 sq.ft.
Rigging:	Una
Price Guide:	$550us
Summary:	An American class. Over 600 boats in circulation. 2 crew.

ALEZAN

Design:	France
Supplier:	Aloa Marine, France Aquaboats Limited, England
Specifications:	*Construction:* GRP *LOA:* 4.50m/13'0 *Beam:* 1.90m/6'2¾ *Displ:* 120kg/264 lbs
Fittings:	Centreboard boat
Sails:	Area 12.1m²/130 sq.ft.
Rigging:	Sloop
Price Guide:	4.600 Fr.F.
Summary:	2/3 crew. General purpose and racing dinghy. Can be trailed.

AQUA BELL

Supplier:	Aqua Bell Limited, England
Specifications:	*Construction:* GRP
	LOA: 2.44m/8'0
	Displ: 68kg/150 lbs
Sails:	Area various
Price Guide:	£100
Summary:	A general purpose dinghy. An auxiliary engine can be fitted.

AQUARIUS

Design:	Jorge L. Garcia, 1970
Supplier:	Aquarius National Association, U.S.A.
Specifications:	*Construction:* GRP
	LOA: 5m/16'5
	Beam: 1.7m/5'7
	Draft: 0.2m/8'' cb up
	Displ: 182kg/400 lbs
Fittings:	Centreboard boat. Aluminium spars. Hiking straps fitted. Positive foam flotation.
Sails:	Area 9.7m^2/105 sq.ft.
Rigging:	Una
Price Guide:	$2,000us
Summary:	Single-hander. Self bailing. Sailed only in the south-east of America.

ALIOS

Design:	Christian Maury, France 1973	
Supplier:	Lanaverre, France	
Specifications:	*Construction:*	Plastic
	LWL:	5.05m/16'7
	LOA:	5.58m/18'4
	Beam:	2.12m/6'11½
	Draft:	0.60m/1'11½
	Displ:	1,000kg/2,205 lbs
	Ballast:	200kg/ 441 lbs
Fittings:	Centreboard boat	
Sails:	Area 15m^2/161 sq.ft.	
Rigging:	Sloop	
Price Guide:	On application	
Summary:	A general purpose dinghy that is safe in all conditions.	

ARROW
USA

Design:	J. Deering, U.S.A.
Supplier:	Arrow Association, U.S.A. Stamm Boat Co., U.S.A.
Specifications:	*Construction:* Wood or GRP *LOA:* 5.49m/18'0 *Beam:* 1.93m/6'4 *Draft:* 1.27m/4'2
Fittings:	Wood or aluminium spars.
Sails:	Area 16.2m^2/175 sq.ft. Spinnaker not official.
Rigging:	Sloop
Price Guide:	On application.
Summary:	2 crew.

BARNEGAT 17

Design:	Howard Siddons, U.S.A.
Supplier:	Barnegat 17 National Association U.S.A.
Specifications:	*Construction:* GRP *LOA:* 5.05m/16'7 *Beam:* 1.83m/6'0 *Draft:* 0.2m/8'' cb up
Fittings:	Aluminium spars. Centreboard boat. Hiking straps fitted.
Sails:	Area 14.4m^2/145 sq.ft. Spinnaker allowed.
Rigging:	Sloop
Price Guide:	On application.
Summary:	2 crew. Sailed on the North-east coast of America.

ALTO

Design:	France
Supplier:	Francqueville, France
Specifications:	*Construction:* Plastic
	LOA: 5.00m/16'4¾
	Beam: 1.45m/4'9
	Displ: 100kg/220 lbs
Fittings:	Aluminium spars.
Sails:	Area 12m^2/130 sq.ft.
Rigging:	Sloop
Price Guide:	5.500 Fr.F.
Summary:	A sleek all-purpose dinghy.

BARNEGAT BAY SNEAKBOX

Design:	Various
Supplier:	Alan Chadwick, U.S.A.
	Barnegat Bay Sneakbox National Association U.S.A.
Specifications:	*Construction:* Wood or grp
	LOA: 3.66, 4.27, 4.57m/12', 14', 15',
	Beam: 1.52m/5'0
	Draft: 1.003m/3'3½
Fittings:	Spars — wood or aluminium
Variations:	In length available
Sails:	Area 14.5m^2/156 sq. ft.
Rigging:	Sloop
Price Guide:	Prices vary.
Summary:	Single-hander. Exclusive American class, sailed mainly in the North-east.

BAY BIRD 7′ 9″ DINGHY

Design:	Annapolis Corporation U.S.A.
Supplier:	Annapolis Sailboat Builders Inc. U.S.A.
Specifications:	*Construction:* GRP
	LOA: 2.36m/7'9
	Beam: 1.3m/4'3
	Displ: 36kg/80 lbs
Fittings:	Aluminium spars. Centreboard boat.
Sails:	Area 4.2m^2/45 sq.ft.
Rigging:	Una
Price Guide:	$570us
Summary:	Single-hander. A popular, general purpose dinghy.

APOLLON

Design:	France
Supplier:	Kirie, France
Specifications:	*Construction:* Plastic
	LOA: 4.40m/14'5
	Beam: 1.80m/5'11
	Displ: 440kg/970 lbs
Fittings:	Aluminium spars
Sails:	Area 11.50m^2/124 sq.ft.
Rigging:	Sloop
Price Guide:	8,487 Fr.F.

AVANT

Design: Matthews & White, U.S.A. 1971

Supplier: Formex Corporation, U.S.A.

Specifications: *Construction:* ABS
LOA: 3.35m/11'0
Beam: 0.91m/3'0
Displ: 39kg/85 lbs

Fittings: Aluminium spars. Daggerboard.

Sails: Area 5.1m^2/55 sq.ft.

Rigging: Una

Price Guide: $220us

Summary: 2 crew. Exclusive American class.

132

BAGHEERA

Design:	France	
Supplier:	Archambault, France	
Specifications:	*Construction:*	Plastic
	LWL:	4.75m/15'7
	LOA:	6.0m/19'8
	Beam:	1.80m/5'11
	Draft:	0.95m/3'1
	Displ:	400kg/882 lbs
	Ballast:	210kg/463 lbs
Fittings:	Aluminium spars.	
Sails:	Area 17.12m^2/184 sq.ft.	
Rigging:	Sloop	
Price Guide:	14,000 Fr.F.	
Summary:	A modern dinghy traditional to the Continental type design. Well finished.	

BEAUFORT

Design:	Ian Proctor, England
Supplier:	Fosrite Plastics Limited England
Rating:	Portsmouth yardstick 96
Specifications:	*Construction:* GRP
	LOA: 5.03m/16'6
	Beam: 1.91m/6'3
	Displ: 200kg/440 lbs
Fittings:	Centreboard boat
Variations:	Auxiliary may be attached.
Sails:	Area 14.7m^2/158 sq.ft. Cruising or racing rigs available. Spinnaker area 16.1m^2/173 sq.ft.
Rigging:	Bermudan sloop
Price Guide:	On application.
Summary:	2/5 crew. Can be trailed.

BEVERLY

Design:	Nathaniel Herreshoff, U.S.A.
Supplier:	Cape Cod Shipbuilding, U.S.A.
Specifications:	*Construction:* GRP
	LOA: 3.51m/11'6
	Beam: 1.37m/4'6
	Draft: 0.15m/6'' cb up
Fittings:	Aluminium spars. Centreboard boat.
Sails:	Area 6.1m^2/66 sq.ft.
Rigging:	Una
Price Guide:	$730us
Summary:	A safe, family dinghy.

BAY BIRD 9' DINGHY

Design:	Annapolis Corporation U.S.A.
Supplier:	Annapolis Sailboat Builders Inc. U.S.A.
Specifications:	*Construction:* GRP
	LOA: 2.74m/9'0
	Beam: 1.37m/4'6
	Displ: 48kg/105 lbs
Fittings:	Aluminium spars. Centreboard boat.
Sails:	Area 4.7m^2/52 sq.ft.
Rigging:	Una
Price Guide:	$720us
Summary:	Single-hander. General purpose, stable dinghy. Larger version of the 7'9.

BIG APPLE

Design:	Sel Yacht Distributors, 1972
Supplier:	Big Apple Association U.S.A.
Specifications:	*Construction:* ABS
	LOA: 4.24m/13'11
	Beam: 1.5m/4'11
	Draft: 0.18m/7'' cb up
	Displ: 84kg/185 lbs
Fittings:	Daggerboard. Aluminium spars. Foam flotation.
Sails:	Area 8.6m^2/93 sq.ft.
Rigging:	Sloop
Price Guide:	$850us
Summary:	An exclusive American class in use mainly in the east. Takes up to 4 crew.

BLOCK ISLAND 25

Design:	U.S.A. 1971
Supplier:	Metalmast Marine U.S.A.
	Block Island Association U.S.A.
Specifications:	*Construction:* GRP
	LOA: 7.82m/25'8
	Beam: 2m/6'7
	Draft: 1.37m/4'6
	Displ: 1,816kg/4,000 lbs
	Ballast: 999kg/2,200 lbs
Fittings:	Aluminium spars.
Variations:	Available also with 2 bunks and head
Sails:	Area 26.3m^2/283 sq.ft.
	Spinnaker area 20.9m^2/225 sq.ft.
Rigging:	Sloop
Price Guide:	$5,000us
Summary:	Trailable and self-baling. Kits available.

BAYMASTER

Design:	Winthrop Warner, U.S.A.
Supplier:	Regatta Plastics U.S.A. Baymaster National Association U.S.A.

Specifications:		
	Construction:	GRP
	LOA:	5.46m/17'11
	Beam:	2.11m/6'11
	Draft:	1.447m/4'9

Fittings:	Aluminium spars. Centreboard boat.
Sails:	Area 13.8m^2/149 sq.ft.
Rigging:	Sloop
Price Guide:	On application
Summary:	2 crew. Self-rescuing. Sailed mainly in the southern states of the U.S.A.

BEETLE CAT

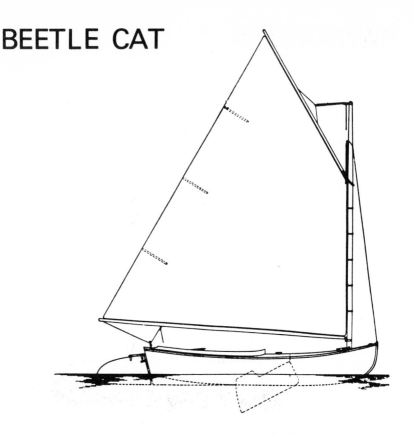

Design:	John Beetle, U.S.A. 1920
Supplier:	Concordia Co. Inc. U.S.A. Beetle Cat Association U.S.A.

Specifications:	*Construction:*	Wood
	LOA:	3.76m/12'4
	Beam:	1.83m/6'0
	Draft:	0.15m/6'' cb up
	Displ:	204kg/450 lbs

Fittings: Centreboard boat. Wooden spars. Hiking straps fitted.

Sails: Area 9.3m^2/100 sq.ft.

Rigging: Gaff

Price Guide: $1,165us

Summary: 2 crew. An American class, very popular in the north-east.

BLANDFORD BELL
CRUSING CANOE

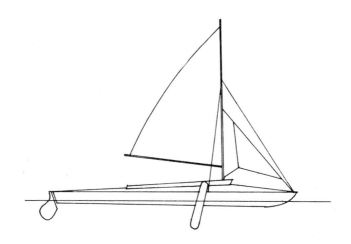

Design: Traditional, U.S.A.

Supplier: Not professionally built

Specifications: *Construction:*   Canvas skinned wood framework
                      LOA: 4.72m/15′6
                      Beam: 0.71m/2′4
                      Draft: 0.43m/1′5
                      Displ: 25kg/56 lbs

Fittings: Rudder-foot paddle operated.

Sails: Area 2.8m^2/30 sq.ft.

BLUENOSE

Design:	W. J. Roue, Canada
Supplier:	McVay Fiberglass Yachts Canada

Specifications:

Construction:	GRP
LOA:	7.16m/23'6
Beam:	1.88m/6'2
Draft:	1.07m/3'6
Displ:	953kg/2,100 lbs
Ballast:	403kg/887 lbs

Fittings:	Aluminium spars. Iron ballast.
Sails:	Area 19.7m^2/212 sq.ft.
Rigging:	Sloop
Price Guide:	$3,300us
Summary:	2 crew boat. Trailable and self-baling.

BROADS YACHT

Design:	Traditional English design.
Supplier:	Various

Specifications:

Construction:	Wood — Carvel
LOA:	6.1m—12.2m/20'—40'
Draft:	Various but shallow
Displ:	Various

Fittings:	Mast in a tall tabernacle
Rigging:	Gaff or Bermudan rigged
Price Guide:	Various
Summary:	A traditional Norfolk Broads yacht — not suitable for sea use.

BLUE CRAB

Design:	Harry R. Sindle, 1971
Supplier:	Newport Boats U.S.A. Blue Crab Association U.S.A.

Specifications:

Construction:	GRP
LWL:	3.00m/9'10
LOA:	3.38m/11'1
Beam:	1.65m/5'5
Draft:	0.08m/3'' cb up
Displ:	68kg/150 lbs

Fittings:	Aluminium spars. Daggerboard. Hiking straps fitted.
Sails:	Area 8.2m^2/88 sq.ft. Spinnaker area 7m^2/75 sq.ft.
Rigging:	Cat or sloop
Price Guide:	$700us
Summary:	An American boat used throughout the Continent. 2—3 crew. Self-rescuing with permanent foam flotation. A general purpose boat.

BLUE CREST

Supplier:	Norman Pearn England
Specifications:	*Construction:* GRP
	LOA: 3.71m/12'2
	Displ: 68kg/150 lbs
Fittings:	Keelboat. Wood trim.
Sails:	Area 7.4m^2/80 sq.ft.
Rigging:	Gunter
Price Guide:	£450
Summary:	Takes up to 4 adults. May be trailed. Outboard cannot be fitted.

BLUE JAY

Design:	Sparkman & Stephens, U.S.A. 1948
Supplier:	McNair Marine Inc. U.S.A. Blue Jay Association U.S.A.

Specifications:

Construction:	Wood or grp
LWL:	3.35m/11'0
LOA:	4.1m/13'6
Beam:	1.57m/5'2
Draft:	0.15m/6'' cb up
Displ:	124kg/275 lbs

Fittings: Centreboard boat. Aluminium or wooden spars. Hiking straps fitted. Teak or mahogany trim.

Sails: Area 8.36m²/90 sq.ft. Spinnaker area 11.6m²/125 sq.ft.

Rigging: Sloop

Price Guide: $1,500us

Summary: 2 crew. An enormously popular boat in the U.S.A. Well suited to racing and day sailing. Ideal for beginners. Kits available.

BOBBIN

Design:	Pearson Bros. U.K. 1969
Supplier:	Pearson Bros. U.K. Bobbin International Association England

Specifications:

Construction:	GRP choice of 2 colours.
LWL:	2.59m/8'6
LOA:	2.74m/9'0
Beam:	1.27m/4'2
Draft:	0.15m/6'' cb up
Displ:	34kg/75 lbs

Fittings:	Centreboard boat. Aluminium spars. Wooden kick-up rudder. Built-in buoyancy.
Variations:	Bobbin II also available — with an 3.35m/11'0 LOA.
Sails:	Area 5.6m^2/60 sq.ft. Terylene
Rigging:	Masthead sloop
Price Guide:	£160/$625us
Summary:	2 crew. Provides at modest cost, safe, simple boating for the whole family. A unique combination of sailboat and surfboard.

BOBTAIL

Design:	England
Supplier:	Norman Pearn England
Specifications:	*Construction:* GRP
	LOA: 2.54m/8'4
	Displ: 50kg/110 lbs
Fittings:	Centreboard boat.
Variations:	Outboard may be fitted.
Sails:	Area 3.7m^2/40 sq.ft.
Rigging:	Gunter
Price Guide:	On application
Summary:	3 crew. Outboard can be fitted. May be trailed and car-topped.

BUTTERBALL

Design:	Richards T. Miller, U.S.A. 1958
Supplier:	Richards T. Miller U.S.A.
Specifications:	*Construction:* Wood
	LOA: 2.9m/9'6
	Beam: 1.75m/5'9
	Draft: 0.14m/5'' cb up
	Displ: 68kg/150 lbs
Fittings:	Centreboard boat. Wooden spars.
Sails:	Area 4.5m^2/49 sq.ft. No spinnaker allowed
Rigging:	Una
Price Guide:	On application.
Summary:	Single-hander. Sailed mainly in the U.S.A. Kits not available.

CACTUS
One design

Design:	Regatta Plastics, U.S.A.
Supplier:	Cactus Association U.S.A.
Specifications:	*Construction:* GRP
	LOA: 3.05m/10'0
	Beam: 1.27m/4'2
	Draft: 0.76m/2'6
Fittings:	Aluminium spars
Sails:	Area 4.8m^2/52 sq.ft. No spinnaker permitted.
Rigging:	Una
Price Guide:	On application
Summary:	Single-hander. Self-rescuing. Kits and plans unavailable.

BUCCANEER

Design:	J. R. Macalpine-Downie, U.S.A. 1969
Supplier:	Marine Products U.S.A. Buccaneer Association U.S.A.
Specifications:	*Construction:* GRP
	LWL: 5.08m/16′8
	LOA: 5.49m/18′0
	Beam: 1.83m/6′0
	Draft: 0.17m/7″ cb up
	Displ: 227kg/500 lbs
Fittings:	Centreboard boat. Aluminium spars. Hiking straps fitted. Foam flotation.
Sails:	Area 16.3m²/175 sq.ft. Spinnaker area 16.5m²/178 sq.ft.
Rigging:	Sloop
Price Guide:	$2,000us
Summary:	2 crew. Sailed on the eastern lakes of the U.S.A.

CANADIAN SABOT

Design: 1931 approx., Canada

Supplier: Canadian Sabot Association Canada

Specifications: *Construction:* Wood and grp
LOA: 2.39m/7'10
Beam: 1.14m/3'9
Draft: 0.1m/4" cb up
Displ: 32kg/70 lbs

Fittings: Daggerboard. Wooden spars.

Sails: Area 4.3m^2/46 sq.ft.

Rigging: Una

Price Guide: $300us

Summary: Single-hander. A traditional day-dinghy design.

CAPE COD KNOCKABOUT

Design: Guerney and Fox, U.S.A. 1911-1958

Supplier: Cape Cod Knockabout Association, U.S.A.

Specifications: *Construction:* GRP or wood
LOA: 5.53m/18'2
Beam: 1.83m/6'0
Draft: 0.23m/9" cb up
Displ: 590kg/1,300 lbs

Fittings: Centreboard boat. Spars — aluminium or wood. Hiking straps fitted. Foam flotation.

Sails: Area 17.5m^2/188 sq.ft.
Spinnaker area 13.9m^2/150 sq.ft.

Rigging: Sloop

Price Guide: $3,320us

Summary: 2—3 crew. Self-rescuing. Kits and plans unavailable.

BULLS'EYE

Design:	Nathaniel Herreshoff U.S.A. 1914
Supplier:	Cape Cod Shipbuilding U.S.A. Bullseye Association U.S.A.
Specifications:	*Construction:* GRP *LOA:* 4.8m/15'9 *Beam:* 1.77m/5'10 *Draft:* 0.75m/2'5 *Displ:* 613kg/1,350 lbs *Ballast:* 340kg/750 lbs
Fittings:	Keelboat. Aluminium spars. Lead ballast. Teak trim. Bulkhead flotation.
Sails:	Area 13m^2/140 sq.ft. Spinnaker permitted.
Rigging:	Sloop
Price Guide:	$2,600us
Summary:	Trailable. 2 crew. Self-rescuing.

BUTTERFLY

Design: John A. Barnett, U.S.A. 1960

Supplier: Barnett Boat Co. U.S.A.

Specifications: *Construction:*   GRP
                   LOA: 3.66m/12'0
                   Beam: 1.37m/4'6
                   Draft: 0.38m/1'3
                   Displ: 62kg/137 lbs

Fittings: Daggerboard. Aluminium spars. Toe rails fitted.
                   Rotating boom.

Sails: Area 7m^2/75 sq.ft. 3–8oz. Dacron.

Rigging: Marconi

Price Guide: $700us

Summary: Single-hander. An American class — over 4,500 boats
                   in circulation. Very safe. Can be righted easily by one
                   person. Hull quick to accelerate and plane.

CAPE COD MERCURY

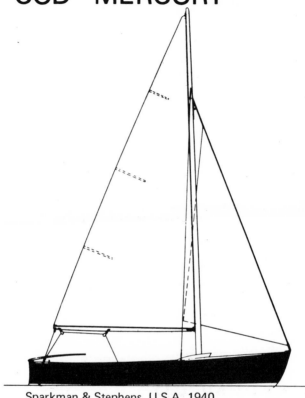

Design:	Sparkman & Stephens, U.S.A. 1940
Supplier:	Cape Cod Shipbuilding U.S.A. Cape Cod Mercury Association U.S.A.

Specifications:

Construction:	GRP
LOA:	4.57m/15'0
Beam:	1.66m/5'5
Draft:	0.75m/2'5" cb down
Displ:	331kg/730 lbs
Ballast:	136kg/300 lbs

Fittings:	Centreboard boat. Aluminium spars. Hiking straps fitted. Positive flotation tanks.
Sails:	Area 11.1m^2/119 sq.ft. Spinnaker area 6.3m^2/68 sq.ft.
Rigging:	Sloop
Price Guide:	$1,600us
Summary:	Very popular on the north-east coast of America. Trailable. Single-hander.

CAPRICE
Canada

Design:	Cuthbertson & Cassian, Canada 1966
Supplier:	Canadian Sailcraft Co. Canada Caprice World Association Canada
Specifications:	*Construction:* GRP *LOA:* 4.47m/14'8 *Beam:* 1.85m/6'1 *Draft:* 0.17m/7'' cb up *Displ:* 114kg/250 lbs
Fittings:	Centreboard boat. Aluminium spars. Hiking straps fitted. Foam flotation.
Sails:	Area 11.4m^2/123 sq.ft. Spinnaker area 15.8m^2/170 sq.ft.
Rigging:	Sloop
Price Guide:	$1,500us
Summary:	2 crew. Self-rescuing.

CHALLENGER

Design:	D. Pryke, England
Supplier:	Seamark-Nunn & Co. England
Rating:	Portsmouth yardstick 120
Specifications:	*Construction:* GRP *LWL:* 3.20m/10'6 *LOA:* 3.35m/11'0 *Beam:* 1.47m/4'10 *Draft:* 0.15m/6'' *Displ:* 68kg/150 lbs
Fittings:	Aluminium spars. Mast height 3.35m/11'0
Sails:	Area 6.4m^2/68 sq.ft.
Rigging:	Gunter
Price Guide:	£205
Summary:	Ideal boat for a small family. Takes 3 adults easily.

CAPE DORY 10

Design:	Andrew C. Vavolotis, U.S.A.
Supplier:	Cape Dory Co. U.S.A.

Specifications:

Construction:	GRP
LOA:	3.2m/10'6
Beam:	1.24m/4'1
Draft:	0.14m/5" cb up
Displ:	68kg/150 lbs

Fittings:	Centreboard boat. Aluminium spars. Mahogany trim. Styrofoam flotation.
Sails:	Area 6.3m^2/68 sq.ft.
Rigging:	Una
Price Guide:	$700us
Summary:	2 crew. An American class. Easy rowing, towing, outboard use. Perfect for clubs and schools.

CAPE DORY 14

Design:	Andrew C. Vavolotis, U.S.A.
Supplier:	Cape Dory Co. Inc. U.S.A.
Specifications:	*Construction:* GRP
	LOA: 4.42m/14'6
	Beam: 1.3m/4'3
	Draft: 0.15m/6'' cb up
	Displ: 91kg/200 lbs
Fittings:	Centreboard boat. Aluminium spars. Kick-up rudder. Mahogany trim.
Sails:	Area 7.9m²/85 sq.ft. No spinnaker.
Rigging:	Una
Price Guide:	$900us
Summary:	An American class. 2 crew. Rows, tows and outboards easily. Very safe for all the family

CAPRI CYCLONE 13

Design:	Frank Butler, U.S.A. 1971
Supplier:	Catalina Yachts U.S.A. Capri Cyclone Association U.S.A.

Specifications:	*Construction:*	GRP hand laid
	LOA:	3.96m/13'0
	Beam:	1.57m/5'2
	Draft:	0.91m/3'0 cb down
	Displ:	59kg/130 lbs

Fittings:	Centreboard boat. Aluminium spars. Foam flotation. Glassed rudder and centreboard.
Sails:	Area 7.4m^2/80 sq.ft.
Rigging:	Una
Price Guide:	$750us
Summary:	Single-hander. Self-bailing. A new class thus restricted in numbers at present. Self-rescuing.

CARAVELLE

Design:	France
Supplier:	Spair Marine France Larsson Trade U.S.A. Doornbos Holland

Specifications:

Construction:	GRP
LWL:	4.03m/13'3
LOA:	4.65m/15'3
Beam:	1.85m/6'0
Draft:	0.25m/10''
Displ:	230kg/429 lbs

Fittings:	Aluminium spars.
Variations:	Provision for oars and up to 6hp engine are included.
Sails:	Area 12.07m^2/132 sq.ft. Spinnaker area 14.70m^2/160 sq.ft.
Rigging:	Sloop
Price Guide:	$1,500/3,990 D.Fl.
Summary:	Takes up to 6 adults. A roomy day-sailer of traditional design.

CARDINAL

Design:	Winthrop Warner, U.S.A.
Supplier:	Regatta Plastics U.S.A. Cardinal Association U.S.A.

Specifications:

Construction:	GRP
LOA:	4.11m/13'6
Beam:	1.78m/5'10
Draft:	0.23m/9" cb up

Fittings:	Centreboard boat. Aluminium spars. Built-in buoyancy.
Sails:	Area 9m²/97 sq.ft. No spinnaker allowed.
Rigging:	Sloop
Price Guide:	On application.
Summary:	Restricted to the States. 2 crew. Kits available but not the plans.

CHAR

Design:	M. S. Redman, England
Supplier:	M. S. Redman Ltd., England
Specifications:	*Construction:* Chine ply
	LOA: 3.35m/11'0
	Displ: 54kg/120 lbs
Fittings:	Centreboard boat. Wooden spars.
Sails:	Area 6m²/65 sq.ft.
Rigging:	Una
Price Guide:	On application
Summary:	2/3 crew. Can be car-topped and trailed. Outboard may be fitted. An ideal tender.

CHARIOTEER

Supplier:	Devon Craft England
Specifications:	*Construction:* GRP
	LOA: 3.66m/12'0
	Displ: 82kg/180 lbs
Fittings:	Aluminium spars.
Sails:	Area 8.4m²/90 sq.ft.
Rigging:	Gunter rig
Price Guide:	£230
Summary:	Takes up to 4 crew. Auxiliary engine can be fitted.

CELEBRITY

Design:	Wester & Evanson, U.S.A. 1952
Supplier:	P. Evanson Yacht Co. U.S.A. Celebrity Association U.S.A.

Specifications:	*Construction:*	GRP
	LOA:	6.02m/19'9
	Beam:	1.93m/6'4
	Draft:	0.25m/10" cb up
	Displ:	363kg/800 lbs

Fittings:	Centreboard boat. Aluminium spars. Teak trim.
Variations:	Keel version also available
Sails:	Area 16m²/172 sq.ft.
Rigging:	Tabernacle rig for ease of stepping mast.
Price Guide:	$2,700us
Summary:	2 crew. Sailed in the east of America. Exceptionally stable, easy to handle and is very roomy. Kits and plans unavailable.

CHIC

Design:	Unknown, 1890
Supplier:	Chic Association U.S.A.
	Peter D. Van Done & Co. U.S.A.

Specifications:	*Construction:*	GRP
	LOA:	3.89m/12'9
	Beam:	1.42m/4'8
	Draft:	0.17m/7"

Fittings:	Wooden spars. Foam flotation.
Sails:	Area 14m^2/151 sq.ft.
Rigging:	Gaff
Price Guide:	$2,000us
Summary:	A popular, traditionally designed dinghy.

CHICKADEE

Design:	Bengt Johnson U.S.A.
Supplier:	Featherweight Marine U.S.A.

Specifications:	*Construction:*	GRP
	LOA:	3.25m/10'8
	Beam:	0.94m/3'1
	Draft:	0.66m/2'2

Fittings:	Wooden spars. Centreboard boat
Sails:	Area 3.7m^2/40 sq.ft.
	Spinnaker area 1.4m^2/15 sq.ft.
Rigging:	Una
Price Guide:	On application
Summary:	Single-hander. Self-rescuing.

CHALLENGER 15

Design:	Fred Ford U.S.A.
Supplier:	Leon F. Irish Co. U.S.A.
	Challenger 15 Association U.S.A.

Specifications:

Construction:	GRP
LWL:	4.27m/14.0
LOA:	4.57m/15'0
Beam:	1.68m/5'6
Draft:	0.17m/7"
Displ:	166kg/365 lbs

Fittings:	Centreboard boat. Aluminium spars. Hiking straps fitted. Positive flotation.
Sails:	Area 13.38m^2/144 sq.ft.
	Spinnaker area 18.6m^2/200 sq.ft.
Rigging:	Sloop
Price Guide:	$1,800us
Summary:	2 crew. An American class. Takes up to 6 adults.

CHORISTER

Supplier:	Harmony Boats U.K.
Specifications:	*Construction:* GRP or wood
	LOA: 2.9m/9'6
	Displ: 45kg/100 lbs
Fittings:	Centreboard boat
Sails:	Area 2.3m^2/25 sq.ft.
Rigging:	Gunter
Price Guide:	£110
Summary:	2 to 4 crew.

CL 11

Design:	Croce & Lofthouse, Canada 1968
Supplier:	C & L Boatworks Canada
	CL 11 Association Canada
Specifications:	*Construction:* GRP
	LOA: 3.43m/11'3
	Beam: 1.48m/4'10
	Draft: 0.2m/8" cb up
	Displ: 77kg/170 lbs
Fittings:	Centreboard boat. Aluminium spars. Hiking straps allowed. Foam flotation.
Sails:	Area 6.5m^2/70 sq.ft.
Rigging:	Sloop
Price Guide:	$825us
Summary:	2 crew. An all purpose boat that also performs well.

CHESAPEAKE BAY LOG CANOE

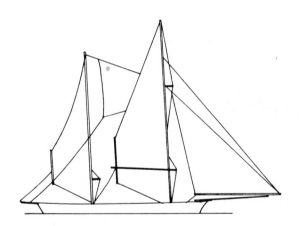

Design:	Traditional, U.S.A.	
Supplier:	Not professionally built	
Specifications:	*Construction:*	Wood
	LOA:	10.97m/36'0
	Beam:	2.13m/7'0
	Draft:	3.05m/10'0
Fitting:	Hollowed log hull. Centreboard boat	
Sails:	Optional areas	
Rigging:	Optional	
Summary:	Traditionally used as an oyster fishing boat	

CL 16

Design:	Croce & Lighthouse, Canada 1967
Supplier:	C & L Boatworks Canada CL 16 Association Canada
Specifications:	*Construction:* GRP *LOA:* 4.88m/16'0 *Beam:* 1.85m/6'1 *Draft:* 0.2m/8" cb up *Displ:* 166kg/365 lbs
Fittings:	Centreboard boat. Aluminium spars. Hiking straps and trapeze allowed. Foam flotation.
Sails:	Area 31.1m^2/141 sq.ft. Spinnaker area 18.6m^2/200 sq.ft. max.
Rigging:	Sloop
Price Guide:	$1,700 us
Summary:	2 crew. Larger version of the CL 11. This boat also performs well.

CLIPPER

Design:	Myron Spaulding, U.S.A. 1940
Supplier:	Clipper National Class Association U.S.A.
Specifications:	*Construction:* Wood *LOA:* 6.1m/20'0 *Beam:* 1.68m/5'6 *Draft:* 0.97m/3'2 *Displ:* 545kg/1,200 lbs *Ballast:* 295kg/650 lbs
Fittings:	Keelboat. Wooden spars.
Sails:	Area 15.8m^2/170 sq.ft. Spinnaker area 13.9m^2/150 sq.ft.
Rigging:	Sloop
Price Guide:	$1,600us
Summary:	Very restricted class on the west coast of America. Used boats only normally for sale. Trailable. Self-bailing. Single-hander

CHIPMUNK

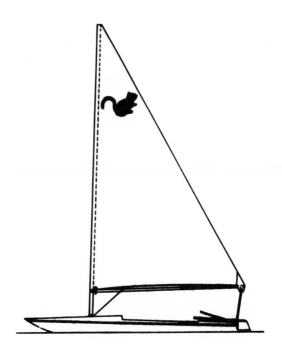

Design:	George O'Day & Ian Proctor England/U.S.A. 1970
Supplier:	Ian Procter England Gemico Corporation U.S.A.
Specifications:	*Construction:* Plastic *LOA:* 3.35m/11'0 *Beam:* 1.22m/4'0 *Draft:* 0.1m/4" cb up *Displ:* 30kg/65 lbs
Fittings:	Centreboard boat. Aluminium spars. Foam flotation.
Sails:	Area 5.2m^2/56 sq.ft.
Rigging:	Una
Price Guide:	$300us
Summary:	1 to 2 crew. Over 3,000 boats in circulation throughout the United States

COAST 13

Design:	Dan Naughton, U.S.A.
Supplier:	George Becker U.S.A.
Specifications:	*Construction:* Wood or grp
	LOA: 4.1m/13'5
	Beam: 1.5m/4'11
	Draft: 0.16m/6'' cb up
Fittings:	Wooden spars
Sails:	Area 9.7m^2/104 sq.ft. Spinnaker not official
Rigging:	Sloop
Price Guide:	On application
Summary:	Single-hander. Sailed only in western U.S.A. Self-rescuing. Kits not available but plans are

COB

Design:	M. S. Redman, England
Supplier:	M. S. Redman Limited England
Specifications:	*Construction:* Chine ply
	LOA: 2.44m/8'0
	Displ: 34kg/75 lbs
Fittings:	Centreboard boat. Wooden spars.
Variations:	Outboard can be fitted.
Sails:	Area 2m^2/21 sq.ft.
Rigging:	Bermudan sloop
Price Guide:	On application
Summary:	2 crew. Can be car-topped. An ideal 'first boat' for sailing and for tender work.

CHUB

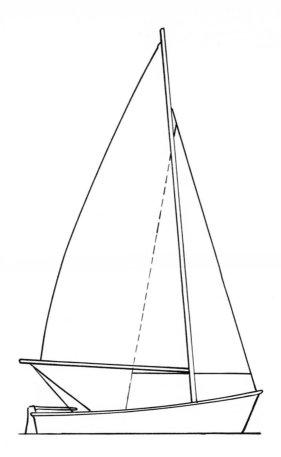

Design:	M. S. Redman England
Supplier:	M. S. Redman Limited England
Specifications:	*Construction:* Chine ply
	LOA: 2.44m/8'0
	Beam: 1.03m/3'4½
	Draft: 0.76m/2'6
	Displ: 41kg/90 lbs
Fittings:	Centreboard boat. Built-in buoyancy. Outboard hatch.
Sails:	Area 3.5m^2/38 sq.ft.
Rigging:	Bermudan sloop
Price Guide:	On application
Summary:	Single-hander. Designed especially to be built at home. Easy to construct.

COLUMBIA 22

Design:	William Crealock U.S.A. 1965
Supplier:	Columbia Yacht Corporation U.S.A. Columbia 22 National Association U.S.A.
Specifications:	*Construction:* GRP
	LOA: 6.71m/22'0
	Beam: 2.49m/8'2
	Draft: 1.07m/3'6
	Displ: 1,362kg/3,000 lbs
	Ballast: 457kg/1,006 lbs
Fittings:	Keelboat. Aluminium spars.
Sails:	Area 20.1m^2/224 sq.ft.
Rigging:	Sloop
Price Guide:	$5,000us
Summary:	Trailable. Self-bailing. 2 crew. Very popular all over the United States. Not in production at present

CONCORDIA SLOOP BOAT

Design:	Robert D. Culler, U.S.A. 1964
Supplier:	Concordia Co. Inc. U.S.A.
Specifications:	*Construction:* Wood
	LOA: 5.38m/17'8
	Beam: 1.52m/5'0
	Draft: 0.46m/1'6
	Displ: 454kg/1,000 lbs
Fittings:	Centreboard boat. Wooden spars. Foam flotation
Sails:	Area 15.4m^2/166 sq.ft.
Rigging:	Sloop
Price Guide:	$3,500us
Summary:	A traditional family daysailer.

C-LARK

Design:	Don Clark, 1964
Supplier:	Clark Boat Co. U.S.A. C-Lark Association U.S.A.
Specifications:	*Construction:* GRP *LWL:* 4.22m/13'10 *LOA:* 4.27m/14'0 *Beam:* 1.75m/5'9 *Draft:* 0.15m/6'' cb up *Displ:* 29kg/312 lbs
Fittings:	Centreboard boat. Aluminium spars.
Sails:	Area 12.4m^2/133 sq.ft. Spinnaker area 13m^2/140 sq.ft.
Rigging:	Sloop
Price Guide:	$1,300us
Summary:	Restricted to America. 2 crew. Engineered for high performance and durability. Very stable.

COMET

Design:	C. Lowndes Johnson, U.S.A. 1932
Supplier:	Comet Class Association U.S.A.
Specifications:	*Construction:* Wood and GRP
	LOA: 4.88m/16'0
	Beam: 0.91m/5'0
	Draft: 0.15m/6'' cb up
	Displ: 107kg/235 lbs
Fittings:	Centreboard boat. Wood and aluminium spars.
Variations:	Buoyancy required in GRP boats.
Sails:	Area 13m^2/140 sq.ft.
	No spinnaker allowed.
Rigging:	Sloop
Price Guide:	$1,750us
Summary:	2 crew. Kits not available but plans are. Sailed mainly on the east coast of America

CORNISH SEA KING

Design:	K. G. Kenchington, England 1973
Supplier:	Calmore Yacht Enterprises England
Specifications:	*Construction:* GRP
	LWL: 3.96m/13'0
	LOA: 4.57m/15'0
	Beam: 1.91m/6'3
	Draft: 0.15m/6''
Fittings:	Centreboard boat. Built-in buoyancy. Aluminium spars.
Sails:	Area 9.75m^2/105 sq.ft.
Rigging:	Ketch
Price Guide:	£375
Summary:	A safe, seaworthy family craft. Also good for fishing purposes

COPPERHEAD

Design:	J. R. Macalpine-Downie, U.S.A. 1970
Supplier:	Sail Manufacturing U.S.A.
Specifications:	*Construction:* GRP
	LOA: 4.19m/13'9
	Beam: 1.35m/4'5
	Draft: 0.1m/4'' cb up
	Displ: 61kg/135 lbs
Fittings:	Centreboard boat. Aluminium spars. Sprayed foam flotation.
Sails:	Area 7.9m^2/85 sq.ft.
Rigging:	Una
Price Guide:	$600us
Summary:	Single-hander. Self-bailing. Sailed in the States only at present

COTTONTAIL

Design:	Robert F. Matteson, U.S.A. 1959
Supplier:	Cottontail Association U.S.A.
Specifications:	*Construction:* GRP
	LOA: 4.84m/15'10
	Beam: 1.5m/4'11
	Draft: 0.28m/11'' cb up
	Displ: 125kg/275 lbs
Fittings:	Centreboard boat. Aluminium spars. Styrofoam flotation.
Sails:	Area $13m^2$/140 sq.ft. Spinnaker area $13m^2$/140 sq.ft.
Rigging:	Sloop
Price Guide:	$1,500us
Summary:	Single-hander. An American class. Trapeze and straps allowed.

CRESCENT

Design:	Richard C. Hill, U.S.A. 1953
Supplier:	M. E. Hill U.S.A. Crescent Sloop Class Association U.S.A.
Specifications:	*Construction:* GRP
	LOA: 7.32m/24'0
	Beam: 2.13m/7'0
	Draft: 1.24m/4'1
	Displ: 1,203kg/2,650 lbs
Fittings:	Keelboat. Aluminium spars. Foam flotation.
Sails:	Area $27.7m^2$/298 sq.ft. Spinnaker area $30.3m^2$/326 sq.ft.
Rigging:	Sloop
Price Guide:	$6,500us
Summary:	3 crew. Restricted to a small number in America. Kits and plans available.

CORONADO 15

Design:	Butler & Edgar, U.S.A. 1967
Supplier:	Capri Sailboats U.S.A. Coronado 15 Association U.S.A.
Specifications:	*Construction:* GRP *LWL:* 4.27m/14'0 *LOA:* 4.65m/15'3 *Beam:* 1.73m/5'8 *Draft:* 0.08m/3'' cb up *Displ:* 175kg/385 lbs
Fittings:	Centreboard boat. Aluminium spars. Foam and air tank flotation. Self-bailers.
Sails:	Area 12.9m^2/139 sq.ft.
Rigging:	Sloop
Price Guide:	$1,275us
Summary:	2 crew. Popular world-wide as an exciting racing sloop or as a comfortable day-sailer.

CROTCH ISLAND PINKY

Design:	Peter V. Van Dine, U.S.A. 1970
Supplier:	Peter V. Van Dine & Co. U.S.A.
Specifications:	*Construction:* GRP
	LOA: 6.45m/21'2
	Beam: 1.96m/6'5
	Draft: 0.51m/1'8
Fittings:	Centreboard boat. Wooden spars.
Sails:	Area 17.3m^2/186 sq.ft.
Price Guide:	$3,000us

CURLEW

Design:	Percy Blandford, England 1965
Supplier:	Percy Blandford England
Specifications:	*Construction:* Single chine plywood
	LOA: 2.74m/9'0
	Beam: 1.22m/4'0
Fittings:	No deck. Wooden spars.
Sails:	Area 4.6m^2/50 sq.ft.
Rigging:	Gunter sloop
Price Guide:	On application.
Summary:	Available in kit form. 1 or 2 crew. Used extensively as tenders to larger vessels.

CRESTWIND

Design:	Peter Milne, England 1971
Supplier:	Sears Roebuck & Co. U.S.A.
Specifications:	*Construction:* GRP
	LOA: 4.25m/13'11
	Beam: 1.52m/5'0
	Draft: 0.18m/7'' cb up
	Displ: 77kg/170 lbs
Fittings:	Centreboard boat. GRP spars. Foam flotation.
Variations:	Outboard can be added for pleasure boating.
Sails:	Area 7.7m^2/83 sq.ft.
Price Guide:	$800us
Summary:	Sturdy, safe and manoeuvrable

CYGNUS

Design:	George Hinterhoeller, U.S.A. 1963
Supplier:	Cygnus National Association Canada Clarkcraft Industries Canada
Specifications:	Construction: GRP *LOA:* 6.1m/20'0 *Beam:* 2.1m/6'10 *Draft:* 0.2m/8" cb up *Displ:* 429kg/945 lbs
Fittings:	Centreboard boat. Aluminium spars.
Sails:	Area $19.2m^2$/207 sq.ft. Spinnaker area $27.9m^2$/300 sq.ft.
Rigging:	Sloop
Price Guide:	$2,500us
Summary:	Found in small numbers world-wide. 2 crew. A day sailer/camper.

DABCHICK

Design:	Jack Koper, U.S.A. 1957
Supplier:	Dabchick International Association, South Africa Dabchick National Association U.S.A.
Specifications:	*Construction:* Wood or GRP *LOA:* 3.66m/12'0 *Beam:* 1.18m/3'10 *Draft:* 0.08m/3" cb up *Displ:* 39kg/85 lbs
Fittings:	Daggerboard. Wooden or aluminium spars. Foam flotation. Self-bailers.
Sails:	Area $5.6m^2$/60 sq.ft. No spinnaker
Rigging:	Sloop
Price Guide:	$595us
Summary:	Single-hander. Popular world-wide. Self-rescuing. Plans available.

CROSBY FAST CAT

Design:	Osterville Marine U.S.A. 1970
Supplier:	Osterville Marine Inc. U.S.A.
Specifications:	*Construction:* GRP
	LOA: 4.34m/14'3
	Beam: 1.93m/6'4
	Draft: 0.48m/1'7
Fittings:	Centreboard boat. Wooden spars. Foam flotation.
Sails:	Area 12.6m^2/136 sq.ft.
Rigging:	Una
Price Guide:	$3,700us
Summary:	A small American class. Self-bailing.

DART

Design:	Trevor Kirby, England
Supplier:	Kirby Marine & Industrial Plastics England
Specifications:	*Construction:* Wood or GRP
	LOA: 4.27m/14'0
	Beam: 1.52m/5'0
	Draft: 0.61m/2'0
	Displ: 91kg/200 lbs
Fittings:	Centreboard boat. Built-in buoyancy. Self-drain cockpit.
Variations:	Variable centreboard and mast positions.
Sails:	Area 9.3m^2/100 sq.ft.
Rigging:	Una
Price Guide:	On application.
Summary:	Ideal for the single-hander enthusiast. Fast, easy to handle. Can be trailed and car-topped. Underwater design means that light and heavy crews are at an equal advantage.

DELUXE SAIL

Design:	American Fiberglass Corporation U.S.A
Supplier:	American Fiberglass Corporation U.S.A.
Specifications:	*Construction:* GRP
	LOA: 2.49m/8'2
	Beam: 1.27m/4'2
	Draft: 0.61m/2'0
	Displ: 37kg/82 lbs
Fittings:	Centreboard boat. Aluminium spars. Foam flotation.
Sails:	Area 3.6m^2/39 sq.ft.
Rigging:	Cat
Price Guide:	$395us
Summary:	Single-hander. An American class. A class, round-chine design that allows comfortable sailing for 2 adults

CUB SCOW

Design:	Robert F. Holmgren, U.S.A. 1967
Supplier:	Seago Corporation U.S.A. Cub Scow Association U.S.A.
Specifications:	*Construction:* GRP *LWL:* 2.74m/9'0 *LOA:* 3.73m/12'3 *Beam:* 1.37m/4'6 *Draft:* 0.08m/3'' cb up *Displ:* 68kg/150 lbs
Fittings:	Centreboard boat. Aluminium spars. Swivel mast.
Sails:	Area 6.97m²/75 sq.ft.
Rigging:	Una
Price Guide:	$750us
Summary:	Single-hander. Self-bailing. Designed to race with the 12' cat-rigged Scow classes.

DAY SAILER

Design:	Uffa Fox, England 1958
Supplier:	O'Day Company U.S.A. Day Sailer Association U.S.A.
Specifications:	*Construction:* GRP *LOA:* 5.11m/16'9 *Beam:* 1.91m/6'3 *Draft:* 0.17m/7'' cb up *Displ:* 261kg/575 lbs
Fittings:	Centreboard boat. Aluminium spars. Positive foam flotation.
Sails:	Area 13.5m^2/145 sq.ft. Spinnaker permitted.
Rigging:	Sloop
Price Guide:	$1,900us
Summary:	2 crew. Popular worldwide. Kits and plans unavailable. Seaworthy and strong. Easily righted. About 7,000 boats in circulation

DEVON DAYBOAT
DEVON YAWL

Design:	Devon Craft Limited England
Supplier:	Devon Craft England
Rating:	Portsmouth yardstick 104
Specifications:	*Construction:* GRP
	LOA: 4.88m/16'0
	Beam: 1.88m/6'2
	Draft: 0.28m/11"
	Displ: 499kg/1,100 lbs
Fittings:	Lead Ballast. Mast 7.74m/24'6 high. ¾ decked
Variations:	Dayboat also available with forward shelter. Auxiliary can be fitted.
Sails:	Area 13.9m^2/150 sq.ft.
Rigging:	Bermudan yawl
Price Guide:	£700 £800
Summary:	Takes up to 6 crew. Designed to fill the gap between the racing dinghy and family tub. Lively in light airs.

DIDDI

Supplier:	Modular Flotation U.K.
Specifications:	*Construction:* GRP
	LOA: 2.44m/8'0
	Displ: 81kg/178 lbs
Fittings:	Centreboard boat. Aluminium spars
Sails:	Area varies
Rigging:	Sloop
Price Guide:	£100
Summary:	2 crew. A true general purpose dinghy.

DINK

Design:	L. S. Herreshoff, U.S.A.
Supplier:	Buzzards Bay Boats U.S.A.
Specifications:	*Construction:* GRP handlaid
	LOA: 2.46m/8'1
	Beam: 1.09m/3'7
	Displ: 40kg/89 lbs
Fittings:	Centreboard boat. Aluminium spars.
Variations:	Outboard may be attached.
Sails:	Area 3.4m^2/37 sq.ft.
Rigging:	Una
Price Guide:	$419us
Summary:	All purpose dinghy. Carries 3 adults.

DEVON DORY

Design:	G. P. Palmer, England
Supplier:	South Devon Boatbuilders England

Specifications:	Construction:	Wood
	LWL:	3.05m/10'0
	LOA:	3.55m/11'8
	Beam:	1.27m/4'2
	Draft:	0.10m/1'4
	Displ:	64kg/140 lbs

Fittings:	Centreboard boat. Wooden spars.
Variations:	4.27m/14' version also available.
Sails:	Area 3.72m^2/40 sq.ft.
Rigging:	Una
Price Guide:	£150
Summary:	Takes 3 crew. Kits available. General purpose dinghy of traditional design, based on flat bottomed, double-ended boats. Very practical.

DOLMEN

Supplier:	Comextra U.K.
Specifications:	*Construction:* GRP
	LOA: 4.06m/13'4
	Displ: 68kg/150 lbs
Fittings:	Aluminium spars.
Sails:	Area 10.2m^2/110 sq.ft.
Price Guide:	£280
Summary:	Takes 4. A general purpose boat.

DOODLE

Design:	Furman L. Shaw Jnr., U.S.A. 1968
Supplier:	Shaw Craft U.S.A.
Specifications:	*Construction:* GRP
	LOA: 4.32m/14'2
	Beam: 1.35m/4'5
	Draft: 0.15m/6'' cb up
	Displ: 79kg/175 lbs
Fittings:	Daggerboard. Aluminium spars. Styrofoam flotation.
Sails:	Area 9.8m^2/105 sq.ft.
Rigging:	Sloop
Price Guide:	$800us
Summary:	Self-bailing. An American class, sailed on the east coast

DISCOVERER

Design:	Joseph V. Puccia, U.S.A. 1966	
Supplier:	Annapolis Sailboat Builders U.S.A.	
	Discoverer Association U.S.A.	
Specifications:	*Construction:*	GRP
	LWL:	4.98m/16'4
	LOA:	5.36m/17'7
	Beam:	1.93m/6'4
	Draft:	0.23m/9'' cb up
	Displ:	295kg/650 lbs
Fittings:	Centreboard boat. Aluminium spars. Teak trim.	
	Positive flotation.	
Sails:	Area 15.3m^2/165 sq.ft.	
	No spinnaker	
Rigging:	Sloop	
Price Guide:	$2,100us	
Summary:	Single-hander. Sailed in the east of America. A stable	
	comfortable day-sailer sloop with excellent perfor-	
	mance. Can be used as an overnight camper	

DOLPHIN 17

Design:	Glen & Murry Corcorran U.S.A. 1972
Supplier:	National Dolphin 17 Association U.S.A.

Specifications:

Construction:	GRP
LOA:	5.11m/16'9
Beam:	1.83m/6'0
Draft:	0.2m/8" cb up

Fittings:	Centreboard boat. Aluminium spars. Air tanks flotation. Self-bailing
Sails:	Area 15.1m^2/163 sq.ft. Spinnaker area 25.1m^2/270 sq.ft.
Rigging:	Sloop
Price Guide:	$2,175us
Summary:	2 to 3 crew. An American class, restricted in numbers

DRASCOMBE DRIVER

Design:	John Watkinson England
Supplier:	Honnor Marine England

Specifications:

Construction:	GRP
LOA:	5.50m/18'0
Beam:	1.88m/6'1½
Draft:	0.43m/1'5
Displ:	360kg/800 lbs

Fittings:	Centreboard boat. Wooden spars. Watemeta engine.
Sails:	Area 12.4m^2/133 sq.ft.
Rigging:	Lug
Price Guide:	£975

DOLPHIN

Supplier:	Fibrocell Limited England
Specifications:	*Construction:* GRP
	LOA: 2.39m/7'10
	Beam: 1.22m/4'0
	Displ: 45kg/100 lbs
Variations:	Outboard may be fitted — up to 4 hp.
Sails:	Area 4.3m^2/46 sq.ft.
Rigging:	Una
Price Guide:	£105
Summary:	2 crew. Can be car-topped.

DOLPHIN SAILER

Design:	England	
Supplier:	H. H. Marine England	
Specifications:	*Construction:*	GRP
	LOA:	1.22m/4'0
	Beam:	2.28m/7'6
	Draft:	0.10m/4''
	Displ:	45kg/100 lbs
Fittings:	Centreboard boat. Built-in buoyancy. Mast 3.66m/12'0 high.	
Sails:	Area 3.7m^2/40 sq.ft.	
Rigging:	Una	
Price Guide:	£100	
Summary:	Ideal for youngsters to learn the rudiments of sailing. Easily rigged.	

DOUGHDISH

Design:	N. G. Herreshoff, U.S.A. 1914	
Supplier:	Doughdish Inc. U.S.A.	
Specifications:	*Construction:*	PVC foam sandwich GRP
	LWL:	3.81m/12'6
	LOA:	4.82m/15'10
	Beam:	1.78m/5'10
	Draft:	0.76m/2'6
	Displ:	681kg/1,500 lbs
	Ballast:	334kg/735 lbs
Fittings:	Lead ballast. Sitka spruce spars.	
Sails:	Area 13m²/140 sq.ft.	
Rigging:	Sloop	
Price Guide:	$3,700us	
Summary:	Carries up to 6 adults. Easy to maintain. High resale value.	

DUET

Supplier:	J. Dunhill U.K.
Specifications:	*Construction:* GRP
	LOA: 3.05m/10'0
	Displ: 59kg/130 lbs
Sails:	Optional
Rigging:	Bermudan sloop
Price Guide:	£160
Summary:	Takes 4.

DUO

Design:	M. Roland, U.S.A.
Supplier:	Duo Association U.S.A.
Specifications:	*Construction:* GRP
	LOA: 4.34m/14'3
	Beam: 1.85m/6'1
	Draft: 1.37m/4'6
Fittings:	Aluminium spars.
Sails:	Area $13m^2$/140 sq.ft.
	Spinnaker allowed.
Rigging:	Sloop
Price Guide:	On application
Summary:	2 crew. Self-rescuing. Trapeze used.

DRASCOMBE DABBER

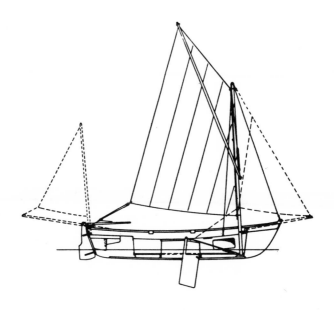

Design:	John Watkinson, England
Supplier:	Honnor Marine England
Est. Rating:	Unknown
Specifications:	*Construction:* GRP
	LWL: 4.27m/14'0
	LOA: 4.72m/15'6
	Beam: 1.79m/5'10
	Draft: 0.20m/8"
	Displ: 120kg/550 lbs
Fittings:	Centreboard boat. Teak trim. Mast 4.30m/14'0 high. Wooden spars.
Variations:	Can be rowed. Outboard may be fitted.
Sails:	Area 10.79m^2/116 sq.ft. (Sprit main) 10.97m^2/118 sq.ft. (Lug main) Dark tan terylene.
Rigging:	Sprit
Price Guide:	£550/$2,200+
Summary:	Design based on the traditional long and straight keeled clinker built beachboats used by fishermen. Tough and versatile.

DRASCOMBE LONGBOAT

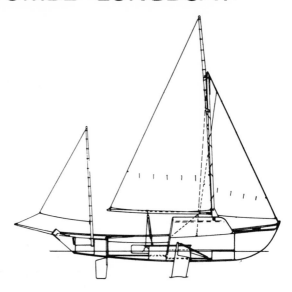

Design:	John Watkinson, England	
Supplier:	Honnor Marine England	
Rating:	Provisional Portsmouth yardstick 111	
Specifications:	*Construction:*	GRP
	LWL:	5.64m/18'6
	LOA:	6.63m/21'9
	Beam:	1.83m/6'7
	Draft:	0.30m/1'0
	Displ:	499kg/1,100 lbs
Fittings:	Keelboat. Teak trim. Wooden spars. Outboard engine.	
Interior:	2 berths. 0.91m^2/3'0 headroom.	
Variations:	Optional canvas shelter. Optional layouts.	
Sails:	Area 13.65m^2/147 sq.ft. (yawl) Tan Terylene	
Rigging:	Yawl standard. Others available.	
Price Guide:	£950/$3,500+	
Summary:	Won the Dayboat of the Show Award at the 1973 London Boat Show. Ideal for owners needing a boat suitable for day cruising with shelter for occasional night stops.	

DRASCOMBE LUGGER

Design: John Watkinson England

Supplier: Honnor Marine, England
John Elliot England

Rating: Provisional Portsmouth yardstick 115

Specifications: *Construction:* Wood or GRP
LOA (GRP): 5.72m/18'9
LOA (Wood): 5.64m/18'6
Beam: 1.91m/6'3
Draft: 0.23m/10''
Displ (Wood): 362.88kg/800 lbs
Displ (GRP): 385.50/850 lbs

Fittings: Centreboard boat. Built-in buoyancy. Wooden spars.

Sails: Area 10.609m^2/113 sq.ft.

Rigging: Yawl

Price Guide: £795/$2,700+

Summary: Handles well under power or sail and makes an ideal inshore fishing boat. Open layout allows a crew of up to 6 adults.

DURAFLOAT 2.40

Supplier:	Clearex Plastics U.K.	
Specifications:	*Construction:*	ABS/plastic
	LOA:	2.39m/7'10
	Beam:	1.22m/3'11¾
	Draft:	0.46m/1'6
	Displ:	41.73kg/92 lbs

Fittings: Centreboard boat. Mast 3.87m/12'8½ high

Variations: Up to 2 hp engine can be fitted.

Sails: Area 2.7m^2/29 sq.ft.

Rigging: Una

Price Guide: £100

Summary: Takes 3. Safe, strong and light.

DURAFLOAT 3.10

Design:	Colin Mudie, England	
Supplier:	Clearex Plastics England	
Specifications:	*Construction:*	ABS plastic polyurethane foam
	LWL:	2.74m/9'0
	LOA:	3.10m/10'2
	Beam:	1.37m/4'6
	Draft:	0.18m/7''
	Displ:	59kg/162 lbs
Fittings:	Centreboard boat. Mast 4.93m/16'2 high.	
Variations:	Up to 6hp engine can be attached.	
Sails:	Area 4.55m^2/49 sq.ft.	
Rigging:	Una	
Price Guide:	£100+	
Summary:	Light, safe and easily transportable dinghy.	

DY 10

Supplier: Daley Yacht & Boat Co. Limited England

Specifications: *Construction:* GRP
LOA: 3.12m/10'3
Beam: 1.35m/4'5
Draft: 0.52m/1'8½

Fittings: Mast — aluminium. Mahogany finish.

Sails: Area 4.8m^2/52 sq.ft.

Rigging: Bermudan

Price Guide: On application.

Summary: A general purpose dinghy for day sailing and fishing. Kits can be supplied. Sturdy and seaworthy.

DYER DHOW 7 9

Design: W. J. H. Dyer, U.S.A. 1946

Supplier: The Anchorage Inc. U.S.A.

Specifications: *Construction:* GRP
LOA: 2.36m/7'9
Beam: 1.22m/4'0
Draft: 0.08m/3" cb up
Displ: 35kg/78 lbs

Fittings: Daggerboard. Wooden spars. Foam flotation.

Sails: Area 3.3m^2/35 sq.ft.

Rigging: Una

Price Guide: $590us

Summary: An enormously popular boat in America. Unsinkable.

DURAFLOAT 3.60

Supplier:	Clearex Plastics England	
Specifications:	*Construction:*	ABS
	LOA:	3.60m/11'8
	Beam:	1.40m/4'8
	Draft:	0.58m/1'11
	Displ:	67kg/160 lbs

Fittings: Centreboard boat. Mast 4.93m/16'2 high

Variations: Outboard may be fitted — up to 10hp.

Sails: Area 4.55m^2/49 sq.ft.

Rigging: Una

Price Guide: £150

Summary: G/P dinghy that can be car-topped and trailed. Takes up to 5 crew.

DUSTER

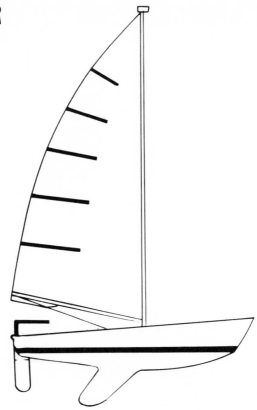

Design:	Owen Merrill, U.S.A.
Supplier:	Thomas Scott U.S.A. Duster Association U.S.A.

Specifications:

Construction:	Wood or GRP
LOA:	4.22m/13'10
Beam:	1.37m/4'6
Draft:	0.08m/3'' cb up
Displ:	100kg/220 lbs

Fittings: Centreboard boat. Wood or aluminium spars. Positive flotation.

Sails: Area 10.9m^2/117sq.ft. No spinnaker allowed.

Rigging: Una

Price Guide: $1,000us

Summary: Single-hander. An American class. Self-rescuing. Trapeze used. Plans available.

DYER DELTA 19

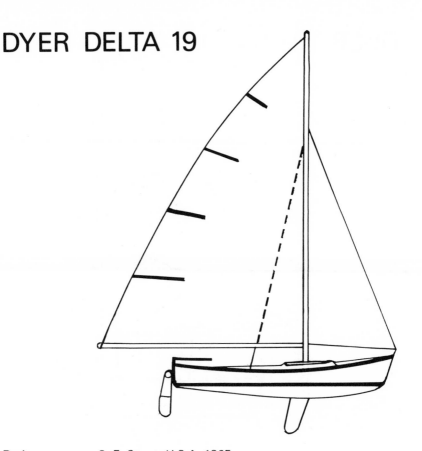

Design:	C. F. Street, U.S.A. 1965
Supplier:	Charles Street, U.S.A. Dyer Delta 19 Association U.S.A. The Anchorage U.S.A.

Specifications:

Construction:	GRP
LOA:	5.72m/18'9
Beam:	1.85m/6'1
Draft:	0.15m/6" cb up
Displ:	250kg/550 lbs

Fittings:	Centreboard boat. Aluminium spars. Positive flotation.
Sails:	Area 17.7m^2/190 sq.ft. Spinnaker area 11.1m^2/120 sq.ft.
Rigging:	Sloop
Price Guide:	$2,500us
Summary:	Only 12 in use in America at present.

DYER DHOW 9'

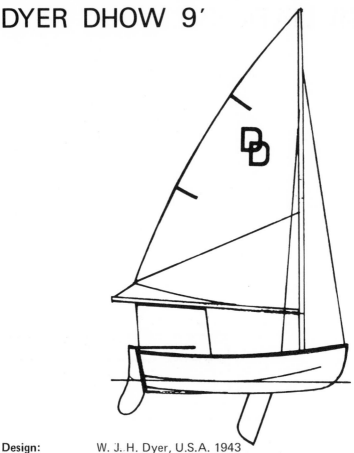

Design:	W. J. H. Dyer, U.S.A. 1943
Supplier:	The Anchorage Inc. U.S.A.
	Dyer Dhow 9' Association U.S.A.

Specifications:

	Construction:	GRP
	LOA:	2.74m/9'0
	Beam:	1.35m/4'5
	Draft:	0.1m/4'' cb up
	Displ:	47kg/104 lbs

Fittings:	Centreboard boat. Spars — wood or aluminium
Sails:	Area 4.2m^2/45 sq.ft.
	No spinnaker allowed.
Rigging:	Una
Price Guide:	$660us
Summary:	Single-hander. Ideal for beginners and for frost-biting.
	Unsinkable.

DYER DHOW 12 ½

Design:	W. J. H. Dyer, U.S.A. 1945
Supplier:	The Anchorage Co. U.S.A. Dyer Dhow 12½ Association U.S.A.
Specifications:	*Construction:* GRP *LOA:* 3.81m/12'6 *Beam:* 1.52m/5'0 *Draft:* 0.13m/5" cb up *Displ:* 89kg/195 lbs
Fittings:	Centreboard boat. Aluminium spars. Positive flotation.
Sails:	Area 8.5m²/91 sq.ft. Spinnaker area 8.4m²/90 sq.ft.
Rigging:	Una
Price Guide:	$1,060us
Summary:	An American class. 2 crew.

EAU VIVE

Design:	J. M. L'Hermenier, France 1967
Supplier:	SEB France William Russell & Co. U.S.A.

Specifications:	*Construction:*	GRP
	LWL:	4.45m/14'7
	LOA:	5.18m/17'0
	Beam:	1.98m/6'6
	Draft:	0.48m/1'7
	Displ:	409kg/900 lbs

Fittings:	Centreboard boat. Aluminium spars. Positive flotation. Self-bailing
Sails:	Area 12.7m^2/137 sq.ft. Spinnaker area 75.6m^2/248 sq.ft.
Rigging:	Sloop
Price Guide:	7,500 Fr. f.
Summary:	2 crew. Straps and trapeze used by crew.

ECONO SAIL

Design:	American Fiberglass Corporation U.S.A.
Supplier:	American Fiberglass Corporation U.S.A.

Specifications:	*Construction:*	GRP
	LOA:	2.13m/7'0
	Beam:	1.27m/4'2
	Displ:	43kg/95 lbs

Fittings:	Centreboard boat. Aluminium spars. Foam flotation.
Sails:	Area 3.3m^2/35 sq.ft.
Rigging:	Una
Price Guide:	$280us
Summary:	Single-hander. A very popular small general purpose dinghy in America

DYER DINK 10

Design:	Philip L. Rhodes, U.S.A. 1934

Supplier:	The Anchorage Co. U.S.A. Dyer Dink Association U.S.A.

Specifications:	*Construction:*	GRP
	LOA:	3.05m/10'0
	Beam:	1.37m/4'6
	Draft:	0.13m/5'' cb up
	Displ:	61kg/135 lbs

Fittings:	Centreboard boat. Aluminium spars. Positive flotation.

Sails:	Area 6.1m^2/66 sq.ft. No spinnaker allowed.

Rigging:	Una
Price Guide:	$850us
Summary:	Sailed all over America. Single-hander.

ELFIN

Supplier:	Robin Elsdale Limited England
Specifications:	*Construction:* GRP and wood
	LOA: 2.52m/8'3
	Displ: 63kg/140 lbs
Sails:	Various
Rigging:	Una
Price Guide:	On application
Summary:	1 or 2 crew. Can be trailed and car-topped

FLIPPER

Design:	Pyle & Quigg, U.S.A. 1965
Supplier:	Lea Craft U.K.
	Newport Boats U.S.A.
	Flipper Association U.S.A.
Specifications:	*Construction:* GRP
	LOA: 2.44m/8'0
	Beam: 1.22m/4'0
	Draft: 0.05m/2'' cb up
	Displ: 34kg/75 lbs
Fittings:	Daggerboard. Aluminium spars. Foam flotation.
Sails:	Area 2.5m^2/27 sq.ft.
	No spinnaker
Rigging:	Una
Price Guide:	£130/$400us
Summary:	Single-hander. Neither kits or plans available. Self-rescuing and self-bailing.

EAST WIND 13

Supplier:	Larship Yachts U.S.A.	
Specifications:	*Construction:*	GRP
	LOA:	4.06m/13'4
	Beam:	1.58m/5'2
	Draft:	0.1m/4''
	Displ:	136kg/300 lbs
Fittings:	Centreboard boat. Kick-up rudder.	
Sails:	Area 9.7m^2(6.9 + 2.8)/104 sq.ft. (74 + 30)	
Rigging:	Sloop	
Price Guide:	$1,000us	
Summary:	Family daysailer.	

FAMILY 15

Supplier:	Richard Dadson, England
Specifications:	*Construction:* Wood
	LOA: 4.57m/15'0
Fittings:	Centreboard boat. Wooden spars.
Variations:	Outboard may be attached.
Sails:	Area 11.1m^2/120 sq.ft.
Rigging:	Bermudan sloop
Price Guide:	£550
Summary:	Can be trailed. Carries up to 5 crew.

FI-GLASS 10

Supplier:	Figlass Limited England
Specifications:	*Construction:* GRP
	LOA: 3.15m/10'4
	Displ: 54kg/120 lbs
Fittings:	Centreboard boat. Aluminium spars.
Variations:	Outboard may be attached.
Sails:	Area 6.3m^2/68 sq.ft.
Rigging:	Gunter
Price Guide:	On application.
Summary:	Can be trailed and car-topped. A general purpose boat.

ELEVEN PLUS

Design:	Eric Parkin, England 1969
Supplier:	Dobson Yacht & Boatbuilders England
Rating:	Portsmouth yardstick 115
Specifications:	*Construction:* Double chine plywood or GRP
	LOA: 3.37m/11'0½
	Beam: 1.39m/4'7
	Draft: 0.18m/7''
	Displ: 66kg/145 lbs
Fittings:	Centreboard boat. Wooden spars. GRP or plywood deck. Stepped mast on foredeck — 5.33m/17'6 high Rolled side-decks.
Variations:	Can be rowed or powered by an outboard.
Sails:	Area 6.5m^2/70 sq.ft.
Rigging:	Bermudan sloop
Price Guide:	On application.
Summary:	2 crew. Suitable for racing and family sailing. Safe, dry seaboat that planes readily.

EL TORO

Design:	MacGregor, U.S.A. 1939
Supplier:	Sidney Co. U.S.A. El Toro International Association U.S.A.
Specifications:	*Construction:* Wood or grp *LOA:* 2.42m/7'11 *Beam:* 1.17m/3'10 *Draft:* 0.08m/3" cb up *Displ:* 36kg/80 lbs
Fittings:	Centreboard boat. Wooden spars. Positive flotation.
Sails:	Area 3.7m^2/40 sq.ft. No spinnaker.
Rigging:	Una
Price Guide:	$300–500us/$300 for kit.
Summary:	Sailed exclusively throughout America. Kits and plans available.

EXPLORER YW

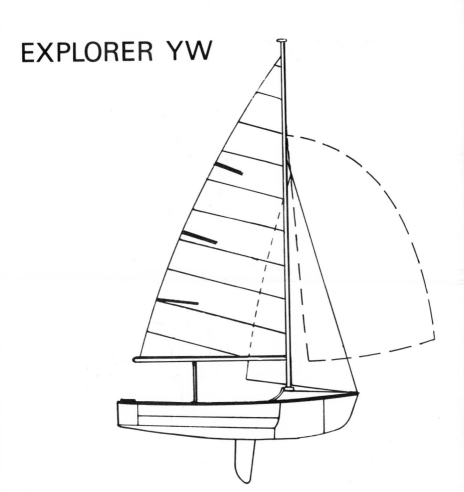

Design:	Jack Holt, England
Supplier:	Jack Holt England
Specifications:	*Construction:* GRP
	LOA: 4.47m/14'9
	Beam: 1.72m/5'8
	Draft: 1.07m/3'6
	Displ: 132kg/290 lbs
Sails:	Area 10.2m²/110 sq.ft.
Rigging:	Sloop
Price Guide:	On application.
Summary:	All purpose, one design boat. Very stable. Ideal for clubs.

FLIPPER SCOW

Design:	Peer Bruun, Denmark
Supplier:	Lakesport Boats Limited Canada Russell Marine Limited England

Specifications:

	Construction:	GRP
	LOA:	3.96m/13'3
	Beam:	1.27m/4'4
	Draft:	0.10m/2'8
	Displ:	70kg/155 lbs

Fittings:	Centreboard boat. Aluminium spars. Built-in buoyancy. Mast 5.49m/18'0 high.
Variations:	Outboard can be fitted.
Sails:	Area $10m^2$/108+ sq.ft. Spinnaker area $7.9m^2$/85 sq.ft.
Rigging:	Bermudan sloop
Price Guide:	£250 £300
Summary:	2 crew. A fast 'fun' dinghy. Trapeze can be fitted. Can be car-topped and trailed. Kits available.

FLITE 12

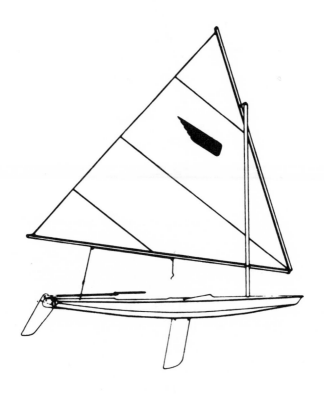

Design:	AMF Alcort U.S.A.
Supplier:	AMF Alcort U.S.A. Flite 12 Association U.S.A.
Specifications:	*Construction:* GRP *LOA:* 3.58m/11'9 *Beam:* 1.17m/3'10 *Displ:* 34kg/75 lbs
Fittings:	Daggerboard. Aluminium spars. Foam flotation.
Sails:	Area 6m^2/65 sq.ft.
Rigging:	Una
Price Guide:	$400us
Summary:	Single-hander.

FLYINGFISH

Design:	Pyle & Quigg, U.S.A. 1967
Supplier:	D. Bruce Connolly U.S.A.
Specifications:	*Construction:* GRP
	LOA: 4.27m/14'0
	Beam: 1.73m/5'8
	Draft: 0.13m/5" cb up
	Displ: 116kg/255 lbs
Fittings:	Centreboard boat. Aluminium spars. Flexible mast.
Sails:	Area 11.1m²/120 sq.ft.
Rigging:	Una
Price Guide:	$1,300us
Summary:	Single-hander. Sailed mainly in the U.S.A. Ideal combination of speed, ease of handling and minimum upkeep. A good travelling boat.

FLYING SCOT

Design:	Gordon K. Douglass, U.S.A. 1957
Supplier:	Customflex Inc., U.S.A. Flying Scot Association U.S.A.
Specifications:	*Construction:* GRP *LOA:* 5.79m/19'0 *Beam:* 2.06m/6'9 *Draft:* 0.2m/8'' cb up *Displ:* 352kg/775 lbs
Fittings:	Centreboard boat. Aluminium spars. Teak trim. Foam flotation.
Sails:	Area 17.7m^2/191 sq.ft. Spinnaker area 18.6m^2/200 sq.ft.
Rigging:	Sloop
Price Guide:	$2,600us
Summary:	Restricted, on the whole, to America. Comfortable and roomy for day-sailing and fast in racing conditions. Strict one-design rules.

FLYING TERN

Design:	E. G. Van de Stadt, Holland 1955
Supplier:	North American Flying Tern Association U.S.A.
Specifications:	*Construction:* GRP
	LOA: 4.27m/14'0
	Beam: 1.6m/5'3
	Draft: 0.1m/4" cb up
	Displ: 130kg/286 lbs
Fittings:	Centreboard boat. Wood and aluminium spars. Air tanks and foam flotation.
Sails:	Area 11.1m^2 (7.4 + 3.7)/120 sq.ft. (80 + 40) Spinnaker area 15.6m^2/168 sq.ft.
Rigging:	Sloop
Price Guide:	$1,175us
Summary:	2 crew. Self-rescuing. Neither kits or plans available. Hiking straps used.

FOAM CREST

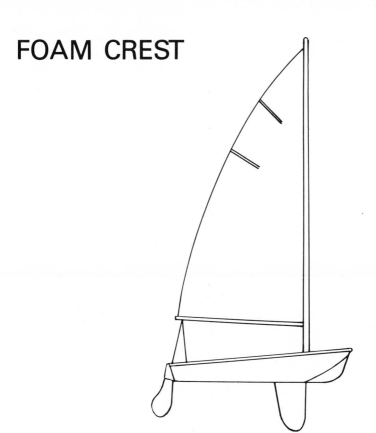

Design:	Percy Blandford, England 1970
Supplier:	Not professionally built.
Specifications:	*Construction:* GRP or single chine plywood
	LOA: 3.66m/12'0
	Beam: 1.52m/5'0
Fittings:	Centreboard boat. Wood or GRP deck. Spars — wooden or metal.
Variations:	Either open or decked dinghy
Sails:	Area 6.1m^2/66 sq.ft. or 7.4m^2/80 sq.ft.
Rigging:	Balanced lug or gunter sloop or Bermudan sloop
Price Guide:	Available in kit form only.
Summary:	2 or 3 crew. V-bottomed frameless, general purpose dinghy.

FORCE 5

Design:	AMF Alcort, U.S.A. 1972
Supplier:	D. Bruce Connolly U.S.A.
Specifications:	*Construction:* GRP
	LOA: 4.25m/13'11
	Beam: 1.47m/4'10
	Displ: 64kg/140 lbs
Fittings:	Daggerboard. Aluminium spars. Foam flotation.
Sails:	Area 8.5m^2/91 sq. ft.
Rigging:	Una
Price Guibe:	$850us

4.45

Design:	Simoun France 1968
Supplier:	Gouteron France New England Sailboat Co. U.S.A. 4.45 International Association France
Specifications:	*Construction:* GRP *LOA:* 4.47m/14'8 *Beam:* 1.75m/5'9 *Draft:* 0.13m/5'' cb up *Displ:* 110kg/242 lbs
Fittings:	Centreboard boat. Aluminium spars.
Sails:	Area $11.1m^2$ (7.7 + 3.4)/120 sq. ft. (83 + 37) Spinnaker area $13m^2$/140 sq.ft.
Rigging:	Sloop
Price Guide:	4,320 Fr. f./$1,100us
Summary:	Sailed mainly in France.

GAUNTLET

Design:	Nathaniel Herreshoff, U.S.A.	
Supplier:	Cape Cod Shipbuilding Co. Limited U.S.A.	
Specifications:	*Construction:*	GRP
	LWL:	5.59m/18'4
	LOA:	6.1m/20'0
	Beam:	1.98m/6'6
	Draft:	1.14m/3'9
	Ballast:	136kg/300 lbs
Fittings:	Keelboat. Aluminium spars.	
Sails:	Area 19.7m^2/212 sq.ft.	
Rigging:	Sloop	
Price Guide:	$2,800 us	
Summary:	An impressive sailing dinghy that carries up to 5 crew.	

GEARY 18

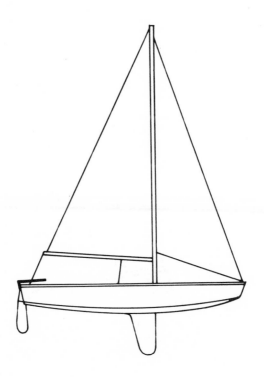

Design:	Ted Geary, U.S.A. 1927
Supplier:	Clark Boat Co. U.S.A. Geary 18 International Y.R.A., U.S.A.
Specifications:	*Construction:* Wood or grp *LOA:* 5.49m/18'0 *Beam:* 1.6m/5'3 *Draft:* 0.15m/6'' cb up *Displ:* 238kg/525 lbs
Fittings:	Centreboard boat. Spars — aluminium or wood. Foam flotation.
Sails:	Area 14.7m^2(10.6 + 4.1)/158 sq.ft. (114 + 44) No spinnaker allowed.
Rigging:	Sloop
Price Guide:	$1,500us
Summary:	Single-hander. Kits and plans available. Self-rescuing Not in production at present.

GEMINI
U.S.A.

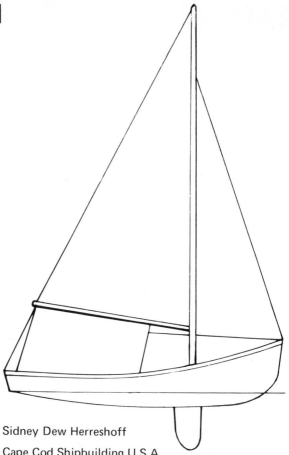

Design: Sidney Dew Herreshoff

Supplier: Cape Cod Shipbuilding U.S.A.
                      Gemini Association U.S.A.

Specifications: *Construction:*   GRP
                      LWL: 4.5m/14'9
                      LOA: 4.9m/16'1
                      Beam: 1.7m/5'7
                      Draft: 0.17m/7" cb up
                      Displ: 200kg/440 lbs

Fittings: Twin centreboards. Aluminium spars. Air and foam
                      flotation.

Sails: Area 13m^2 (8.8 + 4.2)/140 sq.ft. (95 + 45)
                      No spinnaker allowed.

Rigging: Sloop

Price Guide: $1,780us

Summary: 2 crew. Kits and plans unavailable.

GHIBLI

Design:	France.
Supplier:	Gouteron S.a., France
Specifications:	*Construction:* GRP
	LWL: 5.40m/17'8½
	LOA: 6.60m/21'8
	Beam: 2.45m/8'0½
	Draft: 0.80m/2'7½
Fittings:	Centreboard boat. Aluminium spars.
Sails:	Area 20m^2/215 sq.ft.
Rigging:	Sloop
Price Guide:	19,700 Fr. f.

GHOST 13

Design:	George Larsen U.S.A. 1964
Supplier:	Janus Plastics Co. Inc. Ghost 13 National Association U.S.A.
Specifications:	*Construction:* GRP *LOA:* 3.96m/13'0 *Beam:* 1.52m/5'0 *Draft:* 0.15m/6'' cb up *Displ:* 73kg/160 lbs
Fittings:	Centreboard boat. Aluminium spars. Foam flotation. Self-bailers.
Sails:	Area 9.8m^2 (6.5 + 3.3)/105 sq.ft. (70 + 35) Spinnaker area 13m^2/140 sq.ft.
Rigging:	Open
Price Guide:	$900us
Summary:	2 crew. Trapeze and straps used. Sailed only in America at present. Self-rescuing. Kits and plans unavailable. One of the most versatile family sailboats ever developed.

GIG

Design: Seek Brandon, U.S.A. 1967

Supplier: The Dinghy Shop U.S.A.
                      Gig Association U.S.A.

Specifications: *Construction:*   GRP
                      LOA: 2.82m/9'3
                      Beam: 1.45m/4'9
                      Draft: 0.48m/1'7
                      Displ: 66kg/145 lbs

Fittings: Centreboard boat. Aluminium spars. Positive flotation.

Sails: Area 5.2m^2/56 sq.ft.
                      No spinnaker allowed.

Rigging: Una

Price Guide: On application

Summary: Single-hander. General purpose tender.

GLASTRON ALPHA

Design: William Carter, U.S.A.

Supplier: Glastron Alpha Association U.S.A.

Specifications: *Construction:* GRP
LOA: 4.57m/15′0
Beam: 1.27m/4′2
Displ: 77kg/170 lbs

Fittings: Centreboard boat. Alumimium spars. Positive flotation.

Sails: Area 9.1m^2/98 sq.ft.

Rigging: Una

Price Guide: On application

Summary: Single-hander, Sailed only in south-eastern U.S.A. at present.

GRAMPIAN 17

Design: Ian Proctor U.K. 1971

Supplier: Grampian Marine, U.S.A.

Specifications: *Construction:* GRP
LOA: 5.03m/16′6
Beam: 1.88m/6′2
Draft: 0.2m/8′′ cb up
Displ: 250kg/550 lbs

Fittings: Centreboard boat. Aluminium spars. Styrofoam flotation.

Sails: Area 14.1m^2 (10.9 + 3.2)/152 sq. ft. (117 + 35)
Spinnaker area 16.1m^2/173 sq. ft.

Rigging: Sloop

Price Guide: $1,570us

Summary: 2 crew.

GOBLIN

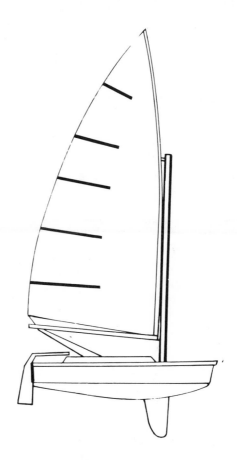

Design: Percy Blandford, England 1962

Supplier: Percy Blandford England

Specifications: *Construction:*   Single chine plywood
                    LOA: 3m/9'10
                    Beam: 1.37m/4'6

Fittings: Wooden spars. Plywood foredeck.

Sails: Area $5.8m^2$/62 sq.ft.

Rigging: Una balance lug or gunter sloop.

Price Guide: On application

Summary: 2 crew. Can be car-topped. Family resemblance to the smaller Gremlin.

GREAT PELICAN

Design:	William H. Short, U.S.A. 1969
Supplier:	Great Pelican Association U.S.A.
Specifications:	*Construction:* Plywood
	LOA: 4.88m/16'0
	Beam: 2.44m/8'0
	Draft: 0.1m/4'' cb up
	Displ: 218kg/480 lbs
Fittings:	Centreboard boat. Wooden spars. Foam flotation.
Sails:	Area 17.4m^2 (12 + 5.4)/187 sq.ft. (129 + 58)
Rigging:	Sloop
Price Guide:	$2,000us
Summary:	2 crew. A small class sailed only in America.

GRUMMAN 17

Design:	Grumman Aircraft Engineering U.S.A.
Supplier:	Grumman Boats U.S.A.
Specifications:	*Construction:* Aluminium
	LOA: 5.18m/17'0
	Beam: 0.91m/3'0
	Displ: 53kg/117 lbs
Fittings:	Centreboard boat. Aluminium spars. Positive flotation.
Sails:	Area 6m^2/65 sq.ft.
Rigging:	Una
Price Guide:	On application.
Summary:	A sailing canoe based on traditional design.

GRENADIER

Design:	New England Sailboat Co. U.S.A. 1971
Supplier:	New England Sailboat Co. U.S.A.
Specifications:	*Construction:* GRP
	LOA: 3.51m/11'6
	Beam: 1.55m/5'1
	Draft: 0.13m/5'' cb up
	Displ: 80kg/177 lbs
Fittings:	Centreboard boat. Aluminium spars. Air tanks and positive foam flotation.
Sails:	Area 7.9m² (6 + 1.9)/85 sq. ft. (65 + 20) Spinnaker area 8.8m²/95 sq. ft.
Rigging:	Sloop
Price Guide:	$800us
Summary:	2 crew. Straps and trapeze used. Can be car-topped. Self-bailing.

GULF COAST 10

Design:	Earl Maudlin, U.S.A. 1969
Supplier:	Gulf Coast Sailboats U.S.A.
Specifications:	*Construction:* GRP
	LOA: 3.05m/10'0
	Beam: 1.37m/4'6
	Draft: 0.15m/6'' cb up
	Displ: 54kg/120 lbs
Fittings:	Daggerboard. Aluminium spars. Air tank flotation.
Variations:	Gulf Coast 14 version also available.
Sails:	Area 4.6m^2/50 sq.ft.
Rigging:	Una
Price Guide:	$495us
Summary:	Single-hander. Sailed only in America, where it is a popular 'fun' dinghy.

GULF COAST 15

Design:	Martin Bludworth, U.S.A. 1968
Supplier:	Gulf Coast Sailboats, U.S.A.
Specifications:	*Construction:* GRP
	LOA: 4.57m/15'0
	Beam: 1.78m/5'10
	Draft: 0.17m/7'' cb up
	Displ: 160kg/350 lbs
Fittings:	Centreboard boat. Aluminium spars. Foam flotation.
Variations:	Gulf Coast 20' version also available, which is a 2-man boat.
Sails:	Area 11.3m^2 (7.6 + 3.7)/122 sq.ft. (82 + 40) Spinnaker area 11.1m^2/120 sq.ft.
Rigging:	Sloop
Price Guide:	$1,235us (15')/$2,400us (20')
Summary:	Single-hander. An American class.

GRUMMAN DINGHY

Design:	Philip Rhodes, U.S.A.
Supplier:	Grumman Boats U.S.A.
Specifications:	*Construction:* Aluminium
	LOA: 2.59m/8'6
	Beam: 1.27m/4'2
	Draft: 0.15m/6''
	Displ: 56kg/124 lbs
Fittings:	Centreboard boat. Aluminium spars.
Variations:	Available also in a rowing version.
Sails:	Area 4.6m^2/50 sq.ft.
Rigging:	Una
Price Guide:	$650
Summary:	Single-hander. Well finished.

HAMPTON

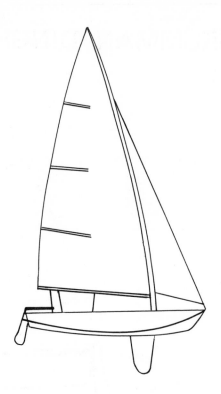

Design:	Vincent J. Serio, U.S.A. 1934

Supplier:	Hampton OD Association, U.S.A.

Specifications:

Construction:	Wood or grp
LOA:	5.49m/18'0
Beam:	1.78m/5'10
Draft:	0.17m/7'' cb up
Displ:	227kg/500 lbs

Fittings: Centreboard boat. Wood or aluminium spars. Self-bailing.

Sails: Area 17.7m^2 (13 + 4.7)/190 sq.ft. (140 + 50) No spinnaker allowed

Rigging: Open

Price Guide: $2,300us

Summary: 2 crew. Straps and trapeze used. Kits and plans available.

GRUMMAN FLYER

Design:	William Shaw, U.S.A. 1966
Supplier:	Rockwell & Newell Inc U.S.A.
Specifications:	*Construction:* Aluminium
	LOA: 4.93m/16'2
	Beam: 2.03m/6'8
	Draft: 0.17m/7" cb up
	Displ: 159kg/350 lbs [
Fittings:	Centreboard boat. Aluminium spars. Positive flotation.
Sails:	Area 13.8m^2/149 sq.ft. Spinnaker area 18.6m^2/200 sq.ft.
Rigging:	Sloop
Price Guide:	On application
Summary:	2 crew. Straps and trapeze used. Self-rescuing.

HANDY CAT 14

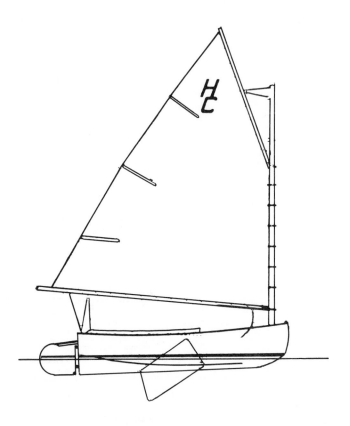

Design:	Merle Hallett, U.S.A.
Supplier:	Cape Dory Co. U.S.A.
Specifications:	*Construction:* GRP
	LWL: 4.06m/13'4
	LOA: 4.27m/14'0
	Beam: 2.03m/6'8
	Draft: 0.3m/1.0
	Displ: 340kg/750lbs
Fittings:	Centreboard boat. Spruce spars. Foam flotation
Sails:	Area 13.1m^2/14.1 sq ft
Rigging:	Una
Price Guide:	$2,700us
Summary:	A dry day sailer, built on traditional cat boat lines. Can be trailed.

HERRESHOFF S

Design:	Nathaniel Herreshoff, U.S.A.
Supplier:	Herreshoff S. National Association, U.S.A.
Specifications:	*Construction:* Wood
	LOA: 8.38m/27'6
	Beam: 2.19m/7'2
	Draft: 1.47m/4'10
Fittings:	Keelboat. Wooden spars.
Sails:	Area 39.6m^2/426 sq.ft.
Rigging:	Sloop
Price Guide:	$4,000us (secondhand)
Summary:	Exclusive American class — most popular on the East coast. 3 crew. Not in production.

HIGHLANDER

Design:	Gordon Douglass, U.S.A. 1951
Supplier:	Douglass & McLeod Inc., U.S.A. Highlander Association, U.S.A.

Specifications:

Construction:	GRP
LWL:	5.87m/19'3
LOA:	6.1m/20'0
Beam:	2.03m/6'8
Draft:	0.2m/8'' cb up
Displ:	377kg/830 lbs

Fittings:	Centreboard boat. Aluminium spars. Positive flotation.
Sails:	Area 20.9m^2/225 sq.ft. Spinnaker area 21.4m^2/230 sq.ft.
Rigging:	Sloop
Price Guide:	$2,800us
Summary:	3 crew allowed. Kits available. A good combination of roominess, stability and performance. Up to 10 adults can be carried.

HOBBITT

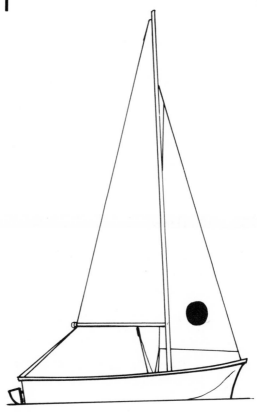

Supplier:	Cumberland Boat Co., England
Specifications:	*Construction:* GRP
	LWL: 3.47m/11'4½
	LOA: 4.0m/13'1½
	Beam: 1.27m/4'2
	Draft: 1.0m/3'3½
	Displ: 61kg/135 lbs
Fittings:	Centreboard boat. 6.5m/21'4 Holt Allen aluminium mast.
Sails:	Area 11.30m^2/122 sq.ft. Terylene
Rigging:	Sloop
Price Guide:	£200
Summary:	Carries 3 adults with comfort. Sails close to the wind and comes about easily.

HUSTLER

Design:	Charles D. Mower, U.S.A.
Supplier:	Hustler Association, U.S.A.
Specifications:	*Construction:* Wood or GRP
	LOA: 5.49m/18'0
	Beam: 1.98m/6'6
	Draft: 0.25m/10'' cb up
Fittings:	Centreboard boat. Wooden spars. Positive flotation.
Sails:	Area 16.7m^2/180 sq.ft.
	No spinnaker allowed.
Rigging:	Una
Price Guide:	On application
Summary:	2 crew. Plans available. Sailed in the north-east of America only

INTERNATIONAL DEVELOPMENT CLASS

Supplier:	International Development Class Association, England
Sails:	Area 15m^2/161 sq. ft.
	Spinnaker area 14m^2/151 sq. ft.
Summary:	Restricted class.

HOBBYSTAR

Design:	Metzeler, Germany
Supplier:	Metzeler, Germany

Specifications:

Construction:	Inflatable Hypalon
LOA:	3.48m/11'5
Beam:	1.32m/4'4

Fittings:	Metal spars. Fitted with a rudder and supplementary keels
Sails:	Area 9.48m^2/102 sq.ft.
Rigging:	Sloop
Price Guide:	£150+
Summary:	Inflatable dinghy. Carries 2—4 adults. Can be sailed seriously.

HOLIDAY

Design:	Harry R. Sindle, U.S.A. 1967

Supplier:	Newports Boats, U.S.A. Holiday Class Association, U.S.A.

Specifications:

Construction:	GRP
LWL:	5.36m/17'7
LOA:	5.94m/19'6
Beam:	2m/6'7
Draft:	0.2m/8" cb up
Displ:	254kg/560 lbs

Fittings: Centreboard boat. Aluminium spars. Positive flotation.

Sails: Area 16.1m^2 (10.4 + 5.7)/173 sq.ft. (112 + 61)
Spinnaker area 20m^2/215 sq.ft.

Rigging: Sloop

Price Guide: $2,100us

Summary: 2–3 crew. Sailed in America only. A well-mannered, good looking family sailboat.

INDIAN

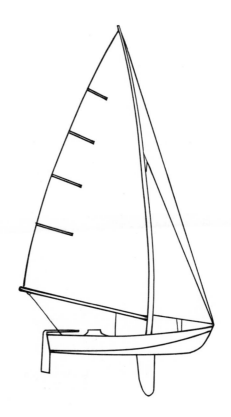

Design:	John Alden, U.S.A. 1921
Supplier:	Indian Class Association, U.S.A.
Specifications:	*Construction:* Wood
	LOA: 6.4m/21'0
	Beam: 1.83m/6'0
	Draft: 0.46m/1'6
Fittings:	Centreboard boat. Wooden spars. Foam flotation.
Sails:	Area 22.3m^2/240 sq.ft.
	Spinnaker area 12.5m^2/135 sq.ft.
Rigging:	Sloop
Price Guide:	$1,000us approx. (secondhand)
Summary:	Not in production currently, so only secondhand boats available. An American class. 3 crew. Plans available

INTERCLUB

Design:	Sparkman & Stephens, Canada	
Supplier:	O'Day, U.S.A.	
Specifications:	*Construction:*	GRP
	LOA:	3.51m/11'6
	Beam:	1.39m/4'7
	Draft:	0.13m/5" cb up
Fittings:	Centreboard boat. Aluminium spars. Positive foam flotation.	
Sails:	Area 6.7m^2/72 sq.ft.	
Rigging:	Una	
Price Guide:	$795us	
Summary:	2 crew. An American class.	

INTERDANE 404

Design:	Peer Bruun, Denmark 1968
Supplier:	Dane-Craft, U.S.A. Interdane 404 Association, U.S.A.

Specifications:

Construction:	GRP
LOA:	4.06m/13'4
Beam:	1.32m/4'4
Draft:	0.1m/4'' cb up
Displ:	70kg/154 lbs

Fittings:	Centreboard boat. Aluminium spars. Foam flotation.
Sails:	Area 10.2m^2 (7.2 + 3)/110 sq.ft. (77 + 33) Spinnaker area 8.2m^2/88 sq.ft.
Rigging:	Sloop
Price Guide:	$990us
Summary:	2 crew. Straps and trapeze used. Easy for the novice to handle yet sensitive to the touch of experienced sailors.

INTERLAKE

Design:	Francis Sweisguth, U.S.A. 1932
Supplier:	Customflex Inc., U.S.A.

Specifications:

Construction:	GRP
LWL:	4.65m/15'3
LOA:	5.49m/18'0
Beam:	1.91m/6'3
Draft:	0.2m/8" cb up
Displ:	295kg/650 lbs

Fittings:	Centreboard boat. Aluminium spars. GRP rudder.
Sails:	Area 16.3m^2/175 sq.ft. 5 oz. Dacron.
Rigging:	Sloop
Price Guide:	$2,275us
Summary:	2 crew. Fine racing qualities and a comfortable, easily managed day-sailer. Exceptional speed in light air. Sailed all over the United States

INTERNATIONAL 21

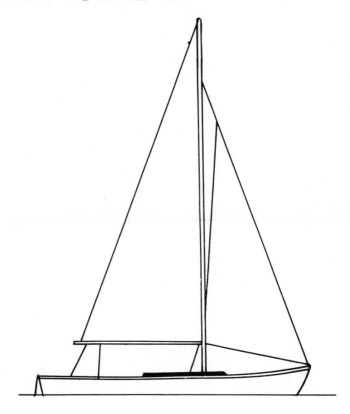

Design:	Hodgdon Brothers, U.S.A.
Supplier:	International 21 Association, U.S.A.
Specifications:	*Construction:* GRP
	LOA: 6.4m/21'0
	Beam: 1.75m/5'9
	Draft: 1.14m/3'9
	Displ: 908kg/2,000 lbs
	Ballast: 499kg/1,100 lbs
Fittings:	Keelboat. Aluminium spars. Flotation tanks.
Sails:	Area 18.6m^2/200 sq.ft.
	Spinnaker area 16.4m^2/177 sq.ft.
Rigging:	Sloop
Price Guide:	On application.
Summary:	2 to 3 crew. Small American class

INTERNATIONAL ONE-DESIGN

Design:	Bjarne Aas, Denmark 1936
Supplier:	Vincent Monte—Sano, U.S.A. International O.D. International Association, U.S.A.

Specifications:	*Construction:*	Wood or GRP
	LOA:	10.19m/33'5
	Beam:	2.06m/6'9
	Draft:	1.62m/5'4
	Displ:	3,042kg/6,700 lbs
	Ballast:	1,861kg/4,100 lbs

Fittings:	Keelboat. Wooden or aluminium spars. Lead ballast.
Sails:	Area 42.8m^2/461 sq.ft. Spinnaker area 42.8m^2/461 sq.ft.
Rigging:	Sloop
Price Guide:	$12,000us
Summary:	4 to 6 crew. Worldwide class restricted in nimbers

JAVELIN

Design:	John Spencer, U.S.A. 1965
Supplier:	John Kennedy, U.S.A.

Specifications:	*Construction:*	Wood
	LOA:	4.27m/14'0
	Beam:	1.68m/5'6
	Draft:	0.13m/5'' cb up
	Displ:	66kg/145 lbs

Fittings:	Centreboard boat. Wood or aluminium spars. Positive flotation. Self-bailing.
Sails:	Area 18.6m^2/200 sq.ft.
Rigging:	Sloop
Price Guide:	On application.
Summary:	2 crew. Straps and trapeze used. About 4,000 in circulation throughout the world.

INTERNATIONAL 210

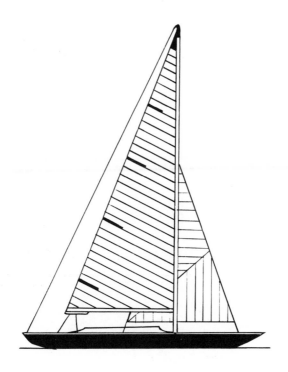

Design:	C. Raymond Hunt, U.S.A. 1949
Supplier:	International 210 Association, U.S.A.
Specifications:	*Construction:* Wood or GRP
	LOA: 9.09m/29'10
	Beam: 1.78m/5'10
	Draft: 1.17m/3'10
	Displ: 1,044kg/2,300 lbs
Fittings:	Keelboat. Wooden spars. Positive flotation.
Sails:	Area 28.3m²/305 sq. ft. Spinnaker area 37.2m²/400 sq. ft.
Rigging:	Sloop
Price Guide:	$4,000 approx. (secondhand)
Summary:	3 crew. Popular American class — most boats purchased secondhand.

JAVELIN

Design:	Uffa Fox, U.K. 1961
Supplier:	Paul Wright, U.K. O'Day, U.S.A. Javelin Class Association, U.S.A.
Specifications:	*Construction:* GRP *LOA:* 4.27m/14'0 *Beam:* 1.73m/5'8 *Draft:* 0.15m/6'' cb up *Displ:* 216kg/475 lbs
Fittings:	Centreboard boat. Aluminium spars. Foam flotation.
Sails:	Area 11.6m^2/125 sq.ft. Spinnaker area 8.4m^2/90 sq.ft.
Rigging:	Sloop
Basic Price:	£600/$1,650us
Summary:	2 crew. Majority sailed in the States. Built for safe, family sailing.

JET 14

Design:	Howard Siddons, U.S.A. 1954
Supplier:	J. M. McClintock & Co., U.S.A.
Specifications:	*Construction:* GRP
	LOA: 4.27m/14'0
	Beam: 1.42m/4'8
	Draft: 0.15m/6'' cb up
	Displ: 129kg/285 lbs
Fittings:	Centreboard boat. Aluminium spars. Air and foam flotation. Self-bailing.
Sails:	Area 10.5m² (8.5 + 2)/113 sq.ft. (91 + 22) Spinnaker area 20m²/215 sq.ft.
Rigging:	Sloop
Price Guide:	$1,365us
Summary:	2 crew. Built only in America. Self-rescuing.

JOLLY BOAT DINGHY

Design:	Seek Brandon, U.S.A. 1936
Supplier:	The Dinghy Shop, U.S.A. Jolly Boat Dinghy National Association, U.S.A.
Specifications:	*Construction:* GRP *LOA:* 2.54m/8'4 *Beam:* 1.27m/4'2 *Draft:* 0.1m/4'' cb up *Displ:* 50kg/110 lbs
Fittings:	Centreboard boat. Aluminium spars. Foam flotation.
Sails:	Area 5.2m^2/56 sq.ft.
Rigging:	Una
Price Guide:	On application
Summary:	Single-hander. A small fun pram dinghy that is safe for youngsters.

JOLLY YARE

Design:	Seek Brandon, U.S.A. 1961
Supplier:	Jolly Yare Association, U.S.A.
Specifications:	*Construction:* GRP *LOA:* 3.86m/12'8 *Beam:* 1.58m/5'2 *Draft:* 0.13m/5'' cb up *Displ:* 79kg/175 lbs
Fittings:	Centreboard boat. Aluminium spars. Positive flotation.
Variations:	Jolly Yare Junior also available — LOA: 3.1m/10'2 — designed in 1964
Sails:	Area 9.4m^2 (6.3 + 3.1)/101 sq.ft. (68 + 33) No spinnaker allowed.
Rigging:	Sloop
Price Guide:	$970us
Summary:	Single-hander.

JETWIND

Design:	Jack Riggleman, U.S.A. 1969
Supplier:	Sears, Roebuck & Co., U.S.A.
	Seawind Sailing Association, U.S.A.
Specifications:	*Construction:* ABS
	LWL: 4.11m/13'6'
	LOA: 4.22m/13'10
	Beam: 1.24m/4'1
	Draft: 0.1m/4" cb up
	Displ: 54kg/120 lbs
Fittings:	Centreboard boat. Aluminium spars. Foam flotation. Double over-lap hull.
Sails:	Area 7.6m^2/82 sq.ft. Polyester.
Rigging:	Una
Price Guide:	$500us
Summary:	Fast, stable and virtually maintenance free.

KENN ELEVEN
REDONDO ELEVEN

Design:	Peter Nethercroft, England
Supplier:	Plycraft, England
Rating:	Portsmouth yardstick 114

Specifications:

Construction:	Hard chine plywood
LOA:	3.35m/11'0
Draft:	0.91m/3'0
Displ:	70kg/155 lbs

Fittings: Centreboard boat. Completely instayed mast. Built-in buoyancy tanks.

Sails: Area 4.6m^2/50 sq.ft. (una)
Area 7m^2/75 sq.ft. (sloop)

Rigging: Bermudan sloop or Una rig.

Price Guide: £150

Summary: Lively and interesting to sail and compares well with other eleven footers. Known as Redondo 11 in America, Kenn 11 in U.K. and Europe.

KID TRAINER

Design:	Christian Maury, France
Supplier:	Comextra, U.K. L. Lanaverre S.A., Holland
Specifications:	*Construction:* GRP *LWL:* 3.78m/12'5 *LOA:* 4.04/13'3 *Beam:* 1.46m/4'9 *Draft:* 0.15m/6'' *Displ:* 89kg/195 lbs
Fittings:	Centreboard boat. Aluminium spars.
Sails:	Area 9.3m^2/100 sq.ft.
Rigging:	Bermudan sloop
Price Guide:	£280
Summary:	2 crew.

KNICKERBOCKER

Design:	Sparkman & Stephens, U.S.A. 1961
Supplier:	Knickerbocker National Association, U.S.A.
Specifications:	*Construction:* GRP
	LOA: 8m/26'3
	Beam: 2m/6'7
	Draft: 1.35m/4'5
Fittings:	Keelboard. Aluminium spars. Positive flotation.
Sails:	Area 31.5m^2/339 sq.ft.
Rigging:	Sloop
Price Guide:	$3,000+
Summary:	An American class.

KOHINOOR

Design:	Murray Wright
Supplier:	Kohinoor Association, U.S.A.
Specifications:	*Construction:* Wood
	LOA: 4.65m/15'3
	Beam: 1.83m/6'0
	Draft: 0.23m/9'' cb up
Fittings:	Centreboard boat. Wooden spars.
Sails:	Area 13.5m^2/145 sq.ft.
	No spinnaker allowed.
Rigging:	Sloop
Price Guide:	$1,600+
Summary:	2 crew. An American class. Sailed only in the north-eastern States

KING FISHER

Design:	Phil Rhodes, American Fiberglass Corporation, U.S.A.
Supplier:	American Fiberglass Corporation, U.S.A.
Specifications:	*Construction:* GRP
	LOA: 3.64m/11'11
	Beam: 1.42m/4'8
	Draft: 0.2m/8'' cb up
	Displ: 114kg/250 lbs
Fittings:	Centreboard boat. Aluminium kick-up rudder. Mast aluminium 5.49m/18'0 high. Foam flotation.
Sails:	Area 7.4m^2/80 sq.ft.
Rigging:	Sloop
Price Guide:	$895us
Summary:	Designed with the novice in mind. Will seat 4 in comfort.

KITE

Design:	Carter Pyle, U.S.A. 1963
Supplier:	Browning Newport Division, U.S.A.
	Kite Association, U.S.A.

Specifications:

Construction:	Epoglass
LWL:	3.33m/10'11
LOA:	3.53m/11'7
Beam:	1.52m/5'0
Draft:	0.13m/5'' cb up
Displ:	93kg/205 lbs

Specifications: Daggerboard. Wooden spars. Flexible instayed mast. Foam flotation.

Sails: Area 7.2m^2/78 sq.ft.
No spinnaker allowed.

Rigging: Una

Price Guide: $960us

Summary: Single-hander. Self-bailing.

KORALLE

Design:	Atlanta Bootsbau Germany
Supplier:	Koralle/East Inc., U.S.A. Koralle Association, U.S.A.
Specifications:	*Construction:* Wood or GRP *LOA:* 4.27m/14'0 *Beam:* 1.42m/4'8 *Draft:* 0.1m/4'' cb up *Displ:* 77kg/170 lbs
Fittings:	Bilgeboards. Spars — wood or aluminium. Positive flotation.
Sails:	Area 8.5 or 10m^2/92 or 108 sq.ft.
Rigging:	Sloop
Price Guide:	On application.
Summary:	Single-hander. Over 14,000 boats built to date.

LAND CAT

Design:	Douglas Deeds, U.S.A. 1972
Supplier:	Gemico Corporation, U.S.A.

Specifications:	Construction:	Plastic
	LOA:	2.44m/8'0
	Beam:	1.83m/6'0
	Displ:	34kg/75 lbs

Fittings:	Centreboard boat. Aluminium spars.
Sails:	Area $5.2m^2$/56 sq.ft.
Rigging:	Una
Price Guide:	$395us
Summary:	Single-hander.

LAPSTRAKE

Supplier:	E. C. Landamore, U. K.

Specifications:	*Construction:*	GRP
	LOA:	2.9m/9'6
	Displ:	86kg/190 lbs

Fittings:	Centreboard boat. Aluminium spars.
Sails:	Area $4.6m^2$/50 sq.ft.
Rigging:	Lug rigged.
Price Guide:	£120
Summary:	A general purpose sailing boat.

KORSAR

Design:	Ernst Lehfeld, U.S.A.
Supplier:	Stanbey Plastics, U.S.A. Korsar Association, U.S.A.
Specifications:	*Construction:* Wood or GRP *LOA:* 4.98m/16'4 *Beam:* 1.7m/5'7 *Draft:* 0.1m/4'' cb up *Displ:* 127kg/280 lbs
Fittings:	Centreboard boat. Spars — wood or aluminium. Positive flotation. Self-bailing.
Sails:	Area 12.8m²/138 sq.ft. Spinnaker area 13.9m²/150 sq.ft.
Rigging:	Sloop
Price Guide:	$1,700us
Summary:	2 crew. About 5,000 boats in ciruclation. Trapeze used.

LIDO 14

Design: W. D. Schock Co., U.S.A.

Supplier: W. D. Schock & Co., U.S.A.
Lido 14 Association, U.S.A.

Specifications:

Construction: GRP
LOA: 4.27m/14'0
Beam: 1.83m/6'0
Draft: 0.13m/5'' cb up
Displ: 141kg/310 lbs

Fittings: Centreboard boat. Aluminium spars. Positive flotation. Hinged mast. Kick-up rudder.

Sails: Area 10.3m^2(7.1 + 3.2)/111 sq.ft. (76 † 35)
No spinnaker allowed.

Rigging: Sloop

Price Guide: $1,295

Summary: Single-hander. An easy-to-sail, comfortable dinghy. Takes up to 4 crew.

LITTLE TOOT

Design:	S. Smith, U.S.A. 1958
Supplier:	Ranger Fibreglass Boats, U.S.A.
Specifications:	*Construction:* GRP
	LOA: 2.54m/8'4
	Beam: 1.32m/4'4
	Draft: 0.1m/4" cb up
	Displ: 45kg/100 lbs
Fittings:	Centreboard boat. Wooden spars. Foam flotation.
Sails:	Area 3.4m^2/37 sq.ft.
Rigging:	Una
Price Guide:	$285us
Summary:	Single-hander. Built and sailed only in America, on the west coast

LONE STAR 13

Design:	Thomas L. Faul, U.S.A. 1964
Supplier:	Marine Products Div. Chrysler Corporation, U.S.A. Lone Star 13 Association, U.S.A.
Specifications:	*Construction:* GRP
	LOA: 3.96m/13'0
	Beam: 1.52m/5'0
	Draft: 0.13m/5'' cb up
	Displ: 152kg/335 lbs
Fittings:	Bilgeboards. Aluminium spars. Foam flotation.
Sails:	Area 8.7m² (4.5 + 4.2)/94 sq. ft. (48 + 45) No spinnaker allowed
Rigging:	Masthead sloop
Price Guide:	$1,200us
Summary:	Sailed in America. An exciting competition boat.

LONE STAR 16

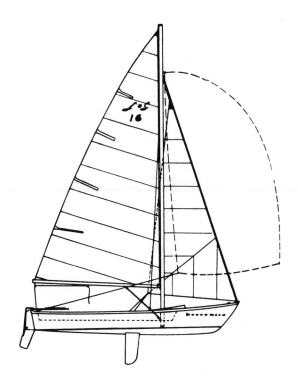

Design:	Thomas L. Faul, U.S.A.
Supplier:	Marine Products Div. Chrysler Corporation, U.S.A.
Specifications:	*Construction:* GRP
	LOA: 4.88m/16'0
	Beam: 1.85m/6'1
	Draft: 0.15m/6'' cb up
Fittings:	Centreboard boat. Aluminium spars. Positive flotation.
Sails:	Area 14.9m²/160 sq.ft.
	Spinnaker area 15.2m²/164 sq.ft.
Rigging:	Sloop
Price Guide:	$1,500
Summary:	3 crew. Roomy cockpit. Grown in popularity because of its exciting performance.

LUDERS 16

Design:	A.E. Luders Jnr., Holland 1945
Supplier:	Arthur L. Bolton, U.S.A. Luders 16 Association, U.S.A.
Specifications:	*Construction:* Plywood or GRP *LOA:* 4.98m/16'4 *Beam:* 1.75m/5'9 *Draft:* 1.22m/4'0 *Displ:* 1,453kg/3,200 lbs *Ballast:* 726kg/1,600 lbs
Fittings:	Keelboat. Wooden or aluminium spars.
Variations:	No class rules for number of crew or weight of boat.
Sails:	Area 24.7m^2/266 sq.ft.
Rigging:	Sloop
Price Guide:	$4,500us
Summary:	Majority of boats in circulation sailed in the U.S.A.

LUDERS 21

Design:	A.E. Luders Jnr., Holland
Suppliers:	Luders 21 Association, U.S.A Ron Rawson Inc., U.S.A.
Specifications:	*Construction:* GRP *LOA:* 6.48m/21'3 *Beam:* 1.7m/5'7 *Draft:* 0.91m/3'0 *Displ:* 511kg/1,125 lbs *Ballast:* 197kg/435 lbs
Fittings:	Keelboat. Aluminium spars. Foam flotation. Lead and GRP ballast.
Sails:	Area 12.6m^2/136 sq.ft. Spinnaker area 9.3m^2/100 sq.ft.
Rigging:	Sloop
Price Guide:	$2,500us
Summary:	3 crew. An American class. Trailable.

LOWELL 19

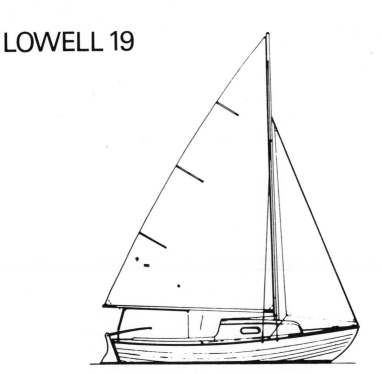

Design:	Pert Lowell, U.S.A. 1934 and 1968
Supplier:	PRM Sailboats Division, U.S.A.
Specifications:	*Construction:* GRP *LWL:* 4.82m/15'10 *LOA:* 5.79m/19'0 *Beam:* 2.13m/7'0 *Draft:* 0.25m/10'' cb up *Displ:* 590kg/1,300 lbs
Fittings:	Centreboard boat. Wooden spars. Mahogany trim. Foam flotation. Self-bailers.
Variations:	Open or with a small cabin.
Sails:	Area 18.6m²/200 sq.ft. Spinnaker area 11.1m²/120 sq.ft.
Rigging:	Sloop
Price Guide:	$3,250us open $3,995 with cabin.
Summary:	2 crew. Ideal for sailing, racing and training. Roomy and safe.

M-16

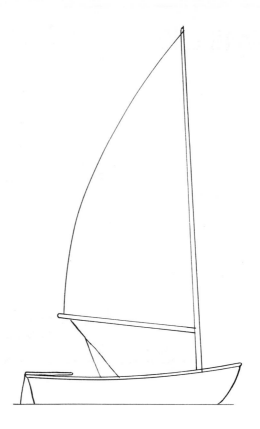

Design: Harry Melges Snr., U.S.A.

Supplier: Melges Boat Works, U.S.A.

Specifications:

Construction:	Wood or GRP	
LOA:	4.88m/16'0	
Beam:	1.68m/5'6	
Draft:	0.76m/2'6	

Fittings: Centreboard boat. Wooden spars. Positive flotation.

Sails: Area 13.9m^2/150 sq.ft.
No spinnaker allowed.

Rigging: Sloop

Price Guide: $2,200

Summary: Carries up to 5 crew.

M- 20

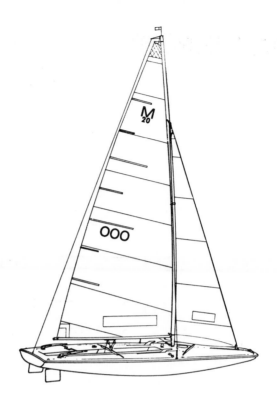

Design:	Harry Melges Snr., U.S.A.
Supplier:	Melges Boat Works, U.S.A. M-20 Association, U.S.A.
Specifications:	*Construction:* GRP *LOA:* 6.1m/20'0 *Beam:* 1.73m/5'8 *Draft:* 0.2m/8'' cb up
Fittings:	Centreboard boat. Spars — wood or aluminium. Positive flotation.
Sails:	Area 15.5m^2/167 sq.ft. Spinnaker area 16.3m^2/175 sq.ft.
Rigging:	Sloop
Price Guide:	$2,600us
Summary:	Carries up to 8 crew. Self-rescuing.

MAC DINGHY

Design:	McClintock-Dubdam, Holland
Supplier:	J. McClintock & Co., U.S.A. Mac Dinghy Association, U.S.A.
Specifications:	*Construction:* GRP *LOA:* 3.05m/10'0 *Beam:* 1.24m/4'1 *Draft:* 0.46m/1'6 *Displ:* 40kg/88 lbs
Fittings:	Centreboard boat. Aluminium spars. Transom motor mount. Air chamber flotation.
Sails:	Area 6m^2/65 sq,ft Spinnaker area 3.7m^2/40 sq. ft.
Rigging:	Sloop
Price Guide:	$650us
Summary:	2 crew. A versatile, responsive performer. Can be car-topped.

MAILBOAT

Design:	Peter Milne and Peter Cook, England 1970	
Supplier:	The Daily Mail, England	
Specifications:	*Construction:*	Polystyrene
	LOA:	2.44m/8'0
	Beam:	1.52m/5'0
Fittings:	Centreboard boat. Metal spars. Varnished wood rudder and tiller.	
Sails:	Area 4.2m^2/45 sq.ft.	
Rigging:	Spritsail sloop	
Price Guide:	On application	
Summary:	2 crew. Can be car-topped	

MARIN

Supplier:	McVay Fiberglass Yachts, Canada Ocqueauteau - Guy, France Navy-Holland, Holland.
Specifications:	*Construction:* GRP *LOA:* 4.88m/16'0 *Beam:* 1.91m/6'3 *Draft:* 0.15m/6'' cb up *Displ:* 193kg/425 lbs *Ballast:* 150kg/330 lbs
Fittings:	Centreboard boat. Aluminium spars. Positive flotation.
Sails:	Area 12.5m^2/135 sq.ft.
Rigging:	Sloop
Price Guide:	
Summary:	2 crew. Self-bailing. Family cruiser.

MARINE TUTOR

Design:	Carl Mungai, England
Supplier:	Capt. F. McNulty & Sons, U.K.
Rating:	Portsmouth yardstick 100
Specifications:	*Construction:* GRP and marine plywood *LOA:* 4.34m/14'3 *Beam:* 1.81m/5'11 *Draft:* 1.07m/3'6 *Displ:* 150kg/330 lbs
Fittings:	Centreboard boat. Mast 6.2m/20'4 high. Built-in buoyancy.
Sails:	Area 11.6m^2/125 sq.ft.
Rigging:	Sloop
Price Guide:	£450
Summary:	Exciting but not too lively for youngsters. Designed specifically for training and family sailing.

MAN O` WAR

Design: J. R. Macalpine-Downie, U.S.A. 1968

Supplier: Marine Products Operations, U.S.A.
Man O' War Association, U.S.A.

Specifications: *Construction:* GRP
LWL: 4.09m/13'5
LOA: 4.57m/15'0
Beam: 1.37m/4'6
Draft: 0.15m/6'' cb up
Displ: 89kg/195 lbs

Fittings: Daggerboard. Aluminium spars. Built-in hiking assists. Foam flotation.

Sails: Area 7.9m^2/85 sq.ft.

Rigging: Una

Price Guide: $700us

Summary: Single-hander. A cat-rigged, planing hull performance sailer. Easy to handle and great fun to sail.

MARLIN MK II

Design:	Ian Proctor England
Supplier:	Small Craft (Blockley), England
Rating:	Portsmouth yardstick 97
Specifications:	*Construction:* GRP
	LWL: 3.66m/12'0
	LOA: 3.98m/13'1
	Beam: 1.68m/5'6
	Draft: 1.12m/3'8
	Displ: 98kg/215 lbs
Fittings:	Round bilged boat. Spruce or alloy spars. Mast 6.4m/21'0 high. Built in buoyancy.
Sails:	Area 9.7m^2/104.5 sq.ft. (racing rig)
	Area 7.1m^2/76.3 sq.ft. (cruising rig)
	Spinnaker area 7.91m^2/85 sq.ft.
Rigging:	Sloop
Price Guide:	£350
Summary:	A general purpose, roomy and stable dinghy. Mk II has a completely new deck layout. Kits available.

MAYFLOWER

Design:	Snark Products Inc. U.S.A.
Supplier:	Snark Products Inc. U.S.A.
Specifications:	*Construction:* Plastic
	LOA: 3.51m/11'6
	Beam: 1.37m/4'6
	Draft: 0.08m/3"
	Displ: 41kg/90 lbs
Fittings:	Daggerboard. Aluminium spars. Foam flotation.
Sails:	Area 7.6m^2/82 sq.ft.
Rigging:	Una
Price Guide:	$450us
Summary:	Carries up to 4 crew. Virtually maintenance free. Easily converted for motoring or rowing.

MARBLEHEAD TRAINER

Design:	E. R. & W. T. Butler, U.S.A. 1959
Supplier:	E. R. Butler & Sons, U.S.A. Marblehead Trainer Association, U.S.A.
Fittings:	*Construction:* Plywood *LOA:* 3m/9'10 *Beam:* 1.32m/4'4 *Draft:* 0.1m/4'' cb up *Displ:* 45kg/100 lbs
Fittings:	Daggerboard. Wooden spars.
Sails:	Area 4.2m^2/45 sq.ft. No spinnaker allowed.
Rigging:	Una
Price Guide:	$255us
Summary:	Single-hander. Sailed mainly in Massachusetts, U.S.A.

MAYFLOWER 10´

Supplier:	K. R. Skentlebury, U.K.
Specifications:	*Construction:* GRP
	LOA: 3.05m/10'0
	Displ: 41kg/90 lbs
Fittings:	Centreboard boat. Aluminium spars.
Sails:	Area 4.6m^2/50 sq.ft.
Rigging:	Bermudan sloop
Price Guide:	£120
Summary:	2 crew. A general purpose dinghy.

MELODY

Design:	William Ashcraft, U.S.A. 1951
Supplier:	Melody Association, U.S.A.
Specifications:	*Construction:* Wood
	LOA: 3.05m/10'0
	Beam: 0.99m/3'3
	Draft: 0.08m/3'' cb up
Fittings:	Centreboard boat. Wooden spars.
Sails:	Area 5.1m^2/55 sq.ft.
	No spinnaker allowed.
Rigging:	Una
Price Guide:	On application.
Summary:	Single-hander. Hiking straps used. No buoyancy added.

MARINER

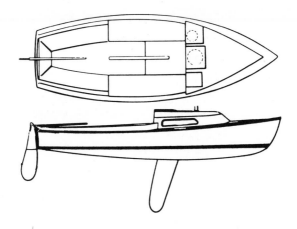

Design:	Philip L. Rhodes, U.S.A. 1963	
Supplier:	O'Day, U.S.A.	
	U.S. Mariner Class Association, U.S.A.	
Specifications:	*Construction:*	GRP
	LOA:	5.84m/19'2
	Beam:	2.13m/7'0
	Draft:	0.2m/8" cb up
	Displ:	636kg/1,400 lbs
Fittings:	Centreboard boat. Aluminium spars. Foam flotation.	
Sails:	Area 17.2m^2/185 sq.ft.	
Rigging:	Sloop	
Price Guide:	$2,600us	
Summary:	2 crew. No restrictions on hiking assists rules.	

MERMAID 14

Design: Roger Hancock, England

Supplier: Mermaid Boats, England

Specifications: *Construction:*   Marine plywood
                      LWL: 4.19m/13'9
                      LOA: 4.27m/14'0
                      Beam: 1.6m/5'3
                      Draft: 1.14m/3'9
                      Displ: 104kg/230 lbs

Fittings: Centreboard boat. Mast $6.1m^2$/20'0 high. Built-in buoyancy.

Variations: Cuddy can be attached for further crew protection.

Sails: Area $9.8m^2$/105 sq.ft.
Spinnaker permitted.

Rigging: Gunter

Price Guide: £250

Summary: 3-4 crew. General purpose dinghy for family cruising or racing. MkII now available in stitch and glue construction

MINI PRAM

Supplier: Monachorum Manufacturers, England

Specifications: *Construction:*   GRP
                      LOA: 2.36m/7'9
                      Displ: 41kg/90 lbs

Fittings: Aluminium spars.

Variations: Outboard may be fitted.

Sails: Area $3.7m^2$/40 sq.ft.

Rigging: Bermudan una

Price Guide: On application

Summary: Single-hander. Can be car-topped and trailed.

MENHIR

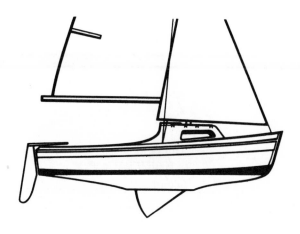

Design:	Christian Maury, France
Supplier:	Comextra, U.K. Lanaverre, Holland

Specifications:	*Construction:*	GRP
	LWL:	4.40m/14'5½
	LOA:	4.75m/15'7
	Beam:	1.92m/6'4
	Draft:	0.03m/1¼''
	Displ:	295kg/650 lbs
	Ballast:	100kg/220 lbs

Fittings:	Centreboard boat. Aluminium spars.
Variations:	Outboard can be fitted.
Sails:	Area 12.1m^2/130 sq.ft.
Rigging:	Various rigs available.
Price Guide:	£750
Summary:	Carries 4 to 5 crew. Can be trailed

MERCURY

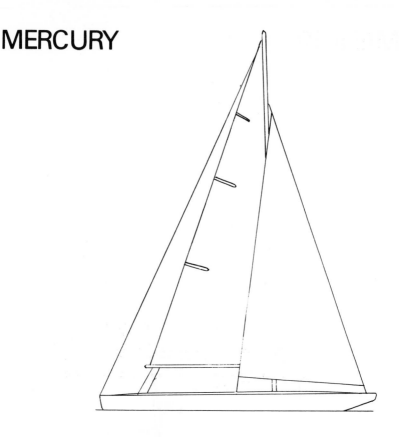

Design:	Ernest Nunes, U.S.A. 1938
Supplier:	Mercury National Association, U.S.A.
Specifications:	*Construction:* Wood or GRP
	LOA: 5.49m/18'0
	Beam: 1.62m/5'4
	Draft: 0.94m/3'1
	Displ: 533kg/1,175 lbs
	Ballast: 288kg/635 lbs
Fittings:	Keelboat. Aluminium spars. Air tank flotation. Self-bailing.
Sails:	Area 16.4m^2/177 sq.ft. Spinnaker area 9.3m^2/100 sq.ft.
Rigging:	Sloop
Price Guide:	$2,000us+
Summary:	2 crew. Popular craft worldwide. Trailable. Kits and plans available.

MINIFISH

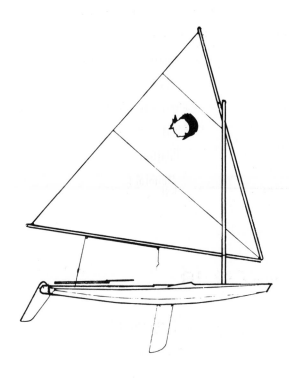

Design:	AMF Alcort, U.S.A.
Supplier:	D. Bruce Connolly, U.S.A.
Specifications:	*Construction:* GRP
	LOA: 3.58m/11'9
	Beam: 1.17m/3'10
	Draft: 0.11m/4½"
	Displ: 34kg/75 lbs
Fittings:	Daggerboard. GRP spars. Sluminium or mahogany trim. Mahogany kick-up rudder. Foam Flotation
Sails:	Area 6m²/65 sq.ft. Dacron
Rigging:	Una
Price Guide:	$400us
Summary:	Can be car-topped. A real performer. Can carry 3 to 4 crew

MINI/YOT

Supplier:	Prettycraft Plastics, England
Specifications:	*Construction:* GRP
	LOA: 2.76m/9'1
	Displ: 41kg/90 lbs
Fittings:	Daggerboard. Aluminium spars.
Variations:	Outboard can be fitted.
Sails:	Area 2.8m^2/30 sq.ft.
Rigging:	Lug rigged.
Price Guide:	On application
Summary:	2 crew. General purpose dinghy that can be car-topped and trailed.

MIRROR 16

Design:	Holt & Bucknell, U.K.
Supplier:	Mirror Boats, U.K.
	James Bliss & Co. U.S.A.
	Mirror 16 Association U.K.
	Mirror 16 Association U.S.A.
Rating:	Portsmouth yardstick 92
Specifications:	*Construction:* Wood with GRP on seams.
	LOA: 4.88m/16'0
	Beam: 1.83m/6'0
	Draft: 1.07m/3'6
	Displ: 118kg/260 lbs
Fittings:	Centreboard boat. Aluminium spars. Mast 5.19m/17'0 high. Built-in buoyancy.
Sails:	Area 16.5m^2 (11.4 + 5.1)/178 sq.ft. (123 + 55) Spinnaker area 11.1m^2/120 sq.ft.
Rigging:	Sloop
Price Guide:	£400/$900us in kit form.
Summary:	2 crew. Kits available. Fast boat suitable for cruising and racing.

MINI TIKI

Supplier:	Iles of Norbury, England	
Specifications:	*Construction:*	GRP
	LOA:	2.92m/9'7
	Beam:q	1.32m/4'4
	Draft:	0.69m/2'3
	Displ:	45kg/100 lbs
Fittings:	Pivotting centreboard. Bendy mast 4.65m/15'3 high. Completely self-draining.	
Sails:	Area 4.9m^2/53 sq.ft.	
Rigging:	Una. Unstayed mast and boom.	
Price Guide:	On application	
Summary:	Single-hander. Easy to sail and very stable. Lively in light airs but suitable for beginners and children. Boom set high.	

MITCHAM 8 and 10

Supplier:	Mitcham Marine, U.K.
Specifications:	*Construction:* GRP
	LOA: 2.44m/8'0
	3.05m/10'0
	Displ: 50kg/110 lbs
	59kg/130 lbs
Fittings:	Centreboard boat. Aluminium spars.
Sails:	Area $3.3m^2$/36 sq.ft.
	Area $3.9m^2$/42 sq.ft.
Rigging:	Lug rigged
Price Guide:	£100 to £130
Summary:	General purpose dinghies.

MONTGOMERY 6-8

Design:	Richard Arthur, U.S.A. 1966
Supplier:	Montgomery Marine Products, U.S.A.
	Montgomery 6–8 Association, U.S.A.
Specifications:	*Construction:* GRP
	LOA: 2.03m/6'8
	Beam: 1.22m/4'0
	Draft: 0.1m/4'' cb up
	Displ: 27kg/60 lbs
Fittings:	Centreboard boat. Aluminium spars. Air flotation tanks.
Variations:	Montgomery 7–11, LOA: 2.42m/7'11 also available.
Sails:	Area $3.7m^2$/40 sq.ft.
Rigging:	Una
Price Guide:	$365us/$440 (7–11)
Summary:	Single-hander. Popular on the west coast of America

MINTO

Design:	W. H. Dole & Ed Hoppen, U.S.A. 1962
Supplier:	Ranger Fibreglass Boats, U.S.A.

Specifications:	*Construction:*	GRP
	LOA:	2.76m/9'1
	Beam:	1.3m/4'3
	Draft:	0.15m/6'' cb up
	Displ:	58kg/127 lbs

Fittings:	Centreboard boat. Wooden spars. Foam flotation.
Sails:	Area 4.5m^2/48 sq.ft.
Rigging:	Una
Price Guide:	$545us
Summary:	Single-hander. Sailed mainly on the west coast of America

MONTGOMERY 10

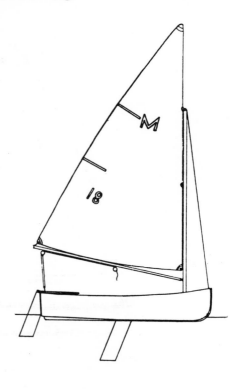

Design:	Jerry Montgomery, U.S.A. 1970
Supplier:	Montgomery Marine Products' U.S.A. Montgomery 10 Association, U.S.A.
Specifications:	*Construction:* GRP
	LOA: 3.05m/10'0
	Beam: 1.55m/5'1
	Draft: 0.1m/4'' cb up
	Displ: 57kg/125 lbs
Fittings:	Centreboard boat. Aluminium spars. Teak trim. Air and foam flotation.
Sails:	Area 5.8m²/62 sq.ft.
Rigging:	Una — Gunter
Price Guide:	$650us
Summary:	Single-hander. A utility dinghy that nevertheless has good sailing characteristics. Easily trailed and cartopped.

MONTGOMERY 12

Design:	Lyle Hess, U.S.A. 1971
Supplier:	Montgomery Marine Products, U.S.A. Montgomery 12 Association, U.S.A.

Specifications:

Construction:	GRP
LOA:	3.73m/12'3
Beam:	1.47m/4'10
Draft:	0.13m/5'' cb up
Displ:	89kg/195 lbs

Fittings:	Centreboard boat. Teak trim. Aluminium spars. Optional bailers.
Sails:	Area 8.5m^2 (5.9 + 2.6)/91 sq.ft. (63 + 28)
Rigging:	Sloop or cat rig
Price Guide:	$995us
Summary:	2 crew. A racing and day-sailing boat. Can be trailed and car-topped easily.

MUSARD

Supplier:	Comextra, England Nautica Corporation, U.S.A.
Specifications:	Construction: *GRP* *LOA:* 3.35m/11'0 *Displ:* 60kg/132 lbs
Fittings:	Centreboard boat.
Variations:	Outboard may be fitted.
Sails:	Area 8.3m^2/89 sq.ft.
Rigging:	Bermudan sloop
Price Guide:	On application
Summary:	2 crew. General purpose dinghy that can be car-topped and trailed.

NADIR

Design:	Chaintiers Nautiques, France 1971
Supplier:	New England Sailboat Co., U.S.A.
Specifications:	*Construction:* GRP *LOA:* 3.81m/12'6 *Beam:* 1.68m/5'6 *Draft:* 0.15m/6" cb up *Displ:* 100kg/220 lbs
Fittings:	Centreboard boat. Aluminium spars. Foam and air tank flotation. Self-bailing.
Sails:	Area 8.5m^2 (6.7 + 1.8)/92 sq.ft. (72 + 20)
Rigging:	Sloop
Price Guide:	$900us
Summary:	2 crew. Most boats to be found in Europe.

MOPPET

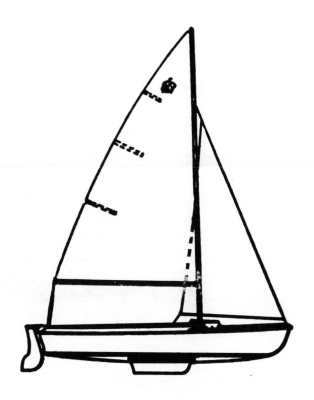

Supplier: McVay Fibreglass Yachts Ltd., Canada

Specifications:

Construction: GRP
LOA: 3.96m/13'0
Beam: 1.7m/5'7
Draft: 0.38m/1'3
Displ: 241kg/530 lbs

Fittings: Keelboat. Aluminium spars. Positive flotation.

Sails: Area 8.9m^2/96 sq.ft.

Rigging: Sloop

Price Guide: On application.

Summary: 2 crew. Sailed only in north-eastern U.S.A.

MOUETTE

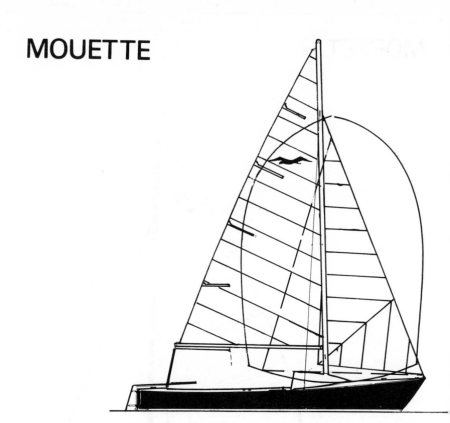

Design: Paceship Canada, 1964

Supplier: Paceship Canada
                      Mouette Association, U.S.A.

Specifications: *Construction:*   GRP
                      LOA: 5.94m/19'6
                      Beam: 2.11m/6'11
                      Draft: 0.3m/1'0
                      Displ: 295kg/650 lbs

Fittings: Centreboard boat. Aluminium spars. Foam flotation.

Sails: Area 14.9m (9.3 + 5.6)/160 sq.ft. (100 + 60)
                      Spinnaker area 7m^2/75 sq.ft.

Rigging: Sloop

Price Guide: $2,450us

Summary: 2 crew.

MUTINEER

Design: J. R. Macalpine-Downie, U.S.A. 1971

Supplier: Chrysler O-D Sail boats, U.S.A.

Specifications: *Construction:*   GRP
                      LWL: 4.29m/14'1
                      LOA: 4.57m/15'0
                      Beam: 1.83m/6'0
                      Draft: 0.2m/8'' cb up
                      Displ: 182kg/400 lbs

Fittings: Centreboard boat. Aluminium spars. Foam flotation. Kick-up rudder. Self-bailed.

Sails: Area 13.9m^2 (9.3 + 4.6)/150 sq.ft. (100 + 50) Spinnaker area 15.6m^2/168 sq.ft.

Rigging: Sloop

Price Guide: $1,510us

Summary: 2 crew. Sailed only in America. A comfortable, sensitive day-sailer.

NARRASKETUCK

Design: Wilbur F. Ketcham, 1935

Supplier: Narrasketuck Association, U.S.A.

Specifications: *Construction:*   Wood
 LOA: 6.17m/20'3
 Beam: 1.98m/6'6
 Draft: 0.3m/1'0

Fittings: Centreboard boat. Spars — wood or aluminium. No flotation.

Sails: Area 21.1m^2/227 sq.ft.

Rigging: Sloop

Price Guide: Secondhand prices vary enormously.

Summary: 2 crew. Not in production so only secondhand boats on the market. Only found in America.

NASSAU DINGHY

Design: Unknown U.S.A., 1960

Supplier: Friend Ship Manufacturing Co., U.S.A.
Nassau Dinghy Association, U.S.A.

Specifications: *Construction:*   GRP
 LOA: 4.22m/13'10
 Beam: 1.22m/4'0
 Draft: 0.46m/1'6
 Displ: 227kg/500 lbs
 Ballast: 114kg/250 lbs

Fittings: Keelboat. Aluminium spars. Built-in buoyancy.

Sails: Area 10.7m^2/115 sq.ft.

Rigging: Sloop

Price Guide: $1,000 secondhand

Summary: Small class restricted to the States. Unlimited crew allowed.

NAIAD

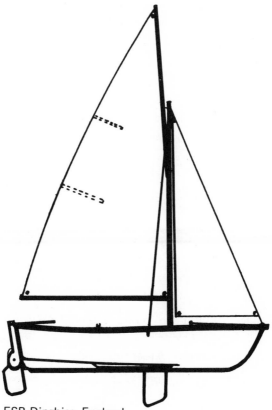

Design:	ESB Dinghies, England
Supplier:	ESB Dinghies Limited, England
Specifications:	*Construction:* GRP
	LWL: 3.66m/12'0
	LOA: 4.03m/13'2½
	Beam: 1.61m/5'2½
	Draft: 0.84m/2'9
	Displ: 1.7kg/330 lbs
Fittings:	Centreboard boat. Spruce spars. Mast height 3.96m/ 13'0
Variations:	7½hp outboard can be attached.
Sails:	Area 7.4m^2/80 sq.ft.
Rigging:	Gunter
Price Guide:	£450
Summary:	Stable and safe. Easily operated rig. Carries up to 5 crew. Short coastal runs made possible by her generously proportioned hull. Can be trailed.

NATIONAL ONE-DESIGN

Design:	William F. Crosby, U.S.A.
Supplier:	Not built professionally in the U.K. National OD Association, U.S.A.
Rating:	Portsmouth yardstick 103
Specifications:	*Construction:* Any
	LWL: 3.20m/10'6
	LOA: 5.18m/17'0
	Beam: 1.73m/5'8
	Draft: 0.61m/2'0
	Displ: 182kg/400 lbs
Fittings:	Centreboard boat. Spars — wood or aluminium. Built-in buoyancy.
Sails:	Area 12.7m^2/137 sq.ft. No spinnaker allowed.
Rigging:	Sloop
Price Guide:	Plans and construction book $25us from class association.
Summary:	2 crew. Self-rescuing. Hiking straps and trapeze allowed. Kits and plans available. Known as17' Dolphin in Europe.

NEPTUNE

Design:	American Fiberglass Corporation, U.S.A. 1971
Supplier:	American Fiberglass Corporation, U.S.A.
Specifications:	*Construction:* GRP
	LOA: 4.27m/14'0
	Beam: 1.73m/5'8
	Draft: 0.41m/1'4
	Displ: 202kg/445 lbs
Fittings:	Centreboard boat. Double hulled GRP. Aluminium spars. Kick-up rudder. Self-bailers.
Sails:	Area 10.7m^2/115 sq.ft.
Rigging:	Sloop
Price Guide:	$1,295us
Summary:	Single-hander, but takes up to 6 adults. A good choice for training schools. Stable and dry.

NAPLES SABOT

Design:	McCulloch, Violette & Campbell, U.S.A.
Supplier:	Naples Sabot Association, U.S.A.
Specifications:	*Construction:* Wood or GRP
	LOA: 2.42m/7'11
	Beam: 1.22m/4'0
	Displ: 43kg/95 lbs
Fittings:	Centreboard boat. Spars — wood, GRP or aluminium Positive flotation.
Sails:	Area 3.5m^2/38 sq.ft. No spinnaker allowed.
Rigging:	Una
Price Guide:	$350 to $600us
Summary:	Single-hander. Hiking straps allowed. Kits and plans available.

NIPPER
U.S.A.

Design: Ray Greene, U.S.A. 1940

Supplier: Ray Greene & Co.,U.S.A.
                     Nipper Association, U.S.A.

Specifications: *Construction:*   GRP
                     LOA: 3.66m/12'0
                     Beam: 1.58m/5'2
                     Draft: 0.15m/6'' cb up
                     Displ: 160kg/350 lbs

Fittings: Centreboard boat. Aluminium spars. Foam flotation.
                     Self-bailing

Sails: Area 9.3m^2/100 sq.ft.

Rigging: Una

Price Guide: $1,150us

Summary: 2 crew. Sailed only in America.

NORDEX BAT

Design: Herbert Peterson, U.S.A.

Supplier: Nordex Boats, U.S.A.

Specifications: *Construction:*   GRP
                     LOA: 3.66m/12'0
                     Beam: 1.37m/4'6
                     Draft: 0.05m/2'' cb up
                     Displ: 68kg/150 lbs

Fittings: Daggerboard. Aluminium spars. Foam flotation.

Sails: Area 6.2m^2/67 sq.ft.

Rigging: Lug

Price Guide: $575us

Summary: Single-hander. Sailed only in eastern U.S.A.

O'DAY 15

Design:	Andrew T. Kostanecki, U.S.A.	
Supplier:	O'Day, U.S.A.	
Specifications:	*Construction:*	GRP
	LOA:	4.55m/14'11
	Beam:	1.78m/5'10
	Draft:	0.17m/7'' cb up
	Displ:	159kg/350 lbs
Fittings:	Centreboard boat. Spars — anodized aluminium. Foam flotation. Self-bailers.	
Sails:	Area 12.5m^2/135 sq.ft.	
Rigging:	Sloop	
Price Guide:	$1,195us	
Summary:	2 crew. Built and sailed only in America to date. Self-rescuing. Planes readily.	

NIPPER

Supplier:	Maxim Marine, England
Specifications:	*Construction:* GRP
	LOA: 2.9m/9'6
	Beam: 1.35m/4'5
	Draft: 0.89m/2'11
	Displ: 73kg/160 lbs
Fittings:	Centreboard boat. Mast 4.57m/15'0 high. Solid foam buoyancy.
Sails:	Area 5.5m^2/59 sq.ft.
Rigging:	Bermudan sloop
Price Guide:	£175
Summary:	2 to 3 crew. Specially designed for minium maintenance. Easy to operate and quick to action. Its speed and performance are outstanding for its size

PIKE

Design:	Theodor Box, U.S.A. 1969
Supplier:	Tedruth Plastics Corporation, U.S.A.
Specifications:	*Construction:* Plastic
	LOA: 3.2m/10'6
	Beam: 1.37m/4'6
	Draft: 0.15m/6'' cb up
	Displ: 100kg/220 lbs
Fittings:	Centreboard boat. Aluminium spars. Foam flotation. Self-bailers.
Sails:	Area 5.3m^2/3.6 + 1.7)/57 sq. ft. (39 + 18)
Rigging:	Sloop
Price Guide:	$775us
Summary:	2 crew. A stable, family dinghy.

OMEGA 14

Design:	Frank Butler and Ted Carpentier, U.S.A.
Supplier:	Omega 14 Association, U.S.A.
Specifications:	*Construction:* GRP
	LOA: 4.14m/13'7
	Beam: 1.62m/5'4
	Draft: 0.91m/3'0
	Displ: 123kg/270 lbs
Fittings:	Centreboard boat. Aluminium spars. Foam flotation.
Sails:	Area 10m^2 (6.3 + 3.7)/108 sq.ft. (68 + 40) No spinnaker allowed.
Rigging:	Sloop
Price Guide:	$995us
Summary:	2 crew. Sailed only in America. Self-bailing.

OD 13

Design:	George O'Day and R. Baker, U.S.A. 1972
Supplier:	Gemica Corporation, U.S.A.
Specifications:	*Construction:* Plastic
	LOA: 3.96m/13'0
	Beam: 1.55m/5'1
	Draft: 0.08m/3" cb up
	Displ: 61kg/135 lbs
Fittings:	Centreboard boat. Aluminium spars. Foam flotation.
Sails:	Area 8.8m^2 (6.5 + 2.3)/95 sq.ft. (70 + 25)
Rigging:	Sloop
Price Guide:	$795us
Summary:	2 to 3 crew.

ORION

Design:	Robert Baker, U.S.A.
Supplier:	Orion Association, U.S.A.
Specifications:	*Construction:* GRP
	LOA: 5.79m/19'0
	Beam: 2.06m/6'9
	Draft: 0.3m/1'0
	Displ: 499kg/1,100 lbs
Fittings:	Centreboard boat. Aluminium spars. Positive flotation.
Variations:	Keelboat or centreboard boat.
Sails:	Area 18.6m^2 (10.8 + 7.8)/200 sq. ft. (116 + 84) Spinnaker area 18.9m^2/203 sq. ft.
Rigging:	Sloop
Price Guide:	$3,000us secondhand
Summary:	2 crew. Sailed only in America.

PACESHIP 12

Design:	Paceship Yachts, Canada
Supplier:	Paceship Yachts, Canada
Specifications:	*Construction:* GRP
	LWL: 3.25m/10'8
	LOA: 3.66m/12'0
	Beam: 1.65m/5'5
	Draft: 0.99m/3'3
	Displ: 136kg/300 lbs
Fittings:	Self-bailing cockpit. Icebox. Positive flotation. Kick-up rudder. Anodized aluminium spars.
Sails:	Area $7.6m^2$/82 sq.ft.
Rigging:	Sloop
Price Guide:	$930us
Summary:	A popular daysailer that is comfortable and easy to handle.

PACESHIP 14

Design:	Bela Molnar, Canada	
Supplier:	Paceship Yachts, Canada	
Specifications:	*Construction:*	GRP
	LWL:	3.35m/11'0
	LOA:	4.11m/13'6
	Beam:	1.78m/5'10
	Draft:	1.12m/3'8 max.
	Displ:	182kg/400 lbs
Fittings:	Self-bailing cockpit. Positive flotation. Icebox. Forward storage. Anodised aluminium spars.	
Variations:	Outboard may be attached.	
Sails:	Area 9.3m^2/100 sq.ft.	
Rigging:	Sloop	
Price Guide:	$1,400us	
Summary:	Can be trailed. Takes up to 4 crew. An ideal compromise of comfort and performance.	

PACESHIP 2-16

Design:	Cuthbertson & Cassran, Canada 1970
Supplier:	Paceship Yachts Limited, Canada
Specifications:	*Construction:* GRP
	LWL: 4.2m/13'9½
	LOA: 4.7m/15'5
	Beam: 1,85m/6'1
	Draft: 0.17m/7'' cb up
	Displ: 227kg/500 lbs
Fittings:	Centreboard boat. Aluminium spars. Foam flotation.
Sails:	Area 10.4m^2/112 sq.ft.
Rigging:	Sloop
Price Guide:	$1,795us
Summary:	Carries up to 5 crew. A big, bold dinghy, that makes an ideal all-round daysailer for families and clubs.

PACIFIC 21

Design:	William Nichols, 1955
Supplier:	Pacific 21 Association, U.S.A.
Specifications:	Construction: GRP
	LOA: 6.4m/21'0
	Beam: 1.52m/5'0
	Draft: 1.07m/3'6
	Ballast: 381kg/840 lbs
Fittings:	Keelboat. Aluminium spars. Positive flotation.
Sails:	Area 17.1m^2/184 sq.ft.
Rigging:	Sloop
Price Guide:	$1,800us secondhand
Summary:	An American class. Hiking straps used.

PEANUT

Design:	Arnold R. Johnson, U.S.A. 1963
Supplier:	Todd Enterprises, U.S.A.
	Peanut Class Association, U.S.A.
Specifications:	Construction: Wood or GRP
	LOA: 2.9m/9'6
	Beam: 1.22m/4'0
	Draft: 0.3m/1'0
	Displ: 30kg/65 lbs
Fittings:	Centreboard boat. Spars — wood or aluminium. Positive flotation.
Sails:	Area 5.1m^2/55 sq.ft.
	No spinnaker allowed.
Rigging:	Una
Price Guide:	$545us
Summary:	Single-hander. Sailed mainly in America. Plans available.

PACESHIP 17

Design:	Cuthbertson & Cassian, Canada 1970	
Supplier:	Paceship Yachts Limited, Canada	
Specifications:	*Construction:*	GRP
	LOA:	5.28m/17'4
	Beam:	2.11m/6'11
	Draft:	0.2m/8'' cb up
	Displ:	238kg/525 lbs
Fittings:	Centreboard boat. Aluminium spars. Foam flotation. Self-bailers.	
Sails:	Area 12.4m²/134 sq.ft.	
Rigging:	Sloop	
Price Guide:	$1,925us	
Summary:	A bold daysailer that carries up to 5 adults.	

PENGUIN

Design:	Philip L. Rhodes, U.S.A.
Supplier:	Ron Rawson, U.S.A. Penguin Association, U.S.A. Beecham Marine, England
Specifications:	*Construction:* Wood or GRP *LOA:* 3.51m/11'6 *Beam:* 1.42m/4'8 *Draft:* 0.08m/3'' cb up *Displ:* 77kg/170 lbs
Fittings:	Centreboard boat. Spars — wood or aluminium.
Variations:	One of a range from 2.29m/7'6 up to 3.51m/11'6. Outboard may be attached.
Sails:	Area 6.7m^2/72 sq.ft.
Rigging:	Una
Price Guide:	On application
Summary:	2 crew. Plans and kits available. Can be trailed and car-topped. About 10,000 boats in circulation world-wide.

PIRATE FISH

Design:	William Bower, U.S.A. 1967
Supplier:	Pirate Fish Association, U.S.A.
Specifications:	*Construction:* GRP *LOA:* 4.62m/15'2 *Beam:* 1.24m/4'1 *Draft:* 0.17m/7'' cb up *Displ:* 61kg/135 lbs
Fittings:	Centreboard boat. Aluminium spars. Positive flotation. Self-bailers.
Variations:	Pirate Fish Junior also available — LOA: 3.38m/11'1
Sails:	Area 7m^2/75sq.ft. . No spinnaker allowed.
Rigging:	Una
Price Guide:	$520us
Summary:	Single-hander. Sailed only in America.

PACESHIP 20

Design:	Cuthbertson & Cassian, Canada 1970	
Supplier:	Paceship Yachts Limited, Canada	
Specifiations:	Construction:	GRP
	LOA:	5.87m/19'3
	Beam:	2.36m/7'9
	Draft:	0.17m/7'' cb up
	Displ:	363kg/800 lbs
Fittings:	Centreboard boat. Aluminium spars. Foam flotation. Self-bailers.	
Variations:	Also available as a weekender with 2 berths.	
Sails:	Area 14.4m²/155 sq.ft.	
Rigging:	Sloop	
Price Guide:	$2,500us	
Summary:	A boat that the whole family can enjoy with the ease of handling and economy of a small boat. Easy to trail, launch and store.	

PELICAN

Design:	Harold S. Glander
Supplier:	Glander Boats Inc. U.S.A.
Specifications:	*Construction:* GRP
	LOA: 3.4m/11'2
	Beam: 1.4m/4'7
	Draft: 0.15m/6'' cb up
	Displ: 64kg/140 lbs
Fittings:	Daggerboard. Aluminium spars.
Sails:	Area 5.8m^2/62 sq.ft.
Rigging:	Una
Price Guide:	$625us
Summary:	2 crew.

PEREGRINE

Design:	Paceships Yachts, Canada 1964	
Supplier:	Paceship Yachts Limited, Canada	
Specifications:	*Construction:*	GRP
	LOA:	4.75m/15'7
	Beam:	1.83m/6'0
	Draft:	0.2m/8'' cb up
	Displ:	193kg/425 lbs
Fittings:	Centreboard boat. Aluminium spars. Foam flotation. Self-bailers.	
Sails:	Area 11.9m^2/128 sq.ft.	
Rigging:	Sloop	
Price Guide:	$1,600us	
Summary:	2 crew.	

PETREL SB-12

Design:	Philip L. Rhodes, U.S.A.
Supplier:	Aluminium Goods, Canada

Specifications:	*Construction:*	Aluminium
	LWL:	3.35m/11'0
	LOA:	3.66m/12'0
	Beam:	1.52m/5'0
	Draft:	0.81m/2'8
	Displ:	77kg/170 lbs

Fittings:	Centreboard boat. Aluminium spars.
Sails:	Area 9.3m^2/100 sq.ft.
Rigging:	Sloop
Price Guide:	On application.
Summary:	4 crew. Exciting, fast, stable and self-rescuing. A stretch formed planing hull.

PIAF

Design:	France
Supplier:	Spair Marine, France
Specifications:	*Construction:* GRP
	LWL: 3.35m/11'
	LOA: 3.75m/12'3½
	Beam: 1.65m/5'5
	Draft: 0.17m/7''
	Displ: 125kg/276 lbs
Fittings:	Centreboard boat. Aluminium spars.
Variations:	Outboard can be attached.
Sails:	Area 8.32m^2/90 sq.ft.
Rigging:	Sloop
Price Guide:	2,000Fr.f.
Summary:	Stable general purpose dinghy.

PINTAIL

Design:	F. S. Ford Jnr., U.S.A. 1964
Supplier:	Molded Fiberglass Boat Co., U.S.A. Pintail Association, U.S.A.
Specifications:	*Construction:* GRP
	LOA: 4.27m/14'0
	Beam: 1.83m/6'0
	Draft: 0.15m/6'' cb up
	Displ: 182kg/400 lbs
Fittings:	Centreboard boat. Aluminium spars. Foam flotation. Self-bailers.
Sails:	Area 11.3m^2 (8.4 + 2.9)/122 sq.ft. (90 + 32) Spinnaker area 9.3m^2/100 sq.ft.
Rigging:	Sloop
Price Guide:	$1,450us
Summary:	2 crew. Sailed only in America.

PIPER

Design:	David Boyd, U.K. 1966
Supplier:	Alexander Robertson, Scotland Piper International Class Association, U.K. Piper National Class Association, U.S.A.
Specifications:	*Construction:* GRP and wood *LWL:* 4.95m/16'3 *LOA:* 7.44m/24'5 *Beam:* 1.91m/6'3 *Draft:* 1.07m/3'6 *Displ:* 1,616kg/3,560 lbs *Ballast:* 953kg/2,100 lbs
Fittings:	Keelboat. Aluminium spars.
Variations:	Outboard can be attached. Also available — Piper OD 'C' type with 3 berths. Same specifications.
Sails:	Area 20.4m^2/220 sq.ft. Spinnaker area 30.2m^2/325 sq.ft.
Rigging:	Sloop
Price Guide:	$6,000us
Summary:	3 crew. Can be trailed. Racing and general purpose dinghy.

PIRANHA 9

Design:	Donald C. Stewart, U.S.A.	
Supplier:	Donald C. Stewart, U.S.A.	
Specifications:	*Construction:*	GRP
	LWL:	2.67m/8'9
	LOA:	2.8m/9'2
	Beam:	1.23m/4'0
	Draft:	0.91m/3'0
	Displ:	57kg/125 lbs
Fittings:	Daggerboard. Double hulled. Aluminium spars. Mahogany trim. Positive flotation.	
Sails:	Area 4.5m^2/48 sq.ft.	
Rigging:	Sloop	
Price Guide:	On application	
Summary:	Single-hander. Self-rescuing. A serious sailing dinghy.	

PIRANHA 13

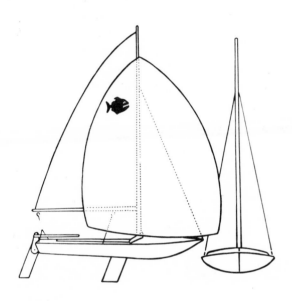

Design:	Donald C. Stewart, U.S.A.
Supplier:	Donald C. Stewart, U.S.A.
Specifications:	*Construction'* GRP
	LWL: 3.35m/11'0
	LOA: 3.96m/13'0
	Beam: 1.42m/4'8
	Draft: 0.97m/3'2
	Displ: 77kg/170 lbs
Fittings:	Centreboard boat. Aluminium spars. Positive flotation.
Sails:	Area 7.8m^2/84 sq.ft. Spinnaker area 11.6m^2/125 sq.ft.
Rigging:	Sloop
Price Guide:	On application
Summary:	2 crew. Self-rescuing and unsinkable. Very stable. Planes well. Takes high winds well.

PLAYMATE

Supplier:	Pearson Brothers Limited, England
Specifications:	*Construction:* GRP
	LOA: 2.13m/7'0
	Beam: 1.24m/4'1
	Draft: 0.51m/1'8
	Displ: 27kg/59 lbs
Fittings:	Centreboard boat. Kick-up rudder. Mast maximum height 3.05m/10'0
Sails:	Area 2.6m^2/28 sq.ft.
Rigging:	Lateen rig
Price Guide:	On application
Summary:	Inexpensive, stable and well-built. Sails well to windward and thus ideal for beginners.

POOLE AB

Design:	H. T. R. Poole, England
Supplier:	H. T. R. Poole Limited, England
Rating:	Portsmouth yardstick 142
Specifications:	*Construction:* GRP
	LOA: 2.59m/8'6
	Beam: 1.32m/4'4
	Draft: 0.84m/2'9
	Displ: 51kg/112 lbs
Fittings:	Centreboard boat. Mast 2.74m/9'0 high. Built-in buoyancy.
Sails:	Area 3.9m^2/42 sq.ft.
Rigging:	Gunter rig
Price Guide:	£180
Summary:	2 crew. A car-top pram dinghy. Suitable for all age groups. Sailed in the Dorset area of the U.K. and Scotland mainly.

PIRATE

Design:	Joseph V. Puccia, U.S.A.
Supplier:	Annapolis Sailboat Builders, U.S.A.
Specifications:	*Construction:* GRP
	LWL: 4.27m/14'0
	LOA: 4.62m/15'2
	Beam: 1.68m/5'6
	Draft: 0.17m/7'' cb up
	Displ: 136kg/300 lbs
Fittings:	Centreboard boat. Aluminium spars. Teak trim. Foam flotation. Self-bailers.
Sails:	Area 13m^2/140 sq.ft.
Rigging:	Sloop
Price Guide:	$1,540us
Summary:	Single-hander. Responsive, snappy performance.

PORPOISE

Supplier:	Frederick C. Mitchell & Sons, England
Specifications:	*Construction:* GRP and wood
	LOA: 2.84m/9'4
	Displ: 73kg/160 lbs
Fittings:	Daggerboard
Variations:	Outboard can be fitted.
Sails:	Area 3.3.m^2/36 sq.ft.
Rigging:	Una
Price Guide:	On application
Summary:	1 to 3 crew. Can be car-topped and trailed General purpose dinghy.

PRAM

Supplier:	Palace Quay Yard, England
Specifications:	*Construction:* Plywood
	LOA: 2.29m/7'6
	Displ: 23kg/50 lbs
Fittings:	Centreboard boat. Wooden spars.
Variations:	7'9 version also available. Outboard may be attached.
Sails:	Area 3.3m^2/35 sq.ft.
Rigging:	Gaff
Price Guide:	On application
Summary:	3 crew. General purpose dinghy. Can be car-topped and trailed.

PUFFER

Design:	AMF Alcort, U.S.A.
Supplier:	D. Bruce Connolly, U.S.A.
Specifications:	*Construction:* GRP
	LOA: 3.81m/12'6
	Beam: 1.47m/4'10
	Draft: 0.09m/3½''
	Displ: 79kg/175 lbs
Fittings:	Centreboard boat. Aluminium spars. Self-bailer.
Sails:	Area 8.4m^2 (5.1 + 3.3)/90 sq.ft. (55 + 35)
Rigging:	Sloop
Price Guide:	$895us
Summary:	2 crew. Sailed only in America. A traditionally designed sloop suitable as a daysailer or trainer.

PUFFIN

Design:	Barry Bucknell, England
Supplier:	Polycell Prout, England
Specifications:	*Construction:* GRP or marine plywood
	LWL: 2.23m/7'4
	LOA: 2.29m/7'6
	Beam: 1.22m/4'0
	Draft: 0.76m/2'6
	Displ: 30kg/65 lbs
Fittings:	Centreboard boat. Mast 3.66m/12'0 high.
Sails:	Area 2.8m^2/30 sq.ft.
Rigging:	Una
Price Guide:	On application
Summary:	1 to 4 crew. Collapsible solid dinghy for car-top use and as a tender. Good for junior racing. Kits available.

PURSAN

Design:	J. M. L'Hermenier, France 1970
Supplier:	William F. Russell & Co., U.S.A.
Specifications:	*Construction:* GRP
	LOA: 3.86m/12'8
	Beam: 1.65m/5'5
	Displ: 81kg/178 lbs
Fittings:	Centreboard boat. Aluminium spars. Positive flotation.
Sails:	Area 8.8m^2/95 sq.ft.
Rigging:	Sloop
Price Guide:	On application
Summary:	2 crew. Trapeze used.

RANA VERSATILE

Supplier:	Rana Boats, U.K.
Specifications:	*Construction:* Wood — clinker
	LOA: 5.03m/16'6
	Displ: 152kg/335 lbs
Fittings:	Wooden spars
Sails:	Area 7.2m^2/77 sq.ft.
Rigging:	Sloop
Price Guide:	£350
Summary:	Carries up to 6 crew. A true daysailer that is sturdy and comfortable.

RANGER 14

Supplier:	M. C. Davies, England
Specifications:	*Construction:* GRP
	LOA: 4.27m/14'0
	Displ: 82kg/180 lbs
Fittings:	Centreboard boat. Wood trim.
Variations:	Outboard may be attached.
Sails:	Area 6.9m^2/74 sq.ft.
Rigging:	Bermudan sloop
Price Guide:	On application
Summary:	Day dinghy. Takes up to 3 crew. Can be trailed.

RANGER CANOE

Design:	Willett Brothers, 1948
Supplier:	Ranger Fiberglass Boats, U.S.A.
Specifications:	*Construction:* GRP
	LOA: 5.18m/17'0
	Beam: 0.89m/2'11
	Draft: 0.1m/4'' cb up
	Displ: 43kg/95 lbs
Fittings:	Centreboard boat. Aluminium spars. Foam flotation.
Sails:	Area 4.8m^2/52 sq.ft.
Rigging:	Una
Price Guide:	$490us
Summary:	Single-hander. Sailed only in America on the west coast. Under 20 in circulation at the present.

RANGER 11

Design:	Raymond H. Richards, U.S.A. 1972
Supplier:	Ranger Fibreglass Boats, U.S.A.
Specifications:	*Construction:* GRP
	LOA: 3.35m/11'0
	Beam: 1.45m/4'9
	Draft: 0.15m/6'' cb up
	Displ: 73kg/160 lbs
Fittings:	Centreboard boat. Aluminium spars.
Sails:	Area 7m^2 (3.9 + 3.1)/75 sq.ft. (42 + 33)
Rigging:	Sloop
Price Guide:	$700us
Summary:	Single-hander. Only a few built to date.

RASCAL

Design:	Ray Greene, U.S.A. 1965
Supplier:	Rascal Association, U.S.A. Ray Greene & Co., U.S.A.

Specifications:

Construction:	GRP
LOA:	4.27m/14'0
Beam:	1.81m/6'0
Draft:	0.15m/6'' cb up
Displ:	170kg/375 lbs

Fittings:	Centreboard boat. Aluminium spars. Positive flotation. Self-bailers.
Sails:	Area 11.8m^2 (7.2 + 4.6)/127 sq.ft. (77 + 50)
Rigging:	Sloop
Price Guide:	$1,640us
Summary:	2 crew. A popular class in America.

RAVEN

Design:	Roger McAleer
Supplier:	Cape Cod Shipbuilding, U.S.A.

Specifications:

Construction:	GRP
LOA:	7.39m/24'3
Beam:	2.13m/7'0
Draft:	0.17m/7'' cb up
Displ:	527kg/1,160 lbs

Fittings:	Centreboard boat. Aluminium spars. Positive flotation. Self-bailers.
Sails:	Area 27.9m^2/300 sq.ft. Spinnaker area 18.6m^2/200 sq.ft.
Rigging:	Sloop
Price Guide:	$3,895us
Summary:	3 crew allowed, trapeze used.

RANGER 12

Supplier:	Ranger Fiberglass Boats, U.S.A.
Specifications:	*Construction:* GRP
	LOA: 3.81m/12'6
	Beam: 1.52m/5'0
	Draft: 0.15m/6'' cb up
	Displ: 102kg/225 lbs
Fittings:	Centreboard boat. Aluminium spars. Foam flotation.
Sails:	Area 9.5m^2 (6.3 + 3.2)/102 sq.ft. (63 + 34)
Rigging:	Sloop
Price Guide:	$925us
Summary:	Sailed only in America. Single-hander.

RAWSON 25

Design: Rawson & Seaborn, U.S.A. 1971

Supplier: Rawson National Association, U.S.A.
Ron Rawson Inc., U.S.A.

Specifications:

Construction:	GRP
LOA:	7.62m/25'0
Beam:	2.13m/7'0
Draft:	1.22m/4'0
Displ:	1,407kg/3,100 lbs
Ballast:	704kg/1,550 lbs

Fittings: Keelboat. Iron ballast.

Sails: Area 29.8m^2/321 sq.ft.
Spinnaker area 23.2m^2/250 sq.ft.

Rigging: Sloop

Price Guide: On application

Summary: 3 crew. Trailable.

R-BOAT

Design: Open design originating in 1920s.

Supplier: R-Boat National Association, U.S.A.

Specifications:

Construction:	Wood
LOA:	12.19m/40'0
Beam:	2.13m/7'0
Draft:	1.78m/5'10
Displ:	4,994kg/11,000 lbs

Fittings: Keelboat. Wooden spars

Sails: Area 54.5^2/587 sq. ft
Spinnaker area 91.8m^2/988 sq. ft.

Rigging: Sloop

Price Guide: Secondhand, approx. $6,000us

Summary: An old open class that maintains its popularity
in the States. Most boats available are secondhand.
5 crew.

RANGER 16

Design:	Gary Mull, 1968	
Supplier:	Ranger Fiberglass.Boats, U.S.A.	
Specifications:	*Construction:*	GRP
	LOA:	5.08m/16'8
	Beam:	1.83m/6'0
	Draft:	0.13m/5" cb up
	Displ:	204kg/450 lbs
Fittings:	Centreboard boat. Aluminium spars. Foam flotation. Self-bailers.	
Sails:	Area 14.4m^2 (9.8 + 4.6)/155 sq.ft. (105 + 50) Spinnaker area 19.5m^2/210 sq.ft.	
Rigging:	Sloop	
Price Guide:	$1,595us	
Summary:	2 crew. Sailed only in America on the west coast.	

REBEL U.S.A.

Design:	Ray Greene, U.S.A. 1940
Supplier:	Ray Greene & Co., U.S.A. Rebel Association, U.S.A.
Specifications:	*Construction:* GRP *LOA:* 4.9m/16′1 *Beam:* 2.03m/6′8 *Draft:* 0.15m/6″ cb up *Displ:* 318kg/700 lbs
Fittings:	Centreboard boat. Aluminium spars. Positive flotation. Self-bailers.
Sails:	Area $15.4m^2$ (11.1 + 4.3)/166 sq.ft. (119 + 47)
Rigging:	Sloop
Price Guide:	$2,440us
Summary:	1—2 crew. Sailed only in America.

RHODES BANTAM

Design:	Philip L. Rhodes, U.S.A. 1946
Supplier:	PIT Fiberglass Inc., U.S.A. Rhodes Bantam Association, U.S.A.
Specifications:	*Construction:* Wood and GRP *LOA:* 4.27m/14′0 *Beam:* 1.68m/5′6 *Draft:* 0.15m/6″ cb up *Displ:* 148kg/325 lbs
Fittings:	Centreboard boat. Spars — wood and aluminium Self-bailers.
Variations:	Flotation optional
Sails:	Area $13m^2$ (9.3 + 3.7)/140 sq.ft. (100 + 40) Spinnaker area $6.5m^2$/70 sq.ft.
Rigging:	Sloop
Price Guide:	$1,300us
Summary:	2 crew. Sailed only in America.

REBCATS COUGAR Mk III

Design:	Roland and Francis Prout
Supplier:	Lofland Sailcraft Inc., U.S.A.
Specifications:	*Construction:* GRP
	LWL: 5.18m/17'0
	LOA: 5.72m/18'9
	Beam: 2.43m/7'11½
	Draft: 0.81m/2'8
	Displ: 272kg/600 lbs
Fittings:	Centreboard boat. Aluminium spars.
Sails:	Area 23.2m^2/250 sq.ft.
Rigging:	Sloop
Price Guide:	On application.
Summary:	2 crew. Fast and easy to sail.

RHODES 18

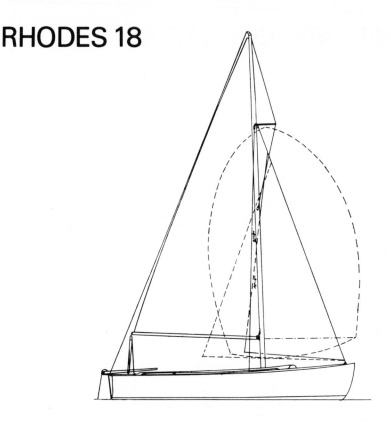

Design:	Philip L. Rhodes, U.S.A.
Supplier:	Cape Cod Shipbuilding Co., U.S.A. Rhodes 18 National Association, U.S.A.

Specifications:	*Construction:*	Wood or GRP
	LOA:	5.49m/18'0
	Beam:	1.91m/6'3
	Draft:	0.81m−1.22m/2'8−4'0
	Displ:	431kg/950 lbs
	Ballast:	136kg/300 lbs

Fittings:	Wooden or aluminium spars. Positive flotation.
Variations:	Available as a keel or centreboard boat.
Sails:	Area 17.1m^2/184sq.ft. Spinnaker area 18.3m^2/197 sq.ft.
Rigging:	Sloop
Price Guide:	$1,990us
Summary:	An exclusive American class. 3 crew allowed.

RHODES 19

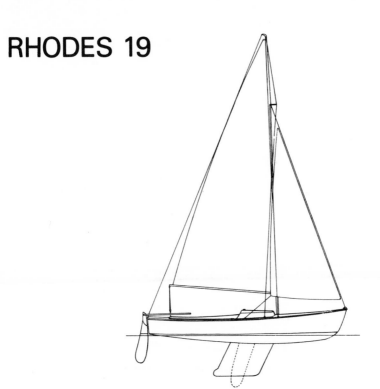

Design:	Philip L. Rhodes, U.S.A. 1959
Supplier:	Rhodes 19 National Association, U.S.A. O'Day, U.S.A.
Specifications:	*Construction:* GRP *LWL:* 5.41m/17'9 *LOA:* 5.84m/19'2 *Beam:* 2.13m/7'0 *Draft:* 0.99m/3'3 *Displ:* 606kg/1,335 lbs
Fittings:	Aluminium spars. Flotation tanks buoyancy.
Variations:	Available as a keel or centreboard boat.
Sails:	Area 16.3m^2/175 sq.ft. Spinnaker area 13.9m^2/150 sq.ft.
Rigging:	Sloop
Price Guide:	$2,500us
Summary:	2 crew. Trailable. A very popular American class, sailed all over the Continent.

ROBIN

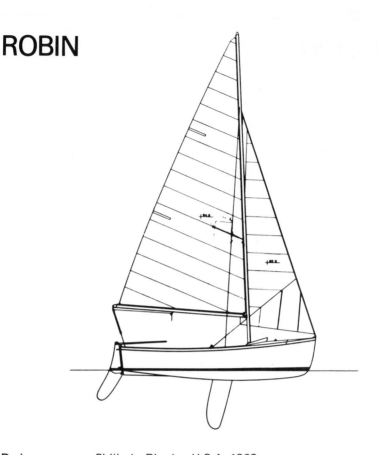

Design:	Philip L. Rhodes, U.S.A. 1962
Supplier:	P. Evanson Boat Co., U.S.A. Robin Association, U.S.A.
Specifications:	*Construction:* GRP *LOA:* 3.3m/10'10 *Beam:* 1.42m/4'8 *Draft:* 0.17m/7'' cb up *Displ:* 68kg/150 lbs
Fittings:	Centreboard boat. Aluminium spars. Teak trim. Kick-up rudder.
Sails:	Area 7.4m^2/80 sq.ft. Spinnaker area optional.
Rigging:	Sloop
Price Guide:	$835us
Summary:	2 crew. Sailed only in America. Kits available. Can be rowed, powered and car-topped.

328

ROOSTER

Design:	Michael P. Smith, 1954
Supplier:	Rooster Association, U.S.A.
Specifications:	*Construction:* Plywood
	LOA: 2.9m/9'6
	Beam: 1.17m/3'10
	Draft: 0.13m/5'' cb up
	Displ: 43.1m/95 lbs
Fittings:	Centreboard boat. Wooden spars. Positive flotation. Bailers.
Sails:	Area 3.4m^2/37 sq.ft.
Rigging:	Lug
Price Guide:	$375us
Summary:	Single-hander. Plans available.

S-12

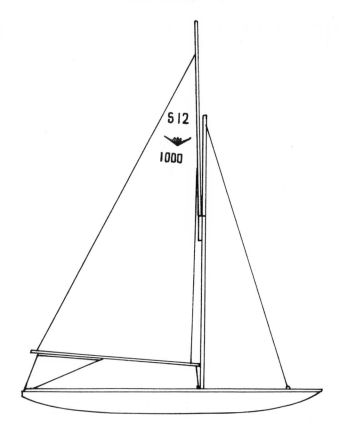

Design:	Russell Swenson, U.S.A. 1961
Supplier:	Alumacraft Boat Co., U.S.A.

Specifications:

Construction:	GRP
LOA:	3.65m/12'0
Beam:	1.219m/4'0
Draft:	0.076m/3" cb up
Displ:	81.3kg/178 lbs

Fittings: Centreboard boat. Aluminium spars. Foam flotation. Self-bailers.

Sails: Area 8.9m^2 (7 + 1.9)/95 sq.ft. (75 + 20)
No spinnaker allowed.

Rigging: Sloop

Price Guide: $600us

Summary: Built only in America at present. Single-hander

SABRE SCOW

Design:	Roger Hewson, Canada 1964
Supplier:	Hewson Marine, U.S.A.
Specifications:	*Construction:* GRP
	LOA: 7.92m²/26'0
	Beam: 1.98m/6'6
	Draft: 0.3m/1'0
	Displ: 381kg/840 lbs
Fittings:	Bilgeboards. Aluminium spars. Positive flotation.
Sails:	Area 25.2m²/272 sq.ft.
	Spinnaker area 37.2m²/400 sq. ft.
Rigging:	Sloop
Price Guide:	On application.
Summary:	3 crew. Very restricted in numbers — most sailed in Canada. Self-rescuing.

SAILFISH 7

Supplier:	Maxim Marine, England
Specifications:	*Construction:* GRP
	LOA: 2.29m/7'6
	Displ: 45kg/100 lbs
Variations:	Outboard may be attached.
Sails:	Area 3.7m^2/40 sq.ft.
Rigging:	Bermudan sloop
Summary:	2 crew. General purpose dinghy that can be car-topped.

SAILFISH 12

Supplier:	Maxim Marine, England
Specifications:	*Construction:* GRP
	LOA: 3.66m/12'0
	Beam: 1.58m/5'2
	Draft: 1.01m/3'4
	Displ: 88.80kg/198 lbs
Fittings:	Centreboard boat. Built-in buoyancy. Aluminium spars.
Sails:	Area 8.36m^2/90 sq.ft.
Rigging:	Bermudan sloop
Price Guide:	£250
Summary:	5 crew. Built specifically for tough, family use. Easy to maintain. Easily sailed.

SAILAWAY

Design: Pearson Bros.,U.K. 1970

Supplier: Pearson Bros., U.K.
Sailaway Association, U.K.

Specifications:

Construction:	GRP
LWL:	3.23m/10'9
LOA:	3.38m/11'1
Beam:	1.52m/5'0
Draft:	0.1m/4'' cb up
Displ:	62kg/130 lbs

Fittings: Centreboard boat. Aluminium spars. Kick-up rudder. Built-in buoyancy.

Sails: Area 6.7m^2 (3.7 + 3)/72 sq.ft. (40 + 32)

Rigging: Sloop

Price Guide: £220/$695us

Summary: 2 crew. Generous beam and deep hull give extra stability plus spaciousness. Popular and easy to handle family dinghy.

SAILOAR-10

Design:	John Lindsay, U.S.A.
Supplier:	Lincoln Fibreglass Inc., U.S.A.
Specifications:	Construction: GRP
	LOA: 3.05m/10'0
	Beam: 1.37m/4'6
	Draft: 0.1m/4" cb up
	Displ: 59kg/130 lbs
Fittings:	Centreboard boat. Aluminium spars. Positive flotation.
Sails:	Area 6m^2/65 sq.ft.
Rigging:	Una
Price Guide:	$700us
Summary:	Single-hander. Sailed only in America.

SALCOMBE YAWL

Design:	J. Stone, England
Supplier:	David Gibbens, England
Rating:	Secondary Portsmouth yardstick 101
Specifications:	Construction: Clinker Mahogany
	LWL: 4.88m/16'0
	LOA: 4.88m/16'0
	Beam: 2.03m/6'8
	Draft: 0.25m/10"
	Displ: 387.4kg/854 lbs
Fittings:	Keelboat. Wooden spars.
Variations:	Outboard may be attached.
Sails:	Area 13.94m^2/150 sq.ft.
Rigging:	Bermudan yawl
Price Guide:	On application
Summary:	2 or 3 crew. A racing and day dinghy that can be trailed. Fast and safe.

SAILFISH

Design:	Bryan & Heyniger, U.S.A. 1947
Supplier:	D. Bruce Connolly, U.S.A.
Specifications:	*Construction:* GRP
	LOA: 4.14m/13'7
	Beam: 0.91m/3'0
	Draft: 0.13m/5'' cb up
	Displ: 44kg/98 lbs
Fittings:	Centreboard boat. Aluminium spars. Foam flotation.
Sails:	Area 7m²/75 sq.ft.
	No spinnaker allowed.
Rigging:	Una
Price Guide:	$475us
Summary:	Single-hander. An extremely popular general purpose dinghy with over 25,000 sailed in America alone. Kits available. Self-rescuing.

SANDPIPER 15

Design:	Mike O'Brien, U.S.A. 1971
Supplier:	Sandpiper 15 Association, U.S.A.
Specifications:	*Construction:* GRP
	LOA: 4.47m/14'8
	Beam: 1.47m/4'10
	Draft: 0.13m/5" cb up
	Displ: 72kg/160 lbs
Fittings:	Centreboard boat. Aluminium spars. Foam flotation.
Sails:	Area 9.3m^2/100 sq.ft.
Rigging:	Lug
Price Guide:	$575 to $995us
Summary:	1 or 2. Sailed exclusively in America. A class restricted in numbers.

SANDSHARK

Design:	Henry Lane Wilson, U.S.A.
Supplier:	Nautical Boat Works, U.S.A.
	Sandshark Association, U.S.A.
Specifications:	*Construction:* GRP
	LOA: 3.66m/12'0
	Beam: 1.37m/4'6
	Draft: 0.1m/4"
	Displ: 68kg/150 lbs
Fittings:	Centreboard boat. Aluminium spars. Positive flotation.
Sails:	Area 9.9m^2/116 sq.ft.
Rigging:	Una
Price Guide:	$600us
Summary:	Single-hander. Sailed only in America

SANDHOPPER

Supplier:	Oliver J. Lee, England Horizon Enterprises, U.S.A.
Rating:	Provisional Portsmouth yardstick 104
Specifications:	*Construction:* GRP *LOA:* 5.79m/19'0 *Displ:* 636kg/1,400 lbs
Fittings:	Keelboat
Variations:	Outboard may be attached.
Sails:	Area 16.1m²/173 sq.ft. +
Rigging:	Bermudan sloop
Price Guide:	On application
Summary:	Takes up to 3 crew. A day and racing dinghy that can be trailed.

SANDPIPER 10

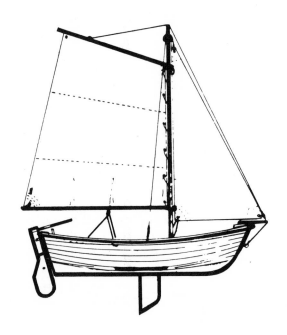

Design:	ESB, England
Supplier:	ESB Co., England

Specifications:	*Construction:*	GRP
	LWL:	3.1m/10'2
	LOA:	3.61m/11'10
	Beam:	1.42m/4'8
	Draft:	0.74m/2'5
	Displ:	95kg/210 lbs

Fittings:	Centreboard boat. Mast 3.66m/12'0 high. Stainless steel fittings. Built-in buoyancy. Non-slip floors.
Variations:	Several versions available.
Sails:	Area 6m^2/66 sq.ft.
Rigging:	Lugger
Price Guide:	£320 deluxe sailing version.
Summary:	A traditionally designed, all purpose dinghy. Well laid out interior.

SAN FRANCISCO PELICAN

Design:	William H. Short, U.S.A. 1958
Supplier:	San Francisco Pelican Association, U.S.A.
Specifications:	*Construction:* Plywood
	LOA: 3.71m/12'2
	Beam: 1.88m/6'2
	Draft: 0.1m/4'' cb up
	Displ: 148kg/325 lbs
Fittings:	Centreboard boat. Wooden spars. Foam flotation.
Sails:	Area 9.7m^2 (6.7 + 3)/105 sq.ft. (72 + 33)
Rigging:	Sloop
Price Guide:	$800us
Summary:	2 crew. Kits and plans available. Self-rescuing.

SCHOCK 25

Supplier:	W. D. Schock Co., U.S.A.
Specifications:	*Construction:* GRP
	LOA: 7.62m/25'0
	Beam: 2.13m/7'0
	Draft: 1.22m/4'0
Fittings:	Centreboard boat. Aluminium spars.
Sails:	Area 20.6m^2/222 sq.ft.
	Spinnaker area 27.9m^2/300 sq.ft.
Rigging:	Sloop
Price Guide:	On application
Summary:	3 crew. Self-rescuing.

SCIMITAR

Design:	Laurent Giles & Partners, England
Supplier:	Gloster Saro Limited, Wales.
Rating:	Portsmouth yardstick 96
Specifications:	*Construction:* GRP
	LOA: 6.17m/20'3
	Beam: 1.91m/6'3
	Draft: 1 0.91m/3'0
Fittings:	Keelboat. Aluminium spars.
Variations:	Adjustable mast position.
Sails:	Area 17.9m^2/193 sq.ft.
Rigging:	Masthead sloop
Price Guide:	On application
Summary:	Excellent all-weather boat. All day, all-round day sailer. Easy to maintain. Can be trailed.

SCAMPER 101

Design:	D. E. Matthews, U.S.A.
Supplier:	Formex Corporation, U.S.A.
Specifications:	*Construction:* ABS
	LOA: 3.35m/11'0
	Beam: 0.91m/3'0
	Draft: 0.1m/4'' cb up
	Displ: 24kg/52 lbs
Fittings:	Centreboard boat. Aluminium spars. Expanded polystyrene flotation.
Sails:	Area 4.2m^2/45 sq.ft.
Rigging:	Una
Price Guide:	$280us approx
Summary:	Single-hander.

SCORPION

Design:	Pargo Inc., U.S.A.
Supplier:	Scorpion Association, U.S.A.
Specifications:	*Construction:* GRP
	LOA: 4.2m/13'9
	Beam: 1.22m/4'0
	Draft: 0.1m/4" cb up
	Displ: 63kg/140 lbs
Fittings:	Centreboard boat. Aluminium spars. Foam flotation. Self-bailers.
Sails:	Area 7m^2/75 sq. ft.
Rigging:	Lug
Price Guide:	$575us
Summary:	Single-hander. Sailed mainly in America — on the east coast. A high performance fun boat.

SCOW

Supplier:	Palace Quay Boat Yard, England
Specifications:	*Construction:* GRP and wood
	LOA: 3.51m/11'6
	Displ: 91kg/200 lbs
Fittings:	Centreboard boat
Variations:	Outboard may be attached.
Sails:	Area 6.5m^2/70 sq.ft.
Rigging:	Gaff
Price Guide:	On application
Summary:	Takes up to 4 adults. A stable, general purpose dinghy. Can be trailed.

SCHOCK DORY

Supplier:	W. W. Schock Co., U.S.A.
Specifications:	*Construction:* GRP
	LOA: 6.1m/20'0
	Beam: 1.73m/5'8
Fittings:	Centreboard boat. Aluminium spars.
Sails:	Area 8.5m^2 (5.6 + 2.9)/91 sq.ft. (60 + 31)
Rigging:	Sloop
Price Guide:	On application.

A SCOW

Design:	John Johnson, U.S.A. 1897
Supplier:	ILYA, U.S.A.
Specifications:	*Construction:* Wood
	LOA: 11.58m/38'0
	Beam: 2.59m/8'6
	Draft: 0.08m/3" cb up
	Displ: 840kg/1,850 lbs
Fittings:	Bilgeboards. Aluminium spars. Foam flotation.
Sails:	Area 51.1m^2 (32.5 + 18.6)/550 sq.ft. (350 + 200) Spinnaker area 111.5m^2/1,200 sq.ft.
Rigging:	Sloop
Price Guide:	$8,000us
Summary:	Only about 30 boats in circulation and all are based in America. Unlimited crew. Traditional design.

MC SCOW

Design:	Harry Melges Snr., U.S.A.
Supplier:	MC Scow Association, U.S.A.
Specifications:	*Construction:* Wood
	LOA: 4.88m/16'0
	Beam: 1.68m/5'6
	Draft: 0.05m/2" cb up
Fittings:	Bilgeboards. Wooden spars. Positive flotation.
Sails:	Area 12.5m^2/135 sq.ft.
Rigging:	Una
Price Guide:	$1,700us+
Summary:	Sailed only in America. Hiking straps used.

SCOUT

Design:	Charles Gorgan, U.S.A.
Supplier:	Seago Corporation, U.S.A.
	Scout Association, U.S.A.

Specificiations:	*Construction:*	GRP
	LOA:	4.06m/13'4
	Beam:	1.91m/6'3
	Draft:	0.28m/11'' cb up
	Displ:	340kg/750 lbs
	Ballast:	113kg/250 lbs

Fittings:	Centreboard boat. Lead ballast. Aluminium spars. Foam flotation.
Sails:	Area 9.3m^2/100 sq.ft.
Rigging:	Una
Price Guide:	$1,530us
Summary:	Single-hander. Built only in America. Ideal for families, resorts, camps and training. Takes up to 6. Speedy in light weathers.

SEA DOG

Design:	Philip L. Rhodes, U.S.A. 1966
Supplier:	Aero Nautical Inc., U.S.A.
Specifications:	*Construction:* GRP
	LOA: 2.9m/9'6
	Beam: 1.24m/4'1
	Draft: 0.13m/5"
	Displ: 61kg/135 lbs
Fittings:	Daggerboard. Aluminium spars. Air chamber flotation.
Sails:	Area 3.9m^2/42 sq.ft.
Rigging:	Una
Price Guide:	$500us
Summary:	2 crew. Built only in America. A stable dinghy. Ideal for youngsters.

SIDEWINDER

Design:	J. R. Macalpine-Downie, 1968
Supplier:	Sail Manufacturing, U.S.A.
	Sail Craft, England
Specifications:	*Construction:* GRP
	LOA: 4.72m/15'6
	Beam: 1.37m/4'6
	Draft: 0.15m/6" cb up
	Displ: 79kg/175 lbs
Fittings:	Centreboard boat. Aluminium spars. Foam flotation Self-bailers.
Sails:	Area 19.2m^2/207 sq. ft.
	Spinnaker area 8.4m^2/90 sq. ft.
Rigging:	Cat or sloop rigged.
Price Guide:	$800–900us
Summary:	2 crew. Built only in the U.S.A. Can be car-topped and trailed. Hiking straps used.

SEA DEVIL

Design:	Lockley Manufacturing, U.S.A. 1964	
Supplier:	Lockley Manufacturing Inc., U.S.A.	
Specifications:	*Construction:*	Plastic
	LOA:	3.66m/12'0
	Beam:	0.99m/3'3
	Draft:	0.08m/3" cb up
	Displ:	36kg/80 lbs
Fittings:	Daggerboard. Aluminium spars. Foam flotation.	
Sails:	Area 6m^2 (5.1 + 0.9)/65 sq.ft. (55 + 10)	
Rigging:	Sloop	
Price Guide:	$230us	
Summary:	1 to 3 crew. Over 15,000 already built — sailed world-wide. Fun for adults, safe for children.	

SEAFARER DINGHY

Design:	Philip L. Rhodes, U.S.A. 1960
Supplier:	Seafarer Fiberglass Yachts Inc., U.S.A.
Specifications:	*Construction:* GRP
	LOA: 2.16m/7'1
	Beam: 1.22m/4'0
	Draft: 0.23m/9"
	Displ: 43kg/95 lbs
Fittings:	Centreboard boat. Aluminium spars. Air tank flotation.
Sails:	Area 2.6m^2/28 sq.ft.
Rigging:	Una
Price Guide:	$395us
Summary:	Single-hander. Easy to handle tender and small family dinghy.

SEAFIRE

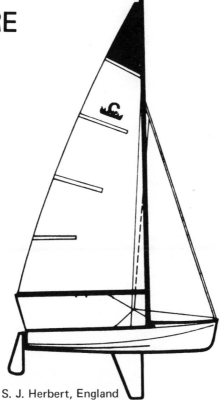

Design: S. J. Herbert, England

Supplier: South Devon Boatbuilders, England

Rating: Portsmouth yardstick 95 (sloop) 98 (una)

Specifications:

Construction:	GRP or marine ply
LWL:	4.11m/13'6
LOA:	4.27m/14'0
Beam:	1.80m/5'11
Draft:	1.17m/3'10
Displ:	86kg/190 lbs

Fittings: Centreboard boat. Mast 6.99m/22'11 high. Built-in buoyancy.

Variations: Flexible mast position for single-handed sailing.

Sails: Area 11.48m^2/120 sq.ft.
Spinnaker are 12.87m^2/135 sq.ft.

Rigging: Sloop or una

Price Guide: £350+

Summary: 2 crew or single-handed. A well balanced fast planing boat that is a delight to sail.

SEA GULL

Design:	Philip L. Rhodes, U.S.A. 1965
Supplier:	Aero Nautical Inc., U.S.A.
Specifications:	*Construction:* GRP
	LOA: 3.66m/12'0
	Beam: 1.45m/4'9
	Draft: 0.15m/6" cb up
	Displ: 109kg/240 lbs
Fittings:	Centreboard boat. Aluminium spars. Foam flotation. Self-bailers.
Sails:	Area 7.8m^2 (5.7 + 2.1)/84 sq.ft. (61 + 23)
Rigging:	Sloop
Price Guide:	$900us
Summary:	Carries 3 crew. Built only in the U.S.A.

SEAGULL

Design:	F. C. Gaines Jnr., U.S.A.
Supplier:	Seagull Association, U.S.A.
Specifications:	*Construction:* GRP
	LOA: 4.42m/14'6
	Beam: 1.27m/4'2
Fittings:	Daggerboard. Aluminium spars. Positive flotation.
Sails:	Area 9.4m^2/102 sq.ft.
Rigging:	Una
Price Guide:	On application
Summary:	Single-hander. Built only in America. Hiking straps used.

SEAGULL

Supplier:	Fibrocell, England
Specifications:	*Construction:* GRP
	LOA: 2.89m/9'6
	Beam: 1.37m/4'2
	Draft: 0.63m/2'1
	Displ: 65.7kg/145 lbs
Fittings:	Centreboard boat. Aluminium spars.
Variations:	Mk I and Mk II available.
Sails:	Area 5.11m^2/55 sq.ft. Spinnaker area 7.06m^2/76 sq.ft. also available.
Rigging:	Sloop, una or gunter
Price Guide:	£80
Summary:	A general purpose, maintenance-free dinghy. Good value for money.

SEA LARK

Design:	Aero Nautical Inc., U.S.A. 1968
Supplier:	Aero Nautical Inc., U.S.A.
Specifications:	*Construction:* GRP
	LOA: 2.33m/7'8
	Beam: 1.17m/3'10
	Draft: 0.1m/4'' cb up
	Displ: 36kg/79 lbs
Fittings:	Daggerboard. Aluminium spars.
Sails:	Area 3.3m^2/35 sq.ft.
Rigging:	Una
Price Guide:	$280us
Summary:	Carries 2 crew. Built only in America.

SEA SCOOTER

Design:	Edwin Monk, U.S.A.
Supplier:	Puget Boat Manufacturing, U.S.A.
Specifications:	*Construction:* GRP
	LOA: 3.18m/10'5
	Beam: 1.42m/4'8
	Displ: 59kg/130 lbs
Fittings:	Daggerboard. Aluminium spars. Air tank flotation.
Sails:	Area 5.6m^2/60 sq.ft.
Rigging:	Una
Price Guide:	$444us
Summary:	Single-hander.

SEA SNARK

Design:	Snark Products, U.S.A.	
Supplier:	Snark Products Inc., U.S.A.	
	Sea Snark Association, U.S.A.	
Specifications:	*Construction:*	Plastic
	LWL:	3.05m/10'0
	LOA:	3.35m/11'0
	Beam:	0.97m/3'2
	Draft:	0.91m/3'0
	Displ:	20kg/45 lbs
Fittings:	Daggerboard. Aluminium spars. Foam flotation.	
Sails:	Area 4.2m^2/45 sq.ft.	
Rigging:	Una	
Price Guide:	$120us	
Summary:	A 'fun' generaly purpose dinghy that has almost reached the 100,000 mark in numbers. Single-hander. Dry, safe, unsinkable.	

SEA SWINGER

Design:	Lockley Manufacturing, U.S.A. 1964
Supplier:	Lockley Manufacturing Inc., U.S.A.
Specifications:	*Construction:* Plastic
	LOA: 3.66m/12'0
	Beam: 0.99m/3'3
	Draft: 0.08m/3'' cb up
	Displ: 36kg/80 lbs
Fittings:	Daggerboard. Aluminium spars. Foam flotation. Self-bailers.
Sails:	Area 4.6m^2/50 sq.ft.
Rigging:	Una
Price Guide:	$200us
Summary:	Carries up to 3 crew. Carefree upkeep.

SESAME

Design:	Allan J. Arnold, U.S.A. 1971
Supplier:	Seahorse Sailboats, U.S.A. Sesame Association, U.S.A.

Specifications:	*Construction:*	GRP
	LWL:	3.58m/11'9
	LOA:	3.66m/12'0
	Beam:	1.37m/4'6
	Draft:	0.08m/3'' cb up
	Displ:	41kg/90 lbs

Fittings:	Centreboard boat. Aluminium spars.
Sails:	Area 9.3m^2 (6.3 + 3)/100 sq.ft. (68 + 32)
Rigging:	Sloop
Price Guide:	$695us
Summary:	Single-hander. Built only in America.

SHETLAND SKIFF

Design:	Traditional, England 1966
Supplier:	Cox Marine, England
Specifications:	*Construction:* GRP
	LOA: 4.65m/15'3
	Beam: 1.64m/5'4
	Draft: 0.32m/1'2
	Displ: 138.8kg/306 lbs
Fittings:	Mahogany trim. Mast 4.42m/14'6 high. Built-in buoyancy.
Sails:	Area 8.08m^2/87 sq.ft.
Rigging:	Gunter
Price Guide:	£300
Summary:	Design based on true Shetland Skiff first sailed 2,000 years ago. A double-ended clinker hull boat. No centre-board — not a racing boat. Light on the helm. Stable and seaworthy. Very roomy.

SHIELDS

Design:	Sparkman & Stephens, U.S.A, 1962
Supplier:	Henry R. Hinckley & Co., U.S.A.
	Shields One-Design Class, U.S.A.
Specifications:	*Construction:* GRP
	LOA: 9.22m/30'3
	Beam: 1.96m/6'5
	Draft: 1.45m/4'9
	Displ: 2,088kg/4,600 lbs
	Ballast: 1,398kg/3,080 lbs
Fittings:	Keelboat. Aluminium spars. Positive flotation.
Sails:	Area 33.4m^2/360 sq.ft.
	Spinnaker area 53.9m^2/580 sq.ft.
Rigging:	Sloop
Price Guide:	$7,500us
Summary:	3 crew. An American class. Can be trailed.

SEVEN / ELEVEN

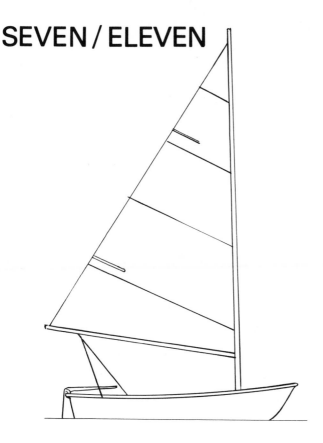

Design:	Robert Baker, U.S.A.	
Supplier:	O'Day, U.S.A.	
Specifications:	*Construction:*	GRP
	LOA:	2.41m/7'11
	Beam:	1.27m/4'2
	Draft:	0.1m/4'' cb up
	Displ:	40kg/89 lbs
Fittings:	Centreboard boat. Aluminium spars. Positive flotation.	
Sails:	Area 3.2m^2/34 sq.ft. No spinnaker allowed.	
Rigging:	Una	
Price Guide:	On application to individual owners.	
Summary:	Not in production. Secondhand boats only in circulation in America.	

SHRIMP

Design:	Vandestadt and McGruer, Canada 1970
Supplier:	Vandestadt and McGruer Ltd., Canada
Specifications:	*Construction:* GRP
	LOA: 2.92m/9'7
	Beam: 1.47m/4'10
	Draft: 0.1m^2/4" cb up
	Displ: 54kg/120 lbs
Fittings:	Centreboard boat. Aluminium spars. Foam flotation. Self-bailers.
Sails:	Area 4.6m^2/50 sq.ft.
Rigging:	Una
Price Guide:	$495us
Summary:	Single-hander. Majority sailed in Canada.

6 METRE

Design:	Open, established 1921
Supplier:	IYRU, England
Specifications:	*Construction:* Open
	LOA: 11.28m/37'0
	Beam: 1.83m/6'0
	Draft: 1.65m/5'5
	Displ: 4,313kg/9,500 lbs
Fittings:	Keelboat
Sails:	Area 42.7m^2/460 sq.ft.
Rigging:	Open
Summary:	5 crew allowed. Write to the IYRU for further information.

SKATE

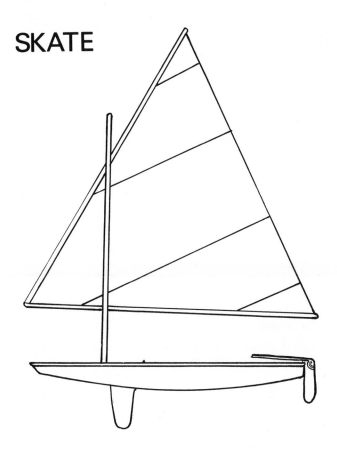

Design:	Wesley Lazott, U.S.A.	
Supplier:	Skate Association, U.S.A.	
Specifications:	*Construction:*	GRP
	LOA:	3.1m/10'2
	Beam:	1.01m/3'4
	Draft:	0.1m^2/4'' cb up
	Displ:	36kg/80 lbs
Fittings:	Centreboard boat. Aluminium spars. Positive flotation.	
Sails:	Area 3.7m^2/40 sq.ft. No spinnaker allowed.	
Rigging:	Una	
Price Guide:	$500us+	
Summary:	Single-hander. Built only in America, and sailed particularly in the north-east. Self rescuing.	

SKIPPER 12

Design:	Peter Milne, U.K. 1968
Supplier:	Richmond Marine, U.K. Intermarine Agency, U.S.A.
Rating:	Portsmouth yardstick 116

Specifications:

Construction:	GRP
LWL:	3.34m/11'0
LOA:	3.66m/12'0
Beam:	1.45m/4'9
Draft:	0.15m/6'' cb up
Displ:	65.77kg/145 lbs

Fittings:	Daggerboard. Aluminium spars. Mast 3.94m/12'11 high. Built-in buoyancy.
Sails:	Area 6.04m^2/65 sq.ft.
Rigging:	Sloop
Price Guide:	£200/$695us
Summary:	2 crew. Over 2,000 boats built. Easy to rig, handle and maintain. Can be car-topped.

SKIPPER 14

Design:	Peter Milne, U.K. 1968
Supplier:	Richmond Marine, U.K. Intermarine Agency, U.S.A.
Rating:	Portsmouth yardstick 116

Specifications:

Construction:	GRP
LWL:	3.96m/13'0
LOA:	4.27m/14'0
Beam:	1.54m/4'11
Draft:	0.15m/6'' cb up
Displ:	83.92kg/185 lbs

Fittings:	Daggerboard. Aluminium spars. Built-in buoyancy. Mast 3.94m/12'11 high.
Sails:	Area 6.50m^2/70 sq.ft.
Rigging:	Sloop
Price Guide:	£250/$895us
Summary:	Carries 2 to 4 crew. Uncomplicated to handle. Can be rigged and launched in minutes. Very versatile.

SKIPJACK

Design: Sindle, Pyle & Moorman, U.S.A. 1964

Supplier: Newport Boats, U.S.A.
Skipjack Association, U.S.A.

Specifications:

Construction:	GRP
LOA:	4.44m/14'7
Beam:	1.6m/5'3
Draft:	0.10m/4'' cb up
Displ:	102.2kg/255 lbs

Fittings: Centreboard boat. Aluminium spars. Foam plus air tank flotation. Self-bailers.

Sails: Area 11.49m^2/125 sq.ft.
Spinnaker area 13.94m^2/150 sq.ft.
Fully battened mainsail.

Rigging: Sloop

Price Guide: $1,500us

Summary: 2 crew. Built only in America. Self-rescuing. Kits and plans unavailable. A well-mannered family sailer.

SKYLARK

Design:	Stephen M. Taylor, Canada (I) 1963 (II) 1964
Supplier:	Canadian Boat Manufacturing Co. Canada Hydro Swift Corporation, U.S.A. Skylark Racing Association, U.S.A.

Specifications:

	Construction:	GRP
	LOA:	4.31m/14'2
	Beam:	1.42m/4'8
	Draft:	0.0508m/2" cb up
	Displ:	under study.

Fittings:	Centreboard boat. Aluminium spars. Foam flotation. Self-bailers. Kick-up rudder.
Variations:	MkI or II available. I — leeboards. II — bilgeboards.
Sails:	Area 9.29m^2/100 sq.ft. No spinnaker allowed. Dacron.
Rigging:	Una
Price Guide:	$795us
Summary:	2 crew. Sailed in America and Canada. Kits/plans unavailable. Bright, stable and responsive.

SLIPPER

Design:	Ray Greene, U.S.A.
Supplier:	Ray Greene & Co. U.S.A. Slipper Association, U.S.A.

Specifications:

	Construction:	GRP
	LOA:	3.66m/12'0
	Beam:	1.58m/5'2
	Draft:	0.15m/6" cb up
	Displ:	159kg/350 lbs

Fittings:	Centreboard boat. Aluminium spars. Foam flotation. Self-bailers.
Sails:	Area 10.2m^2 (9.3 + 0.9)/110 sq.ft. (100 + 10)
Rigging:	Sloop
Price Guide:	$1,155us
Summary:	2 crew. Self-bailing.

SKUNK

Design:	Vandestadt & McGruer, Canada 1968
Supplier:	Vandestadt & McGruer, Canada
Specifications:	*Construction:* GRP
	LOA: 3.377m/11'1
	Beam: 1.647m/5'5
	Draft: 0.127m/5'' cb up
	Displ: 77.2kg/170 lbs
Fittings:	Centreboard boat. Aluminium spars. Foam flotation. Self-bailers.
Sails:	Area 6.503m^2 *(4.6 + 1.9)*/70 sq.ft. (50 + 20) No spinnaker allowed.
Rigging:	Sloop
Price Guide:	$695us
Summary:	2 crew. Kits/plans unavailable. Fills the need of the fisherman, cottage owner and those who wish to sail on a modest income.

SNOWBIRD

Supplier:	W. D. Schock Co., U.S.A.
Specifications:	*Construction:* Wood or GRP
	LOA: 3.66m/12'0
	Beam: 1.52m/5'0
	Draft: 0.1m/4'' cb up
Fittings:	Centreboard boat. Wooden spars. Positive flotation.
Sails:	Area $9.5m^2$/102 sq.ft.
Rigging:	Una
Price Guide:	On application
Summary:	Single-hander. Built only in America.

SPORTYAK I, II, III

Supplier:	Inovac (GB) Limited, England
Specifications:	*Construction:* ABS
	LOA: 2.29m/7'6
	2.59m/8'6
	3.28m/10'9
	Displ: 25kg/54 lbs
	44kg/96 lbs
	75kg/165 lbs
Fittings:	Daggerboard. Various optional fittings available.
Variations:	Outboard can be attached.
Sails:	Area $3.7m^2$, $4.5m^2$, $8.9m^2$/40sq.ft., 48 sq.ft., 96 sq.ft.
Rigging:	Bermudan sloop/Gaff/Lug
Price Guide:	On application.
Summary:	General purpose dinghies that carry from 1 to 4 crew. Can be car-topped and trailed.

SL-140

Design:	Anchor Fiberglass, U.S.A.
Supplier:	Anchor Fiberglass Products, U.S.A.
Specifications:	*Construction:* GRP
	LWL: 2.44m/8'0
	LOA: 4.33m/14'2½
	Beam: 1.17m/3'10
	Draft: 0.09m/3½
	Displ: 61kg/135 lbs
Fittings:	Centreboard boat. Aluminium spars. Deck storage compartment.
Sails:	Area 7m²/75 sq.ft.
Rigging:	Una
Price Guide:	$600us
Summary:	Takes up to 3 crew. Monolithic hull gives greater speed.

SPROG

Design:	H. H. McWilliams, South Africa
Supplier:	Sprog Association, England
Rating:	Portsmouth yardstick 104
Specifications:	*Construction:* Marine plywood
	LWL: 4.19m/13'9
	LOA: 4.27m/14'0
	Beam: 1.3m/4'3
	Draft: 0.91m/3'0
	Displ: 109kg/240 lbs
Fittings:	Centreboard boat. Wooden spars.
Sails:	Area 8.3m^2/89 sq.ft.
Rigging:	Sloop
Price Guide:	Kits vary in price.
Summary:	Available in kit form only. Traditional all-purpose dinghy design.

SQUALL

Design:	Howard Chapelle, U.S.A.
Supplier:	Boston Whaler Inc. U.S.A.
	Squall Association, U.S.A.
Specifications:	*Construction:* GRP
	LOA: 2.84m/9'4
	Beam: 1.35m/4'5
	Draft: 0.15m/6'' cb up
	Displ: 54kg/120 lbs
Fittings:	Centreboard boat. Aluminium spars. Foam flotation.
Sails:	Area 7m^2/75 sq.ft.
Rigging:	Una
Price Guide:	$715us
Summary:	Single-hander. An easily handled, pram dinghy sailed mainly in the north-east of America.

SPARKLER

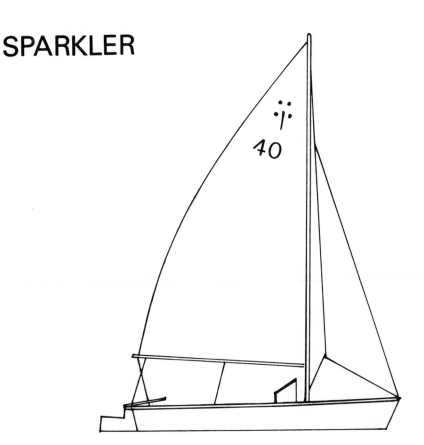

Design:	Bob Ellenbest, U.S.A.
Supplier:	One Design Yachts, U.S.A. Sparkler Association, U.S.A.
Specifications:	*Construction:* GRP *LOA:* 3.353m/11'0 *Beam:* 1.372m/4'6 *Draft:* 0.1016m/4'' cb up *Displ:* 64kg/142 lbs
Fittings:	Daggerboard. Aluminium spars. Positive flotation.
Sails:	Area 7.403m²/79 sq.ft.
Rigging:	Sloop
Price Guide:	$650us approx.
Summary:	Carries 2 crew. Built only in America. Self-rescuing. Hiking straps used.

STARFLITE

Supplier:	I. D. Baret & Co., England
Specifications:	*Construction:* GRP
	LOA: 4.27m/14'0
	Beam: 1.73m/5'8
	Draft: 1.22m/4'0
	Displ: 216kg/475 lbs
Fittings:	Centreboard boat. Aluminium spars. Teak trim. Kick-up rudder.
Sails:	Area 10.4m^2/112 sq.ft.
Rigging:	Sloop
Price Guide:	On application.
Summary:	Very stable dinghy. Takes up to 4 adults.

STINGRAY

Design:	G. Linell, U.S.A.
Supplier:	Arena Craft Products Inc., U.S.A. Stingray Association, U.S.A.
Specifications:	*Construction:* GRP
	LOA: 4.01m/13'2
	Beam: 1.371m/4'6
	Draft: 0.405m/1'4
Fittings:	Centreboard boat. Aluminium spars. Positive flotation.
Sails:	Area 8.861m^2/95 sq.ft. No spinnaker.
Rigging:	Una
Price Guide:	$600us approx.
Summary:	Single-hander. Kits/plans unavailable. Built only in America.

SPINDRIFT

Design:	Hubert, Vandestadt, Canada 1965
Supplier:	Vandestadt & McGruer, Canada
Specifications:	*Construction:* GRP foam sandwich
	LOA: 4.06m/13'4
	Beam: 1.58m/5'2
	Draft: 0.1m/4'' cb up
	Displ: 91kg/200 lbs
Fittings:	Centreboard boat. Aluminium spars. Kick-up rudder. Foam flotation. Self-bailers.
Sails:	Area 9.3m^2 (6.5 + 2.8)/100 sq.ft. (70 + 30)
Rigging:	Sloop
Price Guide:	$995us
Summary:	2 crew. Planes easily. A good all round boat that stands out as good value for money.

STOWAWAY 8

Design: H. H. van der Heide, U.S.A. 1972

Supplier: Sport Skiff Inc., U.S.A.

Specifications: *Construction:* Rubberised nylon.
                     LOA: 2.39m/7'10
                     Beam: 1.12m/3'8
                     Draft: 0.08m/3''
                     Displ: 25kg/55 lbs

Fittings: Centreboard boat. Aluminium spars. Air bag
                     flotation.

Sails: Area 3.5m^2/38 sq.ft.

Rigging: Una

Price Guide: $595us

Summary: 2 crew.

STOWAWAY 10

Design: H. H. van der Heide, U.S.A. 1972

Supplier: Sport Skiff Inc., U.S.A.

Specifications: *Construction:* Rubberised nylon.
                     LOA: 3.1m/10'2
                     Beam: 1.37m/4'6
                     Draft: 0.1m/4'' cb up
                     Displ: 34kg/75 lbs

Fittings: Centreboard boat. Aluminium spars. Air bag flotation.

Sails: Area 5.4m^2/58 sq.ft.

Rigging: Una

Price Guide: $795us

Summary: Carries 3 crew. Built only in America.

STARFISH

Design:	John Fillip, U.S.A.
Supplier:	Canadian Boat Manufacturing Co., Canada
	Fillip Manufacturing Co., U.S.A.

Specifications:

Construction:	GRP
LWL:	3.71m/12'6
LOA:	4.16m/13'8
Beam:	1.219m/4'0
Draft:	0.711m/2'4
Displ:	59.1kg/130 lbs

Fittings:	Centreboard boat. Aluminium spars and trim.
Sails:	Area 7.63m^2/82 sq.ft.
	No spinnaker allowed.
Rigging:	Una
Price Guide:	$900us
Summary:	Single-hander. Self-rescuing. Can be trailed.

SUNBEAM

Design: Alfred Westmacott, England 1922

Supplier: Alfred Westmacott Co., England

Specifications:
Construction: Specified woods.
LWL: 5.33m/17'6
LOA: 8.05m/26'5
Beam: 1.83m/6'0
Draft: 1.14m/3'9

Fittings: Centreboard boat. Wooden spars.

Sails: Area 27.9m^2/300 sq.ft.

Rigging: Bermudan masthead sloop

Price Guide: On application

Summary: The large sail area in comparison with the size of the hull results in remarkable light weather performance, extreme ease of handling and quickness on the helm. Requires skilful sailing, early reefing and care in heavy weather.

SUPER SATELLITE

Design: Ted Carpenter, U.S.A.

Supplier: Catalina Yachts, U.S.A.

Specifications:
Construction: GRP
LOA: 4.27m/14'0
Beam: 1.83m/6'0
Draft: 1.07m/3'6
Displ: 68kg/150 lbs

Fittings: Centreboard boat. Aluminium spars. Positive flotation.

Sails: Area 12.1m^2/130 sq.ft.
No spinnaker allowed.

Rigging: Sloop

Price Guide: Secondhand prices fluctuate.

Summary: 2 crew. Hiking straps used. No longer in production.

SUNFISH

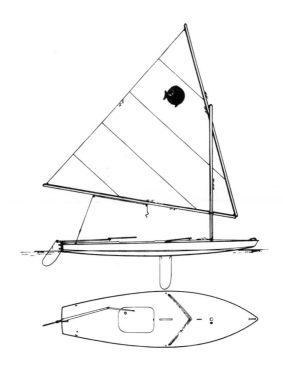

Design:	AMF Alcort, U.S.A.
Supplier:	D. Bruce Connolly, U.S.A.
Specifications:	*Construction:* GRP
	LOA: 4.22m/13'10
	Beam: 1.24m/4'1
	Draft: 0.76m/2'6
	Displ: 63kg/139 lbs
Fittings:	Daggerboard. Aluminium spars. Foam flotation.
Sails:	Area 7m^2/75 sq.ft. No spinnaker allowed. Dacron used.
Rigging:	Una
Price Guide:	$600us
Summary:	Single-hander. Built only in America. Over 60,000 already built. Ideal family boat. Kits available. Perfect for the beginner or advance sailor.

SUNFLOWER

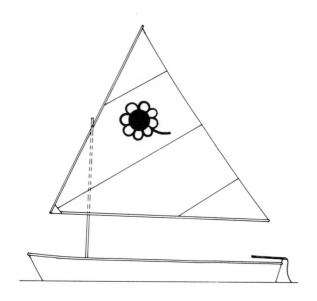

Design:	Snark Products, U.S.A.
Supplier:	Snark Products Inc., U.S.A. Sunflower Association, U.S.A.
Specifications:	*Construction:* Plastic *LWL:* 3.05m/10'0 *LOA:* 3.35m/11'0 *Beam:* 0.97m/3'2 *Draft:* 0.08m/3'' *Displ:* 29kg/63 lbs
Fittings:	Daggerboard. Aluminium spars. Foam flotation. Splash deck.
Sails:	Area 5.1m^2/55 sq.ft.
Rigging:	Una
Price Guide:	$230us
Summary:	Single-hander. Unsinkable. Can be carried and car-topped. Maintenance-free.

SUNSPOT

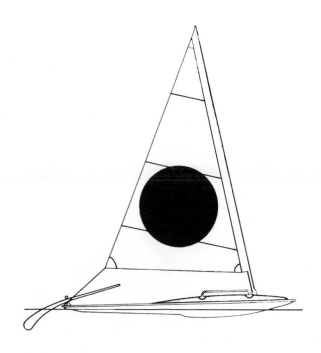

Design:	Colin Mudie, U.S.A.
Supplier:	Sunspot Plastics Inc., Canada Sunspot Association, Canada
Specifications:	*Construction:* Plastic *LOA:* 4.22m/13'10 *Beam:* 1.22m/4'0 *Draft:* 0.2m/8'' cb up *Displ:* 57kg/125 lbs
Fittings:	Bilgekeels. Aluminium spars. Foam flotation. Self-bailers.
Sails:	Area 5.6m^2/60 sq.ft.
Rigging:	Una
Price Guide:	$590us
Summary:	Stable and safe with lots of deck space. Unsinkable and maintenance-free. Recommended for resorts and rentals.

SUPER PORPOISE

Design:	Molded Products Co., U.S.A. 1961
Supplier:	Super Porpoise Association, U.S.A.
Specifications:	*Construction:* GRP
	LOA: 4.47m/14'8
	Beam: 1.24m/4'1
	Draft: 0.5m/2'' cb up
	Displ: 68kg/150 lbs
Fittings:	Centreboard boat. Aluminium spars. Foam flotation. Self-bailers.
Sails:	Area 7.9m^2/85 sq.ft.
Rigging:	Una
Price Guide:	$584us
Summary:	Single-hander. Majority sailed in America.

SUPER SCAMPER

Design:	D. E. Matthews, U.S.A. 1969
Supplier:	Formex Corporation, U.S.A.
Specifications:	*Construction:* ABS
	LOA: 3.35m/11'0
	Beam: 0.91m/3'0
	Draft: 0.1m/4'' cb up
	Displ: 38.6kg/85 lbs
Fittings:	Daggerboard. Aluminium spars. Foam flotation.
Sails:	Area 5.1m²/55 sq.ft.
Rigging:	Una
Price Guide:	$220us
Summary:	2 crew. Over 20,000 sailed in America. Unsinkable, easy to launch, trail and sail. Excellent for the novice or the experienced sailor.

TABUR YAK 3

Supplier: Tabur Marine, U.K.

Specifications:

Construction:	ABS
LOA:	3.2m/10'6
Beam:	1.39m/4'7
Draft:	0.20m/8''
Displ:	83kg/183 lbs

Fittings: Centreboard boats. Aluminium spars. Mast 5.86m/19'3 high. Built-in buoyancy.

Variations: Taburyak 2 (LOA: 2.51m/8'3) also available.

Sails: Area 8.9m^2/96 sq.ft.

Rigging: Bermudan sloop

Price Guide: £200

Summary: Carries up to 5 crew. Suitable for fishing, rowing, sailing and outboard boating.

TANZER 14

Design: Johann Tanzer, Canada 1969

Supplier: Tanzer Industries Ltd., Canada

Specifications:

Construction:	GRP
LOA:	4.1m/13'6
Beam:	1.68m/5'6
Draft:	0.13m/5'' cb up
Displ:	143kg/315 lbs

Fittings: Centreboard boat. Aluminium spars. Foam filled tank flotation. Self-bailing.

Sails: Area 9.5m^2/102sq.ft. (62 + 40)
Spinnaker area 11.15m^2/120 sq.ft. Dacron.

Rigging: Sloop

Price Guide: $1,095us

Summary: 2 crew. A fast, stiff boat with hard chine and generous beam.

SURPRISE

Design: Harry R. Sindle, U.S.A. 1969

Supplier: Newport Boats, U.S.A.
Surprise Association, U.S.A.

Specifications:
Construction:	GRP
LWL:	4.27m/14'0
LOA:	4.44m/14'7
Beam:	1.6m/5'3
Draft:	0.1m/4'' cb up
Displ:	120kg/265 lbs

Fittings: Centreboard boat. Aluminium spars. Foam and air tank flotation. Reinforced transom for outboard motor.

Sails: Area 10.2m^2 (6.2 + 4)/110 sq.ft. (67 + 43) Spinnaker area 13.9m^2/150 sq.ft.

Rigging: Sloop

Price Guide: $1,100us

Summary: 2 or 3 crew — but can carry up to 5 adults. Self-rescuing.

TC 8

Design:	A. E. Scott, U.S.A.	
Specificati⸱ns:	*Construction:*	GRP
	LOA:	2.44m/8'0
	Beam:	1.2m/3'11
	Draft:	0.1m/4''
	Displ:	40.9kg/90 lbs
Fittings:	Centreboard boat. Aluminium spars. Air tank flotation.	
Sails:	Area 3.3m^2/35 sq.ft.	
Rigging:	Una	
Price Guide:	$400us	
Summary:	Single-hander.	

TEN SIX

Supplier:	Wyvern Boats, England	
Specifications:	*Construction:*	Chine
	LOA:	3.2m/10'6
	Displ:	59kg/130 lbs
Fittings:	Centreboard boat.	
Variations:	Outboard may be attached.	
Sails:	Area 8.4m^2/90 sq.ft.	
Rigging:	Various	
Price Guide:	On application.	
Summary:	2 crew. General purpose dinghy. Can be car-topped.	

SUSSEX COB

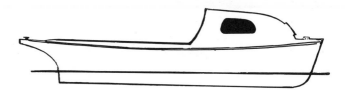

Design:	Pearson Bros., England
Suppliers:	Meeching Boats, U.K.
	Pearson Bros., U.K.

Specifications:

Construction:	GRP
LWL:	4.19m/13'9
LOA:	5.03m/16'6
Beam:	1.73m/5'8
Draft:	0.23m/9'' cb up
Displ:	172kg/380 lbs

Fittings: Centreboard boat. Pine masts and boom. Built-in buoyancy.

Variations: Outboard well and two rowing positions incorporated. Detachable cuddy can be fitted.

Sails: Area 10.22m^2/110 sq.ft. Tan coloured.

Rigging: Gunter or ketch

Price Guide: £500

Summary: Designed for operation from open beaches with a counter stern so that the boat will not swamp when beaching. Versatile and seaworthy. A good fishing vessel.

TERN

Design:	C. Allen, U.S.A.
Supplier:	England Sailboat Co., U.S.A.
Specifications:	*Construction:* Wood or GRP
	LOA: 3.66m/12'0
	Beam: 1.37m/4'6
	Draft: 0.08m/3''
Fittings:	Centreboard boat. Spars — aluminium or wood. Positive flotation.
Sails:	Area 8.2m^2/88 sq.ft. Spinnaker area 6.5m^2/70 sq.ft.
Rigging:	Una
Price Guide:	On application
Summary:	This particular boat built and sailed only in America. Single-hander.

THANET 14

Supplier:	Thanetcraft Ltd., England
Specifications:	*Construction:* GRP
	LOA: 4.34m/14'3
	Displ: 114kg/250 lbs
Fittings:	Centreboard boat.
Variations:	Outboard can be fitted. Thanet 9 also available (LOA: 2.74m/9'0)
Sails:	Area 9.3m^2/100 sq.ft.
Rigging:	Sloop
Price Guide:	On application
Summary:	4 crew. General purpose dinghy that can be trailed.

SWEET 16

Design:	Advance Sailboat Corporation, U.S.A. 1965
Supplier:	Advance Sailboat Co., U.S.A. Sweet 16 Association, U.S.A.
Specifications:	*Construction:* GRP *LWL:* 3.73m/12'3 *LOA:* 4.88m/16'0 *Beam:* 1.83m/6'0 *Draft:* 0.28m/11'' *Displ:* 204kg/450 lbs
Fittings:	Centreboard boat. Aluminium spars. Air and foam flotation. Bailers.
Sails:	Area 11.8m^2/127 sq.ft. Spinnaker area 23.2m^2/250 sq.ft.
Rigging:	Sloop
Price Guide:	$1,540us
Summary:	2 crew. Built only in America. A long, fine bow permits excellent windward performance whilst the wide hull gives good stability.

THUNDERCAT

Design:	Ross Sackett, U.S.A. 1965
Supplier:	Snug Harbour Boat Works, U.S.A. Thundercat Association, U.S.A.
Specifications:	*Construction:* GRP *LOA:* 4m/13'2 *Beam:* 1.6m/5'2 *Draft:* 0.15m/6'' *Displ:* 84kg/185 lbs
Fittings:	Daggerboard. Aluminium spars. Foam flotation.
Sails:	Area 10.22m^2/110 sq.ft.
Rigging:	Una
Price Guide:	$800us
Summary:	An American class.

TOD 15

Design:	W. & J. Tod, England
Supplier:	W & J. Tod (Sales), England
Specifications:	*Construction:* GRP *LOA:* 4.57m/15'0 *Displ:* 186kg/410 lbs
Fittings:	Centreboard boat.
Variations:	Outboard may be attached. Tod 9 (LOA: 9'0) and Tod 12 (LOA: 12'0) also available.
Sails:	Area 11.2m^2/120 sq.ft.
Rigging:	Gunter. Tod 9 — lug-rigged.
Summary:	General purpose dinghy. Takes up to 5 adults. Can be trailed.

TANZER 16

Design:	Johann Tanzer, Canada 1965
Supplier:	Tanzer Industries Ltd., Canada
Specifications:	*Construction:* GRP
	LWL: 4.65m/15'3
	LOA: 4.98m/16'4
	Beam: 1.88m/6'2
	Draft: 0.17m/7'' cb up
	Displ: 204.3kg/450 lbs
Fittings:	Centreboard boat. Aluminium spars. Foam filled tank flotation.
Sails:	Area 13.5m² (9.3 + 4.2)/145 sq. ft. (100 + 45) Spinnaker area 19m²/205 sq. ft.
Rigging:	Sloop
Price Guide:	$1,695us
Summary:	2 crew. A high performance boat that is also comfortable, stable and safe. Ideal for beginners.

TOMBOY

Design:	Morgan Fairest, England
Supplier:	Morgan Fairest, England
Specifications:	*Construction:* ABS
	LOA: 3.12m/10'3
	Displ: 70kg/155 lbs
Fittings:	Daggerboard. Aluminium spars.
Variations:	Outboard can be attached.
Sails:	Area 4.4m^2/47 sq.ft.
Rigging:	Bermudan una
Price Guide:	£140
Summary:	4 or 5 seating capacity. Can be trailed and car-topped.

TOWN CLASS

Design:	Pert Lowell, U.S.A. 1932
Supplier:	Parker Rover Marine, U.S.A.
	Town Class Association, U.S.A.
Specifications:	*Construction:* Wood or GRP
	LOA: 5.03m/16'6
	Beam: 1.75m/5'9
	Draft: 0.18m/7''
	Displ: 353.2kg/800 lbs
Fittings:	Wooden spars. Centreboard boat. Positive flotation.
Sails:	Area 14.1m^2/152 sq.ft.
Rigging:	Sloop
Price Guide:	$2,195us
Summary:	2 crew. Sailed only in the U.S.A.

TECH II

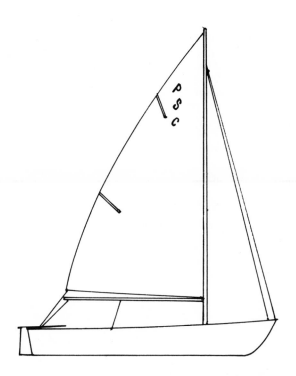

Design:	MIT, U.S.A.
Supplier:	MIT, U.S.A.
Specifications:	*Construction:* GRP
	LOA: 3.8m/12'6
	Beam: 1.52m/5'0
	Draft: 0.1m/4''
Fittings:	Centreboard boat. Aluminium spars. Positive flotation.
Sails:	Area 10m^2/108 sq.ft. No spinnaker allowed.
Rigging:	Una
Price Guide:	On application
Summary:	2 crew. Sailed only in America.

22 SQUARE METER

Design: Open, established 1922

Supplier: 22 Square Meter National Association, U.S.A.

Specifications: *Construction:*   Wood
                       LOA: 9.75m—12.8m/32'—42'
                       Beam: 1,83m—2.13m/6'—7'
                       Draft: 1.32m/4'4
                       Displ: Open
                       Ballast: Open

Fittings: Keelboat. Wooden spars.

Sails: Area 21.9m^2/236 sq.ft.
                       Spinnaker area 46.45m^2/500 sq.ft.

Rigging: Sloop

Price Guide: $8,500us secondhand

Summary: 3 crew. Popular class worldwide.

US MONOTYPE

Design: Howard Snyder, U.S.A.

Supplier: US Monotype Association, U.S.A.

Specifications: *Construction:*   Wood or GRP
                       LOA: 4.32m/14'2
                       Beam: 1.73m/5'8
                       Draft: 0.15m/6''

Fittings: Centreboard boat. Spars — wood or aluminium.
                       Positive flotation.

Sails: Area 8.85m^2/95 sq.ft.

Rigging: Una

Price Guide: $2,000us

Summary: Single-hander. Hiking straps.

THISTLE

Design:	Gordon Douglass, U.S.A. 1946
Supplier:	England's Sailboats, U.S.A. Thistle Association, U.S.A.

Specifications:

	Construction:	Wood or GRP
	LOA:	5.88m/17'0
	Beam:	1.83m/6'0
	Draft:	0.23m/9''
	Displ:	233.8kg/515 lbs

Fittings:	Centreboard boat. Spars — wood and aluminium Bailers.
Variations:	Variable flotation.
Sails:	Area 16.3m^2/175 sq.ft. Spinnaker area 18.6m^2/200 sq.ft.
Rigging:	Sloop
Price Guide:	$2,075us
Summary:	2 crew. A very popular class and general purpose dinghy. Sailed all over America.

THUNDERBIRD

Design:	Ben Seaborn, U.S.A. 1958
Supplier:	Transpacific Marine Co., Taiwan International Thunderbird Class Association, U.S.A.
Est. Rating:	20.6 10R Mk III
Specifications:	*Construction:* Wood or GRP *LWL:* 6.1m/20'0 *LOA:* 7.92m/26'0 *Beam:* 2.29m/7'6 *Draft:* 1.52m/5'0 *Displ:* 1,816kg/4,000 lbs *Ballast:* 694.6kg/1,530 lbs
Fittings:	Keelboat. Cast iron ballast. Spars wood or aluminium. Wood or GRP decking.
Variations:	Can be supplied as a cruiser with 4 berths.
Sails:	Area 33.8m^2/364 sq.ft. Spinnaker area 29.7m^2/320 sq.ft.
Rigging:	Sloop
Price Guide:	$4,500us home built.
Summary:	3 crew. Trailable. Normally supplied in kit form.

TURNABOUT

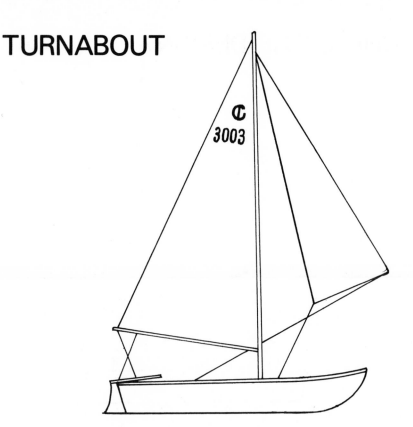

Design:	Harold Turner
Supplier:	Parker River Marine Inc., U.S.A.
Specifications:	*Construction:* Wood or grp
	LOA: 2.9m/9'8
	Beam: 1.6m/5'3
	Draft: 0.08m/3"
Fittings:	Centreboard boat. Wooden spars. Positive flotation.
Sails:	Area 5.57m^2/60 sq.ft.
	Spinnaker area 2.78m^2/30 sq.ft.
Rigging:	Una
Price Guide:	$895us
Summary:	Single-hander. Kits available. Built only in America. Hiking straps used.

UDELL ONE DESIGN

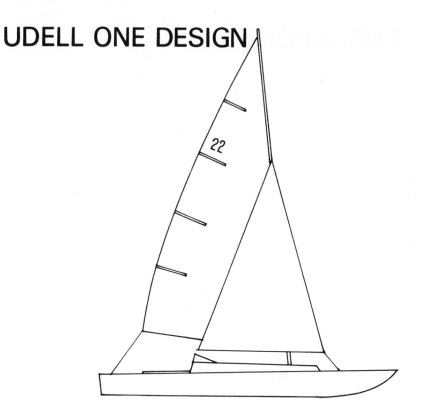

Design:	Knud Reimers, U.S.A. 1954
Supplier:	Raymond Creekmore, U.S.A. Udell National Association, U.S.A.

Specifications:

Construction:	GRP or wood
LOA:	10.97m/36'0
Beam:	1.98m/6'6
Draft:	1.3m/4'4
Displ:	1997.6kg/4,400 lbs
Ballast:	1089.6kg/2,400 lbs

Fittings:	Keelboat. Spars — aluminium or wood
Sails:	Area 21.9m^2/236 sq.ft. Spinnaker area 41.8m^2/450 sq.ft.
Rigging:	Sloop
Price Guide:	$12,500us
Summary:	3 crew. Very small class. Most boats found in the east of America. Trailable.

US ONE DESIGN

Design:	John Alden, U.S.A. 1946
Supplier:	US OD National Association, U.S.A.
Specifications:	*Construction:* Wood
	LOA: 11.48m/37'8
	Beam: 2.13m/7'0
	Draft: 1.63m/5'4
	Displ: 2,860.2kg/6,300 lbs
Fittings:	Keelboat. Wooden spars.
Sails:	Area 35.1m^2/378 sq.ft.
	Spinnaker area 66.3m^2/714 sq.ft.
Rigging:	Sloop
Price Guide:	$4,00us approx.
Summary:	An exclusive American class. Sailed in the north-east. 4 to 5 crew. No buoyancy allowed.

VIPER

Design:	John Fillip, U.S.A. 1967
Supplier:	Fillip Manufacturing Co., U.S.A. Viper Association, U.S.A.
Specifications:	*Construction:* GRP *LOA:* 4.57m/15'0 *Beam:* 1.37m/4'6 *Draft:* 0.10m/4" *Displ:* 97.6kg/215 lbs
Fittings:	Daggerboard. Aluminium spars. Air tank flotation.
Sails:	Area 11.61m^2/125 sq.ft.
Rigging:	Sloop
Price Guide:	$900us
Summary:	1 or 2 crew.

WATERBUG

Design:	Charles Yost, U.S.A. 1971
Supplier:	Waterbug National Association, U.S.A.
Specifications:	*Construction:* Plywood & GRP *LOA:* 3.54m/11'8 *Beam:* 1.22m/4'0 *Draft:* 0.10m/3" *Displ:* 49.94kg/110 lbs
Fittings:	Daggerboard. Aluminium spars. Positive flotation.
Sails:	Area 6.69m^2/72 sq.ft.
Rigging:	Una
Price Guide:	$495us
Summary:	Single-hander. Hiking straps used.

VICTORY

Design:	Ted Carpentier, U.S.A. 1959
Supplier:	Victory National Association, U.S.A.
Specifications:	*Construction:* GRP
	LOA: 6.4m/21'0
	Beam: 1.83m/6'0
	Draft: 0.91m/3'0
	Displ: 681kg/1,500 lbs
	Ballast: 227kg/500 lbs
Fittings:	Keelboat. Aluminium spars. Flotation tanks.
Sails:	Area 18.21m²/196 sq.ft.
Rigging:	Sloop
Price Guide:	$2,200us
Summary:	Can be sailed single-handed. Trailable.

VIKING 170

Design:	Steve Parrot
Supplier:	Viking of America, U.S.A. Viking 170 Association, U.S.A.
Specifications:	*Construction:* GRP *LOA:* 5.13m/16'10 *Beam:* 1.88m/6'2 *Draft:* 0.19m/8"
Fittings:	Centreboard boat. Aluminium spars. Positive flotation.
Sails:	Area 14.77m^2/159 sq.ft.
Rigging:	Sloop
Price Guide:	$950us
Summary:	2 crew.

VINEYARD HAVEN 21

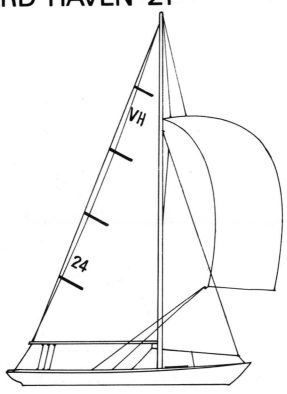

Design:	Erford W. Burt, U.S.A. 1934	
Supplier:	Martha's Vineyard Shipyard Inc., U.S.A.	
	Vineyard National Association, U.S.A.	
Specifications:	*Construction:*	Wood or GRP
	LOA:	6.40m/21'0
	Beam:	1.68m/5'6
	Draft:	1.22m/4'0
	Displ:	1,021.5kg/2,250 lbs
	Ballast:	408.6kg/900 lbs
Fittings:	Keelboat. Wooden spars. Positive flotation. Lead ballast. Self-bailers.	
Sails:	Area 19.6m^2/211 sq.ft.	
	Spinnaker are 25.55m^2/275 sq.ft.	
Rigging:	Sloop	
Price Guide:	$4,400us	
Summary:	An American class. 3 crew allowed. Hiking straps used.	

VITA DINGHY

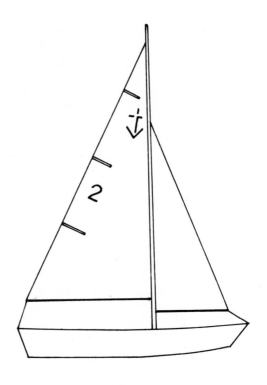

Design:	Joseph C. Dobler, U.S.A. 1965
Supplier:	Vita Dinghy Association, U.S.A.
Specifications:	*Construction:* Plywood or GRP
	LOA: 3.00m/9'10
	Beam: 1.52m/5'0
	Draft: 0.13m/5''
Fittings:	Centreboard boat. Aluminium spars. Positive flotation.
Sails:	Area 6.04m^2/65 sq.ft.
Rigging:	Sloop
Price Guide:	Secondhand boats only available.
Summary:	2 crew. Not in production — secondhand boats only available.

WAHOO

Supplier:	Old Town Canoe Co., U.S.A.
Specifications:	*Construction:* GRP
	LOA: 4.88m/16'0
	Beam: 0.91m/3'0
	Draft: 0.05m/2''
	Displ: 38.6kg/85 lbs
Fittings:	Bilgeboards. Aluminium spars. Foam flotation.
Sails:	Area 6.97m^2/75 sq.ft.
Rigging:	Una
Price Guide:	$695us
Summary:	Single-hander.

WEST ELEVEN `B` TYPE

Design: Geoffrey Sutton, England

Supplier: Weston Marine Centre, England

Rating: Portsmouth yardstick 115

Specifications:

Construction:	GRP
LWL:	2.89m/9'6
LOA:	3.42m/11'3
Beam:	1.40m/4'7
Draft:	0.76m/2'6
Displ:	59kg/130 lbs

Fittings: Centreboard boat. Mast 3.44m/11'4 high. Built-in buoyancy.

Sails: Area 6.97m^2/75 sq.ft.

Rigging: Sloop

Price Guide: £200

Summary: A general purpose sports boat. Clean lines and light weight give her a good sailing performance whilst being roomy and comfortable.

WEYMOUTH FALCON

Design: W. L. Bussell, U.K.

Supplier: W. L. Bussell, U.K.

Specifications:

Construction:	Wood
LOA:	4.88m/16'0
Displ:	204.3kg/450 lbs

Fittings: Centreboard boat. Wooden spars.

Sails: Area 13.47m^2/145 sq.ft.

Rigging: Bermudan sloop

Price Guide: £475

Summary: A general purpose dinghy.

WASP

Design:	ESB, England
Supplier:	ESB Dinghies, England
Specifications:	*Construction:* GRP
	LOA: 2.39m/7'10
	Displ: 45.4kg/100 lbs
Fittings:	Centreboard boat. Aluminium spars.
Sails:	Area 2.97m^2/32 sq.ft.
Rigging:	Una
Price Guide:	£210
Summary:	A general purpose dinghy that is safe and reliable.

WESTWIND

Design: Andre Cornu, France 1972

Supplier: Paceship Yachts, Canada
Westwind National Association, U.S.A.

Specifications:

Construction:	GRP	
LOA:	5.82m/19'1	
Beam:	1.73m/5'9	
Draft:	0.94m/3'1	
Displ:	379kg/835 lbs	
Ballast:	170.3kg/375 lbs	

Fittings: Keelboat. Aluminium spars. Air tank flotation.

Sails: Area 16.54m^2/178 sq.ft.
Spinnaker area 18.58m^2/200 sq.ft.

Price Guide: $2,100us

Summary: 2 crew. Trailable. Self-bailing.

WINARD SABOT

Supplier: Winard Sabot Association, U.S.A.

Specifications:

Construction:	Wood	
LOA:	2.41m/7'11	
Beam:	1.22m/4'0	
Draft:	0.08m/3''	
Displ:	27.3kg/60 lbs	

Fittings: Centreboard boat. Wooden spars.

Sails: Area 3.53m^2/38 sq.ft.

Rigging: Una

Price Guide: On application

Summary: Sailed all over America.

WENSUM

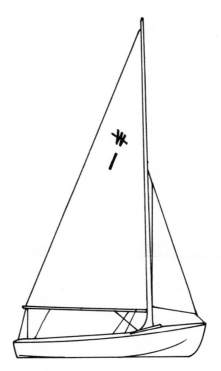

Design:	Percy Blandford, England 1958
Supplier:	Percy Blandford, England
Rating:	Provisional Portsmouth yardstick 130

Specifications:

Construction:	Double chine plywood or GRP
LOA:	3.35m/11'0
Beam:	1.41m/4'8
Draft:	0.10m/4"
Displ:	49.94kg/100 lbs

Fittings:	Centreboard boat. GRP or plywood deck. Wood or metal spars. Air bags or plastic foam buoyancy.
Sails:	Area 6.13m^2 or 7.43m^2/66 or 80 sq.ft.
Rigging:	Sloop or Gunter rigged.
Price Guide:	£200
Summary:	2 or 3 crew. Has a rounded transom. Used as a family boat. Can be trailed.

WHISTLER

Design:	Fred Ford Jnr., U.S.A.
Supplier:	Molded Fiberglass Co., U.S.A. Whistler Association, U.S.A.
Specifications:	*Construction:* GRP *LOA:* 3.35m/11'0 *Beam:* 1.52m/5'0 *Draft:* 0.10m/4" *Displ:* 90.8kg/200 lbs
Fittings:	Centreboard boat. Aluminium spars. Positive flotation.
Sails:	Area 6.87m^2/74 sq.ft.
Rigging:	Sloop
Price Guide:	$300 to S500us secondhand.
Summary:	Not in production at the present time. 2 crew. Sailed in America.

WIANNO SENIOR KNOCKABOUT

Design:	H. Manley Crosby, U.S.A. 1913
Supplier:	Crosby Yacht Building Co. Wianno Senior Knockabout Association, U.S.A.
Specifications:	*Construction:* Wood *LOA:* 7.62m/25'0 *Beam:* 2.44m/8'0 *Draft:* 0.76m/2'6 *Displ:* 1,748kg/3,850 lbs
Fittings:	Centreboard boat. Wooden spars. Self-bailing.
Sails:	Area 34m^2/366 sq.ft.
Rigging:	Gaff
Price Guide:	$6,985us
Summary:	4 crew.

WIDGEON

Design:	Robert Baker, U.S.A. 1963
Supplier:	O'Day, U.S.A.

Specifications:	*Construction:*	GRP
	LWL:	3.51m/11'6
	LOA:	3.76m/12'4
	Beam:	1.52m/5'0
	Draft:	0.13m/5"
	Displ:	129.4kg/285 lbs

Fittings:	Centreboard boat. Aluminium spars. Foam flotation.
Sails:	Area 8.36m^2/90 sq.ft. Spinnaker 5.57m^2/60 sq.ft.
Rigging:	Sloop
Price Guide:	$795us
Summary:	2 crew. Built only in America. Self-rescuing. One of the smallest practical sailboats for adults and family sailing.

WILDFLOWER

Design: Snark Products, U.S.A.

Supplier: Snark Products Inc., U.S.A.

Specifications:

Construction:	Plastic
LOA:	3.51m/11'6
Beam:	1.37m/4'6
Draft:	0.08m/3"
Displ:	40.86kg/90 lbs

Fittings: Daggerboard. Aluminium spars. Foam flotation.

Sails: Area 9.29m^2/100 sq.ft.

Rigging: Sloop

Price Guide: $595us

Summary: A maintenance-free, fun dinghy that can be converted to rowing and motoring.

WITH VITO

Design: Bror With, Norway

Supplier: Bonwitco, England

Specifications:

Construction:	GRP and wood
LOA:	3.12m/10'3
Displ:	95.34kg/210 lbs

Fittings: Centreboard boat. Aluminium spars.

Variations: Outboard can be fitted.

Sails: Area 4.18m^2/45 sq.ft.

Rigging: Sprit

Price Guide: £300

Summary: 2 crew. Can be car-topped and trailed. A beamy training dinghy.

WINDFLITE 14

Design:	AMF Alcort, U.S.A.
Supplier:	D. Bruce Connolly, U.S.A.
Specifications:	*Construction:* GRP
	LOA: 4.22m/13'10
	Beam: 1.24m/4'1
	Draft: 0.10m/4"
	Displ: 63.56kg/140 lbs
Fittings:	Daggerboard. Aluminium spars. Foam flotation.
Sails:	Area 6.97m^2/75 sq.ft.
Rigging:	Lug
Price Guide:	$512us
Summary:	1–2 crew. Built only in America. A maintenance-free fun boat.

WITH VITRESS

Design:	Bror With, Norway
Supplier:	Bonwitco, England
Specifications:	*Construction:* GRP
	LOA: 4.72m/15'6
	Displ: 199.76kg/440 lbs
Fittings:	Centreboard boat. Aluminium spars.
Variations:	Outboard can be fitted.
Sails:	Area 9.48m^2/102 sq.ft.
Rigging:	Bermudan sloop
Price Guide:	£375
Summary:	Takes up to 4 crew. Can be trailed.

WITH VITTING

Design:	Bror With, Norway
Supplier:	Bonwitco, England
Specifications:	*Construction:* GRP
	LOA: 4.42m/14'6
	Beam: 1.78m/5'10
	Draft: 1.07m/3'6
	Displ: 240kg/530 lbs
Fittings:	Centreboard boat.
Variations:	Outboard can be attached.
Sails:	Area 10.5m^2/113 sq.ft.
Rigging:	Sloop
Price Guide:	£375
Summary:	Takes up to 4 crew. Can be trailed.

WINDJAMMER

Design:	Charles Wittholz, U.S.A.
Supplier:	Windjammer Association, U.S.A.
Specifications:	*Construction:* GRP
	LOA: 5.08m/16'9
	Beam: 1.98m/6'6
	Draft: 0.18m/7''
	Displ: 99.88kg/220 lbs
Fittings:	Centreboard boat. Aluminium spars. Positive flotation.
Sails:	Area 14.68m^2/158 sq.ft. No spinnaker allowed.
Rigging:	Sloop
Price Guide:	On application
Summary:	2 crew. Built only in America. Self-rescuing.

WOD

Design:	England
Supplier:	John Fulford, England
Specifications:	*Construction:* GRP
	LOA: 4.01m/13'2
Fittings:	Centreboard boat.
Variations:	Outboard may be attached.
Sails:	Area $7.9m^2$/85 sq.ft.
Rigging:	Bermudan sloop
Price Guide:	£250
Summary:	A general purpose racing dinghy. Can be trailed.

X 21

Design:	Tom Norton, U.S.A. 1971
Supplier:	Christensen Yacht Corp., U.S.A.
	X21 National Association, U.S.A.
Specifications:	*Construction:* GRP
	LOA: 6.4m/21'0
	Beam: 1.98m/6'6
	Draft: 1.07m/3'6
	Displ: 1,090kg/2,400 lbs
	Ballast: 545kg/1,200 lbs
Fittings:	Keelboat. Aluminium spars. Foam flotation. Lead ballast.
Sails:	Area $17.7m^2$/191 sq.ft.
	Spinnaker area $27.9m^2$/300 sq.ft.
Rigging:	Sloop
Price Guide:	$4,250us
Summary:	Trailable. 2 or 3 crew.

WINDMILL

Design:	Clark C. Mills, U.S.A.1953
Supplier:	Advance Sailboat Corporation, U.S.A. Windmill Association, U.S.A.
Specifications:	*Construction:* Wood and GRP *LOA:* 4.72m/15'6 *Beam:* 1.42m/4'9 *Draft:* 0.15m/6'' *Displ:* 89.89m/198 lbs
Fittings:	Daggerboard. Spars — wood or aluminium. Mast 6.25m/20'6 high. Self-bailing.
Variations:	Air or foam flotation.
Sails:	Area 11.06m²/119 sq.ft. No spinnaker allowed.
Rigging:	Sloop
Price Guide:	$400 to $1,200us
Summary:	2 crew. Over 4,000 built already. Kits and plans available. Performs well in light or heavy weather.

Y BOAT

Design:	John Johnson, U.S.A. 1946
Supplier:	Johnson Boat Works, U.S.A.
Specifications:	*Construction:* GRP
	LOA: 5.79m/19'0
	Beam: 2m/6'7
	Displ: 295kg/650 lbs
Fittings:	Centreboard boat. Wooden spars. Foam flotation.
Sails:	Are 16.3m^2/175 sq.ft.
Rigging:	Sloop
Price Guide:	$1,775us
Summary:	Hiking straps used.

YELLOW WHEEL YS 3108

Design:	A. J. Podolski, England
Supplier:	Yellow Wheels, England
Specifications:	*Construction:* GRP
	LOA: 3.12m/10'3
	Beam: 1.37m/4'6
	Draft: 0.08m/3''
	Displ: 22kg/48 lbs
Fittings:	Centreboard boat. Built-in buoyancy. Mast height 2.74m/9'0.
Sails:	Area 14.9m^2/160 sq.ft.
Rigging:	Lug
Price Guide:	£180
Summary:	2 or 3 crew carried. Ideal for beginners, for families, fishing and rentals. Easily trailed.

WOOD PUSSY

Design:	Philip L. Rhodes, U.S.A.
Supplier:	One Design Marine Inc., U.S.A. Wood Pussy Association, U.S.A.
Specifications:	*Construction:* GRP *LOA:* 4.11m/13'6 *Beam:* 1.83m/6'0 *Draft:* 0.18m/7'' *Displ:* 195.22kg/430 lbs
Fittings:	Centreboard boat. Aluminium spars. Positive flotation.
Sails:	Area 9.29m^2/100 sq.ft. No spinnaker allowed.
Rigging:	Una
Price Guide:	$1,395us
Summary:	2 crew. A traditional boat with good stability. Built only in America. Ideal regardless of wind or water.

YEOMAN

Supplier:	E. C. Landamore, England
Specifications:	*Construction:* GRP
	LOA: 6.1m/20'0
	Displ: 636kg/1,400 lbs
Fittings:	Centreboard boat. Aluminium spars.
Sails:	Area 18.6m^2/200 sq.ft.
Rigging:	Bermudan sloop
Price Guide:	£800
Summary:	Carries up to 4 crew.

YW 7'9" UTILITY PRAM

Design:	Yachting World, England
Supplier:	Bell Woodworking, U.K.
Specifications:	*Construction:* Wood
	LOA: 2.36m/7'9
	Displ: 50kg/110 lbs
Fittings:	Centreboard boat.
Sails:	Area optional
Rigging:	Optional
Price Guide:	£100
Summary:	2 crew.

X BOAT

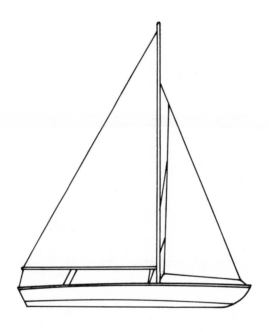

Design:	ILYA, U.S.A. 1934	
Supplier:	ILYA, U.S.A.	
Specifications:	*Construction:*	Wood or GRP
	LOA:	4.88m/16'0
	Beam:	1.85m/6'1
	Draft:	0.05m/2''
	Displ:	227kg/500 lbs
Fittings:	Centreboard boat. Wooden spars. Foam flotation.	
Sails:	Area 10.2m^2 (7.9 + 2.3)/110 sq.ft. (85 + 25)	
Rigging:	Sloop	
Price Guide:	$1,450us	
Summary:	2 crew. Self-rescuing. Hiking straps used. Built only in America.	

Y-FLYER

Design:	Alvin Youngquist, U.S.A. 1941
Supplier:	Jack A. Helms Co., U.S.A. Y—Flyer Association, U.S.A.

Specifications:

Construction:	Plywood & GRP
LOA:	5.54m/18'2
Beam:	1.73m/5'8
Draft:	0.15m/6''
Displ:	227kg/500 lbs

Fittings:	Centreboard boats. Spars — wood or aluminium. Positive flotation.
Sails:	Area 15m^2/161 sq.ft.
Rigging:	Sloop
Price Guide:	$1,900us
Summary:	2 crew. Self-rescuing. Hiking straps allowed.

ZEPHYR

Design:	Thrall & Freitag, U.S.A.
Supplier:	Basin Boatcraft, U.S.A.
Specifications:	*Construction:* Wood
	LOA: 6.1m/20'0
	Beam: 1.22m/4'0
	Draft: 0.81m/2'8
	Displ: Optional
	Ballast: Optional
Fittings:	Keelboat. Wooden spars.
Sails:	Area 10.7m^2/115 sq.ft.
Rigging:	Sloop
Price Guide:	$1,500us
Summary:	An American class. 2 crew. Hiking straps used.

ZIP

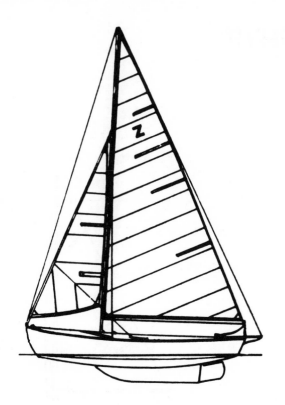

Design:	Harold D. Brainard, U.S.A. 1933
Supplier:	Zip Sloops, U.S.A.
Specifications:	*Construction:* GRP
	LOA: 4.83m/16'0
	Beam: 1.83m/6'0
	Draft: 0.61m/2'0
	Displ: Optional
	Ballast: Optional
Fittings:	Keelboat. Spars — GRP and aluminium. Foam flotation.
Sails:	Area 12.1m^2/130 sq.ft.
Rigging:	Sloop
Price Guide:	$825us
Summary:	2 crew. Trailable. Available in kit form.

GENERAL PURPOSE
AND DAY DINGHIES
multihulls

BAREFOOT 12

Design:	Saunders & Medre, U.S.A. 1970
Supplier:	Barefoot 12 Association, U.S.A.
Specifications:	*Construction:* GRP
	LOA: 3.66m/12'0
	Beam: 2.41m/7'11
	Draft: 0.08m/3''
	Displ: 91kg/200 lbs
Fittings:	Daggerboard. 2 outrigger hulls connected with wood. Aluminium spars.
Sails:	Area 9.3m^2/100 sq.ft.
Rigging:	Una
Price Guide:	$995us
Summary:	Single-hander. Built only in America.

CAL CAT

Design:	Joe Quigg, U.S.A.
Supplier:	Newport Boats, U.S.A.
	Old Salt Sailboat Center, U.S.A.
	Cal Cat Association, U.S.A.
Specifications:	*Construction:* GRP
	LOA: 3.92m/12'10
	Beam: 2.39m/7'10
	Draft: 0.1m/4''
Fittings:	2 symmetrical hulls connected by a bridge deck. Aluminium spars. Positive flotation.
Sails:	Area 9.3m^2/100 sq.ft.
	No spinnaker allowed.
Rigging:	Una
Price Guide:	On application
Summary:	Single-hander. Hiking straps allowed.

ALPHA CAT

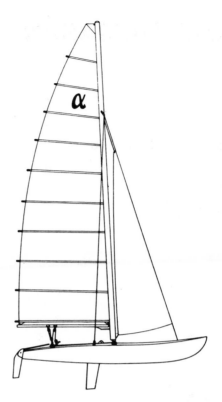

Design:	Tom Roland, U.S.A. 1970
Supplier:	Glastron Boat Co., U.S.A. Alpha Cat Association, U.S.A.
Specifications:	*Construction:* GRP *LOA:* 5.49m/18'0 *Beam:* 3.05m/10'0 *Draft:* 0.15m/6'' *Displ:* 136kg/300 lbs
Fittings:	Daggerboards. 2 symmetrical hulls connected with aluminium. Aluminium spars. Bulkhead flotation.
Sails:	Area 22.6m^2(16.7 + 5.9)/244 sq.ft. (180 + 64)
Rigging:	Sloop
Price Guide:	$2,295us
Summary:	2 crew. Built only in America. Powerful, lightweight exciting sailboat.

CAYAT TRIMARAN

Supplier: Folbot Corporation, U.S.A.

Specifications:
Construction: Wood
LOA: 5.03m/16'6
Beam: 3.91m/12'11

Fittings: Daggerboard

Sails: Area 5.57m^2/60 sq.ft.

Rigging: Una

Price Guide: $506us

FELIX

Design: Pearson Brothers, U.K. 1968

Suppliera: Pearson Brothers, U.K.

Specifications:
Construction: GRP
LOA: 4.32m/14'2
Beam: 1.68m/5'6
Draft: 0.05m/2''
Displ: 68kg/150 lbs

Fittings: Daggerboards. 2 symmetrical hulls connected by aluminium tubes. Aluminium spars. Mast 21'0 high. Air tank flotation.

Sails: Area 9m^2/97 sq.ft.

Rigging: Una

Price Guide: $845us

Summary: Single-hander. Simple rig gives high speeds. Broad planing hulls provide stability and plenty of lift for 2 or 3 people.

AQUA CAT 18

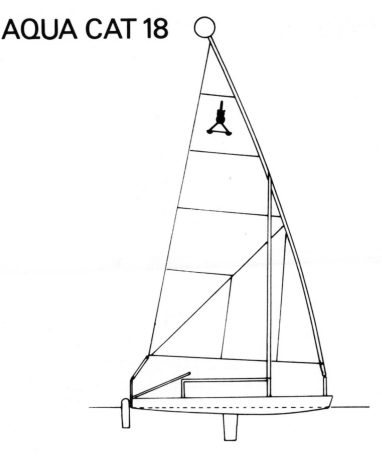

Design:	American Fiberglass Corporation, U.S.A.
Supplier:	American Fiberglass Corporation, U.S.A.

Specifications:

Construction:	GRP
LOA:	5.44m/17'10
Beam:	2.41m/7'11
Draft:	0.15m/6"
Displ:	166kg/365 lbs

Fittings: Daggerboards. 2 symmerical hulls connected by aluminium tubes. Aluminium spars. Positive flotation.

Sails: Area 16.7m^2/180 sq.ft.

Rigging: Una

Price Guide: $900us

Summary: 2 crew. Larger sister to the Aqua Cat. Fast and lively performance.

BUNYIP 20

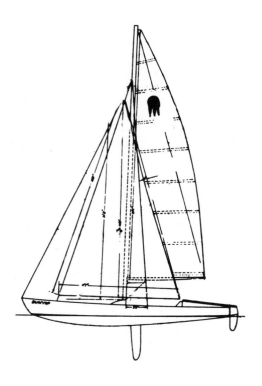

Design:	Lock Crowther, U.S.A. 1965
Supplier:	International Marine Services, U.S.A. Bunyip 20 Association, U.S.A.
Fittings:	*Construction:* Plywood *LOA:* 6.1m/20'0 *Beam:* 3.35m/11'0 *Draft:* 0.3m/1'0
Specifications:	Daggerboard. 3 symmetrical hulls connected by a bridge deck. Aluminium spars. Wood flotation.
Sails:	Area 21.1m^2 (11.2 + 9.9)/227 sq.ft. (120 + 107)
Rigging:	Sloop
Price Guide:	$2,900us
Summary:	2 or 3 crew. Trapeze used.

CATYAK

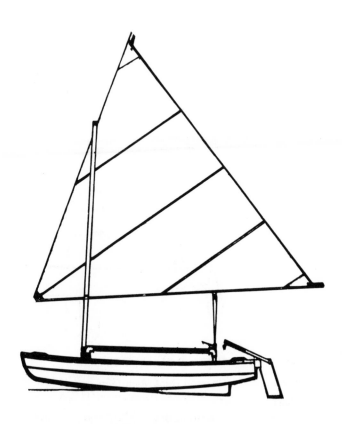

Design:	Frederick Ford, U.S.A. 1973
Supplier:	Dayton Marine Products, U.S.A. Tabur Marine, England
Specifications:	*Construction:* Polyethylene *LOA:* 2.84m/9'4
Sails:	Area 5.11m^2/55 sq.ft.
Rigging:	Una
Price Guide:	£185/$395us
Summary:	A fun multihull dinghy.

CHEETAH CAT

Design:	Robert B. Harris, U.S.A. 1969
Supplier:	Cheetah Boat Manufacturing, U.S.A. Cheetah Cat Association, U.S.A.
Specifications:	*Construction:* GRP and plywood *LOA:* 4.23m/14'1 *Beam:* 2.03m/6'8 *Draft:* 0.2m/8" *Displ:* 141kg/310 lbs
Fittings:	Centreboards boat. 2 symmetrical hulls connected by a bridge deck. Aluminium spars. Styrofoam flotation.
Sails:	Area 17.2m^2 (12.2 + 5)/185 sq.ft. (131 + 54)
Rigging:	Sloop
Price Guide:	$1,795us
Summary:	2 crew. Built only in America.

CHESHIRE

Design:	Frank Meldau, U.S.A. 1967
Supplier:	Cheshire Association, U.S.A.
Specifications:	*Construction:* GRP
	LOA: 4.27m/14'0
	Beam: 1.98m/6'6
	Draft: 0.13m/5''
	Displ: 84kg/185 lbs
Fittings:	Daggerboards. Aluminium spars. 2 symmetrical hulls connected by aluminium tubes. Foam flotation.
Sails:	Area 12.5m^2 (9.7 + 2.8)/135 sq.ft. (105 + 30)
Rigging:	Sloop
Price Guide:	$1,250us
Summary:	Single-hander. Built only in America. Hiking straps used.

DINGO

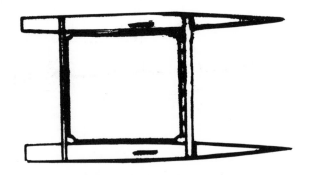

Design:	J. R. MacAlpine Downie
Supplier:	Sail Manufacturing., U.S.A.
Specifications:	*Construction:* GRP
	LOA: 4.52m/14'10
	Beam: 2.19m/7'2
	Displ: 73kg/160 lbs
Fittings:	Centerboards. 2 symmetrical hulls connected by aluminium tubes. Aluminium spars. Positive flotation.
Sails:	Area 11.6m^2/125 sq.ft.
Rigging:	Una
Price Guide:	$995us
Summary:	Single-hander. Hiking straps and trapeze allowed.

DC-14

Design:	MacLear and Harris, U.S.A. 1965
Supplier:	Duncan Sutphen Inc., U.S.A.

Specifications:

Construction:	GRP
LOA:	4.32m/14'2
Beam:	2.13m/7'0
Draft:	0.15m/6''
Displ:	159kg/350 lbs

Fittings:	Daggerboard. 2 symmetrical hulls connected with aluminium. Aluminium spars. Foam flotation.
Sails:	Area 13m^2(9.8 + 3.2)/140 sq.ft. (106 + 34) Spinnaker not official.
Rigging:	Sloop
Price Guide:	$1,240us
Summary:	2 crew. Hiking straps allowed.

GEMINI 18

Design:	American Fiberglass Corporation, U.S.A. 1965
Supplier:	Harvey Cedars Marina, U.S.A.
Specifications:	*Construction:* GRP
	LOA: 5.47m/17'11
	Beam: 2.44m/8'0
	Displ: 166kg/365 lbs
Fittings:	Centreboards. 2 hulls connected with aluminium. Aluminium spars. Foam flotation.
Sails:	Area
Rigging:	Una
Price Guide:	$1,895us
Summary:	2 crew. Secondhand boats also available.

HOBIE MONO-CAT

Design:	Hobie Alter, U.S.A. 1972
Supplier:	Coast Catamarans, U.S.A. Hobie Cat Class Association, U.S.A.
Specifications:	*Construction:* ABS
	LWL: 3.40m/11'2
	LOA: 3.66m/12'0
	Beam: 1.22m/4'0
	Draft: 0.1m/4''
	Displ: 68kg/150 lbs
Fittings:	1 centreboard. 2 asymmetrical hulls joined by a bridge deck. Aluminium spars. Foam flotation.
Sails:	Area 8.4m^2/90 sq.ft.
Rigging:	Una
Price Guide:	$695us
Summary:	Single-hander. Lightweight and easy to handle. Very stable and easy to right. Suitable for a novice as well as experienced skippers.

FLASH CAT

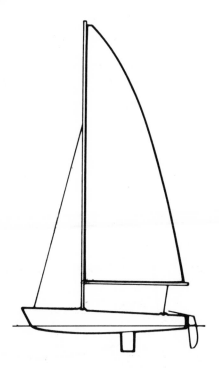

Design:	Greg Gregory, England	
Supplier:	Trowbridge & Sons, England	
Specifications:	*Construction:*	GRP
	LWL:	3.42m/11'3
	LOA:	3.71m/12'2
	Beam:	2.06m/6'9
	Draft:	0.08m/3''
	Displ:	72.58kg/160 lbs
Fittings:	Centreboards. Built-in buoyancy. Mast 6.40m/ 21'0 high. Aluminium spars.	
Sails:	Area 9.12m^2/98 sq.ft.	
Rigging:	Una	
Price Guide:	£300	
Summary:	Kits available. Ideal for family day sailing or for racing Can be trailed and car-topped. Carries up to 4 adults. Easily dismantled.	

FROLICAT

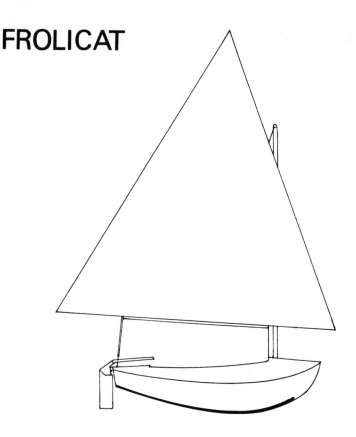

Design:	David Thompson
Supplier:	Fiberdyne Inc., U.S.A.

Specifications:	*Construction:*	GRP
	LOA:	3.25m/10'8
	Beam:	1.83m/6'0
	Draft:	0.36m/1'2
	Displ:	73kg/160 lbs

Fittings: Aluminium spars. Posi-steer rudders — so no centre-board needed.

Sails: Area 7m²/75 sq. ft.

Rigging: Una

Price Guide: On application

Summary: Carries 4 adults. Combines the comfort of a larger boat with the simplicity of sailing boards. Exclusive deep 'V' hulls.

HILU

Design:	AMF Alcort, U.S.A.
Supplier:	D. Bruce Connolly, U.S.A.
Specifications:	*Construction:* GRP
	LOA: 4.27m/14'0
	Beam: 2.39m/7'10
	Draft: 0.15m/6''
	Displ: 34kg/75 lbs
Fittings:	Centreboards. 2 outrigger hulls connected with aluminium. Aluminium spars. Foam flotation.
Sails:	Area 6.04m^2/65 sq.ft.
Rigging:	Una
Price Guide:	$595us
Summary:	Single-hander. Built only in America. A real fun boat that can be assembled and packed in seconds.

HONKER (water)

Design:	Honker Landsailors Corporation, U.S.A. 1972
Supplier:	Honker Landsailors Corporation, U.S.A.
Specifications:	*Construction:* GRP
	LOA: 3.66m/12'0
	Beam: 1.85m/6'1
	Displ: 57kg/125 lbs
Fittings:	3 symmetrical hulls connected with aluminium. Aluminium spars. Foam flotation.
Sails:	Area 4m^2/43 sq.ft.
Rigging:	Una
Price Guide:	$720us
Summary:	1 or 2 crew. A design that is used on land and ice as well as water.

IMS 16

Design:	Bert K. Anderson, U.S.A. 1972
Supplier:	IMS 16 Association, U.S.A.
	International Marine Services, U.S.A.
Specifications:	*Construction:* GRP
	LOA: 4.88m/16'0
	Beam: 2.44m/8'0
	Displ: 84kg/185 lbs
Fittings:	Daggerboards. 2 symmetrical hulls connected by aluminium. Aluminium spars.
Sails:	Area 13.9m^2/150 sq.ft. Spinnaker area optional.
Rigging:	Sloop
Price Guide:	$1,695us
Summary:	1—2 crew. Trapeze used. Built only in America.

HOBIE CAT 14

Design:	Hobie Alter U.S.A. 1970
Supplier:	Coast Catamarans U.S.A. Hobie Cat Class Association U.S.A. M. C. Davies England

Specifications:

Construction:	GRP sandwich
LOA:	4.22m/13'10
Beam:	2.33m/7'8
Draft:	0.1m/4''
Displ:	98kg/215 lbs

Fittings: No centreboard. Kick-up rudders. 2 assymetrical hulls connected with aluminium. Aluminium spars. Mast 6.78m/22'3 high

Sails: Area 11m2/118 sq. ft.

Rigging: Una

Price Guide: S1,195us

Summary: Single-hander. Over 11,000 boats registered worldwide. Perfect for surfing, beaching, day-sailing and racing. Capable of 20 mph+

KENT CATAMARAN

Supplier:	Alan Bell Catamarans, England
Specifications:	*Construction:* Wood
	LOA: 4.27m/14'0
	Displ: 82kg/180 lbs
Fittings:	Centreboard boat.
Sails:	Area 10.2m^2/110 sq.ft.
Rigging:	Una
Price Guide:	On application
Summary:	Single-hander. Can be trailed and car-topped.

MUSKETEER

Design:	J. R. MacAlpine Downie, England 1973
Supplier:	Chrysler Sailboats, U.S.A.
Specifications:	*Construction:* GRP
	LOA: 5.03m/16'6
	Beam: 2.44m/8'0
	Draft: 0.17m/7''
	Displ: 182kg/400 lbs
Fittings:	2 centreboards. 2 symmetrical hulls joined by aluminium tubes. Aluminium spars. Foam flotation.
Sails:	Area 23.2m^2 (14.9 + 8.3)/250 sq.ft. (160 + 90)
Rigging:	Sloop
Price Guide:	$1,400us
Summary:	2—4 crew. Trapeze optional

HOBIE CAT 16

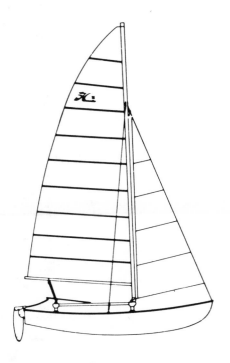

Design:	Hobie Alter, U.S.A. 1970
Supplier:	Coast Catamarans, U.S.A. Hobie Cat Class Association, U.S.A.

Specifications:

	Construction:	GRP sandwich
	LOA:	5.05m/16'7
	Beam:	2.42m/7'11
	Draft:	0.25m/10''
	Displ:	148kg/325lbs

Fittings:	No centreboard. 2 asymmetrical hulls connected with aluminium. Aluminium spars. Foam flotation. Kick-up rudders.
Sails:	Area 20.3m^2(15.2 + 5.1)/218 sq.ft. (163 + 55)
Rigging:	Sloop
Pirce Guide:	$1,695us
Summary:	2 crew. Easily righted, safe and unsinkable hulls. A challenging sail for novices and experienced crew. Capable of 25mph+.

ISOTOPE

Design:	Frank Meldau, U.S.A. 1966
Supplier:	Isotope Association, U.S.A.
Specifications:	*Construction:* GRP
	LWL: 4.27m/14'0
	LOA: 4.88m/16'0
	Beam: 2.29m/7'6
	Draft: 0.15m/6"
	Displ: 102kg/225 lbs
Fittings:	Centreboards. 2 symmetrical hulls connected with aluminium. Aluminium spars. Foam flotation.
Sails:	Area 17.2m^2(13 + 4.2)/185 sq.ft. (140 + 45)
Rigging:	Sloop
Price Guide:	$1,885us
Summary:	Single-hander. Built only in America.

KANGAROO

Design:	Bert Anderson, U.S.A. 1970
Supplier:	International Marine Services, U.S.A. Kangaroo Association, U.S.A.
Specifications:	*Construction:* Wood and grp *LOA:* 5.43m/17'10 *Beam:* 3.45m/11'4 *Draft:* 0.2m/8" *Displ:* 136kg/300 lbs
Fittings:	Daggerboard. 3 symmetrical hulls connected by aluminium. Aluminium spars. Sealed float flotation.
Sails:	Area 21.8m^2(9.9 + 11.9)/235 sq.ft. (107 + 128) Spinnaker area optional.
Rigging:	Sloop
Price Guide:	S2,100us
Summary:	2 crew. Trapeze used. A small class found mainly in America.

KIMBA KAT

Design:	Allan J. Arnold, U.S.A. 1970
Supplier:	Seahorse Sailboats, U.S.A. Kimba Kat Association, U.S.A.
Specifications:	*Construction:* GRP *LWL:* 3.51m/11'6 *LOA:* 3.64m/11'11 *Beam:* 1.68m/5'6 *Draft:* 0.15m/6" *Displ:* 41kg/90 lbs
Fittings:	Skegs. 2 symmetrical hulls connected by aluminium. Aluminium spars. Foam filled bag flotation. Kick-up rudders.
Sails:	Area 9.3m^2 (6.3 + 3)/100 sq.ft. (68 + 32)
Rigging:	Sloop
Price Guide:	$695us+
Summary:	A light, car-top catamaran that has a high performance. Easy to transport.

KONA 14

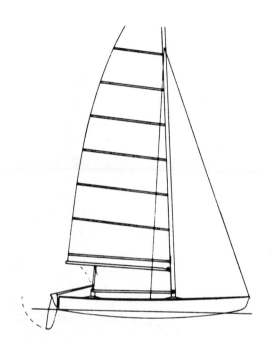

Design:	Lyle Hess, U.S.A. 1971
Supplier:	Fiberform Division U.S. Industries, U.S.A. Kona 14 Association, U.S.A.
Specifications:	*Construction:* GRP *LOA:* 4.29m/14'1 *Beam:* 2m/6'7 *Draft:* 0.2m/8" *Displ:* 68kg/150 lbs
Fittings:	No board required. 2 asymmetrical hulls connected with aluminium. Aluminium spars. Foam flotation
Sails:	Area 11.1m^2/120 sq.ft.
Rigging:	Sloop
Price Guide:	$1,195us
Summary:	2 crew. Trapeze used. Built only in America.

KRAKEN 18

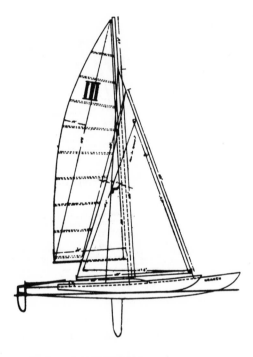

Design:	Lock Crowther, U.S.A. 1967
Supplier:	International Marine Services, U.S.A.
Specifications:	*Construction:* Plywood
	LOA: 5.49m/18'0
	Beam: 3.35m/11'0
	Draft: 0.2m/8"
Fittings:	1 daggerboard. 3 symmetrical hulls joined by a bridge deck. Aluminium spars. Wood flotation.
Sails:	Area 21.1m^2 (11.1 + 10)/227 sq.ft. (120 + 107)
Rigging:	Sloop
Price Guide:	$1,800us
Summary:	2 crew. 2 trapezes used.

KRAKEN 25

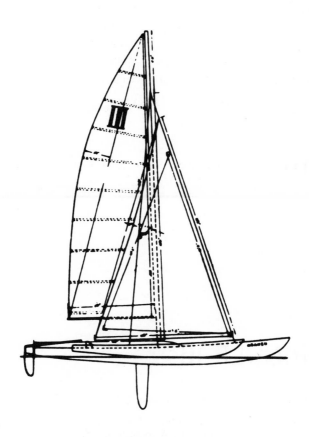

Design: Lock Crowther, U.S.A. 1967

Supplier: International Marine Services, U.S.A.

Specifications: *Construction:*   Wood
                     LOA: 7.62m/25'0
                     Beam: 4.27m/14'0

Fittings: 1 daggerboard. 3 symmetrical hulls joined by a bridge
                     deck. Aluminium spars. Wood flotation.

Sails: Area 27.9m^2/300 sq.ft.

Rigging: Sloop

Price Guide: $3,200us

Summary: 2 or 3 crew. Trapeze used.

OYSTER CATAMARAN

Supplier:	Compton Page Ltd., England
Specifications:	Construction: GRP
	LOA: 2.44m/8'0
	Displ: 49kg/108 lbs
Variations:	Outboard can be attached.
Sails:	Area 3.3m^2/35 sq.ft.
Rigging:	Una

Summary: General purpose catamaran that takes up to 3 adults. Can be car-topped.

PRINDLE 16

Design:	Geoffrey Prindle, U.S.A. 1972
Supplier:	Surfglas Inc., U.S.A.
	Prindle 16 Association, U.S.A.
Specifications:	*Construction:* GRP
	LOA: 4.88m/16'0
	Beam: 2.41m/7'11
	Draft: 0.25m/10''
	Displ: 143kg/315 lbs
Fittings:	No centreboard required. 2 asymmetrical hulls connected by aluminium. Aluminium spars. Foam flotation.
Sails:	Area 17.7m^2(13.9 + 3.8)/190 sq.ft. (150 + 40)
Rigging:	Sloop
Price Guide:	$1,695us
Summary:	2 crew. Trapeze used. Built only in America.

MALIBU OUTRIGGER

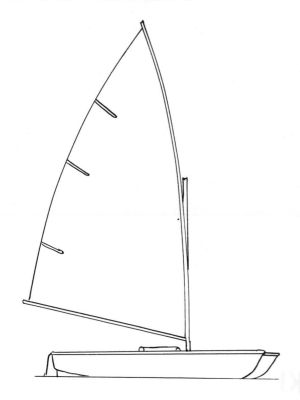

Design:	Warren Seaman, U.S.A.
Supplier:	Browning Marine Division, U.S.A. Malibu Outrigger Association, U.S.A.
Specifications:	*Construction:* Wood *LOA:* 5.72m/18'9 *Beam:* 3.55m/11'8 *Draft:* 0.2m/8''
Fittings:	Daggerboard. Outrigger hulls connected by wood beams. Wooden spars. Positive flotation.
Sails:	Area 17.8m^2/192 sq.ft. No spinnaker allowed.
Rigging:	Una
Price Guide:	On application
Summary:	2 crew. Kits and plans available. Built only in America.

QUICK CAT

Design:	Lindsay Cunningham, U.S.A.
Supplier:	Quick Cat Association, U.S.A.
Specifications:	*Construction:* Wood
	LOA: 4.88m/16'0
	Beam: 1.93m/6'4
	Draft: 0.1m/4"
Fittings:	Centreboards. 2 symmetrical hulls connected by aluminium. Spars — wood or aluminium. Sliding seat. Positive flotation.
Sails:	Area 11.7m^2/126 sq.ft.
Rigging:	Una
Price Guide:	On application
Summary:	Single-hander.

SKEETER CAT

Design:	Furman L. Shaw Junior, U.S.A. 1972
Supplier:	Shaw Craft, U.S.A.
Specifications:	*Construction:* GRP
	LOA: 3.05m/10'0
	Beam: 1.52m/5'0
	Draft: 0.15m/6"
Fittings:	2 symmetrical hulls connected with aluminium. Aluminium spars. Foam flotation.
Sails:	Area 6.04m^2/65 sq.ft.
Rigging:	Una
Price Guide:	$595us
Summary:	Single-hander. Hiking straps used.

MOSQUITO TRIMARAN

Design:	Rodney Garrett and Derek Norfolk, England
Supplier:	Anderson Aerosails Hywood Marine, England
Specifications:	*Construction:* GRP *LOA:* 5.49m/18'0 *Beam:* 3.05m/10'0 *Displ:* 336kg/740 lbs
Fittings:	Mahogany centreboard. Anodised spars.
Sails:	Area 16.3m^2/175 sq.ft. Terylene
Rigging:	Sloop
Price Guide:	On application
Summary:	Retractable outriggers reduce beam to 6' for easy towing and parking. Terylene trampoline side deck extensions.

PHOENIX

Design:	J. R. MacAlpine-Downie, U.S.A.
Supplier:	Sail Manufacturing, U.S.A.
Specifications:	*Construction:* GRP
	LOA: 5.49m/18'0
	Beam: 2.41m/7'11
	Draft: 0.1m/4"
Fittings:	Centreboards. 2 symmetrical hulls connected with aluminium. Aluminium spars. Positive flotation.
Sails:	Area 19m^2/204 sq.ft. Main fully battened.
Rigging:	Sloop
Price Guide:	$1,500us
Summary:	2 crew. Trapeze used.

SCAMPER CAT

Design:	D. Matthew, U.S.A.	
Supplier:	Formex Corporation, U.S.A.	
Specifications:	*Construction:*	Plastic
	LWL:	3.51m/11'6
	LOA:	3.66m/12'0
	Beam:	2.03m/6'8
	Draft:	0.33m/1'1
	Displ:	83.99kg/185 lbs
Fittings:	2 symmetrical hulls connected by aluminium. Aluminium spars. Foam flotation.	
Sails:	Area 6.97m^2/75 sq.ft.	
Rigging:	Una	
Price Guide:	$450us	
Summary:	2 crew. Sails either single-handed or with a group. Unsinkable. Can be car-topped. Tough and sturdy.	

SEA MOTH II

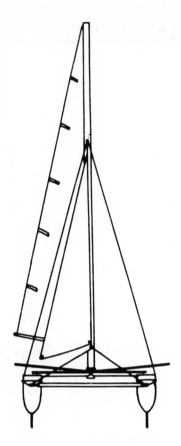

Design:	AMF Alcort, U.S.A.
Supplier:	D. Bruce Connolly, U.S.A.
Specifications:	*Construction:* GRP
	LOA: 4.57m/15'0
	Beam: 1.96m/6'5
	Displ: 68.1kg/150 lbs
Fittings:	2 daggerboards. 2 symmetrical hulls connected by aluminium. Aluminium spars. Air tank flotation.
Sails:	Area 11.6m^2/125 sq. ft.
Rigging:	Sloop
Price Guide:	$1,180us
Summary:	Single-hander. Built only in America. Flies a jib for easier tacking. Fast and easy to handle.

SEA SKATER CAT

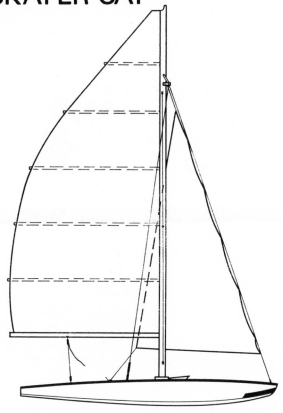

Design:	D. Butcher	
Rating:	Portsmouth yardstick 92	
Specifications:	*Construction:*	GRP and marine ply
	LWL:	3.28m/10'9
	LOA:	3.81m/12'6
	Beam:	1.68m/5'6
	Draft:	0.59m/1'11
	Displ:	63.56kg/140 lbs
Fittings:	Centreboard boat. Mast 5.49m/18'0 high. 2 symmetrical hulls.	
Sails:	Area 11.52m^2/124 sq.ft.	
Rigging:	Sloop	
Price Guide:	On application	
Summary:	1 or 2 crew. A very good light weather performance because of low weight and small wetted surface area.	

SUN CAT

Design:	Clark Mills, U.S.A. 1966
Supplier:	Dilks & Co., U.S.A.
Specifications:	*Construction:* GRP
	LOA: 5.03m/16'6
	Beam: 2.21m/7'3
	Draft: 0.20m/9'' cb up
	Displ: 499kg/1,100 lbs
Fittings:	Twin bilgeboards. Aluminium spars.
Sails:	Area $15.33m^2$/165 sq.ft.
Rigging:	Una
Price Guide:	$2,695us
Summary:	Built only in America

TIGER CUB

Design:	Ron Given, N.Z. 1970
Supplier:	High Performance Sailboat Sales, U.S.A.
	Tiger Cub Association, New Zealand
Specifications:	*Construction:* Plywood or GRP
	LOA: 3.05m/10'0
	Beam: 1.52m/5'0
	Draft: 0.13m/5''
	Displ: 34.05kg/75 lbs
Fittings:	Daggerboards. 2 symmetrical hulls connected with aluminium. Aluminium spars. Air tank flotation.
Sails:	Area $6.97m^2$/75 sq.ft.
Rigging:	Una
Price Guide:	$895us

SEA SPRAY 15

Design:	Allan J. Arnold, U.S.A.
Supplier:	Gen-Mar Incorporated, U.S.A.
Specifications:	*Construction:* GRP
	LOA: 4.57m/15'0
	Beam: 1.96m/6'5
	Draft: 0.56m/1'10
	Displ: 68.1kg/150 lbs
Fittings:	Daggerboards. 2 symmetrical hulls connected with aluminium. Aluminium spars. Positive flotation.
Sails:	Area 12.54m^2/135 sq.ft.
Rigging:	Sloop
Price Guide:	$1,100us
Summary:	Single-hander. Strong, light, high performance catamaran.

SEA SPRAY 18

Design:	Kirke Leonard, U.S.A. 1972
Supplier:	Gen-Mar Incorporated, U.S.A.

Specifications:	*Construction:*	GRP
	LOA:	5.49m/18'0
	Beam:	2.41m/7'11
	Draft:	0.71m/2'4
	Displ:	99.88kg/220 lbs

Fittings: 2 centreboards. 2 symmetrical hulls connected with aluminium Aluminium spars. Foam flotation. Kick-up rudders.

Sails: Area 20.44m^2/220 sq.ft.

Rigging: Sloop

Price Guide: $1,995us

Summary: 2 crew. A well balanced, and easy to tack catamaran.

TRIAD

Design:	Joseph C. Dobler, U.S.A. 1964
Supplier:	Triad Association, U.S.A.
Specifications:	*Construction:* Plywood and GRP
	LOA: 5.79m/19'0
	Beam: 3.86m/12'9
	Draft: 0.25m/10"
Fittings:	Daggerboard. 3 symmetrical hulls connected with wood beams. Aluminium spars. Air tank flotation.
Sails:	Area 29.26m^2/315 sq.ft. (192 + 123) No spinnaker allowed.
Rigging:	Sloop
Price Guide:	On application.
Summary:	2 crew. Trapeze used. Plans available.

TRIKINI 17 Mk II

Design:	Leonard Susman, U.S.A. 1970
Supplier:	Lenman Industries Inc., U.S.A.
Specifications:	*Construction:* GRP
	LOA: 5.13m/16'10
	Beam: 3.61m/11'10
	Draft: 0.18m/7''
	Displ: 136.2kg/300 lbs
Fittings:	Daggerboard. 3 symmetrical hulls connected with aluminium. Aluminium spars. Foam flotation.
Sails:	Area 18.12m^2/195 sq.ft.
Rigging:	Sloop
Price Guide:	$2,395us
Summary:	2 crew. Trapeze used. Built only in America.

TRIKINI `D´

Design:	Leonard Susman, U.S.A. 1970
Supplier:	Lenman Industries Inc., U.S.A.
Specifications:	*Construction:* GRP
	LOA: 10.36m/34'0
	Beam: 7.32m/24'0
	Draft: 0.25m/10''
	Displ: 454kg/1,000 lbs
Fittings:	Daggerboard. 3 symmetrical hulls connected with aluminium. Aluminium spars. Foam flotation.
Sails:	Area 46.45m^2/500 sq.ft. Spinnaker area 74.32m^2/800 sq.ft.
Rigging:	Sloop
Price Guide:	$9,995us
Summary:	2 crew. Trapeze used. 2 only built to date in America.

TRIFOIL

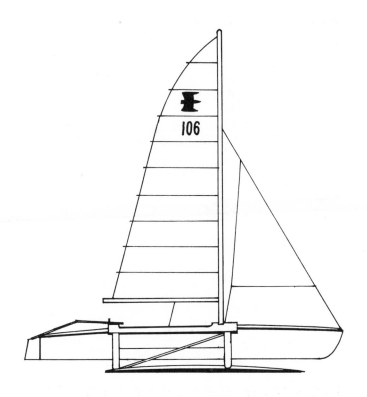

TRIFOIL

Design:	Erick J Manners, England
Supplier:	Erick J. Manners, England
Specifications:	*Construction:* Plywood
	LOA: 6.10m/20'0
	Beam: 3.66m/12'0
Fittings:	Round bottom hulls. Plywood decks. Wood or metal spars.
Sails:	Area 18.12m^2/195 sq.ft. (cruising)
	Area 21.83m^2/235 sq.ft. (racing)
Rigging:	Bermudan sloop
Price Guide:	On application
Summary:	Available world-wide.

TRIUMPH 24

Design: Lasco Marine, U.S.A.

Supplier: Triumph 24 Association, U.S.A.

Specifications:
Construction:	GRP
LOA:	7.32m/24'0
Beam:	4.27m/14'0
Draft:	0.46m/1'6

Fittings: 3 symmetrical hulls connected with a bridge deck. Aluminium spars. Positive flotation.

Sails: Area 22.57m^2/243 sq.ft. No spinnaker allowed.

Rigging: Sloop

Price Guide: $2,200us

Summary: 2 crew. Kits available. Built only in America.

VENTURE CATAMARAN

Design: Roger McGregor, U.S.A. 1970

Supplier: Kincaid & Co. U.S.A.

Specifications:
Construction:	GRP
LOA:	4.57m/15'0
Beam:	2.41m/7'11
Draft:	0.15m/6"
Displ:	99.88kg/220 lbs

Fittings: 2 asymmetric hulls connected by aluminium tubes. Aluminium spars. Foam flotation.

Sails: Area 14.03m^2/151 sq.ft.

Rigging: Sloop

Price Guide: $695us

Summary: Single-hander. Hiking straps used.

TRIKINI 13 Mk II

Design:	Leonard Susman, U.S.A. 1971
Supplier:	Lenman Industries Inc., U.S.A.
Specifications:	*Construction:* GRP
	LOA: 3.96m/13'0
	Beam: 2.74m/9'0
	Draft: 0.18m/7"
	Displ: 72.64kg/160 lbs
Fittings:	Daggerboard. 3 symmetrical hulls connected with aluminium. Aluminium spars. Positive flotation.
Sails:	Area 10.68m^2/115 sq.ft.
Rigging:	Una
Price Guide:	$1,295us
Summary:	Single-hander. Trapeze used. Built only in America.

WALLABY

Design:	Bert K. Anderson, U.S.A. 1972
Supplier:	International Marine Services, U.S.A.
	Wallaby Association, U.S.A.
Specifications:	*Construction:* Wood and GRP
	LOA: 4.27m/14'0
	Beam: 2.90m/9'6
	Draft: 0.15m/6''
Fittings:	Aluminium spars.
Sails:	Area 13.94m^2/150 sq.ft.
Rigging:	Una
Price Guide:	$1,250us
Summary:	Only 3 recorded built to date. Single-hander. Trapeze used.

YW CATAMARAN

Design:	Rod MacAlpine-Downie, England
Supplier:	MacAlpine-Downie, England
Rating:	Portsmouth yardstick 78
Specifications:	*Construction:* Wood or GRP
	LOA: 4.72m/15'6
	Beam: 2.13m/7'0
	Draft: 0.76m/2'6
	Displ: 109kg/240 lbs
Fittings:	Wood or aluminium spars. 2 symmetrical hulls.
Sails:	Area 10.3m^2/175 sq.ft.
Rigging:	Cat
Price Guide:	On application
Summary:	2 crew. Trapeze used. Kits and plans available.

TRIUMPH

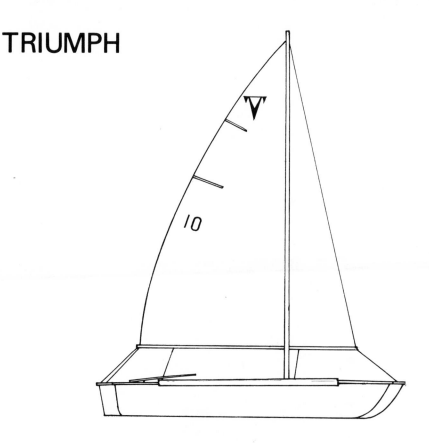

Design:	Snark Products, U.S.A.
Supplier:	Snark Products Inc., U.S.A.
Specifications:	*Construction:* Plastic
	LOA: 2.74m/9'0
	Beam: 1.52m/5'0
	Draft: 0.08m/3"
Fittings:	3 symmetrical hulls connected by a bridge deck. Aluminium spars. Foam flotation. Outboard well.
Sails:	Area 5.57m^2/60 sq.ft.
Rigging:	Una
Price Guide:	$369us
Summary:	Single-hander. A swift, versatile trimaran that is safe and easy to handle. Very stable. Maintenance-free.

461

SKIMMERS AND SAILING SURFBOARDS

BEACHCOMBER

Supplier:	Sailskiff Sportscraft, England
Rating:	Portsmouth yardstick 110
Specifications:	*Construction:* Mahogany and marine ply or GRP
	LOA: 3.96m/13'0
	Beam: 1.14m/3'9
	Draft: 0.46m/1'6
	Displ: 41kg–43kg/90–95 lbs
Fittings:	Marine ply centreboard and rudder. Alloy spars.
Sails:	Area 7.4m²/80 sq. ft. (racing) 6.7m²/72 sq. ft. (cruising). Terylene — blue and white.
Rigging:	Una — jib may be added.
Price Guide:	£176
Summary:	1 or 2 crew. Kits available.

BONITO

Design:	Pearson Bros. U.K. 1965
Supplier:	Pearson Bros. U.K. Lincoln Fibreglass Inc. U.S.A. Bonito Association U.K. Bonito National Association U.S.A.
Est. Rating:	Portsmouth yardstick 104

Specifications:

Construction:	GRP choice of 2 colours.
LWL:	4.27m/14'0
LOA:	4.42m/14'6
Beam:	1.27m/4'2
Draft:	0.08m/3" cb up
Displ:	57kg/125 lbs

Fittings:	Grp spars. Wood centreboard boat.
Sails:	Area 8.2m^2/88 sq.ft. Terylene
Rigging:	Una
Price Guide:	£250/$675us
Summary:	2 crew. Modern hull shape with stem and deep V forward combined with a flat run aft. Easily carried on car top and can be rigged and launched in minutes. Over 4,000 boats in circulation worldwide.

465

GOLDFISH

Design:	F. C. Gaines Jnr., U.S.A.
Supplier:	Goldfish Sailboat Co., U.S.A.
	Goldfish Association, U.S.A.
Specifications:	*Construction:* GRP
	LOA: 4.19m/13'9
	Beam: 1.22m/4'0
	Draft: 0.1m/4" cb up
	Displ: 61kg/135 lbs
Fittings:	Daggerboard. Aluminium spars. Mast $3.05m^2$/10'0 high. Positive flotation.
Sails:	Area $7.4m^2$/80 sq.ft.
	No spinnaker allowed.
Rigging:	Open
Price Guide:	On application
Summary:	Single-hander. An American class. Responds to all the elements. Very safe. Self-rescuing. Hiking straps used

NYMPH

Design:	Percy Blandford, England 1965
Supplier:	Percy Blandford, England
Specifications:	*Construction:* Single chine plywood
	LOA: 3.51m/11'6
	Beam: 1.07m/3'6
	Draft: 0.10m/4"
	Displ: 38.6kg/85 lbs
Fittings:	Flush plywood deck. Wooden spars.
Variations:	Built by amateurs.
Sails:	Area $4.6m^2$/50 sq.ft.
Rigging:	Una
Price Guide:	On application.
Summary:	1 or 2 crew. Toe straps fitted. Can be car-topped. Not usually raced.

FLYING SAUCER

Design:	Andrew Kostanecki, U.S.A. 1966
Supplier:	O'Day, U.S.A. Fenton Hill Marine, England
Specifications:	*Construction:* GRP *LOA:* 4.57m/15'0 *Beam:* 1.58m/5'2 *Draft:* 0.15m/6'' cb up *Displ:* 89kg/195 lbs
Fittings:	Centreboard boat. Aluminium spars. Positive flotation.
Sails:	Area 10.7m^2/115 sq.ft. No spinnaker.
Rigging:	Una
Price Guide:	On application
Summary:	2 crew. Carries up to 3 adults. Can be trailed and car-topped.

OD 11

Design:	George O'Day and Ian Proctor
Supplier:	OD 11 World Association, Israel OD 11 Association, U.S.A. Gemico Corporation, U.S.A.
Specifications:	*Construction:* GRP *LOA:* 3.35m/11'0 *Beam:* 1.22m/4'0 *Draft:* 0.08m/3" cb up *Displ:* 41kg/90 lbs
Fittings:	Daggerboard. Aluminium spars. Foam flotation. Self-bailing.
Sails:	Area 5.2m^2/56 sq.ft. Dacron.
Rigging:	Una
Price Guide:	$495us
Summary:	Single-hander. Self-rescuing.

SAILORSKI 10

Supplier:	E Type Boats Ltd., England
Specifications:	*Construction:* GRP *LOA:* 3.05m/10'0 *Draft:* 0.05m/2" *Displ:* 72.64kg/160 lbs
Fittings:	Centreboard boat. Aluminium spars.
Variations:	Outboard may be attached.
Sails:	Various areas
Rigging:	Bermudan una
Price Guide:	£150
Summary:	2 crew. A general purpose dinghy that can be trailed.

MINISAIL

Design:	Ian Proctor,U.K. 1961
Supplier:	Richmond Marine, U.K. Minisail World Association, U.K.
Rating:	Portsmouth yardstick 110
Specifications:	*Construction:* GRP
	LWL: 3.66m/12'0
	LOA: 3.96m/13'0
	Beam: 1.12m/3'8
	Draft: 0.08m/3'' cb up
	Displ: 43kg/95 lbs
Fittings:	Daggerboard. Aluminium spars. Sliding seat. Built-in buoyancy.
Sails:	Area 7.4m^2/80 sq.ft. White and red or orange sails.
Rigging:	Una
Price Guide:	£200/$495us
Summary:	1 or 2 crew. A fun boat popular worldwide — over 7,000 built to date. An instant boat — just add wind and water. Inexpensive, easy to transport.

SEA BAT

Supplier: Sailskiff Sportscraft Limited, England

Specifications:

Construction:	Mahogany ply or GRP
LOA:	3.51m/11'6
Beam:	0.99m/3'3
Displ:	31.78kg/70 lbs

Fittings: Alloy spars.

Sails: Area $6.69m^2$/72 sq.ft.

Rigging: Una

Price Guide: £140

Summary: Single-hander. Fun and fast, giving speeds up to 14 knots. Light, easily rigged and can be car-topped.

SKI SAIL

Supplier: Chippendale Boats, England

Specifications:

Construction:	GRP and wood
LOA:	4.11m/13'6
Beam:	1.12m/3'9
Displ:	54.48kg/120 lbs

Fittings: Centreboard boat. 2 symmetrical hulls.

Variations: Outboard cannot be fitted.

Sails: Area $7.9m^2$/85 sq.ft.

Rigging: Bermudan catamaran.

Price Guide: £200

Summary: Single-hander. May be car-topped and trailed. Outboard cannot be attached.

TOPPER

Design:	Ian Proctor, England
Supplier:	J. Dunhill. Enterprises, England

Specifications:

Construction:	GRP
LOA:	3.34m/11'0
Beam:	1.16m/3'10
Draft:	0.76m/2'6
Displ:	50kg/110 lbs

Fittings: Centreboard boat. Anodised aluminium spars. Built-in buoyancy.

Sails: Area 5.2m^2/56 sq.ft.

Rigging: Una

Price Guide: £140

Summary: Easy to handle, fast and planes easily whether on calm or choppy water. An international one-design that can boast fleets in the Middle East, Europe and the U.S.A. Maintenance-free.

WINDSURFER

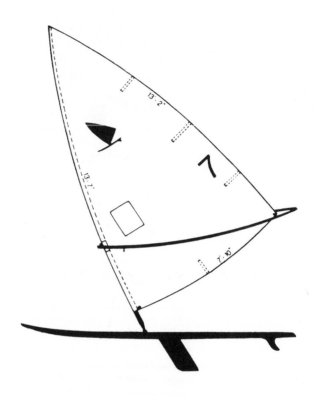

Design: Hoyle Schweitzer, U.S.A. 1968

Supplier: Windsurfer Association, U.S.A.

Specifications:
Construction:	Plastic
LOA:	3.66m/12'0
Beam:	0.66m/2'2
Draft:	0.05m/2''
Displ:	27.2kg/60 lbs

Fittings: Daggerboard. Spars — GRP and wood. Foam flotation. Self-bailers.

Sails: Area 5.2m²/56 sq.ft.

Rigging: Una

Price Guide: $365us

Summary: Single-hander. A sailing surfboard of unusual design—sailed standing upright.

RACERS, CRUISERS AND DUAL PURPOSE BOATS
an introduction

Boats included in this section all have overnight accommodation. They are listed in length overall order, smallest first, with multihulls listed separately. Sizes range from 12' 0 to 82'0.

Most designs listed here are used and marketed for cruising and racing. Builders can normally supply boats in both racing and cruising versions. Motor cruisers and boats designed solely for cruising have comparatively small sail areas and powerful engines and are thus easily handled. They can be separated from other craft but have been included in LOA order in the one section, to enable potential buyers to compare the types of boats available.

Racers and cruisers can be sectioned off, however, according to their size. Small cruisers, up to 20'0, with only two bunks and no sanitary arrangements are suitable for day sailing and overnight stops.

The general rule for boats over 20'0 is that the larger the boat the longer the cruise that can be undertaken because of increased comfort and amenities available. Larger boats carry greater quantities of fuel and fresh water and can provide healthier washing, sanitary and cooking facilities.

Multihulls, both catamarans and trimarans are by their very design roomier than monohulls. As many as 14 adults can be accommodated in separate cabins in larger models. These boats are stable and fast in high winds but because of their relatively large wetted surface area perform less well in light airs. Multihulls can be raced and cruised just as successfully as monohulls.

As illustrated on the following pages there are hundreds of racer/cruisers on the market. To help the first time buyer the most important factors involved in purchasing a boat are identified below.

Final choice should be based on several factors:

1. how much money is available
2. the purpose the boat is bought for
3. how much time is going to be spent with the boat
4. how many people are going to be involved
5. where the boat is going to be sailed and berthed

The amount of money available will determine the size and quality of

473

boat to be purchased. 70% of the amount available should be spent on the basic boat leaving the balance for insurance, moorings, sails and gadgets. Bear in mind that a new boat, as a new car, will have teething troubles. Any minor faults will be ironed out by the time a design reaches its third or fourth year of production. Second-hand models of popular designs are often available. Not always cheaper than new boats because supplied fully equipped, second-hand boats, from established dealers, will have been proved sea-worthy.

Kits and mouldings can be purchased for those who wish to build or complete their own boat. Initial cost is minimal but do not under-estimate the number of weekends and evenings involved in such a task.

Boats built of glass reinforced plastics are easier to maintain and cheaper to purchase than wooden models. Timber boats are individually built over a period of months whilst glass hulls appear from their moulds almost as quickly as cars from the production line. Wooden trims are often used on glass boats to counteract their clinical appearance.

Do not make false economies when purchasing. For example, teak, the hardest wood, though most expensive to use as a trim, is the most reliable. Cheaper woods warp easily and are costly to replace. Insist on stainless steel fittings which are durable and reliable where possible.

Take builders up on offers of trial sails. Regard racing successes with a degree of scepticism. Firms have been known to send out souped-up boats with professional crew with the specific aim of winning trophies to impress potential purchasers.

The functions of the boat must be decided in order of priority before final purchase. If racing is the major preoccupation ask if the boat is eligible for IOR and other major competitions. Is it's racing record good? Is the boat supplied with full racing inventory? Is equipment conveniently situated?

If comfort is more important than performance establish that the boat can house all the family comfortably both at sea and in port. If long cruises are envisaged ensure that there is maximum stowage capacity. Is the boat safe enough for young children? Are the sanitary arrangements adequate? Is the boat safe and seaworthy? are other salient factors.

Decide whether the boat is to be berthed permanently at water, or whether it will be regularly trailed. If the former establish well in advance that there is room at the marina of your choice. Waiting lists for space tend to be long. The nature of the sailing water in your area should also be studied carefully. A deep keel boat will be of no use in a shallow water channel.

Many popular waterways all over the world are permanently crowded. The number of accidents at sea rise each year. For your own and others safety ensure that helmsmen and crew attain an acceptable level of competence before taking to the water.

Racing is the most active, spectacular and widely publicised aspect of owning a large boat. Sponsored round-the-world races and lone voyages across oceans have focused attention on this popular sport.

As with dinghies, most larger boats are raced somewhere, some time, by somebody, though there are boats more specifically designed as racing machines. As the number of boats of a particular class are restricted—a successful class may boast only fifty members—handicapping systems have emerged to ensure competitive racing between different classes.

In the UK and Europe the Portsmouth yardstick is used to handicap smaller craft. Larger craft are classified by tonnage, a system introduced by the Royal Thames Yacht Club. Small cabin craft are measured from 2½ tons upwards. A measurement of about 5 tons is the normal minimum for open sea cruising.

Other systems of handicapping are in use all over the world. Most of these are devised and used locally, particularly in the USA.

Apart from handicap races, level racing, where boats of similar size compete, is increasing in popularity. The Offshore Rating Council, established in the late 1960s, recognises five Level Rating Classes. These are ¼ ton, ½ ton, ¾ ton, 1 ton and 2 ton levels. The names of the measurements are not related to the actual weight of boats but are named after the original Ton Cup class races established in the late 1890s.

Approximate requirements for a boat to qualify under these rules are:

¼ ton	LWL 18'0	2 berths	3/4 crew
½ ton	LWL 21'7	3 berths	4/5 crew
¾ ton	LWL 24'5	4 berths	5/6 crew
1 ton	LWL 27'5	4/5 berths	6/7 crew
2 ton	LWL 32'0	not yet established	

All boats must be issued with an International Offshore Rule Certificate before competing in these classes. New designs are geared towards these international rules, whilst older models are being modified to enable them to compete under IOR.

Cruising and racing are international sports, enjoyed by thousands both in inland and offshore waters. One only has to cast an eye around the world—San Francisco Bay, Sydney Harbour, the Solent, Hong-kong Harbour—to know that the number of boats and enthusiasts are growing regularly each season. To join them is to experience excitement, challenge, the pride and joy of ownership and the comradeship unique to the sailing world.

RACERS/CRUISERS 12´-20´
monohulls

BARBEL I

Design:	M. S. Redman, England
Supplier:	M. S. Redman, England

Specifications:	*Construction:*	Wood
	LWL:	3.28m/10'9
	LOA:	3.66m/12'0
	Beam:	1.22m/4'0
	Draft:	0.3m/1'0
	Displ:	182kg/400 lbs
	Ballast:	68kg/150 lbs

Fittings:	Bilge keel
Interior:	2 berths
Variations:	Optional outboard
Sails:	Area 5.6m^2/60 sq.ft.
Rigging:	Sloop
Price Guide:	£5.00 for plans
Summary:	Plans available from M.S. Redman. A comfortable small cruiser.

SPARROW

Design:	Herb Stewart, U.S.A.	
Supplier:	MS Marine Inc., U.S.A.	
Specifications:	*Construction:*	GRP
	LWL:	3.33m/10'11
	LOA:	3.66m/12'0
	Beam:	1.73m/5'8
	Draft:	0.51m/1'8
	Displ:	159kg/350 lbs
	Ballast:	59kg/130 lbs
Fittings:	Fixed keel	
Interior:	2 berths — 2.03m/6'8 long.	
Sails:	Area 6.8m^2 (3.8 + 3)/73 sq.ft. (32 ±41)	
Rigging:	Sloop	
Price Guide:	$1,395us	
Summary:	A small, convenient overnighter. Self-rescuing and bailing. Can be trailed.	

TERN (UK)

Design:	M. S. Redman, England
Supplier:	M. S. Redman, England
Specifications:	*Construction:* Wood
	LOA: 3.66m/12'0
	Draft: 0.91m/3'0
Fittings:	Centreboard boat
Interior:	2 berths
Variations:	Outboard may be attached
Sails:	Area optional
Rigging:	Bermudan sloop
Price Guide:	On application
Summary:	A compact daysailer. Can be trailed.

BRIGAND

Design:	Cabochard, France
Supplier:	Cabochard, France
Specifications:	*Construction:* GRP
	LOA: 4.20m/13'9
	Beam: 1.82m/5'11½
	Displ: 380kg/838 lbs
Fittings:	Aluminium spars
Interior:	2 berths
Variations:	Outboard attached
Sails:	Area 11m^2/118 sq.ft.
Rigging:	Sloop
Price Guide:	On application
Summary:	A robust weekender with a roomy cockpit.

VOYAGER

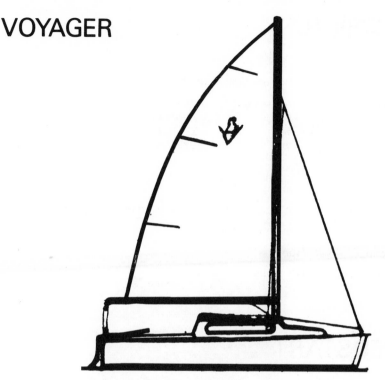

Design:	Redman/McMullen, England 1968
Supplier:	Juxtamare Marine Ltd., England Intermarine Agency, U.S.A.
Est. Rating:	Portsmouth yardstick 129
Specifications:	*Construction:* GRP
	LWL: 3.81m/12'6
	LOA: 4.06m/13'4
	Beam: 1.55m/5'1
	Draft: 0.41m/1'4
	Displ: 236kg/520 lbs
	Ballast: 73kg/160lbs
Fittings:	Twin keel. 1½–4HP outboard. Teak trim. Aluminium spars.
Interior:	2 berths
Sails:	Area 7.4m^2/80 sq.ft.
Rigging:	Sloop
Price Guide:	£580
Summary:	Excellent windward ability. Kits and mouldings available.

TARPON

Design: P. W. Blandford, England

Supplier: Stalbridge Boats Ltd., England

Specifications:

Construction:	Wood
LOA:	4.27m/14'0
Beam:	1.52m/5'0
Displ:	159kg/350 lbs

Fittings: Wood deck

Interior: 2 berths

Variations: Can be supplied also as an open boat

Sails: Area 9.9m^2/106 sq.ft.

Rigging: Gunter

Price Guide: On application

REDSTART

Design: McMullen & Jardine, England 1970

Supplier: Juxtamare Marine, England
Intermarine Agency, U.S.A.

Est. Rating: Portsmouth number 125

Specifications:

Construction:	GRP
LWL:	3.96m/13'0
LOA:	4.42m/14'6
Beam:	1.55m/5'1
Draft:	0.61m/2'0
Displ:	295kg/650 lbs
Ballast:	124kg/273 lbs

Fittings: Lead ballast. GRP deck. Anodised alloy spars. 1.5—4HP outboard. Mahogany trim.

Interior: 2 berths in 1 cabin.

Variations: Optional galley and toilet.

Sails: Area 9.9m^2 (6 + 3.9)/107 sq.ft. (65 + 42)
Spinnaker area 7.43m^2/80 sq.ft.

Rigging: Sloop

Price Guide: £478/$2,200us

BARBEL II

Design:	M. S. Redman, England
Supplier:	M. S, Redman, England
Specifications:	*Construction:* Wood or GRP
	LWL: 3.89m/12'9
	LOA: 4.27m/14'0
	Beam: 1.52m/5'0
	Draft: 0.30m/1'0
	Displ: 240kg/530 lbs
	Ballast: 91kg/200 lbs
Fittings:	Bilge keel
Interior:	2 berths/2 also in cockpit optional. Cooker. Toilet space.
Variations:	Optional outboard.
Sails:	Area 8.18/88.25 sq.ft.
Rigging:	Bermudan sloop
Price Guide:	Plans £5.00 per set.
Summary:	A neatly designed small family cruiser. Can be trailed. Kits and plans available.

TRAILER SAILER 14

Design:	R. T. Hartley, New Zealand
Supplier:	R. T. Hartley, New Zealand
Specifications:	*Construction:* Marine plywood
	LOA: 4.27m/14'0
	Beam: 1.98m/6'6
	Draft: 1.14m/3'9
	Displ: 272kg/600 lbs
Fittings:	Mast height 5.49m/18'0
Interior:	2 berths
Sails:	Area 11.8m^2/127 sq.ft.
Rigging:	Sloop
Price Guide:	
Summary:	A camping dinghy that has 2 permanent berths.

WEST WIGHT POTTER

Design	Stanley Smith, U.S.A. 1960
Supplier:	HMS Marine Inc., U.S.A.

Specifications:

Construction:	GRP
LWL:	3.51m/11'6
LOA:	4.27m/14'0
Beam:	1.6m/5'3
Draft:	0.81m/2'8
Displ:	250kg/550 lbs
Ballast:	34kg/75 lbs

Fittings: Galvanised steel ballast. GRP deck. Aluminium spars.

Interior: 2 berths in 1 cabin.

Variations: 1—5HP outboard

Sails: Area 7.1m^2(4.8 + 2.3)/76 sq.ft. (52 + 24)

Rigging: Sloop

Price Guide: $1,650us

Summary: A traditional small cruiser. Designed for the North Sea. Very sturdy and stable.

SEA SHANTY

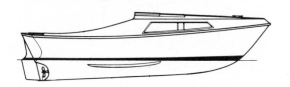

Design:	Norman Pearn, England
Supplier:	Norman Pearn & Co., England
Specifications:	*Construction:* GRP and wood
	LOA: 4.34m/14'3
	Beam: 1.83m/6'0
	Draft: 0.3m/1'0
	Displ: 363kg/800 lbs
Fittings:	Bilge keel. Iron ballast. 1½—5HP inboard engine.
Interior:	2 berths
Sails:	Area 9.3m^2/100 sq.ft.
Rigging:	Gunter
Price Guide:	£1,200
Summary:	Light and roomy cabin. Smaller version of the Sea Shanty 18. Can be trailed.

WEST WIGHT `C' TYPE

Design: Stanley Smith, U.S.A.

Supplier: Ring Marine, England

Specifications:
Construction:	GRP
LWL:	3.58m/11'9
LOA:	4.42m/14'6
Beam:	1.6m/5'3
Draft:	0.81m/2'8
Displ:	245kg/540 lbs

Fittings: Mahogany trim. Drop keel. Self-bailing.

Interior: 2 berths

Variations: Optional outboard. 7HP maximum.

Sails: Area 10.2m^2/110 sq.ft.
Spinnaker area 6.0m^2/65 sq.ft.

Rigging: Sloop

Price Guide: £450

Summary: Designed specifically for the North Sea. Very competent for offshore cruising. Self-bailing — non-sinkable.

CROSSBOW

Design:	John White, England
Supplier:	Adams Martin (Leeds) Ltd., England

Specifications:

Construction:	GRP
LWL:	4.26m/14'0
LOA:	4.52m/14'10
Beam:	1.85m/6'1
Draft:	0.30m/1'0
Displ:	204kg/450 lbs

Fittings:	Centreboard boat.
Interior:	2 berths. Full sitting headroom.
Variations:	Optional outboard
Sails:	Area 10.69m^2/115 sq.ft.
Rigging:	Sloop
Price Guide:	£485+
Summary:	Easily trailed. Stable and dry sailer. Good storage space.

NEWPORT 16

Design:	C. William Lapworth, U.S.A.
Supplier:	Capital Yachts Inc., U.S.A.

Specifications:

Construction:	GRP
LWL:	4.16m/13'8
LOA:	4.75m/15'7
Beam:	1.91m/6'3
Draft:	0.61m/2'0
Displ:	341kg/750 lbs

Fittings:	Iron ballast. GRP deck. Aluminium spars.
Interior:	2 berths in 1 cabin. 1 open toilet.
Variations:	Keel or centreboard models available. Galley optional. Optional HP outboard.
Sails:	Area 12.7m^2/137 sq.ft.
Rigging:	Sloop
Price Guide:	$1,600us
Summary:	A neat, 2-berth cruiser that carries 5 in comfort.

CAPELAN

Design:	Chantiers Beneteau, France
Supplier:	Chantiers Beneteau, France Arie de Boom BV, Holland
Specifications:	*Construction:* GRP *LOA:* 4.50m/14'9 *Beam:* 2.05m/6'9 *Draft:* 0.60m/1'11½ *Displ:* 480kg/1,058 lbs
Fittings:	Aluminium spars
Interior:	2 berths — seating for 4.
Sails:	Area 12.50m^2/135 sq.ft.
Rigging:	Sloop
Price Guide:	8,000 D.Fl.
Summary:	An interesting small cruiser that is easy to handle and maintain.

LE GABIER

Supplier: Chantiers France Navals Ocqueateau, France
                       Navy-Holland, Holland

Specifications: *Construction:*   Polyester
                       LOA: 4.55m/14'11
                       Beam: 1.85m/6'1
                       Draft: 0.45m/1'5½
                       Displ: 520kg/1,146 lbs
                       Ballast: 205kg/452 lbs

Fittings: Aluminium spars

Interior: 2 berths

Variations: Optional power

Sails: Area 10.50m^2 (7.20 + 3.50)/113 sq.ft. (78 + 35)

Rigging: Sloop

Price Guide: On application

Summary: An easy to sail, comfortable overnighter that seats
                       five comfortably.

KELPIE

Design:	C. S. J. Roy, England 1967
Supplier:	West Kirby Marine Services, England
Specifications:	*Construction:* GRP
	LWL: 3.81m/12'6
	LOA: 4.57m/15'0
	Beam: 1.68m/5'6
	Draft: 0.61m/2'0
	Displ: 499kg/1,100 lbs
	Ballast: 204kg/450 lbs
Fittings:	GRP deck. Alloy spars.
Interior:	2 berths. 1.37m/4'6 cockpit. 1.12m/3'8 maximum cabin headroom.
Variations:	Fin or bilge keel. Available also as an open dayboat. Outboard can be fitted.
Sails:	Area: dayboat 11.6m^2/125 sq.ft. weekender 10.7m^2/115 sq.ft.
Rigging:	Sloop
Price Guide:	£490+
Summary:	Suitable for the beginner or the experienced sailor. Easily trailed, launched and recovered. Finished to a very high standard.

491

ION 16

Design:	K. Littledike, England 1972
Suppliers:	Iles of Norbury, England
Specifications:	*Construction:* All ply panels
	LWL: 4.34/14'3
	LOA: 4.65m/15'3
	Beam: 2.08m/6'10
	Draft: 0.91m/3'0
	Displ: 272kg/600 lbs
	Ballast: 45kg/100 lbs
Fittings:	Drop keel. Outboard 4HP. Metal spars.
Interior:	2 berths
Variations:	Optional outboard up to 8HP.
Sails:	Area 10.7m^2/115 sq.ft.
Rigging:	Sloop
Price Guide:	£495
Summary:	Supplied only in kit form — stitch and glue construction.

SUNSPOT 15 MK II

Design:	Arthur Howard, England 1968
Supplier:	Intermarine Ltd., England Intermarine Agency, U.S.A.
Est. Rating:	Portsmouth number 123
Specifications:	*Construction:* GRP *LWL:* 4.09m/13'5 *LOA:* 4.65m/15'3 *Beam:* 1.91m/6'3 *Draft:* 0.57m/1'11 *Displ:* 440kg/900 lbs *Ballast:* 181kg/400 lbs
Fittings:	GRP deck. Built-in buoyancy. Aluminium alloy spars.
Interior:	4 berths (2 + 2). 1.40m/4'7 maximum cabin head-room.
Variations:	Outboard may be fitted. Cooker and toilet may be included.
Sails:	Area 9.76m^2/105 sq.ft.
Rigging:	Sloop
Price Guide:	£800
Summary:	Designed for estuary and coastal sailing. Good for the novice cruiser sailor. Kits and mouldings available.

AMERICAN 16

Design:	American Fiberglass Corporation, U.S.A. 1972
Supplier:	American Fiberglass Corporation, U.S.A. American 16 National Association, U.S.A.

Specifications:	*Construction:*	GRP
	LWL:	4.42m/14'6
	LOA:	4.57m/15'10
	Beam:	1.83m/6'0
	Draft:	0.18m/7'' cb up
	Displ:	270kg/595 lbs

Fittings:	Tabernacle or regular mast available. Aluminium spars. Kick-up aluminium rudder. Double hulled.
Interior:	2 berths/seating.
Sails:	Area 11.6m^2/125 sq.ft. Dacron.
Rigging:	Sloop
Price Guide:	$1,900–2,000us

CABIN 16

Design:	Richard Dadson, England
Supplier:	Richard Dadson, England

Specifications:	*Construction:*	Clinker — mahogany on oak
	LWL:	4.50m/14'9
	LOA:	4.88m/16'0
	Beam:	1.40m/5'10
	Draft:	1.06m/3'6 down
	Displ:	454kg/1,000 lbs
	Ballast:	90kg/200 lbs

Fittings:	Retractable keel.
Interior:	2 berths
Variations:	Optional outboard engine. Available as a cabin sloop, motor cruiser, or as an open fishing boat.
Sails:	Area 11.61m^2/125 sq.ft.
Rigging:	Gunter
Price Guide:	£770
Summary:	Can be trailed. Stout and attractive. One of the few wooden clinker built boats. Still available on the British market.

DS-16

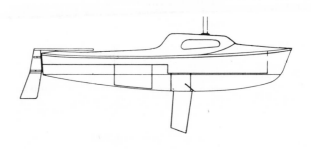

Design:	Diller and Schwill, Canada 1970	
Supplier:	Schwill Yachts Inc., Canada	
Specifications:	*Construction:*	GRP
	LWL:	4.37m/14'4
	LOA:	4.88m/16'0
	Beam:	1.83m/6'0
	Draft:	0.17m/7'' cb up
	Displ:	227kg–318kg/500–700 lbs
	Ballast:	57kg/125 lbs
Fittings:	GRP deck. Aluminium spars. Lead ballast.	
Interior:	2 berths in 1 cabin. Icebox.	
Variations:	Optional HP outboard	
Sails:	Area 14.4m^2(9.8 + 4.6)/155 sq.ft. (105 + 50)	
Rigging:	Sloop	
Price Guide:	$1,895–2,000us	
Summary:	A compact cruiser for two	

MARAUDEUR

Design:	Jean-Jacques Herbulot, France
Supplier:	Spair Marine, France
	Nautica Corporation, U.S.A.

Specifications:	*Construction:*	GRP
	LWL:	4.67m/15'4
	LOA:	4.88m/16'0
	Beam:	1.75m/5'9
	Draft:	0.3m/1'0
	Displ:	279kg/615 lbs
	Ballast:	70kg/154 lbs

Fittings:	GRP deck. Aluminium spars.
Interior:	2 berths. 1 cabin.
Sails:	Area 14.1m^2/152 sq.ft.
Rigging:	Sloop
Price Guide:	7,300 Fr.F.
Summary:	A useful daysailer/overnighter. Good performance.

INVADER

Design:	Oliver J. Lee, England
Supplier:	Oliver J. Lee, England

Specifications:	*Construction:*	
	LOA:	4.9m/16'1
	Draft:	1.01m/3'4

Fittings:	Centreboard boat.
Interior:	3 berths
Variations:	Optional outboard
Sails:	Area 11.5m^2/124 sq.ft.
Rigging:	Sloop
Price Guide:	On application.
Summary:	Can be trailed.

SHARKY

Supplier:	Salterns Yacht Agency, England
Specifications:	*Construction:* GRP
	LWL: 4.24m/13'11
	LOA: 4.88m/16'0
	Beam: 1.68m/5'6
	Draft: 0.46m/1'6
	Displ: 409kg/900 lbs
Fittings:	Bilge keel. Iron ballast. Alloy spars. GRP deck.
Interior:	2 berths. 1.42m/4'8 headroom.
Variations:	Sailing or motor versions available.
Sails:	Area 8.4m^2/90 sq.ft.
Rigging:	Sloop
Price Guide:	£440
Summary:	Good windward performance. Comfortable and sea kindly.

HUNTER 490

Design: Oliver J. Lee, England 1971

Supplier: Hunter Boats Ltd., England

Specifications:

Construction:	GRP	
LWL:	4.25m/13'11½	
LOA:	4.9m/16'1	
Beam:	2m/6'6¾	
Draft:	0.99m/3'3¼	
Displ:	454kg/1,000 lbs	
Ballast:	136kg/300 lbs	

Fittings: Teak trim. Centreboard ballasted. Retractable keel.

Interior: 2/3 berths. 1.22m/4'0 maximum cabin headroom.

Variations: Optional outboard 2—4HP.

Sails: Area 11.2m^2/121 sq.ft. White terylene.

Rigging: Sloop

Price Guide: £795+

Summary: Well-liked by ex-dinghy men who want to keep the family happy without loss of speed and precise hand-ling qualities. Often described as a mini-high-perfor-mance ditch crawler because of retractable keel. Kits and mouldings available.

SHIPMATE SENIOR

Design:	Norman Howard, England 1971	
Supplier:	Small Craft, England	
Specifications:	*Construction:*	GRP
	LWL:	4.32m/14'2
	LOA:	4.96m/16'3
	Beam:	1.91m/6'3
	Draft:	1.08m/3'6½
	Displ:	340kg/750 lbs
	Ballast:	41kg/90 lbs
Fittings:	Centreboard boat. Steel ballast. Anodised spars.	
Interior:	2/3 berths. Sitting headroom.	
Variations:	Shipmate Mk II can also be supplied — as an open dayboat. Outboard can be attached.	
Sails:	Area 9.7m²/104 sq.ft.	
Rigging:	Sloop	
Price Guide:	£675	
Summary:	An ideal weekend cruiser. Easy to trail. Very stable.	

TANZER OVERNIGHTER

Design:	Johann Tanzer, Canada 1969
Supplier:	Tanzer Industries Ltd., Canada
Specifications:	*Construction:* GRP
	LWL: 4.75m/15'7
	LOA: 4.98m/16'4
	Beam: 1.88m/6'2
	Draft: 0.17m/7''
	Displ: 227kg/500 lbs
Fittings:	GRP deck. Aluminium spars. Positive flotation. Kick-up centreboard and rudder.
Interior:	2 berths in 1 cabin
Variations:	Optional HP outboard
Sails:	Area 12.5m^2 (9.3 + 3.2)/135 sq.ft. (100 + 35) Spinnaker area 19m^2/205 sq.ft. Dacron.
Rigging:	Sloop
Price Guide:	$2,000us with sails
Summary:	Fast, stable, well balanced. Easily trailed. Inexpensive and compact.

TRAILER SAILER 16

Design:	R. T. Hartley, New Zealand
Supplier:	R. T. Hartley, New Zealand
Specifications:	*Construction:* Marine plywood
	LWL: 4.57m/15'0
	LOA: 5.0m/16'5
	Beam: 2.23m/7'4
	Draft: 1.24m/4'1
	Displ: 363kg/800 lbs
Fittings:	Mast height 6.4m/21'0
Interior:	2 berths
Sails:	Area 16.7m^2/180 sq.ft. Spinnaker area 10.9m^2/117 sq.ft.
Rigging:	Sloop
Price Guide:	On application
Summary:	A small motor sailer.

FOX TROT

Design:	Yves Mareschal, France
Supplier:	Mermaid Boats (Bosham), England Yachting Selection, France
Specifications:	*Construction:* GRP *LOA:* 5.03m/16'6 *Beam:* 1.98m/6'6 *Draft:* 0.30m/1'0 *Displ:* 305kg/672 lbs *Ballast:* 83kg/184 lbs
Fittings:	Centreboard boat. Self-draining cockpit.
Interior:	2 berths. 1.09m/3'7 headroom.
Variations:	Optional outboard engine.
Sails:	Area 12.72m^2/137 sq.ft. Spinnaker area 16.07m^2/173 sq.ft.
Rigging:	Sloop
Price Guide:	£750+/7,150 Fr.F.
Summary:	Carries 5 or 6 in cockpit under sail comfortably. A dry ride. Can be easily launched and recovered.

PIRANHA

Supplier:	Fairey Marine, England	
Specifications:	*Construction:*	GRP
	LOA:	5.16m/16'11
	Beam:	1.93m/6'4
	Draft:	0.74m–0.61m/2'5–2'0
	Displ:	285kg/627 lbs

Fittings: Iron keel. Anodised aluminium. 6HP Renault couach petrol engine.

Interior: 2 berths

Variations: Swing or fixed keel versions.

Sails: Area 15.8m^2 (9 + 6.8)/170 sq.ft. (97 + 73)

Rigging: Sloop

Price Guide: On application

HURLEY 17

Design: Ian Anderson, England 1965

Supplier: Hurley Yachts, U.S.A.
Hurley Marine, England

Specifications:	*Construction:*	GRP
	LOA:	5.18m/17'0
	Beam:	1.98m/6'6
	Draft:	0.91m/3'0
	Displ:	545kg/1,200 lbs
	Ballast:	227kg/500 lbs

Fittings: Swing keel. GRP deck. Aluminium spars.

Interior: 4 berths in 1 cabin. Marine toilet.

Sails: Area 13m^2 (7 + 6)/140 sq.ft. (75 + 65)

Rigging: Sloop

Price Guide: $1,995us

Summary: A clean-lined, easy to sail cruiser.

LANAVERRE 510

Design:	Christian Maury, France
Supplier:	Yachting France, France Comextra, England Bussum, Holland

Specifications:	*Construction:*	GRP
	LWL:	4.72m/15'6
	LOA:	5.11m/16'9
	Beam:	1.88m/6'2
	Draft:	0.91m/3'0
	Displ:	726kg/1,600 lbs
	Ballast:	82kg/180 lbs

Fittings:	Centreboard boat. Aluminium spars.
Interior:	2 berths
Variations:	Optional 4–6HP auxiliary outboard.
Sails:	Area 11.6m^2/125 sq.ft.
Rigging:	Bermudan sloop
Price Guide:	£850/8,000 Fr.F.
Summary:	Carries up to 5 adults comfortably. Can be trailed.

SEAHAWK

Design:	John A. Bennett, England
Supplier:	Reedcraft Ltd., England

Specifications:

Construction:	GRP
LWL:	4.4m/14'6
LOA:	5.13m/16'11
Beam:	1.98m/6'6
Draft:	0.45m/18''
Displ:	545 kg/1,200 lbs
Ballast:	200kg/440 lbs

Fittings:	Retractable keel. GRP deck. Concrete ballast. Anodised alloy spars.
Interior:	2 berths.
Variations:	4 berth layout available. Outboard longshaft or inboard engine.
Sails:	Area 10.7m^2/126 sq.ft.
Rigging:	Sloop
Price Guide:	Kit from £630
Summary:	Stable and safe. Can be trailed and beached. First class family boat.

CAPE COD CAT

Design:	Charles Wittholz, U.S.A.
Supplier:	Cape Cod Shipbuilding Co., U.S.A.
Specifications:	*Construction:* GRP
	LWL: 5m/16'5
	LOA: 5.18m/17'0
	Beam: 2.41m/7'11
	Draft: 0.51m/1'8 cb up
	Displ: 1,271kg/2,800 lbs
	Ballast: 227kg/500 lbs
Fittings:	GRP deck. Wooden spars. 8HP Palmer gasoline auxiliary. Teak trim.
Interior:	2 berths in 1 cabin. Sink, 1 open toilet.
Sails:	Area 23.2m^2/250 sq.ft. (gaff) Area 22.3m^2/240 sq.ft. (marconi)
Rigging:	Gaff or Marconi rigs.
Price Guide:	$4,900us
Summary:	A traditional design small family cruiser. Ideal for racing or cruising.

LEISURE 17

Design:	A. C. Howard, England 1966
Supplier:	Cobramold Ltd., England
Est. Rating:	Portsmouth number 109 (twin keel model)

Specifications:	*Construction:*	GRP
	LWL:	4.27m/14'0
	LOA:	5.18m/17'0
	Beam:	2.13m/7'0
	Draft:	0.63m/2'1
	Displ:	694kg/1,530 lbs
	Ballast:	250—275kg/550—605 lbs

Fittings:	Bilge keel
Interior:	4 berths. 1.44m/4'9 cabin headroom. Space for cooker and toilet.
Variations:	Optional 5HP outboard. Twin bilge keel model available.
Sails:	Area 12.1m^2/130 sq.ft. Spinnaker area 19.32m^2/208 sq.ft.
Rigging:	Bermudan sloop
Price Guide:	£895ex VAT+
Summary:	Can be trailed. Over 675 sailing worldwide. Well-balanced, light and responsive. Seats 6 adults.

SHE JOEMARINE

Design:	Hants Group, England
Supplier:	South Hants Marine, England

Specifications:	*Construction:*	
	LOA:	5.18m/17'0
	Beam:	1.99m/6'6½
	Draft:	0.51m/1'8

Fittings:	Centreboard boat. Inboard. 2HP upwards.
Sails:	Area
Rigging:	Sloop
Price Guide:	

JAKA

Design:	France	
Supplier:	SEB France	
	Aquaboats, England	
Specifications:	*Construction:*	GRP
	LOA:	5.18m/17'0
	Beam:	2.00m/6'7
	Draft:	1.37m/4'6
	Displ:	400kg/880 lbs
Fittings:	Centreboard boat.	
Interior:	2 berths in 1 cabin	
Variations:	Outboard may be attached.	
Sails:	Area 12.7m^2/137 sq.ft.	
Rigging:	Bermudan sloop	
Price Guide:	9,000 Fr.F.	
Summary:	General purpose boat that can be used for day sailing or racing.	

507

LYSANDER 17

Design:	P. W. Blandford, England
Supplier:	Stalbridge Boats, England
Est. Rating:	Portsmouth number 118
Specifications:	*Construction:* Wood
	LWL: 5.02m/16'6
	LOA: 5.18m/17'0
	Beam: 2.03m/6'8
	Draft: 0.69m/2'3
	Displ: 356kg/784 lbs
	Ballast: 50kg/112 lbs
Fittings:	Bilge keel. Double chine. Wood deck.
Interior:	4 berths. 1.11m/3'8 cabin headroom
Variations:	Outboard can be attached.
Sails:	Area 11.6m²/125 sq.ft.
Rigging:	Bermudan sloop or gunter
Price Guide:	£630
Summary:	Designed with the handling and performance of a dinghy but with the comforts of a cabin and the stability of a larger boat. Kits available. Easily trailed.

MONTGOMERY 17

Design:	Lyle C. Hess, U.S.A. 1973
Supplier:	Montgomery Marine Products, U.S.A.
Specifications:	*Construction:* GRP
	LWL: 4.82m/15'10
	LOA: 5.18m/17'0
	Beam: 2.19m/7'2
	Draft: 1.05m/3'5—1'8
	Displ: 545kg/1,200—1,400 lbs
	Ballast: 182kg/400—550 lbs
Fittings:	GRP deck. Aluminium spars.
Interior:	3 berths in one cabin. Galley area. Enclosed head.
Variations:	Trailable or fixed keel versions
Sails:	Area 14.1m^2 (6.9 + 7.2)/152 sq.ft. (74 + 78)
Rigging:	Sloop
Price Guide:	$2,800
Summary:	Self-righting. Self-rescuing.

SKIPPER MARINER

Design:	Peter Milne, England 1972
Supplier:	Richmond Marine, England
	Intermarine Agency, U.S.A.
Est. Rating:	Portsmouth yardstick 109

Specifications:

Construction:	GRP
LWL:	4.72m/15'6
LOA:	5.18m/17'0
Beam:	2.13m/7'0
Draft:	0.30m/1'0
Displ:	363kg/800 lbs
Ballast:	91kg/200 lbs

Fittings:	Retractable keel. Iron ballast. GRP deck. Aluminium spars. 2HP Mighty Mite gasoline outboard.
Interior:	4 berths in 1 cabin. Full sitting headroom.
Variations:	Galley and toilet optional. Available also as an open dayboat seating 6 adults. **Skipper Mate** also available with inly 2 berths.
Sails:	Area 14.6m^2(9.0 + 5.6)/157 sq.ft. (97 + 60)
Rigging:	Sloop
Price Guide:	£695/$2,600us
Summary:	Based on the Skipper 17 hull, this new design offers more room and fuller accommodation. Comfortable, stable with good windward performance.

ACE OF SAILS

Design:	Cox Marine, England
Supplier:	Cox Marine, England

Specifications:

Construction:	GRP
LOA:	5.26m/17'3
Beam:	2.06m/6'9
Draft:	0.46m/1'6

Fittings:	Fin keel
Interior:	2 berths. 1.3m^2/4'3 headroom
Variations:	Outboard may be fitted.
Sails:	Area 11.4m^2/123 sq.ft.
Rigging:	Sloop
Price Guide:	£715

JOEMARIN 17

Design:	Hans Groop, Finland
Supplier:	Joemarin Oy, Finland Tradewind Yachts, England
Specifications:	*Construction:* GPR *LWL:* 4.8m/15'9 *LOA:* 5.21m/17'1 *Beam:* 2m/6'7 *Draft:* 0.48m/1'7 *Displ:* 450kg/992 lbs *Ballast:* 130kg/287 lbs
Fittings:	Cast iron ballast. Centreboard boat. Sandwich GRP deck. Anodised aluminium spars. Teak trim.
Interior:	2 adult + 2 children's berths
Variations:	Optional HP diesel engine
Sails:	Area 12.1m^2/130 sq.ft. Spinnaker area 14.9m^2/160 sq.ft.
Rigging:	Sloop
Price Guide:	£1,400
Summary:	A sailing yacht that enables a small family to weekend and take holidays in coastal waters. Well-balanced.

SIREN

Design:	Vandestadt & McGruer, Canada 1972
Supplier:	Vandestadt & McGruer, Canada
Specifications:	*Construction:* GRP
	LOA: 5.23m/17'2
	Beam: 2.03m/6'8
	Draft: 0.2m/8'' cb up
	Displ: 272kg/600 lbs
Fittings:	Centreboard boat. Aluminium spars. Foam flotation. Self-bailers. Kick-up rudder.
Interior:	4 bunks. Icebox.
Variations:	Optional toilet and stove.
Sails:	Area 13.5m^2 (7.4 + 6.1)/145 sq.ft. (80 + 65)
Rigging:	Sloop
Price Guide:	$2,100 us
Summary:	2 crew. Sailed mainly in Canada. An ideal weekender with large cockpit and spacious cabin.

ALOUETTE

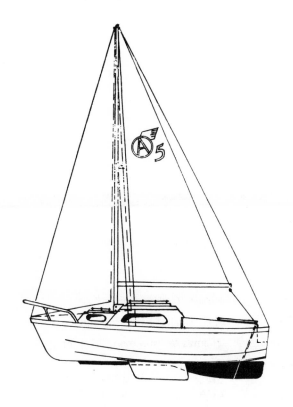

Design:	J. E. Crighton, England
Supplier:	Motivators GRP Products, England
Specifications:	*Construction:* GRP
	LWL: 4.88m/16'0
	LOA: 5.26m/17'3
	Beam: 1.98m/6'6
	Draft: 0.69m/2'3
Fittings:	Keel form T. Auxiliary outboard.
Interior:	3 berths
Sails:	Area 13m^2/140 sq.ft.
Rigging:	Sloop
Price Guide:	On application
Summary:	A compact general purpose cruiser.

MADEIRA SILHOUETTE MK IV

Design:	Robert Tucker, England
Supplier:	J. G. Meakes Ltd., England
Est. Rating:	Thames Measurement 2.3 tons

Specifications:	*Construction:*	GRP
	LWL:	4.27m/14'0
	LOA:	5.26m/17'3
	Beam:	2m/6'7
	Draft:	0.63m/2'1
	Displ:	584kg/1,288 lbs
	Ballast:	204kg/450 lbs

Fittings:	Bilge keel
Interior:	4 berths in 1 cabin. Cooker. Sink. Chemical toilet.
Variations:	Optional 5—8HP inboard.
Sails:	Area 18.1m^2/195 sq.ft. Spinnaker area 10.68m^2/115 sq.ft.
Rigging:	Sloop
Price Guide:	£1,175
Summary:	Good performance yet compact enough for single-handed sailing. 2,500 boats in circulation worldwide making her one of the best proven yachts of her kind to be found today.

PICNIC 17

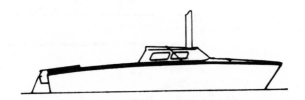

Supplier:	General Boats Co., U.S.A.	
Specifications:	*Construction:*	GRP
	LOA:	5.26m/17'3
	Beam:	2.03m/6'8
	Draft:	0.3m/1'0
	Displ:	363kg/800 lbs
Fittings:	Aluminium spars. Hinged mast.	
Interior:	Can sleep 5. Galley	
Variations:	Outboard or inboard engine.	
Sails:	Area 19m^2/204 sq.ft.	
Rigging:	Sloop	
Price Guide:	$1,985us	
Summary:	An all purpose sturdy boat that will please the family and the sailor.	

PROTON

Design:	Purser/Jardine, England 1973
Supplier:	Juxtamare Marine, England
Specifications:	*Construction:* GRP
	LWL: 4.8m/15'9
	LOA: 5.26m/17'3
	Beam: 2.03m/6'8
	Draft: 1.12m/3'8
	Displ: 681kg/1,500 lbs
	Ballast: 272kg/600 lbs
Fittings:	Fin keel
Interior:	4 berths
Variations:	Optional HP engine
Sails:	Area 12.5m^2/135 sq.ft.
Rigging:	Sloop
Price Guide:	£880+
Summary:	Trailable. Kits and mouldings available.

SILHOUETTE III

Design:	Robert Tucker, England
Supplier:	Hurley Marine, England
Rating:	Portsmouth yardstick 115 (fin)119 (twin)

Specifications:

Construction:	GRP
LWL:	4.27m/14'0
LOA:	5.26m/17'3
Beam:	2m/6'7
Draft:	0.63m/2'1
Displ:	585kg/1,288 lbs

Fittings:	Aluminium spars.
Interior:	2 berths
Variations:	Fin or twin keel models available.
Sails:	Area 15.3m^2/165 sq.ft. Spinnaker 10.7m^2/115 sq.ft.
Rigging:	Bermudan sloop
Price Guide:	£1,100 approx
Summary:	Easily rigged and sailed single-handed. Earlier version of the **Madeira Silhouette IV.**

VENTURE 17

Design:	Roger N. MacGregor, U.S.A.
Supplier:	MacGregor Yacht Corporation, U.S.A.

Specifications:

Construction:	GRP
LWL:	4.88m/16'0
LOA:	5.28m/17'4
Beam:	1.93m/6'4
Draft:	1.37m/4'6
Displ:	409kg/900 lbs
Ballast:	123kg/270 lbs

Fittings:	Cast iron swing keel. GRP deck. Aluminium spars. Positive foam flotation.
Interior:	4 berths in 1 cabin
Sails:	Area 14m^2/151 sq.ft. Spinnaker area 16.7m^2/180 sq.ft.
Rigging:	Sloop
Price Guide:	$1,750us
Summary:	A roomy, mini-yacht designed for sailing comfort, safety and high performance. Carries up to 5 adults.

TABASCO

Design:	France
Supplier:	Spair Marine France
Specifications:	*Construction:* GRP
	LWL: 4.60m/15'1
	LOA: 5.20m/17''½
	Beam: 2.05m/6'8½
	Draft: 0.22m/8½''
	Displ: 450kg/992 lbs
	Ballast: 190kg/419 lbs
Fittings:	6HP engine
Interior:	2 berths
Sails:	Area 15.02m²/162 sq.ft. Spinnaker area 17m²/183 sq.ft.
Rigging:	Sloop
Price Guide:	On application
Summary:	Carries up to 6 adults.

FAMILY 18

Design:	Klepper 1971
Supplier:	Juxtamare Marine England
Est. Rating:	Portsmouth number 109
Specifications:	*Construction:* GRP
	LWL: 4.9m/16'1
	LOA: 5.33m/17'6
	Beam: 2m/6'7
	Draft: 1.09m/3'7
	Displ: 409kg/900 lbs
	Ballast: 190 lbs
Fittings:	Centreboard boat. Alloy spars.
Interior:	4 berths (2 + 2)
Variations:	Optional outboard up to 4HP
Sails:	Area 15.1m^2/163 sq.ft.
	No spinnaker
Rigging:	Bermudan sloop
Price Guide:	£800
Summary:	Stable and easy to handle craft. Kits and mouldings available.

TIBURON

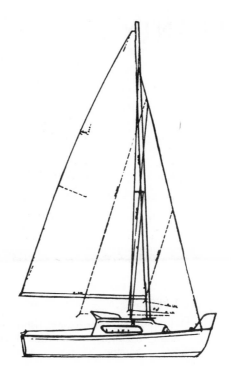

Design:	Jouet of Sartrouville France 1962
Supplier:	P. Jouet & Co. France Carl Zeigler Yacht Agency U.K. European Research & Supply Corp. U.S.A.
Specifications:	*Construction:* GRP *LWL:* 4.7m/15′5 *LOA:* 5.3m/17′6 *Beam:* 2m/6′8 *Draft:* 0.7m/2′4 *Displ:* 617.4kg/1,360 lbs
Fittings:	Built-in buoyancy. Twin keel boat. Outboard engine.
Interior:	4 berths. 1.4m/4′8 headroom.
Sails:	Area 16.63m^2/179 sq.ft.
Rigging:	Auxiliary sloop
Price Guide:	On application
Summary:	Easy to trail. Minimum maintenance required. Lively and responsive to handle

521

SEA SHANTY 18

Design:	Norman Pearn England	
Supplier:	Norman Pearn & Company England	
Specifications:	*Construction:*	GRP
	LWL:	4.42m/14'6
	LOA:	5.41m/17'9
	Beam:	1.98m/6'6
	Draft:	0.46m/1'6
	Displ:	454kg/1,000 lbs
Fittings:	Bilge keel. 5—40HP inboard engine. Wheel steering.	
Interior:	2 berths in 1 cabin. 1.42m/4'8 cabin headroom.	
Variations:	Available in a motor version also	
Sails:	Area 12.2m^2/131 sq.ft.	
Rigging:	Ketch	
Price Guide:	£1,350+	
Summary:	A family boat for offshore fishing and swimming. Shoal draft allows exploration of creeks and coves. Very seaworthy.	

CUB

Supplier:	Copland Boats England	
Specifications:	*Construction:*	GRP
	LOA:	5.49m/18'0
	Draft:	1.07m/3'6
Fittings:	Aluminium spars	
Interior:	2/3 berths	
Variations:	Optional hulls. Optional outboard engine.	
Sails:	Area 11.1m^2/120 sq.ft.	
Rigging:	Sloop	
Price Guide:	On application	
Summary:	Can be trailed.	

TOPAZ MK II

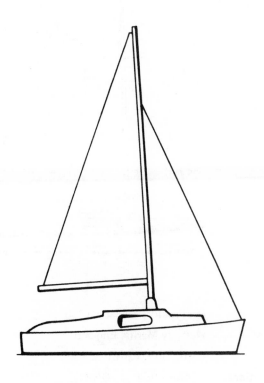

Design:	Leisurecraft Marine England	
Supplier:	Leisurecraft Marine England	
Specifications:	*Construction:*	GRP
	LWL:	4.88m/16'0
	LOA:	5.33m/17'6
	Beam:	1.98m/6'6
	Draft:	0.56m/1'10
Fittings:	Twin keel. 3HP outboard engine.	
Interior:	4 berths (2 + 2)	
Sails:	Area 11.6m^2/125 sq.ft.	
Rigging:	Sloop	
Price Guide:	£950+	
Summary:	Traditional lined, compact family craft.	

NIMROD

Design:	Ian Proctor, England 1968
Supplier:	Westerly Marine England
Rating:	Portsmouth yardstick 100
Specifications:	*Construction:* GRP
	LWL: 4.72m/15'6
	LOA: 5.41m/17'9
	Beam: 1.99m/6'5½
	Draft: 1.22m/4'0
	Displ: 763kg/1,680 lbs
Fittings:	Retractable keel. Mast 6.91m/22'8 high. Anodised aluminium spars. Lead ballast. GRP deck.
Interior:	2 berths in 1 cabin
Variations:	Galley & toilet optional. Optional outboard.
Sails:	Area 12.5m^2/135 sq.ft.
Rigging:	Bermudan sloop
Price Guide:	£ on application/\$2,750us
Summary:	A comfortable cruising weekender with good performance.

BALATON 18

Design:	Hungary
Supplier:	Hungarian Shipyards & Crane Factory, Hungary
	V. G. Waring & Son, England

Specifications:	*Construction:*	GRP
	LWL:	4.60m/15'1
	LOA:	5.48m/18'0
	Beam:	2.13m/7'0
	Draft:	0.75m–1.00m/2'4½–3'3½
	Displ:	820kg/1,808 lbs
	Ballast:	340kg/750 lbs

Fittings:	Sandwich construction deck. Alloy spars.
Interior:	4 berths. 1.45m/4'9 cabin height.
Variations:	Optional outboard engine. Fin or bilge keel models available.
Sails:	Area 16.15m^2/174 sq.ft.
	Spinnaker area 18.00m^2/194 sq.ft.
Rigging:	Bermudan sloop
Basic Price:	On application
Summary:	Designed for use in inshore coastal waters, lakes and estuary cruising.

DORADO

Supplier:	AUI (Leiston) England
Specifications:	*Construction:* Clinker
	LOA: 5.49m/18'0
	Draft: 0.45m/1'6
Fittings:	Bilge keel. Inboard engine.
Interior:	2/3 berths
Sails:	Area 9.3m^2/100 sq.ft.
Rigging:	Gaff
Price Guide:	On application
Summary:	Can be trailed.

DUET

Design:	Dennis Aston, Derek Abra, Roger Hancock U.K. 1973
Supplier:	Mermaid Boats England
Specifications:	*Construction:* Marine plywood
	LOA: 5.49m/18'0
	Beam: 1.98m/6'6
	Draft: 0.38m/1'3
	Displ: 305kg/672 lbs
Fittings:	Wooden spars
Interior:	4 berths (2 full berths)
Variations:	Optional outboard engine
Sails:	Area 13.01m^2/140 sq.ft.
Rigging:	Masthead sloop
Price Guide:	£400+
Summary:	Supplied in kit form only

CHESFORD 18 MS

Design:	Alan Pape England	
Supplier:	Chesford Marine England	
Specifications:	*Construction:*	Clinker
	LWL:	5.05m/16'7
	LOA:	5.49m/18'0
	Beam:	1.90m/6'3
	Draft:	0.61m/2'0
	Displ:	864kg/1,904 lbs
Fittings:	Bilge keel	
Interior:	2 berths	
Variations:	Optional inboard	
Sails:	Area 12.5m^2/134 sq.ft.	
Rigging:	Motor sailer sloop	
Price Guide:	£2,000	
Summary:	A mini motor-sailer that is seakindly and comfortable.	

EDEL

Design:	Edel France 1970
Supplier:	Edel France
	Chichester Yacht Agency England

Specifications:

Construction:	GRP
LOA:	5.46m−7m/18'−23'
Beam:	2.08m−2.5m/6'10−8'2
Draft:	0.48m−0.66m/1'7−2'2
Displ:	1,281kg/2,822 lbs.
Ballast:	180−470kg/396−1,035 lbs

Fittings: Lifting fin keels. 5−6HP engine.

Interior: 4 berths upwards

Variations: II and IV available

Sails: Area 15.1m^2−22.4m^2/162−241 sq.ft.

Rigging: Sloop

Price Guide: £1,700−£2,650

Summary: A good basic design that combines performance with comfort.

FOXCUB

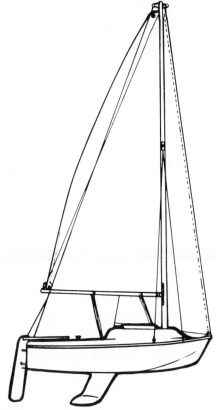

Design:	Uffa Fox England 1971	
Supplier:	Copland Boats England	
Specifications:	*Construction:*	GRP
	LWL:	5.03m/16'6
	LOA:	5.49m/18'0
	Beam:	1.91m/6'3
	Draft:	0.97m or 0.53m/3'2 or 1'9
	Displ:	545kg/1,200 lbs
Fittings:	Alloy spars	
Interior:	4 berths. Chemical toilet.	
Variations:	Fin or bilge keel	
Sails:	Area 12.45m^2/134 sq.ft.	
	Spinnaker area 19.51m^2/210 sq.ft.	
Rigging:	Bermudan sloop	
Price Guide:	£1,200	
Summary:	A small cruiser with a dinghy feel. Easily handled by novices yet a good sail. Kits available.	

GULF COAST 18

Design:	Martin Bludworth U.S.A. 1968
Supplier:	Gulf Coast Sailboats U.S.A.
Specifications:	*Construction:* GRP
	LWL: 4.82m/15'10
	LOA: 5.49m/18'0
	Beam: 1.88m/6'2
	Draft: 0.23m/9" keel up
	Displ: 145kg/320 lbs
Fittings:	Steel swing keel. GRP deck. Aluminium spars. 4HP outboard.
Interior:	2 berths in 1 cabin
Sails:	Area 15.1m^2 (10.2 + 4.9)/163 sq.ft. (110 + 53)
Rigging:	Sloop
Price:	$1,925us
Summary:	A sturdy family daysailer. Good value for money.

MARINER'S MATE

Design:	Alan F. Hill England 1969
Supplier:	Priorycraft England
Specifications:	*Construction:* GRP
	LWL: 4.72m/15'6
	LOA: 5.49m/18'0
	Beam: 2.06m/6'9
	Draft: 0.61m/2'0
	Displ: 1,016kg/2,240 lbs
	Ballast: 408kg/900 lbs
Fittings:	Deep keel boat. Yanmar 8HP inboard auxiliary. Round bilged.
Interior:	2 berths. 1.57m/5'2 cabin headroom. Provision for a stove.
Variations:	Fin or twin keel models. Fisherman version also available.
Sails:	Area 13m^2/140 sq.ft.
Rigging:	Sloop or Gunter
Price Guide:	£1,600
Summary:	Good beam and depth, plus internal ballast, gives this boat good stability.

GOBLET/AMPHORA

Design:	Trevor Kirby England
Supplier:	Brabourne Marine England

Specifications:

Construction:	GRP
LWL:	4.88m/16'0
LOA:	5.49m/18'0
Beam:	2.19m/7'2
Draft:	0.36m–0.91m/1'2–3'0
Displ:	814kg/1,792 lbs

Fittings:	Centreboard. Bilge keel or fin keel. Self-draining cockpit.
Interior:	4 berths
Sails:	Area 12.7m^2/137 sq.ft. Spinnaker area 10m^2/108 sq.ft.
Rigging:	Sloop
Price Guide:	On application
Summary:	Good performance, well-mannered family cruiser. 3,000 lbs of reserve buoyancy available if owner wishes to use storage tanks for this purpose.

TALISMAN MK III

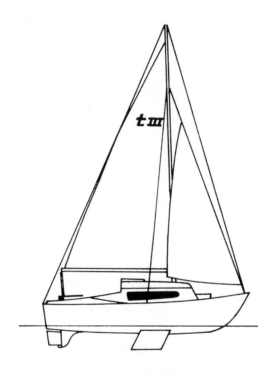

Supplier:	Banham Marine England
Specifications:	*Construction:* GRP
	LWL: 4.88m/16'0
	LOA: 5.49m/18'0
	Beam: 2.03m/6'8
	Draft: 0.53m/1'9
	Displ: 661kg/1,456 lbs
Fittings:	Twin bilge keels. Single chine hull. Metal spars.
Interior:	3/4 berths
Variations:	Optional outboard engine
Sails:	Area 13.9m^2/150 sq.ft. Spinnaker area 18.6m^2/200 sq.ft.
Rigging:	Bermudan sloop
Price Guide:	On application
Summary:	Spacious — good performance — low cost.

VALIANT

Design:	Tom Cox England
Supplier:	Fi-craft Fibreglass Products England
Specifications:	*Construction:* GRP
	LWL: 4.88m/16'0
	LOA: 5.49m/18'0
	Beam: 2.11m/6'11
	Draft: 0.74m—0.99m/2'5—3'3
	Displ: 816kg/1,800 lbs
	Ballast: 363kg/800 lbs
Fittings:	Anodised alloy spars
Interior:	4 berths
Variations:	Twin or fin keel versions available
Sails:	Area 14.49m^2/156 sq.ft.
	Spinnaker area 13.94m^2/150 sq.ft.
Rigging:	Sloop
Price Guide:	£880
Summary:	Comfortable, self contained and capable of outpacing boats of its own size and larger craft. Kits available. Can be trailed.

MINIQUIER

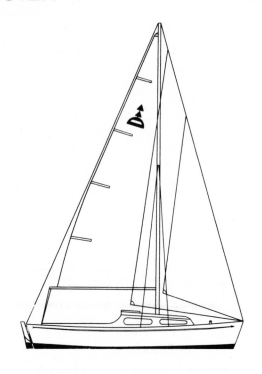

Design:	France 1972	
Supplier:	Uniplaisance France	
Specifications:	*Construction:*	GRP
	LWL:	5.00m/16'5
	LOA:	5.50m/18'0½
	Beam:	2.25m/7'4½
	Draft:	0.75m/2'5½
	Displ:	900kg/1,984 lbs
	Ballast:	400kg/882 lbs
Fittings:	Aluminium spars	
Interior:	3 berths. Galley.	
Sails:	Area 20.53m^2/221 sq.ft.	
Rigging:	Sloop	
Price Guide:	23,400 Fr.f.	
Summary:	A new, well-designed continental type small cruiser.	

ARRAN 18

Design:	C. V. Hughes and H.C. Banham England
Supplier:	Anglia Yachts U.K.
Est. Rating:	Thames measurement 2.8 tons
Specifications:	*Construction:* GRP *LWL:* 4.88m/16'0 *LOA:* 5.54m/18'2 *Beam:* 2.08m/6'10 *Draft:* 0.64m/2'1 *Displ:* 703kg/1,550 lbs *Ballast:* 100kg/220 lbs
Fittings:	Gold anodised spars. Bilge keels. 3.5HP outboard.
Interior:	3 or 4 berths
Variations:	Layout variations available
Sails:	Area 14.86m^2/160 sq.ft. Terylene.
Rigging:	Bermudan sloop
Price Guide:	£875 approx.
Summary:	Stable and comfortable in all weathers. An ideal family yacht. Very safe. Kits and mouldings available.

CORSAIRE

Design:	Jean-Jacques Herbulot France
Specification:	*Construction:* Plywood
	LWL: 4.88m/16'0
	LOA: 5.51m/18'1
	Beam: 1.91m/6'3
	Draft: 0.53m/1'9 cb up
Fittings:	Plywood deck. Aluminium spars.
Interior:	3 berths in 1 cabin
Variations:	Optional outboard
Sails:	Area $16m^2$/172 sq.ft.
Rigging:	Sloop
Price Guide:	On application

HERRESHOFF AMERICA

Design:	Halsy Herreshoff U.S.A. 1971
Supplier:	Nowak & Williams Company U.S.A.
Specifications:	*Construction:* GRP
	LWL: 5.41m/17'9
	LOA: 5.54m/18'2
	Beam: 2.44m/8'0
	Draft: 0.56m/1'10
	Displ: 1,044kg/2,300 lbs
	Ballast: 227kg/500 lbs
Fittings:	Steel ballast. GRP deck. Aluminium spars. 6HP outboard.
Interior:	4 berths in 1 cabin
Variations:	Optional head, stove and sink
Sails:	Area $24.2m^2$/260 sq.ft.
Rigging:	Una
Price Guide:	$5,400us
Summary:	A traditionally designed boat in modern, easy-to-maintain, materials.

DRAGONFLY

Design:	Alan Buchanan England	
Supplier:	Small Craft England	
Specifications:	*Construction:*	Marine ply on 5 frames
	LWL:	5.03m/16'6
	LOA:	5.59m/18'4
	Beam:	2.11m/6'11
	Draft:	0.81m/2'9
	Displ:	908kg/2,000 lbs
Fittings:	Keel boat. Light alloy spars. Self-draining cockpit.	
Interior:	3 berths. 1.22m/4'0 headroom.	
Sails:	Area 15.2m^2/164 sq.ft. Spinnaker area 17.7m^2/190 sq.ft. Terylene.	
Rigging:	Masthead sloop	
Price Guide:	On application	
Summary:	Safe and sturdy sloop for family cruising or passage racing.	

GOLDEN EYE

Design:	Herreshoff U.S.A.
Supplier:	Cape Cod Shipbuilding Company U.S.A.
Specifications:	*Construction:* GRP
	LWL: 4.82m/15'10
	LOA: 5.56m/18'3
	Beam: 1.93m/6'4
	Draft: 0.91m/3'0
	Displ: 1,135kg/2,500 lbs
	Ballast: 599kg/1,320 lbs
Fittings:	GRP deck. Aluminium spars. Lead ballast.
Interior:	2 berths in 1 cabin
Variations:	Optional outboard
Sails:	Area 17.9m^2/193 sq.ft.
Rigging:	Sloop
Price Guide:	$4,900us
Summary:	A useful family cruiser.

SEAFARER

Design:	Alan Buchanan England
Supplier:	Small Craft (Blockley) England
Est. Rating:	Portsmouth number 113
Specifications:	*Construction:* GRP
	LWL: 5.05m/16'7
	LOA: 5.56m/18'3
	Beam: 2.19m/7'2
	Draft: 1.45m/4'9
	Displ: 712kg/1,568 lbs
Fittings:	Steel centreboard. Mahogany trim. Light alloy spars.
Interior:	2 berths
Sails:	Area 13m^2/140 sq.ft. Spinnaker area 17.2m^2/185 sq.ft. Terylene
Rigging:	Sloop
Price Guide:	On application
Summary:	Good for family sailing, hire work and sailing schools. Very stable.

HMS-18

Desing:	Herb Stewart U.S.A. 1970	
Supplier:	HMS Marine Limited U.S.A.	
Specifications:	*Construction:*	GRP
	LWL:	4.9m/16'1
	LOA:	5.59m/18'4
	Beam:	2.39m/7'10
	Draft:	1.22m/4'0
	Displ:	636kg/1,400 lbs
	Ballast:	186kg/410 lbs
Fittings:	Steel ballast. GRP deck. Aluminium spars. 1.5—25HP outboard.	
Interior:	4 berths in 1 cabin. Chemical toilet.	
Sails:	Area 13.5m^2 (7.7 + 5.8)/145 sq.ft. (83 + 62)	
Rigging:	Sloop	
Price Guide:	$2,595us	
Summary:	A sturdy, family cruiser.	

BRADWELL 18

Design:	Ferguson Brothers U.K. 1971
Supplier:	Ferguson Brothers (Bradwell) England

Specifications:

Construction:	GRP
LWL:	5.13m/16'10
LOA:	5.72m/18'9
Beam:	1.91m/6'3
Draft:	0.99m/3'3
Displ:	499kg/1,100 lbs

Fittings:	Mahogany trim. Aluminium anodised spars. Galvanised steel retractable centreboard. Detachable rudder.
Interior:	4 berths in 1 cabin
Sails:	Area 13.7m^2/148 sq.ft.
Rigging:	Sloop
Price Guide:	£1,100

SUNSTAR 18

Design:	Arthur Howard England 1971
Supplier:	Intermarine Limited England Intermarine U.S.A.

Specifications:

Construction:	GRP
LWL:	4.8m/15'9
LOA:	5.72m/18'3
Beam:	2.19m/7'2
Draft:	0.89m/2'11
Displ:	590kg/1,300 lbs
Ballast:	272kg/600 lbs

Fittings:	Lead and iron ballast. GRP deck. Aluminium spars. 4.5HP Sailmaster outboard.
Interior:	4 berths in 1 cabin. Stove. Sink. Chemical toilet. 1.47m/4'10 cabin headroom.
Variations:	5/57 fin keel version also available. Variant II, an alternative model with 2 + 2 berths.
Sails:	Area 15.3m^2(7.9 + 7.4)/165 sq.ft. (85 + 80) Spinnaker area 13.9m^2/150 sq.ft.
Rigging:	Sloop
Basic Price:	£1,100 (kit)/$4,300us

ALACRITY

Design:	Peter Stephenson England 1960
Supplier:	Russell Marine Limited England
	Wells Yachts U.S.A.
Rating:	Portsmouth primary yardstick 110

Specifications:	*Construction:*	GRP
	LWL:	5.18m/17'0
	LOA:	5.64m/18'6
	Beam:	2.11m/6'11
	Draft:	0.56m/1'10
	Displ:	681kg/1,500 lbs
	Ballast:	218kg/480 lbs

Fittings:	GRP deck. Aluminium spars. Iron keels.
Interior:	2—3 berths in 1 cabin
Variations:	Optional interior layouts. Optional outboard engine.
Sails:	Area 14.4m^2/155 sq.ft.
	Spinnaker area 18.6m^2/200 sq.ft.
Rigging:	Bermudan sloop
Price Guide:	£795 approx.
Summary:	Good performance yacht because of the high sail/ ballast weight ratio. Fully self-righting. Several have crossed the Atlantic.

ALBERG TYPHOON

Design:	Carl Alberg U.S.A. 1960
Supplier:	Cape Dory Co. Inc. U.S.A.
Est. Rating:	12.5' MORC
Specifications:	*Construction:* GRP
	LWL: 4.24m/13'11
	LOA: 5.64m/18'6
	Beam: 1.91m/6'3
	Draft: 0.79m/2'7
	Displ: 863kg/1,900 lbs
	Ballast: 409kg/900 lbs
Fittings:	Aluminium spars. GRP deck. 3—6HP optional gasoline outboard.
Interior:	4 berths in 1 cabin. Marine toilet.
Sails:	Area 14.9m^2 (8.9 + 6)/160 sq.ft. (96 + 64)
Rigging:	Sloop
Price Guide:	$3,395us
Summary:	Exceptional daysailer with a big boat feel. Stable and seaworthy

BLACKWATER SLOOP

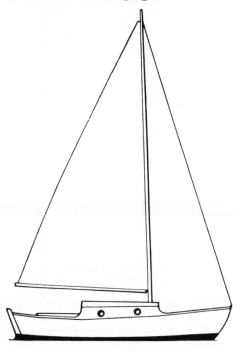

Design:	Dan Webb England	
Supplier:	Dan Webb and Feesey, England	
Specifications:	*Construction:*	Wood — carvel
	LWL:	4.88m/16'0
	LOA:	5.64m/18'6
	Beam:	1.98m/6'6
	Draft:	0.91m/3'0
	Displ:	Optional
	Ballast:	Optional
Fittings:	Fin keel	
Interior:	3/4 berths	
Variations:	4HP engine recommended	
Sails:	Area 12.1m^2/130 sq.ft.	
Rigging:	Bermudan sloop or Gaff	
Price Guide:	£2,500+	
Summary:	A well-mannered, traditional lined cruiser. Can not be trailed.	

HURLEY 18

Design:	Ian Anderson England 1965
Supplier:	Hurley Marine England Hurley Marine Inc. U.S.A.
Rating:	Portsmouth secondary yardstick 109
Specifications:	*Construction:* GRP *LWL:* 4.88m/16'0 *LOA:* 5.64m/18'6 *Beam:* 2.03m/6'8 *Draft:* 0.99m/3'3 *Displ:* 1,067kg/2,350 lbs *Ballast:* 454kg/1,000 lbs
Fittings:	GRP deck. Aluminium spars. Keel boat.
Interior:	3 berths in 1 cabin. Marine toilet.
Variations:	Optional outboard engine
Sails:	Area 16.7m^2(9.3 + 7.4)/180 sq.ft. (100 + 80)
Rigging:	Sloop
Price Guide:	$3,195us
Summary:	A well-mannered, true racing cruiser. Can be trailed.

SAILFISH 18

Design:	Leonardo da Costa Savage
Supplier:	Marim Marine England

Specifications:

Construction:	GRP
LWL:	4.57m/15'0
LOA:	5.64m/18'6
Beam:	2.19m/7'2
Draft:	0.91m/3'0
Displ:	454kg/1,000 approx.
Ballast:	136kg/300 lbs

Fittings:	Drop keel. Anodised aluminium spars. Mahogany and ply rudder.
Interior:	4 berths, +2 in cockpit. Cooker. Chemical toilet.
Variations:	Optional outboard engine
Sails:	Area 16.16m^2/174 sq.ft. (90 + 84) Spinnaker area 16.72m^2/180 sq.ft. Terylene
Rigging:	Bermudan sloop
Price Guide:	£1,100
Summary:	Points well to windward under her 50/50 sail area. A good choice for the dinghyman looking for a larger boat.

SEAGULL

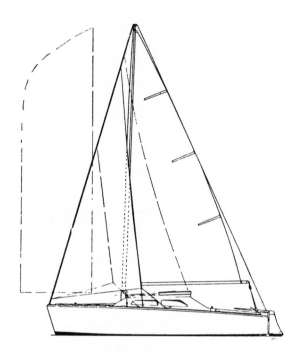

Design:	Ian Proctor England 1958	
Supplier:	Bell Woodworking England	
Rating:	Portsmouth secondary yardstick 109	
Specifications:	*Construction:*	Marine ply
	LWL:	5.26m/17'3
	LOA:	5.64m/18'6
	Beam:	2.06m/6'9
	Draft:	0.43m–1.12m/1'5–3'8
	Displ:	1,017kg/2,240 lbs
Fittings:	Partially retractable bulb keel.	
Interior:	2 berths in 1 cabin	
Sails:	Area 15.8m^2/170 sq.ft.	
Rigging:	Bermudan sloop	
Price Guide:	£1,400	
Summary:	Designed for coastal estuary and inland cruising. Kits available.	

CAPRICE MKII MKIII UK MKIII

Design:	Robert Tucker England 1962
Supplier:	Glen Ridge & Company England Island Plastics England
Rating:	Portsmouth secondary yardstick 118
Specifications:	*Construction:* GRP *LWL:* 4.88m/16'0 *LOA:* 5.79m/19'0 *Beam:* 1.91m/6'3 *Draft:* 1.07–0.76m/3'6–2'6 *Displ:* 762kg/1,680 lbs. *Ballast:* 272kg/600 lbs
Fittings:	Fin keel or twin
Interior:	3 berths
Variations:	Fin or bilge keel options. Optional inboard or outboard.
Sails:	Area 12.54m^2/135 sq.ft.
Rigging:	Sloop
Price Guide:	£1,250
Summary:	An established class with active owners Association. This boat has crossed the Atlantic on several occasions proving her stiff and comfortable ride through water.

CLASSIC

Design:	Arthur Cooksey England
Supplier:	Wayside Marine Craft England

Specifications:

Construction:	GRP
LWL:	4.72m/15'6
LOA:	5.79m/19'0
Beam:	2.19m/7'2
Draft:	0.76m/2'6
Displ:	1,271kg/2,800 lbs

Fittings:	Twin bilge keel
Interior:	4 berths 1.78m/5'10 headroom
Variations:	Optional outboard
Sails:	Area 13m^2/140 sq.ft.
Rigging:	Sloop
Price Guide:	On application
Summary:	Dry and stiff in heavy weather

LYSANDER 19

Supplier:	Stalbridge Boats Limited England

Specifications:

Construction:	Wood
LOA:	5.79m/19'0
Beam:	2.03m/6'8
Draft:	0.69m/2'3
Displ:	458kg/1,008 lbs

Fittings:	Spruce spars
Interior:	5 berths
Sails:	Area 11.6m^2/125 sq.ft.
Rigging:	Sloop
Price Guide:	On application
Summary:	Practical, attractive and versatile. Allows more ambitious exploration of cruising grounds than her smaller sister.

FANTASIE 19

Design:	Robert Tucker England	
Supplier:	Aquaboats England	
Specifications:	*Construction:*	GRP
	LWL:	4.87m/16'0
	LOA:	5.79m/19'0
	Beam:	1.90m/6'3
	Draft:	0.61m/2'0
	Displ:	710kg/1,568 lbs
	Ballast:	247kg/545 lbs
Fittings:	Bilge keel	
Interior:	3 berths	
Variations:	Optional outboard 4—6HP	
Sails:	Area 13.94m^2/150 sq.ft.	
Rigging:	Sloop	
Price Guide:	£800+	
Summary:	Kits available. Can be trailed. A very dry, manoeuvrable craft. Supercedes the Fantasie 575.	

PROJECT 2

Supplier:	Juxtamare Marine England
Specifications:	*Construction:* GRP
	LOA: 5.79m/19'0
	Draft: 0.3m/1'0
Fittings:	Centreboard boat. Wood trim.
Interior:	3 berths
Variations:	Optional outboard engine
Sails:	Area 13.9m^2/150 sq.ft.
Rigging:	Bermudan sloop
Price Guide:	On application
Summary:	Can be trailed.

TANKARD 19

Design:	Oliver J. Lee England
Supplier:	Tankard Yachts England
Specifications:	*Construction:* GRP
	LWL: 4.76m/15'6
	LOA: 5.79m/19'0
	Beam: 2.06m/6'9
	Draft: 0.91m/3'0
	Displ: Optional
	Ballast: 726kg/1,600 lbs
Fittings:	Fin keel. 12HP inboard.
Interior:	2/4 berths. 1.37m/4'6 headroom.
Sails:	Area 15.05m^2/162 sq.ft.
Rigging:	Sloop
Price Guide:	£750 Kit only
Summary:	Designed for offshore coastal cruising. Safe family boat.

HUNTER 19

Design:	Oliver J. Lee England
Supplier:	Channel Yacht Services England
Est. Rating:	Portsmouth number 95
Specifications:	*Construction:* GRP
	LWL: 5.26m/17'3
	LOA: 5.79m/19'0
	Beam: 1.88m/6'2
	Draft: 0.99m/3'3
	Displ: 681kg/1,500 lbs
	Ballast: 363kg/800 lbs
Fittings:	Teak trim. Alloy spars. Keel boat.
Interior:	3 berths + 1
Variations:	Fin or twin keel versions available. Optional outboard engine.
Sails:	Area 14.1m^2/152 sq.ft.
Rigging:	Bermudan sloop. Stainless steel and terylene.
Price Guide:	£975+
Summary:	Cruiser/racer version of the Squib dinghy. High speed and good stability. Ideal daysailer and small cruiser. Kits available.

ROSS HUNTER

Design:	Oliver J. Lee England
Supplier:	Fairhaven Marine U.S.A.

Specifications:

Construction:	GRP
LWL:	5.26m/17'3
LOA:	5.79m/19'0
Beam:	1.88m/6'2
Draft:	0.99m/3'3
Displ:	681kg/1,500 lbs
Ballast:	341kg/750 lbs

Fittings:	Iron ballast. Non-slip surfaces.
Interior:	3 berths. Sitting headroom.
Variations:	Optional outboard.
Sails:	Area 19m^2/204 sq.ft.
Rigging:	Sloop
Price Guide:	£1,000
Summary:	Fast cruiser, attractive appearance and first rate sailing performance.

SEAMASTER SAILER 19

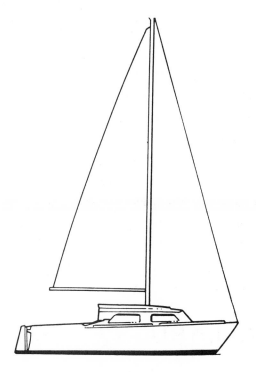

Design:	Laurent Giles & Partners Limited England
Supplier:	Seamaster Limited England
Specifications:	*Construction:* GRP
	LWL: 5.03m/16'6
	LOA: 5.79m/19'0
	Beam: 2.19m/7'2
	Draft: 1.68m/5'6
	Displ: 1,525kg/3,360 lbs
	Ballast: Optional
Fittings:	Anodised alloy spars
Interior:	4 berths
Variations:	Optional keel form
Sails:	Area 17.4m^2/187 sq.ft.
Rigging:	Sloop
Price Guide:	£2,000
Summary:	Smaller sister of the '23'

VOYAGER 19

Supplier: Leisurecraft Marine England

Specifications: *Construction:* GRP
LOA: 5.79m/19'0
Draft: 0.56m/1'10

Fittings:: Bilge keel. Team trim.

Interior: 2/3 berths

Variations: Optional inboard or outboard

Sails: Area 12.5m^2/135 sq.ft.

Rigging: Bermudan sloop

Price Guide: On application

Summary: A neat family cruiser/racer. Can be trailed.

MALLARD

Design: Vince DiMaro U.S.A.

Supplier: Customflex Inc U.S.A.

Specifications: *Construction:* GRP
LWL: 5.74m/18'10
LOA: 5.81m/19'1
Beam: 2.03m/6'8
Draft: 1.07m/3'6
Displ: 522kg/1,150 lbs

Fittings: Centreboard boat. GRP deck. Aluminium spars. GRP kick-up rudder.

Interior: 2 berths

Sails: Area 16.1m^2/173 sq.ft. Dacron

Rigging: Sloop

Price Guide: On application

Summary: Combines the manoeuvrability of the centreboard boat with the stability of the keel boat. Can be sailed single-handed.

LE BOSCO

Design:	France
Supplier:	Ocqueteau Guy France Navy-Holland Holland
Specifications:	*Construction:* GRP *LOA:* 5.85m/19'2 *Beam:* 2.35m/7'8½ *Draft:* 0.75m/2'5½ *Displ:* 1,100kg/2,425 lbs *Ballast:* 410kg/904 lbs
Fittings:	Aluminium spars
Interior:	4 berths
Sails:	Area 16.50m^2/178 sq.ft.
Rigging:	Sloop
Basic Price:	On application
Summary:	A family cruising boat.

MARINER 2+2

Design:	O'Day Company U.S.A.
Supplier:	O'Day U.S.A.
Specifications:	*Construction:* GRP
	LWL: 5.41m/17'9
	LOA: 5.84m/19'2
	Beam: 2.13m/7'0
	Draft: 0.25m/0'10"
	Displ: 592kg/1,305 lbs
	Ballast: 91kg/200 lbs
Fittings:	Lead ballast. GRP deck. Aluminium spars. Positive foam flotation.
Interior:	4 berths. 1 cabin.
Variations:	Galley optional. Toilet optional. Available also as an open dayboat with centreboard.
Sails:	Area 17.2m^2/185 sq.ft.
Rigging:	Sloop
Price Guide:	$2,695us

MS 20

Design:	Olle Enderlein U.S.A. 1970
Supplier:	Oxford Yacht Sales U.S.A.
Specifications:	*Construction:* GRP
	LWL: 5.26m/17'3
	LOA: 5.99m/19'8
	Beam: 2.21m/7'3
	Draft: 0.91m/3'0
	Displ: 1,090kg/2,400 lbs
	Ballast: 409kg/900 lbs
Fittings:	Iron ballast. GRP deck. Aluminium spars. Volvo-Penta diesel.
Interior:	2–3 berths in 2 cabins. Stove.
Variations:	Sea or chemical toilet
Sails:	Area 16.8m^2(9.3 + 7.5)/181 sq.ft. (100 + 81)
Rigging:	Sloop
Price Guide:	$2,500us
Summary:	A neat cruiser that is raced extensively in America.

CONQUEST

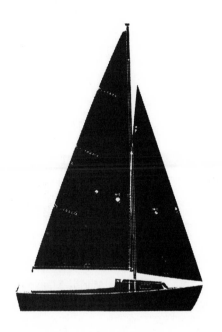

Design:	Paul Coble U.S.A.	
Supplier:	Bristol Yachts U.S.A.	
Specifications:	*Construction:*	GRP
	LWL:	5.21m/17'1
	LOA:	5.86m/19'2½
	Beam:	2.07m/6'9½
	Draft:	0.48m/1'7
	Displ:	795kg/1,750 lbs
Fittings:	GRP deck. Aluminium spars. Lead ballast.	
Interior:	2 berths in 1 cabin	
Variations:	Optional power. Optional galley.	
Sails:	Area 17.3m^2/186 sq.ft.	
Rigging:	Sloop	
Price Guide:	On application	
Summary:	A fast, neatly designed cruiser.	

PRELUDE

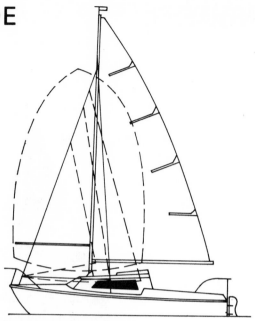

Design:	Ian Proctor England 1970
Supplier:	Rydgeway Marine England
Est. Rating:	Portsmouth number 97
Specifications:	*Construction:* GRP
	LWL: 5.18m/17'0
	LOA: 5.87m/19'3
	Beam: 2.08m/6'10
	Draft: 1.37m/4'6
	Displ: 658kg/1,450 lbs
	Ballast: 229kg/505 lbs
Fittings:	Anodised aluminium spars. Outboard engine.
Interior:	4 berths. Toilet
Variations:	Fin keel, drop keel or twin bilge keels. Optional cooker. De luxe version available.
Sails:	Area 25.5m^2/274 sq.ft. Spinnaker area 14.9m^2/160 sq.ft.
Rigging:	Standard ¾ or masthead rig.
Price Guide:	£1,400
Summary:	Fast between tacks. Light and responsive on the helm. Good all weather qualities. Available at any stage of construction.

LANAVERRE 590

Design:	Christian Maury France
Supplier:	Lanaverre France Comextra England
Rating:	IOR 16' $\pm$ 2 ton Thames measurement
Specifications:	*Construction:* GRP *LWL:* 5.41m/17'9 *LOA:* 5.94m/19'6 *Beam:* 2.06m/6'9 *Draft:* 1.22m/4'0 *Displ:* 544kg/1,200 lbs *Ballast:* 141+kg/310+ lbs
Fittings:	Centreboard boat. Aluminium spars.
Interior:	3/4 berths. 1.47m/4'10 cabin headroom.
Variations:	Fin keel or centreboard boat. Optional 4—9HP auxiliary.
Sails:	Area 16.7m^2/180 sq.ft. Spinnaker area 18.58m^2/200 sq.ft.
Rigging:	Sloop
Price Guide:	£1,225
Summary:	Safe, beamy and ballasted. Unsinkable. Ideal weekender with good performance and exciting sailing. Can be trailed.

MATILDA

Design: Robert Tucker U.S.A. 1970

Supplier: Ouyang Boat Works Limited Canada
Clippercraft Marine Products England

Specifications:

Construction: GRP

LWL: 4.98m/16'4

LOA: 5.94m/19'6

Beam: 2.39m/7'10

Draft: 1.27m/4'2

Displ: 704kg/1,550 lbs

Ballast: 136kg/300 lbs

Fittings: Lead ballast. GRP deck. Aluminium spars. Auxiliary 4–6HP

Interior: 4 berths in 2 cabins. Icebox. Sink.

Variations: Toilet optional

Sails: Area 18.1m^2 (9.8 + 8.3)/195 sq.ft. (105 + 90)
Spinnaker area 23.23m^2/250 sq.ft.

Rigging: Sloop

Price Guide: £1,275/$3,500us less sails

Summary: Ideal boat for shoal waters. Easy to trail and launch. Good performance. Associations active in the U.S.A. and Canada. Kits available.

PRIVATEER

Design: Norman Howard England 1972

Supplier: Small Craft (Blockley) England

Specifications:

Construction:	GRP
LWL:	5.00m/16'5
LOA:	5.98m/19'7½
Beam:	2.08m/6'10
Draft:	0.36m/1'2
Displ:	661.82kg/13 cwts.
Ballast:	200kg/440 lbs

Fittings: Centreboard boat. Anodized light alloy or spruce spars.

Interior: 4 berths. Galley standard. Chemical toilet.

Variations: Optional outboard longshaft

Sails: Area 15.5m^2/167 sq.ft. (Gaff)
Area 14.1m^2/152 sq.ft. (Sloop)

Rigging: Gaff or bermudan cutter

Price Guide: £1,325

Summary: A comfortable and colourful boat. Can be trailed. Sailed and supplied worldwide.

ALIZE

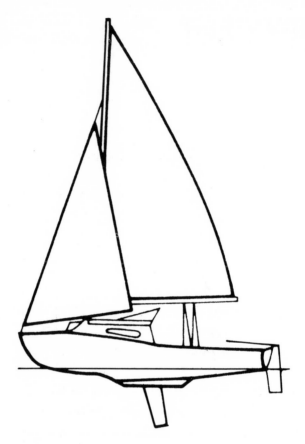

Design:	Jeanneau France
Supplier:	Jeanneau France
Specifications:	*Construction:* Plastic
	LWL: 5.40m/17'8½
	LOA: 6.00m/19'8
	Beam: 2.00m/6'7
	Draft: 0.55m−122m/1'9½−4'
	Displ: 409kg/882 lbs
Fittings:	Aluminium spars
Interior:	2 berths
Sails:	Area 16.60m^2/179 sq.ft.
Rigging:	Sloop
Price Guide:	14,700 Fr.f.
Summary:	An attractive, beamy little cruiser that is a challenge to sail.

O'DAY 20

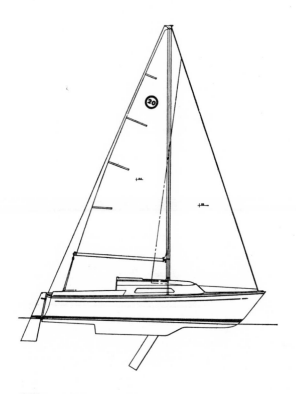

Design:	O'Day U.S.A.
Supplier:	O'Day Company U.S.A.

Specifications:

Construction:	GRP
LOA:	5.99m/19'8
Beam:	2.13m/7'0
Draft:	0.36m/1'2
Displ:	726kg/1,600 lbs
Ballast:	182kg/400 lbs.

Fittings: GRP centreboard boat. Teak trim. Lead ballast Gold anodised spars.

Interior: 4 berths

Variations: Optional outboard bracket mount

Sails: Area 16.2m^2/174 sq.ft.

Rigging: Sloop

Price Guide: $3,000us

SNAPDRAGON 600

Design:	Thames Marine England
Supplier:	Thames Marine England
Rating:	3.63 tons Thames measurement
Specifications:	*Construction:* GRP
	LWL: 5.18m/17'0
	LOA: 6.00m/19'8
	Beam: 2.29m/7'6
	Draft: 0.99m/3'3
	Displ: 1.000kg/2,200 lbs
	Ballast: 453kg/1,000 lbs
Fittings:	8HP outboard engine. Teak trim.
Interior:	4 berths. 1.47m/4'10 cabin headroom.
Variations:	Fin or twin keel versions. Optional hull forms available.
Sails:	Area 16.72m^2/180 sq.ft. Spinnaker area 25.6m^2/275 sq.ft.
Rigging:	Bermudan sloop
Price Guide:	£1,400+
Summary:	Well-balanced hull and simple rig for fast performance and ease of handling. Can be trailed.

SUNDANCE 20

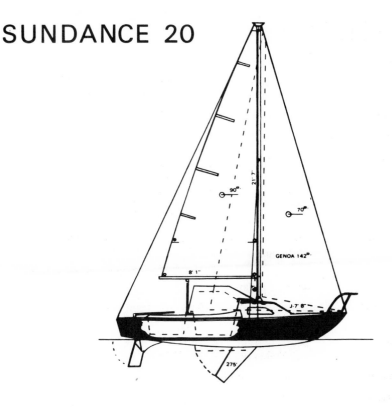

Design:	E. A. Brown U.S.A.	
Supplier:	El-Mar Boat Company U.S.A.	
Specifications:	*Construction:*	GRP
	LWL:	4.77m/15'8
	LOA:	6.02m/19'9
	Beam:	2.06m/6'9
	Draft:	0.28m/11''
	Displ:	590kg/1,300 lbs
	Ballast:	125kg/175 lbs
Fittings:	Aluminium spars. Pivoting keel. Kick-up rudder. Handrails.	
Interior:	2 berths. Icebox.	
Sails:	Area 14.9m²/160 sq.ft. Spinnaker area 20.4m²/220 sq.ft.	
Rigging:	Sloop	
Price Guide:	$2,750us	
Summary:	A good racing overnighter. Can be trailed. Takes up to 6 adults.	

SIGNET 20

Design: Ray Kaufmann U.S.A. 1960

Supplier: Marineways U.K./Newbridgeboats Limited U.K.
Jared C. Halverson U.S.A. (class secretary)

Rating: Secondary Portsmouth yardstick 106

Specifications:

Construction:	GRP
LWL:	4.87m/16'0
LOA:	6.04m/19'10
Beam:	2.03m/6'8
Draft:	0.61m—0.91m/2' or 3'
Displ:	928.7kg/2,146 lbs
Ballast:	363.2kg/800 lbs

Fittings: Bilge keels or single-keel boat. Inboard 4—9HP outboard 5—9HP. GRP deck. Aluminium alloy spars.

Interior: 4 berths. 1.25m/4'1 headroom. Galley. Sink. Icebox. Marine toilet.

Variations: Inboard or outboard engine. Twin keel version available.

Sails: Area 17.42m^2/187 sq.ft.
Spinnaker area 16.7m^2/180 sq.ft.

Rigging: Bermudan sloop

Price Guide: £1,980

GULF COAST 20 W/4

Design: Martin Bludworth U.S.A. 1969

Supplier: Gulf Coast Sailboats U.S.A.

Specifications:

Construction:	GRP
LWL:	4.86m/15'11
LOA:	6.07m/19'11
Beam:	2.11m/6'11
Draft:	0.23m/9" keel up
Displ:	636kg/1,400 lbs
Ballast:	182kg/400 lbs

Fittings: Swing keel. Lead ballast. GRP deck. Aluminium spars. 4HP outboard.

Interior: 4 berths in 1 cabin

Sails: Area 16.3m^2 (10.2 + 6.1)/175 sq.ft. (110 + 65)

Rigging: Sloop

Price Guide: $2,600us

RACERS/CRUISERS 20'-30'
monohulls

BALBOA 20

Design:	Lyle C. Hess, U.S.A. 1968	
Supplier:	Coastal Recreation Inc., U.S.A.	
Est. Rating:	20'5 MORC	
Specifications:	*Construction:*	GRP
	LWL:	5.33m/17'6
	LOA:	6.1m/20'0
	Beam:	2.16m/7'1
	Draft:	1.22m/4'0
	Displ:	772kg/1,700 lbs
	Ballast:	204kg/ 450 lbs
Fittings:	Swing keel. GRP deck. Aluminium spars.	
Interior:	4 berths in 1 cabin.	
Variations	Optional hp outboard. Layouts optional.	
Sails:	Area 16.1m^2/174 sq.ft. Spinnaker area 18.1m^2/194 sq.ft.	
Rigging:	Sloop	
Price Guide:	On application	
Summary:	Can be trailed. Designed for sailing offshore in heavy weather. Roomy and comfortable self-righting. Available through dealers.	

CAL 20

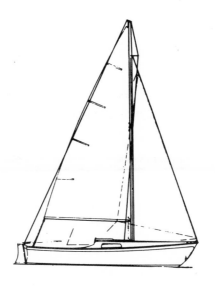

Design:	C. William Lapworth, U.S.A. 1961	
Supplier:	Jensen Marine, U.S.A.	
Specifications:	*Construction:*	GRP
	LWL:	5.49m/18'0
	LOA:	6.1m/20'0
	Beam:	2.13m/7'0
	Draft:	1.01m/3'4
	Displ:	885kg/1,950 lbs
	Ballast:	409kg/900 lbs
Fittings:	Iron ballast. GRP deck. Aluminium spars.	
Interior:	4 berths in 2 cabins. Sitting headroom.	
Variations:	Optional outboard. Optional galley. Optional toilet.	
Sails:	Area 18.2m^2/196 sq.ft. Spinnaker area 21.4m^2/230 sq. ft.	
Rigging:	Sloop	
Price Guide:	$3,850us	
Summary:	A fast ocean racer/family cruiser in cameo. Wide level deck. Hinged mast for easy rigging.	

GIRL FRIEND

Supplier:	Smith & Tucker, England	
Specifications:	*Construction:*	GRP clinker
	LOA:	6.1m/20'0
	Draft:	0.69m/2'3
Fittings:	Bilge keel	
Interior:	4 berths	
Variations:	Optional inboard or outboard engine.	
Sails:	Area 14.9m^2/160 sq.ft.	
Rigging:	Bermudan sloop	
Price Guide:	On application	
Summary:	Can be trailed.	

MISTRAL

Design:	England	
Supplier:	Porthleren Shipyard, England	
Specifications:	*Construction:*	Clinker-wood
	LOA:	6.1m/20'0
	Draft:	1.37m/4'6
Fittings:	Keelboat.	
Interior:	4 berths	
Variations:	Optional inboard engine.	
Sails:	Area 18.6m^2/200 sq.ft.	
Rigging:	Bermudan sloop	
Summary:	Can be trailed.	

FELICITY

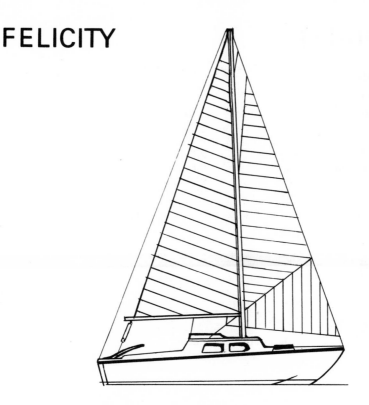

Design:	Ian Anderson, England
Supplier:	Russel Marine Ltd., England
Specifications:	*Construction:* GRP and marine ply
	LWL: 5.03m/16'6
	LOA: 6.1m/20'0
	Beam: 2.15m/7'1
	Draft: 0.59m/1'11
	Displ: 908kg/2,000 lbs
Fittings:	Bilge keels
Interior:	4 berths. 1.22m/4'0 headroom.
Sails:	Area 17.2m^2/185 sq.ft.
	Spinnaker area 19.1m^2/206 sq.ft.
Rigging:	Sloop
Price Guide:	On application.
Summary:	Good family boat. Light and responsive under sail or power. Spacious cockpit. Can be trailed.

PHIALLE

Design: Edward S. Brewer, U.S.A. 1964

Supplier: Edward S. Brewer, U.S.A.

Specifications:
Construction:	Plywood
LWL:	5.26m/17'3
LOA:	6.1m/20'0
Beam:	2.06m/6'9
Draft:	0.66m/2'2
Displ:	953kg/2,100 lbs
Ballast:	272kg/600 lbs

Fittings: Plywood deck. Aluminium spars.

Interior: 3 berths in 1 cabin.

Variations: Optional outboard.

Sails: Area 18.4m^2(11.1 + 7.3)/198 sq.ft. (120 + 78)

Rigging: Sloop

Price Guide: $3,600us

Summary: Kits and plans available.

TMS MOTOR SAILER

Design: Totnes Marine Services, England

Supplier: Totnes Marine Services, England

Specifications:
Construction:	Clinker
LOA:	6.1m/20'0
Draft:	0.56m/1'10

Fittings: Wooden spars

Interior: 2 berths

Variations: Fin or bilge keel models available. Optional inboard motor.

Sails: Area varies

Rigging: Various

Price Guide: On application

Summary: A general purpose motor sailer. Very seaworthy. Can not be trailed.

LE FORBAN

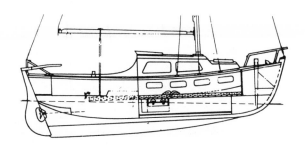

Design: France

Supplier: Chantiers Beneteau France
Fairey Marine, England
Arie de Boom N.V., Holland

Specifications: *Construction:*

LWL:	5.17m/16'11½
LOA:	6.00m/20'0
Beam:	2.30m/7'5
Draft:	0.85m/2'9–2'2
Displ:	1,400kg/3,086 lbs
Ballast:	400kg/882 lbs

Fittings: Anodised aluminium spars. 6 hp Renault Conach petrol auxiliary.

Interior: 3 berths.

Variations: Swing keel or centreboard models available.

Sails: Area 21.20m^{2}226 sq.ft. Terylene.

Rigging: Sloop

Price Guide: On application

Summary: A well-constructed, neatly designed family sloop.

RANGER

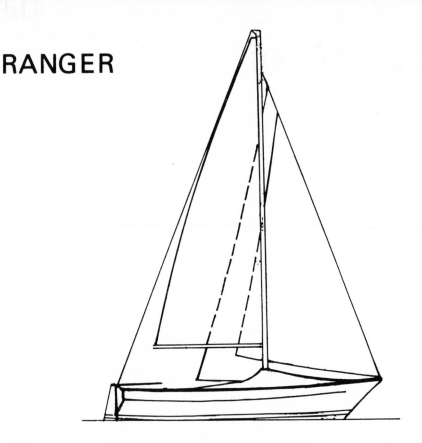

Design:	Raymond H. Richards, U.S.A. 1972
Supplier:	Ranger Fiberglass Manufacturers, U.S.A.

Specifications:

Construction:	GRP
LWL:	4.82m/15'10
LOA:	6.1m/20'0
Beam:	2.39m/7'10
Draft:	0.53m/1'9
Displ:	698kg/1,537 lbs
Ballast:	250kg/550 lbs

Fittings:	GRP deck. Aluminium spars. 5 hp outboard.
Interior:	2 berths in 1 cabin.
Variations:	Optional galley and toilet.
Sails:	Area 19.1m^2(9.8 + 9.3)/206 sq.ft. (106 + 100) Spinnaker area 27.9m^2/300 sq.ft.
Rigging:	Sloop
Price Guide:	$3,100us with sails.
Summary:	Stable, unsinkable and designed for trailers.

SHERIFF

Design: Philippe Harle, France

Supplier: Arcoa-Jouet, France
Dubigeon Normandie, Netherlands
Comextra, England

Rating: 3 tons: Thames measurement

Specifications:

Construction:	GRP
LWL:	4.88m/16'0
LOA:	6.1m/20'0
Beam:	2.29m/7'6
Draft:	0.76m/2'6
Displ:	794kg/1,750 lbs
Ballast:	260kg/573 lbs

Fittings: Keelboat. 4–9 hp outboard engine.

Interior: 2/3 berths. 1.52m/5'0 maximum cabin headroom.

Variations: Optional outboard. Luxury or sports versions available.

Sails: Area 15.8 to 18.6m^2/170 to 200 sq. ft.
Spinnaker area 26m^2/271 sq.ft.

Rigging: Bermudan sloop

Price Guide: £1,650+/14,500 fl.

VIVACITY 20

Design:	D. C. Pollard, England 1962
Supplier:	Russell Marine, England
Rating:	3–4 tons. Thames measurement
Specifications:	*Construction:* GRP
	LWL: 5.62m/18′5
	LOA: 6.10m/20′0
	Beam: 2.13m/7′0
	Draft: 0.71m/2′4
	Displ: 907.2kg/2,000 lbs
	Ballast: 362.88kg/800 lbs
Fittings:	Alloy spars
Interior:	4 berths
Variations:	Fin or twin keel models available. De luxe version available. Optional outboard engine.
Sails:	Area 16.26m^2/175 sq.ft.
Rigging:	Bermudan sloop
Price Guide:	£1,175+
Summary:	Stiff and exciting to sail. Points high. Kits available. Over 1,200 boats in circulation.

SEADRIFT

Design:	Norman Pearn, England
Supplier:	Norman Pearn & Co., England
Rating:	3.99tons. Thames measurement

Specifications:	*Construction:*	GRP and teak
	LWL:	5.11m/16'9
	LOA:	6.12m/20'1
	Beam:	2.39m/7'10
	Draft:	0.61m/2'0
	Displ:	1,916kg/1.88 tons

Fittings:	Twin keel boat. Teak trim. Alloy spars.
Interior:	4 berths. Galley space. Marine toilet.
Sails:	Area 15.51m^2/167 sq.ft.
Rigging:	Sloop
Price Guide:	£3,500
Summary:	All the advantages of family sailing along with single-handed racing when you buy Seadrift. Easily trailed and stored.

CARINITA

Design:	Al Mason, U.S.A.	
Specifications:	*Construction:*	Wood and GRP
	LWL:	5.49m/18'0
	LOA:	6.17m/20'3
	Beam:	2.06m/6'9
	Draft:	1.07m/3'6
	Ballast:	477kg/1,050 lbs
Fittings:	Iron ballast. Deck — wood and GRP. Wooden spars.	
Interior:	4 berths	
Variations:	Optional outboard	
Sails:	Area 17.5m^2/188 sq.ft.	
Rigging:	Sloop	
Price Guide:	$2,500us	

GULF COAST 21

Design:	Martin Bludworth, U.S.A. 1972	
Supplier:	Gulf Coast Sailboats, U.S.A.	
Specifications:	*Construction:*	GRP
	LOA:	6.25m/20'6
	Beam:	2.23m/7'4
	Draft:	0.25m/10'' keel up
	Displ:	726kg/1,600 lbs
	Ballast:	250kg/550 lbs
Fittings:	Steel swing keel. GRP deck. Aluminium spars.	
Interior:	4 berths in 1 cabin.	
Sails:	Area 15.1m^2 (10.2 + 4.9)/163 sq.ft. (110 + 53)	
Rigging:	Sloop	
Price Guide:	$2,595us	
Summary:	Low-priced family cruiser that performs well.	

DS-20

Design:	Diller and Schwill, Canada 1972	
Supplier:	Schwill Yachts Inc., Canada	
Specifications:	*Construction:*	GRP
	LWL:	5.52m/18'1
	LOA:	6.23m/20'5
	Beam:	2.26m/7'5
	Draft:	0.51m/1'8
	Displ:	726kg/1,600 lbs
	Ballast:	250kg/550 lbs
Fittings:	GRP deck. Aluminium spars. Lead ballast.	
Interior:	4 berths in 1 cabin. 1.47m/4'10 headroom.	
Sails:	Area 17.2m^2 (10.2 + 7)/185 sq.ft. (110 + 75)	
Rigging:	Sloop	
Price Guide:	$4,000us	
Summary:	A relatively new boat that is proving popular on the North American continent.	

NEWPORT 20

Design: Gary Mull

Supplier: Capital Yachts.

Specifications:

Construction:	GRP	
LWL:	5.49m/18'0	
LOA:	6.25m/20'6	
Beam:	2.29m/7'6	
Draft:	1.01m/3'4	
Displ:	1,135kg/2,500 lbs	
Ballast:	449kg/990 lbs	

Fittings: Lead ballast. GRP deck. Aluminium spars.

Interior: 5 berths. Galley standard. 1 toilet.

Sails: Area 18.3m^2/197 sq.ft.

Rigging: Sloop

Price Guide: $4,300us

Summary: A well proportioned, good performance small cruiser

FLAMINGO

Design: Francois Sergent, U.S.A.

Supplier: Sergent Boat Works

Specifications:

Construction:	GRP	
LWL:	5.74m/18'10	
LOA:	6.3m/20'8	
Beam:	2.26m/7'5	
Draft:	0.61m/2'0 cb up	
Displ:	999kg/2,200 lbs	
Ballast:	300kg/660 lbs	

Fittings: GRP deck. Aluminium spars. Lead ballast. 3—10 hp outboard auxiliary.

Interior: 4 berths in 1 cabin. Sink with pump. 1 open toilet.

Sails: Area 19m^2/204 sq.ft.

Rigging: Sloop

Price Guide: $6,800us

MATELOT 20

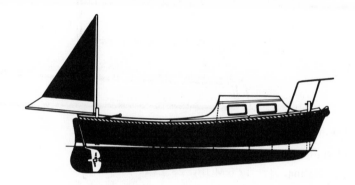

Design:	Cox Marine, England
Supplier:	Cox Marine, England
Specifications:	*Construction:* GRP
	LOA: 6.25m/20'6
	Beam: 2.13m/7'0
	Draft: 0.66m/2'2
	Displ: 1.271kg/2,800 lbs
Fittings:	Centreboard boat. Timber floorboards.
Interior:	2 berths
Sails:	Area 10.7m^2/115 sq.ft.
Rigging:	Sloop
Price Guide:	£1,750+
Summary:	Robust construction. Practical and stimulating performance. Kits available.

SAN JUAN 21

Design:	Don Clarke, U.S.A. 1969
Supplier:	Clarke Boat Co., U.S.A.
Est. Rating:	17'6 MORC 22' CCA
Specifications:	*Construction:* GPR
	LWL: 5.33m/17'6
	LOA: 6.25m/20'6
	Beam: 2.13m/7'0
	Draft: 1.22m/4'0
	Displ: 568kg/1,250 lbs
	Ballast: 182kg/400 lbs
Fittings:	Lead swing keel. GRP deck. Aluminium spars.
Interior:	4 berths in 1 cabin. 1.22m/4'0 cabin headroom
Variations:	Galley and toilet optional Outboard optional
Sails:	Area 17.7m^2 (9.3 + 8.4) /190 sq.ft. (100 + 90)
Rigging:	Sloop
Price Guide:	$2,750us
Summary:	A safe, inexpensive overnighter/cruiser. Roomy cockpit. Racing fleets established in several parts of America.

KINGFISHER 20 PLUS

Design:	R. A. G. Nierop, England 1959
Supplier:	Westfield Engineering Co., England
Rating:	Portsmouth secondary yardstick 112
Specifications:	*Construction:* GRP
	LWL: 5.64m/18'6
	LOA: 6.27m/20'7
	Beam: 2.11m/6'11
	Draft: 0.71m/2'4
	Displ: 1,180kg/2,600 lbs
Fittings:	Twin keel. 6 hp Johnson engine. Self-drain cockpit Alloy spars. Dolphin 12 hp engine.
Interior:	4 berths. 1.47m/4'10 headroom.
Variations:	Available 'unfurnished'
Sails:	Area 16.4m²/177 sq.ft. Spinnaker area 25.1m²/270 sq.ft. Terylene
Rigging:	Bermudan masthead sloop
Price Guide:	£2,100
Summary:	Have been extensively cruised in coastal waters and cross-Channel. Eligible for JOG classification and have been raced very successfully.

LARSHIP 21 OVERNIGHTER

Design:	Larship, U.S.A. 1973	
Supplier:	Larship, U.S.A.	
Specifications:	*Construction:*	GRP
	LWL:	5.49m/18'0
	LOA:	6.27m/20'7
	Beam:	2.13m/7'0
	Draft:	0.56m/1'10
	Displ:	545kg/1,200 lbs
Fittings:	Centreboard boat. Aluminium spars.	
Interior:	4 berths. Galley. Marine toilet.	
Variations:	Layout to specification.	
Sails:	Area 18.2m^2/196 sq.ft.	
Rigging:	Sloop	
Price Guide:	$3,000us	
Summary:	A very new design that will prove extremely popular with sailing families, because of its good performance and spaciousness	

ALOA 21

Design:	J. M. L'hermenier, France 1969
Supplier:	Aloa Marine, France American International Yacht Corporation, U.S.A.
Rating:	17.0' 10R Mk III
Specifications:	*Construction:* GRP *LWL:* 5.44m/17'10 *LOA:* 6.3m/20'8 *Beam:* 2.44m/8'0 *Draft:* 0.99m/3'3 *Displ:* 817kg/1,800 lbs *Ballast:* 300kg/660 lbs
Fittings:	Aluminium spars. GRP deck
Interior:	4 berths in I cabin
Variations:	Optional outboard. Galley and toilet optional
Sails:	Area 16.9m^2/182 sq. ft.
Rigging:	Sloop
Price Guide:	S4,490us
Summary:	Well proportioned small cruiser

ENSENADA 20

Design:	Lyle C. Hess, U.S.A. 1971
Supplier:	Coastal Recreation Inc., U.S.A.

Specifications:	*Construction:*	GRP
	LWL:	5.33m/17'6
	LOA:	6.1m/20'0
	Beam:	2.15m/7'1
	Draft:	1.22m/4'0
	Displ:	726kg/1,600 lbs
	Ballast:	250kg/550 lbs

Fittings:	Swing keel. GRP deck. Aluminium spars.
Interior:	4 berths in 2 cabins.
Variations:	Optional hp outboard.
Sails:	Area 16.2m^2/174 sq.ft. Spinnaker 27.3m^2/294 sq.ft.
Rigging:	Sloop
Price Guide:	$3,495us
Summary:	Raised, flush deck gives more space. Easy to trail. An all round family boat that will give hours of pleasure.

ALLEGRO

Design:	John Westell, England
Supplier:	Honnor Marine, England
Rating:	Provisional Portsmouth yardstick 92

Specifications:	*Construction:*	GRP with cold moulded veneer.
	LWL:	5.61m/18'5
	LOA:	6.32m/20'9
	Beam:	2.13m/7'0
	Draft:	1.14m/3'9
	Displ:	795kg/1,750 lbs

Fittings:	Fixed central ballasted fin or twin lifting fins housed in trunks.
Interior:	2 berths
Sails:	Area 18.5m^2/199 sq.ft.
Rigging:	Sloop
Price Guide:	On application.
Summary:	A light displacement cruisng yacht, with the handling qualities of a good racing dinghy. Easy to trail.

PRIM´VENT

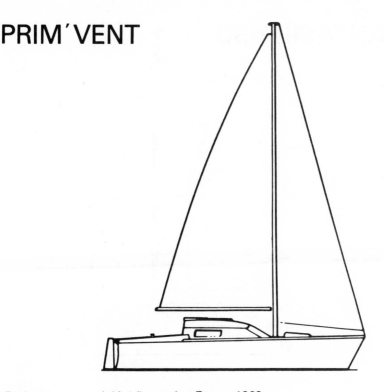

Design:	J. M. L'hemenier, France 1969
Supplier:	Aquaboats, England Andrew Gemeny & Sons, U.S.A.
Est. Rating:	17'0 IOR Mk III. Portsmouth yardstick 95
Specifications:	*Construction:* GRP
	LWL: 5.43m/17'10
	LOA: 6.3m/20'8
	Beam: 2.44m/8'0
	Draft: 0.99m/3'3
	Displ: 817kg/1,800 lbs
	Ballast: 300kg/660 lbs
Fittings:	Keelboat. Iron ballast. GRP deck. Aluminium spars.
Interior:	4 berths in 1 cabin.
Variations:	Optional galley and toilet. Optional outboard.
Sails:	Area 16.9m^2 (9.5 + 7.4)/182 sq.ft. (102 + 80)
Rigging:	Sloop
Price Guide:	On application
Summary:	Popular cruiser/racer worldwide. Can be trailed.

FANTASIE 630

Design:	John Butler, England 1972

Supplier:	Aquaboats Ltd., England

Specificatio₆₅:	*Construction:*	GRP
	LWL:	5.56m/18'3
	LOA:	6.32m/20'9
	Beam:	2.44m/8'
	Draft:	1.02m/3'4
	Displ:	1,374kg/3,030 lbs
	Ballast:	671kg/1,480 lbs

Fittings: Aluminium spars.

Interior: 5 berths. 1.78m/5'10 headroom.

Variations: Fin or twin keel versions available. Optional inboard or outboard.

Sails: Area 19.1m^2(10.2 + 8.9)/206 sq.ft. (110 + 96)
Spinnaker area 27.88m^2/300 sq. ft. +

Rigging: Bermudan sloop

Price Guide: £1,980—£2,175

Summary: Excellent accommodation layout. Kits and mouldings available.

KERLOUAN

Design:	A. Benetêau, France
Supplier:	Chantiers Benetêau, France Fairey Marine, England
Specifications:	*Construction:* GRP *LWL:* 5.32m/17.6 *LOA:* 6.32m/20'9 *Beam:* 2.36m/7'9 *Draft:* 0.91m/3'0 *Displ:* 1,598kg/3,520 lbs *Ballast:* 749kg/1,650 lbs
Fittings:	Anodised aluminium spars, 6 hp Renault conach petrol engine.
Interior:	4 berths. Marine toilet. Galley with sink, water-pump and stove.
Variations:	Swing keel or centreboard models.
Sails:	Area 20.8m^2(11.3 + 9.5)/224 sq.ft. (122 + 102)
Rigging:	Sloop
Price Guide:	£3,900
Summary:	Simple to handle rig and easy to trail cruiser.

LEPE

Supplier:	Aquaboats, England
Specifications:	*Construction:* GRP
	LOA: 6.32m/20'9
	Draft: 0.99m/3'3
Fittings:	Keel boat
Interior:	4 berths
Variations:	Optional outboard engine.
Sails:	Area 16.7m^2/180 sq.ft.
Rigging:	Bermudan sloop
Price Guide:	On application
Summary:	Can be trailed.

ISLANDER 21

Design:	J. H. McGlasson, U.S.A.
Supplier:	Wayfarer Yacht Corporation, U.S.A.
Specifications:	*Construction:* GRP
	LWL: 5.49m/18'0
	LOA: 6.35m/20'10
	Beam: 2.39m/7'10
	Draft: 1.01m/3'4
	Displ: 885kg/1,950 lbs
	Ballast: 454kg/1,000 lbs
Fittings:	Lead ballast. GRP deck. Aluminium spars.
Interior:	4 berths in 2 cabins. Standard galley.
Variations:	Power optional
Sails:	Area 19.3m^2/208 sq.ft.
Rigging:	Sloop
Price Guide:	On application
Summary:	A true family cruiser that is comfortable and sea kindly.

SUNRAY 21

Design:	Arthur Howard, England 1971
Supplier:	Intermarine Limited, England Intermarine Agency, U.S.A.
Est. Rating:	3.35 tons Thames measurement
Specifications:	*Construction:* GRP *LWL:* 5.32m/17'6 *LOA:* 6.30m/20'9 *Beam:* 2.44m/8'0 *Draft:* 0.76m/2'6 *Displ:* 942kg/2,075 lbs *Ballast:* 545kg/1,200 lbs
Fittings:	Lead and iron ballast. GRP deck. Aluminium spars. 5–6 hp outboard. Built-in buoyancy. Teak trim.
Interior:	4 berths in 2 cabins. Stove. Icebox. Sink. 1.78/5'10 cabin headroom
Variations:	Fin or bilge keel models available. Optional toilet.
Sails:	Area 19m^2 (10 + 9)/205 sq.ft. (108 + 97)
Rigging:	Sloop
Basic Price:	£2,040 (kit)/S7,000us
Summary:	A very good performance record against larger boats. Can be lived in aground, on a sandbank, or on a trailer.

Mc VAY 21

Design:	G. W. McVay, U.S.A. 1972
Supplier:	McVay Fiberglass Yachts Ltd., U.S.A.
Specifications:	*Construction:* GRP
	LWL: 5.56m/18'3
	LOA: 6.38m/20'11
	Beam: 2.19m/7'2
	Draft: 0.48m/1'7
	Displ: 788kg/1,735 lbs
	Ballast: 187kg/412 lbs
Fittings:	Cast iron ballast. Twin keels. GRP deck. Aluminium spars.
Interior:	4 berths in one cabin. Sink.
Sails:	Area 15m^2(7.4 + 7.6)/161 sq.ft. (80 + 81)
Rigging:	Sloop
Price Guide:	$3,500us
Summary:	An easy to handle, all purpose small cruiser.

EAGLE

Design:	Halsey Herreshoff, U.S.A. 1973
Supplier:	Nowak & Williams Co., U.S.A.
Specifications:	*Construction:* GRP
	LWL: 5.49m/18'0
	LOA: 6.4m/21'0
	Beam: 2.49m/8'2
	Draft: 0.56m/1'10
	Displ: 1,226kg/2,700 lbs
	Ballast: 318kg/700 lbs
Fittings:	GRP deck. Aluminium spars. Lead ballast.
Interior:	2 berths in 1 cabin.
Variations:	Optional outboard.
Sails:	Area 28.2m^2/304 sq.ft.
Rigging:	Gaff
Price Guide:	$7,995us
Summary:	A traditionally designed, small cruiser that is comfortable and easy to handle.

CLIPPER MK-21

Design:	William Crealock, U.S.A. 1970
Supplier:	Clipper Marine Corporation, U.S.A.

Specifications:

Construction:	GRP
LWL:	5.43m/17'10
LOA:	6.38m/20'11
Beam:	2.21m/7'3
Draft:	1.32m/4'4
Displ:	749kg/1,650 lbs
Ballast:	218kg/480 lbs

Fittings:	Cast iron ballast. Swing keel. GRP deck. Aluminium spars. Mahogany interior.
Interior:	4 berths in 1 cabin. 1.27m/4'2 headroom.
Variations:	Optional toilet. Optional gasoline outboard.
Sails:	Area $17m^2$ (8.9 + 8.1)/183 sq.ft. (96 + 87)
Rigging:	Sloop
Price Guide:	$2,795us
Summary:	Stiff and comfortable under all weather conditions. Can be trailed.

AQUARIUS 21

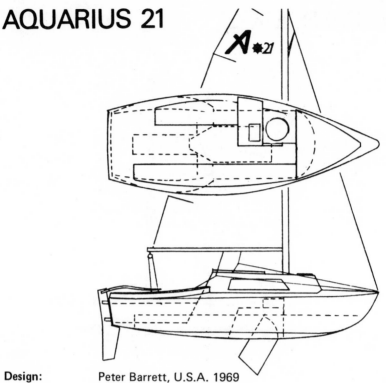

Design: Peter Barrett, U.S.A. 1969

Supplier: Coastal Recreation Inc. U.S.A.

Specifications:

Construction: GRP
LWL: 5.56m/18'3
LOA: 6.4m/21'0
Beam: 2.39m/7'10
Draft: 0.3m/1'0 cb up
Displ: 862kg/1,900 lbs
Ballast: 302kg/665 lbs

Fittings: GRP deck. Aluminium spars. 4 hp Johnson or Evinrude outboard. Headroom 1.8m/5'11

Interior: 4 berths in 1 cabin. Galley and dinette.

Variations: Optional sanitary arrangements.

Sails: Area 16.8m^2 (9.3 + 7.5)/181 sq.ft. (100 + 81) Spinnaker area 24.2m^2/260 sq.ft.

Rigging: Sloop

Price Guide: $2,595us

Summary: Easy to launch and trail. Very versatile. Planes efficiently.

ARMORIC

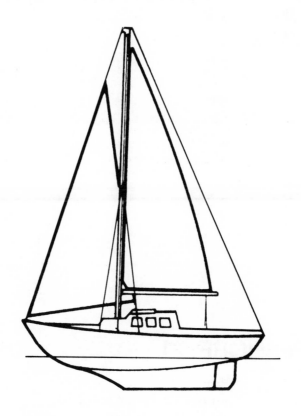

Design:	France	
Supplier:	Blaise, France	
Specifications:	*Construction:*	Plastic
	LWL:	5.00m/16'5
	LOA:	6.40m/21'
	Beam:	2.30m/7'6½
	Draft:	0.80m/2'7½
	Displ:	1,320kg/2,910 lbs
Fittings:	Aluminium spars.	
Interior:	4 berths	
Sails:	Area 23m^2/248 sq.ft.	
Rigging:	Sloop	
Price Guide:	33,000 Fr.f.	

FINESSE 21

Design:	L. Harbottell, England 1950
Supplier:	A. F. Platt Ltd., England
Specifications:	*Construction:* Clinker
	LWL: 5.56m/18'3
	LOA: 6.4m/21'0
	Beam: 2.29m/7'6
	Draft: 0.61m/2'0
Fittings:	Centreboard boat. 5 hp inboard auxiliary.
Interior:	3/4 betths
Sails:	Area 16.7m^2/180 sq.ft.
Rigging:	Bermudan sloop
Price Guide:	£2,200
Summary:	Can be trailed.

OFFSHORE 21

Design:	U.S.A.
Supplier:	Offshore Yachts, U.S.A.
Specifications:	*Construction:* GRP
	LOA: 6.4m/21'0
	Beam: Open
	Draft: Open
	Displ: Open
	Ballast: Open
Fittings:	Keelboat
Interior:	4 berths
Variations:	Optional outboard auxiliary
Sails:	Area varies
Rigging:	Bermudan sloop
Price Guide:	On application
Summary:	Can be trailed.

CORRIBEE 21 MK II

Design:	Robert Tucker, England 1963
Supplier:	Newbridge Boats Ltd., England MTA Marine Sales, U.S.A.
Est. Rating:	Portsmouth secondary yardstick 108
Specifications:	*Construction:* GRP *LWL:* 4.95m/16'3 *LOA:* 6.4m/21'0 *Beam:* 1.83m/6'9 *Draft:* 3.96m/13'0 *Displ:* 908kg/2,000 lbs *Ballast:* 440kg/880 lbs
Fittings:	Keel boat or bilge keels. Mast and boom both heavy alloy, gold anodized.
Interior:	4 berths
Sails:	Area 14.57m^2/156 sq.ft.
Rigging:	Bermudan sloop. (Stainless steel standing rigging. Running of terylene.
Price Guide:	£1,200/$4,000us
Summary:	Easy to handle with high performance. Comfortable accommodation. Kits available.

JOUSTER WESTERLY

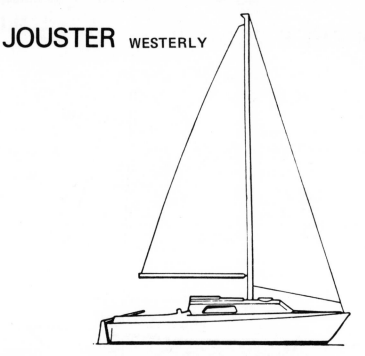

Design:	Laurent Giles & Partners, England 1969
Supplier:	Westerly Marine Construction, England Andrew Gemeny & Sons U.S.A.
Rating:	Portsmouth yardstick 98
Specifications:	*Construction:* GRP *LWL:* 5.56m/18'3 *LOA:* 6.4m/21'0 *Beam:* 2.29m/7'6 *Draft:* 1.07m/3'6 *Displ:* 999kg/2,200 lbs *Ballast:* 431kg/950 lbs
Fittings:	Iron ballast. Finn keel. GRP deck. Aluminium spars.
Interior:	4 berths in 1 cabin.
Variations:	Drop keel model available. Optional galley and toilet. Optional outboard.
Sails:	Area 19.5m^2/210 sq.ft.
Rigging:	Bermudan sloop
Price Guide:	£2,400/$6,200us
Summary:	Fast, safe boat for offshore cruising and club racing. Well-balanced, points well to windward and easily worked single-handed. Kits available.

MUSCADET

Design:	Philippe Harle, France
Supplier:	Aubin Marine, France
Rating:	17'0 IOR Class VI BI

Specifications:

	Construction:	GRP
	LWL:	5.5m/18'0½
	LOA:	6.4m/21'0
	Beam:	2.26m/7'5
	Draft:	1.0m/3'3½
	Displ:	1,250kg/2,756 lbs
	Ballast:	500kg/1,102 lbs

Fittings:	Aluminium spars
Interior:	3/4 berths
Sails:	Area 19.2m^2(10.7 + 8.5)/207 sq.ft. (115 + 92)
Rigging:	Sloop
Price Guide:	22, 600 Fr,f.
Summary:	A well established French racing class that is extremely popular.

SEA-CAT

Design:	Pelle Pettersen, Sweden 1965
Supplier:	Oxford Yacht Sales, U.S.A.
Specifications:	*Construction:* GRP
	LWL: 5.64m/18'6
	LOA: 6.4m/21'0
	Beam: 1.96m/6'5
	Draft: 1.09m/3'7
	Displ: 908kg/2,000 lbs
	Ballast: 303kg/667 lbs
Fittings:	Iron ballast. GRP deck. Aluminium spars. 4 hp auxiliary.
Interior:	4 berths in 1 cabin. Stove. Chemical toilet.
Sails:	Area $16m^2$ (10.5 + 5.5)/172 sq.ft. (113 + 59)
Rigging:	Sloop
Price Guide:	$8,000us

NEWPORT 21-2

Design:	Harry R. Sindle, U.S.A. 1972
Supplier:	Newport Boats, U.S.A.
Specifications:	*Construction:* GRP
	LWL: 5.81m/19'1
	LOA: 6.45m/21'2
	Beam: 2.31m/7'7
	Draft: 0.28m/11" cb up
	Displ: 636kg/1,400 lbs
	Ballast: 182kg/400 lbs composite
Fittings:	Retractable centreboard. GRP deck. Aluminium spars. Foam flotation.
Interior:	4 berths in 1 cabin. Portable toilet.
Variations:	Optional 5 hp outboard. Galley optional.
Sails:	Area $16.9m^2$ (10.4 + 6.5)/182 sq.ft. (112 + 72) Spinnaker area $20m^2$/215 sq.ft.
Rigging:	Sloop
Price Guide:	$2,600us
Summary:	A high performance family daysailer and overnighter. Very seaworthy. Easily trailed.

SNAPDRAGON 21

Design:	Thames Marine, England
Supplier:	Thames Marine, England
Rating:	4 tons Thames measurement
Specifications:	*Construction:* GRP *LWL:* 5.49m/18'0 *LOA:* 6.4m/21'0 *Beam:* 2.21m/7'3 *Draft:* 0.76m/2'6 *Displ:* 998kg/2,200 lbs *Ballast:* 454kg/1,000 lbs
Fittings:	Self drawn cockpit. Air flow system.
Interior:	4 berths. 1.47m/4'10 cabin headroom.
Variations:	Fin or twin keel. Optional 10HP outboard engine.
Sails:	Area 17.18m²/185 sq.ft. Spinnaker area 23.23m²/250 sq.ft.
Rigging:	Bermudan sloop
Price Guide:	£1,600
Summary:	Designed for the family to live in. Can be trailed. Kits available.

VENTURE 21

Design:	Roger N. MacGregor, U.S.A. 1965
Supplier:	MacGregor Yacht Inc., U.S.A.

Specifications:

Construction:	GRP
LWL:	5.64m/18'6
LOA:	6.4m/21'0
Beam:	2.08m/6'10
Draft:	1.68m/5'6
Displ:	545kg/1,200 lbs
Ballast:	182kg/400 lbs

Fittings:	Cast iron swing keel. GRP deck. Aluminium spars. Positive foam flotation.
Interior:	4 berths in 1 cabin
Variations:	Optional galley and toilet.
Sails:	Area 16.3m²/175 sq.ft. Spinnaker area 20.4m²/220 sq.ft.
Rigging:	Sloop
Price Guide:	$2,000us
Summary:	An attractive, good performer.

SPLINTER

Design:	E. G. Van de Stadt, Holland	
Supplier:	G. S. Marine, England	
Rating:	Portsmouth yardstick 98	
Specifications:	*Construction:*	GRP
	LWL:	5.18m/17'0
	LOA:	6.45m/21'2
	Beam:	2.08m/6'10
	Draft:	1.14m/3'9
	Displ:	1,270kg/25 cwt
	Ballast:	408.24kg/900 lbs
Fittings:	Keelboat	
Interior:	3/4 berths	
Variations:	Optional outboard engine.	
Sails:	Area 18.9m^2/203 sq.ft. Spinnaker area 22.30m^2/240 sq.ft.	
Rigging:	Bermudan sloop	
Price Guide:	£1,700	
Summary:	An attractive, thoroughbred racer. Many successes in racing. Can be trailed.	

SANTANA 21

Design:	Seymour Paul, U.S.A. 1969
Supplier:	W. D. Schock Corporation, U.S.A.
Est. Rating:	17'4 MORC
Specifications:	*Construction:* GRP
	LWL: 5.89m/19'4
	LOA: 6.48m/21'3
	Beam: 2.29m/7'6
	Draft: 0.46m/1'6
	Displ: 772kg/1,700 lbs
	Ballast: 250kg/550 lbs
Fittings:	Iron ballast. GRP deck. Aluminium spars.
Interior:	4 berths in 1 cabin. Sink. Stove.
Variations:	Swing or fixed keel models available. Toilet not standard.
Sails:	Area 17.6m^2/189 sq.ft. Spinnaker area 30.4m^2/327 sq.ft.
Rigging:	Sloop
Price Guide:	$2,600us
Summary:	Easy to trail, launch and recover..

VIVACITY 21

Design:	Russell Marine, England 1969
Supplier:	Russell Marine Ltd., England
Specifications:	*Construction:* GRP
	LWL: 5.68m/19'3
	LOA: 6.47m/21'3
	Beam: 2.18m/7'2
	Draft: 0.76m/2'4
	Displ: 1,135kg/2,500 lbs
	Ballast: 499kg/1,100 lbs
Fittings:	Iron and lead ballast. GRP deck. Aluminium spars. 4 to 9 hp outboard auxiliary. Built-in ventilation.
Interior:	4 berths in 2 cabins. 1.37m/4'6 headroom.
Variations:	Fin or twin keel models available. Optional galley and toilet.
Sails:	Area 22.2m^2 (11.5 + 10.7)/239 sq.ft. (124 + 115)
Rigging:	Sloop
Price Guide:	£1,400
Summary:	Fairly quick on the helm and requires careful trimming of the sails. Practical cruising layout. Also known as Vivacity 650.

AUDACITY

Design:	Laurent Giles, England
Supplier:	Laurent Giles, England
Rating:	Portsmouth secondary yardstick 108

Specifications:

Construction:	Cold moulded marine ply
LWL:	5.64m/18'6
LOA:	6.53m/21'5
Beam:	2.21m/7'3
Draft:	0.51m/1'8
Displ:	1,616kg/3,560 lbs

Fittings:	Centreboard boat
Interior:	4 berths. 1.58m/5'2 headroom.
Sails:	Area 18.6m^2/200 sq.ft.
Rigging:	Bermudan sloop
Price Guide:	On application
Summary:	A well-proven, small racer/cruiser that is very popular in the U.K.

LUKE FOX

Supplier:	Whitehall Shipyard, England

Specifications:

Construction:	Clinker
LOA:	6.55m/21'6
Draft:	0.76m/2'6

Fittings:	Bilge keel. Wooden spars.
Interior:	3 berths.
Variations:	Optional inboard engine
Sails:	Area 13m^2/140 sq.ft.
Rigging:	Bermudan sloop
Price Guide:	On application
Summary:	Can be trailed.

VARIANTA

Design: E. G. van de Stadt, Holland

Supplier: Dehler, Holland

Specifications:

Construction:	GRP
LWL:	5.40m/17'8½
LOA:	6.50m/21'4
Beam:	2.10m/6'10½
Draft:	0.70m/2'3½
Displ:	650kg/1,433 lbs
Ballast:	280kg/617 lbs

Interior: 4 berths

Sails: Area 22.05m^2/237 sq.ft.
Spinnaker area 23.00m^2/248 sq.ft.

Rigging: Sloop

Price Guide: 15,980 fl.

Summary: Comfortable. Easy to handle. Can be trailed.

BALLERINA II

Design:	Robert Tucker, England
Supplier:	Penryn Boatbuilding Company, U.K.
Est. Rating:	Thames measurement 3.9 tons. Portsmouth yardstick 116.

Specifications:

Construction:	GRP
LWL:	5.10m/16'9
LOA:	6.56m/21'6
Beam:	2.26m/7'5
Draft:	0.69m/2'3
Displ:	1,017kg/2,240 lbs
Ballast:	362kg/800 lbs

Fittings:	Bilge keel boat.
Interior:	3 or 4 berths.
Variations:	Inboard or outboard auxiliary.
Sails:	Area 18.3m^2/197 sq.ft. Spinnaker area 21.6m^2/232 sq.ft.
Rigging:	Bermudan sloop
Price Guide:	£1,700+
Summary:	Fine windward performance — a well proved cruising sloop

CATALINA 22

Design:	Frank Butler, U.S.A.	
Supplier:	Catalina Yachts, U.S.A.	
Specifications:	*Construction:*	GRP
	LWL:	5.89m/19'4
	LOA:	6.55m/21'6
	Beam:	2.33m/7'8
	Draft:	0.51m/1'8
	Displ:	840kg/1,850 lbs
	Ballast:	250kg/550 lbs

Fittings: Aluminium spars. Teak trim. Self-bailing cockpit.

Interior: 5 berths

Variations: Swing or fixed keel models available. Flip top model available. Optional 3—9 hp gasoline auxiliary.

Sails: Area 20.4m²/220 sq. ft
Spinnaker area 32.7m²/352 sq. ft

Rigging: Sloop

Price Guide: $2,850us

Summary: Ideal family fun cruiser as well as a rugged sea-going racer. Easily trailed.

CINDER

Design:	Tyler Boat Co., England 1961.
Supplier:	Tyler Boat Co., England
Est. Rating:	Portsmouth number 102

Specifications:

	Construction:	GRP
	LWL:	5.49m/18'0
	LOA:	6.55m/21'6
	Beam:	2.13m/7'0
	Draft:	0.99m−0.79m/3'3−2'7
	Displ:	1,657kg/3,650 lbs

Fittings:	Centreboard or keel boat
Interior:	4 berths. 1.4m/4'7 headroom.
Sails:	Area 23.2m^2/250 sq.ft.
Rigging:	Sloop
Price Guide:	On application
Summary:	Easily managed and maintained.

FOUR 21

Design:	John Powell, England 1964
Supplier:	Searider Yachts, England
Est. Rating:	Portsmouth number 114
Specifications:	*Construction:* GRP
	LWL: 5.94m/19'6
	LOA: 6.55m/21'6
	Beam: 2.21m/7'3
	Draft: 0.84m/2'9
Fittings:	Twin bilge keels. Inner GRP moulding. Stainless steel fittings.
Interior:	4 berths. 1.52m/5'0 headroom
Variations:	Outboard or inboard engine.
Sails:	Area 20.4m^2/220 sq.ft. Spinnaker are 30.8m^2/332 sq.ft.
Rigging:	Bermudan sloop
Price Guide:	£3,000
Summary:	A fast cruiser/racer. Can be trailed.

GOLIF

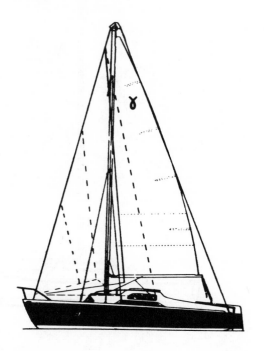

Design:	Jouet of Sartrouville, France
Supplier:	P. Jouet & Cie, France Carl Zeigler England

Specifications:	*Construction:*	GRP
	LWL:	5.99m/19'8
	LOA:	6.55m/21'6
	Beam:	2.29m/7'6
	Draft:	0.97m/3'2
	Displ:	1,090kg/2,400 lbs

Fittings:	To specification
Interior:	4 berths. 1.62m/5'4 headroom.
Variations:	JOG model or crusing with a shallower keel available.
Sails:	Area 20.4m^2/220 sq.ft.
Rigging:	Masthead sloop
Price Guide:	On application
Summary:	Light and manoeuvrable. Can be handled single-handed.

TROTTER

Design:	E. G. van de Stadt, Holland 1962
Supplier:	Marine Plastics, England
Est. Rating:	Portsmouth yardstick 103
Specifications:	*Construction:* GRP
	L'/L: 5.79m/19'0
	LOA: 6.55m/21'6
	Beam: 2.13m/7'0
	Draft: 0.61m/2'0
	Displ: 999kg/2,200 lbs
Fittings:	To specification
Interior:	4 berths. 1.37m/4'6 headroom. Galley. Marine toilet.
Varations:	Optional outboard engine
Sails:	Area 18.4m^2/198 sq.ft.
Rigging:	Bermudan sloop
Price Guide:	On application
Summary:	High performance boat, suitable for offshore racing and cruising.

CS-22

Design:	John Butler, U.S.A. 1970
Supplier:	Canadian Sailcraft Co., Canada

Specifications:	*Construction:*	GRP
	LWL:	5.33m/17'6
	LOA:	6.58m/21'7
	Beam:	2.44m/8'0
	Draft:	0.61m/2'0 cb up
	Displ:	999kg/2,200 lbs
	Ballast:	522kg/1,150 lbs

Fittings:	Cast iron ballast. Balsa core and GRP sandwich deck. Aluminium spars.
Interior:	4 berths in 2 cabins
Variations:	Optional hp outboard. Galley & toilets optional.
Sails:	Area 19.7m^2(7.8 + 11.9)/212 sq.ft. (84 + 128)
Rigging:	Sloop
Price Guide:	$3,000us

ANDERSON 22

Design:	Oliver Lee, England 1973
Supplier:	Anderson, Rigden and Perkins, U.K.
Est. Rating:	Unknown as yet

Specifications:	*Construction:*	GRP
	LWL:	5.87m/19'3
	LOA:	6.63m/21'9
	Beam:	2.31m/7'7
	Draft:	0.56m−1.37m/1'10−4'6
	Displ:	1,180kg/2,600 lbs
	Ballast:	454kg/1,000 lbs

Fittings:	5 hp outboard.
Interior:	4 berths
Variations:	Fin or lifting fin keel options.
Sails:	Area 18.5m^2/199 sq.ft.
Rigging:	Sloop
Price Guide:	£2,090
Summary:	Kits and mouldings available.

WESTERLY PEMBROKE

Design:	Laurent Giles & Partners, England 1974
Supplier:	Westerly Marine, England
Est. Rating:	Unknown as yet

Specifications:	*Construction:*	GRP
	LWL:	5.7m/18'9
	LOA:	6.55m/21'6
	Beam:	2.35m/7'9
	Draft:	0.84m/2'9
	Displ:	1,660kg/3,695 lbs
	Ballast:	726kg/1,600 lbs

Fittings:	Iron twin keels. GRP deck. Aluminium spars. 5 hp Petterdiesel.
Interior:	4 berths in 2 cabins. Sink. Icebox. Pump. Enclosed marine toilet.
Sails:	Area 19.5m^2/210 sq.ft.
Rigging:	Sloop
Price Guide:	£4,000/$8,900us
Summary:	An ideal small, family cruiser. Easily handled. Can be trailed.

VICTOIRE 22

Design:	Holland
Supplier:	Jachtwerf Victoria, Holland
Specifications:	*Construction:* GRP
	LWL: 5.69m/18'8
	LOA: 6.6m/21'8
	Beam: 2.21m/7'3
	Draft: 0.94m/3'1
	Displ: 1,158kg/2,550 lbs
Fittings:	Centreboard boat.
Interior:	4 berths
Variations:	Optional outboard engine
Sails:	Area 16.3m^2/175 sq.ft.
Rigging:	Bermudan sloop
Price Guide:	On application
Summary:	Can be trailed. Comfortable and easy to handle.

TOBY JUG

Design:	Illingworth & Primrose, England
Supplier:	John Illingworth & Association, U.K.
Specifications:	*Construction:* Hard chine.
	LWL: 5.49m/18'0
	LOA: 6.6m/21'8
	Beam: 2.2m/7'3
	Draft: 1.19m/3'11
	Displ: 953.4kg/2,100 lbs
Fittings:	Aluminium spars
Interior:	3 berths. 1.17m/3'10 headroom.
Sails:	Area 18.9m^2/204 sq.ft.
Rigging:	Masthead sloop
Price Guide:	On application
Summary:	Fast and light. Reasonably priced. A new and exciting small cruiser.

ETAP 22

Design:	E. G. van der Stadt, Holland 1972
Supplier:	Etap Yachts, Holland Knoxmore Bagley, England
Specifications:	*Construction:*

	LWL:	5.79m/19'0
	LOA:	6.59m/21'8
	Beam:	2.44m/8'0
	Draft:	1.39m/4'7
	Displ:	1,278kg/2,815 lbs
	Ballast:	520kg/1,146 lbs

Fittings:	Drop keel. 5 hp outboard.
Interior:	4 berths
Variations:	Interior layout to specification
Sails:	Area 10.7m²/115 sq. ft. Spinnaker area 28m²/310 ft.
Rigging:	Sloop
Price Guide:	£3,300
Summary:	Spacious, sturdy with a surprising pull.

O'DAY 22

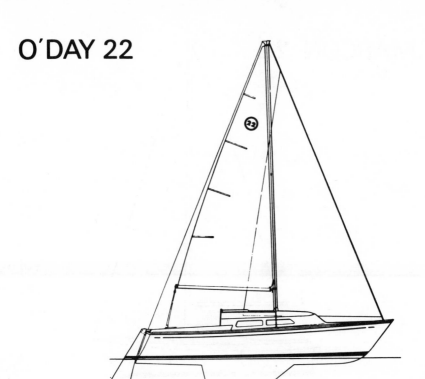

Design:	C. Raymond Hunt Assoc., U.S.A. 1971
Supplier:	O'Day Co., U.S.A.

Specifications:

Construction:	GRP
LWL:	5.79m/19'0
LOA:	6.6m/21'8
Beam:	2.19m/7'2
Draft:	0.59m/1'11
Displ:	817kg/1,800 lbs
Ballast:	272kg/600 lbs

Fittings:	Lead ballast. GRP deck. Aluminium spars. Self-bailing cockpit.
Interior:	4 berths in 2 cabins
Variations:	Optional hp outboard. Optional galley. Toilet optional.
Sails:	Area 18.2m^2/196 sq.ft.
Rigging:	Sloop
Price Guide:	$2,800
Summary:	Trailable and self-righting. Does combine family cruising with budgetary requirements.

MARCON 22

Design:	Alan F. Hill, England
Supplier:	Marine Construction (U.K.), England
Specifications:	*Construction:* GRP
	LWL: 5.49m/18'0
	LOA: 6.63m/21'9
	Beam: 2.39m/7'10
	Draft: 1.3m—0.78m/4'3—2'7
	Ballast: 562kg/1,240 lbs
Fittings:	GRP deck. Light alloy spars.
Interior:	4 berths
Variations:	Fin or twin keel models. Optional inboard or outboard.
Sails:	Area 17.2m^2/185 sq.ft. Terylene.
Rigging:	Bermudan sloop
Price Guide:	£2,600
Summary:	Moderately light displacement plus high aspect fin keel and transom hung rudder gives high performance for this type of boat.

SEAL

Design:	Angus Primrose, England 1969
Supplier:	John Baker (Kenton Forge), England
Est. Rating:	Portsmouth number 100
Specifications:	*Construction:* GRP
	LWL: 5.64m/18'6
	LOA: 6.63m/21'9
	Beam: 2.36m/7'9
	Draft: 1.17m/3'10
	Displ: 1,088kg/2,400 lbs
	Ballast: 363kg/800 lbs
Fittings:	Iron ballast. Gold anodised spars.
Interior:	4 berths. 1.45m/4'9 cabin headroom.
Variations:	De luxe version for cruising also eveilable.
Sails:	Area 17.09m^2/184 sq.ft.
	Spinnaker area 26.94m^2/290 sq.ft.
Rigging:	Sloop
Price Guide:	£2,000
Summary:	Designed for family sailing. Safe and stable with ample room. Kits and mouldings available.

ALACRITY 22
CATALINA 22
JAGUAR 22

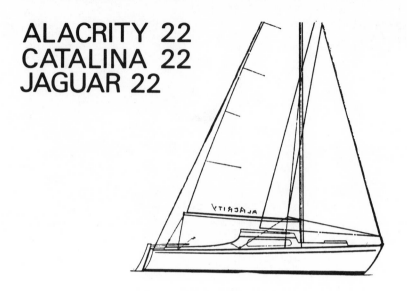

Design:	Frank Butler & Robert Finch, U.S.A. 1970
Supplier:	Russell Marine, U.K. Catalina Yachts Inc., U.S.A.
Rating:	Portsmouth secondary yardstick 107

Specifications:

Construction:	GRP
LWL:	5.90m/19'4
LOA:	6.66m/21'10
Beam:	2.34m/7'8
Draft:	0.51m/1'8 keel up
Displ:	839kg/1,850 lbs
Ballast:	272kg/600 lbs

Fittings:	Steel ballast. GRP deck. Aluminium spars. Outboard auxiliary.
Interior:	5 berths
Variations:	Fin or drop keel or bilge keel options available. Galley and toilets optional.
Sails:	Area 17.65m^2/190 sq.ft. (cruising suit) Area 19.69m^2/212 sq.ft. (racing suit)'
Rigging:	Sloop
Price Guide:	£1,295–£1,620/$2,595us
Summary:	A perfect combination of comfort and performance afloat coupled with reasonable cost. Very high stability. Known as Alacrity in the U.K. Catalina in North America and Jaguar in Europe and Scandinavia.

KESTREL 22

Design:	J. Francis Jones, England 1955
Supplier:	Seaward Yachts, England
Est. Rating:	Portsmouth number 110

Specifications:	*Construction:*	GRP or clinker mahogany on oak
	LWL:	5.99m/19'8
	LOA:	6.65m/21'10
	Beam:	2.15m/7'1
	Draft:	0.69m−1.32m/2'3−4'4
	Displ:	1,220kg/2,688 lbs
	Ballast:	499kg/1,100 lbs

Fittings:	Vire engine.
Interior:	2/4 berths. 1.37m/4'6 headroom.
Variations:	Fin or twin keel versions available.
Sails:	Area 19m^2/205 sq.ft.+
Rigging:	Bermudan sloop
Price Guide:	£2,700
Summary:	Originally designed for the dinghy sailer who wanted something with a roof on it. A very popular class in the U.K.

PANDORA

Design:	E. G. van der Stadt, Holland 1968
Supplier:	Rydgeway Marine, England
Rating:	17'4 IOR

Specifications:	*Construction:*	GRP
	LWL:	5.72m/18'9
	LOA:	6.65m/21'10
	Beam:	2.11m/6'11
	Draft:	0.99m/3'3
	Displ:	1,100kg/2,427 lbs
	Ballast:	444kg/980 lbs

Fittings:	To specification
Interior:	4 berths in 2 cabins. Galley. Toilet. 1.45m/4'9 headroom.
Variations:	Keel alternatives available. Optional outboard engine.
Sails:	Area 17.7m^2/191 sq. ft. Spinnaker area 28.7m^2/309 sq. ft.
Rigging:	Bermudan sloop
Price Guide:	£1,800

BRISTOL 22

Design:	Halsey Herreshoff, U.S.A. 1968
Supplier:	Bristol Yacht Co. U.S.A.

Specifications:	*Construction:*	GRP
	LWL:	5.94m/19'6
	LOA:	6.71m/22'0
	Beam:	2.36m/7'9
	Draft:	0.61m or 1.07m/2'0 or 3'6
	Displ:	1,294kg/2,850 lbs
	Ballast:	522kg/1,150 lbs

Fittings:	Balsa core and GRP deck. Aluminium spars.
Interior:	5 berths in 2 cabins. Icebox. Sink. 1 sea toilet.
Sails:	Area 19.04m^2/205 sq.ft.
Rigging:	Sloop
Price Guide:	$4,238us

KOALA

Design:	Walter F. Rayner Ltd., England 1963	
Supplier:	F. C. Mitchell & Sons, England	
Specifications:	*Construction:*	Mahogany on oak
	LWL:	5.33m/17'6
	LOA:	6.65m/21'10
	Beam:	2.29m/7'6
	Draft:	0.84m/2'9
	Displ:	1,691kg/3,566 lbs
Fittings:	Vire 6 hp auxiliary.	
Interior:	4 berths. 1.52m/5'0 headroom.	
Sails:	Area 16.9m²/182 sq.ft.	
Rigging:	Sloop	
Price Guide:	On application	
Summary:	Comfortable family cruiser with ample power.	

DOUGLAS 22

Design:	Carl A. Alberg, U.S.A. 1963
Supplier:	North American Fiberglass Moulding, Canada
Specifications:	*Construction:* GRP
	LWL: 4.88m/16'0
	LOA: 6.71m/22'0
	Beam: 2.13m/7'0
	Draft: 0.94m/3'1
	Displ: 1,453kg/3,200 lbs
	Ballast: 545kg/1,200 lbs
Fittings:	GRP deck. Aluminium spars. 4.5 or 9 hp outboard.
Interior:	4 berths in 2 cabins.
Sails:	Area 21.9m^2(10.6 + 11.3)/236 sq.ft. (114 + 122)
Rigging:	Sloop
Price Guide:	$5,500us
Summary:	Also known as **North America 22**

CIRRUS

Design:	Laurent Giles, England
Supplier:	Westerly Marine, England
	Andrew Gemeny & Sons, U.S.A.
Est. Rating:	Portsmouth number 105
Specifications:	*Construction:* GRP
	LWL: 5.79m/19'0
	LOA: 6.71m/22'0
	Beam: 2.44m/8'0
	Draft: 1.07m/3'6
	Displ: 1,470.9kg/3,240 lbs
Fittings:	Centreboard boat.
Interior:	4 berths
Variations:	Optional inboard or outboard.
Sails:	Area 19.51m^2/210 sq.ft.
Rigging:	Bermudan sloop
Price Guide:	On application
Summary:	Can be sailed single-handed easily. Attractive lines.

DAUNTLESS 22

Design:	The Dauntless Company, England
Supplier:	The Dauntless Company, England
Specifications:	*Construction:* Mahogany on oak
	LWL: 6.40m/21'0
	LOA: 6.71m/22'0
	Beam: 2.44m/8'0
	Draft: 1.22m/4'0
Fittings:	Drop keel boat, Stuart Turner 5 hp inboard auxiliary.
Interior:	4 berths
Sails:	Area 22.3m^2/240 sq.ft.
Rigging:	Sloop
Price Guide:	£2,000+
Summary:	Kits available.

D & M 22

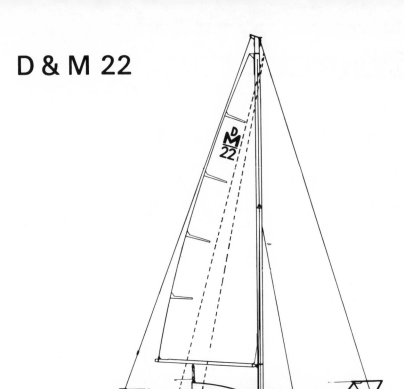

Design:	Sparkman & Stephens, Canada 1972
Supplier:	Douglass & McLeod Inc., U.S.A.
Est. Rating:	18'0 IOR Mk III 17'3 MORC
Specifications:	*Construction:* Balsa core and GRP
	LWL: 5.72m/18'9
	LOA: 6.71m/22'0
	Beam: 2.57m/8'5
	Draft: 1.07m/3'6
	Displ: 1,816kg/4,000 lbs
	Ballast: 817kg/1,800 lbs
Fittings:	Balsa core and GRP deck. Aluminium spars. 5–6 hp outboard. Lead ballast.
Interior:	4 berths in 2 cabins. Sink, Stove. Icebox. Chemical toilet.
Sails:	Area 23.6m^2(10.5 + 13.1)/254 sq.ft. (113 + 141)
Rigging:	Sloop
Price Guide:	$7,300us

ECLIPSE MK II

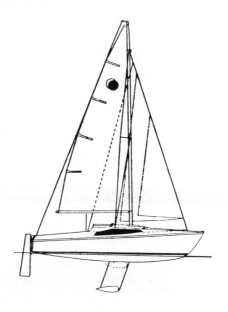

Design:	Ian Proctor, England 1972
Supplier:	Performance Yachts, England
Rating:	17'4 IOR. Portsmouth secondary yardstick 102.

Specifications:	Construction:	GRP
	LWL:	5.89m/19'4
	LOA:	6.71m/22'0
	Beam:	2.34m/7'8
	Draft:	0.53m—1.37m/1'9—4'6
	Displ:	1,088kg/2,400 lbs
	Ballast:	362kg/800 lbs

Fittings:	Retractable keel — hydraulically operated. Lead ballast.
Interior:	4 berths. 1.43m/4'10 headroom.
Variations:	Fixed keel available. Optional outboard.
Sails:	Area 17.37m^2/187 sq.ft.
Rigging:	Sloop. Masthead rig
Price Guide:	£2,250
Summary:	A responsive racer/cruiser with high performance and wide choice of sails.

GALION 22

Design:	Ian Hannay, England
Supplier:	Deacons Boatyard, England Am Tec Imports, U.S.A.

Specifications:

Construction:	GRP
LWL:	6.1m/20'0
LOA:	6.71m/22'0
Beam:	2.21m/7'3
Draft:	0.99m/3'3
Displ:	1,544kg/3,400 lbs
Ballast:	771kg/1,700 lbs

Fittings:	Iron ballast. Finn keel. GRP deck. Aluminium spars.
Interior:	4 berths in 2 cabins. 1.75m/5'9 headroom. Optional galley and toilet.
Variations:	Optional gasoline outboard.
Sails:	Area 19.2m^2/207 sq.ft.
Rigging:	Sloop
Price Guide:	£2,950us
Summary:	Kits available. Comfort for 4 adults below with good headroom. Cockpits seats 6 adults easily.

ITCHEN FERRY

Design:	G. Drummond-Bayne, England 1972
Supplier:	G. D. B. Design Group, England
Est. Rating:	Thames measurement 4.8 tons
Specifications:	*Construction:* GRP
	LWL: 6.40m/21'0
	LOA: 6.71m/22'0
	Beam: 2.39m/7'10
	Draft: 0.86m/2'10
	Displ: 2,743kg/2 tons
	Ballast: 1,778kg/3,920 lbs
Fittings:	GRP and foam sandwich deck. Gold anodised alloy spars.
Interior:	3 berths. Flush sea-toilet. Stove. Sink. 1.83m/6'0 cabin headroom.
Variations:	Optional Stuart Turner 5 hp engine.
Sails:	Area 19.13m^2 (11.33 + 7.80)/206 sq.ft. (122 + 84) [sloop]
Rigging:	Bermudan or gaff.
Price Guide:	£1,950–£1,400 (for kit). £3,500 complete.
Summary:	Based on the original Itchen Ferry built in the 19th century. Strong and comfortable. Kits available.

PT ¼ TON

Design:	Plastrend, U.S.A. 1968
Supplier:	Plastrend Inc., U.S.A.
Est. Rating:	18'0 IOR Mk III 17'0 MORC

Specifications:

Construction:	GRP
LWL:	5.18m/17'0
LOA:	6.71m/22'0
Beam:	2.13m/7'0
Draft:	0.71m/2'4
Displ:	908kg/2,000 lbs
Ballast:	345kg/760 lbs

Fittings:	Cast iron ballast. GRP and wood core deck. Aluminium spars.
Interior:	4 berths in 2 cabins. Sink. Icebox. Chemical toilet. 4'3 headroom.
Variations:	Keel or centreboard models. Optional outboard.
Sails:	Area 17.7m^2 (7.4 + 10.3)/190 sq.ft. (80 + 110)
Rigging:	Sloop
Price Guide:	$5,000us

SHEARWATER

Design:	Dell Quay Yacht Yard, England
Supplier:	Dell Quay Yacht Yard, England
Rating:	Portsmouth number 111

Specifications:

Construction:	Cold moulded marine ply.
LWL:	5.64m/18'6
LOA:	6.71m/22'0
Beam:	2.13m/7'0
Draft:	0.61m–1.22m/2'0–4'0
Displ:	1,525.4kg/1.5 tons

Fittings:	To specification
Interior:	4 berths. 1.68m/5'6 headroom.
Sails:	Area 18.58m^2/200 sq.ft.
Rigging:	Bermudan sloop
Price Guide:	On application

LEISURE 22

Design:	Graham Caddick, England 1971
Supplier:	Cobramold Ltd., England
Specifications:	*Construction:* GRP
	LWL: 6.07m/19'11
	LOA: 6.71m/22'0
	Beam: 2.39m/7'10
	Draft: 0.81m–1.19m/2'8–3'11
	Displ: 1,495kg/3,300 lbs
	Ballast: 635kg/1,400 lbs
Fittings:	Mast height 7.93m/26'0. Cast iron ballast.
Interior:	4/5 berths. 1.73m/5'8 headroom.
Variations:	Twin bilge keels or fin keel. 7–10 hp engine.
Sails:	Area 20.0m^2/225 sq.ft. Spinnaker area 32.5m^2/350 sq.ft.
Rigging:	Sloop
Price Guide:	£2,200
Summary:	Well-balanced, easy to handle and designed to provide dry, comfortable sailing.

NORTHSTAR 22

Design:	Hughes Boatworks, Canada
Supplier:	North Star Yachts, Canada
Specifications:	

	Construction:	Wood
	LWL:	5.94m/19'6
	LOA:	6.71m/22'0
	Beam:	2.31m/7'7
	Draft:	1.83m/6'0
	Displ:	999kg/2,200 lbs
	Ballast:	374.5kg/825 lbs

Fittings:	Cast iron keel — retractable. Self-bailing cockpit.
Interior:	5 berths. 4'3 headroom.
Sails:	Area 20.44m^2/220 sq.ft.
Rigging:	Sloop
Price Guide:	$4,500us
Summary:	A swing keel, trailable racer/cruiser for the family. Ample room for 6 cruising.

RHODES CONTINENTAL

Design:	Philip Rhodes, U.S.A. 1969
Supplier:	General Boats Corp., U.S.A.
Specifications:	*Construction:* GRP
	LWL: 6.1m/20'0
	LOA: 6.71m/22'0
	Beam: 2.44m/8'0
	Draft: 0.46m/1'6
	Displ: 908kg/2,000 lbs
	Ballast: 272kg/600 lbs
Fittings:	Lead ballast. GRP deck. Aluminium spars.
Interior:	4/5 berths in 1 cabin. Galley. Semi-enclosed toilet.
Variations:	Keel or centreboard models. Optional hp outboard.
Sails:	Area 24.6m^2/265 sq.ft.
Rigging:	Sloop
Price Guide:	$3,000us
Summary:	An attractive trailable cruiser that sleeps 4 comfortably.

SAILMASTER 22

Design:	Sparkman & Stephens, Canada
Supplier:	Lion Yachts, U.S.A.
Specifications:	*Construction:* GRP
	LWL: 5.03m/16'6
	LOA: 6.71m/22'0
	Beam: 2.13m/7'0
	Draft: 0.71m/2'4
	Displ: 1,657kg/3,650 lbs
Fittings:	Lead ballast. GRP deck. Aluminium spars.
Interior:	4 berths in 1 cabin. Galley. 1 open toilet.
Variations:	Optional outboard. **Sailmasters** available in other lengths.
Sails:	Area 21.83m^2/235 sq.ft.
Rigging:	Sloop
Price Guide:	$4,200us
Summary:	A nice-lined, good performance racer/cruiser that is good value for money.

SANTANA 22

Design:	Gary Mull, U.S.A. 1965
Supplier:	W. D. Schock Co., U.S.A.
Est. Rating:	20'6 CCA

Specifications:		
	Construction:	GRP
	LWL:	5.69m/18'8
	LOA:	6.71m/22'0
	Beam:	2.39m/7'10
	Draft:	1.07m/3'6
	Displ:	1,180kg/2,600 lbs
	Ballast:	558.4kg/1,230 lbs

Fittings:	Iron ballast. GRP deck. Aluminium spars.
Interior:	4 berths in 1 cabin. Sink. Stove.
Variations:	Toilet not standard.
Sails:	Area 20.16m^2/217 sq.ft.
Rigging:	Sloop
Price Guide:	$4,250us
Summary:	Available through dealers. There is an active class association.

SEAMEW

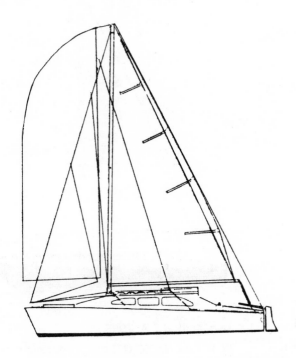

Design:	Ian Proctor, England 1962
Supplier:	Bell Woodworking, England
Est. Rating:	Portsmouth number 106

Specifications:	*Construction:*	Marine plywood
	LWL:	6.4m/21'0
	LOA:	6.71m/22'0
	Beam:	2.23m/7'4
	Draft:	0.53m/1'9
	Displ:	2,542kg/2.5 tons

Fittings:	Partially retractable keel.
Interior:	4/5 berths.
Sails:	Area 18.77m^2/202 sq.ft.
Rigging:	Sloop
Price Guide:	£2,000
Summary:	A larger version of the 'Seagull'. Kits available.

SNAPDRAGON 670

Design: Thames Marine, England 1971

Supplier: Thames Marine, England

Est. Rating: 4¾ ton Thames measurement. Portsmouth number 104

Specifications:
Construction:	GRP
LWL:	5.79m/19'0
LOA:	6.71m/22'0
Beam:	2.44m/8'0
Draft:	1.14m−0.81m/39−2'8
Displ:	1,496kg/3,300 lbs
Ballast:	703kg/1,550 lbs

Fittings: 6HP Vive petrol engine.

Interior: 5 berths. 1.73m/5'8 cabin headroom.

Variations: Fin or twin keel forms available.

Sails: Area 19.04m^2/205 sq.ft.
Spinnaker area 32.52m^2/350 sq.ft.

Rigging: Sloop

Price Guide: £2,700

Summary: Combines living space for five with racing performance. Kits available.

SOUTH COAST 22

Design:	South Coast Seacraft, U.S.A. 1970	
Supplier:	South Coast Seacraft Inc., U.S.A.	
Specifications:	*Construction:*	GRP
	LWL:	5.33m/17'6
	LOA:	6.71m/22'0
	Beam:	2.16m/7'1
	Draft:	0.25m/10''
	Displ:	817.2kg/1,800 lbs
	Ballast:	229.3kg/505 lbs
Fittings:	Cast iron ballast. Balsa core and GRP deck. Aluminium spars.	
Interior:	5 berths in 1 cabin.	
Variations:	Galley and toilets optional.	
Sails:	Area 17.56m^2/189 sq.ft.	
Rigging:	Sloop	
Price Guide:	$3,400us	

PLATE 1

PLATE 2

PLATE 3

PLATE 4

PLATE 5

PLATE 6

PLATE 7

PLATE 8

PLATE 9

PLATE 10

PLATE 11

PLATE 13

PLATE 14

PLATE 15

PLATE 16

PLATE 17

PLATE 18

PLATE 19

PLATE 20

PLATE 21

PLATE 22

PLATE 23

SPARTA

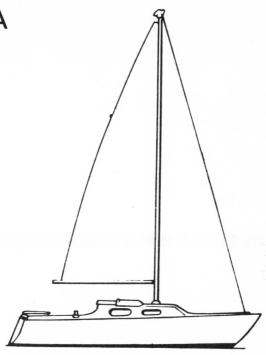

Design: C. J. Butler, England 1972

Supplier: Butler Mouldings, England

Rating: 18' ±IOR Thames measurement 2.95 tons.
Portsmouth number 97

Specifications:

Construction:	GRP
LWL:	5.80m/19'0
LOA:	6.70m/22'0
Beam:	2.16m/7'1½
Draft:	1.84m/4'1
Displ:	1,088kg/2,400 lbs
Ballast:	498kg/1,100 lbs

Fittings: Gold anodised alloy spars. Outboard engine.

Interior: 4 berths. Full galley. Toilet and chart table.

Sails: Area 16.16m^2/174 sq.ft.
Spinnaker area 37.52m^2/350 sq.ft.

Rigging: Sloop

Price Guide: £1,900+

Summary: Conceived as an inexpensive Quarter Ton Cup
Contender, based on the successful Achilles design.
Kits available.

STURGEON

Supplier: Fibocon, Holland

Specifications:

Construction:	GRP
LWL:	5.49m/18'0
LOA:	6.72m/22'0
Beam:	2.28m/7'6
Draft:	0.75m/2'5
Displ:	1,650kg/3,600 lbs
Ballast:	600kg/1,325 lbs

Fittings: Iron ballast. GRP deck. Aluminium spars.

Interior: 4 berths. Galley. 1.55m/5'2 headroom.

Variations: Outboard may be fitted.

Sails: Area 21.30m^2/229 sq.ft.
Spinnaker area 31.00m^2/335 sq.ft.

Rigging: Sloop

Price Guide: 15,100 D.Fl.

VENTURE 222

Design:	Robert N. MacGregor, U.S.A.
Supplier:	MacGregor Yacht Inc., U.S.A.

Specifications:	*Construction:*	GRP
	LWL:	5.54m/18'2
	LOA:	6.71m/22'0
	Beam:	2.23m/7'4
	Draft:	1.37m/4'6
	Displ:	371kg/800 lbs
	Ballast:	227kg/500 lbs

Fittings:	Cast iron swing keel. GRP deck. Aluminium spars.
Interior:	5 berths in 1 cabin. Icebox. Sink.
Variations:	Optional toilet.
Sails:	Area 16.44m^2/177 sq.ft.
Rigging:	Sloop
Price Guide:	$2,600us
Summary:	Easy to trail, launch and rig.

KELLS 22

Design:	Paul A. Lindh, U.S.A. 1971
Supplier:	Kells Corporation, U.S.A.
Specifications:	*Construction:* GRP
	LWL: 5.49m/18'0
	LOA: 6.76m/22'2
	Beam: 2.31m/7'7
	Draft: 0.28m/11'' keel up
	Displ: 840kg/1,850 lbs
	Ballast: 238kg/525 lbs
Fittings:	Swing keel. Cast iron ballast. GRP deck. Aluminium spars.
Interior:	5 berths in 1 cabin.
Variations:	Galley and toilets optional
Sails:	Area 16.8m^2/181 sq.ft.
Rigging:	Sloop
Price Guide:	$2,995us

HERON

Design:	Chas.A. Purbrook Ltd., England 1952	
Supplier:	Chas.A. Purbrook Ltd., England	
Specifications:	*Construction:*	Wood — choice of Iroko, Elm or Mahogany
	LWL:	5.79m/19'0
	LOA:	6.78m/22'3
	Beam:	2.29m/7'6
	Draft:	0.91m–1.62m/3'0–5'4
	Displ:	3,153kg/6,944 lbs
Fittings:	To specification	
Interior:	3/4 berths. 1.68m/5'6 headroom.	
Variations:	Centreboard or bilge keels models available. Various layouts available.	
Sails:	Area 24.5m^2/264 sq.ft.	
Rigging:	Bermudan sloop	
Price Guide:	On application.	
Summary:	Sturdy, seaworthy and comfortable shallow draft cruiser.	

PEARSON 22

Design: William H. Shaw, U.S.A. 1968

Supplier: Pearson Yachts, U.S.A.

Specifications: *Construction:*   GRP
                    LWL: 5.61m/18'5
                    LOA: 6.78m/22'3
                    Beam: 2.31m/7'7
                    Draft: 1.04m/3'5
                    Displ: 1,180kg/2,600 lbs
                    Ballast: 454kg/1,000 lbs

Fittings: Iron ballast. GRP deck. Aluminium spars.

Interior: 4 berths in 1 cabin. 1.22m/4'0 headroom.

Variations: Optional galley and toilet. Optional outboard.

Sails: Area 20.2m^2 (9.8 + 10.4)/217 sq.ft. (106 + 111)

Rigging: Sloop

Price Guide: $4,000us

Summary: A well-proven family cruiser/racer.

OUTLAW

Design: Peter Milne, England 1972

Supplier: Sail Craft, England

Specifications: *Construction:*   GRP
                    LWL: 5.79m/19'0
                    LOA: 6.81m/22'4
                    Beam: 2.39m/7'10
                    Draft: 0.33m/1'1
                    Displ: 1,019.7kg/2,246 lbs
                    Ballast: 227kg/500 lbs

Fittings: Lifting keel

Interior: 5 berths

Sails: Area 24.43m^2/263 sq.ft.

Rigging: Sloop

Price Guide: Not yet known.

MACWESTER ROWAN 22

Design:	C. S. J. Roy, England 1969
Supplier:	Macwester Marine, England
Est. Rating:	Portsmouth number 105
Specifications:	*Construction:* GRP
	LWL: 5.64m/18'6
	LOA: 6.78m/22'3
	Beam: 2.51m/8'3
	Draft: 0.84m/2'9
	Displ: 2,288kg/5,040 lbs
	Ballast: 651.5kg/1,435 lbs
Fittings:	Polyester resin deck. Keelboat. Stuart Turner 5HP engine. Gold anodised spars.
Interior:	5 berths
Variations:	Fin or twin keel boat. Optional inboard.
Sails:	Area 20.9m²/225 sq.ft. Terylene.
Rigging:	Bermudan sloop
Price Guide:	£3,100
Summary:	2 crew. Kits and mouldings available.

VIKING 22

Design:	Cuthbertson & Cassvan, Canada
Supplier:	Ontario Yachts Ltd., Canada
Specifications:	*Construction:* GRP
	LWL: 5.33m/17'6
	LOA: 6.81m/22'4
	Beam: 2.13m/7'0
	Draft: 1.12m/3'9
	Displ: 771.8kg/1,700 lbs
	Ballast: 408.6kg/900 lbs
Fittings:	GRP deck. Cast iron ballast. Aluminium spars.
Interior:	2 berths.
Sails:	Area 18.64m²/200.63 sq.ft.
Rigging:	Sloop
Price Guide:	$3,900us
Summary:	A high performance day sailer. An excellent club boat for fleet racing and training. Easily trailed.

COLVIC 23

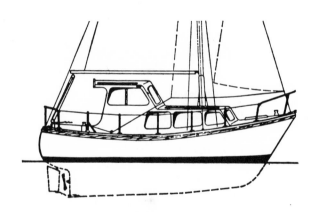

Design:	Colvic Craft, England	
Supplier:	Colvic Craft, England	
Specifications:	*Construction:*	Wood
	LOA:	6.83m/22'5
	Beam:	2.54m/8'4
Interior:	4 berths	
Rigging:	Motor-sailer	
Price Guide:	On application	
Summary:	A neat motor-sailer that is comfortable with adequate power. Kits only.	

ENSIGN

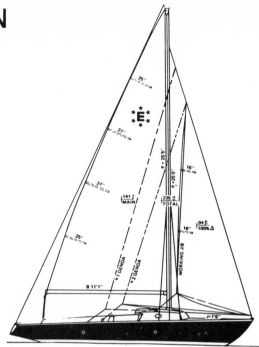

Design: Carl Alberg, U.S.A. 1962

Supplier: Pearson Yachts, U.S.A.
                     Ensign National Association, U.S.A.

Specifications: *Construction:*   GRP
                     LWL: 5.08m/16'9
                     LOA: 6.86m/22'6
                     Beam: 2.13m/7'0
                     Draft: 0.91m/3'0
                     Displ: 908kg/2,000 lbs
                     Ballast: 545kg/1,200 lbs

Fittings: Keelboat. Mahogany trim. Aluminium spars.
                     Stainless steel fittings. Lead ballast.

Variations: Optional head with 2 bunks.

Sails: Area 18.7m^2/201 sq.ft.

Rigging: Sloop

Price Guide: $4,400us

Summary: 2—3 crew. Exclusive American class. Over 1,500
                     boats in circulation. Excellent keel boat for racing
                     in heavy weather.

SEA SPRITE

Design:	Carl Alberg, U.S.A. 1958	
Supplier:	Wickford Shipyard, U.S.A.	
Est. Racing:	16'6 CCA	
Specifications:	*Construction:*	GRP
	LWL:	4.95m/16'3
	LOA:	6.86m/22'6
	Beam:	2.13m/7'0
	Draft:	0.91m/3'0
	Displ:	1,520.9kg/3,350 lbs
	Ballast:	669.65kg/1,475 lbs
Fittings:	GRP deck. Aluminium spars. Lead ballast.	
Interior:	4 berths in 2 cabins. Icebox. Stove. Sink. Marine toilet.	
Variations:	Holding system optional. Optional outboard.	
Sails:	Area 22.95m^2/247 sq.ft. Spinnaker area 30.1m^2/324 sq.ft.	
Rigging:	Sloop	
Price Guide:	$5,000us	
Summary:	A well-tested design that is attractive and practical. Moulded in one rigid unit.	

TANZER 22

Design:	Johann Tanzer, Canada 1970
Supplier:	Tanzer Industries, Canada.
Est. Rating:	18'0 IOR Mk III 17'0 MORC
Specifications:	*Construction:* GRP
	LWL: 5.99m/19'9
	LOA: 6.86m/22'6
	Beam: 2.39m/7'10
	Draft: 1.04m/3'5
	Displ: 1,316.6kg/2,900 lbs
	Ballast: 567.5kg/1,250 lbs
Fittings:	Iron ballast. GRP deck. Aluminium spars. Self-draining cockpit.
Interior:	4 berths in 2 cabins. Icebox. Sink with pump.
Variations:	Fin or keel/CB models available. Optional sea, chemical holding tank. Optional HP outboard with bracket.
Sails:	Area 20.62m^2(10.4 + 10.22)/222 sq.ft. (112 + 110)
Rigging:	Sloop
Price Guide:	$5,300us
Summary:	A very spacious, high performance boat that has a raised deck. There is an active class association.

COLUMBIA 23

Design:	Alan Payne, U.S.A./Australia 1973
Supplier:	Columbia Yachts, U.S.A.
Specifications:	*Construction:* GRP
	LWL: 6.1m/20'0
	LOA: 6.88m/22'7
	Beam: 2.41m/7'11
	Draft: 0.59m/1'11
	Displ: 1044kg/2,300 lbs
	Ballast: 367.7kg/810 lbs
Fittings:	Lead ballast. GRP deck. Aluminium spars. 7½HP outboard gasoline.
Interior:	4 berths in 2 cabins. 1.68m/5'6 headroom.
Variations:	Optional stove and toilet.
Sails:	Area 20.25m^2 (9.29 + 10.96)/218 sq.ft. (100 + 118)
Rigging:	Sloop
Price Guide:	$4,250us
Summary:	Comfortable and stylish, suited to the mobile sailor who needs a versatile boat. Can be trailed.

AQUARIUS 23

Design:	Peter Barrett, U.S.A. 1969	
Supplier:	Coastal Recreation Inc., U.S.A.	
Est. Rating:	22.6' CCA	
Specifications:	*Construction:*	GRP
	LWL:	6.45m/21'2
	LOA:	6.91m/22'8
	Beam:	2.31m/7'11
	Draft:	0.33m/1'1 cb up
	Displ:	1,035kg/2,280 lbs
	Ballast:	360kg/815 lbs
Fittings:	GRP deck. Aluminium spars. 6—9.5HP Evinrude or Johnson outboard.	
Interior:	5 berths in 1 cabin	
Variations:	Optional sanitary arrangements	
Sails:	Area 23m^2(12.8 + 10.2)/248 sq.ft. (138 + 110) Spinnaker area 29.7m^2/320 sq.ft.	
Rigging:	Sloop	
Price Guide:	$3,395us	

OLYMPIC DOLPHIN MKII

Design:	Derek Angus, U.S.A. 1970	
Supplier:	Olympic Yachts, Canada	
Specifications:	*Construction:*	GRP
	LWL:	6.25m/20'6
	LOA:	6.93m/22'9
	Beam:	2.21m/7'3
	Draft:	1.07m/2'6 keel model
		0.66m/2'2 cb model cb up
	Displ:	908kg/2,000 lbs
	Ballast:	363kg/800 lbs keel
		454kg/1,000 lbs cb
Fittings:	GRP deck. Aluminium spars. Self bailing cockpit.	
Interior:	4 berths in 2 cabins. Sink. Icebox. 1 enclosed toilet.	
Variations:	Keel or centreboard models. Optional HP outboard.	
Sails:	Area 19.6m^2(9.1 + 10.5)/211 sq.ft. (98 + 113) Spinnaker area 32.5m^2/350 sq.ft.	
Rigging:	Sloop	
Price Guide:	On application	

PACESHIP PY 23¼ TON

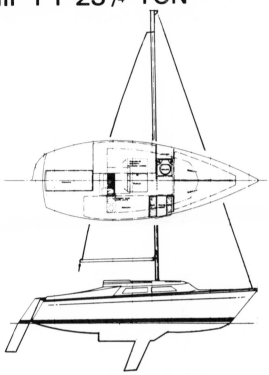

Design:	C. Raymond Hunt Assoc., U.S.A. 1973
Supplier:	Paceship Yachts, Canada.
Est. Rating:	18'0 IOR
Specifications:	Construction: GRP

LWL: 6.02m/19'9
LOA: 6.88m/22'7
Beam: 2.44m/8'0
Draft: 1.45m/4'9
Displ: 1,044kg/2,300 lbs
Ballast: 427kg/940 lbs

Fittings:	GRP deck. Aluminium spars. Centreboard boat.
Interior:	5 berths in 2 cabins. Icebox. Sink. 1 enclosed head.
Sails:	Area 19.7m^2/212 sq.ft.
Rigging:	Sloop
Price Guide:	$5,300us
Summary:	A new 23 footer that will prove popular because of its neat appearance and practical layout.

BAROUDER

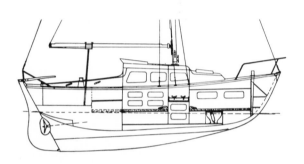

Design:	Beneteau, France 1970
Supplier:	Chantiers Beneteau, France. Fairey Marine, England Arie de Boom BV., Holland
Specifications:	*Construction:* GRP *LWL:* 5.85m/19'3 *LOA:* 7.00m/22'9 *Beam:* 2.49m/8'0 *Draft:* 1.05m/3'4 *Displ:* 2300kg/5,060 lbs *Ballast:* 747kg/1,650 lbs
Fittings:	Anodised aluminium spars. 15HP Renault conach petrol engine.
Interior:	4/5 berths. 1.80m/5'8 headroom. Marine toilet. Galley — sink. Stove. Icebox.
Sails:	Area 26.5m^2/265 sq.ft.
Rigging:	Sloop
Price Guide:	£5,000/26,350 D.Fl.
Summary:	Comfortable racer/cruiser that has a good turn of speed.

‑ISLANDER 23

Design:	William Crealock, U.S.A.
Supplier:	Islander Yachts, U.S.A. Russell Marine, England
Specifications:	*Construction:* GRP *LWL:* 6.12m/20'1 *LOA:* 6.93m/22'9 *Beam:* 2.36m/7'9 *Draft:* 0.84m/2'9 *Displ:* 681kg/1,500 lbs
Fittings:	4 berths
Variations:	Optional outboard
Sails:	Area 19.5m^2/210 sq.ft.
Rigging:	Bermudan sloop
Price Guide:	$7,000us+
Summary:	Can be trailed.

MAPLE LEAF

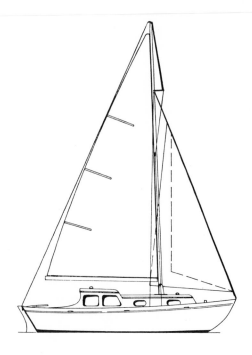

Design:	Chandler & Smith (Boatbuilders), England 1959
Suppliers:	Chandler & Smith (Boatbuilders), England
Specifications:	

Construction:	Mahogany on oak
LWL:	5.51m/18'1
LOA:	6.93m/22'9
Beam:	2.36m/7'9
Draft:	0.76m–1.52m/2'6–5'0
Displ:	2,186kg/4,815 lbs

Fittings:	Shoal draft. ST 4HP engine.
Interior:	3 berths. 1.45m/4'9 headroom.
Sails:	Area 21.4m^2/230 sq.ft.
Rigging:	Sloop
Price Guide:	On application
Summary:	A fast, weatherly and comfortable motor sailer. Can be easily sailed single-handed and the centreboard ensures good windward performance.

BLUE JACKET

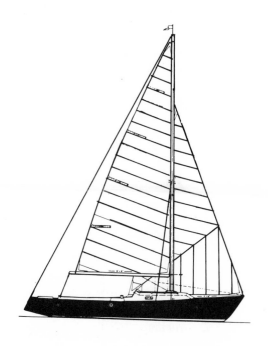

Design:	Cuthbertson & Cassran, Canada 1967	
Supplier:	Paceship, Canada	
Specifications:	*Construction:*	GRP
	LWL:	5.33m/17'6
	LOA:	7.96m/22'10
	Beam:	2.13m/7'0
	Draft:	1.14m/3'9
	Displ:	908kg/2,000 lbs
	Ballast:	409kg/900 lbs
Fittings:	GRP deck. Aluminium spars. Iron ballast.	
Interior:	2 berths in 1 cabin. Sink.	
Variations:	Optional outboard. Optional toilet.	
Sails:	Area 18.6m^2/201 sq.ft.	
Rigging:	Sloop	
Price Guide:	$4,000us	
Summary:	A well established design.	

BINIOU

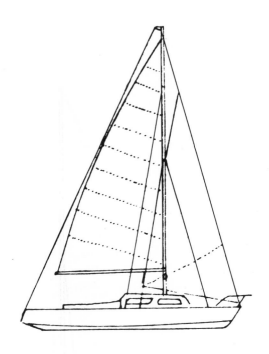

Design:	France
Supplier:	Constantini, France
Specifications:	*Construction:* GRP and balsa core
	LWL: 5.50m/18'0½
	LOA: 7.00m/22'11½
	Beam: 2.30m/7'6½
	Draft: 1.10m/3'7
	Displ: 1,200kg/2,646 lbs
	Ballast: 565kg/1,246 lbs
Fittings:	To specification
Interior:	4 berths. Galley. Enclosed toilet.
Sails:	Area 25.20m^2/271 sq.ft. Spinnaker area 35.40m^2/381 sq.ft.
Rigging:	Sloop
Price Guide:	32,500 Fr.F.

BUCCANEER

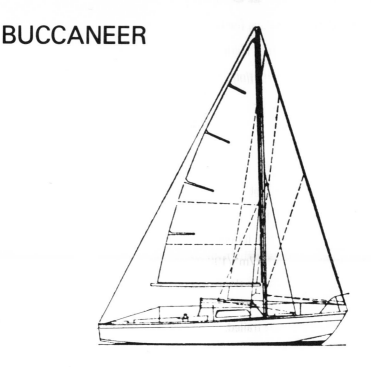

Design:	E. G. Van de Stadt, Holland
Supplier:	Wilgate Limited, England
Specifications:	*Construction:* Wood — hard chine plywood
	LWL: 5.54m/18'2
	LOA: 7.01m/23'0
	Beam: 2.29m/7'6
	Draft: 1.68m/5'6
	Displ: 1,119kg/2,464 lbs
Fittings:	Fin keel
Interior:	3 berths
Variations:	Inboard or outboard auxiliary
Sails:	Area 21.8m^2/235 sq.ft.
	Spinnaker area 29.7m^2/320 sq.ft.
Rigging:	Masthead sloop
Price Guide:	On application
Summary:	Light displacement craft designed for off-shore racing.

CHESFORD 23 MS

Design:	Alan Pape, England	
Supplier:	Chesford Marine, England	
Specifications:	*Construction:*	Clinker
	LWL:	6.48m/21'3
	LOA:	7.01m/23'0
	Beam:	2.29m/7'6
	Draft:	0.76m/2'6
	Displ:	2,288kg/5.040 lbs
	Ballast:	136kg/300 lbs
Fittings:	Bilge keel	
Interior:	4 berths	
Variations:	Optional inboard auxiliary.	
Sails:	Area 17.7m^2/190 sq.ft.	
Rigging:	Bermudan sloop	
Price Guide:	£3,750	
Summary:	Can be trailed.	

GULF COAST 23

Design:	Martin Bludworth, U.S.A. 1969	
Supplier:	Gulf Coast Sailboats, U.S.A.	
Specifications:	*Construction:*	GRP
	LWL:	5.33m/17'6
	LOA:	7.01m/23'0
	Beam:	2.23m/7'4
	Draft:	1.52m/5'0
	Displ:	908kg/2,000 lbs
	Ballast:	250kg/550 lbs
Fittings:	GRP deck. Aluminium spars. 6HP outboard. Iron ballast. Swing keel.	
Interior:	5 berths in 1 cabin	
Variations:	Optional toilet	
Sails:	Area 17.5m^2 (10.2 + 7.3)/188 sq.ft. (110 + 78)	
Rigging:	Sloop	
Price Guide:	$3,295us	

CALIFE

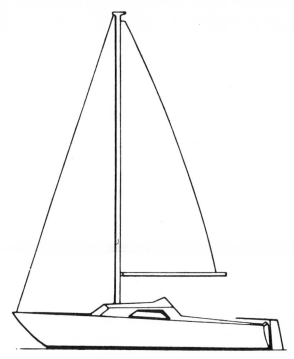

Design:	Philippe Harlé, France 1971
Supplier:	Arcoa-Jouet, France Comextra, England Navy-Holland, Holland
Est. Rating:	17'0 IOR
Specifications:	*Construction:* GRP *LWL:* 5.79m/19'0 *LOA:* 7.01m/23'0 *Beam:* 2.51m/8'3 *Draft:* 1.09m/3'7 *Displ:* 1,353kg/2,980 lbs *Ballast:* 545kg/1,200 lbs
Fittings:	Fin keel
Interior:	4 berths
Variations:	Optional HP inboard or outboard auxiliary
Sails:	Area 19.7m^2/212 sq.ft.
Rigging:	Bermudan sloop
Price Guide:	£3,000
Summary:	Mouldings available.

DAUNTLESS 23 MK IV

Design:	The Dauntless Co., England 1973
Supplier:	The Dauntless Co., England
Est. Rating:	5.5 tons Thames measurement

Specifications:

Construction:	Mahogany on oak
LWL:	6.40m/21'0
LOA:	7.01m/23'0
Beam:	2.51m/8'3
Draft:	0.61m/2'0
Displ:	2,286kg/5,040 lbs
Ballast:	272kg/600 lbs

Fittings:	tuart Turner 5HP inboard. Drop keel.
Interior:	4 berths
Sails:	Area 22.29m^2/240 sq.ft.
Rigging:	Gunter Sloop
Price Guide:	£2,475
Summary:	Traditionally built — warm and roomy. May be sailed single-handed. Hull kits available.

664

ELIZABETHAN 23 MK I & II

Design:	Peter Webster, U.K. 1969
Supplier:	Peter Webster, U.K.
Rating:	Portsmouth primary yardstick 96
Specifications:	*Construction:* GRP
	LWL: 6.64m/18'6
	LOA: 7.00m/23'0
	Beam: 2.18m/7'1
	Draft: 0.77m/2'6
	Displ: 1,727kg/3,808 lbs
	Ballast: 854kg/1,880 lbs
Fittings:	Teak trim. Centreboard boat.
Interior:	4 berths in 2 cabins. 1.37m/4'6 headroom.
Variations:	Optional inboard or outboard.
Sails:	Area 17.74m^2/191 sq.ft.
Rigging:	Sloop
Price Guide:	£2,650
Summary:	A true sailing yacht in miniature with good sailing performance and exceptional stability. Also available part assembled.

GEORGIAN 23

Design:	Alex H. McGruer, U.S.A. 1969
Supplier:	McGruer & Clark Ltd., U.S.A.
Specifications:	*Construction:* GRP
	LWL: 6.1m/20'0
	LOA: 7.01m/23'0
	Beam: 2.44m/8'0
	Draft: 1.07m/3'6
	Displ: 1,975kg/4,350 lbs
	Ballast: 908kg/2,000 lbs
Fittings:	GRP deck. Aluminium spars. Iron ballast.
Interior:	4 berths in 2 cabins. Sink. Stove. 1 marine head.
Sails:	Area 23m^2(11.1 + 11.9)/248 sq.ft. (120 + 128)
Rigging:	Sloop
Price Guide:	On application

H ALCYON 23

Design:	Alan Buchanan, England 1969
Supplier:	Offshore Yachts International, England Imports Co. of America, U.S.A.
Est. Rating:	Thames measurement 4½ tons Portsmouth primary yardstick 103

Specifications:

Construction:	GRP
LWL:	5.64m/18'6
LOA:	7.01m/23'0
Beam:	2.29m/7'6
Draft:	1.12m—0.76m/3'8—2'6
Displ:	1,362kg/3,000 lbs
Ballast:	499kg/1,100 lbs

Fittings:	Fin or bilge keel. Aluminium spars.
Interior:	4 berths in 2 cabins. Sink with pump. Stove. 1 salt water toilet.
Variations:	Optional inboard or outboard
Sails:	Area 20m^2/215 sq.ft.
Rigging:	Sloop
Price Guide:	£2,400
Summary:	Easy to sail, pointing high to windward and responsive to the helm. Over 400 have been built and are being sailed in all parts of the world.

HUNTER 701

Design:	Oliver J. Lee, England 1970
Supplier:	Hunter Boats Ltd., England
Est. Rating:	18.4' IOR

Specifications:

Construction:	GRP
LWL:	6.01m/19'8½
LOA:	7.01m/23'0
Beam:	2.26m/7'5
Draft:	0.76m/2'6
Displ:	1,176kg/2,600 lbs
Ballast:	590kg/1,300 lbs

Fittings:	Anodised aluminium spars. GRP deck.
Interior:	4 berths. 1.37m/4'6 cabin headroom. Galley — stove and toilet.
Variations:	Outboard can be attached.
Sails:	Area 16.80m^2/181 sq.ft.
Rigging:	Stainless steel and synthetic fibres.
Price Guide:	£2,500
Summary:	Fast and seaworthy. Kits available.

IP 23

Design:	W. Waight/Island Plastics Ltd., England 1969
Supplier:	Island Plastics, England
Specifications:	*Construction:* GRP
	LWL: 6.2m/20'4
	LOA: 7.01m/23'0
	Beam: 2.82m/9'3
	Draft: 0.91m/3'0
	Displ: 2,034kg/4,480 lbs
	Ballast: 508kg/1,120 lbs
Fittings:	Fin keel. Inboard 15—25HP diesel.
Interior:	To specifications
Sails:	Area 18.1m^2/195 sq.ft.
Rigging:	Sloop (motor sailer)
Price Guide:	£500 bare hull
Summary:	Supplied only as a bare hull. A competent family motor sailer.

IRWIN 23

Design:	Ted Irwin, U.S.A. 1968
Supplier:	Irwin Yacht & Marine Corp., U.S.A.
Specifications:	*Construction:* GRP
	LWL: 5.64m/18'6
	LOA: 7.01m/23'0
	Beam: 2.44m/8'0
	Draft: 0.74m/2'5 cb up
	Displ: 1,453kg/3.200 lbs
	Ballast: 681kg/1,500 lbs
Fittings:	Lead ballast. GRP and balsa core deck. Aluminium spars. Mast 9.6m/31'6 high.
Interior:	4 berths in 2 cabins
Variations:	Optional toilet. Optional outboard.
Sails:	Area 23.7m^2(11.8 + 11.9)/255 sq.ft. (127 + 128) Spinnaker area 39.7m^2/427 sq.ft.
Rigging:	Sloop
Price Guide:	$7,255us

O'DAY 23

Design:	C. Raymond Hunt Assoc., U.S.A.
Supplier:	O'Day Co., U.S.A.
Est. Rating:	17.4' MORC 19.3' off soundings.
Specifications:	*Construction:* GRP
	LWL: 6.1m/20'0
	LOA: 7.01m/23'0
	Beam: 2.41m/7'11
	Draft: 0.61m/2'0
	Displ: 1,407kg/3,100 lbs
	Ballast: 568kg/1,250 lbs
Fittings:	Iron ballast. GRP deck. Aluminium spars.
Interior:	5 berths in 1 cabin. Galley standard. Pop Top Model. Cabin headroom 1.93m/6'4.
Variations:	Toilets optional. Optional outboard. Pop or fixed top available.
Sails:	Area 22.8m^2/245 sq.ft.
Rigging:	Sloop
Price Guide:	$4,800us

RANGER 23 ¼ TON

Design:	Gary Mull, U.S.A. 1971
Supplier:	Ranger Yachts, U.S.A.
Est. Rating:	18.0' IOR Mk III

Specifications:	*Construction:*	GRP
	LWL:	6.1m/20'0
	LOA:	7.01m/23'0
	Beam:	2.41m/7'11
	Draft:	1.14m/3'9
	Displ:	1,544kg/3,400 lbs
	Ballast:	681kg/1,500 lbs

Fittings:	GRP deck. Aluminium spars.
Interior:	4 berths in 2 cabins. Sink. Fridge. 1 chemical toilet.
Sails:	Area 23.9m²/257 sq.ft.
Rigging:	Sloop
Price Guide:	$6,000us
Summary:	The first U.S. boat designed specifically to the Quarter Ton Rule. Has proved herself on the racing scene.

RUFFIAN 23 ¼ TON

Design:	W.P. Brown, 1972
Supplier:	Weatherly Yachts Ltd., N. Ireland
Rating:	17.9' IOR
Specifications:	*Construction:* GRP
	LWL: 6.1m/20'0
	LOA: 7.01m/23'0
	Beam: 2.59m/8'6
	Draft: 1.45m/4'9
	Displ: 1,298kg/2,860 lbs
	Ballast: 631kg/1,390 lbs
Fittings:	Fin keel. Shrimp 4—7HP engine.
Interior:	5 berths
Sails:	Area 27.9m^2/300 sq.ft.
Rigging:	Sloop
Price Guide:	£3,000

PAGEANT WESTERLY

Design:	Laurent Giles & Partners, England 1969
Supplier:	Westerly Marine Construction, England
	Andrew Gemeny & Sons, England
Rating:	Portsmouth secondary yardstick 112.
Specifications:	*Construction:* GRP
	LWL: 5.79m/19'0
	LOA: 7.03m/23'1
	Beam: 2.44m/8'0
	Draft: 0.86m/2'10
	Displ: 1,952kg/4,300 lbs
	Ballast: 953kg/2,100 lbs
Fittings:	Twin keel. Volvo MD1B 10HP engine.
Interior:	4/5 berths in 2 cabins
Sails:	Area 21.9m^2/236 sq.ft.
Rigging:	Bermudan sloop
Price Guide:	£4,300/$10,750us
Summary:	Capable of fast, comfortable passage making. Exceptionally seaworthy. Kits available.

SEAMASTER SAILER 23

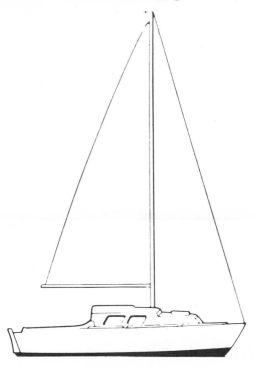

Design: Laurent Giles & Partners, England 1968

Supplier: Seamaster Limited, England

Specifications: *Construction:*   GRP
                     LOA: 7.01m/23'0
                     Beam: 2.44m/8'0
                     Draft: 1.68m/5'6
                     Displ: 2,247kg/4,950 lbs
                     Ballast: 908kg/2,000 lbs

Fittings: 10HP Bukh engine

Interior: 5 berths

Variations: Bilge keel or centreboard boat. Optional power.

Sails: Area 23.2m^2/250 sq.ft.

Rigging: Sloop

Price Guide: £4,000

Summary: Responds readily to all weather sailing. Mouldings
                     available.

SNAPDRAGON

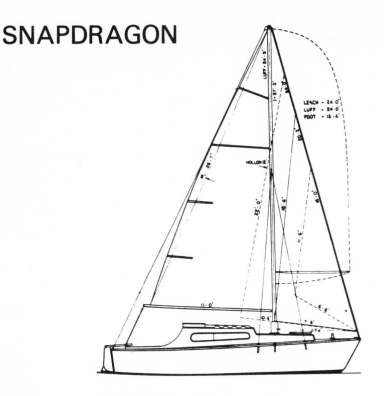

Design:	Thames Structural Plastics, England 1961	
Supplier:	Thames Structural Plastics, England	
Rating:	Portsmouth secondary yardstick 101	
Specifications:	*Construction:*	GRP
	LWL:	6.04m/19'10
	LOA:	7.01m/23'0
	Beam:	2.33m/7'8
	Draft:	0.48m/1'7
	Displ:	1.339kg/2,950 lbs
Fittings:	To specification	
Interior:	4 berths	
Variations:	Centreboard or bilge keels	
Sails:	Area 20.4m²/220 sq.ft.	
Rigging:	Sloop	
Price Guide:	£3,000	
Summary:	Designed for serious fast cruisng with generous accommodation. Kits available.	

VENTURE OF NEWPORT

Design:	Roger N. MacGregor, U.S.A. 1972	
Supplier:	MacGregor Yacht Corp., U.S.A.	
Specifications:	*Construction:*	GRP
	LWL:	5.94m/19'6
	LOA:	7.01m/23'0
	Beam:	2.23m/7'4
	Draft:	0.46m/1'6
	Displ:	908kg/2,000 lbs
	Ballast:	272kg/600 lbs
Fittings:	Cast iron ballast. GRP deck. Aluminium spars.	
Interior:	5 berths in 1 cabin. Icebox. Sink with pump.	
Variations:	Self-contained or sea toilet. 1½–10HP engine.	
Sails:	Area 24.4m^2/263 sq.ft.	
Rigging:	Sloop or cutter	
Price Guide:	$2,900us	
Summary:	Heavily built and stable. Based on the pilot cutters of the late 1800s.	

VIRGO 23

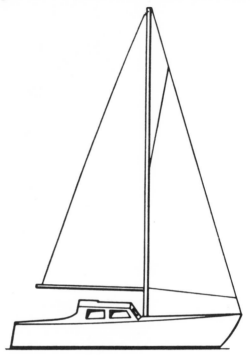

Design:	Newbridge Boats Ltd., England
Supplier:	Newbridge Boats Ltd., England

Specifications:	*Construction:*	GRP
	LWL:	6.05m/19'10
	LOA:	7.01m/23'0
	Beam:	2.54m/8'4
	Draft:	1.22m/4'0
	Displ:	1,996kg/4,400 lbs
	Ballast:	998kg/2,200 lbs

Fittings:	Fin keel. 5—12HP outboard.
Interior:	4 berths. 1.83m/6'0 cabin headroom.
Sails:	Area 23.6m^2/254 sq.ft.
Rigging:	Sloop
Price Guide:	£3,000
Summary:	A fast off-shore cruiser well tested in rough weather. Kits available.

ALBIN-VIGGEN

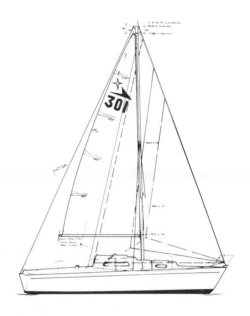

Design:	Per Brohäll, Sweden 1972
Supplier:	Albin Marine, Sweden Albin Marine, England Larsson Trade U.S.A. Inc.

Specifications:

Construction:	GRP
LWL:	6.00m/19'7
LOA:	7.10m/23'3
Beam:	2.24m/7'3
Draft:	1.11m/3'6
Displ:	1.4tons/3,087 lbs
Ballast:	600kg/1,323 lbs

Fittings:	Mast and boom gold anodised aluminium. Roller reefing.
Interior:	4 berths. Practical stateroom.
Sails:	Area 25.4m^2/273 sq.ft. Spinnaker area 43m^2/463 sq.ft. Dacron
Rigging:	Bermudan sloop
Price Guide:	£4,000
Summary:	A family cruiser. Light but responsive on the helm.

GRAMPIAN 23

Design:	Grampian Marine, Canada
Supplier:	Grampian Marine Ltd., Canada
Specifications:	*Construction:* GRP
	LWL: 6.38m/20'11
	LOA: 7.09m/23'3
	Beam: 2.44m/8'0
	Draft: 0.74m/2'5 cb up
	Displ: 1,453kg/3,200 lbs
	Ballast: 469kg/1,033 lbs
Fittings:	GRP deck. Aluminium spars.
Interior:	5 berths in 2 cabins. 5'4 cabin headroom.
Variations:	Centreboard or keelboat options. Optional outboard. Pop top model available.
Sails:	Area 22.8m^2(10.3 + 12.5)/245 sq.ft. (111 + 134)
Rigging:	Sloop
Price Guide:	$5,995us
Summary:	A family boat that is safe, stable and fast. Can be trailed.

LYMINGTON

Design:	Laurent Giles, England 1954
Supplier:	Laurent Giles & Partners, England
Est. Rating:	Portsmouth number 103

Specifications:	*Construction:*	To specification
	LWL:	5.92m/19'5
	LOA:	7.09m/23'3
	Beam:	2.03m/6'8
	Draft:	1.14m/3'9
	Displ:	Variable
	Ballast:	Variable

Fittings:	Variable. No extras.
Interior:	2 berths
Sails:	Area 26m^2/280 sq.ft.
Rigging:	Bermudan sloop
Price Guide:	Varies
Summary:	Price and specifications vary according to design and yard chosen. Suitable for offshore cruising.

REVE DE MER

Design: Finot Group, France 1972

Supplier: Chantiers Mallard, France
F. E. Sparkes Marine, England

Est. Rating: 18' ± IOR

Specifications:
Construction:	Polyester and tubular steel frame
LWL:	5.33m/17'6
LOA:	7.1m/23'3
Beam:	2.47m/8'1¼
Draft:	1.09m—1.4m/3'7—4'7
Displ:	999kg/2,200 lbs

Fittings: Fin keel. Anti-slip decking. Gold anodised alloy spars. 7HP engine.

Interior: 4 berths

Variations: Cruising or high performance models available. The latter has a deeper draught and backstay adjuster.

Sails: Area 25.1m^2/270 sq.ft. Woven tergal sheets. Dacron sails.

Rigging: Sloop

Price Guide: £4,500

Summary: A superbly constructed, responsive racer that is able to cope with all weather situations.

TANKARD 23/710 MK III

Design: Oliver J. Lee, England

Supplier: Tankard Yachts, England

Specifications:
Construction:	GRP or wood
LWL:	5.79m/19'0
LOA:	7.11m/23'4
Beam:	2.19m/7'2
Draft:	1.07m/3'6

Fittings: 12HP inboard

Interior: 4 berths

Variations: Fin or twin keel

Sails: Area 23.2m^2/250 sq.ft.

Rigging: Bermudan sloop

Price Guide: On application

STONE HORSE

Design: S. S. Crocker, U.S.A. 1931

Supplier: Edey & Puff Inc., U.S.A.

Specifications:

	Construction:	GRP and foam sandwich
	LWL:	5.588m/18'4
	LOA:	7.112m/23'4
	Beam:	2.158m/7'1
	Draft:	1.067m/3'6
	Displ:	1, 128.5kg/4,490 lbs
	Ballast:	908kg/2,000 lbs

Fittings: Deck — GRP and foam sandwich. Wooden spars. 5HP auxiliary — westerbeke diesel. Lead ballast.

Interior: 2 berths in 1 cabin + 2 in cockpit.

Sails: Area 31.56m^2/339 sq.ft.

Rigging: Ketch or sloop

Price Guide: $12,800us

Summary: Unsinkable. Speedy, comfortable, easy to handle. Sold direct from Edey & Duff Inc.

CLIPPER 23

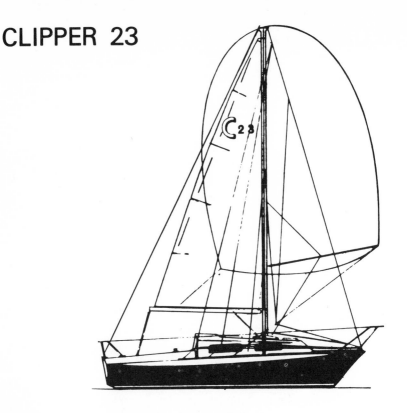

Design:	Alex McGruer, U.S.A. 1969
Supplier:	Challenger Yachts, U.S.A.
Specifications:	*Construction:* GRP
	LWL: 5.64m/18'6
	LOA: 7.14m/23'5
	Beam: 2.44m/8'0
	Draft: 0.91m/3'0
	Displ: 1,362kg/3,000 lbs
	Ballast: 691kg/1,522 lbs
Fittings:	GRP deck. Aluminium spars.
Interior:	4 berths in 2 cabins. Sink with pump
Variations:	Optional inboard or outboard. Optional toilet.
Sails:	Area 20.6m^2 (10.2 + 10.4)/222 sq.ft. (110 + 112)
Rigging:	Sloop
Price Guide:	$5,000us
Summary:	A well-proved offshore racer that will delight all the family.

RELAX 24

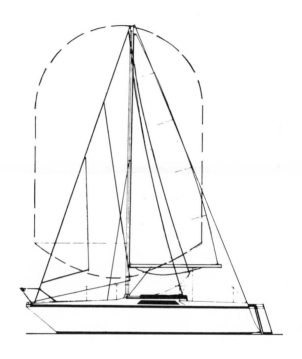

Supplier:	Corail Marine, France	
Est. Rating:	IOR 17'3	
Specifications:	*Construction:*	GRP
	LWL:	5.75m/18'10½
	LOA:	7.15m/23'5½
	Beam:	2.50m/8'2½
	Draft:	1.10m/3'7½
	Displ:	1,000kg/2,204 lbs
	Ballast:	400kg/882 lbs
Fittings:	To specification	
Interior:	2 berths.	
Sails:	Area 26.70m²/287 sq.ft. Spinnaker area 32m²/344 sq.ft.	
Rigging:	Sloop	
Price Guide:	On application	

ARDEN CLANSMAN

Design:	Arden Yachts, U.K.
Supplier:	Arden Yachts, U.K.
Rating:	Portsmouth secondary yardstick 108

Specifications:	*Construction:*	GRP
	LWL:	5.64m/18'6
	LOA:	7.16m/23'6
	Beam:	2.21m/7'3
	Draft:	1.07m/3'6
	Displ:	1,780kg/3,920 lbs

Fittings:	Fin keel. Aluminium alloy spars.
Interior:	4 berths
Variations:	Optional inboard auxiliary.
Sails:	Area 22.5m^2/242 sq.ft. Terylene
Rigging:	Masthead sloop
Price Guide:	£3,400
Summary:	Ballast ratio of 55%. A traditional-lined, attractive sailing cruiser.

BARON 23

Supplier:	Baron Craft, England
Specifications:	*Construction:*
	LOA: 7.16m/23'6
Rigging:	Sloop (motor sailer)
Price Guide:	£2,275

BUCKLER RANGE

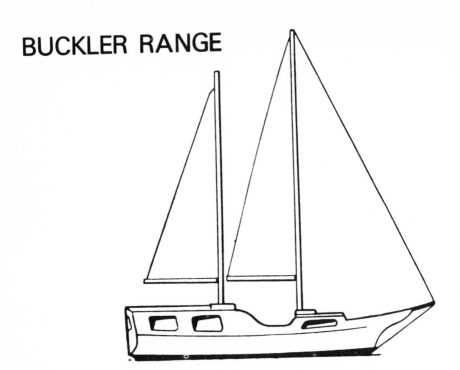

Design:	Buckler Boat Co., England 1973
Supplier:	Buckler Boat Co., England
Specifications:	*Construction:* GRP
	LWL: 5.18m/17'0
	LOA: 7.16m/23'6
	Beam: 15.08m/7'11
	Draft: 1.07m–0.76m/3'6–2'6
	Displ: 1,798kg/3,960 lbs+
	Ballast: Various
Fittings:	Wood trim. Aluminium spars. Keelboat.
Interior:	To specification
Variations:	I and II versions. Rig, hull profile and keel arrangement to specification.
Sails:	Area 16.3m^2–17.9m^2/175–193 sq.ft. Terylene
Rigging:	Ketch, schooner or Bermudan sloop
Price Guide:	On application (from £1,600)
Summary:	A new concept in sailing — basic attractive features but great scope for individuality. Kits available.

HURLEY 24/70

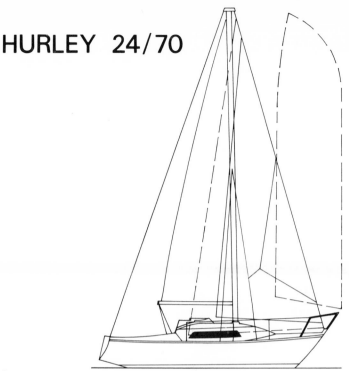

Design:	Ian Anderson, England 1971
Supplier:	Hurley Marine, England Hurley Marine, U.S.A.
Specifications:	*Construction:* GRP *LWL:* 5.79m/19'0 *LOA:* 7.16m/23'6 *Beam:* 2.33m/7'8 *Draft:* 1.07m/3'6 *Displ:* 2,225kg/4,900 lbs *Ballast:* 1,044kg/2,300 lbs
Fittings:	GRP deck. Aluminium spars. 7HP Petter diesel auxiliary.
Interior:	4 berths in 2 cabins. 1.78m/5'10 headroom.
Variations:	Fin or bilge keel models. Outboard model also available.
Sails:	Area 24.9m^2 (11.9 + 13)/268 sq.ft. (128 + 140) Spinnaker area 32.89m^2/354 sq.ft.
Rigging:	Sloop
Price Guide:	£4,500/$7,895us
Summary:	Skeg hull form with modern reverse counter transom that gives a long waterline and low wetted area.

687

KARAWI

Design: E. G. Van de Stadt, Holland

Supplier: Mulder & Rijke BV, Holland

Specifications:

Construction:	GRP
LWL:	6.0m/19'8
LOA:	7.10m/23'6
Beam:	2.55m/8'5
Draft:	0.90m/3'0
Displ:	1,907kg/4,200 lbs
Ballast:	397kg/874

Fittings: GRP deck. Anodised aluminium spars. Teak faced plytrim.

Interior: 4 berths in 2 cabins. Full galley. 1.8 'm/6'0 headroom.

Variations: Optional engine

Sails: Area 23.0m^2/247 sq.ft.

Rigging: Sloop

Price Guide: On application

TEQUILA SPORT

Design: Philippe Harlé, France

Supplier: Gilbert Marine, France
Navy-Holland, Holland
Anderson Marine, England

Est. Rating: 18.0' IOR

Specifications:

Construction:	GRP
LWL:	5.7m/18.70'
LOA:	7.2m/23.62'
Beam:	2.45m/8'0½
Draft:	1.48m/4.86'
Displ:	1,160kg/2,640 lbs
Ballast:	455kg/1,000 lbs

Fittings: To specification

Interior: 2 berths. 1.52m/5'0 cabin headroom.

Sails: Area 25.25m^2/272 sq.ft.
Spinnaker area 40.40m^2/435 sq.ft.

Rigging: Sloop

Price Guide: £3,500

MAGYAR 7

Design:	S. Nemeth
Supplier:	Brabourne (Marine) England (importers)
Est. Rating:	Portsmouth number 111

Specifications:	*Construction:*	Pine on oak
	LWL:	6.17m/20'3
	LOA:	7.16m/23'6
	Beam:	2.29m/7'6
	Draft:	0.69m/2'3
	Displ:	1,401kg/3,086 lbs

Fittings:	Twin keel, double chine boat. Roller reefing gear. Foam bunk mattresses. Self-draining cockpit.
Interior:	4 berths. 1.52m/5'0 headroom.
Sails:	Area 22.8m²/245 sq.ft.
Rigging:	Bermudan sloop
Price Guide:	On application
Summary:	An easily driven hull — very strongly built.

VIVACITY 24/720

Design:	Alan Hill, England 1968
Supplier:	Russell Marine, England Wells Yachts, U.S.A.
Specifications:	*Construction:* GRP *LWL:* 6.32m/20'9 *LOA:* 7.16m/23'6 *Beam:* 2.44m/8'0 *Draft:* 1.22m—'/3'8—2'6 *Displ:* 1,090kg/2,400 lbs *Ballast:* 793kg/1,750 lbs
Fittings:	Iron ballast. GRP deck. Aluminium spars. Maximum 10HP outboard.
Interior:	5 berths in 2 cabins. Sink. Icebox. Stove.
Variations:	Twin keel model also available. Optional toilet.
Sails:	Area 23.70m^2/255 sq.ft.
Rigging:	Sloop
Price Guide:	£3,100
Summary:	A well proved design.

KITTIWAKE 24

Design:	Kenner Boat Co., U.S.A. 1968	
Supplier:	Ray Greene &Co. Inc.,U.S.A.	
Specifications:	*Construction:*	GRP
	LWL:	5.41m/17'9
	LOA:	7.18m/23'7
	Beam:	2.26m/7'5
	Draft:	0.86m/2'10
	Displ:	1,725kg/3,800 lbs
	Ballast:	681kg/1,500 lbs
Fittings:	GRP deck. Aluminium spars.	
Interior:	4 berths in 2 cabins	
Variations:	Optional HP outboard.	
Sails:	Area 20.4m^2(11.9 + 8.5)/220 sq.ft. (128 + 92)	
Rigging:	Sloop	
Price Guide:	$5,995us	

NORTHERN ¼ TON

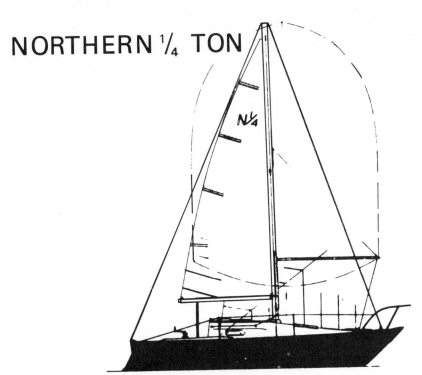

Design:	Cuthbertson & Cassian, Canada 1972
Supplier:	Northern Yacht Ltd., Canada
Rating:	18.0' IOR Mk III
Specifications:	*Construction:* GRP
	LWL: 5.89m/19'4
	LOA: 7.21m/23'8
	Beam: 2.57m/8'5
	Draft: 1.22m/4'0
	Displ: 1,544kg/3,400 lbs
	Ballast: 658kg/1,450 lbs
Fittings:	Lead ballast. GRP and balsa core deck. Aluminium spars.
Interior:	4 berths in 2 cabins. Icebox. Stove. Sink. W/Pump. Enclosed head.
Variations:	Optional hp outboard.
Sails:	Area 18.7m^2 (8.3 + 10.4)/201 sq.ft. (89 + 112)
Rigging:	Sloop
Price Guide:	$6,000
Summary:	Built specifically for Quarter Ton Competition. Clean lined and speedy.

WAARSCHIP QUARTER TONNER

Design:	Akerman & Kremer, Holland 1967
Supplier:	Anson Marine, England
Rating:	18'0 IOR
Specifications:	*Construction:* Marine ply and Mahogany clinker
	LWL: 5.50m/18'4
	LOA: 7.20m/23'8
	Beam: 2.50m/8'2
	Draft: 0.99m/3'3
	Displ: 1,197kg/2,640 lbs
	Ballast: 499kg/1,100 lbs
Fittings:	Fin keelboat. Cast iron ballast. Aluminium spars.
Interior:	4 berths
Variations:	6 hp outboard or inboard engine. 2 versions available — long or short coach roof, and deep or shallow keel. Latter known as **Waarschip Jog.**
Sails:	Area 25.7m²/277 sq. ft. Spinnaker 35m²/375 sq. ft.
Rigging:	Bermudan sloop
Price Guide:	£2,400
Summary:	A good all-rounder. Designed specifically for racing. Can be trailed. Ideal for the dinghy man moving on to his first boat. Kits available.

ACHILLES 24

Design: Oliver J. Lee modified by Chris Butler, England 1972

Supplier: Butler Mouldings, England

Est. Rating: Provisional Portsmouth yardstick 99 18'3 IOR

Specifications:

Construction:	GRP
LWL:	6.096m/20'
LOA:	7.24m/23'9
Beam:	2.15m/7'1
Draft:	1.14m/3'9
Displ:	1,179kg/2,600 lbs

Fittings: Mast — deck stepped, gold anodised. Boom — gold anodised, roller reefing. Rudder — GRP. Fin or triple keel.

Interior: 4 berths — Decking GRP

Variations: Keel boat or bilge keels. Inboard or outboard engine.

Sails: Area 23.2m^2/250 sq. ft.
Spinnaker area 32.5m^2/350 sq. ft.

Rigging: Bermudan sloop

Price Guide: £1,900

Summary: 4 berth cruiser-racer. Versatile. Responsive and easily handled.

CAY

Design: Herreshoff and Glander, U.S.A.

Supplier: Glander Boats Inc., U.S.A.

Specifications:

Construction:	GRP
LWL:	6.02m/19'9
LOA:	7.24m/23'9
Beam:	2.44m/8'0
Draft:	0.91m/3'0
Displ:	3,087kg/6,800 lbs
Ballast:	999kg/2,200 lbs

Fittings: GRP deck. Aluminium spars.

Interior: 4 berths in 2 cabins

Sails: Area 32.5m^2 (17.3 + 15.2)/350 sq.ft. (186 + 164)

Rigging: Sloop

Price Guide: $1,650us for the bare hull

MIRAGE 24 ¼ TON

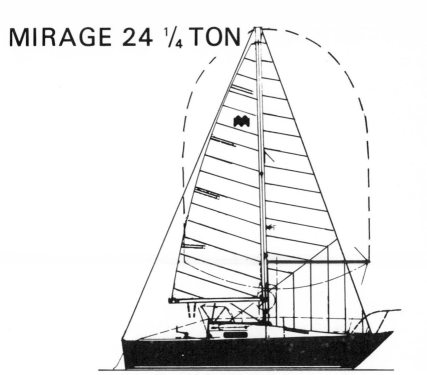

Design:	Cuthbertson & Cassian, Canada 1972
Supplier:	Mirage Yachts Ltd., Canada
Rating:	18' IOR Mk III. 17.4' MORC
Specifications:	*Construction:* GRP
	LWL: 6.12m/20'1
	LOA: 7.26m/23'10
	Beam: 2.57m/8'5
	Draft: 1.22m/4'0
	Displ: 1,680kg/3,700 lbs
	Ballast: 681kg/1,500 lbs
Fittings:	Lead ballast. GRP deck. Aluminium spars.
Interior:	4 berths in 2 cabins. Sink. Stove.
Variations:	Toilet optional
Sails:	Area 20.9m²/225 sq.ft.
Rigging:	Sloop
Price Guide:	$6,500us
Summary:	A relatively new competition boat that is proving very popular in Canada and the U.S.A.

WESTWIND

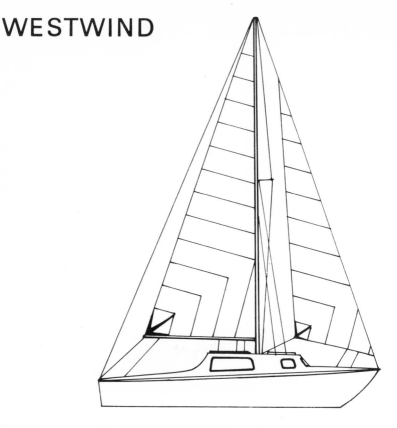

Design:	Ted Hood, U.S.A. 1966-67
Supplier:	Paceship Yachts, Canada
Est. Rating:	20.0′–21.0′ MORC 18.1′–18.6′ CCA
Specifications:	*Construction:* GRP
	LWL: 5.54m/18′2
	LOA: 7.29m/23′11
	Beam: 2.44m/8′0
	Draft: 0.63m/2′1
	Displ: 2,102kg/4,630 lbs
	Ballast: 1,076kg/2,370 lbs
Fittings:	GRP deck. Aluminium spars. Outboard well.
Interior:	3 berths in 2 cabins. Sink. Icebox. Overboard discharge toilet.
Sails:	Area 28.2m²/304 sq. ft.
Rigging:	Sloop
Price Guide:	$6,200us

EYGTHENE 24

Supplier:	Master Marine, Guernsey
Est. Rating:	18'0 IOR

Specifications:

Construction:	GRP
LWL:	6.25m/20'6
LOA:	7.32m/24'0
Beam:	2.95m/9'8
Draft:	1.44m/4'8
Displ:	1.9T/1.9 tons
Ballast:	908kg/2,000 lbs.

Fittings:	Lead ballast
Interior:	Optional layout
Variations:	Optional engine. Optional keelboat.
Sails:	Area 24.44m^2/272 sq.ft.
Rigging:	Sloop
Price Guide:	£4,200+
Summary:	A design that allows a great deal of individuality.

FINESSE 24

Design:	A. F. Platt, England
Supplier:	A. F. Platt Limited, England
Specifications:	*Construction:*
	LWL: 6.5m/21'4
	LOA: 7.32m/24'0
	Beam: 2.46m/8'1
	Draft: 0.76m/2'6
Fittings:	10 hp inboard auxiliary.
Interior:	4/5 berths
Variations:	Bilge keel or keel boat
Sails:	Area 22.3m^2/240 sq.ft.
Rigging:	Bermudan sloop
Price Guide:	£3,800
Summary:	Can be trailed.

SHARK

Design:	George Hinterhoeller, U.S.A. 1959
Supplier:	C & C Yachts, Canada
Est. Rating:	18.8' IOR Mk III
Specifications:	*Construction:* GRP
	LWL: 6.1m/20'0
	LOA: 7.32m/24'0
	Beam: 2.08m/6'10
	Draft: 0.91m/3'0
	Displ: 999kg/2,200 lbs
	Ballast: 306kg/675 lbs
Fittings:	Iron ballast. GRP deck. Aluminium spars.
Interior:	4 berths in 2 cabins. Sink. Icebox. 1 open toilet.
Variations:	Optional outboard
Sails:	Area 17.7m2 (10.8 + 6.9)/190 sq. ft. (116 + 74)
Rigging:	Sloop
Price Guide:	$5,485us
Summary:	An attractive offshore cruiser built to the high standards of C & C.

GIPSY II

Design:	Rodney Warrington Smythe, England 1960
Supplier:	Penryn Boatbuilding Co., England
Specifications:	*Construction:* Hard chine marine ply
	LWL: 5.79m/19'0
	LOA: 7.32m/24'0
	Beam: 2.59m/8'6
	Draft: 0.84m/2'9
	Displ: 1,780kg/3,920 lbs
	Ballast: 454kg/1,000 lbs
Fittings:	Twin bilge
Interior:	4/5 berths. 1.58m/5'2 headroom.
Variations:	Optional power.
Sails:	Area 22.3m^2/240 sq.ft.
Rigging:	Bermudan sloop
Price Guide:	£4,000
Summary:	Comfortable and economic under sail or power. Complete inventory included in basic price. Can be trailed. Kits and mouldings available.

NORTH STAR

Design:	Colin Mudie, England
Supplier:	W. Richardson & Co., England

Specifications:	Construction:	Multi-skin moulded wood
	LWL:	5.56m/18'3
	LOA:	7.32m/24'0
	Beam:	2.21m/7'3
	Draft:	0.99m/3'3
	Displ:	1,525kg/3,360 lbs

Fittings:	To specification
Interior:	4 berths. 1.45m/4'9 headroom.
Sails:	Area 24.7m^2/266 sq.ft.
Rigging:	Masthead sloop
Price Guide:	On application
Summary:	Big cockpit, wide decks and high protective cockpit coamings make this a practical and safe boat for families with children.

SEAFARER SAIL'N TRAIL 24

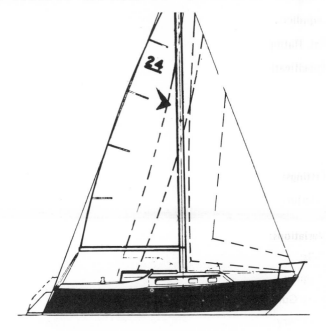

Design:	Philip L. Rhodes, U.S.A. 1970
Supplier:	Seafarer Fiberglass Yachts, U.S.A.
Est. Rating:	17.7' MORC
Specifications:	*Construction:* GRP
	LWL: 6.32m/20'9
	LOA: 7.32m/24'0
	Beam: 2.39m/7'10
	Draft: 0.53m/1'9
	Displ: 1,521kg/3,350 lbs
	Ballast: 681kg/1,500 lbs
Fittings:	Swing keel. Lead ballast. GRP deck. Aluminium spars.
Interior:	5 berths in 2 cabins. 1.45m–1.78m/4'9–5'10 cabin headroom.
Variations:	Optional interiors available. Race or cruising decks available.
Sails:	Area 23.9m^2 (10.3 + 13.6)/257 sq.ft. (111 + 146)
Rigging:	Sloop
Price Guide:	$15,200us
Summary:	Can be trailed.

T-24

Design:	Ted Tyler, U.S.A. 1961
Supplier:	Tylercraft, U.S.A.
Est. Rating:	17.5' IOR Mk III Portsmouth secondary yardstick 95

Specifications:

Construction:	GRP
LWL:	6.1m/20'0
LOA:	7.32m/24'0
Beam:	2.26m/7'5
Draft:	0.61m–1.14m/2'0–3'9
Displ:	1,816kg/4,000 lbs
Ballast:	749kg/1,650 lbs

Fittings:	Iron ballast. GRP deck. Aluminium spars.
Interior:	5 berths in 2 cabins. Sink. Pump. Stove. Icebox. Enclosed sea toilet.
Variations:	Twin or fin keel models available.
Sails:	Area 23.7m^2/255 sq.ft.
Rigging:	Sloop
Price Guide:	On application
Summary:	A popular cruiser/racer worldwide.

WEEKENDER

Design:	Sparkman & Stephens, U.S.A.
Supplier:	Sparkman & Stephens, U.S.A.

Specifications:

Construction:	GRP
LWL:	5.26m/17'3
LOA:	7.37m/24'2
Beam:	1.91m/6'3
Draft:	1.07m/3'6
Displ:	976.1kg/2,150 lbs

Fittings:	GRP deck. Aluminium spars. Iron ballast.
Interior:	4 berths in 2 cabins
Variations:	Power optional. Galley optional.
Sails:	Area 20.3m^2/218 sq.ft.
Rigging:	Sloop
Price Guide:	On application

TRIDENT 24

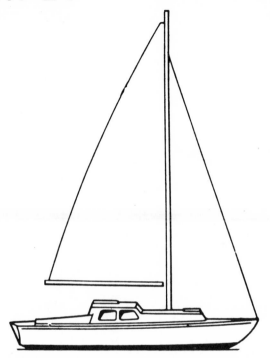

Design:	Alan F. Hill, England
Supplier:	Marine Construction (UK) Ltd., England
Est. Rating:	Portsmouth number 96
Specifications:	*Construction:* GRP
	LWL: 5.79m/19'0
	LOA: 7.32m/24'0
	Beam: 2.26m/7'5
	Draft: 1.12m–0.76m/3'8–2'6
Fittings:	GRP deck
Interior:	4 berths
Variations:	Fin or bilge keel models available
Sails:	Area 22.8m^2/245 sq.ft.
Rigging:	Bermudan sloop
Price Guide:	£4,500
Summary:	Responsive, easy on the helm and safe.

COGNAC

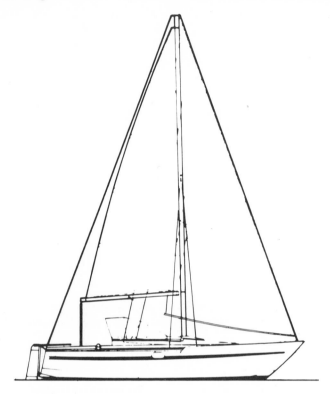

Design:	Phillippe Harlé, France	
Supplier:	Aubin Marine, France	
Est. Rating:	18.7' IOR	
Specifications:	*Construction:*	Wood
	LWL:	5.90m/19'4½
	LOA:	7.35m/24'1½
	Beam:	2.72m/8'11
	Draft:	1.20m−1.40m/3'11−4'7
	Displ:	1,700kg/3,748 lbs
	Ballast:	665kg−760kg/1,466 lbs−1,675 lbs
Fittings:	Wooden spars	
Interior:	5 berths. Marine toilet.	
Sails:	Area 22.65m^2(11.65 + 11.00)/244 sq.ft. (125 + 119)	
Rigging:	Sloop	
Price Guide:	38,800 Fr.f.	

CAL T/4 ¼ TON

Design:	C. William Lapworth, U.S.A. 1972
Supplier:	Jensen Marine, U.S.A.
Est. Rating:	18.0′ IOR Mk III
Specifications:	*Construction:* GRP
	LWL: 6.4m/21′0
	LOA: 7.37m/24′2
	Beam: 2.44m/8′0
	Draft: 1.22m/4′0
	Displ: 1,816kg/4,000 lbs
	Ballast: 908kg/2,000 lbs
Fittings:	GRP deck. Aluminium spars.
Interior:	4 berths in 2 cabins. 1 enclosed toilet.
Sails:	Area 23.8m^2/256 sq.ft.
Rigging:	Sloop
Price Guide:	$6,600us
Summary:	50% ballast ratio. Long waterline plus moderately high ratio sail plan give speed and stability.

SAN JUAN 24 ¼ TON

Design:	Bruce Kirby, U.S.A. 1971
Supplier:	Clark Boat Co., U.S.A.
Est. Rating:	18.0' IOR Mk III 18'8 MORC
Specifications:	*Construction*

LWL:	5.79m/19'0
LOA:	7.37m/24'2
Beam:	2.44m/8'0
Draft:	1.22m/4'0
Displ:	1,498kg/3,300 lbs
Ballast:	726kg/1,600 lbs

Fittings:	Lead ballast. 6HP outboard. Teak trim.
Interior:	4 berths in 2 cabins. Sink. Stove. Chemical toilet.
Sails:	Area 22.4m^2 (9.4 + 13)/241 sq.ft. (101 + 140) Spinnaker area 480 sq.ft.
Rigging:	Sloop
Price Guide:	$5,900us
Summary:	Many racing successes to her name. Beautifully finished interior.

GREENWICH 24

Design:	George Stadel, U.S.A.	
Supplier:	Allied Boat Co., U.S.A.	
Specifications:	*Construction:*	GRP
	LWL:	5.31m/17'5
	LOA:	7.39m/24'3
	Beam:	2.21m/7'3
	Draft:	0.91m/3'0
	Displ:	1,737kg/3,825 lbs
	Ballast:	681kg/1,500 lbs
Fittings:	GRP deck. Aluminium spars. Lead ballast.	
Interior:	5 berths in 2 cabins	
Variations:	Power optional	
Sails:	Area 20.9m^2/225 sq.ft.	
Rigging:	Sloop	
Price Guide:	$7,500us	
Summary:	An old design that is kept alive by popular demand.	

BALATON 24

Design:	Hungary
Supplier:	Hungarian Shipyards and Crane Factory
	V. G. Waring & Son, U.K.

Specifications:

	Construction:	GRP
	LWL:	6.45m/21'2
	LOA:	7.45m/24'4
	Beam:	2.30m/7'6½
	Draft:	1.20m/3'11
	Displ:	580kg/1,279 lbs
	Ballast:	1,650kg/3,638 lbs

Fittings:	Raised deck. Self-draining cockpit.
Interior:	5 berths
Variations:	Inboard or outboard engine. Fin or bilge keel models.
Sails:	Area 25.50m^2/274 sq. ft.
Rigging:	Bermudan sloop
Price Guide:	On application
Summary:	A comfortable, safe and fast cruiser for offshore, estuary or lake cruising.

SPIRIT 24

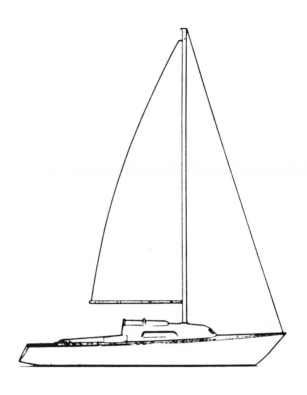

Design:	E. G. Van de Stadt, Holland	
Supplier:	George Stead Yachts, England	
Specifications:	*Construction:*	GRP
	LWL:	5.69m/18'8
	LOA:	7.39m/24'4
	Beam:	2.23m/7'4
	Draft:	1.47m/4'10
Fittings:	Fin keel. 4 hp outboard.	
Interior:	5 berths	
Sails:	Area 26m^2/280 sq.ft.	
Rigging:	Sloop	
Price Guide:	On application	

EXTENSION

Design:	Jac de Ridder, Holland 1973
Supplier:	George Stead Yachts, England
Est. Rating:	19.0' IOR

Specifications:

Construction:	GRP
LWL:	6.09m/20'0
LOA:	7.44m/24'5
Beam:	2.77m/9'1
Draft:	1.55m/5'1
Displ:	908kg/2,000 lbs
Ballast:	454kg/1,000 lbs

Fittings:	Fin keel
Interior:	5 berths
Sails:	Area 24.6m^2/265 sq.ft.
Rigging:	Sloop
Price Guide:	£1,500 hull
Summary:	Available only as a bare hull.

BRISTOL 24

Design:	Paul Coble, U.S.A. 1965
Supplier:	Bristol Yacht Co., U.S.A.
Est. Rating:	17.2' MORC

Specifications:

Construction:	GRP
LWL:	5.5m/18'1
LOA:	7.48m24'7
Beam:	2.44m/8'0
Draft:	1,05m/3'5
Displ:	2,688kg/5,920 lbs
Ballast:	1,135kg/2,500 lbs

Fittings:	Balsa core and GRP deck. Aluminium spars.
Interior:	5 berths in 2 cabins. Sink. Icebox. 1 sea toilet.
Sails:	Area 27.5m^2(14.5 + 13)/296 sq.ft. (156 + 140)
Rigging:	Sloop
Price Guide:	$6,148us

CONTESSA

Design:	Robert Tucker, England
Supplier:	Bridge Boats Ltd., England
Specifications:	*Construction:* Cold moulded mahogany
	LWL: 5.03m/16'6
	LOA: 7.47m/24'6
	Beam: 2.29m/7'6
	Draft: 0.91m/3'0
	Displ: 1,135kg/2,500 lbs
Fittings:	Lead keel
Interior:	4 berths. 1.37m/4'6 headroom
Sails:	Area 18.1m^2/195 sq.ft.
Rigging:	Sloop
Price Guide:	On application.
Summary:	A dry seaworthy hull. Stands up well to her canvas.

MEDUSA

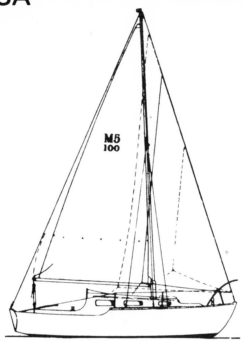

Design:	Maurice Griffiths, England
Supplier:	Carl Ziegler Yacht Agency, England
Est. Racing:	Portsmouth number: 114

Specifications:

Construction:	GRP
LWL:	5.72m/18'9
LOA:	7.47m/24'6
Beam:	2.44m/8'0
Draft:	0.76m/2'6
Displ:	2,136kg/4,704 lbs

Fittings:	Twin keel bpat. Volvo Penta 7 hp diesel auxiliary. Anodised alloy spars.
Interior:	4 berths 1.78m/5'10 headroom.
Sails:	Area 23.7m^2/255 sq.ft. Terylene.
Rigging:	Sloop
Price Guide:	On application
Summary:	Comfortable, easy to handle and cheap to maintain. Can be trailed.

OFFSHORE ¼ TON

Design:	Bernard Olesinski, U.S.A. and France 1973
Supplier:	Offshore Yachts, U.S.A.
Est. Rating:	¼ ton IOR Mk III 5.5m/18'0 IOR

Specifications:	*Construction:*	GRP
	LWL:	6.95m/19'6
	LOA:	7.47m/24'6
	Beam:	2.50m/8'2
	Draft:	1.40m/4'9
	Displ:	1,356kg/3,150 lbs
	Ballast:	574kg/1,310 lbs

Fittings:	Sandwich deck with non-skid surface. Cast iron ballast. 5.5 hp diesel auxiliary. Silver anodised spars.
Interior:	4 berths. 1.47m/5'8 headroom. Galley. Gimalde 2 Stove. Sink. Fresh water pump. Enclosed marine toilet.
Sails:	Area 21.4m^2/230 sq.ft. Spinnaker area 42.6m^2/450 sq.ft.
Rigging:	Sloop
Price Guide:	£4,750
Summary:	A new Quarter Ton Competition design. Kits and mouldings available.

PILOT 6 TON

Design:	Rodney Warrington Smyth, England 1958-59	
Supplier:	Falmouth Boat Construction Ltd., England	
Specifications:	*Construction:*	Pitch pine on oak
	LWL:	6.4m/21'0
	LOA:	7.47m/24'6
	Beam:	2.64m/8'8
	Draft:	1.17m/3'10
	Displ:	5,085kg/11,200 lbs
Fittings:	Watermeta Ford engine	
Interior:	4 berths 1.91m^2/6'3 headroom	
Sails:	Area 26.5m^2/285 sq.ft.	
Rigging:	Masthead sloop	
Price Guide:	£3,900	
Summary:	An economic motor sailer. Good size galley with ample storage space.	

SNAPDRAGON 747

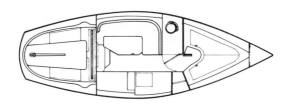

Design:	Thames Marine, England, 1972
Supplier:	Thames Marine, England
Est. Rating:	Portsmouth number 106
Specifications:	*Construction:* GRP
	LWL: 6.25m/20'6
	LOA: 7.47m/24'6
	Beam: 2.44m/8'0
	Draft: 0.76m/2'6
	Displ: 1,680kg/3,700 lbs
	Ballast: 704kg/1,550 lbs
Interior:	5 berths
Variations:	Bilge or keelboat models available. Optional inboard engine.
Sails:	Area 20.4m^2/220 sq.ft.
Rigging:	Bermudan sloop
Price Guide:	£4,000
Summary:	Can be trailed. Kits available.

CONTEST 25

Design:	Dick Zaal, Holland 19
Supplier:	Conyplex NV, Holland Interyacht, England Holland Yachts Inc., U.S.A.
Est. Rating:	Provisional Portsmouth number 101 IOR ± 18'
Specifications:	*Construction:* GRP *LWL:* 6.10m/20'0 *LOA:* 7.54m/24.67' *Beam:* 2.50m/8.25' *Draft:* 1.25m/4.10' *Displ:* 2,350kg/5,160 lbs *Ballast:* 950kg/2,100 lbs
Fittings:	7 hp Vire engine. Gold anodised, sound deadened mast.
Interior:	5 berths. Cabin height 1.80m/6'0
Variations:	Volvo Penta diesel engine as an alternative
Sails:	Area 25.2m^2/271 sq.ft.
Rigging:	Sloop. Stainless steel and terylene standing and running rigging.
Price Guide:	£6,700
Summary:	Planned with ¼ Ton competitions in mind, still comfortable for family racing or cruising.

SANTANA 25 ¼ TON

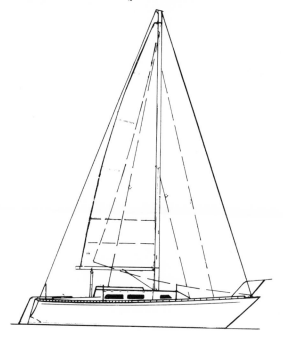

Design:	Chad Turner, U.S.A. 1972
Supplier:	W. D. Schock Corporation, U.S.A.
Est. Rating:	18.0' IOR

Specifications:

Construction:	GRP
LWL:	5.94m/19'6
LOA:	7.49m/24'7
Beam:	2.39m/7'10
Draft:	1.24m/4'1
Displ:	1,839kg/4,050 lbs
Ballast:	817kg/1,800 lbs

Fittings:	Iron ballast. GRP deck. Aluminium spars.
Interior:	4 berths in 2 cabins. Icebox. Sink. Toilet.
Variations:	Swing keel model also available.
Sails:	Area 24.3m²/262 sq.ft. Spinnaker area 40m²/431 sq.ft.
Rigging:	Sloop
Price Guide:	$6,950us
Summary:	One of the largest Quarter Ton boats afloat.

VENTURE 224

Design:	Roger N. MacGregor, U.S.A.
Supplier:	MacGregor Yacht Corporation, U.S.A.

Specifications:

Construction:	GRP
LWL:	6.5m/21'4
LOA:	7.49m/24'7
Beam:	2.41m/7'11
Draft:	1.52m/5'0
Displ:	953kg/2,100 lbs
Ballast:	261kg/575 lbs

Fittings:	Iron swing keel. GRP deck. Aluminium spars.
Interior:	5 berths in 1 cabin. Icebox. Sink. Pump. Headroom 1.85m/6'1
Variations:	Optional toilet. 1½–10 hp outboard.
Sails:	Area 21.5m^2/231 sq.ft.
Rigging:	Sloop
Price Guide:	$3,000us
Summary:	Designed to combine maximum comfort with easy single-handed sailing and high performance.

ALBIN 25

Design:	Sweden
Supplier:	Albin Marine, U.K.
	Albin Marine, Sweden

Specifications:

Construction:	GRP
LOA:	7.62m/25'0
Draft:	0.71m/2'4

Fittings:	Bilge keel
Interior:	4 berths
Sails:	Area 8.4m^2/90 sq.ft.
Rigging:	Bermudan sloop
Price Guide:	£6,000

FAMILY FOUR

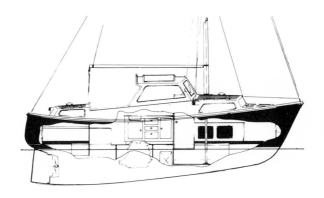

Supplier:	Jachtbonw Steyn b.v., Holland
Specifications:	*Construction:*

LOA:	7.50m/24'7½
Beam:	2.80m/9'2
Draft:	0.90m/2'11½
Displ:	2,000kg/4,409 lbs
Ballast:	Optional

Fittings:	Volvo Penta 25PK diesel engine
Interior:	2 berths
Variations:	Available as a motor cruiser only
Sails:	Area optional
Rigging:	Sloop
Price Guide:	38,500 fl.

JAKON-KRUISER I & II

Design:	Holland	
Supplier:	Jachtwerf Volendam, Holland	
Specifications:	*Construction:*	Steel
	LWL:	6.10m/20'
	LOA:	7.50m–8.10m/24'7½–26'7
	Beam:	2.24m–2.45m/7'4–8'0½
	Draft:	1.05m/3'5
	Displ:	1,764 lbs
	Ballast:	800–1,500kg/1764lbs – 3,307lbs
Interior:	4 berths	
Sails:	Area 23m^2 and 25.2m^2/248 and 271 sq.ft. Spinnaker area 35m^2 and 41.5m^2/377 and 447 sq.ft.	
Rigging:	Sloop	
Price Guide:	16,000 and 21,000 D.Fl.	

ERICSON 25 ¼ TON

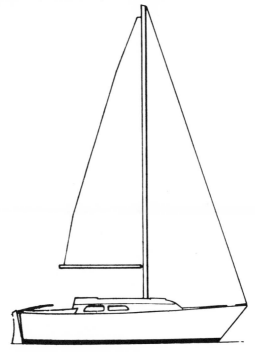

Design: Bruce King, U.S.A. 1972

Supplier: Ericson Yachts Inc., U.S.A.
Hamble Marine, U.K.
Nordmarine, Italy

Est. Rating: 18.0' IOR Mk III

Specifications:

Construction:	GRP
LWL:	6.35m/20'10
LOA:	7.52m/24'8
Beam:	2.44m/8'0
Draft:	0.61m/2'0
Displ:	2,452kg/5,400 lbs
Ballast:	1,135kg/2,500 lbs

Fittings: GRP deck. Aluminium spars.

Interior: 4—5 berths in 2 cabins. 1.68m/5'6 headroom

Variations: Optional 6—8HP outboard

Sails: Area 24.6m^2 (9.8 + 14.8)/265 sq.ft. (105 + 160)

Rigging: Sloop

Price Guide: £5,650/$7,700us

LISTANG ¼ TON

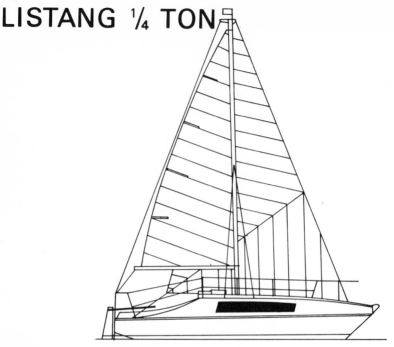

Design:	Feltz, 1969
Supplier:	Juxtamare Marine, U.K. Intermarine Agency, U.S.A.
Est. Rating:	18—19' IOR Mk III
Specifications:	*Construction:* GRP *LWL:* 5.81m/19'1 *LOA:* 7.52m/24'8 *Beam:* 2.49m/8'2 *Draft:* 1.22m/4'0 *Displ:* 1,362kg/3,000 lbs *Ballast:* 272kg/600 lbs
Fittings:	Keelboat. Cast iron ballast. GRP and balsa core deck. Aluminium spars.
Interior:	6 berths in 2 cabins
Variations:	Cruising or racing models available
Sails:	Area 21.5m^2(9.4 + 12.1)/231 sq.ft. (101 + 130)
Rigging:	Sloop
Price Guide:	£4,675/$6,500—7,800us
Summary:	Exceptional ability in bad weather. Kits and mouldings available.

CARAVEL

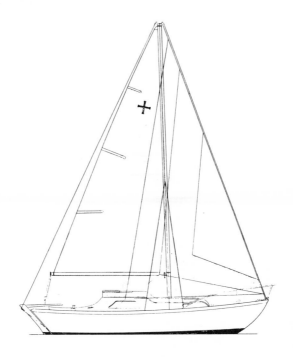

Design:	David Cheverton, England 1965
Supplier:	David Cheverton Ltd., England
Est. Rating:	Portsmouth number 101

Specifications:	*Construction:*	Mahogany on laminated frames
	LWL:	5.79m/19'0
	LOA:	7.54m/24'9
	Beam:	2.44m/8'0
	Draft:	1.16m/3'8
	Displ:	3,051kg/6,720 lbs

Fittings:	Penta 6 hp diesel auxiliary.
Interior:	4 berths
Sails:	Area 25.2m^2/271 sq.ft. Terylene.
Rigging:	Bermudan sloop
Price Guide:	£4,200
Summary:	Capable of offshore passages in all weathers. A very comfortable and easily handled sea-going boat.

WHITE SQUAW

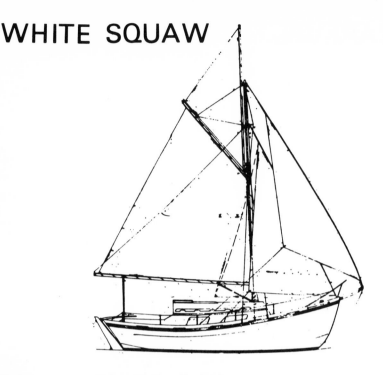

Design:	Robert Tucker, England
Supplier:	Bridge Boats, England
Specifications:	*Construction:* Wood
	LWL: 5.79m/19'0
	LOA: 7.54m/24'9
	Beam: 2.8m/9'2
	Draft: 0.91m/3'0
	Displ: 2,034kg/4,480 lbs
	Ballast: 661kg/1,456 lbs
Fittings:	To specification
Interior:	5 berths
Variations:	Engine, fuel and water capacity all optional
Sails:	Area 30.7m²/330 sq.ft.
Rigging:	Gaff cutter
Price Guide:	£4,000+
Summary:	The top sail cutter is a very flexible rig and allows a large amount of canvas without excessive mast height or vast wardrobe of sails. Built originally for work around the western approaches and thus very tough and able boat.

CAPE 25

Design:	Cape Dory Co., U.S.A. 1972
Supplier:	Cape Dory Co. Inc., U.S.A.

Specifications:

Construction:	GRP
LWL:	5.49m/18'0
LOA:	7.57m/24'10
Beam:	2.21m/7'3
Draft:	0.91m/3'0
Displ:	1,748kg/3,850 lbs
Ballast:	681kg/1,500 lbs

Fittings:	Lead ballast. GRP deck. Aluminium spars.
Interior:	4 berths in 2 cabins
Variations:	Optional stove. Optional outboard.
Sails:	Area 21.2m^2 (12.8 + 8.4)/228 sq.ft. (138 + 90)
Rigging:	Sloop
Price Guide:	$6,995us
Summary:	A pleasant combination of safety, comfort and good looks.

CAPE DORY 25

Design:	Cape Dory Co., U.S.A. 1974	
Supplier:	Cape Dory Co., U.S.A.	
Specifications:	*Construction:*	GRP
	LWL:	18'0
	LOA:	24'10
	Beam:	7'3
	Draft:	3'0
	Displ:	3,850 lbs
	Ballast:	1,500 lbs
Fittings:	Lead ballast. Teak trim. Self-bailing cockpit.	
Interior:	4 berths. Marine toilet.	
Sails:	Area 228 sq.ft.	
Rigging:	Sloop	
Price Guide:	$4,500us	
Summary:	A well-finished, beautifully lined boat that has been completely designed with the yachtsman in mind.	

DELANTA

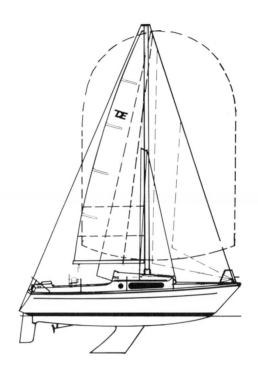

Design:	E. G. van der Stadt, Holland 1973
Supplier:	Dehler Jachtboun b.v., Holland
Specifications:	*Construction:* GRP
	LWL: 6.10m/20'
	LOA: 7.60m/24'11
	Beam: 2.48m/8'2
	Draft: 1.25m/4'1
	Displ: 1,500kg/3,307 lbs
	Ballast: 600kg/1,323 lbs
Fittings:	Aluminium spars. Vire 7 hp inboard engine. Sandwich GRP deck.
Interior:	5 berths. Enclosed toilet.
Sails:	Area 30.1m^2/324 sq.ft. Spinnaker area 40.3m^2/434 sq.ft.
Rigging:	Sloop
Price Guide:	35,880 fl.

MORGAN 24

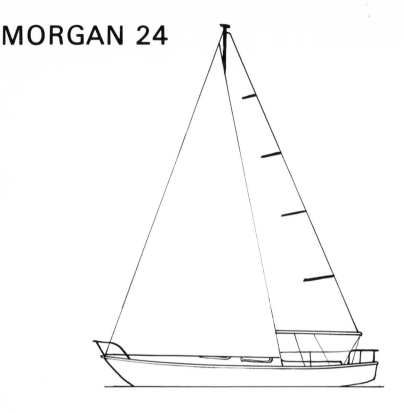

Design:	Charles E. Morgan Jnr
Supplier:	Morgan Yacht Corporation, U.S.A. Peter Webster Ltd., England

Specifications:

	Construction:	GRP
	LWL:	6.55m/21'6
	LOA:	7.6m/24'11
	Beam:	2.44m/8'0
	Draft:	1.93m/6'4
	Displ:	2,225kg/4,900 lbs
	Ballast:	863kg/1,900 lbs

Fittings:	GRP deck. Aluminium spars. Lead ballast.
Interior:	4 berths in 2 cabins. Galley standard.
Variations:	Auxiliary power optional
Sails:	Area 28.8m^2/310 sq.ft.
Rigging:	Sloop
Price Guide:	$8,000us

CAL 25

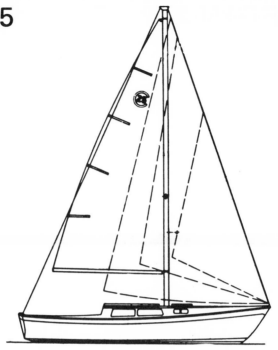

Design:	C. William Lapworth, U.S.A. 1965
Supplier:	Jensen Marine, U.S.A.
Specifications:	*Construction:* GRP
	LWL: 6.1m/20'0
	LOA: 7.62m/25'0
	Beam: 2.44m/8'0
	Draft: 1.22m/4'0
	Displ: 1,816kg/4,000 lbs
	Ballast: 771.8kg/1,700 lbs
Fittings:	Lead ballast. GRP deck. Aluminium spars. Spade rudder.
Interior:	5 berths in 2 cabins. Galley — icebox, sink, stove. 6'4 headroom.
Variations:	Optional outboard and galley
Sails:	Area 26.57m^2/286 sq.ft.
Rigging:	Masthead sloop
Price Guide:	$8,500us
Summary:	Over 300 boats now in the water. There is a strong class association. Fast with a long waterline.

NORTHERN 25

Design:	Northern Yachts, Canada 1970
Supplier:	Northern Yachts Ltd., Canada
Rating:	21.0' IOR Mk III.
Specifications:	*Construction:* GRP
	LWL: 5.79m/19'0
	LOA: 7.62m/25'0
	Beam: 2.44m/8'0
	Draft: 1.22m/4'0
	Displ: 2,179kg/4,800 lbs
	Ballast: 1,044kg/2,300 lbs
Fittings:	Lead ballast. Fiberglass & balsa core deck. Aluminium spars. Outboard.
Interior:	5 berths in 2 cabins. Icebox. Stove and w/pumps. Enclosed head.
Sails:	Area 28.3m^2(13 + 15.3)/305 sq.ft. (140 + 1?5)
Rigging:	Sloop
Price Guide:	$7,500
Summary:	Beautifully finished and comfortable racer/cruiser.

WING 25

Design:	Colin Mudie (hull) E.G. van der Stadt (superstructure) England and Holland
Supplier:	A. V. Robertson, Scotland Reedcraft, England
Specifications:	*Construction:* GRP
	LWL: 5.49m/18'0
	LOA: 7.62m/25'0
	Beam: 2.44m/8'0
	Draft: 1.09m/3'7
Fittings:	Fin keel. 6½ hp Lister diesel engine.
Interior:	4 berths in 2 cabins. 1.83m/6'0 headroom.
Sails:	Area 23.7m^2/255 sq.ft.
Rigging:	Bermudan masthead sloop
Price Guide:	£4,500
Summary:	Can be trailed. Shallow draft and generous beam for maximum comfort makes this a good family cruiser.

MIDSHIP 25

Design:	Robert Finch, U.S.A.

Supplier:	Midship Yacht Co., U.S.A.

Specifications:

Construction:	GRP
LWL:	6.76m/22'2
LOA:	7.62m/25'0
Beam:	2.44m/8'0
Draft:	0.36m/1'2
Displ:	1,770.6kg/3,900 lbs
Ballast:	431.3kg/950 lbs

Fittings: Aluminium spars. Cast iron ballast.

Interior: 5 berths. 5'9 headroom.

Variations: Optional power. Retractable or fixed keel models.

Sails: Area 24.15m^2/260 sq.ft.

Rigging: Sloop

Price Guide: $7,000us

Summary: Modern hull design plus spaciousness. Thoroughly tank tested hull.

731

NORTH STAR 500

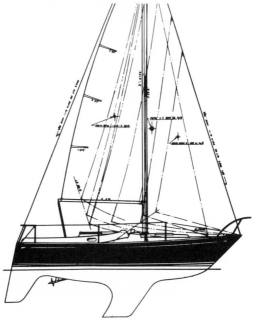

Design: Sparkman & Stephens, Canada 1973

Supplier: North Star Yachts, Canada
Hughes Boat Works Ltd.

Rating: 18'0 IOR Mk III

Specifications:
Construction:	GRP	
LWL:	6.17m/20'3	
LOA:	7.62m/25'0	
Beam:	2.74m/9'0	
Draft:	1.52m/5'0	
Displ:	1,951kg/4,298 lbs	
Ballast:	776kg/1,710 lbs	

Fittings: Fin keel. Lead ballast. GRP deck with balsa core. Aluminium spars. Auxiliary 30 hp Universal Atomic 4 gasoline.

Interior: 3 berths. 2 cabins. Sink. Icebox. Pot pourri recirculating toilet.

Sails: Area 26.8m^2/289 sq.ft.

Rigging: Sloop

Price Guide: £5,700/$12,500us

Summary: A new competition boat.

SEARIDER 25

Design:	L. H. James, England 1963	
Supplier:	Searider Yachts, England	
Est. Rating:	Portsmouth number 110	
Specifications:	*Construction:*	GRP
	LWL:	6.25m/20'6
	LOA:	7.62m/25'0
	Beam:	2.36m/7'9
	Draft:	0.91m/3'0
	Displ:	2,270kg/5,000 lbs
Fittings:	30 hp diesel.	
Interior:	5 berths. 1.83m/6'0 headroom.	
Variations:	Twin or fin keel	
Sails:	Area 26.01m^2/280 sq.ft.	
Rigging:	Sloop	
Price Guide:	£4.300	
Summary:	Sails or motors at 6 knots.	

C & C 25

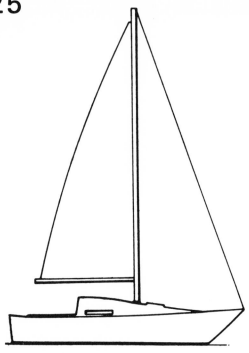

Design:	C & C Design Group, Canada 1972
Supplier:	C & C Yachts Manufacturing, Canada
Est. Rating:	20.5' IOR Mk III 20.8' MORC
Specifications:	*Construction:* GRP
	LWL: 6.3m/20'8
	LOA: 7.64m/25'1
	Beam: 2.62m/8'7
	Draft: 1.14m/3'9
	Displ: 1,880kg/4,140 lbs
	Ballast: 949kg/2,090 lbs
Fittings:	Lead ballast. Balsa core and GRP deck. Aluminium spars.
Interior:	5 berths in 2 cabins
Sails:	Area 28.4m^2(12.4 + 16)/306 sq.ft. (133 + 173)
Rigging:	Sloop
Price Guide:	$8,750us
Summary:	Available through dealers.

LA PAZ 25

Design:	Lyle C. Hess, U.S.A.
Supplier:	Coastal Recreation Inc., U.S.A.

Specifications:

Construction:	GRP
LWL:	7.11m/23'4
LOA:	7.64m/25'1
Beam:	2.44m/8'0
Draft:	0.61m/2'0
Displ:	2,088kg/4,600 lbs
Ballast:	545kg/1,200 lbs

Fittings: Shoal draft keel. 25HP Volvo engine. GRP deck. Teak trim.

Interior: 6 berths. 1.93m/6'4 headroom. Enclosed head with shower.

Sails: Area 22.8m²/245 sq.ft.

Rigging: Sloop

Price Guide: On application

Summary: Designed specifically for family cruising with self-tending jib, inboard engine and spacious interior. Can be trailed. 600 mile cruising range under power.

TIGER WESTERLY

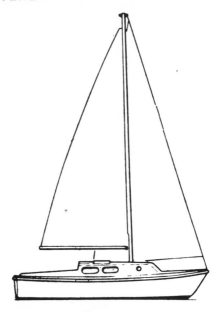

Design:	John Butler, England 1969
Supplier:	Westerly Marine Construction, England Andrew Gemeny & Sons, U.S.A.
Est. Rating:	19.2' MORC

Specifications:

Construction:	GRP
LWL:	6.65m/21'10
LOA:	7.64m/25'1
Beam:	2.67m/8'9
Draft:	1.3m/4'3
Displ:	2,390kg/5,264 lbs
Ballast:	1,017kg/2,240 lbs

Fittings:	Fin keel. Iron ballast. GRP spars.
Interior:	6 berths in 2 cabins. Sink. Icebox. 1 enclosed marine toilet.
Variations:	Optional inboard or outboard
Sails:	Area 26.8m^2/288 sq.ft.
Rigging:	Bermudan sloop
Price Guide:	£4,800/$11,750us
Summary:	A good, dry seaboat that points high. Can be sailed single-handed. Can be trailed. Kits available.

TOP HAT

Design:	Illingworth & Primrose, England
Supplier:	Illingworth & Primrose, England
Est. Rating:	Portsmouth number 94
Specifications:	*Construction:* Cold moulded marine ply
	LWL: 6.4m/21'0
	LOA: 7.64m/25'1
	Beam: 2.44m/8'0
	Draft: 1.3m/4'3
	Displ: 2,583kg/5,690 lbs
Fittings:	To specifications
Interior:	4 berths. 1.83m/6'0 headroom
Variations:	Modifications to layout available
Sails:	Area 26.6m^2/286 sq.ft.
Rigging:	Masthead sloop
Price Guide:	£4,600+
Summary:	Designed to suit both the cruising and racing man. Spacious accommodation.

WESTERLY 25

Design:	D. A. Rayner, England 1964
Supplier:	Westerly Marine Construction, England
Rating:	Portsmouth secondary yardstick 107
Specifications:	*Construction:* GRP
	LWL: 6.4m/21'0
	LOA: 7.64m/25'1
	Beam: 2.26m/7'5
	Draft: 0.76m/2'6
	Displ: 1,797kg/3,595 lbs
Fittings:	6 hp Johnson engine on retractable carriage. Burma teak trim. Self-drain cockpit.
Interior:	4 berths. 1.78m/5'10 headroom.
Sails:	Area 25.6m^2/276 sq.ft.
Rigging:	Bermuda sloop.
Price Guide:	£4,200
Summary:	A real racing craft that can navigate shallow waters and be trailed behind a car.

CHAPPIQUIDICK

Design:	Edward S. Brewer, U.S.A. 1969
Supplier:	Edward S. Brewer, U.S.A.
Specifications:	*Construction:* GRP
	LWL: 7.32m/24'0
	LOA: 7.7m/25'3
	Beam: 3.66m/12'0
	Draft: 0.91m/3'0 cb up
	Displ: 4,585kg/10,100 lbs
	Ballast: 908kg/2,000 lbs
Fittings:	Lead ballast. GRP deck. Aluminium spars.
Interior:	4 berths in 1 cabin. Standard galley.
Variations:	Optional diesel auxiliary
Sails:	Area 48.5m^2/522 sq.ft.
Rigging:	Sloop
Price Guide:	On application

HUGHES 25

Design:	Howard Hughes, Canada
Supplier:	Hughes Boat Works, Canada
Specifications:	*Construction:* GRP
	LWL: 5.79m/19'0
	LOA: 7.67m/25'2
	Beam: 2.29m/7'6
	Draft: 0.99m/3'3
	Displ: 1,589kg/3,500 lbs
	Ballast: 726kg/1,600 lbs
Fittings:	Teak trim. Magnesium alloy hardware. 6 hp outboard auxiliary.
Interior:	5 berths. 1.45m/4'9 headroom.
Variations:	Choice of interior layouts
Sails:	Area 27.9m²/300 sq. ft. Spinnaker area 44m²/474 sq. ft.
Rigging:	Sloop
Price Guide:	$12,000us
Summary:	Stiff, light and responsive. Well equipped. Safe and easy to handle. Also known as **North Star 25**.

FISHER 25

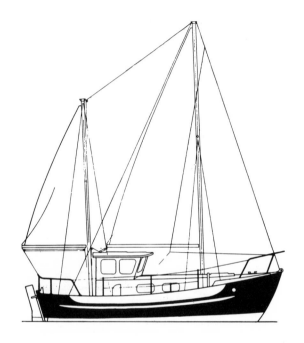

Design:	Fairways Marine, England 1974	
Supplier:	Fairways Marine, England	
Specifications:	*Construction:*	GRP
	LWL:	6.38m/21'0
	LOA:	7.72m/25'3
	Beam:	2.83m/9'4
	Draft:	1.11m/3'9
	Displ:	4,984.9kg/10,980 lbs
Fittings:	Aft cockpit. Wheelhouse.	
Interior:	5 berths	
Variations:	Optional diesel power	
Sails:	Various areas	
Rigging:	Ketch	
Price Guide:	£8,400	
Summary:	Supplied with complete inventory.	

FREEWARD 25

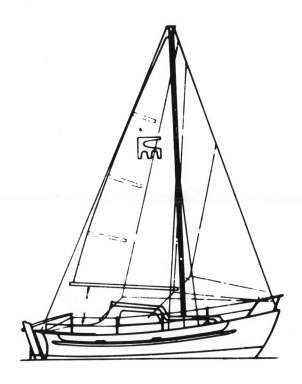

Design:	Gordon Wyatt, England 1972
Supplier:	Fairways Marine, England
Specifications:	*Construction:* GRP
	LWL: 6.4m/21'0
	LOA: 7.7m/25'3
	Beam: 2.84m/9'4
	Draft: 1.14m/3'9
	Displ: 4,540kg/10,000 lbs
	Ballast: 2,043kg/4,500 lbs
Fittings:	Finn keel. Volvo MD2B 25 hp diesel inboard.
Interior:	4/5 berths
Sails:	Area 21.8m^2/235 sq.ft.
Rigging:	Sloop (motor sailer)
Price Guide:	£7,000
Summary:	A popular motor-sailer, well equipped for her price.

VERTUE

Design:	Laurent Giles & Partners, England 1936
Supplier:	Laurent Giles & Partners, England

Specifications:	*Construction:*	As required
	LWL:	6.55m/21'6
	LOA:	7.70m/25'3
	Beam:	2.19m/7'2
	Draft:	1.37m/4'6
	Displ:	4,576kg/10,080 lbs
	Ballast:	Optional

Fittings:	To specification
Interior:	2—5 berths
Sails:	Area 35.3m^2/380 sq.ft.
Rigging:	Bermudan sloop
Price Guide:	Write for quotation
Summary:	One of the most successful cruising yachts ever designed. Great sea-going qualities — she has crossed every ocean of the world. Built to individual specification.

AMPHIBI-CON

Design:	Mount Desert Yachts, U.S.A.
Supplier:	Burr Brothers, U.S.A.

Specifications:	*Construction:*	GRP
	LWL:	6.6m/21'8
	LOA:	7.75m/25'5
	Beam:	2.36m/7'9
	Draft:	0.74m/2'5 cb up
	Displ:	1,770.6kg/3,900 lbs
	Ballast:	499.4kg/1,100 lbs

Fittings:	Wooden deck. Aluminium spars.
Interior:	4 berths in 2 cabins.
Variations:	Optional gasoline auxiliary. Galley optional
Sails:	Area 24.7m^2/266 sq.ft.
Rigging:	Sloop
Price Guide:	$8,000us
Summary:	Well-established boat.

TOMAHAWK 25

Design:	Alan Hull, England 1970
Supplier:	Marine Construction (UK) England
Est. Rating:	Portsmouth number 94
Specifications:	*Construction:* GRP
	LWL: 6.1m/20'0
	LOA: 7.72m/25'4
	Beam: 2.59m/8'6
	Draft: 1,42m or 0.91m/4'8 or 3'0
	Displ: 2,300kg/5,066 lbs
Fittings:	GRP deck. Gold anodised spars.
Interior:	5 berths
Variations:	Fin or twin keel models
Sails:	Area 26.7m^2/287 sq.ft.
Rigging:	Bermudan masthead sloop
Price Guide:	£4,800
Summary:	Light on the helm, sensitive and well balanced. Kits available.

LILL SCAMPI ¼ TON

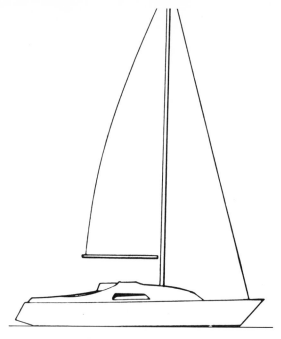

Design:	Peter Norlin, Sweden
Supplier:	Solna Marin AB, Sweden David Smithells, England

Specifications:

Construction:	GRP
LWL:	5.89m/19'4
LOA:	7.72m/25'4
Beam:	2.54m/8'4
Draft:	1.37m/4'6
Displ:	Optional
Ballast:	Optional

Fittings:	Foam sandwich deck. Cast iron fin keel. Aluminium spars. Teak trim.
Interior:	Cooker. 1 enclosed toilet.
Variations:	Optional engine
Sails:	Area optional
Rigging:	Sloop
Price Guide:	£4,600
Summary:	A well-mannered comfortable boat that is very attractive.

IRWIN 25

Design:	Ted Irwin, U.S.A. 1968
Supplier:	Irwin Yacht & Marine Corp., U.S.A.
Est. Rating:	19.0'—19.5' MORC

Specifications:

Construction:	GRP
LWL:	6.23m/20'6
LOA:	7.75m/25'5
Beam:	2.44m/8'0
Draft:	1.22m—0.81m/4'0—2'8
Displ:	2,452kg/5,400 lbs
Ballast:	829kg/1,825 lbs
	999kg/2,200 lbs

Fittings:	Lead ballast. GRP and balsa core deck. Aluminium spars. Mast 10.46m/34'4 high.
Interior:	6 berths in 2 cabins. Full galley. 1.75m/5'9 cabin headroom. 1 enclosed toilet.
Variations:	Keel or keel/centreboard options. Optional outboard.
Sails:	Area 28.1m^2(13.6 + 14.5)/302 sq.ft. (146 + 156) Spinnaker area 47m^2/506 sq.ft.
Rigging:	Sloop
Price Guide:	$9,200us
Summary:	Roomy and safe.

CONTESSA 26

Design:	David Sadler, England 1965
Supplier:	J. J. Taylor & Sons, Canada J. C. Rogers, England
Est. Rating:	20.6′ MORC IOR 20′ approx.
Specifications:	*Construction:* GRP *LWL:* 6.4m/21′0 *LOA:* 7.77m/25′6 *Beam:* 2.29m/7′6 *Draft:* 1.22m/4′0 *Displ:* 2,452kg/5,400 lbs *Ballast:* 1,044kg/2,300 lbs
Fittings:	Iron ballast. GRP deck. Aluminium spars.
Interior:	4 berths in 2 cabins
Variations:	Optional gasoline or diesel auxiliary. Various interior layouts available.
Sails:	Area 28.2m^2(13 + 15.2)/304 sq.ft. (140 + 164)
Rigging:	Sloop
Price Guide:	£3,900/$8,800
Summary:	Balanced and seaworthy, true racing yachts that has proved herself in many competitions. Kits and mouldings available.

ESSEX 26

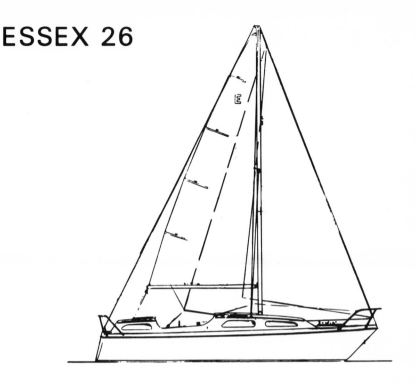

Design:	Essex Co. U.S.A. 1971
Supplier:	Essex Co. Ltd., U.S.A.

Specifications:	*Construction:*	GRP
	LWL:	7.01m/23'0
	LOA:	7.77m/25'6
	Beam:	2.41m/7'11
	Draft:	0.59m/1'11
	Displ:	1,362kg/3,000 lbs
	Ballast:	602kg/1,325 lbs

Fittings:	GRP deck. Aluminium spars. Lead ballast.
Interior:	6 berths in 3 cabins
Variations:	Optional outboard
Sails:	Area 24.2m^2 (11.1 + 13.1)/260 sq.ft. (120 + 140)
Rigging:	Sloop
Price Guide:	$6,000us
Summary:	Available through dealers.

HUSTLER 25 .5

Design: Holman & Pye, England 1972

Supplier: Island Boat Sales, England

Est. Rating: 19' ± IOR

Specifications: *Construction:*

LWL:	6.48m/21'3
LOA:	7.77m/25'6
Beam:	2.64m/8'8½
Draft:	1.47m/4'10
Displ:	2,390kg/5,264 lbs
Ballast:	1,180kg/2,600 lbs

Fittings: Fin keel. Inboard Petter 5 hp.

Interior: 5 berths

Sails: Area 26.5m^2/285 sq.ft.

Rigging: Sloop.

Price Guide: £5,000

COLUMBIA 26 MKII

Design: William H. Tripp Jnr, U.S.A.

Supplier: Columbia Yacht Corp., U.S.A.

Est. Rating: 19.9' IOR Mk III

Specifications: *Construction:*   GRP

LWL:	6.55m/21'6
LOA:	7.8m/25'7
Beam:	2.59m/8'6
Draft:	1.32m–0.97m/4'4–3'2
Displ:	2,679kg/5,900 lbs
Ballast:	1,158kg/2,550 lbs
	1,453kg/3,200 lbs

Fittings: Fin keel. GRP deck. Aluminium spars. 9.5 hp OMC outboard. Lead ballast. Teak trim.

Interior: 5 berths

Variations: Shoal draft model also available.

Sails: Area 28.8m^2/310 sq.ft. Dacron

Rigging: Sloop

Price Guide: $7,500us

Summary: Large uncluttered deck makes for pleasant sailing and handling. Over 1,000 built to date.

MAXI

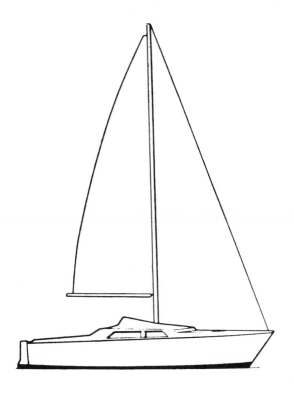

Design:	Pelle Petterson, Sweden	
Supplier:	Pelle Petterson AB, Sweden	
	Pelle Petterson (UK), England	
Specifications:	*Construction:*	GRP
	LWL:	6.71m/22'0
	LOA:	7.77m/25'6
	Beam:	2.49m/8'2
	Draft:	1.37m/4'6
	Displ:	1,627kg/3,584 lbs
Fittings:	Centreboard boat. Teak trim. 14 hp inboard engine.	
Interior:	5 berths	
Sails:	Area 25.1m^2/270 sq.ft.	
Rigging:	Sloop	
Price Guide:	£5,400+	
Summary:	Open plan Scandinavian interior design.	

BALBOA 26

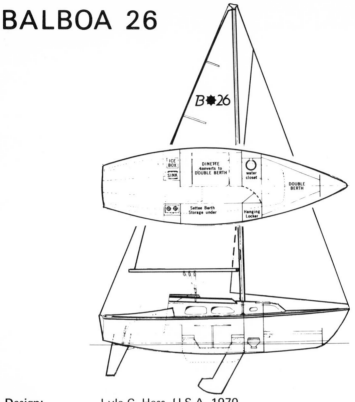

Design: Lyle C. Hess, U.S.A. 1970

Supplier: Coastal Recreation Inc., U.S.A.

Specifications:
Construction:	GRP
LWL:	6.25m/20'10
LOA:	7.8m/25'7
Beam:	2.44m/8'0
Draft:	1.52m/5'0
Displ:	1,634kg/3,600 lbs
Ballast:	545kg/1,200 lbs

Fittings: Swing keel. Teak trim. GRP and plywood deck. Aluminium spars. 9.5 hp Evinrude or Johnson outboard.

Interior: 5 berths in 2 cabins. 1 enclosed head.

Sails: Area 27.2m^2 (12.5 + 14.7)/293 sq.ft. (135 + 158)

Rigging: Sloop

Price Guide: $5,795us

Summary: Heavy, strong construction. Can be trailed and launched from any ramp. Self-righting. Stiff and safe.

ANNAPOLIS 26

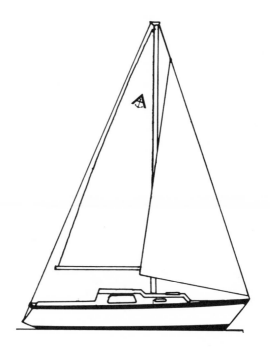

Design:	John Holmes, U.S.A. 1970
Supplier:	Tidewater Boats Inc., U.S.A.

Specifications:

Construction:	GRP
LWL:	6.1m/20'0
LOA:	7.82m/25'8
Beam:	2.44m/8'0
Draft:	1.22m/4'0
Displ:	2,225kg/4,900 lbs
Ballast:	908kg/2,000 lbs

Fittings:	Aluminium spars. GRP deck. 5 hp Petter diesel engine.
Interior:	5 berths in 2 cabins. 1 enclosed toilet. 1.70m/5'7 headroom.
Sails:	Area 27.2m^2(11.7 + 15.5)/126 + 167)
Rigging:	Sloop
Price Guide:	$7,950us
Summary:	Good sailing performance combined with rugged construction that is easily maintained.

CLIPPER Mk-26

Design:	William Crealock, U.S.A. 1972	
Supplier:	Clipper Marine Corporation, U.S.A.	
Specifications:	*Construction:*	GRP
	LWL:	6.2m/20'4
	LOA:	7.85m/25'9
	Beam:	2.41m/7'11
	Draft:	1.62m–1.22m/5'4–4'0
	Displ:	1,090kg–1,208kg/2,400–2,660 lbs
	Ballast:	245kg–363kg/540–800 lbs
Fittings:	Cast iron ballast. GRP deck. Aluminium spars.	
Interior:	5 berths in 2 cabins	
Variations:	Swing keel and fixed keel models available. Optional gasoline outboard.	
Sails:	Area 24m^2 (10.8 + 13.2)/258 sq.ft. (116 + 142)	
Rigging:	Sloop	
Price Guide:	$5,500us	
Summary:	Incorporates quality, performance, safety and comfort. A perfect family cruising sailboat.	

FOLKBOAT INTERNATIONAL

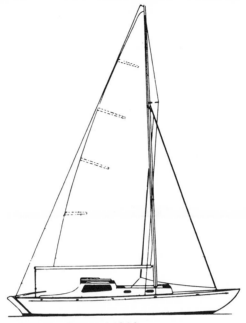

Design:	Tord Sunden, Finland 1966
Supplier:	City Centre Boatyard, England Oxford Yacht Sales, U.S.A.
Est. Rating:	18.6' MORC Portsmouth secondary yardstick 100 and 96 stripped.

Specifications:

Construction:	GRP
LWL:	6.02m/19'9
LOA:	7.85m/25'9
Beam:	2.26m/7'5
Draft:	1.22m/4'0
Displ:	2,157kg/4,750 lbs
Ballast:	1,249kg/2,750 lbs

Fittings:	GRP deck. Aluminium spars. 6 hp outboard.
Interior:	4 berths in 2 cabins
Variations:	Optional toilet.
Sails:	Area 26m^2 (16 + 10)/280 sq.ft. (172 + 108)
Rigging:	Sloop
Price Guide:	£4,500/$8,500us
Summary:	Clean lined boat that has proved itself in many long-distance races.

HAIDA 26

Design:	Ray Richards, U.S.A. 1965
Supplier:	Gove's Cove Yacht Basin, U.S.A.
Est. Rating:	23.6' CCA

Specifications:	*Construction:*	GRP
	LWL:	6.4m/21'0
	LOA:	7.85m/25'9
	Beam:	2.51m/8'3
	Draft:	1.37m/4'6
	Displ:	1,952kg/4,300 lbs
	Ballast:	817kg/1,800 lbs

Fittings:	Iron ballast. GRP deck. Aluminium spars.
Interior:	4 berths in 2 cabins. Standard galley. 1 enclosed toilet.
Variations:	Optional outboard
Sails:	Area 30.7m^2/330 sq.ft.
Rigging:	Sloop
Price Guide:	$7,800us

ATLANTA

Design:	Fairey/Uffa Fox, England
Supplier:	Fairey Marine, England
Est. Rating:	Portsmouth secondary yardstick 100

Specifications:	*Construction:*	Hot moulded marine ply
	LWL:	7.47m/24'6
	LOA:	7.92m/26'0
	Draft:	1.75m/5'9
	Displ:	2,034kg/4,480 lbs

Fittings:	All main ballast retractable.
Interior:	6 berths
Sails:	Area 22.7m^2/244 sq.ft.
Rigging:	Ketch
Price Guide:	£5,100
Summary:	A very effective sea-going cruiser.

MYSTERE

Design:	F. R. Parker, England 1970
Supplier:	Langstone Marine, England
Est. Rating:	Portsmouth number 98
Specifications:	*Construction:* GRP
	LWL: 5.64m/18'6
	LOA: 7.85m/25'9
	Beam: 2.59m/8'6
	Draft: 0.84m–1.37m/2'9–4'6
	Displ: 2,293kg/5,050 lbs
	Ballast: 1,017kg/2,240 lbs
Fittings:	To specification
Interior:	6 berths
Variations:	Bilge keel or keelboat. Optional inboard engine.
Sails:	Area 16.7m²/180 sq. ft.
Rigging:	Bermudan sloop
Price Guide:	£5,450
Summary:	Can be trailed.

KAISER 26

Design:	John Kaiser, U.S.A.	
Supplier:	John Kaiser Associates, U.S.A.	
Specifications:	*Construction:*	GRP
	LWL:	5.94m/19'6
	LOA:	7.87m/25'10
	Beam:	2.39m/7'10
	Draft:	1.22m/4'0
	Displ:	2,815kg/6,200 lbs
	Ballast:	1,226kg/2,700 lbs
Fittings:	Twin keel. Lead ballast. GRP deck. Aluminium spars.	
Interior:	4 berths in 2 cabins. Standard galley.	
Variations:	Optional 40 hp auxiliary.	
Sails:	Area 30.7m^2/330 sq.ft.	
Rigging:	Sloop	
Price Guide:	$9,800us	

SOUTH COAST ONE DESIGN

Design:	C. A. Nicholson, England 1955	
Supplier:	Burnes Shipyard, England	
Specifications:	*Construction:*	Mahogany
	LWL:	6.4m/21'0
	LOA:	7.9m/25'11
	Beam:	2.39m/7'10
	Draft:	1.6m/5'3
	Displ:	4,210kg/9,274 lbs
Fittings:	To specification	
Interior:	4 berths	
Sails:	Area 26.1m^2/281 sq.ft.	
Rigging:	Bermudan sloop	
Price Guide:	£4,800	
Summary:	Particularly stiff in hard weather. A comfortable ride.	

BOWMAN 26

Design:	Holman & Pye, England
Supplier:	Bowman Boats England
Specifications:	*Construction:* GRP
	LOA: 7.92m/26'0
	Draft: 1.22m/4'0
Fittings:	Fin keel
Interior:	5 berths
Variations:	Optional inboard
Sails:	Area 22.8m^2/245 sq.ft.
Rigging:	Bermudan sloop
Price Guide:	On application
Summary:	Can not be trailed.

BRISTOL 26

Design:	Halsey Herreshoff, U.S.A.
Supplier:	Bristol Yacht Co., U.S.A.
Est. Rating:	20.3' MORC
Specifications:	*Construction:* GRP
	LWL: 6.66m/21'10
	LOA: 7.92m/26'0
	Beam: 2.44m/8'0
	Draft: 0.87m/2'10 cb
	1.17m/3'10 keel
	Displ: 2,588kg/5,700 lbs
	Ballast: 1,090kg/2,400 lbs
Fittings:	Aluminium spars. Deck of balsa core and GRP. Optional outboard.
Interior:	6 berths in 2 cabins
Variations:	Keel or centreboard boats available.
Sails:	Area 30.4m^2 (14.8 + 15.6)/327 sq.ft. (159 + 168)
Rigging:	Sloop
Price Guide:	$7,320us
Summary:	Available through dealers. Also known as **Courier**.

CUTLASS 26

Design: Norway

Supplier: Yachts International, England

Specifications: *Construction:* GRP
LOA: 7.92m/26'0
Beam: 2.8m/9'2
Draft: 0.99m/3'3

Fittings: 75 hp Volvo Penta MD21 engine. Aluminium spars. Wood trim.

Interior: 5 berths

Variations: Available as a pure power cruiser, as well as the sailing version.

Sails: Area 26m^2 (18.4 + 7.6)/280 sq.ft. (198 + 82)

Rigging: Bermudan sloop

Price Guide: £7,350

Summary: An all-weather cruiser, that is convenient and comfortable.

ECUME DE MER

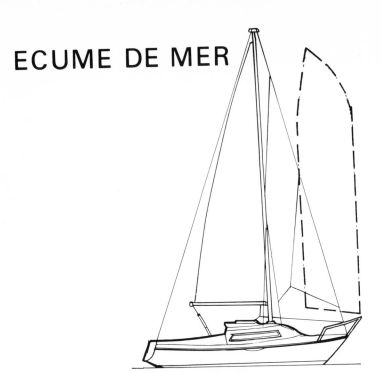

Design: Finot Group, France 1970

Supplier: Chantier Mallard, France
F. E. Sparkes, England

Est. Rating: 18.0' IOR

Specifications:

Construction:	GRP
LWL:	5.87m/19'3
LOA:	7.93m/26'0
Beam:	2.64m/8'9
Draft:	1.24m—1.52m/4'1—5'0
Displ:	1,816kg/4,000 lbs
Ballast:	731kg/1,610 lbs

Fittings: Fin keel. 5 or 9 hp engine.

Interior: 5 or 6 berths.

Variations: Cruising or racing versions available. Flush deck available.

Sails: Area 24m^2/258 sq.ft.

Rigging: Sloop

Price Guide: £5,500

Summary: Rigid hull. Adjustable backstay that gives perfect control in all conditions. Superb windward performance.

GRAMPIAN 26

Design: Alex McGruer, Canada 1970

Supplier: Grampian Marine, Canada

Specifications:

Construction:	GRP
LWL:	6.63m/21'9
LOA:	7.92m/26'0
Beam:	2.54m/8'4
Draft:	1.3m—0.91m/4'3—3'0
Displ:	2,542kg/5,600 lbs
Ballast:	1,180kg/2,600 lbs

Fittings: GRP deck. Aluminium spars.

Interior: 5 berths in 2 cabins. Flush marine toilet.

Variations: Optional outboard. Keel or keel/centreboard options.

Sails: Area 30.2m²/14.5 + 15.7)/325 sq.ft. (156 + 169)

Rigging: Sloop

Price Guide: $8,995us

Summary: Over 400 built. Good value for money.

GULF COAST 26

Design:	Martin Bludworth, U.S.A. 1971
Supplier:	Gulf Coast Sailboats, U.S.A.
Specifications:	*Construction:* GRP
	LOA: 7.92m/26'0
	Beam: 2.44m/8'0
	Draft: 0.53m/1'9 cb up
	Displ: 2,043kg/4,500 lbs
	Ballast: 965kg/2,125 lbs
Fittings:	Cast iron ballast. GRP deck. Aluminium spars.
Interior:	5 berths in 2 cabins.
Sails:	Area 28.7m^2(13.2 + 15.5)/309 sq.ft. (142 + 167)
Rigging:	Sloop
Price Guide:	$6,495us

MIC MAC SLOOP

Design:	G. W. MacVay, Canada 1968
Supplier:	MacVay Fiberglass Yachts, Canada
Specifications:	*Construction:* GRP
	LWL: 6.2m/20'4
	LOA: 7.92m/26'0
	Beam: 2.19m/7'2
	Draft: 1.12m/3'8
	Displ: 2,270kg/5,000 lbs
	Ballast: 1,135kg/2,500 lbs
Fittings:	Cast iron ballast. GRP deck. Aluminium spars.
Interior:	4 berths in one cabin. Sink. Stove. Icebox. Enclosed sea toilet or holding tank.
Sails:	Area 26.7m^2(14.6 + 12.1)/287 sq.ft. (157 + 130)
Rigging:	Sloop
Price Guide:	$8,000us
Summary:	Available through dealers.

KINGFISHER 26

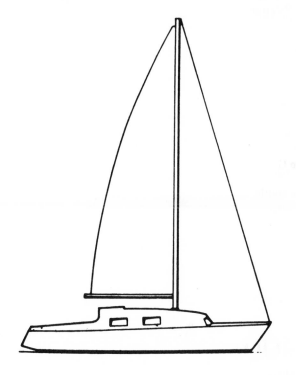

Design:	R. A. G. Nierop, England
Supplier:	Westfield Engineering Co., England
Est. Rating:	Portsmouth number 107

Specifications:		
	Construction:	GRP
	LWL:	6.4m/21'0
	LOA:	7.92m/26'0
	Beam:	2.33m/7'8
	Draft:	0.99m/3'3

Fittings:	Bilge keel
Interior:	4 berths
Variations:	Optional inboard up to 33 hp.
Sails:	Area 24.2m^2/260 sq.ft.
Rigging:	Bermudan sloop
Price Guide:	£4,000
Summary:	Can be trailed

SHE S27 ¼ TON

Design:	Sparkman & Stephens, U.S.A. 1971
Supplier:	South Hants Marine, England
Est. Rating:	18.0' IOR Mk III

Specifications:

Construction:	GRP
LWL:	5.87m/19'3
LOA:	7.92m/26'0
Beam:	2.59m/8'6
Draft:	1.45m/4'9
Displ:	2,497kg/5,500 lbs
Ballast:	1,022kg/2,250 lbs

Fittings:	Lead ballast. GRP and balsa sandwich deck. Aluminium spars. 5 hp Stuart Turner gasoline.
Interior:	5/6 berths in 2 cabins. Stove. 1 sea toilet.
Sails:	Area $25.6m^2$ (11.1 + 14.4)/275 sq.ft. (120 + 155)
Rigging:	Sloop
Price Guide	£5,850/$11,560us
Summary:	One of the best-designed and fastest boats of its size in the world. Also known as **She 26.**

SCOD

Supplier:	Burne's Shipyard, England

Specifications:

Construction:	Carvel
LOA:	7.92m/26'0
Draft:	1.6m/5'3

Fittings:	Keelboat. Inboard engine.
Interior:	4 berths
Sails:	Area $26.1m^2$/281 sq.ft.
Rigging:	Bermudan sloop
Price Guide:	£4,600

MACWESTER 26

Design:	C. S. J. Roy, England 1964	
Supplier:	Macwester Marine Co. Ltd., England	
Est. Rating:	Portsmouth number 103	
Specifications:	*Construction:*	GRP
	LWL:	6.4m/21'0
	LOA:	7.92m/26'0
	Beam:	2.8m/9'2
	Draft:	0.84m/2'9
	Displ:	3,051kg/6,720 lbs
Fittings:	To specification	
Interior:	4 berths. 1.83m/6'0 headroom.	
Variations:	Optional inboard auxiliary	
Sails:	Area 28m^2/301 sq.ft.	
Rigging:	Masthead sloop	
Price Guide:	£4,500	
Summary:	Designed to give maximum amount of accommodation and deck space, plus good cruising/sailing performance. Can be trailed.	

T-26

Design: Ted Tyler, U.S.A. 1970

Supplier: Tylercraft, U.S.A.

Specifications:

Construction:	GRP
LWL:	6.55m/21'6
LOA:	7.92m/26'0
Beam:	2.44m/8'0
Draft:	0.76m—1.22m/2'6—4'0
Displ:	2,270kg/5,000 lbs
Ballast:	999kg/2,200 lbs

Fittings: Iron ballast. GRP deck. Aluminium spars. 13 hp outboard.

Interior: 5 berths in 2 cabins. Sink. Icebox. Enclosed toilet.

Variations: Twin or fin keel models.

Sails: Area 34.6m^2/372 sq. ft.

Rigging: Sloop

Price Guide: $10,500us

MIC MAC SCHOONER

Design: G. W. McVay, Canada 1972

Supplier: Macvay Fiberglass Yachts, Canada

Specifications:

Construction:	GRP
LWL:	6.15m/20'2
LOA:	7.98m/26'2
Beam:	2.19m/7'2
Draft:	1.07m/3'6
Displ:	2,361kg/5,200 lbs
Ballast:	1,044kg/2,300 lbs

Fittings: Cast iron ballast. GRP deck. Aluminium spars. Auxiliary 5HP Westerbeke diesel.

Interior: 4 berths in 2 cabins. Sink. Stove. Icebox. Enclosed sea toilet.

Sails: Area 26.5m^2 (9.8 + 9.3 + 7.4)/285 sq. ft. (105 +100 + 80)

Rigging: Schooner

Price Guide: $12,500

SNAPDRAGON 26

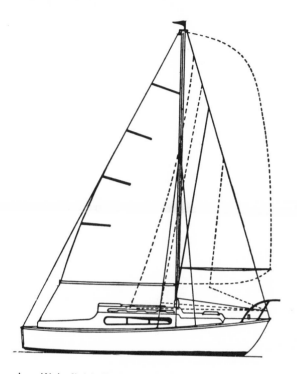

Design: Len Wakefield, England 1966

Supplier: Thames Marine, England

Est. Rating: Portsmouth number 100

Specifications:
	Construction:	GRP
	LWL:	6.6m/21'8
	LOA:	7.92m/26'0
	Beam:	2.59m/8'6
	Draft:	0.76m/2'6
	Displ:	2,043kg/4,500 lbs
	Ballast:	908kg/2,000 lbs

Fittings: Iron twin keels. GRP deck. Aluminium spars.

Interior: 5 berths in 1 cabin. Galley. 1 enclosed toilet.

Variations: Optional outboard.

Sails: Area 23.7m²/255 sq.ft.

Rigging: Sloop

Price Guide: £5,200

TARTAN 26½ TON

Design;	Thomas A. Norton, U.S.A. 1972
Supplier:	Tartan Marine, U.S.A.
Est. Rating:	21.7' IOR Mk III 21.2' MORC

Specifications:	*Construction:*	GRP
	LWL:	6.86m/22'6
	LOA:	7.92m/26'0
	Beam:	2.44m/8'0
	Draft:	1.37m/4'6
	Displ:	2,361kg/5,200 lbs
	Ballast:	999kg/2,200 lbs

Fittings:	Lead ballast. GRP deck. Aluminium spars. 12 hp Kermath diesel.
Interior:	4 berths in 1 cabin. Stove. Icebox. Sink. 1 enclosed toilet.
Sails:	Area 28.2m^2 (11.7 + 16.5)/304 sq.ft. (126 + 178)
Rigging:	Sloop
Price Guide:	$13,500us
Summary:	A handsome ½ ton competitor. Available through dealers.

WESTERLY CENTAUR

Design:	Laurent Giles, England 1968
Supplier:	Westerly Marine Construction, England Andrew Gemeny & Sons, U.S.A.
Rating:	Portsmouth primary yardstick 95
Specifications:	*Construction:* GRP *LWL:* 6.5m/21'4 *LOA:* 7.92m/26'0 *Beam:* 2.57m/8'5 *Draft:* 0.91m/3'0 *Displ:* 3,042kg/6,700 lbs *Ballast:* 1,271kg/2,800 lbs
Fittings:	Twin keels. Volvo Penta MD2B 5 hp. Aluminium spars.
Interior:	6 berths in 2 cabins. Sink. Icebox. Pump. 1 enclosed marine toilet.
Variations:	Two interior arrangements available.
Sails:	Area 27.3m^2/294 sq.ft.
Rigging:	Sloop
Basic Price:	£4,900
Summary:	Kits available. Built to withstand the rigours of offshore cruising.

WESTERLY CHIEFTAIN

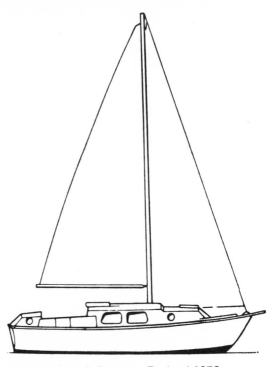

Design: Laurent Giles & Partners, England 1972

Supplier: Westerly Marine, England
Andrew Gemeny & Sons, U.S.A.

Specifications:

Construction:	GRP
LWL:	6.5m/21'4
LOA:	7.92m/26'0
Beam:	2.57m/8'5
Draft:	0.91m/3'0
Displ:	3,095kg/6,817 lbs
Ballast:	1,271kg/2,800 lbs

Fittings: Twin keel. Volvo MD2B 25 hp inboard engine.

Interior: 5 berths

Sails: Area 27.3m^2/294 sq.ft.

Rigging: Sloop

Price Guide: £5,700

Summary: Kits available.

YANKEE 26 ¼ TON

Design:	Sparkman & Stephens, U.S.A. 1973
Supplier:	Yankee Yachts Inc., U.S.A.
Est. Rating:	18.0' IOR Mk III

Specifications:

Construction:	GRP
LWL:	6.3m/20'8
LOA:	7.92m/26'0
Beam:	2.64m/8'8
Draft:	1.45m/4'9
Displ:	2,422kg/5,335 lbs
Ballast:	976kg/2,150 lbs

Fittings:	Lead ballast. GRP deck. Aluminium spars. 7 hp Westerbeke via gasoline auxiliary.
Interior:	5/6 berths in 2 cabins. Ice-chest. Sink.
Variations:	Supplied with or without power.
Sails:	Area 27.8m^2 (11.8 + 16)/299 sq.ft. (127 + 172)
Rigging:	Sloop
Price Guide:	$11,750–10,000us

NYMPHET

Design:	C. R. Holman, England
Supplier:	C. R. Holman, England
Specifications:	*Construction:* Wood
	LWL: 6.1m/20'0
	LOA: 7.98m/26'2
	Beam: 2.27m/7'5½
	Draft: 1.27m/4'2
	Displ: 2,878kg/6,339 lbs
Fittings:	STP 5MC 4 hp or Albin engine. Self-drain cockpit.
Interior:	4 berths. 1.6m/5'3 headroom.
Variations:	Alternative layouts available
Sails:	Area 27.6m^2/297 sq.ft.
Rigging:	Sloop
Price Guide:	On application
Summary:	Good performance and capable of being driven hard.

CAPITAN 26

Design:	Sparkman & Stephens, Canada
Supplier:	Chris-Craft Corporation, U.S.A.
Specifications:	*Construction:* GRP
	LWL: 5.79m/19'0
	LOA: 8m/26'3
	Beam: 2.49m/8'2
	Draft: 1.22m/4'0
	Displ: 1,952kg/4,300 lbs
	Ballast: 831kg/1,830 lbs
Fittings:	GRP deck. Aluminium spars. Iron ballast.
Interior:	2 berths in 1 cabin. Standard galley.
Variations:	Auxiliary power optional
Sails:	Area 28m^2/301 sq.ft.
Rigging:	Sloop

PEARSON 26

Design:	William H. Shaw, U.S.A. 1970
Supplier:	Pearson Yachts, U.S.A.
Specifications:	*Construction:* GRP
	LWL: 6.6m/21'8
	LOA: 7.98m/26'2
	Beam: 2.64m/8'8
	Draft: 1.22m/4'0
	Displ: 2,452kg/5,400 lbs
	Ballast: 999kg/2,200 lbs
Fittings:	Iron ballast. GRP deck. Aluminium spars.
Interior:	5 berths in 1 cabin. Sea toilet. 1.73m/5'8 cabin headroom.
Variations:	Optional galley.
Sails:	Area 29.5m^2 (12.7 + 17.5)/318 sq.ft. (137 + 189)
Rigging:	Masthead sloop
Price Guide:	$6,840us
Summary:	Fast and manoeuvrable offshore racer. Introduced at the 1970 New York Boat Show. 600 built to date.

CAPRI 26/CAPRI 30

Design:	Sparkman & Stephens, Canada
Supplier:	Chris Craft Corporation,U.S.A.
Specifications:	*Construction:* GRP
	LWL: 6.1m–7.62m/20'–25'
	LOA: 8m–9.14m/26'3–30'
	Beam: 2.49m–2.94m/8'2–9'8
	Draft: 1.22m–1.14m/4'0–3'9
	Displ: 2,179kg–533kg/4,800llbs–1,174 lbs
	Ballast: 831kg/1,830 lbs
Fittings:	Iron ballast. GRP deck. Aluminium spars.
Interior:	4/5 berths in 2 cabins. Standard galley.
Variations:	Auxiliary power optional
Sails:	Area 28m^2–44.2m^2/301 sq. ft.–476 sq. ft.
Rigging:	Sloop
Price Guide:	$10,500us+
Summary:	Modern design that has proved adequate and popular with many.

CHANNEL ROVER

Design:	Bill O'Brien, England
Supplier:	O'Brien & Spencer, Ltd., England
Specifications:	*Construction:*
	LWL: 7.2m/23'7½
	LOA: 8.0m/26'3
	Beam: 4.5m/14'9
	Draft: 1.82m/5'11½
Fittings:	Drop keel. Twin diesel auxiliaries.
Variations:	Optional inboard or outboard.
Sails:	Area 33m^2/355 sq.ft.
Rigging:	Sloop (motor sailer)
Price Guide:	On application

SANTANA 26

Design:	Seymour Paul, U.S.A. 1971
Supplier:	W. D. Schock Corporation, U.S.A.
Est. Rating:	IOR 21.4'
Specifications:	

Construction:	GRP
LWL:	6.43m/21'1
LOA:	7.98m/26'2
Beam:	2.41m/7'11
Draft:	1.52m—1.68m/5'0—5'6
Displ:	1,884kg/4,150 lbs
Ballast:	802kg/1,767 lbs

Fittings:	Iron ballast. GRP deck. Aluminium spars.
Interior:	6 berths in 1 cabin. Stove. Icebox. Sink. Icebox 1 marine toilet.
Variations:	Swing or fixed keel models
Sails:	Area 30.1m²/324 sq.ft. Spinnaker area 48.3m²/520 sq.ft.+
Rigging:	Sloop
Price Guide:	$8.750us
Summary:	A comfortable cruiser with complete inventory of equipment.

DEFENDER 27

Design: J. Gaubert & A. Mauric, Holland 1969

Supplier: Jachtwerf F. Dekker & Zouen, Holland

Specifications:

Construction: Sandwich GRP
LWL: 5.80m/19'1
LOA: 8.00m/26'3
Beam: 2.50m/8'2
Draft: 1.26m/4'1
Displ: 2,000kg/4,400 lbs
Ballast: 850kg/1,880 lbs

Fittings: Sandwich GRP deck. Aluminium spars. Fin keel.

Interior: 3 berths. Full galley with stove and sink. 1 enclosed toilet.

Variations: Optional 12 hp engine.

Sails: Area 27m^2/291 sq.ft.
Spinnaker area 44m^2/474 sq.ft.

Rigging: Sloop

Price Guide: £4,600+/32,400 fl.

Summary: Kits available.

8 METRE

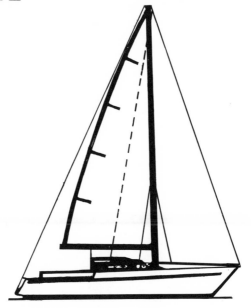

Design:	E. G. van de Stadt, Holland 1969
Supplier:	Tyler Boat Co., England (Kits)
	Jack Parles International Marine, England (boats)

Specifications:

	Construction:	GRP
	LWL:	7.09m/23'3
	LOA:	8.00m/26'3
	Beam:	2.41m/8'0
	Draft:	1.30m/4'3
	Displ:	2,540kg/5,600 lbs
	Ballast:	1,100kg/2,425 lbs

Fittings: To individual specification. Iron ballast. GRP deck.

Interior: 4 berths in 2 cabins. Sink. Stove. 1 enclosed toilet.

Variations: Optional inboard

Sails: Area 28.50m^2/306.78 sq.ft.
Spinnaker area 44.50m^2/479 sq.ft.

Rigging: Sloop

Price Guide: £1,600+

Summary: Home builder kit or complete boat. A safe and economical family cruiser that sets high standards of comfort. Good looking. Also know as **Offshore 8.**

EVENTIDE

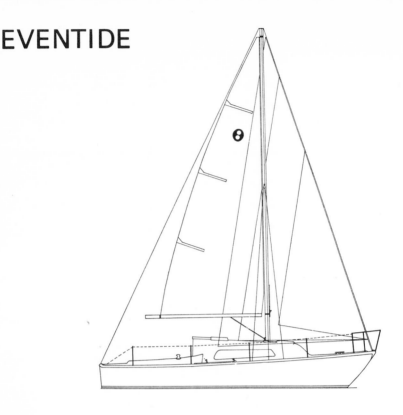

Design:	Maurice Griffiths, England 1962
Supplier:	Hartwell Boat Builders, England
Est. Rating:	Portsmouth number 112

Specifications:

Construction:	GRP
LWL:	6.71m/22'0
LOA:	8.00m/26'3
Beam:	2.44m/8'0
Draft:	0.64m/2'1
Displ:	1,634kg/3,600 lbs

Fittings:	Bilge keel
Interior:	4/6 berths. 1.72m/5'8 headroom.
Sails:	Area 25.6m^2/275 sq.ft. Spinnaker area 40.7m^2/438 sq.ft.
Rigging:	Sloop
Price Guide:	£5,200
Summary:	A successful and seaworthy family sailing cruiser.

PUMA 26

Design:	Holman & Pye
Supplier:	Puma France
Est. Rating:	19.5' IOR
Specifications:	*Construction:* GRP
	LWL: 6.42m/21'1
	LOA: 8.00m/26'3
	Beam: 2.80m/9'2
	Draft: 1.45m/4'9
	Displ: 2,750kg/6,063 lbs
	Ballast: 1,120kg/2,469 lbs
Fittings:	Aluminium spars.
Interior:	4 berths
Sails:	Area 41.51m^2/447 sq.ft.
Rigging:	Sloop
Price Guide:	68,760 Fr.f.
Summary:	Well equipped and built for competitive racing.

RANGER 26

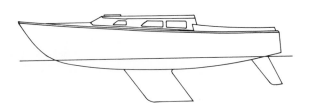

Design:	Gary Mull, U.S.A. 1969
Supplier:	Ranger Yachts, U.S.A.
Est. Rating:	21.6' IOR Mk III 25.6' CCA
Specifications:	*Construction:* GRP
	LWL: 6.63m/21'9
	LOA: 8m/26'3
	Beam: 2.64m/8'8
	Draft: 1.32m/4'4
	Displ: 2,660kg/5,860 lbs
	Ballast: 931kg/2,050 lbs
Fittings:	Iron ballast. GRP deck. Aluminium spars.
Interior:	5 berths in 2 cabins. Sink. Icebox. Standard marine toilet. 1.73m/5'8 cabin headroom.
Sails:	Area 29.9m^2/322 sq.ft.
Rigging:	Sloop
Price Guide:	$7,600us
Summary:	Superbly finished with ample locker space and storage.

COLUMBI 27′ MOTOR SAILER

Design:	Viksund Boats, Norway
Supplier:	Viksund Båt A/S, Norway Viksund Boats U.K.
Specifications:	*Construction:* GRP *LOA:* 8.05m/26′5 *Beam:* 2.85m/9′4 *Draft:* 1.10m/3′7 *Displ:* 3.5 tonnes/7,716 lbs *Ballast:* 1,000kg/2,205 lbs
Fittings:	Inboard Volvo Penta MD2B 25 hp or MD3B 36 hp engine.
Interior:	6 berths
Variations:	Can be supplied as a motor-boat or with a steadying rig only (sloop)
Sails:	Area 25m^2/269 sq.ft.
Rigging:	Ketch
Price Guide:	£6,500
Summary:	Built to satisfy the needs of Norwegian fishermen — thus safe and sturdy.

INVICTA MKIII

Design:	E. G. Van de Stadt, Holland 1962
Supplier:	Tyler Boat Co., England
Rating:	Portsmouth primary yardstick 94

Specifications:

Construction:	GRP
LWL:	6.3m/20'8
LOA:	8.06m/26'5
Beam:	2.23m/7'4
Draft:	1.2m/3'11
Displ:	2,327kg/5,125 lbs
Ballast:	1,047kg/2,307 lbs

Fittings:	8 hp ST engine.
Interior:	3/4 berths. 1.75m/5'9 headroom.
Sails:	Area 32m^2/344 sq.ft.
Rigging:	Masthead sloop
Price Guide:	£4,900
Summary:	A well-established racing machine.

WARSASH

Design:	Frederick R. Parker, England
Supplier:	Russell Marine; England

Specifications:

Construction:	GRP
LWL:	5.99m/19'8
LOA:	8.13m/26'8
Beam:	2.21m/7'3
Draft:	1.22m/4'0
Displ:	2,034kg/4,480 lbs

Fittings:	Lead ballast
Interior:	4 berths. 1.42m/4'8 headroom.
Variations:	Optional engine
Sails:	Area 21.7m^2/234 sq.ft.
Rigging:	Bermudan sloop
Price Guide:	£5,900
Summary:	Fast and reasonably priced. Similar to the **Folkboat** design. Large cockpit and ample accommodation space. Deep keel boat.

NOVA

Design:	John Westell, England 1971
Supplier:	Penryn Boat Building, England
Specifications:	*Construction:* GRP
	LWL: 6.73m/22'1
	LOA: 8.13m/26'8
	Beam: 2.77m/9'1
	Draft: 1.3m/4'3
	Displ: 3,387kg/7,460 lbs
	Ballast: 1,362kg/3,000 lbs
Fittings:	Wood trim. Fin keelboat. Saab 10 hp inboard emgine.
Interior:	5 berths
Sails:	Area 33.4m^2/360 sq.ft.
Rigging:	Bermudan sloop
Price Guide:	£5,800
Summary:	Can be trailed. Kits and mouldings available.

DIAMOND MKII

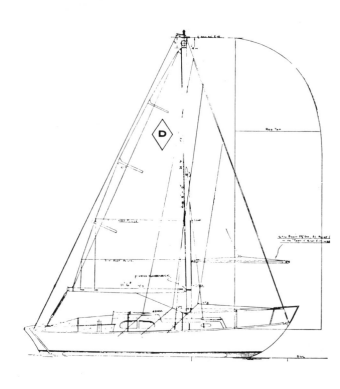

Design:	Alan Buchanan, England 1964	
Supplier:	Stebbings (Burnham) Ltd., England	
Specifications:	Construction:	GRP
	LWL:	6.18m/20'2
	LOA:	8.12m/26'8
	Beam:	2.31m/7'7
	Draft:	1.24m/4'1
	Displ:	3,051kg/6,720 lbs
Fittings:	Stainless steel fittings.	
Interior:	4 berths. 1.78m/5'10 headroom.	
Sails:	Area 26.9m^2/289 sq.ft. Terylene.	
Rigging:	Bermudan sloop	
Price Guide:	£5,600	
Summary:	Light on the helm. Can be sailed single-handed.	

CORONADO 27

Design:	William H. Tripp Jnr., U.S.A.
Supplier:	Coronado Yachts, U.S.A. Playvisa Coronado Yachts, England
Est. Rating:	20.8' IOR Mk III
Specifications:	*Construction:* GRP *LWL:* 6.71m/22'0 *LOA:* 8.13m/26'8 *Beam:* 2.59m/8'6 *Draft:* 1.33m or 1.07m/4'5 or 3'6 *Displ:* 2,837kg/6,250 lbs *Ballast:* 1,158kg/2,550 lbs
Fittings:	GRP deck. Aluminium spars.
Interior:	5 berths. 1.83m/6' headroom.
Variations:	Shoal draft model also available. Optional auxiliary.
Sails:	Area 28.1m^2/302 sq.ft.
Rigging:	Sloop
Price Guide:	$9,852us
Summary:	Exceptional performance on all points of sail. Well-planned galley. Good value for money.

SEAHAWK RANGE

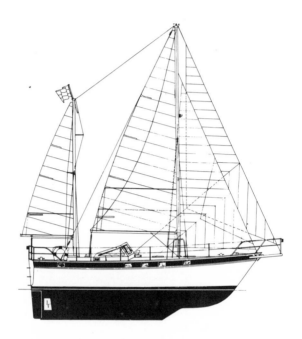

Design: Jachtbouw Noord, Holland

Supplier: Jachtbouw Noord, Holland

Specifications: *Construction:*   Wood
                     LOA: 8.10m—12.00m/26'7—39'4½
                     Beam: 2.56m—3.10m/8'4½—10'2
                     Draft: 1.05m—1.40m/3'5—4'7
                     Displ: 2,700—9,000kg/5,952 lbs—19,841 lbs

Fittings: To specification

Interior: 4—8 berths

Variations: A range of motor sailing and cruising yachts available
                     finished to individual specifications.

Sails: Area from 24.2m^2—60.9m^2/260 sq.ft.—656 sq.ft.

Rigging: Sloop or ketch

Price Guide: 19,800—72,650 DM

Summary: Built to high standards. Character, individual boats.

NICHOLSON 26

Design:	Camper & Nicholson, England
Supplier:	Camper & Nicholson, England Burne's Shipyard Ltd., England Camper Nicholson, U.S.A.
Est. Rating:	Portsmouth number 97
Specifications:	*Construction:* GRP *LWL:* 6.1m/20'0 *LOA:* 8.1m/26'7 *Beam:* 2.29m/7'6 *Draft:* 1.52m/5'0 *Displ:* 4,281kg/9,430 lbs
Fittings:	Teak woodwork. All fittings of stainless steel. Keel boat.
Interior:	4 berths. 1.83m/6'0 headroom.
Sails:	Area 27.3m^2/294 sq.ft.
Rigging:	Bermudan sloop
Price Guide:	£6,000
Summary:	Handles well and within the compass of the average family crew. Handsome, powerful and well appointed. Can not be trailed.

787

BIANCA 26

Design:	Paul Elvström & Jan Kaerulf, Denmark 1973

Supplier: Bianca Yacht A/S, Denmark

Specifications:

Construction:	GRP
LWL:	6.10m/20'0
LOA:	8.10m/26'7
Beam:	2.60m/8'6
Draft:	1.50m/4'11
Displ:	1,800kg/3,968 lbs

Fittings: Aluminium spars. Sandwich deck.

Interior: 4/5 berths

Sails: Area optional

Rigging: Masthead rig.

Price Guide: 69,500 D.Kr.

Summary: A family cruiser.

ERICSON 27

Design:	Bruce King, U.S.A. 1971
Supplier:	Ericson Yachts Inc., U.S.A. Hamble Marine, U.K. Nordmarine, Italy
Est. Rating:	19.6' IOR Mk III

Specifications:

Construction:	GRP
LWL:	6.25m/20'6
LOA:	8.16m/26'9
Beam:	2.74m/9'0
Draft:	1.2m/3'11
Displ:	2,996kg/6,600 lbs
Ballast:	1,317kg/2,900 lbs

Fittings:	Fin keel. GRP deck — non-skid. Aluminium spars.
Interior:	5 berths in 2 cabins. 1.85m/6'1 headroom.
Variations:	Optional toilet. Optional hp auxiliary.
Sails:	Area 30m^2 (13 + 17)/ 323 sq.ft. (140 + 183)
Rigging:	Sloop
Price Guide:	£7,500/$8,995us
Summary:	Pleasingly proportioned, efficient yacht.

TARANTELLE 27

Design:	Philippe Harlé, France 1973
Supplier:	Arcoa-Jouet, France Comextra, England
Est. Rating:	21.5' IOR
Specifications:	*Construction:* GRP *LWL:* 7.24m/23'9 *LOA:* 8.15m/26'9 *Beam:* 2.87m/9'5 *Draft:* 1.52m/5'0 *Displ:* 2,237kg/4,928 lbs *Ballast:* 840kg/1,850 lbs
Fittings:	Fin keel. Gold anodised spars. Teak trim.
Interior:	5 berths in 2 cabins. Galley. Enclosed toilet.
Variations:	Optional inboard or outboard engine.
Sails:	Area 44.1m^2/475 sq.ft.
Rigging:	Sloop
Price Guide:	£5,850
Summary:	A new French design that performs well.

CATALINA 27 ½ TON

Design:	Robert Finch and Frank Butler, U.S.A. 1970
Supplier:	Catalina Yachts Inc., U.S.A.
Est. Rating:	20.5′ MOR Mk III 20.6′ MORC 23.8′ MORF & CCA
Specifications:	*Construction:* GRP
	LWL: 6.63m/21′9
	LOA: 8.18m/26′10
	Beam: 2.69m/8′10
	Draft: 1.22m/4′0
	Displ: 2,565kg/5,650 lbs
	Ballast: 1,180kg/2,600 lbs
Fittings:	Lead ballast. GRP deck. Aluminium spars.
Interior:	6 berths in 2 cabins
Variations:	Optional auxiliary. Optional galley and toilets. **Catalina 27** also available — smaller sail plan.
Sails:	Area 31.9m^2 (14 + 17.9)/343 sq.ft. (151 + 192)
Rigging:	Sloop
Price Guide:	$7,600us
Summary:	A very competitively priced boat that has a full inventory supplied. Sailplan and hull shape give a good performance. Known as **Jaguar 27** in Europe with slight alterations.

JAGUAR 27

Design:	Bob Finch and Frank Butler, U.S.A. 1971
Supplier:	Jaguar Yachts, Holland
Est. Rating:	21.5' IOR. 7.50 tons Thames Measurement

Specifications:	*Construction:*	GRP
	LWL:	6.63m/21'9
	LOA:	8.18m/26'10
	Beam:	2.72m/8'11
	Draft:	1.23m/4'0½
	Displ:	2,542kg/5,600 lbs
	Ballast:	1,180kg/2,601 lbs

Fittings:	Alloy spars. GRP and plywood deck. 10 hp engine.
Interior:	6 berths in 2 cabins. 1.88m/6'2 cabin headroom.
Sails:	Area 28.4m^2/306 sq.ft. Spinnaker area 52.5m^2/565 sq.ft.
Rigging:	Sloop
Price Guide:	£4,000/32,900 fl.
Summary:	Exceptionally good to windward and able to cope with short steep seas. Good value for money. 800 built already. Known as **Catalina 27** in the U.S.A. with minor alterations.

HALCYON CLIPPER 27

Design:	Alan Buchanan, England 1970
Supplier:	Offshore Yachts International, England

Specifications:

Construction:	GRP
LWL:	6.1m/20'0
LOA:	8.21m/26'11
Beam:	2.68m/8'9
Draft:	1.3m—0.94m/4'3—3'1
Displ:	3,051kg/6,720 lbs
Ballast:	1,352kg/2,979 lbs

Fittings:	Wood trim. GRP deck. Aluminium spars.
Interior:	5 berths in 2 cabins. Sink with pump. Stove and oven. Icebox.
Variations:	Fin or bilge keel versions available.
Sails:	Area 24m^2/258 sq.ft. Spinnaker area 52m^2/560 sq.ft.
Specifications:	Bermudan sloop
Price Guide:	£4,820
Summary:	Also know as **Offshore Halycon Clipper 27.**

LUTH

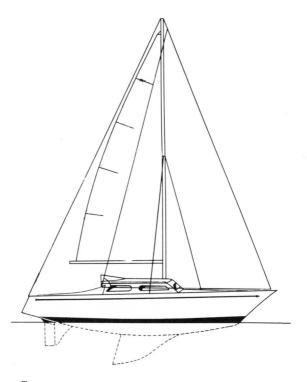

Design:	France	
Supplier:	Costantini, France	
Est. Rating:	18'6 IOR	
Specifications:	*Construction:*	GRP
	LWL:	5.83m/19'1½
	LOA:	8.20m/26'11
	Beam:	2.72m/8'11
	Draft:	1.40m/4'7
	Displ:	1,700kg/3,748 lbs
	Ballast:	800kg/1,764 lbs
Fittings:	To specification	
Interior:	5 berths. Galley. 1 Marine toilet.	
Sails:	Area 34.10m²/367 sq.ft.	
Rigging:	Sloop	
Price Guide:	57,500 Fr.f.	

BAL-MACWESTER 27

Design:	C. S. J. Roy, England 1970
Supplier:	Built by Bal-Marine, England Supplies by Rotomarine, England Macwester Marine
Est. Rating:	Portsmouth number 101

Specifications:	*Construction:*	GRP
	LWL:	6.86m/22'6[
	LOA:	8.23m/27'0
	Beam:	2.8m/9'2
	Draft:	1.12m/3'8
	Displ:	3,396.6kg/7,480 lbs
	Ballast:	1,105.6kg/2,436 lbs

Fittings:	Twin keel. Inboard Saab 18HP diesel. Alloy spars.
Interior:	4/5 berths
Sails:	Area 30.7m^2/330 sq.ft.
Rigging:	Sloop
Price Guide:	£6,500
Summary:	Also known simply as **Macwester 27.**

CALYPSO

Design:	A. D. Truman Ltd., England	
Supplier:	A. D. Truman Ltd., England	
Specifications:	*Construction:*	Mahogany on oak
	LWL:	7.32m/24'0
	LOA:	8.23m/27'0
	Beam:	2.54m/8'4
	Draft:	0.89m/2'11
	Displ:	3,178kg/7,000 lbs
Fittings:	To specification	
Interior:	4 berths. 1.83m/6'0 headroom.	
Sails:	Area from 30.7m^2/330 sq.ft.	
Rigging:	Bermudan sloop or ketch (motor sailer)	
Price Guide:	£6,000+	
Summary:	Easily handled.	

CUTLASS 27

Design: Eric White and Alan Hill, England

Supplier: Marine Construction, England

Est. Rating: Portsmouth number 97

Specifications:

Construction:	GRP	
LWL:	6.1m/20'	
LOA:	8.23m/27'	
Beam	2.33m/7'8	
Draft:	1.37m/4'6	
Displ:	2,949kg/6,496 lbs	
Ballast:	1,476kg/3,250 lbs	

Fittings: Alloy spars. Lead ballast.

Interior: 4 berths

Sails: Area 26.9m^2/290 sq.ft. Terylene.

Rigging: Bermudan sloop

Price Guide: On application

Summary: Good windward qualities. Easy on the helm and capable in heavy weather.

FLUSH POKER

Design:	M. Joubert, France 1972
Supplier:	Jeanneau, France Anderson Marine, England
Est. Rating:	19.1′ IOR
Specifications:	*Construction:*

	LWL:	6.4m/21′0
	LOA:	8.2m/27′0
	Beam:	2.87m/9′5
	Draft:	1.65m/5′5
	Displ:	1.998kg/4,400 lbs

Fittings:	Fin keel
Interior:	4—6 berths
Sails:	Area 38.3m^2/412 sq.ft. Spinnaker area 55m^2/592 sq.ft.
Rigging:	Sloop
Price Guide:	On application
Summary:	A new French boat designed on Continental lines.

FOLKDANCER

Design:	F. R. Parker, England
Supplier:	Hurley Marine, England Wells Yachts, U.S.A.
Est. Rating:	Portsmouth number 96

Specifications:	*Construction:*	GRP
	LWL:	5.99m/19'8
	LOA:	8.23m/27'0
	Beam:	2.29m/7'6
	Draft:	1.22m/4'0
	Displ:	2,288kg/5,040 lbs
	Ballast:	1,135kg/2,500 lbs

Fittings:	Iron ballast. GRP deck. Aluminium spars. 5HP auxiliary.
Interior:	6 berths in 2 cabins. Standard galley.
Sails:	Area 27.5m^2/296 sq.ft.
Rigging:	Sloop
Price Guide:	On application.

HALCYON 27

Design:	Alan Buchanan, England 1962
Supplier:	Offshore Yachts International, England Imports Co. of America, U.S.A.
Est. Rating:	Portsmouth number 100

Specifications:

Construction:	GRP
LWL:	6.17m/20'3
LOA:	8.23m/27'0
Beam:	2.33m/7'8
Draft:	1.22m/4'0
Displ:	2,724kg/6,000 lbs
Ballast:	1,362kg/3,000 lbs

Fittings:	Fin keel. Aluminium spars. Wickstrom 7 hp inboard.
Interior:	4 berths. Sink with pump. Stove. Icebox. 1 marine toilet.
Sails:	Area 26.9m^2/290 sq.ft. Spinnaker area 552 sq.ft.
Rigging:	Sloop
Price Guide:	£4,800
Summary:	A genuine performer when handled by experts but still manageable for the novice. Kits and mouldings available.

KERRY MKII

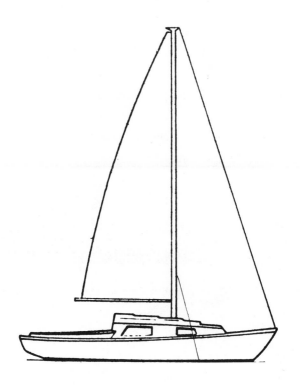

Design:	G. O'B. Kennedy, Ireland 1968
Supplier:	Kennedy International Boats, Ireland
Specifications:	*Construction:*

LWL:	6.4m/21'0
LOA:	8.23m/27'0
Beam:	2.51m/8'3
Draft:	1.32m/4'4
Displ:	2,642kg/5,820 lbs
Ballast:	1,117kg/2,460 lbs

Fittings:	Fin keel. Farymann 10 hp diesel inboard.
Sails:	Area 33.4m^2/360 sq.ft.
Rigging:	Sloop
Price Guide:	£6,000

NEWPORT 27S ½ TON

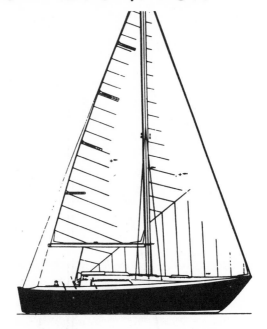

Design:	Cuthbertson & Cassian, U.S.A.
Supplier:	Capital Yachts Inc. U.S.A.
Rating:	21.7' MORC 24.7' CCA

Specifications:

Construction:	GRP
LWL:	6.81m/22'4
LOA:	8.23m/27'0
Beam:	2.8m/9'2
Draft:	1.3m/4'3
Displ:	2,724kg/6,000 lbs
Ballast:	1,090kg/2,400 lbs

Fittings:	Lead ballast. Balsa core & Fiberglass deck. Aluminium spars. Universal Atomic 4 gasoline.
Interior:	5 berths in 2 cabins.
Variations:	Outboard
Sails:	Area 32.9m^2 (14.8 + 18.1)/354 sq.ft. (159 + 195)
Rigging:	Sloop
Price Guide:	$1,100 I.B. $9,000 O.B.
Summary:	Lightweight, yet very strong. Really will satisfy the racing and family man.

O'DAY 27 ½ TON

Design:	Alan P. Gurney, U.S.A. 1972
Supplier:	O'Day Co., U.S.A.
Rating:	21.5' IOR Mk III. 21.6' MORC

Specifications:	*Construction:*	GRP
	LWL:	6.93m/22'9
	LOA:	8.23m/27'0
	Beam:	2.74m/9'0
	Draft:	1.22m/4'0
	Displ:	2,270kg/5,000 lbs
	Ballast:	1,012kg/2,230 lbs

Fittings:	Lead ballast. GRP deck. Aluminium spars.
Interior:	5 berths in 2 cabins. Sink. W/pump.
Variations:	Optional stove; toilets. Optional auxiliary inboard or outboard.
Sails:	Area 31.6m^2/340 sq.ft.
Rigging:	Sloop
Price Guide:	$8,000

PHILIPA 27

Design:	Robert Clark, England
Supplier:	Philip & Son, England
Specifications:	*Construction:* Wood
	LWL: 6.25m/20'6
	LOA: 8.23m/27'0
	Beam: 2.67m/8'9
	Draft: 1.37m/4'6
Fittings:	Fin keel. Volvo MD16 10 hp inboard engine.
Sails:	Area 32.5m^2/350 sq.ft.
Rigging:	Sloop
Price Guide:	On application

BRISTOL 27

Design:	Carl Alberg, U.S.A. 1965
Supplier:	Bristol Yacht Co., U.S.A.
Specifications:	*Construction:* GRP
	LWL: 6.02m/19'9
	LOA: 8.28m/27'2
	Beam: 2.44m/8'0
	Draft: 1.22m/4'0
	Displ: 2,996kg/6,600 lbs
	Ballast: 1,169kg/2,575 lbs
Fittings:	Balsa core and GRP deck. Aluminium spars. 30HP Universal Atomic 4 gasoline engine.
Interior:	4—5 berths in 2 cabins.
Sails:	Area 31.7m^2 (16 + 15.7)/341 sq.ft. (172 + 169)
Rigging:	Sloop
Price Guide:	$10,000us

SAFARI

Design: Michel Dufour, France 1969

Supplier: Michel Dufour, France
Michel Dufour, U.S.A.
Carl Ziegler Yacht Agency, England

Est. Rating: 19.8' IOR Mk III

Specifications: *Construction:*   GRP
                  LWL: 6.50m/21'6
                  LOA: 8.25m/27'0
                  Beam: 2.76m/9'2
                  Draft: 1.30m/4'4
                  Displ: 2.7 tons/5,954 lbs
                  Ballast: 1 ton/2,204 lbs

Fittings: Iron ballast. GRP sandwich deck. Aluminium spars.
10HP Volvo MDIB diesel auxiliary.

Interior: 5 berths in 2 cabins. 1.77m/5'10 headroom. Stove.
Icebox. Sink. Water pump. 1 sea toilet.

Sails: Area 28.?m^2(14.3 + 14.3)/308 sq.ft. (154 + 154)
Spinnaker area 55m^2/590 sq.ft.

Rigging: Sloop. Stainless steel and terylene.

Price Guide: £9,420/65,700 Fr.f./$14,850us

Summary: A fine lined weekend cruiser.

SNAPDRAGON 27 Mk II

Design:	Thames Marine, England 1969	
Supplier:	Thames Marine, England	
Est. Rating:	Portsmouth number 103	
Specifications:	*Construction:*	GRP
	LWL:	6.93m/22'9
	LOA:	8.23m/27'0
	Beam:	2.59m/8'6
	Draft:	0.84m/2'9
	Displ:	2,497kg/5,500 lbs
	Ballast:	999kg/2,200 lbs
Fittings:	12HP Yanmar diesel engine.	
Interior:	6 berths	
Variations:	Fin or twin keel boat.	
Sails:	Area 25.1m^2/270 sq.ft.	
Rigging:	Bermudan sloop	
Price Guide:	£5,400	
Summary:	Kits available.	

VANCOUVER 27

Design:	Robert B. Harris, U.S.A. 1973
Supplier:	Harris and Heacock, U.S.A.

Specifications:	*Construction:*	GRP and balsa/foam sandwich
	LWL:	6.99m/22'11
	LOA:	8.23m/27'0
	Beam:	2.64m/8'8
	Draft:	1.32m/4'4
	Displ:	3,950kg/8.700 lbs
	Ballast:	1,725kg/3,800 lbs

Fittings:	GRP deck. Aluminium spars. Yanmar TS80 diesel auxiliary.
Interior:	3 berths in 2 cabins. Stove. Icebox. Sink. Enclosed toilet.
Sails:	Area 35.2m^2/379 sq.ft.
Rigging:	Sloop
Price Guide:	$275us plans only
Summary:	Supplied in kit form.

BIANCA 27

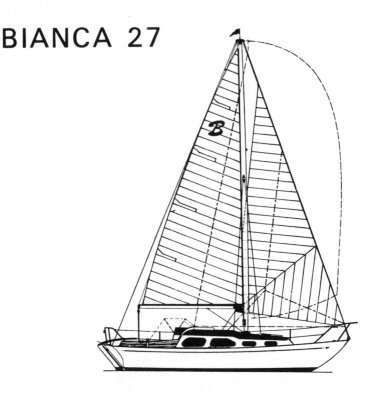

Design:	H. Christiansen, Denmark
Supplier:	Bianca Yachts A/S, Denmark
Specifications:	*Construction:* GRP
	LWL: 6.20m/20'4
	LOA: 8.25m/27'1
	Beam: 2.44m/8'
	Draft: 1.40m/4'7
	Displ: 3.250kg/7.165 lbs
	Ballast: 1,450kg/3,197 lbs
Fittings:	Mahogany trim. GRP deck. Stainless steel rudder fittings. Aluminium spars.
Interior:	4/5 berths. Galley — stove. Sink. Iceboxes.
Sails:	Area 31.6m^2/340 sq.ft. Spinnaker area 48.5m^2/522 sq.ft.
Rigging:	Masthead rig
Price Guide:	81,200 D.Kr.
Summary:	Spacious, comfortable and with good sailing qualities.

R6

Design: Paul H. H. Rhodes MRINA, England 1965

Supplier: Paul H. H. Rhodes, England

Specifications:

Construction:	Mahogany on elm and iroko
LWL:	6.4m/21'0
LOA:	8.25m/27'1
Beam:	2.36m/7'9
Draft:	1.27m/4'2
Displ:	3,254kg/7,168 lbs

Fittings: ST 4–8 hp engine. Under deck tiller.

Interior: 4 berths. 1.85m/6'1 headroom.

Sails: Area 30.2m^2/325 sq.ft.

Rigging: Auxiliary sloop

Price Guide: On application

Summary: Fast and perfectly balanced on all points of sailing. Large galley.

SABRE 27

Design:	Alan Hill, England 1967	
Supplier:	Marine Construction, England	
Specifications:	*Construction:*	GRP
	LWL:	6.76m/22'2
	LOA:	8.25m/27'1
	Beam:	2.74m/9'0
	Draft:	1.42m–0.91m/4'8–3'0
	Displ:	3,087kg/6,800 lbs
Fittings:	Gold anodised spars.	
Interior:	4 berths	
Variations:	Twin or fin keel models available	
Sails:	Area 28.8m^2/310 sq.ft.	
Rigging:	Bermudan masthead sloop	
Price Guide:	£6,000+	
Summary:	A complete family boat that is also speedy enough to win open races. Kits and mouldings available.	

SANTANA 27

Design: Gary Mull, U.S.A. 1966

Supplier: W. D. Schock Corporation, U.S.A.

Est. Rating: 26.2' CCA

Specifications:

Construction:	GRP
LWL:	6.86m/22'6
LOA:	8.25m/27'1
Beam:	2.74m/9'0
Draft:	1.3m/4'3
Ballast:	1,044kg/2,300 lbs

Fittings: Iron ballast. GRP deck. Aluminium spars.

Interior: 6 berths in 1 cabin. Icebox. Sink. Water pump. Marine toilet.

Variations: Optional power

Sails: Area 32.3m^2/348 sq.ft.

Rigging: Sloop

Price Guide: $9,250us

Summary: A true cruiser — supplied with a full inventory.

811

VEGA

Design: Per Brohall, Sweden 1967

Supplier: Albin Marine AB, Sweden.
Albin Marine AB, England
Larsson Trade, U.S.A.

Est. Rating: 23.0' IOR Mk III

Specifications:

Construction:	GRP
LWL:	7.01m/23'0
LOA:	8.25m/27'1
Beam:	2.46m/8'1
Draft:	1.12m/3'8
Displ:	2,311kg/5,090 lbs
Ballast:	917kg/2,020 lbs

Fittings: GRP deck. Aluminium spars. 10 hp Volvo diesel auxiliary.

Interior: 4/6 berths in 2 cabins. Sink, fresh and sea water pumps. Standard sea toilet.

Sails: Area 31.9m^2/343 sq.ft.

Rigging: Sloop

Price Guide: £6,000

Summary: Family cruiser with good windward performance. Performance rivals larger boats. An all-weather boat. Modern and luxurious.

ADMIRAL 27

Design:	R. D. Carlson, U.S.A.
Supplier:	Durabilt Corporation, U.S.A.
Est. Rating:	23.1′ IOR
Specifications:	*Construction:* GRP
	LWL: 7.62m/25′0
	LOA: 8.27m/27′1½
	Beam: 2.44m/8′0
	Draft: 0.59m/1′11 up
	Displ: 1,952kg/4,300 lbs
	Ballast: 726kg/1,600 lbs
Fittings:	Aluminium spars. 10 hp outboard — gasoline. Retractable keel — centreboard.
Interior:	4 to 6 berths. 1.83m/6′ headroom.
Sails:	Area 31.2m^2/336 sq.ft. Spinnaker area 47.4m^2/510 sq.ft.
Rigging:	Sloop
Price Guide:	$8,000us
Summary:	Ideal for inland and coastal sailing as easily trailed.

H-BOAT

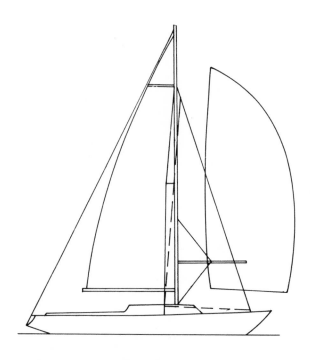

Design:	Hans Groop, Finland 1967
Supplier:	Artetno, Finland
Specifications:	*Construction:* GRP

LWL:	6.30m/20'8
LOA:	8.28m/27'2
Beam:	2.18m/7'2
Draft:	1.30m/4'3
Displ:	1,450kg/3,197 lbs
Ballast:	735kg/1,620 lbs

Fittings:	Sandwich deck. Teak trim.
Interior:	4 berths
Sails:	Area 24.5m^2/264 sq. ft. Spinnaker area 35m^2/377 sq. ft.
Rigging:	Sloop
Price Guide:	Fmk. 34,400
Summary:	Sailed extensively in Scandinavia and Europe.

C&C 27 ½ TON

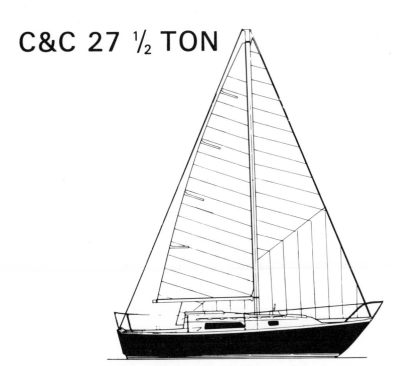

Design:	C & C Design Group, Canada 1970
Supplier:	C & C Yachts Manufacturing, Canada Anstey Yachts, England
Est. Rating:	21.3' IOR Mk III 22.5' MORC Portsmouth number 93

Specifications:

Construction:	GRP
LWL:	6.76m/22'2
LOA:	8.31m/27'3
Beam:	2.8m/9'2
Draft:	1.3m/4'3
Displ:	2,352kg/5,180 lbs
Ballast:	1,140kg/2,512 lbs

Fittings:	Lead ballast. Balsa core and GRP deck. Aluminium spars. 30 hp Atomic 4 gasoline auxiliary.
Interior:	5 berths in 2 cabins. 1.83m/6'0 headroom.
Sails:	Area 32.3m^2 (13.9 + 18.4)/348 sq.ft. (150 + 198)
Rigging:	Sloop
Price Guide:	$13, 495us
Summary:	Built to very high standards to perform whether as an all-out racer or as a temporary home.

PINTAIL

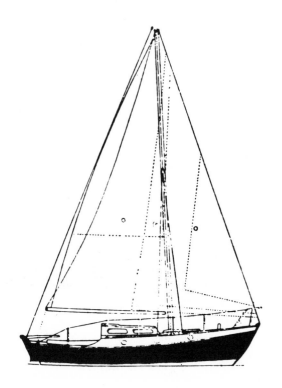

Design:	Purbrook Rossiter, England 1962
Supplier:	Purbrook Rossiter, England
Specifications:	*Construction:* GRP and wood
	LWL: 7.01m/23'0
	LOA: 8.31m/27'3
	Beam: 2.67m/8'9
	Draft: 1.07m/3'6
	Displ: 5.288kg/11,648 lbs
Fittings:	Alloy spars. Bilge keel.
Interior:	4/5 berths
Sails:	Area 32.5m^2/350 sq.ft.
Rigging:	Sloop
Price Guide:	£9,850
Summary:	Well-balanced, stiff and dry. Handles easily and will come about under mainsail or jib only.

DUFOUR 27

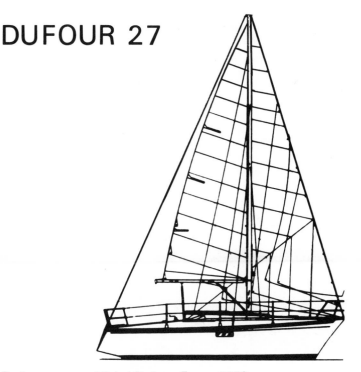

Design:	Michel Dufour, France 1972
Supplier:	Michel Dufour SA, U.S.A. Michel Dufour, France Carl Ziegler Yacht Agency, England
Specifications:	

	Construction:	GRP
	LWL:	6.12m/20'4
	LOA:	8.31m/27'3
	Beam:	2.8m/9'2
	Draft:	1.47m/4'10
	Displ:	2,397kg/5,280 lbs
	Ballast:	899kg/1,980 lbs

Fittings:	GRP and foam sandwich deck. Aluminium spars. Cast iron and lead ballast. 10HP Volvo MDB diesel engine.
Interior:	5 berths in 2 cabins. 1.83m/6'0 headroom. Galley — stove, sink, icebox. Marine toilet.
Sails:	Area 28.8m^2 (13.9 + 14'9)/310 sq.ft. (150 + 160)
Rigging:	Sloop
Price Guide:	£8,500/$14,500us
Summary:	A boat of excellent racing potential with high aspect modern rig and a hull of low wetted surface area.

CONTEST 27

Design:	Dick Zaal, Holland 1972
Supplier:	Conyplex NV, Holland Interyacht, England Holland Yacht Inc., U.S.A.
Est. Rating:	IOR type 'A' ± 19' type 'B' ± 20'2

Specifications:

Construction:	GRP
LWL:	6.60m/21.75'
LOA:	8.35m/27.35'
Beam:	2.75m/9.00'
Draft:	1.35m—1.63m/4.43'—5.33'
Displ:	2,665—2,800kg/5,863—6,160 lbs
Ballast:	1,185—1,320kg/2,607—2,904 lbs

Fittings:	Internal halyards, anchor well. 2 Speed winches. Volvo Penta MDIB engine.
Interior:	5 berths. Well planned deck and cockpit. Lined throughout. Teak finish.
Variations:	Choice of 'A' or 'B'. 'A' — more emphasis on cruising and comfort. 'B' — a deeper keel and more sail area — 6 berths in 3 cabins.
Sails:	Area 32.0m^2/344 sq.ft. ('A' type) Area 34.6m^2/373 sq.ft. ('B' type)
Rigging:	Sloop
Price Guide:	£7,500/'A' S17,000us, 'B' S18,000us
Summary:	Smart racer and comfortable cruiser. A splendid sea boat.

VERL 27

Design:	Robert Clark, England 1973
Supplier:	Verlvale Ltd., England
Est. Rating:	20.3′ IOR

Specifications:	*Construction:*	GRP
	LWL:	6.6m/21′7
	LOA:	8.32m/27′3½
	Beam:	2.59m/8′6·
	Draft:	1.37m/4′6
	Displ:	2,118kg/4,660 lbs
	Ballast:	840kg/1,850 lbs

Fittings:	GRP deck. Anodised aluminium spars. Vire 7 hp petrol engine.
Interior:	5 berths. Full galley.
Sails:	Area 33.44m^2/360 sq.ft.
Rigging:	Sloop
Price Guide:	£5,200
Summary:	A fast seaworth yacht. Kits and mouldings available.

KENT 8M

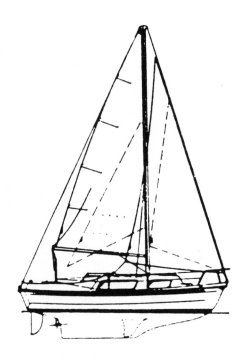

Design:	Paerryman
Supplier:	Porter & Haylett Ltd., England
Specifications:	*Construction:* GRP
	LWL: 7.05m/23'1½
	LOA: 8.23m/27'4
	Beam: 2.64m/8'8
	Draft: 0.96m/3'2
	Displ: 2,770kg/6,200 lbs
	Ballast: 1,050kg/2,370 lbs
Fittings:	Fin keel. Perkins 4/108 49shp Diesel engine. Anodised aluminium spars.
Interior:	5 berths
Variations:	Ordinary and de luxe versions available.
Sails:	Area 31.7m^2/341 sq.ft.
Rigging:	Sloop
Price Guide:	£6,980

CAL T/2 ½ TON

Design:	C. William Lapworth, U.S.A. 1972
Supplier:	Jensen Marine, U.S.A.
Est. Rating:	21.7′ IOR Mk III

Specifications:

Construction:	GRP
LWL:	6.81m/22′4
LOA:	8.36m/27′5
Beam:	2.74m/9′0
Draft:	1.37m/4′6
Displ:	2,452kg/5,400 lbs
Ballast:	1,135kg/2,500 lbs

Fittings:	GRP deck. Aluminium spars.
Interior:	5—6 berths in 2 cabins. Standard galley. 1.83m/6′ headroom.
Variations:	Optional HP outboard
Sails:	Area 32.4m^2/349 sq.ft.
Rigging:	Sloop
Price Guide:	$11,300us
Summary:	A highly successful racer/cruiser. Spacious, luxurious interior. Based on the proven Cal 27 hull.

FISHERMAN 27

Design:	A. Burnard, England
Supplier:	Fairey Marine, England
Specifications:	*Construction:* Hot moulded wood.
	LOA: 8.36m/27'5
	Beam: 2.67m/8'9
Fittings:	Wooden spars. Deck and superstructure either wood or metal.
Interior:	4 berths
Variations:	Optional inboard.
Sails:	Sloop 17.7m^2/190 sq.ft.
	Mizzen 9.8m^2/105 sq.ft.
Rigging:	Sloop or mizzen only
Price Guide:	On application
Summary:	Very full bodied with a rounded stern. Motor sailing comfort.

REGENT

Supplier:	Comextra, England
Specifications:	*Construction:* GRP
	LOA: 8.38m/27'6
	Draft: 1.4m/4'7
Fittings:	Keelboat
Interior:	5 berths
Variations:	Optional inboard or outboard engine
Sails:	Area 35.3m^2/380 sq.ft.
Rigging:	Bermudan sloop
Price Guide:	On application
Summary:	Can not be trailed.

HONEY BEE

Design:	A. K. Balfour, Scotland
Supplier:	City Centre Boatyard, Scotland
Specifications:	*Construction:* Mahogany strip plank/carvel
	LWL: 6.4m/21'0
	LOA: 8.38m/27'6
	Beam: 2.44m/8'0
	Draft: 1.68m/5'6
	Displ: 4,322kg/9,520 lbs
Fittings:	To specification
Interior:	4/6 berths. 1.83m/6'0 headroom.
Sails:	Area 28.7m²/309 sq.ft.
Rigging:	Masthead sloop
Price Guide:	On application
Summary:	Practical and attractive design. A well-lit interior.

MORGAN 27

Design:	Morgan Yacht Corp., U.S.A. 1971
Supplier:	Morgan Yacht Corp., U.S.A. Peter Webster Ltd., England
Rating:	23.6' IOR Mk III 22.7' MORC
Specifications:	*Construction:* GRP *LWL:* 7.62m/25'0 *LOA:* 8.38m/27'6 *Beam:* 3m/9'10 *Draft:* 1.37m/4'6 *Displ:* 3,178kg/7,000 lbs *Ballast:* 1,498kg/3,300 lbs
Fittings:	GRP deck. Aluminium spars.
Interior:	7 or 5 berths in 1 or 2 cabins. Galley standard. 1 enclosed toilet.
Variations:	Auxiliary gasoline optional
Sails:	Area 34.7m^2(14.4 + 20.3)/373 sq.ft. (155 + 218)
Rigging:	Sloop
Price Guide:	£ on application/$10,000

SOUTHERLY 28

Design:	John Bennett, U.K.
Supplier:	Southern Yacht & Charter Co., England

Specifications:

	Construction:	GRP
	LWL:	7.32m/24'0
	LOA:	8.38m/27'6
	Beam:	2.74m/9'0
	Draft:	0.76m/2'6
	Displ:	3,814kg/3.75 tons
	Ballast:	1,322kg/1.3 tons

Fittings:	Centreboard boat. Anodised alloy spars. Self-draining cockpit. 25 hp Volvo Penta MD2B diesel engine.
Interior:	5 berths. Galley. Enclosed toilet.
Sails:	Area 22.7m^2/244.8 sq.ft.
Rigging:	Sloop
Price Guide:	£6,500
Summary:	Sails well to windward and gives a good power performance

COMMANDO

Design:	Illingworth & Primrose, England 1962
Supplier:	Blanks Boatyard, England
Specifications:	*Construction:* Cold moulded mahogany
	LWL: 6.25m/20'6
	LOA: 8.46m/27'9
	Beam: 2.51m/8'3
	Draft: 1.07m/3'6
	Displ: 2,797kg/6,160 lbs
Fittings:	To specification
Interior:	4 berths 1.78m/5'10 headroom.
Sails:	Area 24.7m^2/266 sq.ft.
Rigging:	Sloop (motor sailer)
Price Guide:	On application
Summary:	A comfortable craft capable of good performance under sail or power.

JAVA

Design:	Walter F. Rayner Ltd., England
Supplier:	Peters Boatyard Ltd., England
Specifications:	*Construction:* Mahogany on oak
	LWL: 6.48m/21'3
	LOA: 8.46m/27'9
	Beam: 2.59m/8'6
	Draft: 1.22m/4'0
	Displ: 3,732kg/8,221 lbs
Fittings:	To specification
Interior:	4 berths
Variations:	Optional vedette or Saab auxiliary.
Sails:	Area 27.2m^2/293 sq.ft.
Rigging:	Sloop
Price Guide:	On application
Summary:	A power sloop

TANZER 28 ½ TON

Design:	Johann Tanzer, Canada 1972
Supplier:	Tanzer Industries Ltd., Canada
Est. Rating:	21.7' IOR Mk II
Specifications:	*Construction:* GRP — hand laid
	LWL: 7.16m/23'6
	LOA: 8.41m/27'7
	Beam: 3m/9'10
	Draft: 1.24m/4'1
	Displ: 2,951kg/6,500 lbs
	Ballast: 1,090kg/2,400 lbs
Fittings:	Iron ballast. GRP deck. Aluminium spars. Flush deck.
Interior:	6 berths in 2 cabins. Stove. Icebox. Sink and pump. Fire extinguisher. Portable chemical and enclosed head.
Variations:	Gasoline or diesel auxiliary.
Sails:	Area 32.1m^2 (13.5 + 18.6)/345 sq.ft. (145 + 200) Spinnaker area 68.7m^2/740 sq.ft.
Rigging:	Sloop
Price Guide:	$15,500us
Summary:	Larger version of the Tanzer 22. Beamy and spacious. Supplied with a full inventory.

DUTCHY

Design:	W. de Vries Leutsch Jnr, Holland
Supplier:	Jachtwerf Zuider Zee, Holland
Specifications:	*Construction:* Steel — sand blasted
	LWL: 6.30m/20'9
	LOA: 8.43m/27'9
	Beam: 2.62m/8'7
	Draft: 1.10m/3'8
	Displ: 3,559kg/7,840 lbs
Fittings:	Wooden spars.
Interior:	5 berths — layout to specification
Sails:	Area 26.5m^2/285 sq.ft. Dacron
Rigging:	Masthead sloop
Price Guide:	Variable
Summary:	Very seaworthy. Easy to handle.

828

EAST ANGLIAN

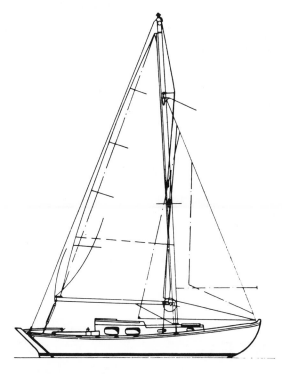

Design:	Alan Buchanan, England 1957
Supplier:	Dixon Kerly Ltd., England
Specifications:	*Construction:* Mahogany on oak
	LWL: 6.4m/21'0
	LOA: 8.46m/27'9
	Beam: 2.44m/8'0
	Draft: 1.37m/4'6
	Displ: 3,763kg/8,288 lbs
	Ballast: 1,627kg/3,584 lbs
Fittings:	To specification
Interior:	3 berths. 1.83m/6'0 headroom.
Variations:	Optional 4 hp auxiliary.
Sails:	Area 25.6m^2/275 sq.ft.
Rigging:	Sloop
Price Guide:	£7,000
Summary:	A beautifully finished, classic cruiser. Very spacious.

SERAPH

Design:	Vermeulen Jachtwerf, Holland
Supplier:	Vermeulen Jachtwerf, Holland

Specifications:

Construction:	*Ply*
LWL:	6.4m/21'0
LOA:	8.46m/27'9
Beam:	2.97m/9'9
Draft:	1.47m/4'10
Displ:	4,068kg/8,960 lbs

Fittings:	Volvo Penta diesel engine. Steel reinforced.
Interior:	4 berths. 1.88m/6'2 headroom.
Sails:	Area 41.8m^2/450 sq.ft.
Rigging:	Sloop
Price Guide:	On application
Summary:	Based on traditional Dutch design. Exceptionally roomy below. Efficient windward sailing.

TRINTEL

Design:	E. G. van de Stadt, Holland
Supplier:	Jachtwerf Ann Wever, Holland Clyde Chandlers, Scotland

Specifications:

Construction:	Steel
LWL:	6.5m/21'4
LOA:	8.46m/27'9
Beam:	2.44m/8'0
Draft:	1.3m/4'3
Displ:	4,576kg/10,080 lbs

Fittings:	10 hp Albin engine.
Interior:	5 berths. 1.91m/6'3 headroom
Sails:	Area 31.6m^2/340 sq.ft.
Rigging:	Auxiliary Bermudan ketch
Price Guide:	£7,000
Summary:	Comfortable, easily handled cruising sloop, with little maintenance as there are no seams.

VARNE 27

Design:	Duncan M. Stuart, England 1973
Supplier:	Varne Marine Ltd., England
Specifications:	*Construction:* GRP — hand laid
	LWL: 6.40m/21'0
	LOA: 8.45m/27'9
	Beam: 2.74m/9'0
	Draft: 1.30m/4'3
	Displ: 2,812kg/6,200
	Ballast: 1,177kg/2,595 lbs
Fittings:	GRP and sandwich core deck. Lead ballast. 12 hp Farryman ASOM diesel engine. Gold anodised and spruce spars.
Interior:	Oven. Twin sink. Marine flush toilet—enclosed with shower.
Sails:	Area 31.94m^2(18 + 14)/344 sq.ft. (149 + 195)
Rigging:	Sloop
Price Guide:	£7,120
Summary:	Kits available. A new boat just coming into its own as a popular cruiser.

NORMANDY

Design: Laurent Giles, England

Supplier: Laurent Giles & Partners, England

Specifications: *Construction:* To specification
LWL: 6.55m/21'6
LOA: 8.48m/27'10
Beam: 2.39m/7'10
Draft: 1.6m/5'3
Displ: 4,068kg/8,960 lbs

Fittings: To specification

Interior: 4/5 berths

Sails: Area 31.9m^2/343 sq.ft.

Rigging: Bermudan sloop

Price Guide: £7,500

Summary: Roomy, good value for money, cruiser.

APACHE UK

Design: Edward S. Brewer & Assoc., U.S.A. 1972

Supplier: Ouyang Boat Works, Canada

Est. Rating: 23.5' IOR

Specifications: *Construction:* Balsa core and GRP
LWL: 7.47m/24'6
LOA: 8.53m/28'0
Beam: 2.87m/9'5
Draft: 1.32m/4'4
Displ: 3,064m/6,750 lbs
Ballast: 1,362kg/3,000 lbs

Fittings: Aluminium spars. Deck of balsa core and GRP Teak trim.

Interior: 5 berths in 2 cabins. Galley. 1.85m/6'1 headroom.

Variations: Optional gasoline or diesel auxiliary

Sails: Area 34.5m^2(14.8 + 19.7)/372 sq.ft. (160 + 212)

Rigging: Masthead rig

Price Guide: $9,500us

Summary: A fast cruising/racing boat with an exceptionally long waterline.

YANKEE 28
¹/₂ TON

Design:	Robert Finch, U.S.A. 1971
Supplier:	Yankee Yachts Inc., U.S.A.
Est. Rating:	21.7′ IOR Mk III

Specifications:	*Construction:*	GRP
	LWL:	6.68m/21′11
	LOA:	8.46m/27′9
	Beam:	2.59m/8′6
	Draft:	1.42m/4′8
	Displ:	2,951kg/6,500 lbs
	Ballast:	1,249kg/2,750 lbs

Fittings:	GRP and balsa core deck. Teak trim. Aluminium or wood spars. 30 hp Universal Atomic 4 gasoline.
Interior:	6 berths in 2 cabins. Icebox. Sink
Variations:	Optional toilet
Sails:	Area 33.3m² (13.7 + 19.6)/358 sq.ft. (147 + 211)
Rigging:	Sloop
Price Guide:	$15,250us
Summary:	Beautifully finished inside and out. High aspect sail plan and high ballast to displacement ratio gives excellent performance.

VOLLENHOVENS BOLJACHT

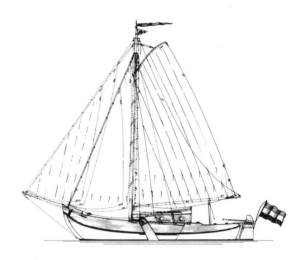

Design:	J. K. Gipon, Holland	
Supplier:	Kooijman en de Vries Jachtbouw BV, Holland	
Specifications:	*Construction:*	Wood
	LOA:	8.50m/27'10½
	Beam:	3.10m/10'2
	Draft:	0.65m/2'1½
	Displ:	5,500kg/12,125 lbs
Fittings:	Teak trim.	
Interior:	6 berths. Sink. Toilet.	
Variations:	Fittings and finish to individual specification	
Sails:	Area 32.3m² (22.8 + 9.5)/348 sq.ft. (245 + 103)	
Rigging:	Sloop	
Price Guide:	69,500 D.Fl.	
Summary:	A boat designed on traditional lines.	

ALOHA 28

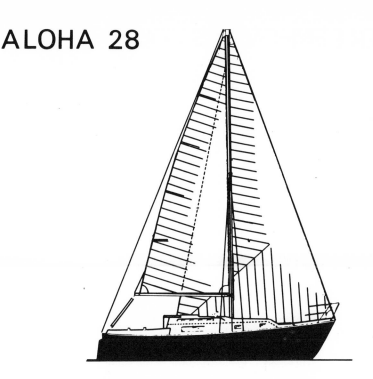

Design:	Edward S. Brewer & Assoc., U.S.A. 1972
Supplier:	Ouyang Boat Works, Canada
Est. Rating:	23.5' IOR
Specifications:	*Construction:* Balsa core and GRP
	LWL: 7.47m/24'6
	LOA: 8.53m/28'
	Beam: 2.87m/9'5
	Draft: 1.32m/4'4
	Displ: 3,064kg/6,750 lbs
	Ballast: 1,362kg/3,000 lbs
Fittings:	Aluminium spars. Deck of balsa core and GRP. Teak trim.
Interior:	5 berths in 2 cabins. Galley. 1.85m/6'1 headroom.
Variations:	Optional gasoline or diesel auxiliary
Sails:	Area 34.5m^2(14.8 + 19.7)/372 sq.ft. (160 + 212)
Rigging:	Masthead rig
Price Guide:	$9,500us
Summary:	A fast cruising/racing boat with an exceptionally long waterline.

BRISTOL HALF-TON

Design:	Halsey Herreshoff, U.S.A. 1972
Supplier:	Bristol Yacht Co., U.S.A.
Est. Rating:	21.7' IOR Mk III
Specifications:	*Construction:* GRP
	LWL: 7.32m/24'0
	LOA: 8.53m/28'0
	Beam: 2.9m/9'6
	Draft: 1.62m/5'4
	Displ: 2,996kg/6,600 lbs
	Ballast: 1,362kg/3,000 lbs
Fittings:	Balso core and GRP deck. Aluminium spars. 10HP Farryman diesel engine.
Interior:	5 berths in 2 cabins
Sails:	Area 34.5m^2(14.4 + 20.1)/371 sq.ft. (155 + 216)
Rigging:	Sloop
Price Guide:	$14,847us
Summary:	Designed specifically for ½ ton Competition. Available through dealers.

PASSATORE

Design:	J. M. Finot, France
Supplier:	F. E. Sparkes Marine, England
Specifications:	*Construction:*
	LWL: 6.28m/20'7½
	LOA: 8.53m/28'0
	Beam: 3.05m/10'0
	Draft: 1.7m/5'7
Fittings:	Fin keel. Farymann diesel 10HP auxiliary.
Sails:	Area 111.6m^2/1201 sq.ft.
Rigging:	Sloop
Price Guide:	On application

ATLANTA 28

Design:	C. S. J. Roy, England 1972	
Supplier:	Atlanta Marine, England	
Specificatiᴏns:	*Construction:*	GRP
	LWL:	6.71m/22'0
	LOA:	8.53m/28'0
	Beam:	2.8m/9'2
	Draft:	1.42m/4'8
	Displ:	3,305kg/7,280 lbs
	Ballast:	908kg/2,000 lbs
Fittings:	Fin keel. Inboard. 10HP diesel engine.	
Interior:	5 berths. Full galley. 1 enclosed toilet.	
Sails:	Area 42.7m^2/460 sq.ft.	
Rigging:	Sloop	
Price Guide:	£5,500	
Summary:	Kits and mouldings available. A well-balanced family cruiser.	

CORONADO 28

Design:	Coronada Yachts, U.S.A. 1973
Supplier:	Coronada Yachts, U.S.A. Playvisa Coronado Yachts, England
Specifications:	*Construction:* GRP *LWL:* 6.76m/22'2 *LOA:* 8.53m/28'0 *Beam:* 2.59m/8'6 *Draft:* 1.47m/4'10 *Displ:* 3,087kg/6,800 lbs *Ballast:* 1,271kg/2,800 lbs
Fittings:	Lead ballast. Teak trim. Aluminium spars.
Interior:	6 berths
Sails:	Area 33.4m^2/359 sq.ft.
Rigging:	Sloop. Stainless steel.
Price Guide:	$11,995us
Summary:	Stiff in heavy weather and easy to sail. Ideal family cruising boat.

GALION 28

Design:	Ian Hannay, England
Supplier:	Deacons Boatyard, England
	Am Tec Imports, U.S.A.

Specifications:		
	Construction:	GRP
	LOA:	8.53m/28'0
	Beam:	2.74m/9'0
	Draft:	1.09m−1.39m−1.7m/3'7−4'7−5'7

Fittings:	GRP deck
Interior:	6 berths in 2 cabins. Standard galley.
Variations:	Twin or 2 keel options. Optional gasoline auxiliary.
Sails:	Area 31.7m^2/341 sq.ft.
Rigging:	Bermudan sloop
Price Guide:	£4,900+

GREAT DANE 28

Design:	Aage Utzon, Denmark 1965
Supplier:	Klaus Baess, Denmark Danyachts, U.S.A.

Specifications:

Construction:	GRP
LWL:	6.5m/21'4
LOA:	8.53m/28'0
Beam:	2.49m/8'2
Draft:	1.37m/4'6
Displ:	3,859kg/8,500 lbs
Ballast:	1,771kg/3,900 lbs

Fittings:	GRP deck. Aluminium spars. 25HP Volvo MD-2B diesel engine. Lead ballast. Teak trim.
Interior:	5 berths in 2 cabins. 1.88m/6'2 headroom.
Sails:	Area 36.7m^2 (20 + 16.7)/395 sq.ft. (215 + 180)
Rigging:	Sloop
Price Guide:	$17,500us f.o.b. Denmark
Summary:	Family cruiser built to Lloyd's specifications. Very roomy. High standard Danish workmanship.

840

HALMATIC 8.80

Design:	Camper & Nicholsons, England 1969
Supplier:	Camper & Nicholsons, England 1969 Wells Yachts, U.S.A.

Specifications:	*Construction:*	GRP
	LWL:	7.03m/23'1
	LOA:	8.53m/28'0
	Beam:	2.74m/9'0
	Draft:	0.91m/3'0
	Displ:	3,541kg/7,800 lbs
	Ballast:	1,312kg/2,890 lbs

Fittings:	Bilge keel
Interior:	5 berths. 1.89m/6'0 headroom.
Variations:	Optional inboard engine.
Sails:	Area 27.3m^2/294 sq.ft.
Rigging:	Sloop
Price Guide:	£7,300
Summary:	Can be trailed. A very modern motor sailer that can cope with most offshore conditions comfortably.

NEWPORT 28

Design: Cuthbertson & Cassian, U.S.A. 1973

Supplier: Capital Yachts Inc., U.S.A.

Specifications: *Construction:*   GRP
                      LWL: 7.01m/23'0
                      LOA: 8.53m/28'0
                      Beam: 2.9m/9'6
                      Draft: 1.37m/4'6
                      Displ: 3,178kg/7,000 lbs
                      Ballast: 1,362kg/3,000

Fittings: Lead ballast. GRP deck. Aluminium spars.

Interior: 7 berths in 2 cabins

Variations: Optional HP gasoline inboard or outboard.

Sails: Area 35.8m^2/385 sq.ft.

Rigging: Sloop

Price Guide: $13,000us

OFFSHORE 28

Design:	A. E. Luders Jr, Holland 1972
Supplier:	Cheoy Lee, Hong Kong Lion Yachts, U.S.A.

Specifications:	*Construction:*	GRP
	LWL:	6.71m/22'0
	LOA:	8.53m/28'0
	Beam:	2.8m/9'2
	Draft:	1.07m/3'6
	Displ:	3,602kg/7,935 lbs

Fittings:	GRP deck. Wood or aluminium spars. Auxiliary 30HP Universal Atomic 4 diesel.
Interior:	5 berths in 2 cabins. Sink. Icebox. One enclosed set toilet.
Variations:	Teak overlay deck optional
Sails:	Area 35m^2(16.7 + 18.3)/377 sq.ft. (180 + 197)
Rigging:	Sloop
Price Guide:	$13,500us

SABRE 28 ½ TON

Design:	Roger Hewson, U.S.A. 1971
Supplier:	Hewson Marine Inc., U.S.A.
Est. Rating:	21.7' IOR Mk III 22.3' MORC

Specifications:	*Construction:*	GRP
	LWL:	6.71m/22'10
	LOA:	8.53m/28'0
	Beam:	2.74m/9'0
	Draft:	1.3m/4'3
	Displ:	3,133kg/6,900 lbs
	Ballast:	1,317kg/2,900 lbs

Fittinga:	Lead ballast. GRP and balsa core deck. 30HP Atomic 4 gasoline. Aluminium spars.
Interior:	6 berths in 2 cabins. Stove. Sink. Icebox. 1 sea toilet.
Sails:	Area 36.3m^2 (16.6 + 19.7/391 sq.ft. (179 + 212)
Rigging:	Sloop
Price Guide:	$14,000us
Summary:	Available through dealers.

WESTERLY 28

Design:	John Butler, England
Supplier:	Westerly Marine Construction, England Andrew Gemeny & Sons, U.S.A.

Specifications:	*Construction:*	GRP
	LWL:	6.71m/22'0
	LOA:	8.53m/28'0
	Beam:	2.74m/9'0
	Draft:	1.37m/4'6
	Displ:	3,178kg/7,000 lbs
	Ballast:	1,225.8kg/2,700 lbs

Fittings:	Lead ballast. GRP deck. Aluminium spars.
Interior:	6 berths in 2 cabins. Galley standard.
Variations:	Optional power
Sails:	Area 35.39m^2/381 sq.ft.
Rigging:	Sloop
Price Guide:	£6,900

P 28

Design:	H. Hallberg, Sweden 1959
Supplier:	Larssen Trade AB, Sweden Thomas Nelson, England

Specifications:

Construction:	Mahogany on ash
LWL:	6.27m/20'7
LOA:	8.53m/28'0
Beam:	2.31m/7'7
Draft:	1.27m/4'2
Displ:	2,803kg/6,175 lbs

Fittings:	Albin engine
Interior:	4 berths. 1.8m/5'11 headroom
Sails:	Area 31.1m^2/335 sq.ft.
Rigging:	Bermudan sloop
Price Guide:	On application
Summary:	Ideal family cruiser which can be raced competitively as well. Originally designed for the Pacific.

SPIRIT 28

Design:	E. G. van de Stadt, Holland	
Supplier:	George Stead Yachts, England	
Specifications:	*Construction:*	GRP
	LWL:	6.88m/22'7
	LOA:	8.53m/28'0
	Beam:	2.82m/9'3
	Draft:	1.80m/5'1
Fittings:	Fin keel. Couach 15HP inboard engine	
Interior:	4/5 berths	
Sails:	Area 40.88m^2/440 sq.ft.	
Rigging:	Sloop	
Price Guide:	£7,300+	

MORGAN OUT ISLAND 28

Design:	Morgan Yacht Corp.	
Supplier:	Morgan Yacht Corp. Peter Webster Ltd., England	
Specifications:	*Construction:*	GRP
	LWL:	7.26m/23'10
	LOA:	8.67m/28'5
	Beam:	2.82m/9'3
	Draft:	1.07m/3'6
	Displ:	3,632kg/8,000 lbs
	Ballast:	1,362kg/3,000 lbs
Fittings:	Lead ballast. GRP deck. Aluminium spars. Auxiliary 18HP Atomic 4 gasoline.	
Interior:	6/7 berths in 2 cabins. Sink. Water pump. Icebox. Stove. 1 enclosed head.	
Sails:	Area 33.8m^2(16.7 + 17.1)/364 sq.ft. (180 + 184)	
Rigging:	Sloop	
Price Guide:	£8,200/$16,000 us	

VICTOIRE 28

Design:	Jachtwerf Victoria, Holland
Supplier:	Jachtwerf Victoria, Holland
Specifications:	*Construction:* GRP
	LOA: 8.53m/28'0
	Draft: 1.35m/4'5
Fittings:	Bilge keel. Other fittings to specification.
Interior:	5 berths. Layout to specification.
Variations:	Optional inboard engine.
Sails:	Area 35.67m^2/384 sq.ft.+
Rigging:	Various
Price Guide:	On application
Summary:	Can not be trailed.

SERENDIPITY

Supplier:	Seaglass Ltd., England
Specifications:	*Construction:* GRP
	LOA: 8.56m/28'1
	Draft: 1.4m/4'7
Fittings:	Keel boat. Inboard engine.
Interior:	4/5 berths
Sails:	Area 26.66m^2/287 sq.ft.
Rigging:	Bermudan sloop
Price Guide:	On application
Summary:	Can not be trailed.

GULF COAST 29

Design:	Martin Bludworth, U.S.A. 1969
Supplier:	Gulf Coast Sailboats, U.S.A.
Specifications:	*Construction:* GRP
	LWL: 6.71m/22'0
	LOA: 8.69m/28'6
	Beam: 2.74m/9'0
	Draft: 1.32m/4'4
	Displ: 2,542kg/5,600 lbs
	Ballast: 1,021kg/2,250 lbs
Fittings:	Cast iron ballast. GRP deck. Aluminium spars.
Interior:	5 berths in 2 cabins
Sails:	Area 32.1m^2(16.3 + 15.8)/356 sq. ft.(176 + 170)
Rigging:	Sloop
Price Guide:	$7,495us

ARMAGNAC

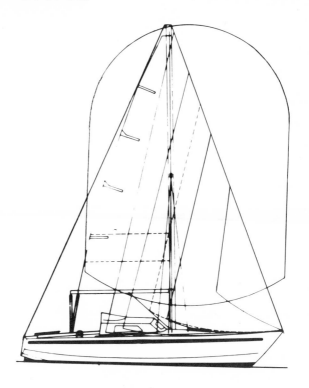

Design:	Phillippe Harlé, France
Supplier:	Aubin Marine, France
Specifications:	*Construction:* GRP
	LWL: 6.80m/
	LOA: 8.55m/28'0½
	Beam: 2.80m/9'2
	Draft: 1.37m—1.60m/4'6—5'3
	Displ: 2,200kg/4,850 lbs
	Ballast: 1,200kg/2,646 lbs
Fittings:	10 CV maximum auxiliary.
Interior:	5 berths. Galley. Sink.
Sails:	Area 25.10m^2 (13.60 + 11.50)/270 sq.ft. (146 + 124)
Rigging:	Sloop
Price Guide:	59,650 Fr.f.
Summary:	A popular French design seen most in the Meditteranean.

TRAPPER

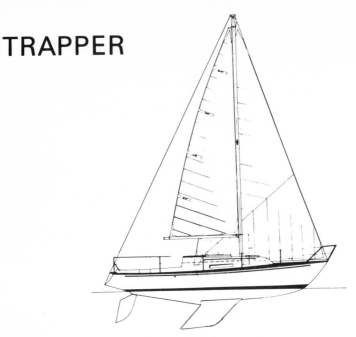

Design:	Cuthbertson & Cassian, Canada
Supplier:	C & C. Yachts, Canada Anstey Yachts Ltd., England
Est. Rating:	20.5' IOR

Specifications:

Construction:	GRP
LWL:	6.71m/22'0
LOA:	8.59m/28'2
Beam:	2.54m/8'4
Draft:	1.42m/4'8
Displ:	2,157kg/4,755 lbs
Ballast:	1,034kg/2,250 lbs

Fittings:	Fin keel. Iron ballast. GRP deck. Gold anodised aluminium spars.
Interior:	4 berths. 1.52m/5' headroom. Sink. Stove. Marine toilet.
Variations:	Optional engine
Sails:	Area 25.59m^2/274.82 sq.ft.
Rigging:	Sloop
Price Guide:	£5,000
Summary:	Designed for the owner who intends to sail and use the boat — extremely practical. An eyecatcher from both the appearance and performance points of view. Kits available.

VIKING 28 ½ TON

Design:	Cuthbertson & Cassian, Canada 1967
Supplier:	Ontario Yacht Co. Ltd., Canada
Est. Rating:	21.7'/22.3' IOR Mk III
Specifications:	*Construction:* GRP
	LWL: 6.71m/22'0
	LOA: 8.59m/28'2
	Beam: 2.57m/8'5
	Draft: 1.37m/4'6
	Displ: 2,158.7kg/4,755 lbs
	Ballast: 1,021.5kg/2,250 lbs
Fittings:	Cast iron ballast. GRP and balsa core deck. Aluminium spars. 6HP Vire gasoline.
Interior:	4 berths in 2 cabins. Stove. Icebox. Sink. Water pump. 1 chemical toilet.
Variations:	Inboard or outboard.
Sails:	Area 29.91m^2 (14.03 + 15.89)/322 sq.ft. (151 + 171)
Rigging:	Sloop
Price Guide:	$10,400–11,625us
Summary:	A well established design that performs well.

THOLENSE SCHOW

Design:	A van Ovdgaarden, Holland	
Supplier:	C. H. Hitters, Holland	
	J. G. Meakes Ltd., England	
Specifications:	*Construction:*	Steel
	LWL:	6.93m/22'9½
	LOA:	8.59m/28'2½
	Beam:	2.79m/9'2½
	Draft:	1.27m/4'2
	Displ:	6,508.5kg/6.4 tons
Fittings:	BMC Vedette engine	
Interior:	5 berths	
Sails:	Area 35.3m²/380 sq.ft.	
Rigging:	Motor sailer	
Price Guide:	£8,000+	
Summary:	A traditional Dutch motor sailer. Ideal for family or single-handed cruising. Very spacious.	

TWISTER

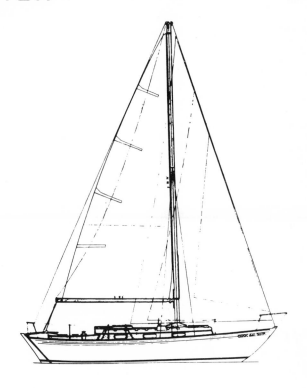

Design: C. R. Holman, England

Supplier: J. W. & A. Upham, England

Est. Rating: Portsmouth number 95

Specifications:

Construction:	GRP
LWL:	6.55m/21'6
LOA:	8.61m/28'3
Beam:	2.46m/8'1
Draft:	1.52m/5'0
Displ:	4,576.3kg/4.5 tons

Fittings: Keelboat 10HP Albin engine.

Interior: 4/5 berths. 1.83m/6'0 headroom.

Sails: Area 39.48m^2/425 sq.ft.

Rigging: Bermudan sloop

Price Guide: £8,200

Summary: Finished to a very high standard. Can be trailed.

DEFENDER

Design:	Sparkman & Stephens, Canada
Supplier:Yach	Columbia Yacht Corporation, U.S.A.
Specifications:	*Construction:* GRP
	LWL: 6.86m/22'6
	LOA: 8.69m/28'6
	Beam: 2.44m/8'0
	Draft: 1.22m/4'0
	Displ: 3,813.6kg/8,400 lbs
	Ballast: 1,870.48kg/4,120 lbs
Fittings:	GRP deck. Aluminium spars. Lead ballast.
Interior:	6 berths in 2 cabins. Standard galley.
Variations:	Optional 30HP auxiliary
Sails:	Area 35.39m^2/381 sq.ft.
Rigging:	Sloop
Price Guide:	$13,500us

WAARSCHIP ½ TONNER

Design:	Akerman & Kremer, Holland 1970/1971
Supplier:	Awson Marine, England
Est. Rating:	21.6' IOR
Specifications:	*Construction:* GRP
	LWL: 6.40m/21'0
	LOA: 8.69m/28'6
	Beam: 2.94m/9'9
	Draft: 1.65m/5'5
	Displ: 3,050.8kg/6,720 lbs
	Ballast: 1,371.08kg/3,020 lbs
Fittings:	Fin keel. RCA Dolphin 12HP engine.
Interior:	6 berths
Sails:	Area 42.07m^2/452.9 sq.ft.
Rigging:	Sloop
Price Guide:	£6,600
Summary:	Kits available.

IRWIN 28 MkIII ½ TON

Design:	Ted Irwin, U.S.A. 1973
Supplier:	Irwin Yacht & Marine Corp., U.S.A.
Est. Rating:	21.7' IOR Mk III 21.5'–22.0' MORC
Specifications:	*Construction:* GRP
	LWL: 7.01m/23'0
	LOA: 8.67m/28'5
	Beam: 2.74m/9'0
	Draft: 1.37m–0.91m/4'6–3'0
	Displ: 3,541kg/7,800 lbs
	Ballast: 1,362kg/3,000–3,200 lbs
Fittings:	Balsa core and GRP deck. Aluminium spars. 30HP Universal Atomic 4 gasoline auxiliary.
Interior:	5 berths in 1 cabin.
Variations:	Fin keel or keel/centreboard options.
Sails:	Area 35m² (14.4 + 20.6)/377 sq.ft. (155 + 222)
Rigging:	Sloop
Summary:	Designed for all-out racing.

KING'S CRUISER 29

Design:	Tord Sunden, Finland
Supplier:	Turun Veneveistamo, Finland Ballena Marine, England
Rat. Rating:	21.6' IOR Portsmouth number 93

Specifications:	*Construction:*	GRP
	LWL:	7.06m/23'2
	LOA:	8.69m/28'6
	Beam:	2.49m/8'2
	Draft:	1.5m/4'11
	Displ:	2,996kg/6,600 lbs
	Ballast:	1,398kg/3,080 lbs

Fittings:	Iron ballast. GRP deck. Aluminium spars. Volvo Penta MD1 diesel auxiliary.
Interior:	4 berths in 2 cabins.
Sails:	Area 48.1m^2 (23.8 + 24.3)/518 sq.ft. (256 + 262)
Rigging:	Sloop.
Basic Price:	£7,900

PARKWOOD 28

Design:	W. de Vries Leutsch Jnr, Holland 1964	
Supplier:	Parkwood Marine Yacht Builders, Wales	
Specifications:	*Construction:*	Steel/Mahogany
	LWL:	6.8m/22'4
	LOA:	8.69m/28'6
	Beam:	2.6m/8'7
	Draft:	1.12m/3'8
	Displ:	3.66 tonnes/3.6 tons
Fittings:	Lister 13HP engine	
Interior:	5 berths 1.9m/6'2 headroom.	
Sails:	Area 35m^2/377 sq.ft.	
Rigging:	Bermudan masthead sloop	
Price Guide:	On application	
Summary:	Designed for the family man. Can be sailed single-handed. Easy to maintain.	

PETER DUCK

Design:	Laurent Giles Ltd., England 1946
Supplier:	Laurent Giles & Partners Ltd., England
Specifications:	*Construction:* Iroko on oak
	LWL: 7.62m/25'0
	LOA: 8.69m/28'6
	Beam: 2.74m/9'0
	Draft: 1.14m/3'9
	Displ: 5,848kg/12,880 lbs
Fittings:	BMC captain 31HP inboard engine.
Interior:	4 berths 1.83m/6'0 headroom.
Sails:	Area 30.2m^2/325 sq.ft.
Rigging:	Auxiliary Bermudan ketch
Price Guide:	
Summary:	Comfortable and well built. Standard price includes a good inventory.

CHANCE P29/25 ½ TON

Design:	Britton Chance Jnr, Canada 1973
Supplier:	Paceship Yachts, Canada Robertsons of Sandbank, England.
Est. Rating:	21.7′ IOR Mk III
Specifications:	*Construction:* GRP and balsa core *LWL:* 7.85m/25′9 *LOA:* 8.71m/28′7 *Beam:* 2.84m/9′4 *Draft:* 1.55m/5′1 *Displ:* 3,405kg/7,500 lbs *Ballast:* 942.05kg/2,075 lbs
Fittings:	Balsa core. GRP deck. Aluminium spars. 30HP Atomic 4 auxiliary.
Interior:	5/6 berths in 2 cabins. Galley — stove, sink, icebox, Freshwater pump.
Sails:	Area 33.91m²/365 sq.ft.
Rigging:	Sloop
Price Guide:	£ on application/$22,700us
Summary:	A boat that will stand the test of time on and off the race circuit. It will please from an aesthetic, practical and competition point of view.

ERICSON 29 ½ TON

Design:	Bruce King, U.S.A. 1969
Supplier:	Ericson Yachts Inc., U.S.A. Hamble Marine, U.K. Nordmarine, Italy
Est. Rating:	20.6' IOR Mk III 24.6' CCA

Specifications:

Construction:	GRP and oiled teak
LWL:	6.71m/22'0
LOA:	8.71m/28'7
Beam:	2.82m/9'3
Draft:	1.32m/4'4
Displ:	3,859kg/8,500 lbs
Ballast:	1,771kg/3,900 lbs

Fittings:	GRP deck. Aluminium spars. Lead ballast.
Interior:	6 berths in 2 cabins
Variations:	Optional make and HP auxiliary
Sails:	Area 37.5m^2 (16.7 + 20.8)/404 sq.ft. (180 + 224)
Rigging:	Sloop
Price Guide:	£9,500/$12,495us
Summary:	One of the fastest auxiliary type boats around.

RANGER 29

Design:	Gary Mull, U.S.A. 1970	
Supplier:	Ranger Yachts, U.S.A.	
Est. Rating:	21.2' IOR Mk III	
Specifications:	*Construction:*	GRP
	LWL:	7.01m/23'0
	LOA:	8.71m/28'7
	Beam:	2.84m/9'4
	Draft:	1.35m/4'5
	Displ:	3,042kg/6,700 lbs
	Ballast:	1,421kg/3,130 lbs
Fittings:	GRP deck. Aluminium spars. 30HP Universal gasoline auxiliary.	
Interior:	5 berths in 2 cabins. Sink. Icebox. 1 chemical toilet. 6' cabin headroom.	
Sails:	Area 37.1m^2/399 sq.ft.	
Rigging:	Sloop	
Price Guide:	$14,000us	
Summary:	Spacious cockpit. Available through dealers.	

SEAFARER 29k

Design: McCurdy & Rhodes, U.S.A. 1972

Supplier: Seafarer Fiberglass Yachts, Inc.

Est. Rating: 20.0' IOR Mk III

Specifications:

Construction:	GRP	
LWL:	6.48m/21'3	
LOA:	8.74m/28'8	
Beam:	2.74m/9'0	
Draft:	1.52m/5'0	
Displ:	2,860.2kg/6,300 lbs	
Ballast:	1,135kg/2,500 lbs	

Fittings: Keelboat. Lead ballast. GRP deck. Aluminium spars.

Interior: 5 berths in 2 cabins. Icebox. Sink. Sea toilet. 1.83m/ 6'0 headroom.

Variations: Centreboard model also available — known as **Seafarer 29.** Cruising or racing decks available.

Sails: Area 33.17m^2(15.2 + 17.93)/357 sq. ft.(164 + 193)

Rigging: Sloop or ketch

Price Guide: $9,000us

JOEMARIN 29

Design:	Britton Chance & Finnish Design Group, Finland 1974
Supplier:	Joemarin Oy, Finland Tradewind Yachts, England
Specifications:	*Construction:* GRP *LWL:* 7.82m/25'8 *LOA:* 8.76m/28'9 *Beam:* 2.84m/9'4 *Draft:* 1.66m/5'5½ *Displ:* 3,859kg/8,500 lbs *Ballast:* 1,224kg/2,695 lbs
Fittings:	Volvo MD6 12HP diesel engine.
Interior:	6 berths. Washing space with standing room.
Sails:	Area 325.2m^2/3,500 sq.ft.
Rigging:	Sloop
Price Guide:	On application
Summary:	A totally designed functional sailing boat. Completed by a new production method.

863

PACESHIP P29

Design:	Cuthbertson & Cassian, Canada 1971
Supplier:	Paceship Yachts, Canada
Est. Rating:	22.6' IOR Mk III 23.2' MORC
Specifications:	*Construction:* GRP
	LWL: 6.71m/22'0
	LOA: 8.79m/28'10
	Beam: 2.77m/9'1
	Draft: 0.94m/3'1
	Displ: 2,951kg/6,500 lbs
	Ballast: 1,430kg/3,150 lbs
Fittings:	Lead ballast. GRP deck. Aluminium spars. 33HP Universal Atomic 4 gasoline.
Interior:	6 berths in 2 cabins. Icebox. Sink. Fridge. Monomatic enclosed toilet.
Sails:	Area 33.7m^2/363 sq.ft.
Rigging:	Sloop
Price Guide:	$14,500us

OHLSON 8.8

Design:	Einar Ohlson, Sweden 1970
Supplier:	Campbell/Shehan Inc., U.S.A. Ohlson, Sweden Michael Pocock, England
Est. Rating:	22.5' IOR

Specifications:

Construction:	GRP
LWL:	7.52m/24'8
LOA:	8.81m/28'11
Beam:	2.87m/9'5
Draft:	1.58m/5'2
Displ:	2,996kg/6,600 lbs
Ballast:	1,248.5kg/2,750 lbs

Fittings:	Lead ballast. GRP deck. Aluminium spars. 12HP Farryman auxiliary.
Interior:	6 berths in 2 cabins. Icebox. Stove. Groco enclosed sea toilet.
Sails:	Area 14.6m^2/157 sq.ft.
Rigging:	Sloop
Price Guide:	£7,200/$18,700us

TRINTELLA 1

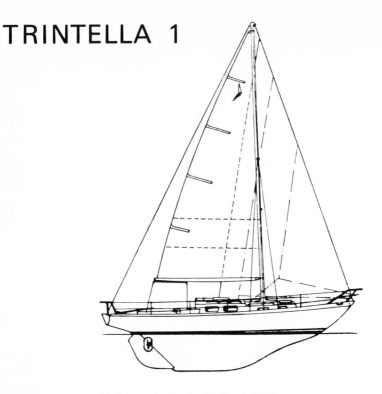

Design:	E. G. van de Stadt, Holland 1967
Supplier:	Jachtwerf Anne Wever NV, Holland Stangate Marine Ltd., England
Specifications:	*Construction:* GRP *LWL:* 6.50m/21′4 *LOA:* 8.81m/28′11 *Beam:* 2.51m/8′3 *Draft:* 1.32m/4′4 *Displ:* 3,836.3kg/8,450 lbs. *Ballast:* 1,747.9kg/3,850 lbs
Fittings:	Iron ballast. Teak and GRP deck. Aluminium spars. 10HP Albin auxiliary.
Interior:	5 berths in 1 cabin. Sink. Pump. Stove. Raritan marine toilet.
Sails:	Area 35.77m^2 (19.51 + 16.26)/385 sq.ft. (210 + 175) Spinnaker area 59m^2/635 sq.ft.
Rigging:	Sloop
Price Guide:	58,500 D.Fl.
Summary:	One of a series. Also known as **Victory 30**.

ALOA 29 ½ TON

Design:	Finot France, 1972
Supplier:	Aloa Marine, France American International Yacht Corporation, U.S.A.
Est. Rating:	21.7' IOR Mk III
Specifications:	*Construction:* GRP *LWL:* 6.55m/21'6 *LOA:* 8.84m/29'0 *Beam:* 3.3m/10'10 *Draft:* 1.63m/5'4 *Displ:* 2,951kg/6,500 lbs *Ballast:* 999kg/2,200 lbs
Fittings:	Aluminium spars. GRP deck. 10HP Renault RC9D diesel engine.
Interior:	5 berths in 2 cabins.
Sails:	Area 41.3m^2 (16.7 + 24.6)/445 sq.ft. (179 + 265)
Rigging:	Sloop
Price Guide:	84,000 F.fr. S19,900us
Summary:	Smaller sister of the Aloa.

CASCADE 29

Design:	Robert A. Smith, U.S.A., 1961
Supplier:	Yacht Constructors Inc., U.S.A.

Specifications:	*Construction:*	GRP
	LWL:	7.32m/24'0
	LOA:	8.84m/29'0
	Beam:	2.49m/8'2
	Draft:	1.45m/4'9
	Displ:	3,405kg/7,500 lbs
	Ballast:	1,071kg/2,360 lbs

Fittings:	Cast iron ballast. GRP and plywood deck. Aluminium spars.
Interior:	6 berths in 2 cabins.
Sails:	Area 37.6m^2 (20.8 + 16.8)/405 sq.ft. (224 + 181)
Rigging:	Sloop
Price Guide:	$1,775 for the bare hull

KESTELOO

Design:	E. G. van de Stadt, Holland
Supplier:	SMS Yacht Builders, England

Specifications:	*Construction:*	Steel
	LWL:	6.78m/22'3
	LOA:	8.84m/29'0
	Beam:	2.74m/9'0
	Draft:	1.55m or 1.32m/5'1 or 4'4
	Displ:	Optional
	Ballast:	Optional

Fittings:	To specification
Interior:	To specification
Sails:	Variable
Rigging:	Various rigs available
Price Guide:	From £1,350
Summary:	Hulls for completion.

CAL 29

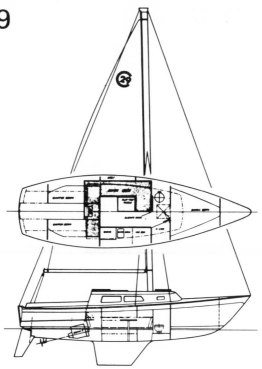

Design:	C. William Lapworth, U.S.A. 1968
Supplier:	Jensen Marine, U.S.A.

Specifications:

Construction:	GRP
LWL:	7.32m/24'0
LOA:	8.84m/29'0
Beam:	2.82m/9'3
Draft:	1.37m/4'6
Displ:	3,632kg/8,000 lbs
Ballast:	1,521kg/3,350 lbs

Fittings:	Lead ballast. Aluminium spars.
Interior:	6 berths in 2 cabins. Standard galley.
Variations:	Optional HP gasoline auxiliary. **Cal 2—29** model also available.
Sails:	Area 40.3m^2/434 sq.ft.
Rigging:	Sloop
Price Guide:	$17,200—19,000us
Summary:	Light displacement, long waterline provides speed while her ventral fin provides control off the wind.

NICHOLSON 30

Design:	Camper & Nicholsons, England 1972
Supplier:	Camper & Nicholsons, England Camper Nicholson, U.S.A.
Est. Rating:q	21.7' IOR
Specifications:	*Construction*

LWL:	24'0
LOA:	8.84m/29'0
Beam:	2.98m/9'9½
Draft:	1.73m/5'8
Displ:	3,305kg/7,280 lbs
Ballast:	1,271kg/2,800 lbs

Fittings:	Fin keel. Volvo MD16 inboard auxiliary.
Interior:	4/5 berths
Sails:	Area 46.4m^2/499 sq.ft.
Rigging:	Sloop
Price Guide:	£9,700

SNAPDRAGON 890

Design:	Thames Marine, England 1971
Supplier:	Thames Marine, England Peek Yachting International, Holland Wells Yachts Inc., U.S.A.
Est. Rating:	Portsmouth number 99
Specifications:	*Construction:* GRP

LWL:	7.32m/24'6
LOA:	8.90m/29'0
Beam:	2.89m/9'6
Draft:	0.99m/3'3
Displ:	3,630kg/8,000 lbs
Ballast:	1,590kg/3,500 lbs

Fittings:	Iron twin keels. GRP deck. Aluminium spars.
Interior:	6 berths in 2 cabins. 1.88m/6'2 headroom. Galley standard. 1 enclosed toilet.
Variations:	Optional diesel engine
Sails:	Area 29.5m^2(17.8 + 11.5)/317 sq.ft. (192 + 125) Spinnaker area 46.5m^2/500 sq.ft.
Rigging:	Sloop
Price Guide:	£7,500

ELIZABETHAN 29

Design:	C. R. Holman, England 1960	
Supplier:	Peter Webster Ltd., England	
Rating:	Portsmouth primary yardstick 94	
Specifications:	*Construction:*	GRP
	LWL:	6.09m/20'0
	LOA:	8.84m/29'0
	Beam:	2.28m/7'6
	Draft:	1.27m/4'2
	Displ:	3,305kg/7,280 lbs
Fittings:	Fare Gota engine	
Interior:	4 berths. 1.78m/5'10 headroom.	
Sails:	Area 29.7m^2/320 sq.ft.	
Rigging:	Masthead sloop	
Price Guide:	£6,800	
Summary:	Good performance. Capable of being driven hard.	

NORTHERN 29

Design:	Sparkman & Stephens, Canada 1970	
Supplier:	Northern Yachts, Ltd.	
Specifications:	*Construction:*	GRP
	LWL:	6.78m/22'3
	LOA:	8.84m/29'0
	Beam:	2.74m/9'0
	Draft:	1.37m/4'6
	Displ:	3,519kg/7,750 lbs
	Ballast:	1,703kg/3,750 lbs
Fittings:	Lead ballast. GRP and balsa core deck. Aluminium spars. 36HP Atomic 4 gasoline.	
Interior:	6 berths in 2 cabins. Icebox. Stove. Sink. Water pumps. Enclosed head.	
Sails:	Area 35.7m^2(15 + 20.7)/384 sq.ft. (161 + 223)	
Rigging:	Sloop	
Price Guide:	$15,500us	

OHLSON 29

Design:	Einar Ohlson, Sweden 1970
Supplier:	Vinga Marine, Sweden Atlanta Marine, England
Est. Rating:	IOR 6.50m/21.53'
Specifications:	*Construction:* GRP *LWL:* 6.70m/22'0 *LOA:* 8.85m/29'0 *Beam:* 2.70m/8'11 *Draft:* 1.60m/5'3 *Displ:* 3.14tonnes/3.1 tons *Ballast:* 1.26 tonnes/1.23 tons
Fittings:	Foam sandwich deck. Volvo Penta
Interior:	5 berths
Variations:	Can be supplied cheaper in a basic sailaway form.
Sails:	Area 31.8m^2/342 sq.ft.
Rigging:	Sloop
Price Guide:	£7,875
Summary:	A popular cruiser for the open sea, speedy and comfortable for all the family.

SHAKO

Design:	Finot Group, France
Supplier:	George Stead Yachts, England

Specifications:

Construction:	GRP
LWL:	6.6m/21'8
LOA:	8.84m/29'0
Beam:	3.30m/10'10
Draft:	1.62m/5'4

Fittings:	Fin keel. 9HP couach inboard.
Sails:	Area 46m^2/495 sq.ft.
Rigging:	Sloop
Price Guide:	

LEGEND

Design:	E. G. van de Stadt Holland
Supplier:	Burnes Shipyard England

Specifications:

Construction:	GRP
LWL:	6.76m/22'2
LOA:	8.92m/29'3
Beam:	2.69m/8'10
Draft:	1.68m/5'6

Fittings:	Finn keel. Brit Sprite/Albin 10HP inboard.
Interior:	5 berths
Sails:	Area 42.3m^2/455 sq.ft.
Rigging:	Sloop
Price Guide:	£6,000

TRISKEL

Design:	Constantini France	
Supplier:	Constantini France	
Est. Rating:	18'0 RORC 21'0IOR	
Specifications:	*Construction:*	Wood
	LWL:	6.70m/21'11½
	LOA:	8.90m/29'2½
	Beam:	2.72m/8'11
	Draft:	1.34m/4'4½
	Displ:	2,800kg/6,173 lbs
	Ballast:	1,350kg/2,976 lbs
Fittings:	To specification	
Interior:	5 berths. Galley. Marine toilet.	
Sails:	Area 40.10m^2/432 sq.ft. Spinnaker area 52.50m^2/565 sq.ft.	
Rigging:	Sloop	
Price Guide:	55,900 Fr.f.	

T-29

Design:	Ted Tyler U.S.A. 1969
Supplier:	Tylercraft U.S.A.
Est. Rating:	22.3′ IOR Mk III

Specifications:

Construction:	GRP
LWL:	7.01m/23′0
LOA:	8.92m/29′3
Beam:	2.59m/8′6
Draft:	0.86m–1.37m/2′10–4′6
Displ:	2,860kg/6,300 lbs
Ballast:	1,294kg/2,850 lbs

Fittings:	Iron ballast. GRP deck. Aluminium spars.
Interior:	6 berths in 2 cabins. Pump. Sink. Icebox. Stove. Enclosed marine toilet and shower.
Variations:	Twin or fin keel. Optional inboard or outboard.
Sails:	Area 34.7m^2/374 sq.ft.
Rigging:	Sloop
Price Guide:	$11,500us

ELIZABETHAN 30 MK III

Design:	David Thomas England 1969/1973
Supplier:	Peter Webster Limited England Henri Wanquiez France
Est. Rating:	21.4′ IOR

Specifications:

Construction:	GRP
LWL:	7.32m/24′0
LOA:	8.99m/29′6
Beam:	2.82m/9′3
Draft:	1.52m/5′0
Displ:	3,305kg/3.25 tons
Ballast:	1,688kg/3,718 lbs

Fittings:	Keel boat. Teak trim. GRP deck. Alloy spars.
Interior:	5 berths. 1.83m/6′0 headroom. 10HP engine recommended.
Sails:	Area 34m^2/366 sq.ft.
Rigging:	Bermudan rig
Price Guide:	£7,250

FINNSAILER 29

Design: Turku Boatyard Finland 1970

Supplier: Turun Veneveistämo Finland
Ballena Marine England

Specifications:

Construction:	GRP	
LWL:	7.98m/26'2	
LOA:	8.92m/29'3	
Beam:	2.8m/9'2	
Draft:	1.01m/3'4	
Displ:	4,068kg/8.960 lbs	
Ballast:	903kg/1,390 lbs	

Fittings: Bilge keel

Interior: 6 berths

Sails: Area 25.1m^2/270 sq.ft.

Rigging: Bermudan sloop

Price Guide: £10,400

Summary: Based on traditional Baltic Sea pilot craft.

LA CRUISER

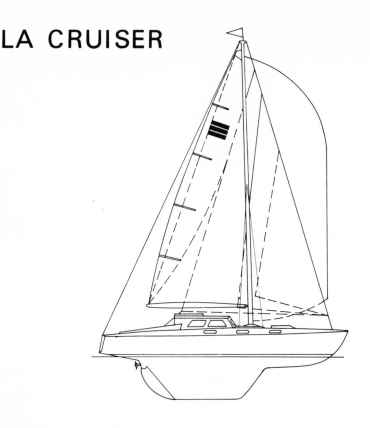

Design:	Knud Olsen Denmark
Supplier:	A/S Borresens Baadebyggeri Denmark
Est. Rating:	21.6' MORC
Specifications:	*Construction:* Plywood and GRP
	LWL: 7.62m/25'0
	LOA: 8.97m/29'5
	Beam: 2.44m/8'0
	Draft: 1.52m/5'0
	Displ: 2,815kg/6,200 lbs
	Ballast: 1,300kg/2,837 lbs
Fittings:	Iron ballast. Plywood and GRP deck. Wooden spars. 10HP Volvo Penta diesel auxiliary.
Interior:	4 berths in 2 cabins. Galley — sink. Icebox.
Sails:	Area 30m^2 (18 + 12)/323 sq.ft. (194+ 129)
Rigging:	Sloop
Price Guide:	109,000 Danish Krone

PRIVATEER UK

Design:	Rodney Warrington Smyth U.K.
Supplier:	Falmouth Boat Construction Ltd England
Specifications:	*Construction:* Oak, pitch pine and teak
	LWL: 6.71m/22'0
	LOA: 8.99m/29'6
	Beam: 2.82m/9'3
	Draft: 1.68m/5'6
	Displ: 5,085kg/11,200 lbs
Fittings:	Watermeta Ford egnine
Interior:	4 berths. 1.85m/6'1 headroom.
Sails:	Area 39.9m^2/430 sq.ft.
Rigging:	Auxiliary Bermudan sloop
Price Guide:	On application
Summary:	A fast, graceful auxiliary sloop built to Lloyds specifications. Gives lasting value.

WANDERER

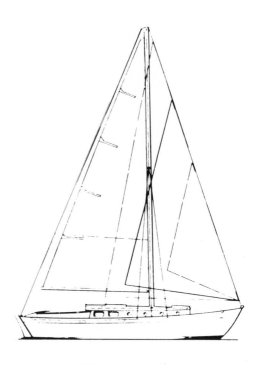

Design:	Laurent Giles & Partners England 1963	
Supplier:	Laurent Giles & Partners England	
Specifications:	*Construction:*	To specification
	LWL:	7.47m/24'6
	LOA:	8.99m/29'6
	Beam:	2.84m/9'4
	Draft:	1.52m/5'0
	Displ:	6,610kg/6.5 tons
Fittings:	To individual requirements	
Interior:	5 berths. Full headroom.	
Sails:	Area 40.7m^2/438.5 sq.ft.	
Rigging:	Bermudan sloop	
Price Guide:	£8,500	
Summary:	Built to a very high standard of craftsmanship.	

WESTWALKRUISER

Design:	Holland
Supplier:	Jachtwerf Volendam Holland
Specifications:	*Construction:* Steel — sandblasted
	LWL: 7.47m/24'6
	LOA: 8.99m/29'6
	Beam: 2.64m/8'8
	Draft: 1.22m/4'0
	Ballast: 1,362kg/3,000 lbs
Fittings:	Mahogany trim. 10HP diesel engine — Sabb.
Interior:	5 berths. Galley. 1.88m/6'2 headroom. 1 enclosed toilet.
Variations:	Numerous accessories can be fitted.
Sails:	Area 35.7m²/384 sq.ft.
Rigging:	Sloop
Price Guide:	48,500 D.Fl.
Summary:	An efficient and comfortable sailing boat. A very handsomely finished interior that will satisfy the most traditional tastes.

881

CARTER 30

Design:	Dick Carter U.S.A. 1974
Supplier:	Carter Offshore U.S.A. Carter Offshore England
Est. Rating:	21.7' IOR Mk III

Specifications:

Construction:	GRP
LWL:	7.01m/23'0
LOA:	9.07m/29'9
Beam:	3.07m/10'1
Draft:	1.52m/5'0
Displ:	3.314kg/7,300 lbs
Ballast:	1,353kg/2,980 lbs

Fittings:	Lead keel. Farymann A30H diesel engine. Teak trim. Silver anodised spars.
Interior:	3 berths. Galley — sink. Stove. Wilcox Crittenden toilet.
Sails:	Area 35.7m^2/384 sq.ft.
Rigging:	Sloop
Price Guide:	£10,250/$20,100us

LUDERS 30

Design:	A. E. Luders Jnr Holland 1971
Supplier:	Cheoy Lee Hong Kong Lion Yachts U.S.A.

Specifications:

Construction:	GRP
LWL:	6.71m/22'0
LOA:	9.09m/29'10
Beam:	2.76m/9'1
Draft:	1.45m/4'9
Displ:	4,495kg/9,900 lbs
Ballast:	1,703kg/3,750 lbs

Fittings:	GRP deck. Lead ballast. Aluminium spars. 30HP Atomic 4 gasoline auxiliary.
Interior:	4/6 berths in 2 cabins
Variations:	Teak overlay on deck optional
Sails:	Area 39.5m^2 (19.4 + 20.1)/425 sq.ft. (209 + 216)
Rigging:	Sloop
Price Guide:	On application

UNTERELBE

Supplier: Jachtwerf Saaman b.v. Holland

Specifications: *Construction:*   Steel
                     LWL: 8.02m/26'4
                     LOA: 9.00m/29'6½
                     Beam: 3.00m/9'9
                     Draft: 0.85m/2'9½
                     Displ: 5,500kg/12,125 lbs
                     Ballast: 1,500kg/3,307 lbs

Fittings: Diesel engine

Interior: 4 berths. Full galley.

Sails: Area 19.20m^2/207 sq.ft.

Price Guide: 65,000 D.Fl.

SCAMPI ½ TON

Design:	Peter Norlin Sweden 1969
Supplier:	Solna Marine AB Sweden David Smithells England American International Yacht Corp. U.S.A.
Est. Rating:	21.7' IOR Mk III 21.5'−22.1' MORC

Specifications:

Construction:	GRP
LWL:	6.93m/22'9
LOA:	9.02m/29'7
Beam:	2.97m/9'9
Draft:	1.45m/4'9
Displ:	2,996kg/6,600 lbs
Ballast:	1,179kg/2,596 lbs

Fittings:	Iron ballast. Teak trim. GRP deck. Aluminium spars. 12 HPFerrymann diesel auxiliary.
Interior:	5/7 berths in 2 cabins. Sink. Stove. Icebox. Seaclo toilet.
Sails:	Area 30m^2(15 + 15)/322 sq.ft. (161 + 161) Spinnaker area 63.2m^2/680 sq.ft.
Rigging:	Sloop
Price Guide:	£8,600
Summary:	Combines the comfort of a cruising boat with the speed and efficiency of a racing yacht.

ACHILLES 9 METER

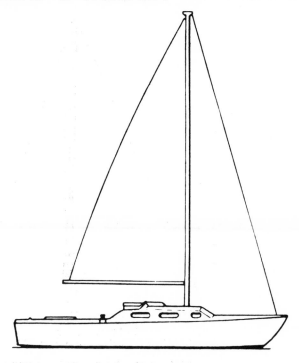

Design:	C. J. Butler England 1973
Supplier:	Butler Mouldings England
Est. Rating:	Portsmouth secondary yardstick 94
Specifications:	*Construction:*

LWL:	7.87m/25'10
LOA:	9.09m/29'10
Beam:	2.72m/8'11
Draft:	1.52m/5'0
Displ:	2,633kg/5,800 lbs
Ballast:	1,180kg/2,600 lbs

Fittings:	Fin keel. 10HP Volvo MDIB auxiliary.
Interior:	6 berths
Sails:	Area 25.1m^2/270 sq.ft.
Rigging:	Sloop
Price Guide:	£5,995
Summary:	Kits available.

CAPE COD BLUECHIP

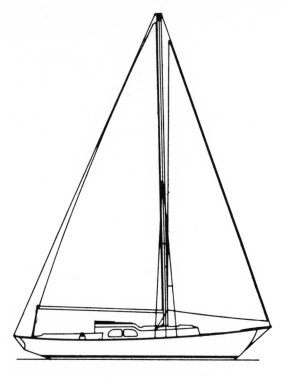

Design:	Sidney Dew Herreshoff U.S.A. 1961
Supplier:	Cape Cod Shipbuilding U.S.A.

Specifications:	*Construction:*	GRP
	LWL:	7.06m/23'2
	LOA:	9.09m/29'10
	Beam:	2.9m/9'6
	Draft:	1.52m/5'0
	Ballast:	1,476kg/3,250 lbs

Fittings:	Lead ballast. GRP deck. Aluminium spars. 22HP gasoline auxiliary.
Interior:	4—6 berths in 2 cabins. Standard galley.
Variations:	Optional make of auxiliary.
Sails:	Area 43.2m²/465 sq.ft.
Rigging:	Sloop
Price Guide:	$16,200us
Summary:	Also known as **Blue Chip**.

PEARSON 30

Design:	William H. Shaw U.S.A. 1971
Supplier:	Pearson Yachts U.S.A.
Est. Rating:	24.1' IOR Mk III

Specifications:

Construction:	GRP
LWL:	7.62m/25'0
LOA:	9.09m/29'10
Beam:	2.9m/9'6
Draft:	1.52m/5'0
Displ:	3,777kg/8,320 lbs
Ballast:	1,616kg/3,560 lbs

Fittings:	Lead ballast. GRP deck. Aluminium spars. 22HP gasoline auxiliary.
Interior:	6 berths in 2 cabins. Sink. Icebox. Sea toilet. 1.85m/6'1 headroom.
Sails:	Area 41.2m^2(18.3 + 22.9)/444 sq.ft. (197 + 247)
Rigging:	Sloop
Price Guide:	$13,730us
Summary:	A fast offshore racer/cruiser. Long waterline with high aspect ratio.

CAL 3-30 ¾ TON

Design:	C. William Lapworth, U.S.A. 1973
Supplier:	Jensen Marine, U.S.A.
Est. Rating:	24.5' IOR 29'11 MORC
Specifications:	*Construction:* GRP
	LWL: 8.05m/26'5
	LOA: 9.12m—9.2m/29'11—30'2
	Beam: 3.1m/10'2
	Draft: 1.68m/5'6
	Displ: 4,767kg/10,500 lbs
	Ballast: 2,270kg/5,000 lbs
Fittings:	GRP deck. Aluminium spars. 30HP Universal Atomic 4 gasoline auxiliary.
Interior:	6 berths in 2 cabins. Standard galley.
Sails:	Area 44m^2(18 + 26)/474 sq.ft. (194 + 280)
Rigging:	Sloop
Price Guide:	$21,000us

CHANCE 30/30 ¾

Design:	Britton Chance Jnr., U.S.A.
Supplier:	Allied Boat Co. Inc., U.S.A.
Est. Rating:	23.6'1OR Mk III 24.2'MORC 29.3'CCA
Specifications:	*Construction:* GRP
	LWL: 7.62m/25'0
	LOA: 9.12m/29'11
	Beam: 3.05m/10'0
	Draft: 1.6m/5'3
	Displ: 5,085kg/11,200 lbs
	Ballast: 2,497kg/5,500 lbs
Fittings:	Lead ballast. Balsa core and GRP deck. Aluminium spars. Palmer M-60 gasoline auxiliary.
Interior:	5 berths in 2 cabins.
Sails:	Area 44.9m^2 (17.7 + 27.3)/483 sq. ft. (189 + 294)
Rigging:	Sloop.
Price Guide:	S18,000us
Summary:	Available also in a 9.32m/30'7 LOA for IOR racing.

BALLAD

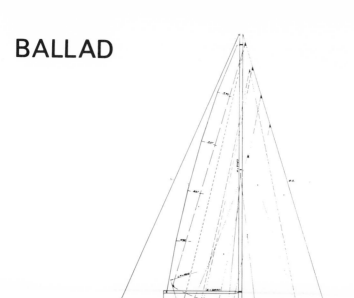

Design:	Rolf Magnusson Sweden 1972
Supplier:	Albin Marine Sweden Albin Marine U.K. Larsson Trade U.S.A.
Est. Rating:	21.7 IOR Mk III
Specifications:	*Construction:* GRP *LWL:* 6.88m/22'7 *LOA:* 9.12m/29'11 *Beam:* 2.94m/9'8 *Draft:* 1.55m/5'1 *Displ:* 3,303kg/7,276 lbs *Ballast:* 1,551kg/3,417 lbs
Fittings:	Anodised aluminium spars. Lead ballast. Stainless steel rudder. GRP deck. 10HP Volvo diesel engine.
Interior:	6 berths in 2 cabins. Galley. 1 enclosed toilet.
Variations:	2 interior versions available.
Sails:	Area 43m^2/463 sq.ft. Spinnaker area 70m^2/753 sq.ft.
Rigging:	Sloop
Price Guide:	£9,620/$19,500us
Summary:	Fast cruiser fitting into the Half-Ton Cup class. Very luxurious.

COLUMBIA 30 ³/₄ TON

Design:	William H. Tripp Jnr U.S.A.
Supplier:	Columbia Yacht Corp. U.S.A.
Est. Rating:	24.7' IOR Mk. III
Specifications:	

Construction:	GRP
LWL:	8.08m/26'6
LOA:	9.12m—9.17m/29'11 or 30'1
Beam:	2.9m/9'6
Draft:	1.75m or 1.19m/5'9 or 3'11
Displ:	4,767kg/10,500 lbs
Ballast:	2,315kg/5,100 lbs

Fittings:	GRP deck. Aluminium spars. 27HP Palmer P-60 gasoline auxiliary. Lead ballast.
Interior:	6 berths. 1.91m/6'3 headroom.
Variations:	Shoal draft model also available.
Sails:	Area 47.8m² or 42.9m²/515 or 462 sq.ft.
Rigging:	Sloop. Standard or short rig.
Price Guide:	$17,600us
Summary:	A powerful hull and sailplan. Spacious interior.

CORONADO 30

Design:	Coronado Yachts U.S.A.
Supplier:	Coronado Yachts U.S.A. Playvisa Coronado Yachts England
Est. Rating:	23.6' IOR Mk III 38.5' CCA

Specifications:

	Construction:	GRP
	LWL:	7.62m/25'0
	LOA:	9.12m/29'11
	Beam:	3.07m/10'1
	Draft:	1.6m/5'3
	Displ:	3,859kg/8,500 lbs
	Ballast:	1,226kg/2,700 lbs

Fittings:	GRP deck. Aluminium spars. 30/27HP Univ Atomic 4/Palmer P-60 gasoline auxiliary.
Interior:	6 berths
Variations:	Available also in shoal draft keel model.
Sails:	Area 38.2m²/411 sq.ft. Dacron.
Rigging:	Sloop
Price Guide:	$14,995us
Summary:	Carefully planned luxurious interior. Outstanding performance.

891

GRAMPIAN 30

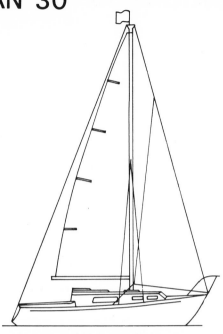

Design:	Alex McGruer, Canada 1970
Supplier:	Grampian Marine Limited Canada
Est. Rating:	25.5' IOR Mk III 23.4' MORC

Specifications:

Construction:	GRP
LWL:	7.77m/25'6
LOA:	9.12m/29'11
Beam:	2.9m/9'6
Draft:	0.99m/3'3 cb up
Displ:	3,904kg/8.600 lbs
Ballast:	1,757kg/3,870 lbs

Fittings: GRP sandwich deck. Aluminium spars. Lead ballast. 30HP Universal Atomic 4 gasoline.

Interior: 6/7 berths in 2 cabins. 6'4 headroom.

Sails: Area 36.2m^2(17.7 + 18.5)/390 sq.ft. (190 + 200)

Rigging: Sloop

Price Guide: $14,500us

Summary: Long waterline, beamy, spaciousness — add up to a very impressive racer/cruiser.

IRWIN COMPETITION 30 ³/₄ TON

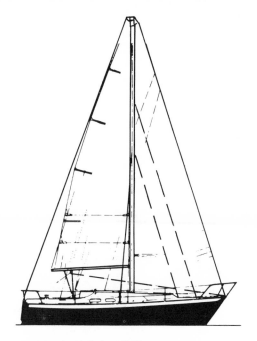

Design:	Ted Irwin U.S.A. 1972
Supplier:	Irwin Yacht and Marine Corporation U.S.A.
Est. Rating:	24.5' IOR Mk III 25.0' MORC
Specifications:	*Construction:* GRP
	LWL: 8.21m/26'11
	LOA: 9.12m/29'11
	Beam: 3.1m/10'2
	Draft: 1.62m/5'4
	Displ: 4,540kg/10,000 lbs
	Ballast: 2,088kg/4,600 lbs
Fittings:	Lead ballast. GRP and balsa core deck. Aluminium spars. 30H Р Atomic 4 gasoline auxiliary.
Interior:	4 berths in 2 cabins
Variations:	Optional toilet
Sails:	Area 43.9m² (17.8 + 26'1)/473 sq.ft. (192 + 281)
Rigging:	Sloop
Price Guide:	$16,500us
Summary:	Measures up to the ¾ ton racing rules.

MORGAN 30/2

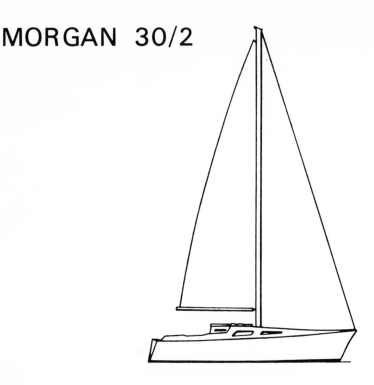

Design:	Morgan Yacht Corp. U.S.A. 1972
Supplier:	Morgan Yacht-Corp. U.S.A.
	Peter Webster Ltd. England

Specifications:

Construction:	GRP
LWL:	8.38m/27'6
LOA:	9.12m/29'11
Beam:	3.45m/11'4
Draft:	1.6m/5'3
Displ:	4,540kg/10,000 lbs
Ballast:	2,270kg/5,000 lbs

Fittings:	Lead ballast. GRP deck. Aluminium spars. Aux. 30HP Atomic 4 gasoline.
Interior:	6 berths in 2 cabins. Sink. W/pump. Icebox. Stove. 1 enclosed head.
Sails:	Area 46.7m^2 (19.4 + 27.3)/503 sq.ft. (209 + 294)
Rigging:	Sloop
Price Guide:	£10,250/$16,500
Summary:	Incorporates all the good thins about the **Morgan 30** plus much more.

NORTH STAR 1000 $^1/_2$

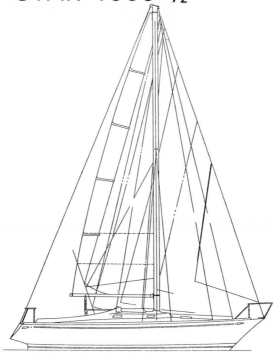

Design:	Sparkman & Stevens U.S.A. 1973
Supplier:	Hughes Boat Works Ltd. Canada Knoxmore Bagley England
Est. Rating:	21.7' IOR

Specifications:

Construction:	GRP
LWL:	6.91m/22'8
LOA:	9.12m/29'11
Beam:	2.9m/9'6
Draft:	1.6m/5'3
Displ:	3,632kg/8,000 lbs
Ballast:	1,684kg/3,710 lbs

Fittings:	Fin keel. Lead ballast. GRP with balsa core deck. Aluminium spars. Aux: 30HP Universal Atomic 4.
Interior:	5 berths in 2 cabins. Stove. Sink. Icebox. Recirculating toilet.
Sails:	Area 37.1m^2/399 sq.ft.
Rigging:	Sloop
Price Guide:	£8,500+ without engine/$17,500

PION ½

Design:	E. G. Van de Stadt, Holland 1972
Supplier:	E. G. Van de Stadt BV, Holland
Est. Rating:	21.7' IOR Mk III

Specifications:

Construction:	GRP
LWL:	7.14m/23'5
LOA:	9.12m/29'11
Beam:	2.94m/9'8
Draft:	1.68m/5'6
Displ:	3,854kg/8,490 lbs
Ballast:	1,526kg/3,362 lbs

Fittings:	Cast iron ballast. GRP deck. Aluminium spars. 10HP Arona diesel auxiliary.
Interior:	5 berths in 2 cabins. Sink. Stove. 1 sea toilet.
Sails:	Area 48.5m^2 (19.2 + 29.3)/522 sq.ft. (207 + 315)
Rigging:	Sloop
Price Guide:	$16,160us

YANKEE 30 MK II ¾ TON

Design:	Sparkman & Stephens U.S.A. 1970
Supplier:	Yankee Yachts U.S.A.
Est. Rating:	24.5' MORC 23.9' IOR

Specifications:

Construction:	GRP
LWL:	7.47m/24'6
LOA:	9.12m/29'11
Beam:	2.74m/9'0
Draft:	1.65m/5'5
Displ:	4,540kg/10,000 lbs
Ballast:	2,202kg/4,850 lbs

Fittings:	Lead ballast. Teak trim. GRP & balsa core deck. Wood or aluminium spars. Westerbeke Pilot 10 diesel.
Interior:	5 berths in 2 cabins. Icebox. Sink. Stove. Enclosed head.
Sails:	Area 42.6m^2 (17.4 + 25.2)/458 sq.ft. (187 + 271)
Rigging:	Sloop
Basic Price:	$19,000us
Summary:	A very powerful and proficient boat. Finished well.

RACERS/CRUISERS 20´- 30´
multihulls

CRACKSMAN

Design:	Michael Henderson, England 1960
Supplier:	Newbridge Boats, England
Specifications:	*Construction:* GRP
	LWL: 4.88m/16'0
	LOA: 6.10m/20'0
	Beam: 2.44m/8'0
	Draft: 0.25m/10"
	Displ: 409kg/900 lbs
Fittings:	Swing keel
Interior:	3—4 berths
Variations:	Open dayboat version also available
Sails:	Area 18.6m^2/200 sq.ft.
Rigging:	Una
Price Guide:	£1,000 — £1,200
Summary:	A stable catamaran that combines speed with comfort. Single-hander. Ideal for beginners. Kits and mouldings available.

BUCCANEER Mk II

Design:	Lock Crowther, U.S.A. 1970
Supplier:	International Marine Services, U.S.A.
Specifications:	*Construction:* GRP over wood
	LWL: 7.39m/24'3
	LOA: 7.62m/25'0
	Beam: 5.79m/19'0
	Draft: 0.35m/1'2
Fittings:	3 symmetrical hulls connected with aluminium crossarms. Aluminium spars. 7.5 hp Johnson outboard. Self-bailing cockpit.
Interior:	3—4 berths in 1—2 cabins. Stove. Icebox. Sink and pump. 1 head.
Sails:	Area 35.3m^2/380 sq.ft.+
Rigging:	Sloop
Price Guide:	$8,900us
Summary:	There is an active class association.

HIRONDELLE

Design:	Chris Hammond, England 1968
Supplier:	Pennington Yachts, England Symons Sailing Inc., U.S.A.
Est. Rating:	Provisional Portsmouth yardstick 84
Specifications:	*Construction:* GRP *LWL:* 6.1m/20'0 *LOA:* 6.91m/22'8 *Beam:* 3.05m/10'0 *Draft:* 0.38m/1'3 *Displ:* 1,226kg/2,700 lbs
Fittings:	Twin centreboards
Interior:	4 berths
Sails:	Area 23.2m^2/250 sq.ft.
Rigging:	Sloop
Price Guide:	£3,900
Summary:	A cruising catamaran for the family man. Light and easily handled. Kits available.

BUCCANEER 24

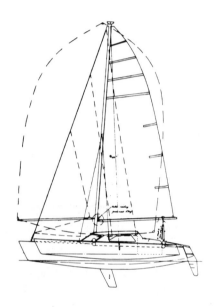

Design:	Lock Crowther, U.S.A. 1968
Supplier:	International Marine Services, U.S.A.
Specifications:	*Construction:* GRP over wood
	LWL: 7.01m/23'0
	LOA: 7.32m/24'0
	Beam: 5.79m/19'0
	Draft: 0.38m/1'3
Fittings:	3 symmetrical hulls connected with aluminium cross-arms. Aluminium spars. 5 hp seagull outboard auxiliary.
Interior:	2–3 berths in 1 cabin
Sails:	Area 37.3m^2 (17.6 + 19.7)/402 sq.ft. (190 + 212)
Rigging:	Sloop
Price Guide:	$8,500us

CROSS TRIMARAN RANGE

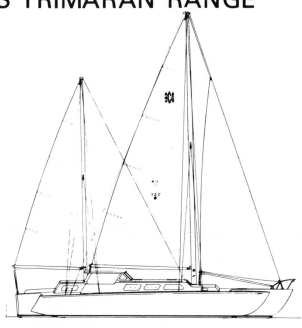

Design: Norman A. Cross, from 1963—1972

Supplier: Norman A. Cross, U.S.A.

Specifications: *Construction:* Plywood and GRP or GRP
                     LOA: 7.32m—15.16m/24'—49'9
                     Beam: 4.27m—8.23m/14'—27'
                     Draft: 0.86m—1.42m/2'10—4'8
                     Displ: 953kg—10,896kg/2,100—24,000 lbs

Fittings: 3 symmetrical hulls connected with plywood beams. Spars — wood or aluminium. Auxiliary outboards from 5 hp outboard to 55 hp inboard. Fin keel.

Interior: 3 berths to 10 berths

Variations: Range available — 7.32m/24', 7.92m/26', 8.53m/ 28', 9.14m/30', 9.45m/31', 10.36m/34', 10.67m/ 35', 10.97m/36', 36R', 11.58m/38', 12.8m/42', 42Mk II, 14.02m/46', 14.94m/49', 15.24m/50'.

Sails: Total areas range from 22.3m^2/240 sq.ft. to 83.6m^2/900 sq. ft.

Rigging: Various

Price Guide: Plans available for all. Prices range from $60 to $600. Approximate cost for home building from $11,800 to $18,000.

HIRONDELLE 24

Design:	Chris Hammond, England 1970
Supplier:	Pennington Yachts, England Symons Sailing Inc., U.S.A.
Specifications:	*Construction:* GRP *LWL:* 6.1m/20'0 *LOA:* 7.32m/24'0 *Beam:* 3.05m/10'0 *Draft:* 0.38m/1'3 *Displ:* 1,226kg/2,700 lbs
Fittings:	Balsa core deck. 2 symmetrical hulls joined by a bridge deck. Aluminium spars. 9.9 hp Chrysler outboard engine.
Interior:	4–5 berths in 3 cabins. 1.75m/5'9 headroom.
Sails:	Area 23.2m^2(11 + 12.2)/250 sq.ft. (118 + 132) Spinnaker are 37.2m^2/400 sq.ft.
Rigging:	Sloop
Price Guide:	$8,900us
Summary:	Very spacious. Winner of many trophies. Cannot be trailed.

BROWN 25 TRI

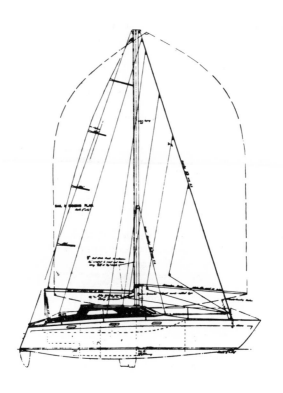

Supplier:	Border Marine, U.K.	
Specifications:	*Construction:*	GRP and wood
	LOA:	7.62m/25'0
Fittings:	Centreboard boat. 3 symmetrical hulls.	
Interior:	2 berths	
Variations:	Optional outboard engine	
Sails:	Various sail plans available	
Rigging:	Bermudan sloop	
Price Guide:	On application	
Summary:	Can be trailed.	

Pi-25 TRIMARAN

Design:	Arthur Piver, England
Supplier:	Cox Marine, England Symons Sailing, U.S.A.
Specifications:	*Construction:* Fiberglassed plywood *LWL:* 7.16m/23'6 *LOA:* 7.62m/25'0 *Beam:* 2.44m/8'0 *Draft:* 0.56m/1'10 *Displ:* 610kg/1,344 lbs
Fittings:	Alloy spars. Stainless steel fittings. Crescent 8 outboard auxiliary.
Interior:	3 berths. 1.62m/5'4 headroom.
Variations:	Fixed wing version available for deep-sea sailing.
Sails:	Terylene
Price Guide:	On application
Summary:	A de luxe trimaran with cambered decks, reverse sheer, low chine centre hull and chined floats.

SUPER BUC

Design:	U.S.A. 1972
Supplier:	International Marine Services, U.S.A.
Specifications:	*Construction:* Wood *LWL:* 7.62m/25'0 *LOA:* 7.87m/25'10 *Beam:* 5.79m/19'0 *Draft:* 0.3m/1'0
Fittings:	3 symmetrical hulls connected with aluminium tubes. Aluminium spars. Self-bailing cockpit.
Interior:	2 berths in 1 cabin. Stove. Icebox. Sink. 1 enclosed head.
Sails:	Area 50m^2/527 sq.ft.
Price Guide:	$12,000us

TELSTAR TRIMARAN

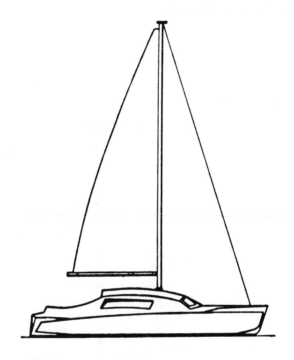

Design:	Tony Smith, England 1970
Supplier:	A. J. S. Sandwich Yacht, U.K.
Specifications:	*Construction:* GRP
	LWL: 7.32m/24'0
	LOA: 7.92m/26'0
	Beam: 4.57m/15'0
	Draft: 1.45m/4'9
	Displ: 1,525kg/3,360 lbs
Fittings:	Centreboards. GRP and balsa core deck. Gold anodised spars.
Interior:	5 berths
Variations:	Optional inboard or outboard engine.
Sails:	Area 27.9m^2/300 sq.ft.
Rigging:	Sloop
Price Guide:	£4,500
Summary:	Can be trailed. Kits available.

HEAVENLY TWINS
CATAMARAN

Design:	P. M. Patterson, England 1971
Supplier:	P. T. Yachts, England
Specifications:	*Construction:*

LWL:	6.55m/21'6
LOA:	7.98m/26'2
Beam:	4.19m/13'9
Draft:	0.69m/2'3

Fittings:	Twin keel. Seafarer 12 hp inboard auxiliary.
Interior:	6 berths
Sails:	Area 27.4m^2/295 sq.ft.
Rigging:	Sloop or cutter
Price Guide:	£7,200

BOBCAT

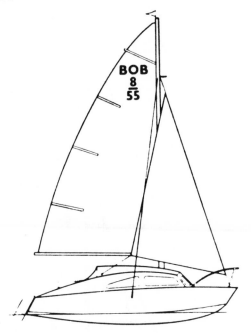

Design:	Bill O'Brien, England
Supplier:	Bobcats Limited, England BOB Cruising Cat Association, England
Est. Rating:	Provisional Portsmouth number 98
Specifications:	*Construction:* GRP and marine ply *LOA:* 8.08m/26'6 *Beam:* 4.27m/14'0 *Draft:* 0.63m/2'1 *Displ:* 2,034kg/4,480 lbs
Fittings:	Centreboards. 2 symmetrical hulls connected by marine ply
Interior:	6 berths
Variations:	Optional inboard or outboard auxiliary.
Sails:	Area 35.3m^2/380 sq.ft.
Rigging:	Sloop
Price Guide:	£7,000+
Summary:	Can be sailed single-handed. Very stable.

RANGER 27 CATAMARAN

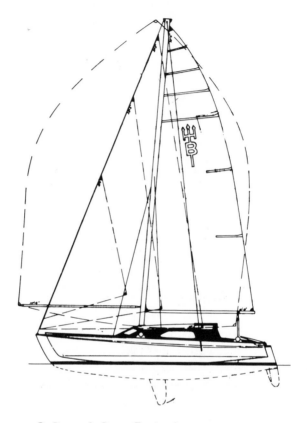

Supplier:	G. Prout & Sons, England
Est. Rating:	Provisional Portsmouth number 90
Specifications:	*Construction:* GRP
	LOA: 8.23m/27'0
	Draft: 0.56m/1'10
Fittings:	Keelboat
Interior:	4–6 berths
Variations:	Optional outboard engine
Sails:	Area 29.3m^2/315 sq.ft.
Rigging:	Bermudan sloop
Price Guide:	On application
Summary:	Cannot be trailed.

CATALAC 29

Design:	John Winterbotham, England 1971
Supplier:	Tom Lock Cats, England Ocean Catamarans, U.S.A.
Est. Rating:	Provisional Portsmouth number 92
Specifications:	*Construction:* GRP *LOA:* 8.92m/29'3 *Beam:* 4.27m/14'0 *Draft:* 0.69m/2'3 *Displ:* 3,051kg/6,720 lbs
Fittings:	2 symmetrical hulls connected with monocoque construction. Steep V hulls — no keels. Aluminium spars.
Interior:	5 berths in 4 cabins
Variations:	Optional outboard
Sails:	Area 41.8m^2/450 sq.ft.
Rigging:	Sloop
Price Guide:	£7,500
Summary:	A safe, handy and swift cruising cat. Kits and mouldings available.

BUCCANEER 28

Design: Lock Crowther, U.S.A. 1973

Supplier: International Marine Services, U.S.A.

Specifications:

Construction:	GRP over wood
LWL:	8.15m/26'9
LOA:	8.61m/28'3
Beam:	6.55m/21'6
Draft:	0.53m/1'9

Fittings: 3 symmetrical hulls connected with aluminium crossarms. Aluminium spars. 9 hp Johnson outboard.

Interior: 4 berths in 2 cabins

Sails: Area $56.7m^2$ (25.6 + 31.1)/610 sq. ft (275 + 335)

Rigging: Sloop

Price Guide: New — price unfixed.

RACERS/CRUISERS 30' - 40'
monohulls

ALICUDI

Design:	Brabourne Marine, England
Supplier:	Brabourne Marine, England
Specifications:	*Construction:* GRP and mahogany
	LWL: 7.62m/25'0
	LOA: 9.14m/30'0
	Beam: 2.74m/9'0
	Draft: 0.99m/3'3
	Displ: 3,632kg/8,000 lbs
Fittings:	To specification
Interior:	5 berths in 2 cabins
Sails:	Area 25.5m^2/275 sq.ft.
Rigging:	Sloop (motor sailer)
Price Guide:	On application
Summary:	Luxurious boat with good performance under motor or sail.

BRISTOL C30

Design:	Halsey Herreshoff, U.S.A.1970
Supplier:	Bristol Yacht Co., U.S.A.
Specifications:	*Construction:* GRP
	LWL: 6.91m/27'8
	LOA: 9.14m/30'0
	Beam: 2.79m/9'2
	Draft: 1.37m—1.01m/4'6—3'4 cb
	Displ: 3,814kg/8,400 lbs
Fittings:	Balsa core and GRP deck. Aluminium spars. 25 hp Volvo MD2B diesel engine.
Interior:	6 berths in 2 cabins
Variations:	Keel or centreboard boats available
Sails:	Area 34.4m^2(16.9 + 17.5)/370 sq.ft. (182 + 188)
Rigging:	Sloop
Price Guide:	$14,900us
Summary:	Price includes sails and diesel engine.

912

ACADIAN 30 Mk II

Supplier:	Paceship Yachts, Canada
Est. Rating:	CCA 23'–23.5' (sloop) 23'–24' (yawl)
Specifications:	*Construction:* GRP
	LWL: 6.4m/21'0
	LOA: 9.14m/30'0
	Beam: 2.59m/8'6
	Draft: 1.32m/4'4
	Displ: 3,178kg/7,000 lbs
	Ballast: 1,544kg/3,400 lbs
Fittings:	Teak deck. Aluminium spars. Universal Atomic 4 engine.
Interior:	5/6 berths. 1.83m/6'0 headroom. Galley. Icebox. Stove. Enclosed head.
Sails:	Area 35.2m^2/378.8 sq.ft. (sloop)
	Area 36.6m^2/394.5 sq.ft. (yawl)
Rigging:	Sloop or yawl
Price Guide:	$14,250–14,500us

CAMPAIGNER

Design:	David Cheverton, England 1963
Supplier:	David Cheverton & Partners Ltd., England

Specifications:

Construction:	Mahogany on laminated frames
LWL:	7.32m/24'0
LOA:	9.14m/30'0
Beam:	2.74m/9'0
Draft:	1.52m/5'0
Displ:	4,881kg/4.80 tons

Fittings:	To specification
Interior:	5 berths. 1.85m/6'1 headroom
Sails:	Area 39m^2/420 sq.ft.
Rigging:	Auxiliary masthead sloop
Price Guide:	On application
Summary:	Eligible for all offshore and handicap racing events.

CAPE 30

Design:	Ted Hood, U.S.A.
Supplier:	Cape Dory Co. Inc., U.S.A.

Specifications:

Construction:	GRP
LWL:	6.15m/20'2
LOA:	9.14m/30'0
Beam:	2.82m/9'3
Draft:	1.37m/4'6
Displ:	4,249kg/9,359 lbs
Ballast:	1,498kg/3,300 lbs

Fittings:	Lead ballast. GRP deck. Aluminium spars. 18 hp Atomic 4 gasoline auxiliary.
Interior:	5 berths in 2 cabins. Sink. Icebox. Stove. 1 marine toilet.
Sails:	Area 185.2m^2/408 sq. ft.
Rigging:	Sloop
Price Guide:	$23,900us
Summary:	Designed for speed, comfort and quality.

CLAYMORE 30

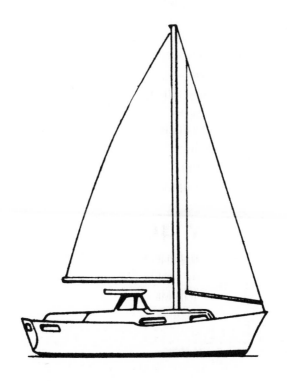

Design:	Alan F. Hill, England
Supplier:	Marine Construction, England

Specifications:	*Construction:*	GRP
	LWL:	7.32m/24'0
	LOA:	9.14m/30'0
	Beam:	3.12m/10'3
	Draft:	1.24m/4'1
	Displ:	6,407kg/6.3 tons

Fittings:	GRP deck. Anodised light alloy spars.
Interior:	5 berths
Sails:	Area 16m^2/172 sq.ft. (ketch) Area 20.4m^2/220 sq.ft. (sloop)
Rigging:	Sloop or ketch (motor-sailer)
Price Guide:	£14,000+
Summary:	Built for deep-sea cruising comfort. Not suitable for trailing.

COMET FRANCE

Design: Finot Group & van de Stadt, France 1971

Supplier: Builders: Sipla, Italy
Sparkes Marine, U.K.

Specifications:

Construction:		GRP
LWL:		6.81m/22'4
LOA:		9.14m/30'0
Beam:		3.05m/10'0
Draft:		1.71m/5'7
Displ:		3,254kg/7,168 lbs
Ballast:		1,203kg/2,650 lbs

Fittings: Fin keel. 10—15 hp engine.

Interior: 5/6 berths.

Sails: Area various

Rigging: Various

Price Guide: £10,100

Summary: Designed for family cruising comfort.

EASTERLY 30 ³⁄₄ TON

Design: Mike Brennan, U.S.A. 1967

Supplier: Easterly Yachts, U.S.A.

Est. Rating: 24.0' IOR Mk III

Specifications:

Construction:		GRP
LWL:		7.11m/23'4
LOA:		9.14m/30'0
Beam:		2.76m/9'1
Draft:		1.22m/4'0
Displ:		3,178kg/7,000 lbs
Ballast:		999kg/2,200 lbs

Fittings: Balsa core and GRP deck. Aluminium spars. Lead ballast. 30 hp Atomic Four gasoline auxiliary.

Interior: 5 berths in 2 cabins.

Sails: Area 35.3m² (17.2 + 18.1)/380 sq.ft. (185 + 195)

Rigging: Sloop

Price Guide: $14,750us

Summary: Eligible for ¾ ton racing.

COMPETITION 30

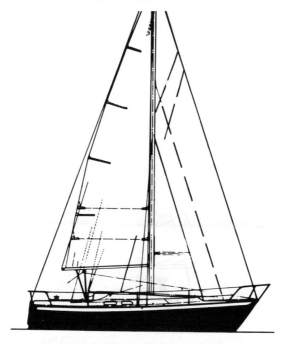

Design:	Ted Irwin, U.S.A.
Supplier:	Irwin Yacht & Marine Corp., U.S.A.
Est. Rating:	¾ ton under IOR Mk III
Specifications:	*Construction:* GRP
	LWL: 8.21m/26'11
	LOA: 9.14m/30'0
	LWL: 3.1m/10'2
	Draft: 1.6m/5'3
	Displ: 4,540kg/10,000 lbs
Fittings:	30HP auxiliary
Interior:	6 berths. Enclosed toilet compartment.
Sails:	Area 54.8m^2/590 sq.ft.
Rigging:	Sloop
Price Guide:	$16,800us
Summary:	Designed specifically for ¾ ton racing under the IOR Mk III rules. Practical layout that will please serious racing crews.

DARTSAILER RANGE

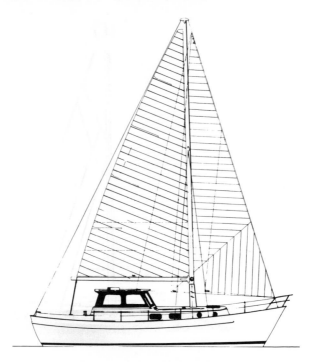

Design: W. de Vries Leutsch, Laurent Giles & Parters, Mclear and Harris, England and Holland.

Supplier: Holland Boat Co., Holland

Specifications:

Construction:	GRP
LWL:	7.86m/25'10
LOA:	9.15m/30'0
Beam:	3.00m/9'10
Draft:	1.25m/4'3
Displ:	7,000kg/15,435 lbs
Ballast:	2,000kg/4,410 lbs

Fittings: Self-draining cockpit. Mahogany trim.

Interior: 4/5 berths. 1.90m/6'3 headroom.

Sails: Area 37.10m^2/399 sq.ft.

Rigging: Varies

Price Guide: 77,500 fl.

Summary: A range based on standard hulls and designs but each boat finished to individual specifications.

DESTINY

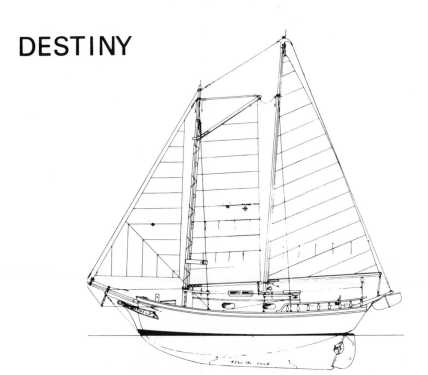

Design:	James. D. Rosborough, Canada 1965
Supplier:	James D. Rosborough, Canada
Specifications:	*Construction:* Wood
	LWL: 7.92m/26'0
	LOA: 9.14m/30'0
	Beam: 3.35m/11'0
	Draft: 1.35m/4'5
	Displ: 6,174kg/13,600 lbs
	Ballast: 999kg/2,200 lbs
Fittings:	Fiberglassed wood deck. Wooden spars. 50 hp Perkins diesel engine.
Interior:	4—6 berths in 1 cabin. 1.88m/6'2 headroom.
Variations:	Layout to specification
Sails:	Area 45.5m^2/490 sq.ft. 9.2oz. Dacron.
Rigging:	Ketch or to specification.
Price Guide:	$33,500us
Summary:	A boat of true character — traditional lines. A boat to live on.

HILLYARD

Design:	David Hillyard, England
Supplier:	David Hillyard Ltd., England
Est. Rating:	Portsmouth numbers 106, 109

Specifications:

Construction:	Mahogany on oak
LOA:	9.14m—12.19m/30'—40'
Beam:	2.59m—3.43m/8'6—11'3
Draft:	1.07m—1.52m/3'6—5'0
Displ:	8,130kg—12,190kg/17,920 lbs —26,880 lbs

Fittings:	All craft are fully equipped
Interior:	Layouts to specification. 4 to 6 berths.
Variations:	To specification between general measurements centre or aft cockpit.
Sails:	Area from 31.1m^2/335 sq.ft.
Rigging:	Sloop or cutter
Price Guide:	On application £8,000—19,000
Summary:	Double enders that have a world-wide reputation for reliability and comfort. Available as an 8 tonner, 9 tonner, 12 tonner and 16 tonner.

R-30

Design:	James D. Rosborough, Canada 1970
Supplier:	James D. Rosborough, Canada

Specifications:

Construction:	Wood
LWL:	7.37m/24'2
LOA:	9.14m/30'0
Beam:	2.69m/8'10
Draft:	1.12m/3'8 keel
Displ:	4,472kg/9.850 lbs
Ballast:	908kg/2,000 lbs

Fittings:	Lead ballast. Fiberglassed wood deck. Wooden spars. 7 hp Torpedo diesel.
Interior:	4 berths in 1 cabin. Stove. Sink. Icebox. 1 toilet.
Sails:	Area 32m^2(16.8 + 7.9 + 7.3)/344 sq. ft. (181+85 + 78)
Rigging:	Ketch
Price Guide:	$15,500us
Summary:	Embodies simplicity, ease of handling, sea-keeping ability and good turn of speed.

FISHER 30

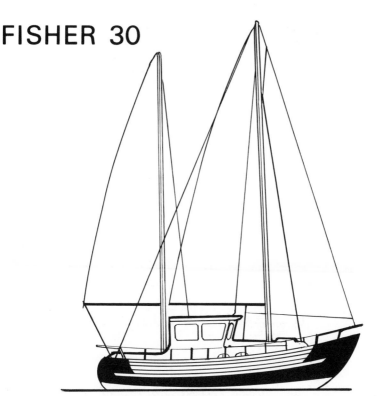

Design:	Gordon Wyatt, England 1970
Supplier:	Fairways Marine, England Offsounding Yachts, U.S.A.

Specifications:	*Construction:*	GRP
	LWL:	7.62m/25'0
	LOA:	9.14m/30'0
	Beam:	2.82m/9'3
	Draft:	1.3m/4'3
	Displ:	6,600kg/14,560 lbs
	Ballast:	3305kg/7,280 lbs

Fittings:	Saab 22HP inboard diesel
Interior:	5/6 berths
Variations:	De luxe version also available.
Sails:	Area 30.7m^2/330 sq.ft. (sloop)
Rigging:	Sloop or ketch
Price Guide:	£11,000–12,000
Summary:	A traditional designed motor-sailer that is supplied with a comprehensive inventory.

HURLEY 30/90

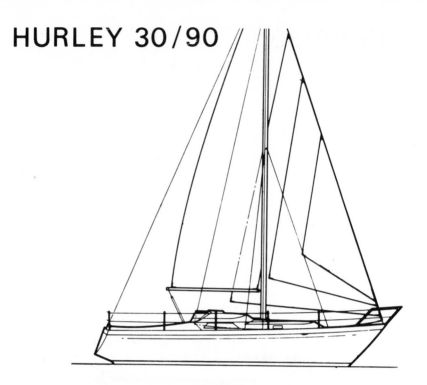

Design:	Ian Anderson, England 1972
Supplier:	Hurley Marine, England Hurley Marine, U.S.A.
Est. Rating:	IOR 21.7'

Specifications:

Construction:	GRP
LWL:	7.32m/24'0
LOA:	9.14m/30'0
Beam:	2.97m/9'9
Draft:	1.45m/4'9
Displ:	3,859kg/8,500 lbs
Ballast:	1,725kg/3,800 lbs

Fittings:	GRP deck. Fin keel. Aluminium spars. 10 hp Volvo Penta MDIB diesel auxiliary.
Interior:	6 berths in 2 cabins. 1.9m/6'2 headroom.
Sails:	Area 35m^2(13.2 + 21.8)/377 sq.ft. (142 + 235) Spinnaker area 66.89m^2/720 sq.ft.
Rigging:	Sloop
Price Guide:	£8,800
Summary:	Kits and mouldings available.

ISLANDER 30 ¾ TON

Design:	Robert Finch, U.S.A. 1970
Supplier:	Islander Yachts, U.S.A.
Est. Rating:	24.5' IOR Mk III

Specifications:	*Construction:*	GRP
	LWL:	7.49m/24'7
	LOA:	9.14m/30'0
	Beam:	3.05m/10'0
	Draft:	1.52m/5'0
	Displ:	3,904kg/8,600 lbs
	Ballast:	1,589kg/3,500 lbs

Fittings:	Lead ballast. GRP deck. Aluminium spars. 25 hp Palmer gasoline engine.
Interior:	6 berths in 2 cabins. Standard galley.
Sails:	Area 40.8m²/439 sq.ft.
Rigging:	Sloop
Price Guide:	$14,995us
Summary:	Magnificent interior finished with mahogany to a very high standard. Easy to handle, very stable.

KEMROCK CHANNEL

Design:	Kemrock Fibreglass Ltd.
Supplier:	Kemrock Fibreglass Ltd., England

Specifications:	Construction:	GRP
	LWL:	8.69m/28'6
	LOA:	9.14m/30'0
	Beam:	3.05m/10'0
	Draft:	1.07m/3'6

Fittings:	Wood finish. 50 hp inboard auxiliary.
Interior:	5 berths
Variations:	Keel boat or bilge keel
Sails:	Area 43.2m^2/465 sq.ft.
Rigging:	Bermudan sloop
Price Guide:	On application
Summary:	Cannot be trailed.

HUSTLER 30

Design:	Holman & Pye, England 1969
Supplier:	Island Boat Sales, England
Est. Rating:	$\pm$ 21.0' IOR

Specifications:	Construction:	GRP
	LWL:	6.91m/22'8
	LOA:	9.14m/30'0
	Beam:	2.8m/9'2
	Draft:	1.68m or 1.39m/5'6 or 4'7
	Displ:	3,450kg/7,600 lbs
	Ballast:	1,589kg/3,500 lbs

Fittings:	Fin keel. Penta MD1B 10 hp inboard.
Interior:	6 berths
Sails:	Area 33.4m^2/359 sq.ft.
Rigging:	Sloop
Price Guide:	£11,000
Summary:	Kits and mouldings available.

KINGFISHER 30

Design:	R. A. G. Nierop
Supplier:	Westfield Engineering Co. Ltd., England
Specifications:	*Construction:* GRP
	LWL: 7.62m/25'0
	LOA: 9.14m/30'0
	Beam: 2.74m/9'0
	Draft: 1.2m/3'11
	Displ: 3,966kg/8,736 lbs
Fittings:	Twin bilge keel. Alloy spars. Self-drain cockpit. Watermeta Sea Wolf 30 hp engine.
Interior:	6 berths. Centre cockpit.
Variations:	Available 'unfurnished'
Sails:	Area 29.7m²/320 sq. ft.
Rigging:	Bermudan masthead sloop
Price Guide:	£6,900
Summary:	Luxurious cruiser for the family.

MG 30

Design:	Morgan Giles Ltd., England
Supplier:	Morgan Giles Ltd., England

Specifications:	*Construction:*	GRP
	LWL:	6.42m/21'1
	LOA:	9.14m/30'0
	Beam:	2.67m/8'9
	Draft:	1.43m/4'8½
	Displ:	3,966kg/8,736 lbs

Fittings:	Metal spars. Deck stepped mast. 10 hp Albin engine.
Interior:	4 berths 1.81m/5'11 headroom.
Sails:	Area 33.4m^2/360 sq.ft.
Rigging:	Bermudan masthead sloop
Price Guide:	On application
Summary:	Efficient and easy to handle. Now built in GRP from a timber prototype.

N-30 PHASE II

Design:	Gary Mull, U.S.A. 1971
Supplier:	Capital Yachts Inc., U.S.A.
Est. Rating:	24.5' IOR Mk III

Specifications:	*Construction:*	GRP with balsa core
	LWL:	7.62m/25'0
	LOA:	9.14m/30'0
	Beam:	3.2m/10'6
	Draft:	1.45m/4'9
	Displ:	3,632kg/8,000 lbs
	Ballast:	1,180kg/2,600 lbs

Fittings:	Lead keel. GRP deck. Aluminium spars. Gasoline auxiliary.
Interior:	7 berths in 2 cabins. 1.91m/6'3 headroom.
Sails:	Area 38.9m^2/419 sq.ft.
Rigging:	Sloop
Price Guide:	$16,000us
Summary:	Also known as **Newport 30 Phase II.** Redesigned to qualify for ¾ ton racing. One of the best performance boats on the market.

PILOT 9 TON

Design:	Rodney Warrington-Smyth, England 1962
Supplier:	Falmouth Boat Construction, England
Specifications:	*Construction:* Pitch pine on oak
	LWL: 7.32m/24'0
	LOA: 9.14m/30'0
	Beam: 2.82m/9'3
	Draft: 1.37m/4'6
	Displ: 6,102kg/13,440 lbs
Fittings:	Perkins 4/99 diesel engine
Interior:	4/5 berths. 1.91m/6'3 headroom.
Sails:	Area 37.2m^2/400 sq.ft. +
Rigging:	Motor sailer masthead sloop or ketch rig
Price Guide:	On application
Summary:	Easily managed rig. Very powerful. Based on the Pilot 6 ton design. Good storage space.

PT Mk II ¾ TON

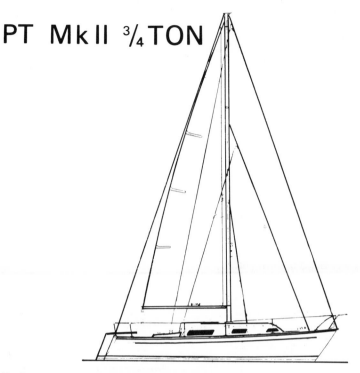

Design:	Plastrend, U.S.A. 1970
Supplier:	Plastrend, U.S.A.
Est. Rating:	24.5' IOR Mk III 25.0' MORC

Specifications:

Construction:	GRP with steel core
LWL:	8.23m/27'0
LOA:	9.14m/30'0
Beam:	2.97m/9'9
Draft:	1.6m/5'3
Displ:	4,540kg/10,000 lbs
Ballast:	2,406kg/5,300 lbs

Fittings:	Lead ballast. GRP deck. Aluminium spars. 18 hp Volvo.
Interior:	7 berths in 2 cabins. Sink. Waterpump. Icebox. 1 chemical toilet. 1.85m/6'1 headroom.
Sails:	Area 43.3m^2(16.7 + 26.6)/466 sq.ft. (180 + 286) Spinnaker area 83.6m^2/900 sq.ft.
Rigging:	Sloop
Price Guide:	$17,000us
Summary:	A real racing machine, yet matching up to rigorous expectations for cruising.

SEADOG

Design:	Reg Freeman, England 1965
Supplier:	Reg Freeman, England
Est. Rating:	Portsmouth number 103

Specifications:

Construction:	GRP
LWL:	7.32m/24'0
LOA:	9.14m/30'0
Beam:	2.74m/9'0
Draft:	1.07m/3'6
Displ:	5,797kg/12,768 lbs
Ballast:	1,780kg/3,920 lbs

Fittings:	Bilge keel
Interior:	5 berths
Variations:	Optional inboard engine
Sails:	Area 41.3m^2/444 sq.ft.
Rigging:	Ketch
Price Guide:	£12,000
Summary:	Full keel verions also available — known as **Deep Sea Dog.** Cannot be trailed.

SHE D 30

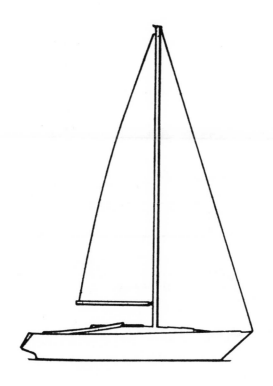

Design:	Sparkman & Stephens, U.S.A.
Supplier:	South Hants Marine, England
Specifications:	*Construction:* GRP
	LOA: 9.1m/30'0
	Beam: 2.87m/9'5
	Draft: 1.75m/5'9
Fittings:	Flush decks
Rigging:	Sloop
Price Guide:	
Summary:	A flat out racing yacht. Top quality and top price.

SOVEREL 30 Mk III

Design: Walt Walters & Bill Soverel, U.S.A. 1969 Mk III 1972

Supplier: Soverel Marine Inc., U.S.A.

Est. Rating: 26.2' IOR Mk III 24.5' MORC

Specifications:

Construction:	Ply fibreglass
LWL:	7.925m/26'0
LOA:	9.144m/30'
Beam:	2.90m/9'6
Draft:	1.12m/3'8 cb up
Displ:	4,540kg/10,000 lbs
Ballast:	2,270kg/5,000 lbs

Fittings: Keel or centreboard boat. Volvo engine — 30 hp. Anodised aluminium mast and boom. Deck of stainless steel and marinium.

Interior: 6 berths in 2 cabins.

Variations: Mk I and II available. Mk II longer mast, larger rig and 1,000 lbs more ballast. Mk III beamier.

Sails: Area 43.66m^2/470 sq. ft. 6 oz. Dacron.

Rigging: Cutter

Price Guide: $17,500us Mk III

Summary: Slender and stiff with a large sail plan. Great on all points and under all wind conditions. Sold direct. from Soverel Marine.

TARTAN 30 ³⁄₄ TON

Design: Olin Stephens, U.S.A.

Supplier: Tartan Marine Co. Ohio, U.S.A.

Est. Rating: IOR 24.2' Mk III 29.10' MORC 28.2' CCA

Specifications:

Construction:	Tensil-cor-GRP
LWL:	7.39m/24'3
LOA:	9.14m/30'
Beam:	3.05m/10'
Draft:	1.5m/4'11
Displ:	3,973kg/8,750 lbs
Ballast:	1,725kg/3,800 lbs

Fittings: Lead ballast. 30HP Universal Atomic 4 engine gas. Teak trim. GRP deck. Wooden spars.

Interior: 6 berths in 2 cabins. 1.96m/6'5 headroom. Enclosed head. Sink. Stove. Icebox.

WIBO 930

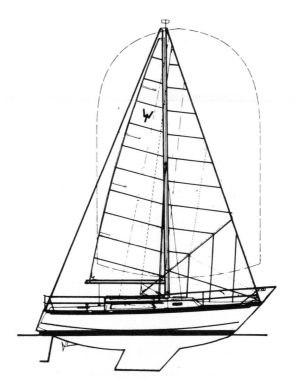

Design:	E. G. Van de Stadt, Holland
Supplier:	Bebs Marine Ltd., England
Specifications:	*Construction:* Steel
	LOA: 9.14m/30'0
Fittings:	Teak and mahogany trim
Interior:	5 berths. 1.93m/6'4 headroom.
Rigging:	Sloop.
Price Guide:	£5,725

WATERWITCH

Design:	Maurice Griffiths, England
Supplier:	Hartwell Boat Builders, England
Specifications:	*Construction:* Hard chine marine ply.
	LWL: 7.92m/26'0
	LOA: 9.14m/30'0
	Beam: 2.46m/8'1
	Draft: 0.91m/3'0
	Displ: 3,405kg/7,500 lbs
Fittings:	Bilge keel. 8 hp engine.
Interior:	5 berths. 1.83m/6'0 headroom.
Sails:	Area 38.1m^2/410 sq.ft.
Rigging:	Sloop
Price Guide:	£7,200
Summary:	Easy to identify with dinghy hauled up on two davits athwart the stern. A very seaworthy boat that has made numerous extensive cruises combatting very inclement weather especially in the Pacific.

ZULU

Supplier:	Staniland & Co. Ltd., England
Specifications:	*Construction:* Carvel
	LOA: 9.14m/30'0
Fittings:	Keelboat
Interior:	4 berths
Variations:	Optional inboard engine
Sails:	Area 32.5m^2/350 sq.ft.
Rigging:	Bermudan sloop
Price Guide:	
Summary:	Can not be trailed.

OPTIMA

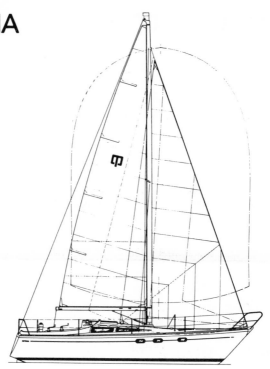

Design:	E. G. van de Stadt, Holland
Supplier:	Dehler, Holland
Specifications:	

	Construction:	GRP
	LWL:	7.35m/24'1½
	LOA:	9.20m/30'2
	Beam:	3.00m/9'10
	Draft:	1.55m/5'1
	Displ:	3,600kg/7,937 lbs

Fittings:	To specification
Interior:	Layout to individual requirements
Variations:	Optional power
Sails:	Area 43.8m^2/471 sq.ft. Spinnaker area 62.4m^2/672 sq.ft.
Rigging:	Sloop
Price Guide:	56,880 fl.
Summary:	A highly individual boat with tremendous character.

C & C 30 ¾ TON

Design:	C & C Design Group, Canada 1970
Supplier:	C & C Yachts Manufacturing, Canada Anstey Yachts, England
Est. Rating:	24.5′ IOR Mk III
Specifications:	*Construction:* GRP *LWL:* 7.54m/24′9 *LOA:* 9.17m/30′1 *Beam:* 3.07m/10′1 *Draft:* 1.52m/5′0 *Displ:* 3,496kg/7,700 lbs *Ballast:* 1,662kg/3,660 lbs
Fittings:	Lead ballast. Balsa core and GRP deck. Aluminium spars. 30HP Atomic 4 gasoline auxiliary.
Interior:	6 berths in 2 cabins. Stove. Sink & pump. 1 enclosed toilet.
Sails:	Area 42.6m^2 (18.2 + 24.4)/459 sq.ft. (196 + 263)
Rigging:	Sloop
Price Guide:	$20,995us
Summary:	A ¾ ton racer.

SYSTEM 30

Design:	Sparkman & Stephens, U.S.A.
Supplier:	Whitney Operations, U.S.A.
Specifications:	*Construction:* GRP *LWL:* 6.71m/22′0 *LOA:* 9.17m/30′1 *Beam:* 2.59m/8′6 *Draft:* 1.42m/4′8 *Displ:* 3,027kg/6,667 lbs
Fittings:	GRP deck. Aluminium spars. Lead ballast. 12 hp auxiliary.
Interior:	5 berths in 2 cabins. Galley standard.
Sails:	Area 59.5m^2/640 sq.ft.
Rigging:	Sloop
Price Guide:	$18,900us

HUSKY

Design:	West Norway Shipbuilding Association, Norway
Supplier:	Lars Hausberg, Norway

Specifications:

Construction:	Iroko on oak
LWL:	8.15m/26'9
LOA:	9.2m/30'2
Beam:	2.97m/9'9
Draft:	1.39m/4'7
Displ:	6,100kg/13,400 lbs

Fittings:	Teak deck. Perkins 4/107 engine.
Interior:	4/6 berths
Sails:	Area 33.4m^2/360 sq.ft.
Rigging:	Sloop
Price Guide:	On application
Summary:	First class performance under sail or power. Immensely strong.

YANKEE 30 Mk III ¾ TON

Design:	Sparkman & Stephens, U.S.A. 1973
Supplier:	Yankee Yachts Inc., U.S.A.
Est. Rating:	24.3'—24.5'
Specifications:	*Construction:* GRP
	LWL: 7.62m/25'0
	LOA: 9.17m/30'1
	Beam: 2.74m/9'0
	Draft: 1.65m/5'5
	Displ: 4,540kg/10,000 lbs
	Ballast: 2,202kg/4,850 lbs
Fittings:	Lead ballast. Teak trim. GRP and balsa core deck. Aluminium spars. 10HP Westerbeke Pilot diesel auxiliary.
Interior:	5 berths in 2 cabins. Stove. Sink. Icebox. 1 enclosed toilet.
Sails:	Area 43.1m^2/464 sq.ft.
Rigging:	Sloop
Price Guide:	$18,000us
Summary:	Sleek and roomy. Beautifully finished. Powerful high aspect ration sail plan.

WESTERLY 30

Design:	Denys Rayner, England
Supplier:	Westerly Marine Construction, England Andrew Gemeny & Son, U.S.A.
Specifications:	*Construction:* GRP
	LWL: 7.85m/25'9
	LOA: 9.2m/30'2
	Beam: 2.64m/8'8
	Draft: 0.91m/3'0
	Displ: 3,814kg/8,400 lbs
	Ballast: 1,634kg/3,600 lbs
Fittings:	Iron ballast. GRP deck. Aluminium spars.
Interior:	6 berths in 2 cabins. Galley standard.
Variations:	Power optional
Sails:	Area 38.4m^2/413 sq.ft.
Rigging:	Sloop
Price Guide:	On application

ALBERG 30

Design:	Carl A. Alberg, Canada 1963
Supplier:	Whitby Boat Works, Canada
Est. Rating:	22.5'–22.7' IOR Mk III

Specifications:

	Construction:	GRP
	LWL:	6.6m/21'8
	LOA:	9.22m/30'3
	Beam:	2.66m/8'9
	Draft:	1.3m/4'3
	Displ:	4,086kg/9,000 lbs
	Ballast:	1,498kg/3,300 lbs

Fittings:	Deck GRP with balsa core. Teak trim. Aluminium spars. Iron ballast. 30 hp Universal Atomic 4 gasoline.
Interior:	4 berths in 2 cabins. Galley. Brydon Boy toilet.
Sails:	Area 38.1m^2 (20.5 + 17.6)/410 sq.ft. (221 + 189)
Rigging:	Sloop
Price Guide:	$15,500us
Summary:	Stiff, dry with a sea-kindly motion. She is a rugged boat and yet so comfortable.

SELECTA

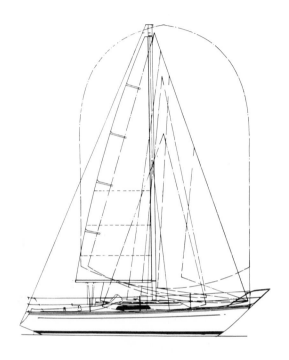

Design:	E. G. van de Stadt, Holland
Supplier:	Fibocon bv, Holland
Specifications:	*Construction:* GRP
	LWL: 7.00m/22'11½
	LOA: 9.23m/30'3½
	Beam: 2.90m/9'6
	Draft: 1.50m/4'11
	Displ: 3,760kg/8,289 lbs
	Ballast: 1,430kg/3,153 lbs
Fittings:	Teak trim. Renault DTN40 35 hp petrol. GRP deck. Aluminium alloy spars.
Interior:	6 berths. Full galley. Enclosed toilet.
Sails:	Area 40.30m^2/434 sq.ft. Spinnaker area 67.60m^2/728 sq.ft.
Rigging:	Sloop
Price Guide:	57,700 fl.
Summary:	A sturdy, seaworthy sailing vessel.

940

ARPEGE ½ TON

Design:	Michel Dufour, France 1966
Supplier:	Michel Dufour, France Michel Dufour, U.S.A. Carl Ziegler Yacht Agency, U.K.
Est. Rating:	21.2' IOR Mk III 20.7' MORC Provisional Portsmouth yardstick 93

Specifications:

	Construction:	GRP
	LWL:	6.71m/22'0
	LOA:	9.25m/30'4
	Beam:	3.02m/9'11
	Draft:	1.35m/4'5
	Displ:	3,632kg/8,000 lbs
	Ballast:	1,385kg/3,050 lbs

Fittings:	Fiberglassed sandwich deck. Keel boat. Aluminium spars. 25 hp Volvo MD2B diesel auxiliary.
Interior:	6 berths in 2 cabins. Galley. Marine toilet.
Sails:	Area 35.1m^2 (17 + 18.1)/378 sq.ft. (183 + 195)
Rigging:	Bermudan sloop. S/S and Terylene.
Price Guide:	£10,675/$18,000us
Summary:	Good cruising performance and racing record. Stiff and seaworthy. Over 900 boats built.

COSTANTINI 30

Design:	Costantini, France
Supplier:	Costantini, France
Specifications:	*Construction:* GRP
	LWL: 6.90m/22'8
	LOA: 9.25m/30'4
	Beam: 3.02m/9'11
	Draft: 1.72m/5'8
	Displ: 2,700kg/5,952 lbs
	Ballast: 1,350kg/2,976 lbs
Fittings:	Mast height 1.80m/5'11. Vire Mark VII de 7CV engine.
Interior:	5 berths. Galley. 1 enclosed marine toilet.
Sails:	Area 45.10m^2/485 sq. ft.
	Spinnaker area 65.00m^2/700 sq.ft.
Rigging:	Sloop
Price Guide:	118,500 Fr.f.
Summary:	A delight to sail whether under power or sail.

SHE SCANDINAVIAN

Design:	Sparkman & Stephens, U.S.A.
Supplier:	South Hants Marine, England
Specifications:	*Construction:* GRP
	LOA: 9.28m/30'4½
	Beam: 2.70m/8'10½
	Draft: 1.66m/5'5½
Fittings:	Fin keel. Volvo 12 hp inboard engine.
Interior:	5 berths
Sails:	Area 39m^2/420 sq.ft.
Rigging:	Sloop
Price Guide:	£7,000

SHE S31B ½ TON

Design: Sparkman & Stephens, U.S.A.

Supplier: South Hants Marine, England

Est. Rating: 21.7' IOR Mk III Portsmouth number 88

Specifications:

Construction:	GRP
LWL:	6.71m/22'0
LOA:	9.24m/30'4
Beam:	2.69m/8'10
Draft:	1.68m/5'6
Displ:	3,496kg/7,700 lbs
Ballast:	1,544kg/3,400 lbs

Fittings: Fin keel. GRP and balsa sandwich deck. Aluminium spars. 12 hp Albin gasoline auxiliary.

Interior: 5 berths in 2 cabins. Gas stove. 1 Lavac toilet.

Sails: Area 27.9m^2/300 sq.ft.

Rigging: Bermudan sloop

Price Guide: £7,800/$17,000us

Summary: An attractive and comfortable ½ ton racer.

943

BRABANT

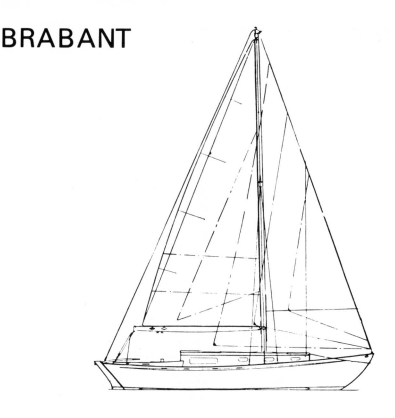

Design:	A. H. Buchanan Ltd., England 1958	
Supplier:	Stebbings (Burnham), England	
Specifications:	*Construction:*	Steel
	LWL:	7.31m/24'0
	LOA:	9.3m/30'6
	Beam:	2.72m/8'11
	Draft:	1.4m/4'7
	Displ:	5,115kg/11,267 lbs
Fittings:	Hull imported from Holland	
Interior:	5 berths	
Sails:	Area 37.1m^2/400 sq.ft.	
Rigging:	Bermudan sloop	
Price Guide:	On application	
Summary:	A fast family cruiser that sails at a comfortable heel even in the highest winds.	

BRISE DE MER

Design:	Groupe Finot, France 1973
Supplier:	Leguen et Hemidy, France
Est. Rating:	IOR 22'0
Specifications:	*Construction:* Aluminium
	LWL: 7.14m/23'5
	LOA: 9.30m/30'6
	Beam: 3.17m/10'5
	Draft: 0.95m/3'1
	Displ: 3,870kg/8,532 lbs
Fittings:	Aluminium spars
Interior:	6 berths
Sails:	Maximum area 44.80m^2/482 sq.ft.
Rigging:	Sloop
Price Guide:	100,000 Fr.f.
Summary:	An impressive performer. Very attractive shape and layout.

JAVELIN 30

Design:	Frederick R. Parker, England 1971
Supplier:	Marine Construction, England

Specifications:

Construction:	GRP
LWL:	6.71m/22'0
LOA:	9.3m/30'6
Beam:	2.74m/9'0
Draft:	1.52m/5'0
Displ:	3,051kg/6,720 lbs

Fittings:	Fin keel. Gold anodised spars. Iron rudder. 12 hp engine.
Interior:	3—5 berths.
Sails:	Area 25.7m^2/277 sq.ft. Spinnaker area 70.6m^2/760 sq.ft.
Rigging:	Masthead sloop
Price Guide:	£2,600
Summary:	Supplied in kit form. Designed specifically for cheap completion by owners. The class has won many races in the small racing class.

MACWESTER 30 WIGHT

Design:	C. S. J. Roy, England 1970
Supplier:	Macwester Marine, England
Specifications:	*Construction:* GRP
	LWL: 7.16m/23'6
	LOA: 9.3m/30'6
	Beam: 2.88m/9'4½
	Draft: 0.99m/3'3
	Displ: 4,068kg/8,960 lbs
Fittings:	Light alloy spars.
Interior:	6/7 berths
Variations:	Also known as **Macwester 30' Yawl.**
Sails:	Area 36.2m²/390 sq.ft.
Rigging:	Yawl
Price Guide:	On application
Summary:	Embodies all the best features of the **Macwester 26** and **28**, but the redesigned hull and longer waterline makes this a much more powerful vessel.

947

PHANTOM 30

Design: | H. Streuer

Supplier: | Yachtbau Genzel GmbH, Holland

Est. Rating: | IOR ± 21.7'

Specifications: | *Construction:*
LWL: | 7.40m/24'3½
LOA: | 9.30m/30'6
Beam: | 2.84m/9'4
Draft: | 1.35m/4'5
Displ: | 3,500kg/7,716 lbs
Ballast: | 1,400kg/3,086 lbs

Price Guide:

RAWSON 30

Design: | Bill Garden, U.S.A. 1958

Supplier: | Ron Rawson Inc., U.S.A.

Specifications: | *Construction:* | GRP
LWL: | 6.71m/22'0
LOA: | 9.3m/30'6
Beam: | 2.74m/9'0
Draft: | 1.52m/5'0
Displ: | 5,448kg/12,000 lbs
Ballast: | 2,270kg/5,000 lbs

Fittings: | Concrete and steel ballast. GRP deck. Aluminium spars. 27 hp International P60 gasoline.

Interior: | 5 berths in 2 cabins. Sink. Waterpump. Icebox. Enclosed toilet.

Sails: | Area 38.1m^2 (20.9 + 17.2)/410 sq.ft. (225 + 185)

Rigging: | Sloop

Price Guide: | $19,000us

Summary: | Available through dealers and sold direct.

COMMANDER 31

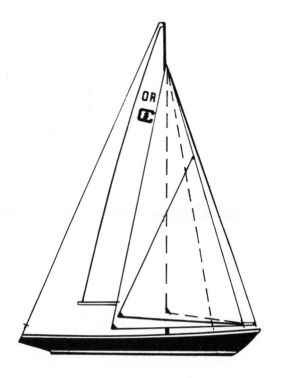

Design:	Jan Kærulf, Denmark
Supplier:	Bianca Yacht A/S, Denmark
Est. Rating:	Class 4 IOR

Specifications:

Construction:	GRP
LWL:	6.70m/21'11½
LOA:	9.32m/30'7
Beam:	2.70m/8'10½
Draft:	1.65m/5'5
Displ:	3,500kg/7,716 lbs
Ballast:	1,600kg/3,527 lbs

Fittings:	GRP sandwich deck. Stainless steel fittings. Teak trim.
Interior:	5/6 berths. Galley. Enclosed toilet.
Sails:	Area 41m^2/441 sq.ft. Spinnaker area 60m^2/646 sq.ft.
Rigging:	Sloop
Price Guide:	94,000 D.Kr.

SEAWIND 30

Design:	Thomas S. Gilmer, U.S.A.	
Supplier:	Allied Boat Co., U.S.A.	
Specifications:	*Construction:*	GRP
	LWL:	7.32m/24'0
	LOA:	9.3m/30'6
	Beam:	2.82m/9'3
	Draft:	1.27m/4'2
	Displ:	5,484kg/12,080 lbs
	Ballast:	1,907kg/4,200 lbs

Fittings: Lead ballast. Palmer M-60 gasoline. GRP deck. Aluminium spars.

Interior: 5 berths in 2 cabins. Sink. Stove. Oven. Icebox. Sea toilet.

Sails: Area 46.5m^2/500 sq.ft. (ketch)
Area 42.9m^2/462 sq.ft. (sloop)

Rigging: Ketch or sloop

Price Guide: $22,700us

Summary: A well-established design. Safe and seaworthy.

WING 30

Design:	M. J. Sutcliffe, England	
Supplier:	A. V. Robertson, England	
Specifications:	*Construction:*	GRP
	LWL:	7.32m/24'0
	LOA:	9.32m/30'7
	Beam:	3.05m/10'0
	Draft:	1.37m/4'6

Fittings: Fin keel. Perkins 4.107 inboard engine.

Interior: 6 berths

Sails: Area 36.2m^2/390 sq.ft.

Rigging: Ketch

Price Guide: On application

FRIENDSHIP 30

Design:	Marbridge Associates, U.S.A.
Supplier:	Bruno & Stillman, U.S.A.
Specifications:	*Construction:* GRP
	LWL: 7.62m/25'0
	LOA: 9.35m/30'8
	Beam: 3.05m/10'0
	Draft: 1.37m/4'6
	Displ: 5,675kg/12,500 lbs
	Ballast: 1,816kg/4,000 lbs
Fittings:	30 hp gasoline auxiliary.
Interior:	4 berths. 1.81m/5'11 headroom
Variations:	Finish to individual specification.
Sails:	Area 80.1m^2/862 sq.ft.
Rigging:	Schooner
Price Guide:	On application
Summary:	Sea-kindly, stable and surprisingly fast. Comfortable and easy to handle.

951

HURLEY 9.5

Design:	G. K. Colyer, England
Supplier:	Hurley Marine, England Hurley Marine, U.S.A.
Specifications:	*Construction:*
	LWL: 6.84m/22'5
	LOA: 9.35m/30'8
	Beam: 3.1m/10'2
	Draft: 1.22m/4'0
Fittings:	Finn keel. Thorneycroft 90 inboard.
Interior:	To specification
Sails:	Area 25.8m^2/278 sq.ft.
Rigging:	Ketch
Price Guide:	£10,000+
Summary:	A powerful motor ketch that is comfortable and sound.

FRERS 31 ½ TON

Design:	German Frers, Argentina 1973
Supplier:	Frers North American, U.S.A.
Est. Rating:	21.7' IOR Mk III
Specifications:	*Construction:* GRP with foam core
	LWL: 7.85m/25'9
	LOA: 9.4m/30'10
	Beam: 3.15m/20'4
	Draft: 1.5m/4'11
	Displ: 3,995kg/8,800 lbs
	Ballast: 1,861kg/4,100 lbs
Fittings:	GRP with balsa core deck. Aluminium spars. Lead ballast. 20HP Westerbeke Pilot diesel auxiliary.
Interior:	5—7 berths in 2 cabins
Sails:	Area 36.5m^2/393 sq.ft.
Rigging:	Sloop
Price Guide:	$24,500us
Summary:	An interesting new range of boats imported in from the Argentine.

KRITI 31

Supplier:	Corail Marine, France	
Specifications:	*Construction:*	GRP
	LWL:	7.20m/23'7½
	LOA:	9.38m/30'9
	Beam:	3.35m/11'0
	Draft:	1.50m/4'11
	Displ:	4,060kg/8,951 lbs
	Ballast:	1,150kg/2,535 lbs
Fittings:	9—18CV engine	
Interior:	4, 6 or 8 berths	
Variations:	2 versions — racing or cruising	
Sails:	Area 45m^2/484 sq.ft.	
	Spinnaker area 60m^2/646 sq.ft.	
Rigging:	Sloop	
Price Guide:	On application	

OFFSHORE 31

Design:	Herreshoff, U.S.A.
Supplier:	Cheoy Lee, Hong Kong Lion Yachts, U.S.A.

Specifications:	*Construction:*	GRP
	LWL:	7.16m/23'6
	LOA:	9.4m/30'10
	Beam:	2.69m/8'10
	Draft:	1.14m/3'9
	Displ:	4,881kg/10,750 lbs
	Ballast:	1,884kg/4,150 lbs

Fittings:	Iron ballast. GRP deck. Wood or aluminium spars. Auxiliary Atomic 4 gasoline.
Interior:	4 berths in 2 cabins. Sink. Icebox. 1 enclosed sea toilet.
Sails:	Area 33.7m^2(16.8 + 9.7 + 7.2)/363 sq.ft. (181 + 104 + 78)
Rigging:	Ketch
Price Guide:	On application

BALATON 31

Design:	Cardell, Sweden
Supplier:	Hungarian Shipyards & Crane Factory, Hungary V. G. Waring & Son, U.K.

Specifications:	*Construction:*	GRP
	LWL:	7.35m/24'1
	LOA:	9.45m/31'0
	Beam:	2.96m/9'9½
	Draft:	1.60m/5'3
	Displ:	3,650kg/8,047 lbs
	Ballast:	1,500kg/3,307 lbs

Fittings:	GRP and sandwich deck. Farymann 30A engine. Mahogany and teak trim. Light alloy spars.
Interior:	5 berths
Sails:	Area 46m^2/495 sq.ft. Spinnaker area 70m^2/753 sq.ft.
Rigging:	Sloop
Price Guide:	On application.

GOLDFISH 31 MOTSAILER

Supplier: Viksund Båt A/S, Norway
Viksund Boats, U.K.

Specifications:

Construction:	GRP
LOA:	9.40m/30'10
Beam:	3.20m/10'6
Draft:	1.20m/3'11
Displ:	4,500kg/9,920 lbs
Ballast:	2,000kg/4,409 lbs

Fittings: Volvo Penta MD3b 36 hp diesel engine.

Interior: 8 berths

Variations: Motor boat or sailing version with a steadying ketch rig supplied.

Sails: Area 42m^2/452 sq. ft.

Rigging: Ketch

Price Guide: £10,300

Summary: Built to satisfy the needs of Norwegian fishermen—therefore sturdy, safe and comfortable. Spacious and practical. Easily handled by a single person.

955

COLVIC CRAFT 31

Design:	John Bennett & Associates, England
Supplier:	Ardleigh Laminated Plastics, England

Specifications:	*Construction:*	GRP
	LWL:	8.53m/28'0
	LOA:	9.45m/31'0
	Beam:	3.05m/10'0
	Draft:	1.22m/4'0
	Displ:	7,119kg/7 tons

Fittings:	Aluminium spars
Interior:	6 berths
Sails:	Area 27.4m^2/295 sq.ft.
Rigging:	Ketch
Price Guide:	£11,000
Summary:	A powerful motor ketch.

CONCORDIA 31

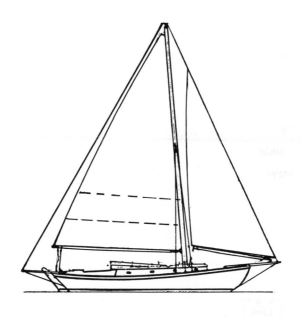

Design:	Harris & Howland, U.S.A. 1938

Supplier:	Concordia Co. Inc., U.S.A.

Specifications:	*Construction:*	Wood
	LWL:	7.62m/25'0
	LOA:	9.45m/31'0
	Beam:	2.84m/9'4
	Draft:	1.52m/5'0
	Displ:	9,534kg/21,000 lbs
	Ballast:	2,361kg/5,200 lbs

Fittings:	Iron ballast. Wooden deck. Wooden spars. 31 hp Gray gasoline auxiliary.

Interior:	4 berths in 2 cabins

Sails:	Area 49.2m^2/530 sq.ft.

Rigging:	Sloop

Price Guide:	$21,000us

EUROPA 10

Design:	John Bennett Assoc., England
Supplier:	Porter & Haylett Ltd., England
Est. Rating:	Portsmouth number 112
Specifications:	*Construction:*

LWL: 8.54m/28'0
LOA: 9.45m/31'0
Beam: 3.05m/10'0
Draft: 1.22m/4'0

Fittings:	Finn keel. 38 hp inboard.
Interior:	6 berths
Sails:	Area 58.8m^2/633 sq.ft.
Rigging:	Ketch
Price Guide:	£11,500
Summary:	Racer/cruiser of character.

HACATHIAN

Design:	Maurice Griffiths, England
Supplier:	M. F. Sales Ltd., England
Specifications:	*Construction:* Steel

LOA: 9.45m/31'0
Beam: 2.74m/9'0
Draft: 1.07m/3'6
Displ: 6,100kg/13,440 lbs

Fittings:	Trim of mahogany and Lima
Interior:	5 berths. 1.85m/6'1 headroom.
Sails:	Area 37.2m^2/400 sq.ft.
Rigging:	Ketch
Price Guide:	£8,000+
Summary:	Developed from the **Waterwich** class.

ELIZABETHAN 31

Supplier:	Peter Webster Ltd., England
Specifications:	*Construction:* GRP
	LWL: 7.37m/24'2
	LOA: 9.45m/31'0
	Beam: 2.84m/9'4
	Draft: 1.40m/4'7½
	Displ: 5,339kg/11,700 lbs
Fittings:	Teak trim. GRP deck. Alloy spars.
Interior:	5/6 berths
Variations:	Ketch carries a more powerful engine
Sails:	Area 33.6m²/362 sq.ft. (ketch)
	Area 35.1m²/378 sq.ft. (sloop)
Rigging:	Ketch or sloop
Price Guide:	£7,500
Summary:	A fast, family cruising yacht with a large amount of space below decks. Ketch built on the standard sloop hull.

959

LIZ 31 MS

Supplier:	Peter Webster, England
Specifications:	*Construction:* GRP
	LOA: 9.45m/31'0
	Draft: 1.42m/4'8
Fittings:	Keelboat
Interior:	6 berths
Variations:	Optional inboard engine
Sails:	Area 43m^2/463 sq.ft.
Rigging:	Ketch
Price Guide:	£10,000+
Summary:	Can be trailed.

NORTH SEA 24

Design:	C. R. Holman, England 1964
Supplier:	Tucker Brown & Co., England
Specifications:	*Construction:* Wood
	LWL: 7.32m/24'0
	LOA: 9.45m/31'0
	Beam: 2.74m/9'0
	Draft: 1.7m/5'7
	Displ: 5,634kg/12,410 lbs
Fittings:	Albinco Cadet 10 hp engine.
Interior:	5/6 berths. 1.83m/6'0 headroom.
Sails:	Area 40.6m^2/437 sq.ft.
Rigging:	Masthead sloop
Price Guide:	£9,000
Summary:	A cruiser/racer of proven ability. The design developed from the **Holman 31** and **Holman 37.**

IW 31

Design:	Sparkman & Stephens, U.S.A. 1968
Supplier:	IW-Varvet, Sweden South Hants Marine, England
Est. Rating:	21.7' IOR
Specifications:	

	Construction:	GRP
	LWL:	6.7m/22'0
	LOA:	9.3m/31'0
	Beam:	2.70m/9'0
	Draft:	1.60m/5'3
	Displ:	3,600kg/7,920 lbs
	Ballast:	1,600kg/3,520 lbs

Fittings:	10 hp diesel engine. Volvo MDI. Sandwich deck. Alloy spars.
Interior:	5 berths. Sink. Pump. Icebox. Pantry. Foot pump. Toilet.
Variations:	Optional engine on racing version.
Sails:	Area 36m^2/388 sq.ft.
Rigging:	Sloop
Price Guide:	£8,600 ex VAT
Summary:	A neat cruiser of some character.

WESTERLY BERWICK

Design:	Laurent Giles, England 1973
Supplier:	Westerly Marine, England Andrew Gemeny & Sons, U.S.A.
Specifications:	*Construction:* GRP *LWL:* 7.62m/25'0 *LOA:* 9.45m/31'0 *Beam:* 2.90m/9'6 *Draft:* 1.37m/4'6 *Displ:* 3,814kg/8,400 lbs *Ballast:* 1,816kg/4,000 lbs
Fittings:	Twin keel boat. Gold anodised spars. 25 hp Ford Watermeta inboard diesel.
Interior:	6 berths. Galley — stove, sink, icebox.
Sails:	Area 35.9m^2/386 sq.ft. (ketch) Area 39.2m^2/422 sq.ft. (sloop)
Rigging:	Sloop or ketch
Price Guide:	£7,750—8,350
Summary:	A functional, well-priced boat. Good value for money.

IRWIN 31

Design:	Ted Irwin, U.S.A.
Supplier:	Irwin Yacht and Marine Corporation, U.S.A.
Specifications:	*Construction:* GRP *LWL:* 6.78m/22'3 *LOA:* 9.47m/31'1 *Beam:* 2.92m/9'7 *Draft:* 2.39m/7'10 *Displ:* 4,358kg/9,600 lbs *Ballast:* 1,725kg/3,800 lbs
Fittings:	Lead ballast. GRP deck. Aluminium spars.
Interior:	6 berths in 2 cabins. Standard galley.
Variations:	Optional 30 hp auxiliary.
Sails:	Area 42.7m^2/460 sq.ft.
Rigging:	Sloop
Price Guide:	$19,500us

S-31

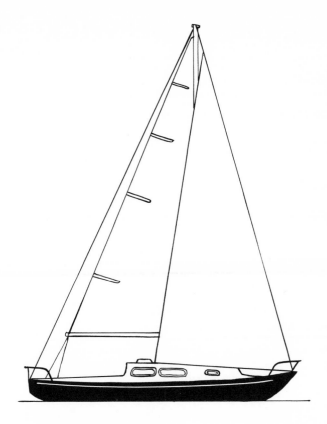

Design:	John Brandymayer, Canada,
Supplier:	Spencer Boats, Canada
Est. Rating:	26.8′ CCA
Specifications:	*Construction:* GRP

LWL:	7.32m/24′0
LOA:	9.45m/31′0
Beam:	2.80m/9′2
Draft:	1.52m/5′0
Displ:	4,086kg/9,000 lbs
Ballast:	1,407kg/3,100 lbs

Fittings:	Lead ballast. GRP deck. Aluminium spars.
Interior:	6 berths in 2 cabins. Galley. 1 enclosed toilet.
Variations:	Auxiliary power optional
Sails:	Area 41.8m^2/450 sq.ft.
Rigging:	Sloop
Price Guide:	On application

COMPASS 31

Design:	E. Bjorn Jansen, 1969
Supplier:	Built by Lisberg Maritime. Interyacht, England

Specifications:		
	Construction:	GRP
	LWL:	7.77m/25'6
	LOA:	9.5m/31'2
	Beam:	3.1m/10'2
	Draft:	1.4m/4'7
	Displ:	5,085kg/1,200 lbs
	Ballast:	2.034kg/4,480 lbs

Fittings:	Fin keel. 31 hp Captain Newage auxiliary.
Interior:	5/6 berths
Sails:	Area 43.3m^2/466 sq.ft.
Rigging:	Ketch
Price Guide:	£14,750
Summary:	Kits and mouldings available.

WESTERLY PENTLAND

Design:	Laurent Giles, England 1973
Supplier:	Westerly Marine, England
Est. Rating:	10.35 tons Thames Measurement
Specifications:	*Construction:* GRP
	LWL: 7.62m/25'0
	LOA: 9.5m/31'0
	Beam: 2.9m/9'6
	Draft: 1.1m/3'7
	Displ: 4,960kg/10,163 lbs
	Ballast: 2,012kg/4,440 lbs
Fittings:	Anodised aluminium spars. Twin keels. 25 hp Ford Watermeta diesel engine.
Interior:	6 berths in 3 cabins 1.91m^2/6'3 headroom. Galley. Marine head & washbasin.
Sails:	Area 45.1m^2/534 sq.ft. (ketch) Area 40.2m^2/529 sq.ft. (sloop)
Rigging:	Sloop or ketch
Price Guide:	£8,250–8,500
Summary:	Based on the successful **Westerly Renown**.

CONTEST 31 HT

Design:	Dick Zaal, Holland 1972
Supplier:	Conyplex NV, Holland Interyacht, England Holland Yachts, U.S.A.
Est. Rating:	21.3′ IOR
Specifications:	*Construction:* GRP *LWL:* 7.15m/23′5 *LOA:* 9.5m/31′2 *Beam:* 3.15m/10′4 *Draft:* 1.45m/4′9 *Displ:* 4,465kg/9,843 lbs *Ballast:* 1,900kg/4,189 lbs
Fittings:	Fin keel. Volvo Penta MD2B 25 hp inboard. Anodised aluminium spars.
Interior:	6 berths. Galley. 1.95m/6′4 headroom. Marine toilet.
Sails:	Area 433 sq. ft. Spinnaker 76m²/817 sq. ft.
Rigging:	Sloop
Price Guide:	£10,750
Summary:	Very spacious design that makes her ably suited to offshore racing.

SEAFARER 31

Design:	W. H. Tripp Jnr, U.S.A.
Supplier:	Seafarer Fiberglass Yachts Inc., U.S.A.
Est. Rating:	20.5' IOR Mk III

Specifications:	*Construction:*	GRP
	LWL:	6.81m/22'4
	LOA:	9.5m/31'2
	Beam:	2.49m/8'10
	Draft:	1.52m/5'0
	Displ:	3,973kg/8,750 lbs
	Ballast:	1,544kg/3,400 lbs

Fittings:	Lead ballast. GRP deck. Aluminium spars.
Interior:	4/6 berths in 2 cabins. Sink. Icebox. Enclosed toilet.
Variations:	Mk I or II versions available.
Sails:	Area 34.6m^2/372 sq.ft.
Rigging:	Sloop or yawl
Price Guide:	$10,500–14,500us

CONTEST 31

Design:	Van Essen, Holland 1971
Supplier:	Conyplex NV, Holland Holland Yachts Inc., U.S.A. Interyacht, England
Est. Rating:	22.0' IOR Mk III
Specifications:	*Construction:* GRP *LWL:* 7.6m/24'11 *LOA:* 9.55m/31'4 *Beam:* 2.84m/9'4 *Draft:* 1.24m/4'1 *Displ:* 3,805kg/8,380 lbs *Ballast:* 1,603kg/3,530 lbs
Fittings:	Lead ballast. GRP deck. Aluminium spars.
Interior:	6 berths in 3 cabins
Variations:	Optional 25 hp auxiliary.
Sails:	Area 34.6m^2 (15.5 + 19.1)/372 sq.ft. (167 + 205)
Rigging:	Sloop
Price Guide:	£9,200/$21,000us
Summary:	A fast cruiser that is close winded and very manoeuvrable.

VICTORIA

Design:	Holland
Specifications:	*Construction:* Mahogany on oak *LWL:* 7.32m/24'0 *LOA:* 9.55m/31'4 *Beam:* 2.69m/8'10 *Draft:* 1.3m/4'3 *Displ:* 3,904kg/8,600 lbs
Fittings:	Palmer 22 hp engine.
Interior:	4 berths
Sails:	Area 39.9m^2/430 sq. ft.
Rigging:	Optional
Price Guide:	On application
Summary:	Wide beam and ample ballast give good stability.

TERN

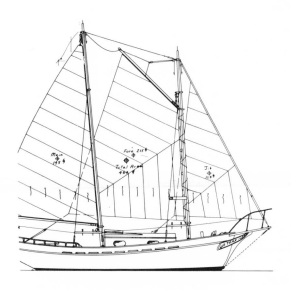

Design:	James D. Rosborough, Canada 1967
Supplier:	James D. Rosborough, Canada
Specifications:	*Construction:* Wood
	LWL: 7.39m/24'3
	LOA: 9.53m/31'3
	Beam: 2.94m/9'8
	Draft: 1.52m/5'0
	Displ: 6,174kg/13,600 lbs
	Ballast: 908kg/2,000 lbs
Fittings:	Lead ballast. Fiberglassed wood deck. Aluminium spars. 30 hp Perkins diesel.
Interior:	4/6 berths in 1 cabin. Gas stove. Sink. Icebox. 1 toilet.
Variations:	Layout to specification
Sails:	Area 42.7m^2 (13.3 + 9.7 + 19.7)/460 sq.ft. (143 + 104 + 213)
Rigging:	To specification
Price Guide:	$19,900us
Summary:	A boat of old world charm and distinction. Sail rig — tremendously powerful.

GALAXY ¾ TON

Design:	William H. Tripp Jnr., U.S.A. redesigned 1971
Supplier:	Metalmast Marine, U.S.A.
Specifications:	*Construction:* GRP
	LWL: 7.42m/24'4
	LOA: 9.58m/31'5
	Beam: 3.08m/10'1½
	Draft: 1.52m/5'0
	Displ: 4,086kg/9,000 lbs
Fittings:	Lead ballast. GRP deck. Aluminium spars.
Interior:	6 berths in 2 cabins
Variations:	Optional diesel auxiliary
Sails:	Area 46.5m^2(18.1 + 28.4)/501 sq.ft. (195 + 306)
Rigging:	Sloop
Price Guide:	$19,900us
Summary:	Redesigned to comply with IOR ¾ ton racing rules.

RUSTLER

Design:	C. R. Holman, England
Supplier:	Russell Anstey Yachts, England
Specifications:	*Construction:* GRP
	LWL: 7.32m/24'0
	LOA: 9.58m/31'5
	Beam: 2.74m/9'0
	Draft: 1.68m/5'6
	Displ: 5,593kg/12,320 lbs
Fittings:	Teak trim. Keel boat. Wortham Blake Fisherboy Mk III engine.
Interior:	5/6 berths. 1.83m/6'0 headroom. Sit in chart table fitted.
Sails:	Area 48.7m^2/524 sq.ft.
Rigging:	Sloop
Price Guide:	On application
Summary:	Good performance in light and heavy weather. Can be trailed.

DEFENDER 32

Design:	J. Gaubert & A. Mauric, France 1969
Supplier:	Jachtwerf F. Dekker en Zonen, Holland
Specifications:	*Construction:* GRP
	LWL: 6.96m/22'10
	LOA: 9.60m/31'6
	Beam: 3.00m/9'10
	Draft: 1.45m/5'3
	Displ: 3,200kg/7,056 lbs
	Ballast: 1,450kg/3,197 lbs
Fittings:	Sandwich GRP deck. Aluminium spars. Fin keel.
Interior:	4 berths. Galley — water pump. 1 enclosed toilet.
Variations:	25 hp engine optional.
Sails:	Area 39.30m^2/423 sq.ft.
	Spinnaker area 68m^2/732 sq. ft.
Rigging:	Sloop
Price Guide:	£8,000+/57,250 fl.

SHE 9.5 TRAVELLER ½ TON

Design:	Sparkman & Stephens, U.S.A.
Supplier:	South Hants Marine, England
Est. Rating:	21.5' IOR Mk III

Specifications:	Construction:	GRP
	LWL:	6.71m/22'0
	LOA:	9.58m/31'5
	Beam:	2.69m/8'10
	Draft:	1.68m/5'6
	Displ:	3,587kg/7,900 lbs
	Ballast:	1,498kg/3,300 lbs

Fittings:	Iron ballast. GRP and balsa sandwich deck. Aluminium spars. 12 hp Albin 12 gasoline auxiliary.
Interior:	5/6 berths in 2 cabins. Stove. 1 Lavac toilet.
Sails:	Area 33.4m^2 (13.9 + 19.5)/360 sq.ft. (150 + 210)
Rigging:	Sloop
Price Guide:	£8,400/$18,700us
Summary:	Top quality finish. Easy to maintain. Kits available.

FLEUR DE MER

Design:	France 1974
Supplier:	F. E. Sparkes Marine, England (Lancing 3836)

Specifications:	Construction:	GRP
	LOA:	9.6m/31'6
	Beam:	3.51m/11'6
	Draft:	1.50m−1.73m/4'11−5'8
	Displ:	403kg/888 lbs

Fittings:	Teak trim
Interior:	Galley — fully equipped. Toilet and showers.
Variations:	Shoal or draft models available.
Sails:	Area 54.7m^2/589 sq.ft.
Rigging:	Sloop
Price Guide:	£13,600
Summary:	6½ knots cruising speed.

GOLDENHIND 31

Design:	Maurice Griffiths, England 1963
Supplier:	Terry Erskine Yachts, England

Specifications:

Construction:	Hard chine marine ply
LWL:	8.15m/26'9
LOA:	9.6m/31'6
Beam:	2.69m/8'10
Draft:	1.07m/3'6
Displ:	4,068kg/8,960 lbs
Ballast:	1,861kg/4,100 lbs

Fittings:	Hull, decks and coachroof all nylon sheathed for protection.
Interior:	5 berths. 1.88m/6'2 headroom. Galley.
Variations:	Optional inboard motor. Sloop or ketch models available.
Sails:	Area 34.4m^2/370 sq.ft. (cruising suit) Area 39.6m^2/426 sq.ft. (racing rig)
Rigging:	Bermudan sloop
Price Guide:	£8,500–9,300
Summary:	Well suited to family sailing.

CARENA 32 GHOSTER

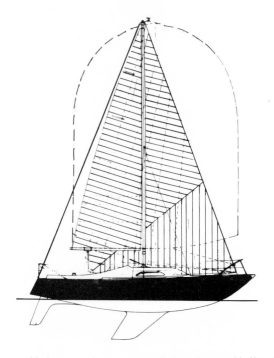

Design:	H. Lemstra-bureau voor Scheepbonw, Holland
Supplier:	Scheepswerf Porsius, Holland
Specifications:	*Construction:* Pre-moulded marine ply
	LWL: 7.00m/22'11½
	LOA: 9.63m/31'7
	Beam: 3.12m/10'3
	Draft: 1.66m/5'5½
	Displ: 2,700kg/5,952 lbs
	Ballast: 1,100kg/2,425 lbs
Fittings:	Cast iron keel. Plywood deck. Aluminium spars.
Interior:	1 Wilcox Crittenden toilet. Pump. Stove.
Variations:	Optional power. Many options can be included.
Sails:	Area 47.10m^2/507 sq.ft. Spinnaker area 60m^2/646 sq. ft.
Rigging:	Sloop
Price Guide:	85,550 fl.

ERICSON 32

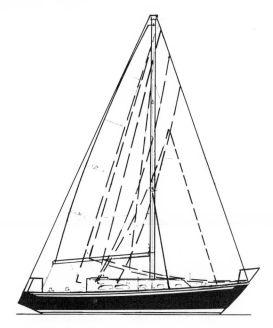

Design:	Bruce King, U.S.A. 1968
Supplier:	Ericson Yachts Inc., U.S.A. Hamble Marine, U.K. Nordmarine, Italy
Est. Rating:	23.5' IOR Mk III 27.4' CCA

Specifications:

Construction:	GRP
LWL:	7.32m/24'0
LOA:	9.62m/31'7
Beam:	2.94m/9'8
Draft:	1.5m/4'11
Displ:	3,995kg/8,800 lbs
Ballast:	1,816kg/4,000 lbs

Fittings:	Fin keel. GRP deck — non-skid. Aluminium spars. Lead ballast. 30 hp Universal Atomic 4 gasoline.
Interior:	6 berths in 2 cabins.
Sails:	Area 42m^2(19m + 23m)/452 sq.ft. (205 + 247)
Rigging:	Sloop
Price Guide:	£ on application/$17,495us
Summary:	Easily maintained. Good all-weather ability.

MACWESTER WIGHT SERIES II

Design:	C. S. J. Roy, England
Supplier:	Macwester Marine, England

Specifications:	*Construction:*	GRP
	LWL:	8.53m/28'0
	LOA:	9.67m/31'9
	Beam:	2.89m/9'5
	Draft:	0.99m/3'3
	Displ:	4,136.8kg/9,120 lbs
	Ballast:	1,490kg/3,285 lbs

Fittings:	Twin keel. BMC Captain diesel engine. GRP deck. Gold anodised alloy spars.
Interior:	7 berths. Lavac toilet. Sink. Stove. Water pump.
Sails:	Area 36.23m^2/390 sq. ft. (ketch) Area 35.3m^2/380 sq. ft. (sloop)
Rigging:	Ketch or sloop
Price Guide:	£7,900—£8,500
Summary:	Kits and mouldings available.

PT 32 $^3/_4$ TON

Design:	Andy Green, U.S.A. 1973
Supplier:	Composite Technology Inc., U.S.A.
Est. Rating:	24.5' IOR Mk III

Specifications:	*Construction:*	GRP and steel
	LWL:	8.33m/27'4
	LOA:	9.68m/31'9
	Beam:	3m/9'10
	Draft:	1.65m/5'5
	Displ:	4,722kg/10,400 lbs
	Ballast:	2,452kg/5,400 lbs

Fittings:	Lead ballast. GRP deck. Aluminium spars. 25 hp Universal Atomic auxiliary.
Interior:	5/7 berths in 2 cabins. Sink. Water pump. Icebox. 1 enclosed chemical toilet.
Sails:	Area 45.3m^2/488 sq.ft.
Rigging:	Sloop
Price Guide:	$18,000us
Summary:	Sold direct.

NANTUCKET CLIPPER

Design:	Alan Buchanan, England 1969
Supplier:	Offshore Yachts International, England
Specifications:	*Construction:* GRP
	LWL: 6.4m/21'0
	LOA: 9.65m/31'8
	Beam: 2.76m/9'1
	Draft: 1.3m/4'3
	Displ: 3,741kg/8,240 lbs
	Ballast: 1,221kg/2,690 lbs
Fittings:	Teak trim. Keelboat. GRP deck. Gold anodised spars. Balanced spade GRP rudder.
Interior:	5 berths
Sails:	Area 34.2m^2/368 sq.ft. (yawl)
	Area 33.6m^2/362 sq.ft. (sloop)
	Spinnaker area 63.2m^2–66.9m^2/680–720 sq.ft.
Rigging:	Sloop or yawl
Price Guide:	£6,900
Summary:	Stability ensured by high ballast ratio of 41%. Modest draft reduces berthing and navigation problems. Kits and mouldings available.

DOUGLAS 32

Design:	Edward S. Brewer, U.S.A.
Supplier:	Douglas Boat Works, Canada Pacific Ocean Yachts, Jersey
Est. Rating:	22.0' IOR

Specifications:

Construction:	GRP or aluminium
LWL:	6.91m/22'9
LOA:	9.70m/31'10
Beam:	2.82m/9'3
Draft:	1.41m/4'8
Displ:	4,427kg/9,750 lbs
Ballast:	1,703kg/3,750 lbs

Fittings:	Teak trim. Fin keel. 22 hp Palmer auxiliary. Aluminium spars.
Interior:	4/5 berths. 1.90m/6'3 headroom. Galley — Icebox. Sink. Water system. Stove. Marine toilet with pump.
Sails:	Area 42.7m²/460 sq. ft. Spinnaker area 69.7m²/750 sq. ft.
Rigging:	Sloop
Price Guide:	$22,500us
Summary:	Rugged reliability combined with impeccable workmanship. Sailed particularly in the Caribbean.

RIVAL 32

Design:	Peter Brett Assoc., RINA, England 1966
Supplier:	Marine Construction (UK), England

Specifications:

Construction:	GRP
LWL:	7.47m/24'6
LOA:	9.7m/31'10
Beam:	2.94m/9'8
Draft:	1.42m/4'8
Displ:	5,288kg/11,648 lbs

Fittings:	GRP deck. Anodised light alloy spars. 25 hp engine.
Interior:	6 berths
Sails:	Area 31.5m²/339 sq.ft.
Rigging:	Masthead sloop
Price Guide:	£9,000
Summary:	Well planned and eminently serviceable. Cannot be trailed. Kits and mouldings available.

PACESHIP 32

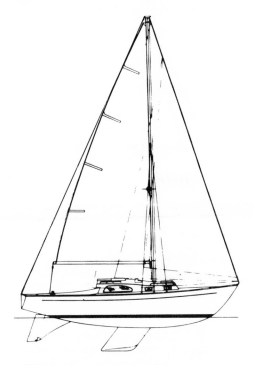

Design:	William H. Tripp Jnr., U.S.A.
Supplier:	Paceship Yachts, Canada

Specifications:

Construction:	GRP
LWL:	7.47m/24'6
LOA:	9.7m/31'10
Beam:	3.2m/10'6
Draft:	1.42m/4'8
Displ:	3,632kg/8,000 lbs
Ballast:	1,544kg/3,400 lbs

Fittings:	Iron ballast. GRP deck. Aluminium spars. 30 hp Universal Atomic 4 gasoline.
Interior:	6 berths in 2 cabins. Sink. Stove, w/oven. Enclosed Monomatic toilet.
Sails:	Area 46m^2 (24.1 + 21.9)/495 sq.ft. (159 + 236)
Rigging:	Sloop
Price Guide:	$25,000us
Summary:	An older design that has withstood the test of time.

CORONADO 32 MkII

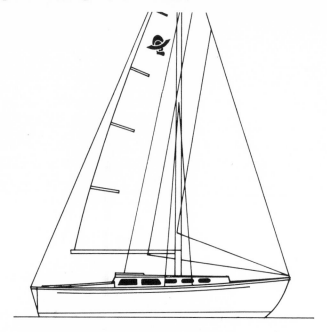

Design:	William H. Tripp Jnr, U.S.A.
Supplier:	Coronado Yachts, U.S.A. Playvisa Coronado Yachts, England

Specifications:

Construction:	GRP
LWL:	8.15m/26'9
LOA:	9.73m/31'11
Beam:	2.87m/9'5
Draft:	1.78m—1.19m/5'10—3'11
Displ:	5,448kg/12,000 lbs
Ballast:	2,315kg/5,100 lbs

Fittings:	Lead ballast. GRP deck. Aluminium spars. 27 hp Palmer P-60 gasoline auxiliary.
Interior:	6 berths. 1.93m/6'4 headroom.
Variations:	Shoal draft model also available.
Sails:	Area 37.9m^2/408 sq.ft.
Rigging:	Sloop
Price Guide:	$22,232us
Summary:	Plenty of room for privacy for guests. **The** boat for adventurous sailors.

BREWER 32

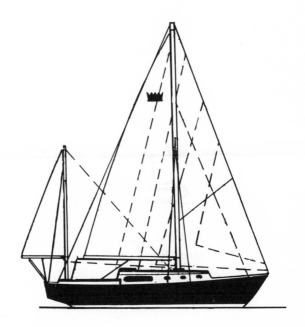

Design:	Edward S. Brewer, U.S.A.
Supplier:	Edward S. Brewer, U.S.A.

Specifications:

Construction:	GRP
LWL:	7.32m/24'0
LOA:	9.74m/31'11½
Beam:	3.04m/9'11½
Draft:	1.6m/5'3
Displ:	4,022kg/8,860 lbs
Ballast:	1,634kg/3,600 lbs

Fittings:	Wooden deck. Aluminium spars. Iron ballast.
Interior:	6 berths in 2 cabins. Galley included.
Variations:	Optional auxiliary power
Sails:	Area 45.1m²/4·86 sq.ft.
Rigging:	Yawl
Price Guide:	On application

CENTURION

Design:	Kim Holman, France 1969
Supplier:	Wauquiez, France
Est. Rating:	IOR 22.3'–23'

Specifications:

Construction:	GRP
LWL:	7.32m/24'0
LOA:	9.75m/32'0
Beam:	3.00m/9'10
Draft:	1.78m/5'10
Displ:	4,800kg/10,700 lbs
Ballast:	2,000kg/4,409 lbs

Fittings:	Lead ballast. GRP deck. Aluminium spars. Teak trim.
Interior:	6 berths in 2 cabins. Standard galley. 1.88m/6'2 headroom. 1 enclosed toilet.
Variations:	Optional diesel auxiliary. Taller mast optional with larger rig.
Sails:	Area 44.8m^2/482 sq. ft. Spinnaker are 776.9m^2/828 sq. ft.
Rigging:	Sloop
Price Guide:	On application
Summary:	A very fast auxiliary cruiser/racer. Strongly built to a high standard for long offshore cruising.

IRWIN 32

Design:	Ted Irwin, U.S.A. 1969
Supplier:	Irwin Yacht and Marine Corp., U.S.A.
Est. Rating:	24.5' MORC

Specifications:

Construction:	GRP
LWL:	7.62m/25'0
LOA:	9.75m/32'0
Beam:	2.94m/9'8
Draft:	1.52m—1.07m/5'0—3'6
Displ:	5,221kg/11,500 lbs
Ballast:	2,270kg/5,000 lbs

Fittings:	GRP and balsa core deck. Lead ballast. Aluminium spars. 30 hp Atomic 4 gasoline auxiliary.
Interior:	6 berths in 2 cabins
Variations:	Keel or keel/centreboard options
Sails:	Area 45.7m^2 (22.5 + 23.2)/492 sq.ft. (242 + 250)
Rigging:	Sloop or yawl
Price Guide:	$18,000us
Summary:	Dual purpose, character boat — ideal for cruising or racing

NICHOLSON 32 Mk X

Design:	Camper & Nicholsons Ltd., England 1962 Mk X 1971
Supplier:	Camper & Nicholsons Ltd., England Camper & Nicholsons Ltd., U.S.A.
Est. Rating:	Thames measurement 10 tons

Specifications:

Construction:	GRP
LWL:	7.31m/24'0
LOA:	10.05m/32'0
Beam:	2.81m/9'3
Draft:	1.68m/5'6
Displ:	6,200kg/6.15 tons
Ballast:	3,092kg/6,810 lbs

Fittings:	Inboard engine/diesel or gasoline optional. Keel boat.
Interior:	5 berths. 6' headroom.
Variations:	Alternatives in layout, finish and engine available.
Sails:	Area 55m²/594 sq. ft. 8 oz. Vectis.
Rigging:	Masthead auxiliary. Bermudan sloop.
Price Guide:	£11,500/$20,000us
Summary:	Value for money. Fast for passage cruising yet very roomy for cruising.

WESTSAIL 32

Design:	Colin Archer et alia, U.S.A. approx. 1900
Supplier:	Westsail Corporation, U.S.A.

Specifications:	*Construction:*	GRP
	LWL:	8.38m/27'6
	LOA:	9.75m/32'0
	Beam:	3.35m/11'0
	Draft:	1.52m/5'0
	Displ:	8,853kg/19,500 lbs
	Ballast:	2,996.4kg/6,600 lbs

Fittings: Lead ballast. GRP deck. Aluminium spars. 25 hp Volvo MD2B diesel auxiliary.

Interior: 6 berths in 2 cabins. Sink. Water pump.

Sails: Area 58.43m^2 (28.15 + 16.44 + 13.84)/629 sq.ft. (303 + 177 + 149)

Rigging: Ketch

Price Guide: $27,000us

Summary: A very ruggedly constructed boat that also has a great deal of character. Very seaworthy.

CHANCE P32/28

Design:	Britton Chance Jnr., U.S.A.
Supplier:	Paceship Yachts, Canada Chantier Henri Wanquiez, France Robertsons of Sandbank, Scotland
Est. Rating:	IOR 24.5'—25.5'
Specifications:	*Construction:* GRP *LWL:* 8.46m/27'9 *LOA:* 9.78m/32'1 *Beam:* 3.05m/10'0 *Draft:* 1.75m/5'9 *Displ:* 5,459.35kg/12,025 lbs *Ballast:* 2,124.72kg/4,680 lbs
Fittings:	GRP deck. Teak trim. Aluminium spars. 30 hp Universal Atomic 4 gasoline auxiliary.
Interior:	4 berths in 2 cabins. 1.8m/5'11 headroom. Stainless steel sink. Icebox. Enclosed toilet.
Variations:	Diesel auxiliary optional
Sails:	Area 42.55m^2/458 sq.ft.
Rigging:	Sloop
Price Guide:	£ on application/$28,500us
Summary:	Light on the helm, well-balanced and fast.

SHE C32

Design:	Sparkman & Stephens, U.S.A.
Supplier:	South Hants Marine, England
Est. Rating:	22.0' IOR Mk III

Specifications:

Construction:	GRP
LOA:	9.78m/32'1
Beam:	2.87m/9'5
Draft:	1.68m/5'6
Displ:	3,532.2kg/7,800 lbs
Ballast:	1,589kg/3,500 lbs

Fittings:	Fin and skeg keel. GRP and balsa sandwich deck. Aluminium spars. Teak trim. 8 hp Yanmar YS8 diesel.
Interior:	6 berths in 2 cabins. Stove. Lavac sea-toilet.
Sails:	Area 36.23m^2/390 sq.ft.
Rigging:	Sloop
Price Guide:	£8,750/$18,750us
Summary:	Kits available.

BARBARY

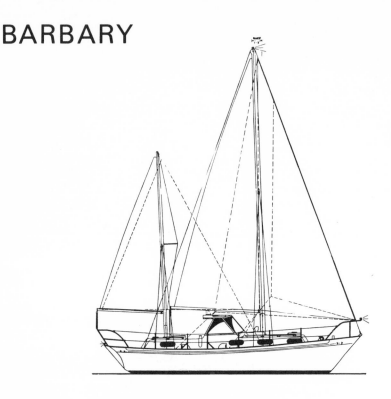

Design:	Walter F. Rayner, England 1969
Supplier:	Walter F. Rayner Ltd., England F. C. Mitchell & Sons, England
Est. Rating:	TM 11.5 tons
Specifications:	*Construction:* GRP *LWL:* 7.62m/25'0 *LOA:* 9.88m/32'0 *Beam:* 3.15m/10'4 *Draft:* 1.45m/4'9 *Displ:* 6.102kg/1,344 lbs *Ballast:* 2,473.4kg/5,448 lbs
Fittings:	Wood trim. Fin keel. Mercedes Benz 42 hp diesel auxiliary.
Interior:	6 berths. 1.90m/6'3 headroom.
Sails:	Area 44.6m^2/480 sq.ft.
Rigging:	Ketch or sloop
Price Guide:	£14,000 ex VAT

SCHOKKER

Design:	Holland		
Supplier:	Koojiman ende Vries Jachtbouw bv, Holland		
Specifications:	*Construction:*	GRP	
	LOA:	9.84m/32'3½	
	Beam:	3.30m/10'10	
	Draft:	0.65m/2'1½	
Fittings:	To specification		
Interior:	Layout optional		
Sails:	Area 45.5m^2/489 sq.ft.		
Price Guide:	89,000 fl.		
Summary:	A traditional design built in modern materials.		

IRWIN 32 ½ TON

Design:	Ted Irwin, U.S.A. 1972
Supplier:	Irwin Yacht & Marine Corp., U.S.A.
Specifications:	*Construction:* GRP
	LWL: 7.92m/26'0
	LOA: 9.91m/32'6
	Beam: 3.05m/10'0
	Draft: 1.2m/3'11
	Displ: 5,902kg/13,000 lbs
	Ballast: 1,816kg/4,000 lbs
Fittings:	Lead ballast. GRP and balsa core deck. Aluminium spars. 30 hp Atomic 4 gasoline auxiliary.
Interior:	6 berths in 3 cabins
Variations:	Optional toilet
Sails:	Area 42.9m^2/462 sq.ft. (sloop) Area 49.1m^2/529 sq.ft. (ketch)
Rigging:	Sloop or ketch. Stainless steel and Dacron.
Price Guide:	$19,800us
Summary:	Centre cockpit arrangement makes for easy handling by two persons.

CAL 33

Design:	C. William Lapworth, U.S.A. 1971
Supplier:	Jensen Marine, U.S.A.
Est. Rating:	27.1' IOR Mk III

Specifications:	*Construction:*	GRP
	LWL:	8.38m/27'6
	LOA:	9.95m/32'8
	Beam:	3.15m/10'4
	Draft:	1.83m/6'0
	Displ:	4,903.2kg/10,800 lbs
	Ballast:	2,179.2kg/4,800 lbs

Fittings:	GRP deck. Aluminium spars. 25 hp auxiliary.
Interior:	6 berths in 2 cabins. Full wrap around seating aft.
Sails:	Area 49.79m^2/536 sq.ft.
Rigging:	Sloop
Price Guide:	$21,500us
Summary:	Hand laid-up GRP construction gives maintenance free use in all seasons. Galley situated up forward.

CAPE CARIB 33

Design: Edward S. Brewer & Associates, U.S.A. 1970

Supplier: Cape Cod Shipbuilding Co., U.S.A.
                       Pacific Ocean Yachts, Jersey

Specifications: *Construction:*   GRP
                       LWL: 7.19m/23'7
                       LOA: 9.95m/32'8
                       Beam: 2.82m/9'3
                       Draft: 1.42m/4'8
                       Displ: 4,540kg/10,000 lbs
                       Ballast: 1,589kg/3,500 lbs

Fittings: Lead ballast. GRP and balsa core deck with teak over-
                       lay. Aluminium spars. 25 hp Volvo Penta MO2B diesel
                       auxiliary.

Interior: 5 berths in 2 cabins. 1 enclosed toilet.

Sails: Area 47.5m^2(16.9 + 21.9 + 8.5)/511 sq.ft. (182 +
                       236 + 93)

Rigging: Ketch

Price Guide: $17,200us

Summary: Available through dealers and sold direct.

GIB' SEA 33

Design:	Phillippe Harlé, France 1974
Supplier:	Olivier Gibert, France
Specifications:	*Construction:* GRP
	LOA: 10m/32'10
	Beam: 3.45m/11'4
Fittings:	To specification
Interior:	7 berths
Rigging:	Sloop
Price Guide:	On application

PEARSON 33

Design:	William H. Shaw, U.S.A. 1969
Supplier:	Pearson Yachts, U.S.A.

Specifications:

	Construction:	GRP
	LWL:	7.87m/25'10
	LOA:	10.03m/32'11
	Beam:	3.05m/10'0
	Draft:	1.22m/4'0
	Displ:	4,962kg/10,930 lbs
	Ballast:	1,907kg/4,200 lbs

Fittings:	Lead ballast. GRP deck. Aluminium spars. 30 hp gasoline auxiliary.
Interior:	6 berths in 2 cabins. Sink. Icebox. Sea toilet. 1.88m/6'2 headroom.
Variations:	Racing or cruising versions available.
Sails:	Area 45.7m^2 (21.9 + 23.8)/492 sq.ft. (236 + 256)
Rigging:	Masthead sloop
Price Guide:	$21,000us
Summary:	Safety, speed and comfort — the three watchwords behind the basic design of this boat.

OFFSHORE 33

Design:	Cheoy Lee, Hong Kong 1971
Supplier:	Cheoy Lee, Hong Kong Lion Yachts, U.S.A.

Specifications:	*Construction:*	GRP
	LWL:	9.3m/30'6
	LOA:	10.03m/32'11
	Beam:	3.1m/10'2
	Draft:	1.12m/3'8
	Displ:	4,759kg/10,482 lbs
	Ballast:	1,589kg/3,500 lbs

Fittings:	Iron ballast. GRP deck. Wood spars. Auxiliary 30 hp Palmer M60 gasoline.
Interior:	9 berths in 2 cabins. Sink. Icebox. 1 enclosed sea toilet.
Sails:	Area 48.5m^2/522 sq.ft.
Rigging:	Ketch
Price Guide:	On application
Summary:	Another top quality boat from Cheoy Lee.

ELIZABETHAN 33

Design: David Thomas, England 1973

Supplier: Peter Webster, England
Morgan Yacht Corp., U.S.A.

Specifications:
Construction:	GRP
LWL:	7.62m/25'0
LOA:	10.06m/33'
Beam:	2.84m/9'4
Draft:	1.39m/4'7
Displ:	5,593kg/12,320 lbs
Ballast:	2,369.5kg/5,219 lbs

Fittings: 10 hp Bukh engine.

Interior: 1.91m/6'3 headroom

Sails: Area 46.3m^2/498 sq.ft.

Rigging: Ketch or sloop

Price Guide: £9,500

Summary: Kits and mouldings available.

MORGAN OUT ISLAND 33

Design: Morgan Yacht Corp., U.S.A. 1972

Supplier: Morgan Yacht Corp. U.S.A.
                     Peter Webster Ltd., England

Specifications: *Construction:*   GRP
                     LWL: 8.38m/27'6
                     LOA: 10.06m/33'0
                     Beam: 3.61m/11'10
                     Draft: 1.2m/3'11
                     Displ: 6,583kg/14,500 lbs
                     Ballast: 2,270kg/5,000 lbs

Fittings: Lead ballast. GRP deck. Aluminium spars. Auxiliary
                     30 hp Atomic 4 gasoline.

Interior: 7 berths in 2 cabins. Sink. Water pump. Icebox.
                     Stove. 1 enclosed head.

Sails: Area 48.8m^2 (23.1 + 25.7)/525 sq.ft. (249 + 276)

Rigging: Sloop

Price Guide: £13,500/$22,500us.

PEARSON 10M

Design:	William H. Shaw, U.S.A.
Supplier:	Pearson Yachts, U.S.A.

Specifications:

Construction:	GRP
LWL:	8.89m/29'2
LOA:	10.07m/33'0½
Beam:	3.35m/11'0
Draft:	1.8m/5'11
Displ:	5,648kg/12,441 lbs
Ballast:	2,472kg/5,445 lbs

Fittings:	Lead ballast. GRP and balsa core deck. 30 hp gasoline 4 cylinder engine. Aluminium alloy spars.
Interior:	5/7 berths. 1.88m/6'1½ headroom. Galley. Toilet.
Variations:	Optional equipment
Sails:	Area 48.7m^2/524 sq.ft.
Rigging:	Sloop
Price Guide:	$19,500us
Summary:	Available through dealers.

RANGER 33 1TON

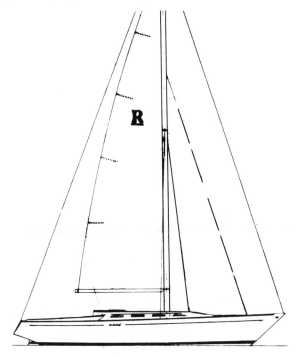

Design:	Gary Mull, U.S.A. 1970
Supplier:	Ranger Yachts, U.S.A.
Est. Rating:	26.6' IOR Mk III 31.5' CCA

Specifications:

Construction:	GRP
LWL:	8m/26'3
LOA:	10.11m/33'2
Beam:	2.92m/9'7
Draft:	1.52m/5'0
Displ:	4,767kg/10,500 lbs
Ballast:	2,043kg/4,500 lbs

Fittings:	Lead ballast. 30 hp Universal gasoline auxiliary. GRP deck. Aluminium spars.
Interior:	6 berths in 2 cabins. Sink. Icebox. 1 enclosed toilet.
Sails:	Area 49.1m^2/529 sq.ft.
Rigging:	Sloop
Price Guide:	$18,600us
Summary:	7 knot cruising speed. Comfort plus performance.

BUSHNELL 33

Design: Leonard J. Bushnell, England

Supplier: John Bushnell (Engineering) Ltd., England

Specifications:

Construction:	Mahogany on oak
LWL:	9.14m/30'0
LOA:	10.16m/33'4
Beam:	3.15m/10.4
Draft:	0.99m/3'3

Fittings: To specification

Interior: 4 berths

Sails: Area 39.9m^2/430 sq.ft.

Rigging: Sloop (motor sailer)

Price Guide: On application

Summary: Designed and constructed for experienced yachtsmen. Can be sailed single-handed. All fittings of gun-metal or stainless steel.

FASTNET 34

Design:	Groupe Finot, France 1973	
Supplier:	Fastnet Marine, U.K.	
Est. Rating:	IOR Classe IV	
Specifications:	*Construction:*	GRP
	LWL:	8.50m/27'11
	LOA:	10.19m/33'5
	Beam:	3.4m/11'2
	Draft:	4,373kg/9,632 lbs
	Displ:	4,277kg/9,420 lbs
	Ballast:	1,589kg/3,500 lbs
Fittings:	Fin keel. Farymann 18CV engine. Flush deck.	
Interior:	6 berths. 1.930m/6'4 headroom.	
Sails:	Area 60m^2/645.84 sq.ft.	
Rigging:	Sloop	
Price Guide:	£13,800	
Summary:	A roomy, good-looking boat.	

NORLIN 34

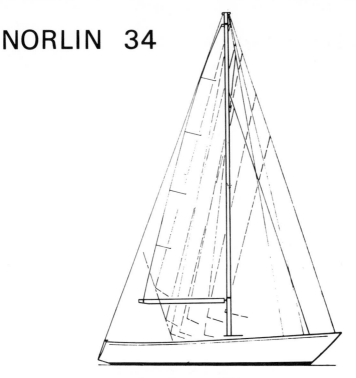

Design:	Peter Norlin, Sweden 1971
Supplier:	Solna Marine, Sweden Vikens Varu, Sweden David Smithells, England Scampi Yachts, U.S.A.
Est. Rating:	26.0' IOR Mk III

Specifications:

Construction:	GRP
LWL:	8.15m/26'9
LOA:	10.21m/33'6
Beam:	3.35m/11'0
Draft:	1.88m/6'2
Displ:	4,500kg/9,900 lbs
Ballast:	2,300kg/5,075 lbs

Fittings:	Fin keel. 12 hp inboard.
Interior:	To specification
Sails:	Area 66.6m^2/717 sq.ft.
Rigging:	Sloop
Price Guide:	£17,500
Summary:	A boat that embodies the basics of Swedish design. Clean and attractive.

COLUMBIA 34 MkII 1 TON

Design:	William H. Fripp Jnr., U.S.A.
Supplier:	Columbia Yacht Corp., U.S.A.
Est. Rating:	27.1' IOR Mk III

Specifications:

Construction:	GRP
LWL:	8.36m/27'5
LOA:	10.24m/33'7
Beam:	3.05m/10'0
Draft:	1.68m−1.14m/5'6−3'9
Displ:	5,448kg/12,000 lbs
Ballast:	2,134 kg/4,700 lbs

Fittings:	GRP deck. Aluminium spars. 27 hp Palmer P-60 gasoline auxiliary.
Interior:	7 berths. 2.13m/7'0 headroom.
Variations:	Shoal draft model also available.
Sails:	Area 48.87m^2/526 sq.ft.
Rigging:	Sloop
Price Guide:	$23,000us
Summary:	The high ratio of sail area to wetted surface and of ballast to displacement contribute a great deal to this yachts speed and stability. An ideal cruiser.

GRAMPIAN 34

Design:	Grampian Marine, Canada 1973	
Supplier:	Grampian Marine Ltd., Canada	
Specifications:	*Construction:*	GRP
	LWL:	8.08m/26'6
	LOA:	10.23m/33'7
	Beam:	3.05m/10'0
	Draft:	1.52m/5'0
	Displ:	5,448kg/12,000 lbs

Fittings: GRP deck. Aluminium spars. 30 hp Universal Atomic 4 gasoline auxiliary.

Interior: 7 berths in 3 cabins. 1 or 2 enclosed heads.

Sails: Area 48.5m^2/522 sq.ft. (sloop)
Area 47.6m^2/512 sq.ft. (ketch)

Rigging: Sloop or ketch

Price Guide: $22,950us

Summary: Centre cockpit and split rig make this boat distinctive. Built to high standards of craftsmanship and safety.

VIKING 33 1TON

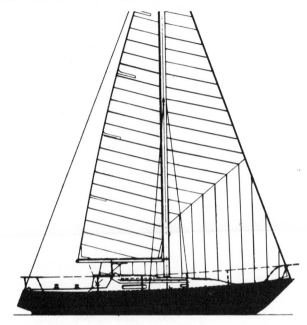

Design:	Cuthbertson & Cassran, Canada 1971
Supplier:	Ontario Yachts Co. Ltd., Canada
Est. Rating:	27.5m' IOR Mk III

Specifications:

	Construction:	GRP
	LWL:	8.28m/27'2
	LOA:	10.24m/33'7
	Beam:	3m/9'10
	Draft:	1.68m/5'6
	Displ:	3,999kg/8,807 lbs
	Ballast:	2,048kg/4,512 lbs

Fittings:	Lead ballast. Balsa core and GRP deck. Aluminium spars. 30 hp Universal Atomic 4 gasoline.
Interior:	5 berths in 2 cabins. Stove. Sink. Water pump. Icebox. 1 chemical toilet.
Sails:	Area 47.19m^2 (18.58 + 28.61)/508 sq.ft. (200 + 308)
Rigging:	Sloop
Price Guide:	$21,500us
Summary:	A bold 1 TON racer that will also double as a comfortable family cruiser.

KING'S CRUISER 33

Design:	Turun Veneveistämo OY, Finland	
Supplier:	Ballena Marine, England	
Est. Rating:	24.7' IOR	
Specifications:	*Construction:*	GRP
	LWL:	8.00m/26'3
	LOA:	10.24m/33'7½
	Beam:	3.12m/10'3
	Draft:	1.58m/5'2
	Displ:	4,608kg/10,150 lbs
	Ballast:	2,304kg/5,075 lbs
Fittings:	Fin keel. Volvo Penta MD2B 25 hp engine.	
Interior:	6 berths	
Sails:	Area 40m² (17.4 + 22.6)/430 sq.ft. (187 + 243)	
Rigging:	Sloop	
Price Guide:	£13,500	

ALOA 34

Design: J. M. L'Hermenier, France 1970

Supplier: Aloa Marine, France
American International Yacht Corporation, U.S.A.

Est. Rating: 23.7' IOR Mk III

Specifications:

Construction:	GRP	
LWL:	7.42m/24'4	
LOA:	10.31m/33'10	
Beam:	3.3m/10'10	
Draft:	1.68m/5'6	
Displ:	4,086kg/9,000 lbs	
Ballast:	1,634kg/3,600 lbs	

Fittings: Aluminium spars. GRP deck. Flush deck. 24 hp Volvo MD2 diesel.

Interior: 6–8 berths in 2 cabins

Variations: 4 versions available.

Sails: Area 34.9m^2(21.4 + 13.5)/376 sq.ft. (231 + 145)

Rigging: Sloop

Price Guide: $24,950us

Summary: A boat with many racing successes to its name.

OFFSHORE 34

Design:	Ian Anderson MRINA, England
Supplier:	Offshore Yachts International, England
Est. Rating:	12 tons Thames Measurement IOR ¾ ton.

Specifications:

	Construction:	GRP
	LWL:	8.31m/27'3
	LOA:	10.36m/34'0
	Beam:	3.35m/11'0
	Draft:	1.83m/6'0
	Displ:	7.316kg/7.2 tons
	Ballast:	3,048kg/ 3 tons

Fittings:	Mercedes OM636 36 hp diesel engine. Silver anodised alloy spars.
Interior:	5 berths. Galley — stove, sink, cold box. Enclosed SL400 toilet.
Sails:	Area 45.31m^2/489 sq.ft.
Rigging:	Sloop
Price Guide:	On application

RIVAL 34

Design:	Peter Brett, England 1971
Supplier:	Southern Boatbuildings Co., England
Specifications:	*Construction:* GRP
	LWL: 7.57m/24'10
	LOA: 10.36m/34'0
	Beam: 2.94m/9'8
	Draft: 1.78m–1.42m/5'10–4'8
	Displ: 5,400kg/11,900 lbs
Fittings:	Fin keel. Volvo MD2B 25 hp inboard.
Interior:	8 berths. Galley. Icebox. Sink. Stove. Lavac toilet.
Sails:	Area 51.1m^2/550 sq.ft.
Rigging:	Sloop
Price Guide:	£10,350

VICTOIRE 34

Design:	BV Jachtwerf Victoria, Holland 1974
Supplier:	BV Jachtwerf Victoria, Holland

Specifications:	*Construction:*	GRP
	LWL:	8.35m/27'4½
	LOA:	10.38m/34'0½
	Beam:	3.24m/10'8
	Draft:	1.60m/5'4
	Ballast:	2,400kg/5,291 lbs

Fittings:	25 hp engine. Volvo Penta.
Interior:	6 berths
Sails:	Area 47.8m²/515 sq.ft. Spinnaker area 12.71m²/136.8 sq.ft.
Rigging:	Sloop
Price Guide:	On application
Summary:	A newly designed boat that will soon make her mark because of performance and appearance

JOEMARIN 34

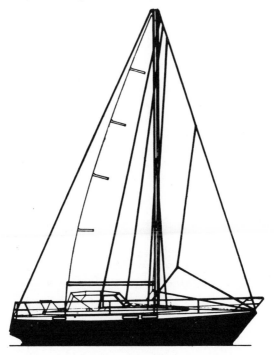

Design:	Hans Groop, Finland 1972	
Supplier:	Joemarin Oy, Finland Tradewind Yachts, England	
Specifications:	*Construction:*	GRP
	LWL:	8.70m/28'6½
	LOA:	10.40m/34'1½
	Beam:	3.15m/10'4
	Draft:	1.45m/4'9
	Displ:	5m³/11, 200 lbs
	Ballast:	2,238kg/4,930 lbs
Fittings:	Full keel. 47 hp diesel engine.	
Variations:	Interior to individual requirements.	
Sails:	Area 50m²/538 sq.ft.	
Rigging:	Sloop	
Price Guide:	£15,700	
Summary:	A true motor sailer, combining many of the new concepts in design.	

OHLSON 35

Design:	Einar Ohlson, Sweden 1970
Supplier:	Campbell/Sheehan Inc., U.S.A. Michael Pocock & Partners
Rating:	25'3 IOR Mk III
Specifications:	*Construction:* GRP *LWL:* 7.32m/24'0 *LOA:* 10.52m/34'6 *Beam:* 3.15m/10'4 *Draft:* 1.8m/5'11 *Displ:* 4,722kg/10,400 lbs *Ballast:* 1,952kg/4,300 lbs
Fittings:	Lead ballast. GRP deck. Aluminium spars. 25 hp Volvo MD2B diesel.
Interior:	6 berths in 2 cabins. Icebox. Stove. Groco enclosed sea toilet.
Sails:	Area 43.4m^2 (18.7 + 24.7)/467 sq.ft. (201 + 266)
Rigging:	Sloop
Price Guide:	£14,850/$31,700us
Summary:	Sophisticated deep draft yacht equally suitable for crusing or IOR racing. Generous beam. Kits available.

1012

CHALLENGER 35

Design:	Challenger Yachts, U.S.A. 1973
Supplier:	Challenger Yacht Corp., U.S.A.
Specifications:	*Construction:* GRP
	LWL: 9.14m/30'0
	LOA: 10.56m/34'8
	Beam: 3.51m/11'6
	Draft: 1.32m/4'4
	Displ: 6,583kg/14,500 lbs
	Ballast: 1,906.8kg/4,200 lbs
Fittings:	Lead ballast. GRP and plywood deck. Aluminium spars. 55 hp Perkins 4-107 diesel auxiliary.
Interior:	6 berths in 2 cabins. Fridge. Stove. 1 enclosed head.
Sails:	Area 50.17m^2/540 sq.ft.
Rigging:	Sloop
Price Guide:	$25,850us

ERICSON 35

Design:	Bruce King, U.S.A. 1969
Supplier:	Ericson Yachts Inc., U.S.A. Hamble Marine, U.K. Nordmarine, Italy
Est. Rating:	25.6' IOR Mk II 29.6' CCA

Specifications:

Construction:	GRP
LWL:	7.87m/25'10
LOA:	10.56m/34'8
Beam:	3.3m/10'10
Draft:	1.5m/4'11
Displ:	5,266kg/11,600 lbs
Ballast:	2,270kg/5,000 lbs

Fittings:	Fin keel. GRP deck. Aluminium spars. 30 hp Universal Atomic 4 gasoline. Lead ballast.
Interior:	6 berths in 2 cabins. 1 enclosed sea toilet.
Sails:	Area 49.5m^2 (21.6 + 27.9)/533 sq.ft. (232 + 301)
Rigging:	Sloop
Price Guide:	£15,000/$22,495us
Summary:	Fine bow, shallow fin keel add up to high performance. Tank tested.

ROGGER

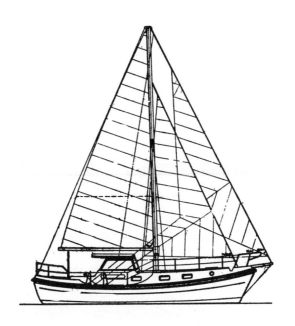

Design:	Eista-Werf. BV, Holland 1974
Supplier:	Eista-Werf, Holland Stangate Marine, England
Specifications:	*Construction:* GRP *LOA:* 10.67m/35'0 *Beam:* 3.45m/11'4 *Draft:* 1.22m/4'0 *Displ:* 8,944kg/19,700 lbs *Ballast:* 2,238kg/4,930 lbs
Fittings:	Flush deck design. Perkins 4-236 72hp diesel engine.
Interior:	5/7 berths
Variations:	Alternative models available - aft cabin, or aft cockpit and wheelhouse.
Sails:	Area 51.1m^2/550 sq.ft.
Rigging:	Bermudan cutter
Price Guide:	£19,900 +

SAGITTA 35

Supplier:	Vanek, France
	Interyacht, England
Specifications:	*Construction:* GRP
	LWL: 7.77m/25'6
	LOA: 10.67m/35'0
	Beam: 3.05m/10'
	Draft: 1.83m/6'
	Displ: 5,000kg/11,023 lbs
	Ballast: 2,600kg/5,732 lbs
Fittings:	Keelboat
Interior:	7 berths
Variations:	Optional inboard.
Sails:	Area 42.5m²/457 sq.ft.
Rigging:	Bermudan sloop
Price Guide:	127,000 Fr.f.
Summary:	Cannot be trailed.

SUPER SOVEREIGN

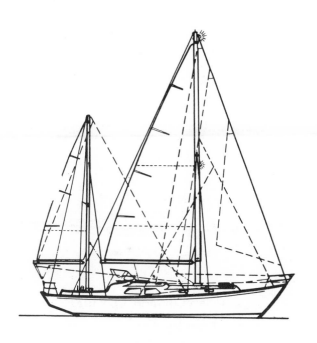

Supplier:	J. W. & A. Uphams, England	
Specifications:	*Construction:*	GRP or wood
	LOA:	10.67m/35'0
	Draft:	1.52m/5'0
	Displ:	optional
	Ballast:	optional
Fittings:	Keelboat	
Interior:	5/6 berths	
Variations:	Optional inboard engine.	
Sails:	Area 54.6m^2/588 sq.ft.	
Rigging:	Ketch	
Price Guide:	On application.	
Summary:	Cannot be trailed.	

CAL 35

Design:	C. William Lapworth, USA 1973
Supplier:	Jensen Marine, USA

Specifications:	*Construction:*	GRP
	LWL:	8.76m/28'9
	LOA:	10.69m/35'1
	Beam:	3.35m/11'0
	Draft:	1.42m/4'8
	Displ:	6,810kg/15,000 lbs
	Ballast:	2,270kg/5,000 lbs

Fittings:	Iron ballast. Teak finish. GRP deck. Aluminium spars. Perkins diesel auxiliary.
Interior:	5 berths in 2 cabins
Sails:	Area 50.7m²/546 sq.ft.
Rigging:	Sloop
Price Guide:	$38,500us
Summary:	Designed as a serious cruising boat. Plenty of room for 5.

DUFOUR 35

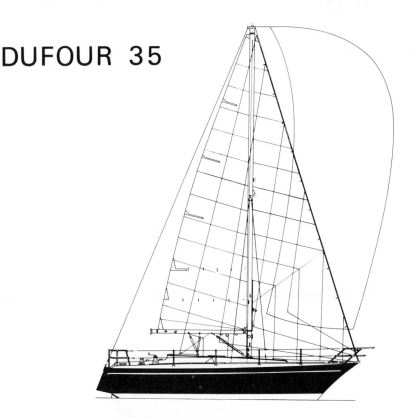

Design:	Michel Dufour, France 1971
Supplier:	Michel Dufour SA, USA Michel Dufour, France
Est. Rating:	26.8′ IOR Mk III
Specifications:	*Construction:* GRP *LWL:* 8.48m/27′10 *LOA:* 10.74m/35′3 *Beam:* 3.45m/11′4 *Draft:* 1.81m/5′11 *Displ:* 5,707kg/12,570 lbs *Ballast:* 2,803kg/6,174 lbs
Fittings:	Fin keel. Fiberglass sandwich deck. Aluminium spars. 25 hp Volvo MD 2B diesel engine.
Sails:	Area 50.4m^2(22.1 + 28.3)/542 sq.ft. (237 + 305) Spinnaker 93m^2/1000 sq.ft.
Rigging:	Sloop. Stainless steel and terylene.
Price Guide:	£20,750/$36,000us
Summary:	An elegant and exceptional boat, with a unique interior layout that gives vast amounts of space. Wide, uncluttered decks.

NICHOLSON 35

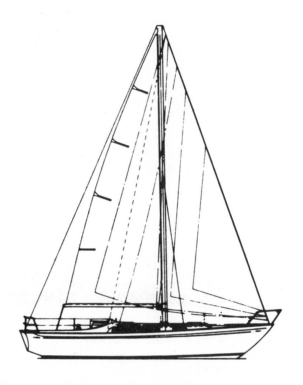

Design:	Camper & Nicholsons, England 1970
Supplier:	Camper & Nicholsons, England
	Camper & Nicholson, USA
Est. Rating:	Portsmouth number: 90 24.7' IOR

Specifications:

Construction:	GRP
LWL:	8.15m/26'9
LOA:	10.74m/35'3
Beam:	3.18m/10'5
Draft:	1.68m/5'6
Displ:	7,264kg/16,000 lbs
Ballast:	3,301kg/7,270 lbs

Fittings:	GRP deck. Aluminium spars. Auxiliary: 40 hp Perkins diesel.
Interior:	6 berths in 2 cabins. Icebox. Sink. Toilet.
Sails:	Area 64m^2/698 sq.ft.
Rigging:	Sloop
Price Guide:	£16,500

TRINTELLA III

Design:	E G Van de Stadt, Holland 1968
Supplier:	Stangate Marine, England Jachtwerf Anne Wever, Holland

Specifications:

Construction:	GRP
LWL:	8.61m/28'3
LOA:	10.74m/35'3
Beam:	3.2m/10'6
Draft:	1.4m/4'7
Displ:	7,264kg/16,000 lbs
Ballast:	2,797kg/6,160 lbs

Fittings: Iron or lead ballast. GRP and teak deck. Aluminium spars. 50 hp Perkins 4-107 auxiliary.

Interior: 7 berths in 2 cabins. Stove. Sink. Fridge. Enclosed Raritan toilet.

Variations: IIIA also available — more spacious interior.

Sails: Area 63.2m^2(25.1 + 38.1)/680 sq.ft. (270 + 410) Spinnaker 82m^2/882 sq.ft.

Rigging: Sloop

Price Guide: £19,000/132,000 Hfl.

Summary: A relatively new boat that has proved extremely popular world-wide.

LUDERS 36

Design:	A E Luders Jnr., Holland 1970
Supplier:	Cheoy Lee, Hong Kong Lion Yachts, USA
Specifications:	*Construction:* GRP *LWL:* 7.62m/25'0 *LOA:* 10.82m/35'6 *Beam:* 3.12m/10'3 *Draft:* 1.6m/5'3 *Displ:* 6,810kg/15,000 lbs *Ballast:* 238kg/525 lbs
Fittings:	Lead ballast. GRP deck. Wood or aluminium spars. 30 hp Palmer M-60 gasoline auxiliary.
Interior:	6 berths in 2 cabins
Variations:	Teak overlay on deck optional.
Sails:	Area 55.4m^2(28.2 + 27.2)/596 sq.ft. (304 + 292)
Rigging:	Sloop
Price Guide:	On application.

PASSAGE 36

Design:	Passage Marine, U.S.A.	
Supplier:	Passage Marine, U.S.A.	
Est. Rating:	27.5' IOR	
Specifications:	*Construction:*	GRP and core
	LWL:	8.84m/29'0
	LOA:	10.84m/35'7
	Beam:	3.58m/11'9
	Draft:	1.91m/6'3
	Displ:	6,878kg/15,150 lbs
	Ballast:	3,360kg/7,400 lbs
Fittings:	GRP and core deck. Lead ballast. Farryman R30M 15 hp diesel auxiliary. Aluminium alloy spars.	
Interior:	5 berths. Icebox. Stove. Pump. Wilcox Crittenden Imperial toilet. Shower.	
Sails:	Area 56.8m^2/611.5 sq.ft.	
Rigging:	Sloop	
Price Guide:	$55,000us	

MORGAN ONE TON

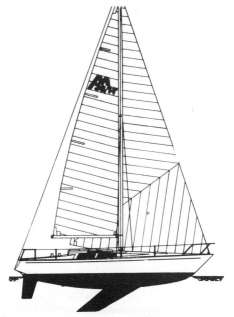

Design:	Morgan Yacht Corp., U.S.A. 1973
Supplier:	Morgan Yacht Corp., U.S.A. Peter Webster, England
Rating:	27'5 IOR

Specifications:

Construction:	GRP
LWL:	9.14m/30'0
LOA:	10.9m/35'9
Beam:	3.58m/11'9
Draft:	1.91m/6'3
Displ:	6,356kg/14,000 lbs
Ballast:	2,769kg/6,100 lbs

Fittings:	Lead ballast. Deck GRP sandwich. Aluminium spars. Auxiliary 35 hp Westerbeke 4-107 diesel.
Interior:	5 berths in 2 cabins. Stainless steel sink. Icebox. Stove. with oven. 1 enclosed toilet.
Variations:	Interior options available for extended cruises.
Sails:	Area 58.2m^2(24.7 + 33.5)/626 sq.ft. (266 + 360)
Rigging:	Sloop
Price Guide:	£17,200/$30,000
Summary:	Long waterline, streamlined fin keel, and heavy ballast/displacement ratio make this a fine performance boat.

MORGAN OUT ISLAND 36

Design:	Morgan Yacht Corp., U.S.A. 1972
Supplier:	Morgan Yacht Corp., U.S.A.
	Peter Webster Ltd., England

Specifications:

Construction:	GRP
LWL:	8.53m/28'0
LOA:	10.92m/35'10
Beam:	3.48m/11'5
Draft:	1.14m/3'9
Displ:	7,264kg/16,000 lbs
Ballast:	3,405kg/7,500 lbs

Fittings: Lead ballast. GRP deck. Aluminium spars.
Auxiliary 30 hp Atomic 4 gasoline.

Interior: 6 berths in 3 cabins. Sink. Water pump. Icebox. Stove.
2 enclosed heads.

Sails: Area 56.7m^2(24.7 + 32)/610 sq.ft. (266 + 344)

Rigging: Sloop

Price Guide: £16,800/$30,000

Summary: The cruising version of the one ton.

CONTEST 36

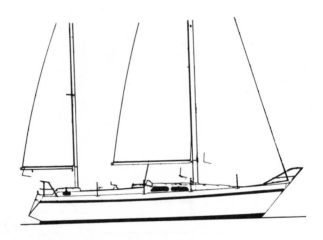

Design: Dick Zaal, Holland 1973

Supplier: Conyplex NV, Holland
Interyacht, England
Holland Yachts, USA

Est. Rating: 27.5' IOR

Specifications:
Construction:	GRP
LWL:	8.80m/28'10
LOA:	10.95m/35'11
Beam:	3.40m/11'2
Draft:	1.90m - 1.50m/6'3 - 4'11

Fittings: Volvo MD2B/3B Penta diesel auxiliary. Teak trim.

Interior: Pressure water. Stove. Toilet.

Variations: Optional second toilet.

Sails: Area 58.10m²/627 sq.ft. sloop
60.27m²/647 sq.ft. ketch

Rigging: Sloop or ketch

Price Guide: £19,000 +

Summary: Available in several versions — it is still being developed
and the builders reserve the right to make alterations to
design, specification and price.

ATLANTIC CLIPPER

Design:	Maurice Griffiths, England 1968
Supplier:	Dart Marina, England

Specifications:

Construction:	GRP
LWL:	7.77m/25'6
LOA:	10.97m/36'0
Beam:	2.94m/9'8
Draft:	1.91m/6'3
Displ:	5,593kg/12,320 lbs
Ballast:	2,420kg/5,330 lbs

Fittings:	Aluminium spars. GRP deck. Teak trim. Perkins 108 47 hp auxilliary.
Interior:	6 berths. Full galley. 1.90m/6'3 headroom. Flushing toilet.
Variations:	Cruising or motor sailing versions.
Sails:	Area 56.2m²/605 sq.ft. Spinnaker 43.7m²/470 sq.ft.
Rigging:	Ketch
Price Guide:	£11,500
Summary:	Good in light winds. Easy to handle under reduced sail in heavy winds. Kits and mouldings available.

CONTESSA 36

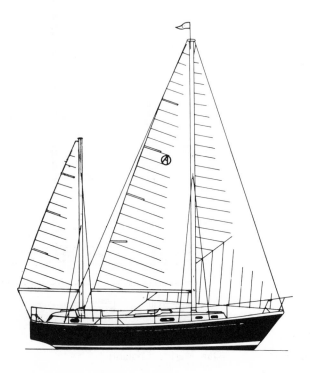

Design:	Arthur Edmunds, U.S.A. 1973	
Supplier:	Allied Boat Co., U.S.A.	
Specifications:	*Construction:*	GRP
	LWL:	8.38m/27'6
	LOA:	10.97m/36'0
	Beam:	3.35m/11'0
	Draft:	1.37m/4'6
	Displ:	6,538kg/14,400 lbs
	Ballast:	2,270kg/5,000 lbs
Fittings:	Lead ballast. GRP with balsa core deck. Aluminium spars. 27hp Westerbeke 4-97 diesel auxiliary.	
Interior:	6 berths in 3 cabins. 2 enclosed heads.	
Sails:	Area 56.1m² (23.4 + 24 + 8.7)/604 sq.ft. (252 + 258 + 94)	
Rigging:	Ketch	
Price Guide:	$33,800us	
Summary:	Cruising comfort at its best. Available through dealers.	

DICKERSON 36

Design:	Ernest Tucker, U.S.A. 1972
Supplier:	Dickerson Boatbuilders, U.S.A.

Specifications:

Construction:	GRP or wood
LWL:	8.18m/26'10
LOA:	10.97m/36'0
Beam:	3.18m/10'5
Draft:	1.22m/4'0
Displ:	5,448kg/12,000 lbs
Ballast:	1,816kg/4,000 lbs

Fittings: Aluminium spars. Teak trim. Deck of fiberglassed plywood. 30hp Universal Atomic 4 gasoline engine.

Interior: 4–5 berths in 1–2 cabins. Galley. Enclosed toilet.

Variations: Interior to individual specifications.

Sails: Area 45.3m^2(20.8 + 13.4 + 11.1)/488 sq.ft. (224 + 144 + 120)

Rigging: Ketch

Price Guide: $23,900us +

Summary: Specifically designed for luxurious cruising.

ROAMER

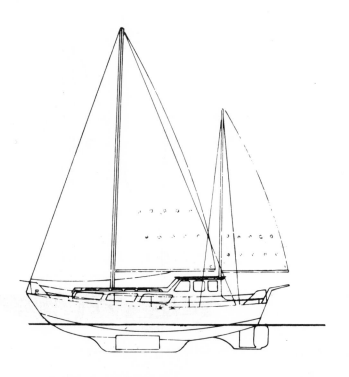

Design:	J B M Engineering Ltd., England	
Supplier:	J B M Engineering Ltd., England	
Specifications:	*Construction:*	Steel
	LOA:	10.97m/36'0
	Beam:	3.20m/10'6
	Draft:	1.14m/3'9
	Displ:	8,644kg/19,040 lbs
Fittings:	Centre ballast keel. Anodised stainless steel spars.	
Interior:	8 berths. Galley — stove. Blake Lavac sea toilet. Shower optional.	
Variations:	Twin keel version also available. Optional power. Optional interior fittings.	
Sails:	Area 43m² (20 + 13.7 + 9.3)/463 sq.ft. (215 + 148 + 100)	
Rigging:	Ketch	
Price Guide:	On application.	

TYRRELL

Design: John Tyrrell, Ireland

Supplier: John Tyrrell & Sons, Ireland

Specifications:
Construction:	Iroko on oak
LWL:	9.14m/30'0
LOA:	10.97m/36'0
Beam:	3.35m/11'0
Draft:	1.52m/5'0

Fittings: Parsons Pike engine. Bridge deck.

Interior: 6 berths

Sails: Area 44.6m^2/480 sq.ft.

Rigging: Bermudan ketch

Price Guide: On application.

Summary: Spacious and comfortable with excellent performance whether under sail or power. Easily handled. Very seaworthy.

ISLANDER 36 1TON

Design:	Alan P. Gurney, U.S.A. 1971	
Supplier:	Islander Yachts, U.S.A.	
Est. Rating:	28.5′ IOR Mk III	
Specifications:	*Construction:*	GRP
	LWL:	8.61m/28′3
	LOA:	10.99m/36′1
	Beam:	3.4m/11′2
	Draft:	1.85m/6′1
	Displ:	5,902kg/13,000 lbs
	Ballast:	2,642kg/5,820 lbs
Fittings:	GRP deck. Lead ballast. Aluminium spars. 25hp Palmer gasoline auxiliary. Wood trim. Wide deck walkways.	
Interior:	6 berths in 2 cabins. Galley.	
Variations:	2 layouts — cruising and racing.	
Sails:	Area 54.6m^2(23.2 + 31.4)/588 sq.ft. (250 + 338)	
Rigging:	Sloop	
Price Guide:	$21,995us	
Summary:	Racer/cruiser — very spacious. Exceptionally stiff under all weather conditions.	

VENTURA 37 SLOOP

Design:	Gerhard Gilgenast, Holland	
Supplier:	Hanjo-Yachtbau GmbH, Holland	
Specifications:	*Construction:*	Wood
	LWL:	9.18m/30'1½
	LOA:	11m/36'1
	Beam:	3.42m/11'2½
	Draft:	1.80m/5'11
	Displ:	6,200kg/13,669 lbs
Fittings:	To specification	
Interior:	To specification	
Sails:	Area 51.3m^2/552 sq.ft.	
Rigging:	Sloop	
Price Guide:	On application.	
Summary:	Finished to individual specification.	

COLUMBIA 36 MkII

Design:	William Crealock, U.S.A. 1973
Supplier:	Columbia Yacht Corporation, U.S.A.

Specifications:	*Construction:*	GRP
	LWL:	8.61m/28'3
	LOA:	11.02m/36'2
	Beam:	3.2m/10'6
	Draft:	1.6m/5'3
	Displ:	5,993kg/13,200 lbs
	Ballast:	2,088kg/4,600 lbs

Fittings:	Lead ballast. GRP deck. Aluminium spars. Palmer M-60 gasoline auxiliary.
Interior:	6 berths in 2 cabins. Standard galley and 1 enclosed toilet.
Sails:	Area 51.8m^2/557 sq.ft.
Rigging:	Sloop
Price Guide:	$23,995us
Summary:	One of the classic yachts to have been launched. Brought back into production with only minor modifications to original design.

NORLIN 37

Design:	Peter Martin, Sweden 1972
Supplier:	Solna Marine AB, Sweden David Smithells, England
Est. Rating:	27.5' IOR Mk. III
Specifiactions:	*Construction:*
	LWL: 9.00m/29'6
	LOA: 11.03m/36'2
	Beam: 3.60m/12'0
	Draft: 1.96m/6'5
	Displ: 7,700kg/16,940 lbs.
	Ballast: 3,700kg/8,140 lbs.
Fittings:	Fin keel. 20 hp engine.
Interior:	1.90m/6'1 headroom.
Sails:	Area 85.0m^2/.913 sq.ft. Spinnaker area 131m^2/1410 sq.ft.
Rigging:	Sloop
Price Guide:	£20,500
Summary:	A sleek cruiser/racer, typical of the Scandinavian school of design.

BANJER

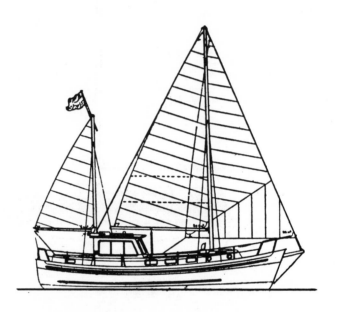

Design:	Lefeber, Holland
Supplier:	Eista Werf BV Holland Stangate Marine England Impex Enterprises USA

Specifications:	*Construction:*	GRP
	LWL:	10.1m/33'0
	LOA:	11.1m/36'6
	Beam:	3.51m/11'6
	Draft:	1.4m/4'7
	Displ.	12,204kg/26,880 lbs.
	Ballast:	4,068kg/8,960 lbs.

Fittings:	Fin keel
Interior:	7 berths. 8.2m/6'6 headroom.
Variations:	Optional inboard 72—120 hp.
Sails:	Area 27.9m²/300 sq.ft.
Rigging:	Ketch
Price Guide:	£28,000

SWAN 37

Design:	Sparkman & Stephens, USA
Supplier:	Nautor Oy Wilh, Finland
	Dave Johnson, England

Specifications:		
	Construction:	GRP
	LWL:	8.33m/27'4
	LOA:	11.13m/36'6
	Beam:	3.30m/10'10
	Draft:	1.88m/6'2

Fittings:	Fin keel. 25 hp inboard engine.
Sails:	Area 72.8m^2/784 sq.ft.
Rigging:	Sloop
Price Guide:	£23,000

CARTER ONE-TON

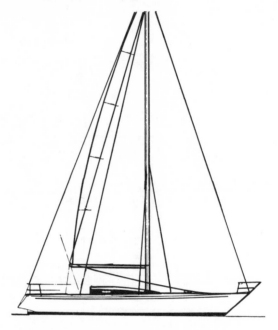

Design:	Dick Carter, USA 1972
Supplier:	Carter Offshore Inc., USA Carter Offshore Ltd., England
Est. Rating:	27.5' IOR Mk III

Specifications:

Construction:	GRP
LWL:	8.66m/28'5
LOA:	11.28m/37'0
Beam:	3.63m/11'11
Draft:	1.93m/6'4
Displ.	6,946kg/15,300 lbs.
Ballast:	2,838kg/6,250 lbs.

Fittings:	Lead ballast. Balsa core and GRP deck. Aluminium spars. Perkins 4—170 diesel auxiliary.
Interior:	7 berths in 2 cabins. Galley and toilets standard.
Sails:	Area: 58.5m^2/630 sq.ft.
Rigging:	Sloop
Price Guide:	£22,200/S45,600 US
Summary:	Light, airy interior with a classic offshore accommodation plan.

FISHER 37

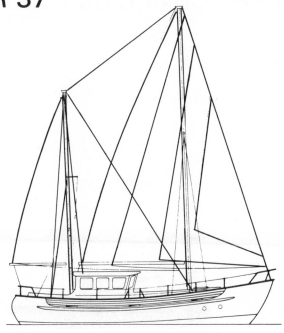

Design:	Gordon Wyatt, England 1972
Supplier:	Fairways Marine, England Offsounding Yachts, USA
Est. Rating:	19 tons Thames measurement
Specifications:	

	Construction:	Wood
	LWL:	9.91m/32'6
	LOA:	11.28m/37'0
	Beam:	3.66m/12'0
	Draft:	1.6m/5'3
	Displ:	14.2 tonnes/31,360 lbs
	Ballast:	6.1 tonnes/13,440 lbs

Fittings:	Finn keel — cast iron ballast. Aluminium spars.
Interior:	6/7 berths. Marine toilet.
Variations:	Optional. Lister or Perkins inboard. Aft cabin version available.
Sails:	Area 53.4m^2/575 sq.ft.
Rigging:	Ketch
Price Guide:	£22,500 +
Summary:	Sturdy motor-sailer.

IRWIN COMPETITION 37 1TON

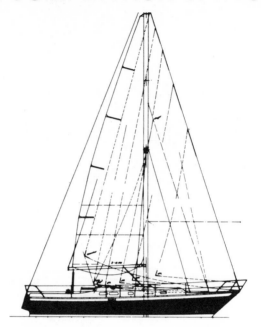

Design:	Ted Irwin, U.S.A. 1972
Supplier:	Irwin Yacht and Marine Corp., U.S.A.
Rating:	27.5' IOR Mk III
Specifications:	*Construction:* GRP
	LWL: 8.94m/29'4
	LOA: 11.28m/37'0
	Beam: 3.55m/11'8
	Draft: 1.91m/6'3
	Displ: 6,992kg/15,400 lbs.
	Ballast: 3,314kg/7,300 lbs.
Fittings:	Lead ballast. GRP and balsa core deck. Aluminium spars. 30 hp Universal Atomic 4 gasoline auxiliary.
Interior:	7 berths in 2 cabins.
Variations:	Optional toilet.
Sails:	Area 58.3m²/628 sq.ft. (23.4 + 34.9) (252 + 376)
Rigging:	Sloop
Price Guide:	$27,950us
Summary:	Designed for 1 Ton Competition based on the popular '37'

RANGER 1 TON

Design:	Gary Mull, U.S.A. 1973
Supplier:	Ranger Yachts, U.S.A.
Est. Rating:	27.5' IOR Mk III. 27.5' MORC

Specifications:

Construction:	GRP
LWL:	8.63m/28'4
LOA:	11.28m/37'0
Beam:	3.45m/11'4
Draft:	1.83m/6'0
Displ:	6901kg/15,200 lbs.
Ballast:	3,314kg/7,300 lbs.

Fittings:	Lead ballast. GRP deck. Aluminium spars. 30 hp Universal Atomic 4 gasoline
Interior:	6/8 berths in 2 cabins. Sink. Icebox.
Variations:	Optional toilet
Sails:	Area 58.2m^2 (23.1 + 35.1)/627 sq. ft. (249 + 378)
Rigging:	Sloop
Price Guide:	$30,300us
Summary:	Long water-line, large sail plan and slightly wider beam are the most prominent features of this boat.

SOVEREL 37

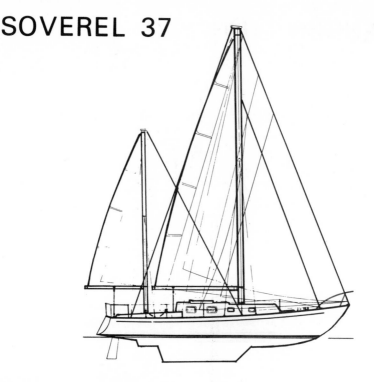

Design:	Bill Soverel, U.S.A. 1970
Supplier:	Soverel Marine Inc., U.S.A.
Est. Rating:	31.0' IOR Mk III
Specifications:	*Construction:* GRP
	LWL: 9.45m/31'0
	LOA: 11.28m/37'0
	Beam: 2.845m/9'4
	Draft: 1.066m/3'6
	Displ: 5,448kg/12,000 lbs
	Ballast: 1,716kg/4,000 lbs lead
Fittings:	Keel or centreboard boat. Centreboard of GRP and lead. GRP spade rudder. Anodised aluminium spars. Universal engine.
Interior:	6 berths in 2 cabins. Sea toilet.
Sails:	Area 48.6sq.m(20.1 + 28.5)/523 sq.ft. (216 + 307) 6 oz. Dacron.
Rigging:	Sloop or ketch. Stainless steel rigging.
Price Guide:	$25,000us
Summary:	Fast, sturdy, requiring the minimum of maintenance. Sold direct from Soverel Marine.

NELSON 37

Design:	Thomas Nelson Yachts, UK
Supplier:	Thomas Nelson Yachts, UK Nelson Marine, Denmark

Specifications:

Construction:	GRP and balsa sandwich
LWL:	9.25m/30'4
LOA:	11.40m/37'4½
Beam:	3.40m/11'2
Draft:	1.60m/5'3
Displ:	8.00T/16,800 lbs
Ballast:	2.90T/5,600 lbs

Fittings:	Lead ballast. Perkins Borg Warner marine diesel 72HP. GRP and balsa core deck. Teak overlay deck. Gold anodised spars.
Interior:	6/8 berths. Galley — stove, fridge/freezer. Pressure water. 2 toilets.
Sails:	Area 51.40m^2/553 sq.ft.
Rigging:	MS sloop
Price Guide:	£30,000
Summary:	De-luxe motor sailer. Good performance yet safe and seaworthy. 550 mile range.

1043

ERICSON 37

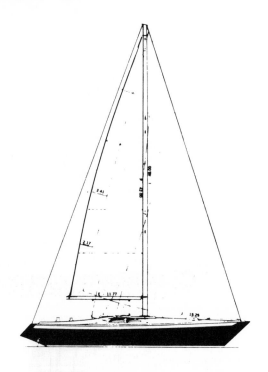

Design:	Ericson Yachts, U.S.A. 1973
Supplier:	Ericson Yachts, U.S.A. Hamble Marine, UK Nordmarine, Italy
Est. Rating:	27.5' IOR Mk III

Specifications:

	Construction:	GRP
	LWL:	8.69m/28'6
	LOA:	11.41m/37'5
	Beam:	3.45m/11'4
	Draft:	1.75m/5'9
	Displ:	7,264kg/16,000 lbs
	Ballast:	3,632kg/8,000 lbs

Fittings:	GRP deck. Aluminium spars. 27 hp Palmer P-60 gasoline auxiliary. Teak trim.
Interior:	6/8 berths in 2 cabins. 1.90m/6'3 headroom.
Sails:	Area 56.9m^2 (22.9 + 34)/613 sq.ft. (247 + 366)
Rigging:	Sloop
Price Guide:	£23,000/$32,700us

GIB'SEA 37

Design:	M Joubert, France 1974
Supplier:	Olivier Gibert, France
Specifications:	*Construction:* GRP
	LOA: 11.40m/37'5
	Beam: 3.80m/12'5½
	Draft: optional
	Displ: optional
	Ballast: optional
Fittings:	To specification.
Interior:	9 berths
Sails:	Area optional
Rigging:	Ketch
Price Guide:	On application.

SEAFARER 38C

Design:	Philip L Rhodes, U.S.A. 1971
Supplier:	Seafarer Fiberglass Inc., U.S.A.

Specifications:

Construction:	GRP
LWL:	8m/26'3
LOA:	11.51m/37'9
Beam:	3.2m/10'6
Draft:	1.37m/4'6
Displ:	7,491kg/16,500 lbs
Ballast:	2,497kg/5,500 lbs

Fittings:	Lead ballast. 72HP Universal Unimite gasoline. GRP deck. Aluminium spars.
Interior:	4/6 berths in 2 cabins. Ice box. Pressure water system. Sea toilet.
Sails:	Area 45.1m^2/485 sq.ft.
Rigging:	Sloop or ketch.
Price Guide:	$23,500us
Summary:	Cruiser of quality and character. Very reasonably priced.

CONTEST 38

Design:	Dick Zaal, Holland 1972
Supplier:	Conyplex NV, Holland Holland Yachts Inc., U.S.A. Interyacht, England
Est. Rating:	26.0' IOR Mk III
Specifications:	*Construction:* GRP *LWL:* 8.47m/27'8 *LOA:* 11.58m/38'0 *Beam:* 3.42m/11'3 *Draft:* 1.98m/6'6 *Displ:* 7,650kg/16,850 lbs *Ballast:* 3,300kg/7,280 lbs
Fittings:	Lead ballast. GRP deck. Aluminium spars. 36HP Volvo gasoline auxiliary.
Interior:	6 berths in 3 cabins. 1.91m/6'3 headroom.
Variations:	Optional toilet.
Sails:	Area 60.2m^2(25 + 35.2)/648 sq.ft. (269 + 379)
Rigging:	Sloop
Price Guide:	£19,000/$41,000us
Summary:	First class performance and appearance.

TAILWIND

Design:	L. Bergstrom, B. Lindell & S. O. Ridder, Sweden 1973
Supplier:	Hurley Marine, England Hurley Marine, U.S.A.
Est. Rating:	IOR 30.5'

Specifications:

Construction:	GRP
LWL:	9.10m/29'10
LOA:	11.65m/38'2
Beam:	3.65m/11'11
Draft:	1.98m/6'6
Displ:	6,706kg/14,784 lbs
Ballast:	2,624kg/5,824 lbs

Fittings:	Flush deck. 20hp Bikh BV ME diesel engine.
Interior:	6/9 berths. Galley — cooker, oven, sinks. Ample storage.
Sails:	Area 61.6m²/663 sq.ft.
Rigging:	Sloop
Price Guide:	£25,750
Summary:	Fast. Elegantly designed. Part-built versions also available. Also known as **Hurley Tailwind.**

YANKEE 38 1TON

Design:	Sparkman & Stephens, U.S.A. 1972
Supplier:	Yankee Yachts, U.S.A.
Est. Rating:	27.5' IOR Mk III
Specifications:	*Construction:* GRP and balsa core
	LWL: 8.76m/28'9
	LOA: 11.63m/38'2
	Beam: 3.58m/11'9
	Draft: 1.91m/6'3
	Displ: 7,264kg/16,000 lbs
	Ballast: 3,326kg/7,327 lbs
Fittings:	Lead ballast. GRP and balsa core deck. Aluminium spars. 25hp Westerbeke 4-91 diesel.
Interior:	8 berths in 3 cabins. Icebox. Sink. Stove. Enclosed head.
Sails:	Area 59.2m^2(23.9 + 35.3)/637 sq.ft. (257 + 380)
Rigging:	Sloop
Price Guide:	$46,000us
Summary:	One of the few Sparkman & Stephens one ton designs in full production. Built for speed, strength and comfort.

ROBB 38

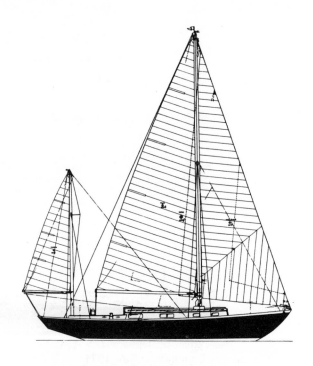

Design:	Arthur Robb, England
Supplier:	Arthur Robb, England Lion Yachts, U.S.A.

Specifications:	*Construction:*	Wood. Teak optional
	LWL:	7.77m/25'6
	LOA:	11.66m/38'3
	Beam:	3.2m/10'6
	Draft:	1.22m/4'0
	Displ:	7,496kg/16,512 lbs

Fittings:	Roller fitted bronze case and centreboard.
Interior:	4/6 berths. 1.88m/6'2 headroom.
Variations:	Layout, engine to specification.
Sails:	Area 62.8m^2/676 sq.ft.
Rigging:	Yawl and optional
Price Guide:	£24,000 +
Summary:	Individually built to a standard design. Comfortable, fast cruiser with minimum draft.

MISTRESS 39

Design:	Art Edmunds, U.S.A. 1971
Supplier:	Allied Boat Co. Inc., U.S.A.
Specifications:	*Construction:* GRP
	LWL: 9.1m/29'10
	LOA: 11.76m/38'7
	Beam: 3.66m/12'0
	Draft: 1.37m/4'6
	Displ: 9,443kg/20,800 lbs
	Ballast: 2,542kg/5,600 lbs
Fittings:	Lead ballast. Deck: balsa core and GRP. Aluminium spars. Westerbeke 4-107 diesel.
Interior:	6 berths in 3 cabins. Stove. W/oven. Icebox. 2 skipper heads.
Sails:	Area 65m^2(26.3 + 29.6 + 9.1)/700 sq.ft. (283 + 319 + 98)
Rigging:	Ketch
Price Guide:	$38,000
Summary:	Very strong hull. Centre cockpit. One of the most popular boats of its type on the market. Lovely and responsive.

CAL 39

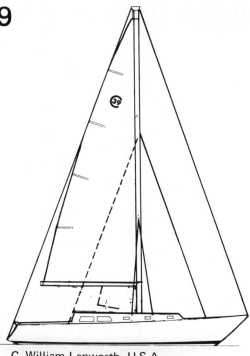

Design:	C. William Lapworth, U.S.A.	
Supplier:	Cal-Boats, U.S.A.	
Est. Rating:	32.6' IOR Mk III	
Specifications:	*Construction:*	GRP
	LWL:	9.53m/31'3
	LOA:	11.78m/38'8
	Beam:	3.55m/11'8
	Draft:	1.83m/6'0
	Displ:	6,628kg/14,600 lbs
	Ballast:	2,996kg/6,600 lbs
Fittings:	Iron ballast. GRP deck. Aluminium spars. Short raked keel.	
Interior:	7 berths in 2 cabins. Standard galley. Layout designed for extended cruising.	
Variations:	Optional gasoline auxiliary.	
Sails:	Area 72.7m^2/783 sq.ft.	
Rigging:	Sloop	
Price Guide:	$31,000us	
Summary:	Designed with IOR rules in mind. Short raked keel is her most prominent feature designed to minimise wetted surface area.	

FRERS 39 1TON

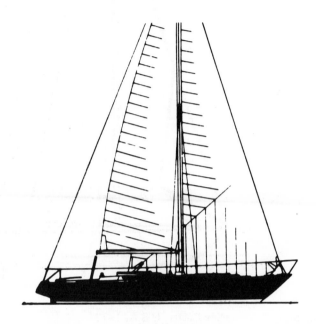

Design:	German Frers, Argentina 1973
Supplier:	Frers North American, U.S.A.
Est. Rating:	27.5' IOR Mk III
Specifications:	*Construction:* GRP with foam core
	LWL: 9.53m/31'3
	LOA: 11.81m/38'9
	Beam: 3.51m/11'6
	Draft: 1.93m/6'4
	Displ: 7,854kg/17,300 lbs
	Ballast 3,859kg/8,500 lbs
Fittings:	GRP with balsa core deck. Aluminium spars. Lead ballast. 40hp Westerbeke 4-107 diesel auxiliary.
Interior:	5/7 berths in 2 cabins.
Sails:	Area 59m^2/635 sq.ft.
Rigging:	Sloop
Price Guide:	$43,000us
Summary:	One of an interesting new range of boats imported from the Argentine.

CARTER 39

Design:	Dick Carter, U.S.A. 1972
Supplier:	Carter Offshore Inc., U.S.A.
	Carter Offshore Ltd., England
Est. Rating:	30.0' IOR Mk III

Specifications:

Construction:	GRP
LWL:	9.14m/30'0
LOA:	11.89m/39'0
Beam:	3.89m/12'9
Draft:	2.06m/6'9
Displ:	8,513kg/18,750 lbs
Ballast:	3,337kg/7,350 lbs

Fittings:	Lead ballast. Balsa core and GRP deck. Aluminium spars. Perkins 4-107 diesel auxiliary.
Interior:	7 berths in 2 cabins. Galley and toilets standard.
Variations:	Available in a coachroof version or a flush deck model.
Sails:	Area 68.2m²/734 sq.ft.
Rigging:	Bermudan sloop
Price Guide:	£25,000–26,000/$55,000us
Summary:	Sold direct from manufacturer, and through agents.

1054

PEARSON 390

Design:	William H. Shaw, U.S.A. 1971
Supplier:	Pearson Yachts, U.S.A.

Specifications:	*Construction:*	GRP
	LWL:	10.26m/33'8
	LOA:	11.89m/39'0
	Beam:	3.96m/13'0
	Draft:	1.3m/4'3
	Displ:	9,352kg/20,600 lbs
	Ballast:	3,405kg/7,500 lbs

Fittings:	Lead ballast. GRP deck. Aluminium spars. 37hp diesel auxiliary.
Interior:	6 berths in 3 cabins. Stove. Sink. Icebox. 2 sea toilets. Showers.
Sails:	Area 61.6m²/663 sq.ft.
Rigging:	Masthead sloop
Price Guide:	$40,000us
Summary:	Big and roomy both above and below deck. Designed for cruising and comfort.

FRERS 40

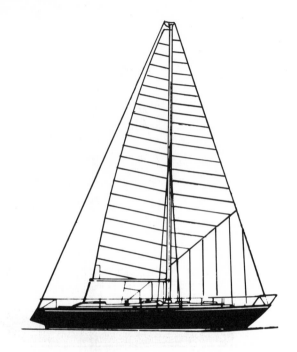

Design: German Frers, Argentina 1973

Supplier: Frers North American, U.S.A.

Est. Rating: 28.1' IOR Mk III

Specifications:

Construction:	GRP	
LWL:	9.88m/32'5	
LOA:	11.99m/39'4	
Beam:	3.53m/11'7	
Draft:	1.91m/6'3 keel. 1.5m/4'11 keel/cb	
Displ:	8,172kg/18,000 lbs	
Ballast:	3,995kg/8,800 lbs	

Fittings: GRP with balsa core deck. Aluminium spars. Lead ballast. 40hp Westerbeke 4-107 diesel auxiliary.

Interior: 8 berths in 3 cabins.

Sails: Area 59.5m^2/640 sq.ft.

Rigging: Sloop

Price Guide: $44,500us

Summary: One of a range of interesting boats imported from the Argentine.

SWAN 40

Design:	Sparkman & Stephens, U.S.A.
Supplier:	Nautor Oy Wilh, Finland
	Dave Johnson, England

Specifications:

Construction:	GRP
LWL:	8.69m/28'6
LOA:	12.04m/39'6
Beam:	3.30m/10'10
Draft:	1.96m/6'5

Fittings:	Fin keel. 25hp inboard engine.
Interior:	
Sails:	Area 84.8m²/913 sq.ft.
Rigging:	Sloop
Price Guide:	On application.

OFFSHORE 40

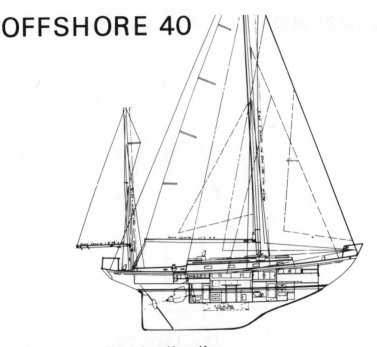

Design:	Cheoy Lee, Hong Kong
Supplier:	Cheoy Lee, Hong Kong Lion Yachts, U.S.A. Satterns Yacht Agency, England
Specifications:	*Construction:* GRP *LWL:* 8.53m/28'0 *LOA:* 12.12m/39'9 *Beam:* 3.28m/10'9 *Draft:* 1.83m/6'0 *Displ:* 9,080kg/20,000 lbs *Ballast:* 3,587kg/7,900 lbs
Fittings:	Iron ballast. GRP deck (teak overlay). Wood or aluminium spars. Auxiliary: 30hp Atomic 4 gasoline. Teak trim.
Interior:	6 berths in 3 cabins. Sink. Icebox. 2 enclosed sea toilets.
Variations:	Choice of two cabin layouts.
Sails:	Area 65.6m^2(32.5 + 25.2 + 7.9)/706 sq.ft. (350 + 271 + 85)
Rigging:	Sloop or yawl.
Price Guide:	£36,000/$ on application.
Summary:	Finished to a very high standard of workmanship. Very luxurious interior.

KETTENBURG 40

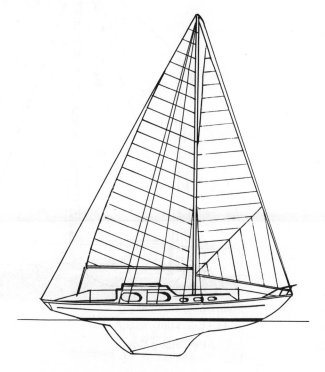

Design:	Kettenburg Marine, U.S.A.
Supplier:	Kettenburg Marine, U.S.A.
Specifications:	

	Construction:	Wood
	LWL:	8.23m/27'0
	LOA:	12.14m/39'10
	Beam:	3.15m/10'4
	Draft:	1.62m/5'4
	Displ:	6,356kg/14,000 lbs
	Ballast:	2,270kg/5,000 lbs

Fittings:	Lead ballast. GRP covered deck. Wooden spars.
Interior:	6 berths in 2 cabins. Standard galley.
Variations:	Optional power.
Sails:	Various areas.
Rigging:	Sloop
Price Guide:	On application.
Summary:	A powerful hull and spacious interior make this a popular boat.

MIDSHIPMAN 40

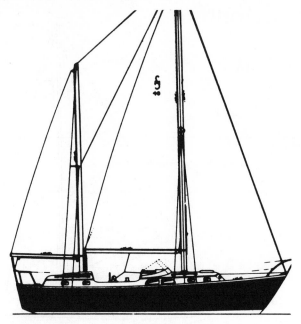

Design:	A. E. Luders Jnr., U.S.A. 1972
Supplier:	Cheoy Lee, Hong Kong Lion Yachts, U.S.A.

Specifications:

Construction:	GRP
LWL:	9.91m/32'6
LOA:	12.14m/39'10
Beam:	4.22m/13'10
Draft:	1.37m/4'6
Displ:	9,080kg/20,000 lbs
Ballast:	2,724kg/6,000 lbs

Fittings: Lead ballast. Deck — GRP. Teak trim. Wood or aluminium spars. 37hp Perkins 4-107 diesel auxiliary.

Interior: 6 berths in 3 cabins. Stove. Sink. Icebox. 2 enclosed sea toilets.

Sails: Area 67.6m^2(24.7m^2 + 30.4 + 12.5)/728 sq.ft. (266 + 327 + 135)

Rigging: Ketch or sloop.

Price Guide: On application.

Summary: Centre cockpit and aft cabin design. Modern design blended with traditional touches to give a comfortable and attractive boat.

RACERS/CRUISERS 30´- 40´
multihulls

IROQUOIS MkII

Design: J. R. MacAlpine Downie, England 1969

Supplier: Sail Craft, England
Thunderbird Products Corporation, U.S.A.

Est. Rating: Portsmouth number 81

Specifications:

Construction:	Moulded GRP
LOA:	9.14m/30'0
Beam:	4.11m/13'6
Draft:	0.41m/1'4
Displ:	2,542kg/5,600 lbs

Fittings: Centreboards. Balsa core deck. 2 symmetrical hulls joined by a bridge deck. Aluminium spars. 12.9 or 25 hp/Chrysler or Johnson outboard.

Interior: 8 berths in 5 cabins. Shower optional.

Variations: Mk IIa also available — longer LOA.

Sails: Area 33.6m^2 (17.2 + 16.4)/362 sq.ft. (185 + 177) Spinnaker area 41.8m^2/450 sq.ft.

Rigging: Sloop

Price Guide: £8,000/$19,900us

Summary: Tacks readily under all conditions and points like a motor boat. Can be trailed. Kits and mouldings available.

NIMBLE TRIMARAN

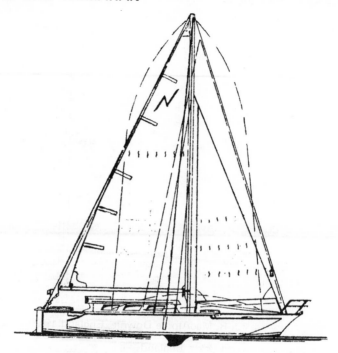

Design:	Arthur Piver, England
Supplier:	Contour Craft, England
Est Rating:	Portsmouth number 86
Specifications:	*Construction:* Fiberglassed plywood
	LWL: 8.53m/28'0
	LOA: 9.14m/30'0
	Beam: 5.49m/18'0
	Draft: 0.61m/2'0
	Displ: 1,017kg/2,240 lbs
Fittings:	Crescent 8 outboard engine
Interior:	4/6 berths. 1.91m/6'3 headroom.
Variations:	A de luxe version also available
Sails:	Area 30.2m^2/325 sq.ft.
Rigging:	Bermudan sloop
Price Guide:	On application
Summary:	Low price plus spacious accommodation. The vast deck space makes admirable play area for children.

OCEANIC CATAMARAN

Design:	Bill O'Brien, England
Supplier:	South Coast Catamarans, England
Specifications:	*Construction:* GRP sheathed marine ply
	LWL: 8.59m/28'2
	LOA: 9.14m/30'0
	Beam: 4.27m/14'0
	Draft: 0.61m/2'0
	Displ: 3,763kg/8,288 lbs
Fittings:	Twin hull. 2 Penta diesel engines.
Interior:	7 berths. 1.98m/6'6 headroom.
Sails:	Area 65m^2/700 sq.ft.
Rigging:	Ketch
Price Guide:	£11,500
Summary:	Roomy with a fine performance. Easily handled from the cockpit. Cannot be trailed

KRAKEN 33 Mk IV

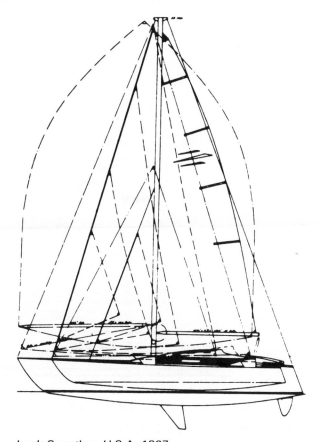

Design:	Lock Crowther, U.S.A. 1967
Supplier:	International Marine Services, U.S.A.
Specifications:	*Construction:* GRP and plywood
	LWL: 9.14m/30'0
	LOA: 10.06m/33'0
	Beam: 7.01m/23'0
	Draft: 0.53m/1'9
Fittings:	3 symmetrical hulls joined by wood box beams. Aluminium spars. 20hp optional outboard.
Interior:	4 berths in 2 cabins
Sails:	Area 63.2m^2/680 sq.ft.
Rigging:	Sloop
Price Guide:	$23,000–28,000us

BUCCANEER 33

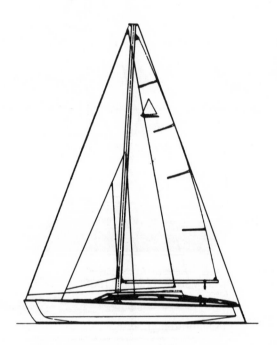

Design:	Lock Crowther, U.S.A. 1973
Supplier:	International Marine Services, U.S.A.
Specifications:	*Construction:* GRP and wood or sandwich foam
	LWL: 9.6m/31'6
	LOA: 10.13m/33'3
	Beam: 7.16m/23'6
	Draft: 0.61m/2'0
Fittings:	3 symmetrical hulls connected by aluminium cross arms. Aluminium spars. 10 hp Honda air-cooled diesel engine.
Interior:	5—6 berths in 2 cabins
Sails:	Area 67.5m^2 (28.1 + 39.4)/727 sq.ft. (302 + 425)
Rigging:	Sloop
Price Guide:	$18,500us
Summary:	Available through dealers. Cruising trimaran.

SNOW GOOSE 34

Design:	Prout Marine, England 1969
Supplier:	Prout Marine, England
Est. Rating:	Portsmouth number 83
Specifications:	*Construction:* GRP
	LWL: 9.14m/30'0
	LOA: 10.36m/34'0
	Beam: 4.57m/15'0
	Draft: 0.81m/2'8
	Displ: 3,632kg/8,000 lbs
Fittings:	Teak trim. GRP deck. Alloy anodised spars. Volvo MD2B 25 hp diesel engine.
Interior:	6 berths
Variations:	Optional inboard or outboard
Sails:	Area 34.5m^2/371 sq.ft. Spinnaker area 111.5m^2/1,200 sq.ft.
Rigging:	Cutter
Price Guide:	£14,200
Summary:	Very efficient catamaran to windward. Stable and strong.

CHEROKEE 35

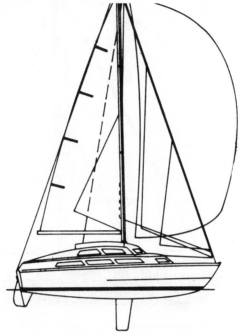

Design: MacAlpine-Downie, U.S.A. 1973

Supplier: Symons Sailing, U.S.A.
Sail Craft, U.K.

Specifications:

Construction:	GRP
LWL:	9.45m/31'0
LOA:	10.67m/35'0
Beam:	5.18m/17'0
Draft:	0.66m/2'2
Displ:	6,102kg/13,440 lbs

Fittings: Centreboards. Balsa core deck. 2 symmetrical hulls connected with a bridge deck. Aluminium spars.

Interior: 8 berths in 4 cabins. 1.93m/6'4 headroom. 1 shower.

Variations: Optional diesel outboard

Sails: Area 57.1m^2(29.3 + 27.8)/615 sq.ft. (315 + 300)

Rigging: Bermudan sloop

Price Guide: £18,000/$38,500us

Summary: Cruising catamaran. Can be sailed single-handed. Interior allows for a great deal of privacy. Kits and mouldings available.

LODESTAR TRIMARAN

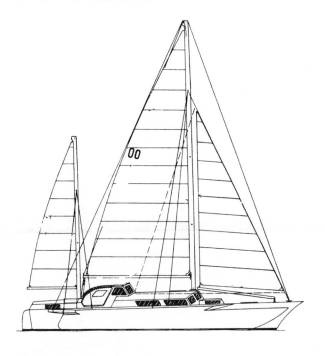

Design:	Arthur Piver, England
Supplier:	Cox Marine, England Symons Sailing Inc., U.S.A.

Specifications:

	Construction:	Fiberglassed plywood
	LWL:	10.06m/33'0
	LOA:	10.67m/35'0
	Beam:	6.1m/20'0
	Draft:	0.76m/2'6
	Displ:	2,034kg/4,480 lbs

Fittings:	Crescent 25 hp outboard
Interior:	8/9 berths. 1.96m/6'5 headroom
Variations:	A de luxe version. **Pi 35** is also available.
Sails:	Area 35.8m^2/385 sq.ft.
Rigging:	Sloop
Price Guide:	On application
Summary:	Ideal for trans-ocean voyages. Attractive price for size and quality of vessel.

POLYNESIAN CONCEPT

Design:	CSK, U.S.A. 1970
Supplier:	W. D. Schock Co., U.S.A.
Specifications:	*Construction:* GRP
	LOA: 11.28m/37'0
	Beam: 5.18m/17'0
	Draft: 0.48m/1'7
	Displ: 2,497kg/5,500 lbs
Fittings:	Daggerboards. 2 symmetrical hulls joined by a bridge deck. Aluminium spars. Inboard engine.
Interior:	7 berths in 3 cabins. 1 enclosed toilet.
Sails:	Area 74.8m^2 (26.8 + 48)/805 sq.ft. (289 + 516)
Rigging:	Sloop
Price Guide:	$36,000us
Summary:	A cruising catamaran.

RACERS/CRUISERS 40′+
monohulls

BOWMAN 40

Design:	Laurent Giles, England 1974	
Supplier:	Emsworth Marine Sales, England	
Specifications:	*Construction:*	GRP
	LWL:	9.30m/30'5
	LOA:	12.19m/40'0
	Beam:	3.38m/11'1
	Draft:	1.62m/5'3
	Displ:	10.6 tonnes/10.5 tons
	Ballast:	4,540kg/10,000 lbs
Fittings:	Full keel boat. Mercedes OM636 engine.	
Interior:	Optional layout 6/7 berths	
Sails:	Area 70.50m^2/761 sq.ft.	
Rigging:	Sloop	
Price Guide:	On application	
Summary:	A combination of tradition and modernisation.	

NORTH STAR 80/20

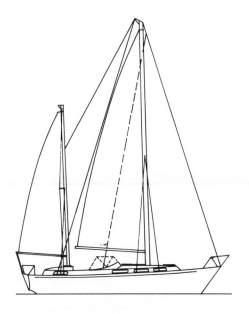

Design:	Sparkman Stevens, U.S.A. 1973
Supplier:	Hughes Boat Works, Canada Knoxmore Bagley, England
Specifications:	*Construction:* GRP *LWL:* 9.45m/31'0 *LOA:* 12.19m/40'0 *Beam:* 4.06m/13'4 *Draft:* 1.45m/4'9 *Displ:* 11,168kg/24,600 lbs *Ballast:* 4,086kg/9,000 lbs
Fittings:	Extended fin keel. Lead ballast. GRP with balsa core deck. Aluminium spars. Auxiliary 52 hp Westerbeke 4-154 diesel.
Interior:	7 berths in 3 cabins. Refrigerator. Stove with oven. Hot and cold pressure water. 2 recirculating toilets.
Sails:	Area 73.3m^2/786 sq.ft.
Rigging:	Sloop
Price Guide:	£25,000/$50,000us

STANDFAST 40

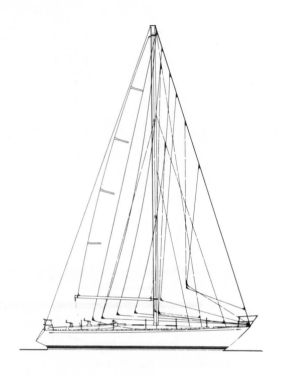

Design:	Frans Maas, Holland 1972
Supplier:	Frans Maas bv, Holland Chichester Yacht Agency, England

Specifications:

Construction:	Sandwich GRP
LWL:	9.90m/32'6
LOA:	12.20m/40'0½
Beam:	4.0m/13'1
Draft:	2.25m/7'5
Displ:	9,500kg/20,950 lbs
Ballast:	4,000kg/8,820 lbs

Fittings:	Sandwich GRP deck. Teak trim. Volvo Penta MD2B 25 hp engine. Aluminium spars.
Interior:	6 berths. Cooker. Fire extinguishers.
Sails:	Area 104m^2/834 sq.ft.
Rigging:	Sloop
Price Guide:	£26,000

TRINTELLA IV

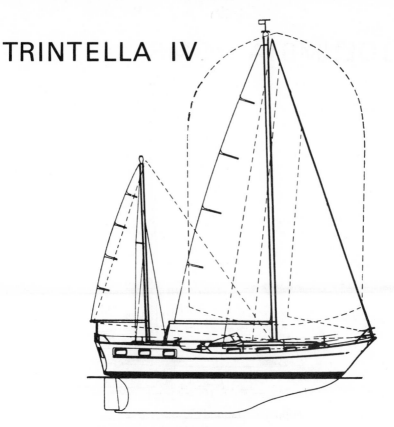

Design: E. G. van de Stadt, Holland

Supplier: Jachtwerf Anne Wever bv, Holland
Aberdair Marine, Scotland

Specifications: *Construction:*   GRP
LWL: 9.80m/32'2
LOA: 12.2m/40'0½
Beam: 3.5m/11'6
Draft: 1.50m/4'11
Displ: 10,500kg/23,148 lbs
Ballast: 4,300kg/9,480 lbs

Fittings: Perkins 4.236 62 hp diesel engine. Aluminium spars.

Interior: 6 berths. Full galley. 2 toilets. 1 shower.

Sails: Area 61.8m^2/665 sq.ft.
Spinnaker area 79m^2/850 sq.ft.

Rigging: Sloop or ketch

Price Guide: £31,300/190,000 fl.

Summary: Fully equipped. Also known as **Victory 40.** Mouldings
available.

COLUMBIA 41 MS

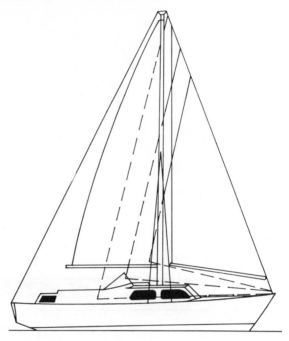

Design:	Tripp and Columbia, U.S.A. 1972
Supplier:	Columbia Yacht Corporation, U.S.A.

Specifications:

Construction:	GRP
LWL:	9.75m/32'0
LOA:	12.34m/40'6
Beam:	3.43m/11'3
Draft:	1.93m—1.5m/6'4—4'11
Displ:	9,307kg/20,500 lbs
Ballast:	3,859kg/8,500 lbs

Fittings:	Lead ballast. GRP deck. Aluminium spars. 65 hp Universal Unimite 4 gasoline auxiliary.
Interior:	8 berths in 3 cabins.
Variations:	Shoal draft model also available.
Sails:	Area 59.3m^2/638 sq.ft. (sloop) Area 59.6m^2/642 sq.ft. (ketch)
Rigging:	Sloop or ketch
Price Guide:	$39,995us
Summary:	A beautiful long distance motor-sailer. Roomy, fast with rugged construction.

NORLIN 41

Design:	Peter Norlin, Sweden, 1972
Supplier:	Solna Marine AB, Sweden David Smithells, England Scampi Yachts, U.S.A.
Est. Rating:	34.5 IOR Mk III
Specifications:	*Construction:* GRP *LWL:* 10.60m/34'9½ *LOA:* 12.35m/40'6½ *Beam:* 3.92m/12'10¼ *Draft:* 1.97m/6'5½ *Displ:* 9,000kg/19,841 lbs *Ballast:* 4,000kg/8,818 lbs
Fittings:	Fin keel
Interior:	Headroom 1.90m/6'1
Sails:	Area 108.0m^2/1,163 sq.ft. Spinnaker area 159m^2/1,711 sq.ft.
Rigging:	Sloop
Price Guide:	£29,800

RIVAL 40

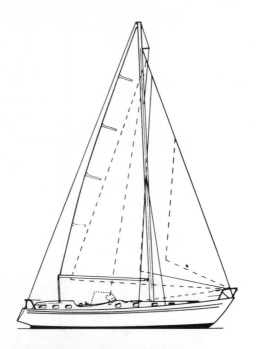

Design:	Peter Brett, England 1973
Supplier:	Southern Boatbuilding Co., England
Specifications:	*Construction:* GRP
	LWL: 9.98m/32'7
	LOA: 12.40m/40'7
	Beam: 3.72m/12'2
	Draft: 1.80m/5'9
	Displ: 10,170kg/22,400 lbs
Fittings:	Fin keel. Perkins 4236M diesel engine. Iron ballast keel. Gold anodised alloy spars. S/S fittings.
Interior:	7/9 berths. Headroom 1.83m/6'0. Galley — fridge, 2 sinks, stove and oven. Lavac toilet. Shower.
Variations:	Optional hp engine.
Sails:	Area 61.3m^2(31.2 + 30.1)/656 sq.ft. (334 + 322) Spinnaker are 99.4m^2/1,070 sq.ft.
Rigging:	Sloop or ketch
Price Guide:	£7,000–22,000
Summary:	Available for home completion.

TARTAN 41

Design:	Olin Stephens, U.S.A. 1972
Supplier:	Tartan Marine, U.S.A. Interyacht, England
Est. Rating:	IOR Mk III 31.8'
Specifications:	*Construction:* GRP *LWL:* 9.88m/32'5 *LOA:* 12.38/40'7$\frac{5}{8}$ *Beam:* 3.73m/12'3 *Draft:* 1.93m/6'4 *Displ:* 8,104kg/17,850 lbs *Ballast:* 4,091kg/9,010 lbs
Fittings:	Lead ballast. GRP deck. Aluminium spars.
Interior:	Westerbeke Pilot 20 diesel engine. 8 berths in 3 cabins. Pressure water. Stove. Icebox. Sink. 1 enclosed head.
Sails:	Area 67.4m^2/725 sq.ft.
Rigging:	Sloop
Price Guide:	£ on application/$45,000us

CUTTYHUNK 41

Design: Alan Pape, England 1974

Supplier: John Sears Ltd., England

Specifications:
Construction:	Wood
LWL:	9.45m/31'0
LOA:	12.50m/41'0
Beam:	1.83m/6'0
Draft:	1.83m/6'0
Displ:	13,393kg/13.17 tons
Ballast:	4,805kg/4.725 tons

Fittings: To specification

Interior: To specification

Sails: Area 74.3m^2/800 sq.ft.

Rigging: Sloop

Price Guide: £30,000

Summary: An extremely refined and elegant yacht, specifically designed for comfortable living on board for long periods.

DICKERSON 41

Design:	Ernest Tucker, U.S.A. 1973	
Supplier:	Dickerson Boatbuilders Inc., U.S.A.	
Specifications:	*Construction:*	GRP
	LWL:	9.65m/31'8
	LOA:	12.5m/41'0
	Beam:	3.81m/12'6
	Draft:	1.37m/4'6
	Displ:	10,442kg/23,000 lbs
	Ballast:	4,020kg/8,500 lbs
Fittings:	Fiberglass plywood deck. Aluminium spars. Mahogany trim. 37 hp Westerbeke Four 107 engine.	
Interior:	6—8 berths in 2 cabins. 2 enclosed toilets.	
Sails:	Area 69.7m^2/750 sq.ft.	
Rigging:	Ketch	
Price Guide:	$30,000us+	
Summary:	Sold direct from the manufacturers.	

GULFSTAR 41

Design:	Gulf Star Inc., U.S.A. 1972
Supplier:	Gulf Star Inc., U.S.A.

Specifications:

Construction:	GRP
LWL:	10.06m/33'0
LOA:	12.5m/41'0
Beam:	3.66m/12'0
Draft:	1.47m/4'10
Displ:	9,534kg/21,000 lbs
Ballast:	3,178kg/7,000 lbs

Fittings: Lead ballast. GRP deck. Aluminium spars. 50 hp 4-107 Perkins diesel.

Interior: 5 berths in 3 cabins. 2 sea toilets. U-shaped galley.

Sails: Area 66.7m^2 (31.6 + 35.1)/718 sq.ft. (340 + 378)

Rigging: Sloop

Price Guide: $36,900us

Summary: Available through dealers.

SWAN 41

Design:	Sparkman & Stephens, U.S.A. 1973	
Supplier:	Nautor, Finland Dave Johnson, U.K. Palmer Johnson Inc, U.S.A.	
Specifications:	*Construction:*	GRP
	LWL:	9.22m/30'3
	LOA:	12.50m/41'0
	Beam:	3.64m/11'11
	Draft:	1.98m/6'6
	Displ:	8,100kg/17,750 lbs
	Ballast:	4,400kg/9,700 lbs
Fittings:	Fin keel. Perkins 4-108M 37 hp engine.	
Interior:	Optional interior layouts available	
Sails:	Area 68.8m^2/740 sq.ft.	
Rigging:	Sloop	
Price Guide:	£40,000	

ISLANDER 41

Design:	Alan P. Gurney, U.S.A. 1972
Supplier:	Islander Yachts, U.S.A.
Est. Rating:	34.1'− 33.5' IOR Mk III

Specifications:

Construction:	GRP and balsa core
LWL:	10.56m/34'8
LOA:	12.55m/41'2
Beam:	3.96m/13'0
Draft:	1.98m/6'6
Displ:	9,988kg/22,000 lbs
Ballast:	4,404kg/9,700 lbs

Fittings:	GRP and balsa core deck. Aluminium spars. Lead ballast. 50 hp Atomic gasoline auxiliary. Flush foredeck.
Interior:	8 berths in 3 cabins. 2 toilets.
Sails:	Area 82.6m^2 (34.5 + 48.1)/889 sq.ft. (371 + 518)
Rigging:	Sloop
Price Guide:	$34,450us
Summary:	Designed to qualify under the IOR rules. Luxurious. Stable.

MORGAN OUT ISLAND 41

Design:	Morgan Yacht Corp., U.S.A. 1971
Supplier:	Morgan Yacht Corp., U.S.A. Peter Webster Ltd., England

Specifications:

Construction:	GRP
LWL:	10.36m/34'0
LOA:	12.57m/41'3
Beam:	4.22m/13'10
Draft:	1.27m/4'2
Displ:	10.896kg/24,000 lbs
Ballast:	4,767kg/10,500 lbs

Fittings:	GRP deck. Aluminium spars. Auxiliary diesel.
Interior:	6 to 8 berths in 3 cabins, galley standard. 2 enclosed toilets.
Variations:	Walk-through version available.
Sails:	Area 72m^2 (33.3 + 38.7)/775 sq.ft. (358 + 417)
Rigging:	Sloop
Price Guide:	£24,000/$40,000
Summary:	Available through dealers in the U.S.A.

SOVEREL 41

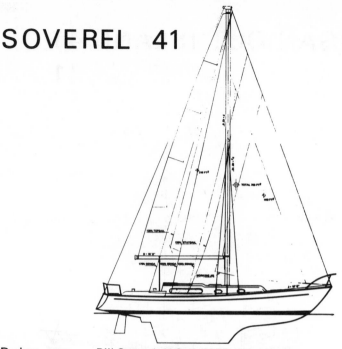

Design:	Bill Soverel, U.S.A. 1972
Supplier:	Soverel Marine Inc., U.S.A.
Est. Rating:	37.3' IOR Mk III
Specifications:	*Construction:* GRP
	LWL: 10.67m/35'0
	LOA: 12.602m/41'4
	Beam: 3.353m/11'0
	Draft: 1.524m/5'0 cb up
	Displ: 8,172kg/18,000 lbs
	Ballast: 4,086kg/9,000 lbs lead
Fittings:	Keel or centreboard boat. Mast 55' high. Anodised aluminium spars. Spade GRP rudder.
Interior:	6 berths in 2 cabins. Teak interior panelling. Marine toilet.
Variations:	Diesel engine optional
Sails:	Area 73.9m^2 (29.3 + 44.6)/795 sq.ft. (315 + 480) 8 oz Dacron. Spinnaker 1.2 oz Dacron
Rigging:	Cutter or yawl
Price Guide:	$40,000
Summary:	Speedy, swift and well-balanced. Pure hull lines that give her a traditional beauty. Sold direct from Soverel Marine.

TREWES PRIVATEER RANGE

Design:	S. M. van der Meer, Holland	
Supplier:	Trewes International, Holland	
Specifications:	*Construction:*	Steel
	LWL:	9.15m—17.70m/30'0—58'1
	LOA:	12.70m—22.56m/41'8—75'0
	Beam:	3.60m—5.25m/11'10—17'2
	Draft:	1.55m—2.10m/5'0—6'9
Fittings:	Engines from 75—195 hp	
Interior:	To individual specifications	
Variations:	A range of custom finished yachts. 11.58m/38', 13.41m/44', 14.33m/47', 16.15m/53', 17.07m/56', 17.98m/59' and 22.86m/75' models available.	
Sails:	Areas from $56.30m^2$—$123.85m^2$/605 — 1,333 sq.ft.	
Rigging:	Ketch	
Price Guide:	On application.	

NICHOLSON 42

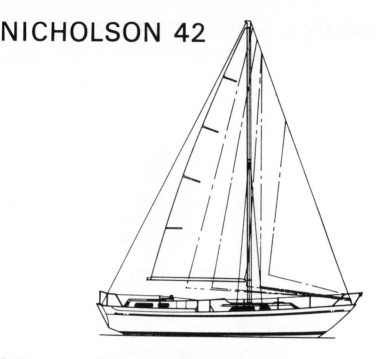

Design:	Camper & Nicholsons, England 1973
Supplier:	Camper & Nicholsons, England Camper & Nicholsons, U.S.A.
Est. Rating:	Thames measurement 20 tons
Specifications:	*Construction:* GRP *LWL:* 8.89m/29'2 *LOA:* 12.75m/41'10 *Beam:* 3.72m/12'2½ *Draft:* 1.68m/5'6 *Displ:* 10,100kg/22,400 lbs *Ballast:* 4,000kg/8,960 lbs
Fittings:	Deck — GRP and balsa core. Lead ballast. Teak trim. Gold anodised alloy spars. Perkins 4.236 diesel 62 hp engine.
Interior:	6 berths. Full galley. 2 toilet compartments and showers. Full headroom throughout.
Sails:	Area 84m^2/897 sq.ft.
Rigging:	Sloop or ketch
Price Guide:	£37,900
Summary:	A comfortable cruiser that combines highest standards of workmanship with true sailing ability.

CHANCE 36

Design:	Britton Chance Jnr, U.S.A. 1971
Supplier:	Paceship Yachts, Canada
Est. Rating:	35.8' IOR Mk III

Specifications:

Construction:	GRP
LWL:	11.05m/36'3
LOA:	12.78m/41'11
Beam:	3.53m/11'7
Draft:	2.44m/8'0
Displ:	11,123kg/24,500 lbs
Ballast:	5,562kg/12,250 lbs

Fittings:	Lead ballast. GRP deck. Aluminium spars. 35 hp Volvo Penta MD3B diesel auxiliary.
Interior:	8 berths in 3 cabins. 2 enclosed toilets with showers.
Sails:	Area 84.6m^2(33.7 + 50.9)/911 sq.ft. (363 + 548)
Rigging:	Sloop
Price Guide:	On application

CARTER 42

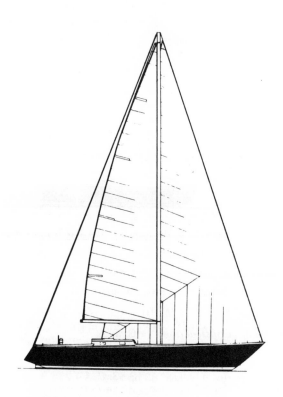

Design:	Dick Carter, U.S.A. 1974
Supplier:	Carter Offshore, U.S.A. Carter Offshore, England
Specifications:	*Construction:* GRP *LOA:* 12.80m/42'0
Variations:	Racing or cruising versions available
Price Guide:	On application.
Summary:	Built in Sweden

WHITBY 42

Design:	Edward S. Brewer, Canada 1971	
Supplier:	Whitby Boat Works Ltd., Canada	
Specifications:	*Construction:*	GRP and balsa core
	LWL:	9.95m/32'8
	LOA:	12.80m/42'0
	Beam:	3.96m/13'0
	Draft:	1.52m/5'0
	Displ:	10,669kg/23,500 lbs
	Ballast:	3,632kg/8,000 lbs
Fittings:	Lead ballast. 63 hp Perkins 4.236 diesel engine. GRP and balsa core deck. Aluminium spars.	
Interior:	8 berths in 3 cabins. 2 sinks. Fridge/freezer. 2 sea toilets with holding tank.	
Sails:	Area 81.3m^2(30 + 35.2 + 16.1)/875 sq.ft (323 + 379 + 173)	
Rigging:	Ketch	
Price Guide:	$49,500us	
Summary:	A big, bold cruising ketch that is spacious and seaworthy. Sold direct from builder.	

PHILIP 43

Design:	Holman & Pye, England 1973
Supplier:	Philip & Son, England
Est. Rating:	30.7′ IOR
Specifications:	*Construction:* GRP
	LWL: 10.058m/33′0
	LOA: 12.87m/42′2½
	Beam: 3.03m/12′10½
	Draft: 2.059m/6′9
	Displ: 9.43 tonnes/9.4 tons
Fittings:	GRP deck. Lead ballast. Silver anodised spars. Perkins 4.108 Lowline diesel engine.
Interior:	8 berths. Sink. Stove. Toilet. Shower. Fresh water tank.
Sails:	Area 91.2m^{2}982 sq.ft.
Rigging:	Sloop
Price Guide:	£26,400
Summary:	Mouldings available

SPANKER 12.8

Design:	E. G. van de Stadt, Holland 1973
Supplier:	Southern Ocean Shipyard, England
Est. Rating:	Thames measurement 23 tons
Specifications:	*Construction:* GRP
	LWL: 10.31m/33'10
	LOA: 12.88m/42'3
	Beam: 3.73m/12'3
	Draft: 2.16m/7'1
	Displ: 10,973kg/24,416 lbs
	Ballast: 4,086kg/9,000 lbs
Fittings:	Fin keel. 37 hp Perkins 4-108 inboard. Alloy spars.
Interior:	6/8 berths. Galley. Marine toilet and shower.
Variations:	Shallow draft version available
Sails:	Area 98.1m²1,056 sq.ft. Spinnaker area 139m²1,496 sq.ft.
Rigging:	Sloop or ketch.
Price Guide:	£35,000
Summary:	An ideal cruiser/racer. Combines the best features of both types of boat. Mouldings available.

FRERS 43

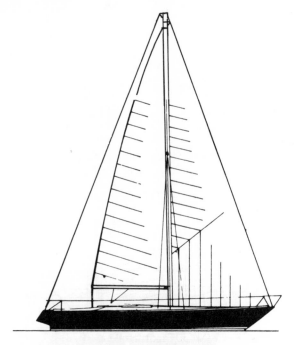

Design:	German Frers, Argentina 1973
Supplier:	Frers North American, U.S.A.
Est. Rating:	32.0' IOR Mk III

Specifications:		
	Construction:	GRP with foam core
	LWL:	10.67m/35'0
	LOA:	13.11m/43'0
	Beam:	3.71m/12'2
	Draft:	2.11m/6'11
	Displ:	9,534kg/21,000 lbs
	Ballast:	4,767kg/10,500 lbs

Fittings:	Wood and GRP deck. Aluminium spars. Lead ballast. 40 hp Westerbeke 4.107 diesel engine.
Interior:	8 berths in 3 cabins
Sails:	Area 68.7m^2/740 sq.ft.
Rigging:	Sloop
Price Guide:	$82,000us
Summary:	One of an interesting range of new boats imported from the Argentine.

1094

CAPE NORTH 43

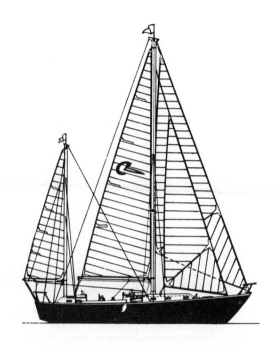

Design: Edward S. Brewer & Associates, U.S.A. 1972

Supplier: Cape Yachts, Hong Kong

Specifications:

Construction:	GRP
LWL:	10.77m/35'4
LOA:	13.16m/43'2
Beam:	3.89m/12'9
Draft:	1.93m/6'4
Displ:	11,259kg/24,800 lbs
Ballast:	5,221kg/11,500 lbs

Fittings: Lead ballast. GRP and balsa core deck. Aluminium spars. 35 hp Perkins 4.107 diesel auxiliary.

Interior: 7 berths in 3 cabins

Sails: Area 83.2m^2 (35.8 + 47.4)/895 sq.ft. (385 + 510)

Rigging: Sloop

Price Guide: On application

Summary: Sold direct from Hong Kong.

GULFSTAR 43

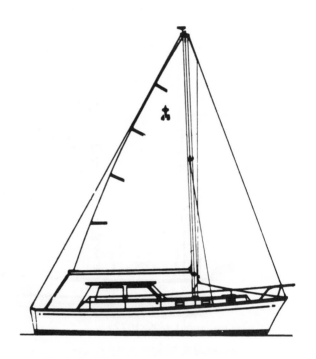

Design:	Gulfstar Inc., U.S.A.
Supplier:	Gulfstar Inc., U.S.A.
Specifications:	*Construction:* GRP
	LWL: 11.94m/39'2
	LOA: 13.21m/43'4
	Beam: 4.24m/13'11
	Draft: 1.07m/3'6
	Displ: 9,534kg/21,000 lbs
Fittings:	To specification
Interior:	To specification
Variations:	2 models available
Sails:	Area various
Rigging:	Various
Price Guide:	On application

HEDONISTE 44

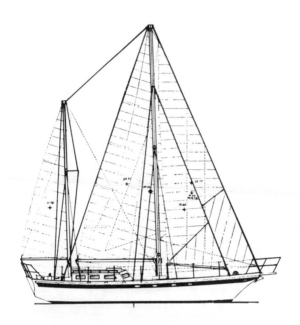

Design: Peter Ibold, U.K. 1972

Supplier: Arma Marine Engineering, U.K.

Specifications:

Construction:	Steel
LWL:	10.0m/32'9
LOA:	13.25m/43'6
Beam:	3.82m/12'6
Draft:	1.75m/5'9
Displ:	12,857kg/28,345 lbs
Ballast:	3,500kg/7,716 lbs

Fittings: 72 hp Perkins diesel engine. Teak deck. Alloy spars.

Interior: 4 permanent berths in 2 cabins.

Variations: To own specification

Sails: Area 46.01m^2 (29.7 + 16.3)/495 sq.ft. (320 + 175)

Rigging: Ketch. 1 x 19 stainless steel — standard. Running—Terylene.

Price Guide: £27,600+

Summary: All are custom built. Kits and steel hulls available.

NICHOLSON 45

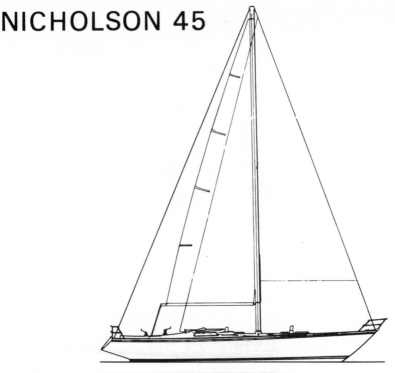

Design:	Camper & Nicholson, England 1971
Supplier:	Camper & Nicholson, England Camper & Nicholson, France Camper & Nicholson, U.S.A.
Est. Rating:	30.8' IOR
Specifications:	*Construction:* GRP *LWL:* 9.75m/33'3 *LOA:* 13.31m/43'8 *Beam:* 3.63m/12'3 *Draft:* 2.15m/7'1 *Displ:* 11,187kg/24,640 lbs *Ballast:* 4,576kg/10,080 lbs
Fittings:	Fin keel. Perkins 4.108 56 hp engine.
Interior:	8 berths
Sails:	Area 57.4m^2/618 sq.ft.
Rigging:	Sloop
Price Guide:	£35,000+
Summary:	A magnificent cruiser/racer, built to high standards of safety and craftsmanship.

GULFSTAR 44

Design:	Gulfstar Inc., U.S.A. 1972
Supplier:	Gulfstar Inc. U.S.A.

Specifications:

Construction:	GRP
LWL:	12.04m/39'6
LOA:	13.41m/44'0
Beam:	4.27m/14'0
Draft:	1.07m/3'6
Displ:	10,215kg/22,500 lbs
Ballast:	1,816kg/4,000 lbs

Fittings: Lead ballast. GRP deck. Teak trim. Aluminium spars. 130 hp 6.354 Perkins diesel auxiliary.

Interior: 8 berths in 3 cabins. 2 sea toilets. Fully equipped galley. Hot and cold water system.

Sails: Area 66.9m^2(35 + 31.9)/720 sq.ft. (377 + 343)

Rigging: Sloop or ketch

Price Guide: $44,900

Summary: A very reliable offshore motor-sailer.

MOODY 44

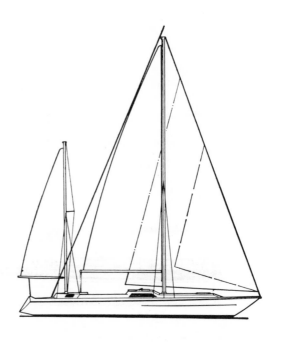

Design:	Laurent Giles & Partners Ltd., U.K. 1970
Supplier:	A. H. Moody & Son, U.K. Halmatic Hulls, England

Specifications:

Construction:	GRP — hull manufactured by Halmatic Ltd.
LWL:	10.36m/34'0
LOA:	13.41m/44'0
Beam:	3.83m/12'7
Draft:	1.98m/6'6
Displ:	13,211kg/29,100 lbs
Ballast:	4,799kg/10,570 lbs

Fittings:	Fin keel. 40½ hp inboard.
Interior:	6 berths
Sails:	Area 75.2m²/810 sq.ft.
Rigging:	Ketch
Price Guide:	On application.

FINNROSE 45

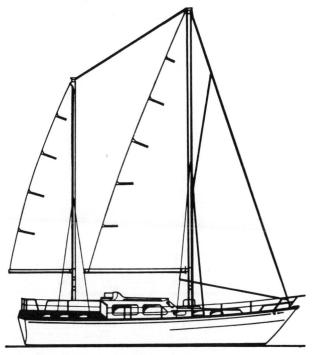

Design:	Angus Primrose, England
Supplier:	Turun veneveistämo, Finland Ballena Ltd., England

Specifications:

Construction:	GRP
LWL:	11.07m/36'4
LOA:	13.72m/45'0
Beam:	4.42m/14'6
Draft:	1.83m/6'0
Displ:	16,271kg/35,840 lbs

Fittings:	Keel boat. Perkins 4.236M diesel auxiliary. Mahogany trim.
Interior:	9 berths
Sails:	Area 81m^2/870 sq.ft.
Rigging:	Ketch
Price Guide:	£45,000+
Summary:	An easy to handle ketch-rigged motor sailer. Well suited to extensive cruises.

IRWIN 45

Design: Ted Irwin, U.S.A. 1970

Supplier: Irwin Yacht & Marine Corp., U.S.A.

Specifications:

Construction:	GRP
LWL:	9.75m/32'0
LOA:	13.72m/45'0
Beam:	3.51m/11'6
Draft:	1.98m/6'6
Displ:	10,442kg/23,000 lbs
Ballast:	4,540kg/10,000 lbs

Fittings: GRP and balsa core deck. Lead ballast. Aluminium spars. 40 hp Perkins 4.107 diesel auxiliary.

Interior: 8 berths in 3 cabins. 2 toilets.

Variations: Keel or keel/centreboard options. Optional toilets.

Sails: Area 81.9m²/882 sq.ft. (sloop)
Area 84.1m²/905 sq.ft. (ketch)

Rigging: Sloop or ketch

Price Guide: $51,900us

Summary: Centre cockpit design that combines attractive appearance with practical considerations.

ISLANDER 40 MS

Design:	Charley Davies, U.S.A. 1972
Supplier:	Islander Yachts, U.S.A.
Specifications:	*Construction:* GRP
	LWL: 9.91m/32'6
	LOA: 13.77m/45'2
	Beam: 4.01m/13'2
	Draft: 1.45m/4'9
	Displ: 9,988kg/22,000 lbs
	Ballast: 2,724kg/6,000 lbs
Fittings:	Lead ballast. GRP deck. Aluminium spars. 100 hp Chrysler diesel.
Interior:	7 berths in 3 cabins. 2 sea toilets.
Sails:	Area 74.9m^2 (27.9 + 30.8 + 16.2)/806 sq.ft. (300 + 332 + 174)
Rigging:	Ketch
Price Guide:	$36,995us
Summary:	1,600 mile range. Can be handled by a man and wife team. Comfortable and elegant.

1103

CAL 2-46

Design: C. William Lapworth, U.S.A.

Supplier: Jensen Marine, U.S.A.

Specifications:
Construction:	GRP
LWL:	11.43m/37'6
LOA:	13.87m/45'6
Beam:	3.81m/12'6
Draft:	1.52m/5'0
Displ:	15,254kg/15 tons
Ballast:	3,632kg/8,000 lbs

Fittings: Lead ballast. Aluminium alloy spars. Perkins 4.236 auxiliary 85 hp. Self-bailing cockpit. GRP deck.

Interior: 5 berths. Galley — double sink. Icebox. Hot and cold water system. 2 enclosed heads.

Sails: Area 69.1m^2/744 sq.ft. (sloop)
Area 80.3m^2/864 sq.ft. (ketch)

Rigging: Sloop or ketch

Price Guide: $65,750us

Summary: A traditional hull design combined with a modern spade rudder for easy steering control. Stable and seakindly.

CAPE CLIPPER 46

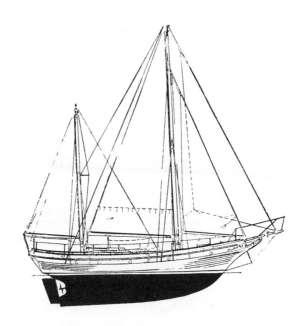

Design:	William Garden, U.S.A. 1974
Supplier:	R. Fung & Co. Ltd., U.S.A. Pacific Ocean Yachts, Jersey.

Specifications:	*Construction:*	Wood
	LWL:	10.21m/33'6
	LOA:	13.89m/45'7
	Beam:	4.06m/13'4
	Draft:	1.75m/5'9
	Displ:	14,528kg/32,000 lbs
	Ballast:	3,904kg/8,600 lbs

Fittings:	To specification
Interior:	Alternative layouts available
Sails:	Area 79.2m^2/853 sq.ft.
Rigging:	Clipper
Price Guide:	On application
Summary:	Strongly built. Dry and comfortable. Easily sailed.

BLUENOSE VESSEL 46

Design:	James D. Rosborough, Canada
Supplier:	James D. Rosborough, Canada

Specifications:

Construction:	Wood — oak
LWL:	10.74m/35'3
LOA:	13.92m/45'8
Beam:	4.04m/13'3
Draft:	1.80m/5'11
Displ:	21,356kg/47,040 lbs
Ballast:	5,448kg/12,000 lbs

Fittings: Black spruce woods. Perkins 85 hp diesel auxiliary. GRP deck.

Interior: 6—8 berths

Sails: Area 78m^2/840 sq.ft. (ketch)
Area 89.2m^2/960 sq.ft. (schooner)
Area 148.6m^2/1,600 sq.ft. (brigantine) Dacron.

Rigging: Ketch, schooner or brigantine.

Price Guide: $41,800

Summary: Traditional craftsmanship combined with modern design to give a real sea-going graceful vessel.

PRIVATEER

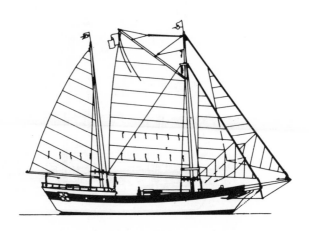

Design:	James D. Rosborough, Canada
Supplier:	James D. Rosborough, Canada

Specifications:

Construction:	Wood
LWL:	10.74m/35'3
LOA:	13.92m/45'8
Beam:	4.04m/13'3
Draft:	1.8m/5'11
Displ:	19,068kg/42,000 lbs
Ballast:	5,448kg/12,000 lbs

Fittings: Iron ballast. Fiberglassed wood deck. Wooden spars. 85 hp Perkins diesel.

Interior: 6–8 berths in 3 cabins. Stove. Sink. Fridge. 2 toilets.

Variations: Layout to specification

Sails: Area 78m^2(37.4 + 21.4 + 19.2)/840 sq.ft. (403 + 230 + 207)

Rigging: Ketch

Price Guide: $52,250us

Summary: Low cost, easy upkeep and constant resale value make this an excellent investment.

ERICSON 46

Design:	Bruce King, U.S.A. 1971
Supplier:	Ericson Yachts, U.S.A. Hamble Marine, U.K. Nordmarine, Italy
Est. Rating:	36.5′ IOR Mk II

Specifications:	*Construction:*	GRP
	LWL:	10.67m/35′0
	LOA:	13.97m/45′10
	Beam:	4.04m/13′3
	Draft:	2.19m/7′2
	Displ:	14,301kg/31,500 lbs
	Ballast:	7,419kg/16,500 lbs

Fittings:	GRP deck. Aluminium spars. Lead ballast. 40 hp Perkins 4.107 diesel engine.
Interior:	7—8 berths in 3 cabins
Sails:	Area 98.8m^2(40.3 + 58.5)/1,064 sq.ft. (434 + 630)
Rigging:	Sloop
Price Guide:	£ on application/$64,995us
Summary:	Has achieved brilliant racing successes since its first appearance.

BOWMAN 46

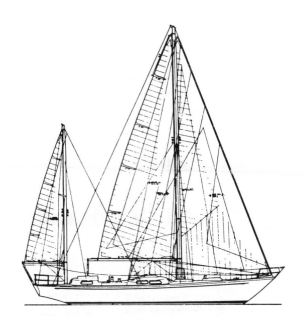

Design: Holman and Pye, England 1971

Supplier: Emsworth Marine Sales, England

Specifications:

Construction:	GRP	
LWL:	9.71m/31'10½	
LOA:	14.02m/46'0	
Beam:	3.95m/12'11½	
Draft:	2.13m—2.51m/7'0—8'3	
Displ:	10,669kg/23,500 lbs	
Ballast:	5,013.5kg/9,426 lbs	

Fittings: Fin keel or centre board boat. Mercedes OM636 42 hp inboard.

Interior: 8 berths

Sails: Area 77.1m^2/830 sq.ft.

Rigging: Sloop or yawl

Price Guide: £27,000

Summary: Mouldings available.

BEAUFORT 14

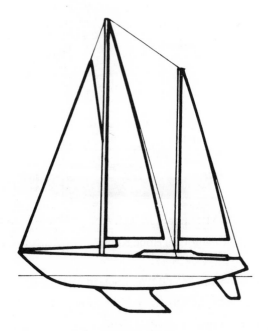

Design:	Jean-Jacques Herbelot, France 1973
Supplier:	Essor Naval du Midi, France

Specifications:

Construction:	GRP
LWL:	12.20m/40'0
LOA:	14.20m/46'7
Displ:	9,000kg/19,841 lbs
Ballast:	4,000kg/8,818 lbs

Fittings:	To specification
Interior:	To specification
Sails:	Area 100m^2/1,076 sq.ft.
Rigging:	Ketch
Price Guide:	269,370 Fr.f.

OFFSHORE 47

Design:	A. F. Luders Jr., U.S.A.
Supplier:	Cheoy Lee, Hong Kong Lion Yachts, U.S.A.
Est. Rating:	32.0' IOR Mk III

Specifications:

Construction:	GRP
LWL:	10.06m/33'0
LOA:	14.25m/46'9
Beam:	3.66m/12'0
Draft:	2.03m/6'8
Displ:	12,258kg/27,000 lbs
Ballast:	4,540kg/10,000 lbs

Fittings:	Lead ballast. GRP deck (teak overlay). Wood or aluminium spars. 50 hp Perkins 4.107 diesel.
Interior:	8 berths in 3 cabins. Sink. Icebox. 2 enclosed sea toilets.
Sails:	Area 92.7m^2 (35.7 + 43.1 + 13.9)/998 sq.ft. (384 + 464 + 150)
Rigging:	Ketch
Price Guide:	On application
Summary:	Built to very high standards. Finished in teak.

NICHOLSON 48

Design:	Camper & Nicholson, England 1971
Supplier:	Camper & Nicholsons, England Camper Nicholson, U.S.A.
Est. Rating:	29.7' IOR
Specifications:	*Construction:*

LWL:	10.16m/33'4
LOA:	14.53m/47'8
Beam:	3.94m/12'11
Draft:	1.68m/5'6
Displ:	14,237kg/31,360 lbs
Ballast:	5,085kg/11,200 lbs

Fittings:	Fin keel boat. Perkins inboard 72 hp
Interior:	7/8 berths
Sails:	Area 97.7m^2/1,052 sq.ft.
Rigging:	Ketch
Price Guide:	£47,300

RADIANT

Design:	Arthur Robb, England
Supplier:	Arthur Robb, England
Specifications:	*Construction:* Wood or steel
	LWL: 11.28m/37'0
	LOA: 14.53m/47'8
	Beam: 3.94m/12'11
	Draft: 2.32m/7'7½
	Displ: 16,526kg/36,400 lbs
Fittings:	50 hp diesel. Silver spruce spars. Lead keel.
Interior:	11 berths. 1.96m–1.85m/6'5–6'1 headroom.
Variations:	Numerous extras and fittings available
Sails:	Area 96m^2/1,033 sq.ft.
Rigging:	Ketch
Price Guide:	On application
Summary:	Powerful fast hull with flush decks and large deck-level cockpit. 640 miles range. Rig easily handled by two.

NORTH STAR 48

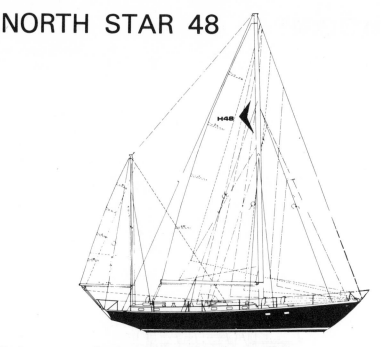

Design: Sparkman & Stephens, Canada 1970

Supplier: Northern Yachts, Canada

Specifications:

Construction:	GRP
LWL:	10.06m/33'0
LOA:	14.68m/48'2
Beam:	3.61m/11'10
Draft:	1.98m/6'6
Displ:	13,620kg/30,000 lbs
Ballast:	7,128kg/15,700 lbs

Fittings: Lead ballast. GRP deck. Aluminium spars. Westerbeke 4.107 diesel engine

Interior: 9 berths in 3 cabins. Galley standard: stove. 2 enclosed toilets. Shower. 2.03m/6'8 headroom.

Variations: Optional gasoline or diesel

Sails: Area 97.4m^2 (40.2 + 46.5 + 10.7)/1,048 sq.ft. (433 + 500 + 115)

Rigging: Ketch or yawl

Price Guide: $70,000us

Summary: All the comforts of a motor sailer along with an honest sailing performance. Excellent visibility. Great speed potential. Also known as **Hughes 48.**

VICTORY 48

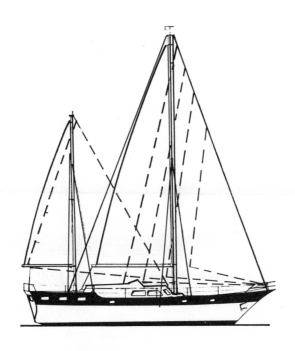

Design:	E. G. van de Stadt, Holland	
Supplier:	Tyler Boat Co. England	
Specifications:	*Construction:*	GRP
	LWL:	11m/36'1
	LOA:	14.71m/48'3
	Beam:	4.06m/13'4
	Draft:	1.68m/5'6
	Displ:	Optional
	Ballast:	Optional
Fittings:	Keelboat	
Interior:	7 berths. 1 enclosed toilet.	
Sails:	Area optional	
Rigging:	Ketch	
Price Guide:	On application	
Summary:	Also known as **Trintella V.**	

CASTLE 48

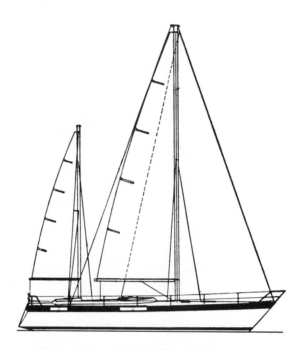

Design:	E. G. van de Stadt, Holland 1973
Supplier:	Castlemain Marine, U.K.
Specifications:	*Construction:* GRP
	LWL: 12.12m/39'8
	LOA: 14.85m/48'8
	Beam: 4.02m/13'2
	Draft: 2.00m/6'7
	Displ: 14,483kg/31,900 lbs
	Ballast: 5,993kg/13,200 lbs
Fittings:	Alloy spars. Diesel engine.
Interior:	8 berths. Plenty of storage space. 1.90m/6'3 head-room. 2 toilets and showers. Hot and cold water system.
Sails:	Area 114.7m^2/1,235 sq.ft.
Rigging:	Ketch. Stainless steel rigging.
Price Guide:	On application
Summary:	First class performance. Built in the Channel Islands.

AQUARIUS

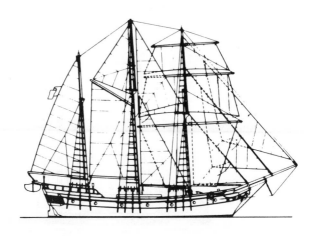

Design: James D. Rosborough, Canada 1971

Supplier: James D. Rosborough, Canada

Specifications:

Construction:	Wood	
LWL:	13.82m/45'4	
LOA:	15.34m/50'4	
Beam:	4.8m/15'9	
Draft:	1.91m/6'3	
Displ:	34,504kg/76,000 lbs	
Ballast:	7,264kg/16,000 lbs	

Fittings: Fiberglassed wood deck. Wooden spars. 130 hp Perkins diesel engine.

Interior: 12 berths in 6 cabins

Variations: Layout to individual requirements.

Sails: Area 218.3m^2/2,350 sq.ft.

Rigging: Brig or brigantine

Price Guide: $84,000us

Summary: Heavy and dependable. A real character boat that is very roomy.

S-51

Design:	John Brandymayer, U.S.A.	
Supplier:	Spencer Boats, U.S.A.	
Est. Rating:	40.0' IOR Mk III	
Specifications:	*Construction:*	GRP
	LWL:	11.43m/37'6
	LOA:	15,54m/51'0
	Beam:	4.01m/13'2
	Draft:	2.26m/7'5
	Displ:	13,620kg/30,000 lbs
	Ballast:	5,902kg/13,000 lbs
Fittings:	Lead ballast. GRP deck. Aluminium spars.	
Interior:	10 berths in 3 cabins. Galley. 2 enclosed toilets.	
Variations:	Optional gasoline auxiliary.	
Sails:	Area 98.9m^2/1,064 sq.ft.	
Rigging:	Optional	
Price Guide:	On application	

WHITE LADY 51

Design:	Henrik Aas, Norway	
Supplier:	Hogden Brothers, U.S.A.	
Specifications:	*Construction:*	GRP
	LWL:	12.09m/39'8
	LOA:	15.60m/51'2
	Beam:	4.01m/13'2
	Draft:	1.68m/5'6
	Displ:	18,160kg/40,000 lbs
	Ballast:	4,994kg/11,000 lbs
Fittings:	GRP deck with balsa core. Perkins 4.236 diesel engine.	
Interior:	7/8 berths. Enclosed toilet with shower. Galley — 2 sinks, stove, fridge/freezer.	
Sails:	Area 82.7m^2/890 sq.ft.	
Price Guide:	On application	

COLUMBIA 52

Design:	William H. Tripp Jnr, U.S.A. 1972
Supplier:	Columbia Yacht Corp., U.S.A.
Est. Rating:	41.3′ IOR Mk III
Specifications:	*Construction:* GRP
	LWL: 11.99m/39′4
	LOA: 15.85m/52′0
	Beam: 3.96m/13′0
	Draft: 2.44m/8′0
	Displ: 17,252kg/38,000 lbs
	Ballast: 9,307kg/20,500 lbs
Fittings:	GRP deck. Aluminium spars. 50 hp Perkins diesel auxiliary.
Interior:	Various layouts available
Variations:	Available as racer/cruiser model or with a flush deck.
Sails:	Area 111.9m^2/1,205 sq.ft.
Rigging:	Sloop
Price Guide:	$75,000us
Summary:	A very fast 52′0 with fine entry that enhances windward performance. Available through dealers.

SEADANCER 52

Design:	Maclear and Harris, U.S.A.
Supplier:	A. H. Moody & Son, England moulded by Halmatic, England
Specifications:	*Construction:* GRP *LWL:* 13.97m/45'10 *LOA:* 15.95m/52'4 *Beam:* 4.65m/15'3 *Draft:* 1.75m/5'9 *Displ:* 17,288kg/38,080 lbs
Fittings:	Teak deck
Interior:	8 berths in 4 cabins. Complete galley. 2 toilets with showers. Freshwater system.
Sails:	Various areas
Rigging:	Choice of rigs
Price Guide:	On application
Summary:	A luxury motor sailer designed for good performance whether under sail or power.

MORGAN CUSTOM 54

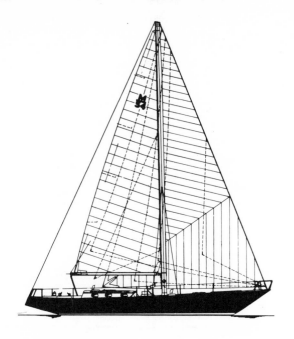

Design:	Charles E. Morgan Jnr, U.S.A. 1969
Supplier:	Morgan Yacht Corporation, U.S.A. Peter Webster Limited, England
Est. Rating:	41'2 IOR Mk III
Specifications:	*Construction:* GRP *LWL:* 11.35m/37'3 *LOA:* 16.38m/53'9 *Beam:* 3.81m/12'6 *Draft:* 2.33m or 1.73m/7'8 or 5'8 *Ballast:* 7,718kg/17,000 lbs
Fittings:	Lead ballast. GRP deck. Aluminium spars.
Interior:	9 berths in 3 cabins. Galley standard. 1 enclosed toilet.
Variations:	Keel or centreboard models available. Auxiliary: optional hp.
Sails:	Area 107.3m^2/1,155 sq.ft.
Rigging:	Sloop
Price Guide:	$75,000 to $79,000us

NICHOLSON 55

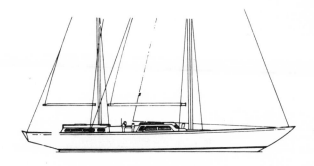

Design:	Camper & Nicholson, England 1973
Supplier:	Camper & Nicholsons, England Camper Nicholson, U.S.A.
Est. Rating:	40.1–40.5' IOR
Specifications:	*Construction:* GRP *LWL:* 11.94m/39'2 *LOA:* 16.59m/54'5 *Beam:* 4.37m/14'4 *Draft:* 2.51m/8'3 *Displ:* 17,288kg/38,080 lbs
Fittings:	Wood deck. Aluminium spars. Lead ballast.
Interior:	Custom built — up to 11 berths
Variations:	Optional diesel. 3 toilets optional
Sails:	Area 144.9m^2/1,560 sq.ft.
Rigging:	Sloop or yawl
Price Guide:	£65,000
Summary:	A pure racing version is also available. Can not be trailed.

ISLANDER 55

Design:	Bruce King, U.S.A.
Supplier:	Wayfarer Yacht Corporation, U.S.A.

Specifications:		
	Construction:	GRP
	LWL:	10.97m/36'0
	LOA:	16.66m/54'8
	Beam:	4.27m/14'0
	Draft:	1.75m/5'9
	Displ:	17,252kg/38,000 lbs
	Ballast:	7,264kg/16,000 lbs

Fittings:	Lead ballast. GRP deck. Aluminium spars. 85 hp auxiliary.
Interior:	10 berths in 4 cabins. Standard galley.
Sails:	Area 110m^2/1,184 sq.ft.
Rigging:	Sloop
Price Guide:	$9,450 for bare hull only.
Summary:	Supplied only in kit form. About the largest boat to be supplied in this fashion. Not a difficult boat to work on.

COLITALIA 56

Design:	Bill Tripp/Carlo Bertolotti, 1974	
Supplier:	Carl Ziegler Yacht Agency, England	
Specifications:	*Construction:*	GRP
	LWL:	12.8m/42'0
	LOA:	17m/55'7
	Beam:	3.96m/13'0
	Draft:	2.44m/8'0
	Displ:	20,980kg/47,000 lbs
	Ballast:	9,820kg/22,000 lbs.
Fittings:	Fin keel. 115 hp diesel Perkins.	
Interior:	8 berths	
Sails:	Area 118m^2/1,225 sq.ft.	
Rigging:	Ketch	
Price Guide:	$160,000us	
Summary:	An exceptionally stable and robust motor sailer. Roomy.	

MADAKET 55

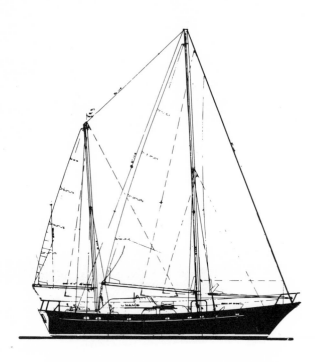

Design:	Steve Seaton, U.S.A.	
Supplier:	Buzzard Bay Boats, U.S.A.	
Specifications:	*Construction:*	GRP
	LWL:	13.11m/43'0
	LOA:	17.02m/55'10
	Beam:	4.57m/15'0
	Draft:	1.37m/4'6
Fittings:	Aluminium spars. Perkins 4.354 diesel engine.	
Interior:	Choice of interior layout. Stove. Fridge/freezer. Hot and cold system. 3 heads with showers.	
Sails:	Area 122. 2m^2/1,315 sq.ft.	
Rigging:	Ketch	
Price Guide:	$110,000us	

CALLISTO 17M

Design:	R. Thill, France, 1973	
Supplier:	Simac-Plaisance, France	
Specifications:	*Construction:*	GRP
	LWL:	12.80m/42'
	LOA:	17.28m/56'8½
	Beam:	4.42m/14'6
	Displ:	18,000kg/39,683 lbs
Fittings:	Teak trim	
Interior:	To specification	
Sails:	Area 168m^2/1,808 sq.ft.	
Rigging:	Ketch	
Price Guide:	On application	

TREEMTER

Design:	S. M. van der Meer, Holland
Supplier:	D. A. D. Munro, England
Specifications:	*Construction:* GRP
	LWL: 13.06m/42'10
	LOA: 17.4m/57'1
	Beam: 4.7m/15'6
	Draft: 1.9m/6'3
Interior:	Accommodation layout to specification
Sails:	Area 69.7m^2 (48.8 + 20.9)/750 sq.ft. (525 + 225)
Rigging:	Sloop
Price Guide:	On application

BEAUFORT 18

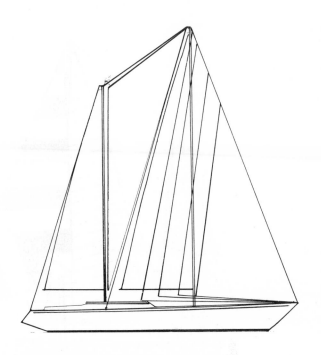

Supplier:	Essor Naval du Midi, France	
Specifications:	*Construction:*	GRP
	LWL:	14.60m/47'10¾
	LOA:	17.70m/58'1
	Beam:	4.92m/16'2
	Draft:	2.20m/7'2½
	Displ:	20,000kg/44,092 lbs
	Ballast:	7,000kg/15,432 lbs
Fittings:	To specification	
Interior:	8 berths	
Sails:	Area 150m^2/1,615 sq.ft.	
Rigging:	Ketch	
Price Guide:	456,000 Fr.f.	

BOOTHBAY CHALLENGER

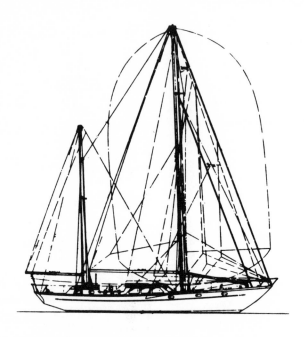

Design: John G. Alden, U.S.A. 1968

Supplier: John G. Alden, U.S.A.

Est. Rating: 42.0' IOR Mk III

Specifications:

Construction:	GRP
LWL:	12.5m/41'0
LOA:	17.85m/58'7
Beam:	4.62m/15'2
Draft:	1.62m/5'4 cb up
Displ:	26,332kg/58,000 lbs
Ballast:	5,221kg/11,500 lbs

Fittings: GRP deck. Aluminium spars. 130 hp Perkins 6.354 diesel engine.

Interior: 8 berths in 4 cabins

Sails: Area 144m^2(58.8 + 62.6)/1,550 sq.ft. (633 + 674)

Rigging: Sloop

Price Guide: $291,000us

VAGABOND

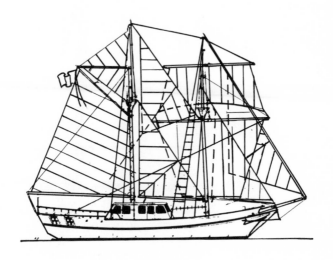

Design:	James D. Rosborough, Canada
Supplier:	James D. Rosborough, Canada
Specifications:	*Construction:* White oak
	LWL: 16m/52'6
	LOA: 19.66m/64'6
	Beam: 5.18m/17'0
	Draft: 2.19m/7'2
	Displ: 55,933kg/123,200 lbs
Fittings:	Choice of decking. Spruce spars.
Interior:	To individual specification
Sails:	Area 212m^2/2,282 sq.ft.
Rigging:	Rig to specification — brigantine
Price Guide:	$100,000us
Summary:	Very big but still easy to handle and maintain.

OCEAN 71

Design:	E. G. van de Stadt, Holland 1969
Supplier:	South Ocean Shipyard, England
Est. Rating:	70 tons Thames measurement 55.5' IOR
Specifications:	*Construction:* GRP
	LWL: 16.99m/55'9
	LOA: 21.64m/71'0
	Beam: 5.31m/17'5
	Draft: 2.44m/8'0
	Displ: 29,056kg/64,000 lbs
	Ballast: 9,307kg/20,500 lbs
Fittings:	Keelboard. Lead ballast. GRP deck. Perkins 115 hp diesel engine.
Interior:	12/15 berths. Galley. Washbasin. Chubb safe.
Variations:	Optional inboard power
Sails:	Area 200.8m^2/2,162 sq.ft. Spinnaker area 288m^2/3,100 sq.ft.
Rigging:	Ketch
Price Guide:	£125,000
Summary:	Cannot be trailed.

DISCOVERY

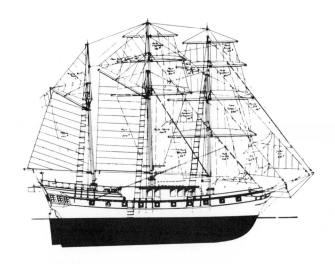

Design:	James D. Rosborough, Canada 1972
Supplier:	James D. Rosborough, Canada
Specifications:	*Construction:* Wood
	LWL: 21.84m/71'8
	LOA: 24.38m/80'0
	Beam: 6.5m/21'4
	Draft: 2.97m/9'9
	Displ: 81,720kg/180,000 lbs
	Ballast: 22,700kg/50,000 lbs
Fittings:	Fiberglassed wood. Wooden spars. 160 hp Perkins diesels (2)
Interior:	16 berths in 10 cabins
Sails:	Area 383.7m^2/4,130 sq.ft.
Rigging:	To specification
Price Guide:	$126,000us
Summary:	A very large boat that provides all the desired space for comfortable life at sea or in port.

RACERS/CRUISERS 40'+
multihulls

VICTRESS TRIMARAN

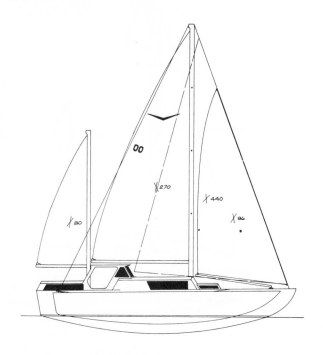

Design:	Arthur Piver, England
Supplier:	Contour Craft, England

Specifications:	*Construction:*	GRP plywood
	LWL:	11.43m/37'6
	LOA:	12.19m/40'0
	Beam:	6.71m/22'0
	Draft:	0.84m/2'9
	Displ:	3,305kg/3¼ tons

Fittings:	To specification
Interior:	5–9 berths. 1.96m/6'5 headroom.
Variations:	Optional inboard engine
Sails:	Area 41.4m^2/446 sq.ft.
Rigging:	Trimaran Bermudan ketch
Price Guide:	On application
Summary:	Sailing speed of 20 knots+.

SOLARIS 42

Design: Terence Compton, England 1971

Supplier: Solaris Marine, England
Symons Sailing Inc., U.S.A.

Specifications:

Construction:	GRP	
LWL:	11.28m/37'0	
LOA:	12.57m/41'3	
Beam:	5.41m/17'9	
Draft:	0.99m/3'3	
Displ:	7,627kg/16,800 lbs	

Fittings: Balsa core deck. 2 symmetrical hulls connected by a bridge deck. Aluminium spars. 84 hp twin Mercededs OM636 diesel.

Interior: 8 berths in 4 cabins

Sails: Area 60.9m^2/656 sq.ft.

Rigging: Ketch

Price Guide: £35,700/$78,000us

Summary: A cruising catamaran — well-established design.

TRIMAR 42 TRIMARAN

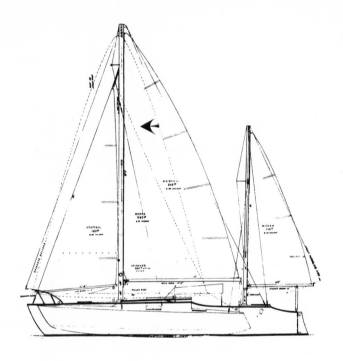

Design:	Louis Macouillard, England
Supplier:	Tri-Craft Ltd., England
Specifications:	*Construction:* GRP
	LWL: 12.19m/40'0
	LOA: 12.80m/42'0
	Beam: 6.40m/21'0
	Draft: 0.91m/3'0
	Displ: 3,305kg/3.25 tons
Fittings:	15 hp Westerbeke engine. Flush deck.
Interior:	8 berths. 1.93m^2/6'4 headroom
Sails:	Area 53.4m^2/575 sq.ft.
Rigging:	Bermudan ketch
Price Guide:	On application
Summary:	Designed with load carrying capacity in mind without detriment to performance. 25 knots under sail. Supplied comprehensively equipped.

SPINDRIFT 45

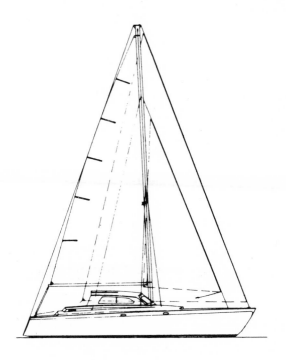

Design:	Lock Crowther, U.S.A. 1972	
Supplier:	International Marine Services, U.S.A.	
Specifications:	*Construction:*	GRP foam sandwich
	LWL:	12.04m/39'6
	LOA:	13.72m/45'0
	Beam:	7.01m/23'0
	Draft:	0.63m/2'1
Fittings:	2 symmetrical hulls connected by plywood beams. Aluminium spars. 40 hp outboard or twin 15 hp diesel.	
Interior:	6—11 berths in 5 cabins	
Sails:	Area 128m^2 (50 + 78)/1,378 sq.ft. (538 + 840)	
Rigging:	Sloop	
Price Guide:	$55,000us	
Summary:	A cruising catamaran. Available through dealers.	

CROSS 50

Design:	Norman A. Cross, U.S.A.
Supplier:	Norman A. Cross, U.S.A.
Specifications:	*Construction:* Wood
	LWL: 13.92m/45'8
	LOA: 15.16m/49'9
	Beam: 8.23m/27'0
	Draft: 1.42m/4'8
	Displ: 10,896kg/24,000 lbs
Fittings:	55 hp. Round bottomed, double diagonal ply hulls. Fin keel.
Interior:	10 berths. 1.91m/6'3 headroom.
Sails:	Area 83.6m²/900 sq.ft.
Rigging:	Ketch
Price Guide:	$20,000 approx. for home building
Summary:	Designed specifically for home completion.

SPINDRIFT 51

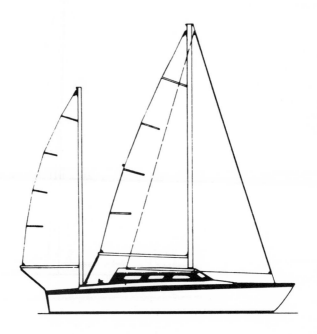

Design:	Lock Crowther, U.S.A. 1970
Supplier:	International Marine Services, U.S.A.

Specifications:	*Construction:*	GRP foam sandwich
	LWL:	13.72m/45'0
	LOA:	15.54m/51'0
	Beam:	7.32m/24'0
	Draft:	0.69m/2'3

Fittings:	2 symmetrical hulls connected by plywood/wood beams. Aluminium spars. 50 hp optional diesel.
Interior:	8–10 berths in 6 cabins
Sails:	Area 157.9m^2 (47.4 + 88.2 + 22.3)/1,700 sq.ft. (510 + 950 + 240)
Rigging:	Ketch
Price Guide:	$70,000us
Summary:	A cruising catamaran. Available through dealers.

DINGHIES ALSO AVAILABLE

NAME	LOA	SUPPLIER
A LION	5.49m	McNair Marine, U.S.A.
ALPHA Mk II	—	Bossoms Boatyard, England
B LION	6.1m	McNair Marine, U.S.A.
BUCKEYE	3.86m	William Mychenberg, U.S.A.
CATFISH	4.01m	D. Bruce Connolly, U.S.A.
COLUMBIA 21	6.6m	Columbia Yacht Corporation, U.S.A.
DYER DHOW 7'11	2.42m	The Anchorage Inc., U.S.A.
EVERSON 12	3.66m	Everson and Sons, England
EVERSON 14	4.27m	Everson and Sons, England
EXPLORER	5.18m	Talman Bigelow, U.S.A.
FALCON	4.77m	McVay Fibreglass Yachts, Canada
GEMINI	3.96m	Stoneham Shaw, England
GRANTA LEAF	2.9m	Granta Boats, England
GRANTA THD	2.59m	Granta Boats, England
JACKSNIPE	4.72m	Jack Holt, England
JOLLY ROGER	2.54m	Lincoln Fibreglass Co., U.S.A.
KADET	3.4m	Sailing Dynamics, U.S.A.
KORALLE JNR	3.61m	Koralle/East Inc., U.S.A.
LEHMAN 12	3.66m	W. D. Schock Co., U.S.A.
MAC 17	5.05m	J. M. McClintock & Co., U.S.A.
MACH 11	4.22m	Snark Products Inc., U.S.A.
MARLOW 12	3.66m	J. G. Meakes, England

NAME	LOA	SUPPLIER
MAYFLOWER 14	4.27m	K. R. Skentlebury, England
MAYLAND RAMBLER	4.19m	Popular Boats, England
MERMAID Mk II	3.35m	Roger Hancock, England
MINUET	5.59m	McVay Fibreglass Yachts, Canada
MISSILE	4.27m	Snyder and Ellenbest, U.S.A.
MOBJACK	5.18m	Nautical Boat Works, U.S.A.
NEWPORT 21	6.25m	Newport Boats, U.S.A.
NORD 12	3.66m	Nordex Boats, U.S.A.
NORDEX HAWK	3.66m	Nordex Boats, U.S.A.
OSPRAY	4.77m	O'Day Co., U.S.A.
PIONEER	2.84m	Polycell Prout, England
PIONEER	5.18m	Talman Bigelow, U.S.A.
POOLE SPRAT	2.59m	Latham and Son, England
PRETTYCRAFT 9	2.74m	Prettycraft Plastics, England
RAINBOW	7.37m	Annapolis Boat Rentals, U.S.A.
REDHEAD	5.26m	Barron Sailboat Distributors, U.S.A.
S-14	4.27m	Alumacraft Boat Co., U.S.A.
SAGA BATSMAN	4.27m	J. G. Meakes, England
SCAMP	3.71m	Scamp Association, U.S.A.
SCAMPER 60	3.35m	Formex Corporation, U.S.A.
C SCOW	6.1m	ILYA, U.S.A.
D SCOW	6.1m	Johnson Boat Works, U.S.A.
E SCOW	8.53m	E Scow Association, U. S.A.
M SCOW	4.88m	M Scow Association, U.S.A.
W SCOW	4.27m	W Scow Association, U.S.A.

NAME	LOA	SUPPLIER
SEAL	2.9m	American Fiberglass Corp, U.S.A.
SEA PUPPY	2.44m	Aero-Nautical Inc., U.S.A.
SHARK V	4.22m	Shark V World Association, England
SHELDUCK	4.88m	Southbrook Marine, England
SHETLANDER	4.27m	Small Craft, England
SILEX	2.21m	Comextra, England
SPRITE	3.01m	O'Day Co., U.S.A.
S.S.	5.03m	Hampton Shipyards, U.S.A.
SUPER SWIFT	3.66m	O'Day Co., U.S.A.
SURFSAILER	4.22m	Ray Greene & Co. Inc., U.S.A.
SWIFT	3.15m	O'Day Co., U.S.A.
TAHOE 10	3.05m	HMS Marine, U.S.A.
TEPCO 12	3.71m	Essex Plastics Co., England
THRIAL	9.14m	Tyler Boat Co., England
THUNDERBIRD PRAM	2.3m	Snug Harbour Boat Works, U.S.A.
TIGER CAT	5.18m	Pearson Yachts, U.S.A.
TOM THUMB	2.44m	Morgan Fairest, England
TORCH	3.96m	A. P. Broomfield, England
TV 50 DINGHY	3,43m	TV Times, England
TWERP catamaran	2.33m	Bill Shipsides (Marine), England
TYPHOON	4.42m	R. Moore and Sons, England
VIKING 140	4.27m	Viking of America, U.S.A.
WATERCAT 10	3.05m	McNabb Rongier (Devs.), England

NAME	LOA	SUPPLIER
WATERCAT 12	3.66m	McNabb Rongier (Devs.), England
WOOTTON O.D.	3.96m	John Fulford, England
WULFRUN 9	2.74m	Leisurecraft Marine, England
WULFRUN CUB	2.13m	Leisurecraft Marine, England

ALSO AVAILABLE 20-30'

LOA	BEAM	DRAFT	SAIL AREA	BERTHS	PRICE

COLUMBIA 22 — Columbia Yacht Corporation, U.S.A.

LOA	BEAM	DRAFT	SAIL AREA	BERTHS	PRICE
6.71m/22'0	2.36m/7'9	0.97m/3'2	21.6m^2/232sq.ft	4	o/a

WESTERLY WARWICK — Westerly Marine, England

LOA	BEAM	DRAFT	SAIL AREA	BERTHS	PRICE
6.55m/21'6	2.36m/7'9	0.84m/2'9	19.5m^2/210sq.ft	4	$8900us

WESTERLY 22 — Westerly Marine Construction, England

LOA	BEAM	DRAFT	SAIL AREA	BERTHS	PRICE
6.55m/21'6	2.26m/7'5	0.84m/2'9	19.5m^2/210sq.ft	4	o/a

CAL 21 — Jensen Marine, U.S.A.

LOA	BEAM	DRAFT	SAIL AREA	BERTHS	PRICE
6.25m/20'6	2.03m/6'8	1.3m/4'3	18.2m^2/196sq.ft	4	$3700us

CRYSTAL — Stebbings (Burnham) Ltd., England

LOA	BEAM	DRAFT	SAIL AREA	BERTHS	PRICE
6.81m/22'4	2.29m/7'6	1.07m/3'6	20.9m^2/225sq.ft	4	o/a

MORGAN 22 — Morgan Yacht Corp., U.S.A. / Peter Webster Ltd., England

LOA	BEAM	DRAFT	SAIL AREA	BERTHS	PRICE
6.86m/22'6	2.44m/8'0	0.56m/1'10	22.1m^2/238sq.ft	4	$4500

PACESHIP 23 — Paceship Yachts, Canada

LOA	BEAM	DRAFT	SAIL AREA	BERTHS	PRICE
6.93m/22'9	2.29m/7'6	1.07m/3'6	20.9m^2/225sq.ft	3	o/a

MAGNIFIK 23 — Juxtamare Marine, England

LOA	BEAM	DRAFT	SAIL AREA	BERTHS	PRICE
6.99m/22'11	—	0.97m/3'2	17m^2/183sq.ft	4	o/a

HURLEY 23 — Hurley Marine, U.S.A. / Hurley Marine, England

LOA	BEAM	DRAFT	SAIL AREA	BERTHS	PRICE
7.01m/23'0	2.33m/7'8	0.91m/3'0	15.6m^2/168sq.ft	4	o/a

LOA	BEAM	DRAFT	SAIL AREA	BERTHS	PRICE

JAGUAR 23/PUMA 23 — Jaguar Yachts, England

LOA	BEAM	DRAFT	SAIL AREA	BERTHS	PRICE
7.01m/23'0	2.29m/7'6	1.14m/3'9	19.2m^2/207sq.ft	–	o/a

SAN CLEMENTE 23 — South Coast Seacraft, U.S.A.

LOA	BEAM	DRAFT	SAIL AREA	BERTHS	PRICE
7.01m/23'0	2.44m/8'0	1.17m/3'10	21.5m^2/231sq.ft	5	o/a

SPARTAN — Harry King & Sons, England

LOA	BEAM	DRAFT	SAIL AREA	BERTHS	PRICE
7.06m/23'2	1.98m/6'6	1.22m/4'0	22.8m^2/245sq.ft	4	o/a

TUCKER 23 — R. Sinclair, England

LOA	BEAM	DRAFT	SAIL AREA	BERTHS	PRICE
7.06m/23'2	–	0.76m/2'6	19.5m^2/210sq.ft	4	o/a

COMPROMIS 720 — Jachtwerf Zaadnoordijk bv, Holland

LOA	BEAM	DRAFT	SAIL AREA	BERTHS	PRICE
7.20m/23'7½	–	–	Various	–	19,800fl

HUSKY 24 — Yachthaven Ltd., England

LOA	BEAM	DRAFT	SAIL AREA	BERTHS	PRICE
7.32m/24'0	2.59m/8'6	0.61m/2'0	16.4m^2/176sq.ft	4	o/a

IRWIN 24 — Irwin Yacht & Marine Corporation, U.S.A.

LOA	BEAM	DRAFT	SAIL AREA	BERTHS	PRICE
7.32m/24'0	2.44m/8'0	1.07m/3'6	25.5m^2/275sq.ft	4	o/a

SIANI — Theo Smith & Co., England

LOA	BEAM	DRAFT	SAIL AREA	BERTHS	PRICE
7.32m/24'0	–	1.14m/3'9	16.7m^2/180sq.ft	4	o/a

JOG CAPRICA — Comextra, England

LOA	BEAM	DRAFT	SAIL AREA	BERTHS	PRICE
7.45m/24'5	–	1.22m/4'0	24.2m^2/260sq.ft	5	o/a

HELMS 25 — Jack A. Helms, U.S.A.

LOA	BEAM	DRAFT	SAIL AREA	BERTHS	PRICE
7.60m/24'11	2.44m/8'0	0.51m/1'8	21.9m^2/236sq.ft	5	$7000us

LOA	BEAM	DRAFT	SAIL AREA	BERTHS	PRICE

ANNA POLIS 25

Tidewater Boats, U.S.A.

7.62m/25'0	1.96m/6'5	1.07m/3'6	$20.9m^2$/225sq.ft	4	o/a

FURZEY 25

Latham & Son, England

7.62m/25'0	—	—	$32.5m^2$/350sq.ft	4	o/a

MORGAN 25

Morgan Yacht Corp.
Peter Webster Ltd., England

7.62m/25'0	2.44m/8'0	0.84m/2'9	$28.8m^2$/310sq.ft	5	$7500us

VERSATILITY

Rye Yacht Centre, England

7.62m/25'0	—	0.91m/3'0	Various	4	o/a

WESTERLY WINDRUSH

Westerly Marine, England
Andrew Gemeney, U.S.A.

7.64m/25'1	2.26m/7'5	0.76m/2'6	$25.6m^2$/276sq.ft	4	o/a

LB 26

Limhamms Batindustri AB, Sweden
A. H. Moody & Sons, England

7.80m/25'7	2.85m/9'4	0.85m/2'9½	Various	—	o/a

SHANNON catamaran

O'Brien & Spencer Ltd., England

8.00m/26'3	4.5m/14'9	0.68m/2'3	$40m^2$/431sq.ft	—	o/a

STELLA

Tucker Brown & Co., England

7.85m/25'9	2.29m/7'6	1.17m/3'10	$31.4m^2$/338sq.ft	—	o/a

SPINNER Mk III

Henderson Pumps & Equipment Ltd.,
England

8.33m/27'4	2.97m/9'9	1.42m/4'8	$39m^2$/420sq.ft	6	o/a

	LOA	BEAM	DRAFT	SAIL AREA	BERTHS	PRICE

CAL 27 Jensen Marine, U.S.A.

| 8.36m/27'5 | 2.74m/9'0 | 1.37m/4'6 | 32.5m^2/350sq.ft | 5 | $11350us |

BORDER REIVER Eyemouth Boatbuilding Company, U.K.

| 8.53m/28'0 | — | 0.76m/2'6 | 5.57m^2/60sq.ft | 4 | o/a |

MACWESTER 28 Macwester Marine, England

| 8.61m/28'3 | — | 1.42m/4'8 | 30.7m^2/330sq.ft | 5 | £6200 |

IRWIN 28 Irwin Yacht & Marine Corp., U.S.A.

| 8.67m/28'5 | 2.44m/8'0 | 1.37m/4'6
0.91m/3'0 | 36.6m^2/394sq.ft | 5 | $13750us |

RANGER De Visser Boatyard Hammonds & Oakwood, England

| 8.72m/28'6 | 2.44m/8'0 | 1.22m/4'0 | 31m^2/334sq.ft | 4 | o/a |

FURZEY 29 Latham & Son Ltd., England

| 8.84m/29'0 | — | — | 37.2m^2/400sq.ft | 5 | £7500 |

SAPPHIRE Mk II Tri. Simpson Marine, England

| 9.07m/29'9 | 6.71m/22'0 | 0.66m/2'2 | 46.5m^2/500sq.ft | — | o/a |

AQUA 30 Aqua Fibre International, England

| 9.12m/29'11 | — | — | 33.5m^2/361sq.ft | 5 | o/a |

ALSO AVAILABLE 30-40'

LOA	BEAM	DRAFT	SAIL AREA	BERTHS	PRICE

OCEAN BIRD TRIMARAN — Honnor Marine, England

9.14m/30'0	7.01m/23'0	0.66m/2'2	48.3m^2/520sq.ft	5	£11,000

PRIOR 30 — R. J. Prior & Son, England

9.14m/30'0	—	1.52m/5'0	36.4m^2/392sq.ft	5	o/a

SONATA — Ryton Engineering Co., England

9.14m/30'0	—	1.75m/5'9	37.2m^2/400sq.ft	5	o/a

TRIFORM SERIES — Erick J. Manners, England

9.14m/30'	5.79m/19'	0.51m/20'	30m^2/323sq.ft	6	o/a

ARISTOCAT 30 — Ocean Catamarans, U.S.A. / Transcat Marine, England

9.3m/30'6	4.27m/14'0	0.43m/1'5	46m^2/495sq.ft	7	£10,175

MACWESTER 30 auxiliary sloop — Macwester Marine, England

9.3m/30'6	2.87m/9'5	0.99m/3'3	35.3m^2/380sq.ft	6	o/a

BROWN 31' TRI — Border Marine, U.K.

9.45m/31'0	—	—	Various	4	o/a

9 METER MS — Hurley Marine, England

9.45m/31'0	—	1.14m/3'9	21m^2/226sq.ft	6	o/a

MISS SILVER — James A. Silver, England

9.45m/31'0	—	1.17m/3'10	27.9m^2/300 sq.ft	6	o/a

RANGER 31 CATAMARAN — G. Prout & Sons Ltd., England

9.45m/31'0	—	0.58m/1'10	29.3m^2/315sq.ft	4/6	o/a

LOA	BEAM	DRAFT	SAIL AREA	BERTHS	PRICE

TORNADO 31 — Playvisa Coronada Yachts, England

LOA	BEAM	DRAFT	SAIL AREA	BERTHS	PRICE
9.45m/31'0	—	—	Various	—	o/a

VENTURE 31 — Torbay Boat Construction, England

LOA	BEAM	DRAFT	SAIL AREA	BERTHS	PRICE
9.45m/31'0	—	1.35m/4'5	40.7m^2/438sq.ft	5	o/a

WESTERLY 31 — Westerly Marine Construction, England

LOA	BEAM	DRAFT	SAIL AREA	BERTHS	PRICE
9.45m/31'0	—	1.22m/4'0	41.1m^2/442sq.ft	6	o/a

SOVEREIGN — Uphams of Brixham, England

LOA	BEAM	DRAFT	SAIL AREA	BERTHS	PRICE
9.60m/31'6	2.87m/9'5	1.32m/4'4	24.3m^2/262sq.ft	4/5	o/a

WIGHT CLASS — Macwester Marine, England

LOA	BEAM	DRAFT	SAIL AREA	BERTHS	PRICE
9.60m/31'6	2.94m/9'8	1.01m/3'4	36.2m^2/390sq.ft	—	o/a

GREEN HIGHLANDER — Illingworth & Associates, England

LOA	BEAM	DRAFT	SAIL AREA	BERTHS	PRICE
9.65m/31'8	—	1.78m/5'10	Optional	6/8	o/a

ATLANTA 32 — Atlanta Marine, England

LOA	BEAM	DRAFT	SAIL AREA	BERTHS	PRICE
9.75m/32'0	3.05m/10'0	1.22m/4'0	44.6m^2/480sq.ft	5	£9,500

ANASTASIA — Bruce Bingham, U.S.A.

LOA	BEAM	DRAFT	SAIL AREA	BERTHS	PRICE
9.75m/32'0	3.35m/11'0	1.4m/4'7	58.5m^2/630sq.ft	4	plans $5.00

CAPE 32 — Cape Yachts, Hong Kong

LOA	BEAM	DRAFT	SAIL AREA	BERTHS	PRICE
9.75m/32'0	2.82m/9'3	1.42m/4'8	47.5m^2/511sq.ft	5	o/a

CONTESSA 32 — J. J. Taylor & Sons, Canada
J. C. Rogers, England

LOA	BEAM	DRAFT	SAIL AREA	BERTHS	PRICE
9.75m/32'0	2.90m/9'6	1.65m/5'6	52.2m^2/562sq.ft	6	£8,000

LOA	BEAM	DRAFT	SAIL AREA	BERTHS	PRICE

HORIZON David Simmonds, England

| 9.75m/32'0 | 3.2m/10'6 | 1.3m/4'3 | 31.8m^2/342sq.ft | — | o/a |

INCHCAPE 32' Eyemouth Boat Building Co., England

| 9.75m/32'0 | — | 0.91m/3'0 | 29.7m^2/320sq.ft | 4/6 | o/a |

NEPTUNE Johnson, Sons & Jago Ltd., England

| 9.98m/32'0 | 3.05m/10'0 | 1.22m/4'0 | | 5 | £15,000 |

NORTH AMERICAN 32 North American Fiberglass Mldg. Ltd., U.S.A.

| 9.75m/32'0 | 2.84m/9'4 | 1.42m/4'8 | 42.7m^2/460sq.ft | 5 | $25,000 |

PIONEER 10 METRE South Ocean Shipyard, England

| 9.75m/32'0 | 3m/9'10 | 1.8m/5'11 | 37.2m^2/400sq.ft | 4/5 | £9,800 |

SOVEREIGN 32 J. W. & A. Upham Ltd., England

| 9.7m/32'0 | 3.2m/10'6 | 1.5m/5'0 | 35.1m^2/420sq.ft | 4/5 | £15,000 |

L 32 Klaus Baess, Denmark

| 9.83m/32'3 | 2.87m/9'5 | 1.45m/4'9 | 46.5m^2/500sq.ft | 5 | o/a |

FALKLAND K. R. Skentlebury & Son Ltd., England

| 9.91m/32'6 | 3.15m/10'4 | 1.42m/4'9 | 37.35m^2/402sq.ft | — | £14,700 |

ISLANDER 32 Wayfarer Yacht Corp., U.S.A.

| 9.91m/32'6 | 3.05m/10'0 | 1.37m/4'6 | 44.2m^2/476sq.ft | 6 | $18,800us |

LOA	BEAM	DRAFT	SAIL AREA	BERTHS	PRICE

ROGGER

Eista Werf bv, Holland
Stangate Marine, England

LOA	BEAM	DRAFT	SAIL AREA	BERTHS	PRICE
9.91m/32'6	3.45m/11'4	1.22m/4'0	37.2m^2/400sq.ft	—	£18,000

RENOWN WESTERLY

Westerly Marine Construction,
England
Andrew Gemeney & Sons, U.S.A.

LOA	BEAM	DRAFT	SAIL AREA	BERTHS	PRICE
9.91m/32'6	2.9m/9'6	1.37m/4'6	40.9m^2/440sq.ft	6	£8,300

CARTER 33 ½ TON

Carter Offshore Inc., U.S.A.
Carter Offshore Ltd., England

LOA	BEAM	DRAFT	SAIL AREA	BERTHS	PRICE
9.93m/32'7	3.35m/11'0	1.68m/5'6	37.62m^2/405sq.ft	7	£12,500

VAGABOND

Fibocon, Holland

LOA	BEAM	DRAFT	SAIL AREA	BERTHS	PRICE
9.97m/32'8½	3.15m/10'4	1.48m/4'10	36.25m^2/390sq.ft	7	o/a

KING'S AMETYST

Gdanska Stocznia Jachtowa Gdansk,
Poland
Tubornet Ltd., England

LOA	BEAM	DRAFT	SAIL AREA	BERTHS	PRICE
9.98m/32'9	2.59m/8'6	1.68m/5'6	41.4m^2/446sq.ft	5	o/a

SEACRACKER 8 TON

Tyler Boat Co., England

LOA	BEAM	DRAFT	SAIL AREA	BERTHS	PRICE
10.01m/32'10	2.8m/9'2	1.4m/4'7	—	5/6	o/a

TRINTELLA 11A

Jachtwerf Anne Wever NV, Holland
Stangate Marine, England

LOA	BEAM	DRAFT	SAIL AREA	BERTHS	PRICE
10.01m/32'10	2.80m/9'2	1.41m/4'8	37.9m^2/408sq.ft	6	o/a

CHALLENGER 32

Challenger Yacht Corp., U.S.A.

LOA	BEAM	DRAFT	SAIL AREA	BERTHS	PRICE
10.03m/32'11	3.4m/11'2	1.47m/4'10	42.7m^2/460sq.ft	6	$23,500us

LOA	BEAM	DRAFT	SAIL AREA	BERTHS	PRICE

CHANCE 29 — 1 TON   Paceship Yachts, Canada

| 10.03m/32'11 | 2.84m/9'4 | 2.06m/6'9 | 49.3m^2/531sq.ft | 6 | $22,250us |

CLIPPER 33   Cheoy Lee, Hong Kong
Lion Yachts, U.S.A.

| 10.03m/32'11 | 3.05m/10'0 | 1.22m/4'0 | 52.8m^2/568sq.ft | 6 | o/a |

GREYHOUND 33   Doornbos, Holland
Ambena Nantik GmbH, Germany

| 10.05m/32'11½ | 3.20m/10'6 | 1.70m/5'7 | 56.3m^2/606sq.ft | 5 | 66,340 DM. |

CONTEST 33   Conyplex NV, Holland
Holland Yachts Inc., U.S.A.
Interyacht, England

| 10.06m/33'0 | 3.15m/10'4 | 1.6m/5'3 | 40.6m^2/437sq.ft | 6 | £11,100 |

DEB 33   Deacons Boatyard Ltd., England
Tyler Boat Co., England

| 10.05m/33'0 | 3.33m/10'11 | 1.09m/3'7 | 60.39m^2/650sq.ft | 6 | o/a |

FANDANGO 33   Arcoa-Jouet S.A., France
Comextra, England

| 10.06m/33'0 | 3.15m/10'4 | 1.7m/5'7 | 42.7m^2/460sq.ft | 7 | 12,700 Fr.f. |

FJORD MS 33   A/S Fjord Plast, Norway
Eastwood Yacht Co., England
Fjord Boats, U.S.A.

| 10.03m/33'0 | 3.21m/10'6½ | 1.35m/4'5 | 39.9m^2/430sq.ft | 6 | £12,000 |

ISIS   Bridge Boats, England

| 10.06m/33'0 | — | 1.22m/4'0 | 37.2m^2/400sq.ft | 4/7 | o/a |

LOA	BEAM	DRAFT	SAIL AREA	BERTHS	PRICE

K-33 TRI Derek Kelsall Limited, England

| 10.06m/33'0 | – | 0.61m/2'0 | 46.5m²/500sq.ft | 6 | o/a |

LUDERS 33 Cheoy Lee, Hong Kong
Allied Boat Co., Inc., U.S.A.

| 10.06m/33'0 | 3.05m/10'0 | 1.52m/5'0 | 49.1m²/529sq.ft | 6 | $25,995us |

NAUTICAL 33 Emsworth Marine Sales, England

| 10.06m/33'0 | – | 1.27m/4'2 | 30.7m²/330sq.ft | 6 | o/a |

NEPTUNIAN MOTOR SAILER
Johnson & Jago, England

| 10.06m/33'0 | 3.05m/10'0 | 1.22m/4'0 | 36.2m²/390sq.ft | 4 | £15,000 |

NORDFARER 33 Dell Quay Sales, England

| 10.06m/33'0 | 3.05/10'0 | 1.4m/4'7 | 35.9m²/386sq.ft | – | o/a |

OFFSHOREMAN Peel Engineering Co., Isle of Man

| 10.06m/33'0 | – | 1.45m/4'9 | 41.8m²/450sq.ft | 5/7 | o/a |

PELAGIAN 33 C. S. J. Roy, England

| 10.06m/33'0 | 2.9m/9'6 | 1.75m/5'9 | 33.4m²/360sq.ft | 6 | £13,600 |

TAVANA Glander Boats Inc., U.S.A.

| 10.06m/33'0 | 3.05m/10'0 | 0.91m/3'0 | 51.37m²/553sq.ft | 6 | o/a |

TAVOY Benson Cruiser Station, England

| 10.06m/33'0 | – | 1.22m/4'0 | Optional | 6 | o/a |

UNIVERSAL Universal Shipyards (Solent),
England

| 10.06m/33'0 | – | – | Various | – | o/a |

1156

LOA	BEAM	DRAFT	SAIL AREA	BERTHS	PRICE

NAUTICAT 33　　　　　　　Siltala Yachts, Finland
Thames Nelson Yacht Agency,
England

| 10.1m/33'2 | 3.26m/10'8 | 1.25m/4'1 | 42m^2/452sq.ft | 4 | £15,500 |

CAPE　　　　　　　Mariner's Boatyard, England

| 10.16m/33'4 | 3.05m/10'0 | 1.42m/4'8 | 44.68m^2/481sq.ft | 5 | o/a |

SPAULDING 33　　　　　　　Spaulding 33 Association, U.S.A.

| 10.16m/33'4 | 2.743m/9'0 | 1.65m/5'5 | 40.88m^2/440sq.ft | 6 | o/a |

ROB　　　　　　　Saaman Yachtbuilders, Holland
Durrels Boat Agency, England

| 10.20m/33'5 | 3.30m/10'10 | 1.50m/4'11 | 48.30m^2/532sq.ft | 6 | £13,000 |

33' NORSEMAN　　　　　　　Aberdour Marine, Scotland

| 10.21m/33'6 | — | 1.37m/4'6 | 31.6m^2/340sq.ft | 4/5 | o/a |

DUFOUR 34　　　　　　　Michel Dufour, France
Michel Dufour, U.S.A.
Carl Ziegler Yacht Agency, U.K.

| 10.25m/33'7 | 3.28m/10'9 | 1.78m/5'10 | 54.10m^2/582sq.ft | 6 | £17,400 |

PALMER JOHNSON 34　　　　Palmer Johnson Inc., U.S.A.

| 10.24m/33'7 | 3.07m/10'1 | 1.78m/5'10 | 44.9m^2/483sq.ft | 7 | $32,500us |

S & S 34　　　　　　　Hurrell and Johnson Ltd., England

| 10.24m/33'7 | — | 1.80m/5'11 | 44.8m^2/482sq.ft | 7 | o/a |

LOA	BEAM	DRAFT	SAIL AREA	BERTHS	PRICE

SINGOALLA

Albin Marine, Sweden
Albin Marine, England
Larsson Yachts, U.S.A.

| 10.26m/33'8 | 3.30m/10'10 | 1.56m/5'2 | 55.74m²/600sq.ft | 8 | o/a |

SEAFARER 34

Seafarer Fiberglass Yachts, U.S.A.

| 10.29m/33'9 | 3.05m/10'0 | 1.14m/3'9 | 49.14m²/529sq.ft | 4/6 | $18,000us |

TARTAN 34

Sparkman & Stephens, U.S.A.
Tartan Marine Co., U.S.A.

| 10.36m/34'0 | 3.10m/10'2 | 2.54m/8'4 | 47.01m²/506sq.ft | 6 | $24,000us |

H/50

Whisstocks Boatyard, England

| 10.44m/34'3 | — | 1.52m/5'0 | 43.2m²/465sq.ft | 6 | o/a |

GAMBLING 34

KMV Kristiansand, Norway
Knoxmore Bagley, England

| 10.46m/34'4 | 3.10m/10'2 | 1.8m/5'11 | 53m²/570sq.ft | 6 | £17,200 |

SAGITTA

Bianca Yacht A/S, Denmark

| 10.52m/34'6 | 3.05m/10'0 | 1.83m/6'0 | | 6 | 224,000d.kr |

SHE D35

South Hants Marine, England

| 10.52m/34'6 | 3.05m/10'0 | 1.83m/6'0 | 41.81m²/450sq.ft | 6 | £17,600 |

SEABREEZE 35

Allied Boat Co. Inc., U.S.A.

| 10.52m/34'6 | 3.12m/10'3 | 1.17m/3'10 | 51.1m²/550sq.ft | 6 | $28,000us+ |

ALC 35

A. Le Comte Co., Holland
A. Le Comte Co., U.S.A.

| 10.54m/34'7 | 3.05m/10'0 | 1.68m/5'6 | 45.1m²/485sq.ft | 6/8 | o/a |

LOA	BEAM	DRAFT	SAIL AREA	BERTHS	PRICE

C&C 35 C & C Yachts Manufacturing, Canada
Anstey Yachts, England

| 10.54m/34'7 | 3.22m/10'7 | 1.6m/5'3 | 53.51m²/576sq.ft | 6 | $24,450us |

ELIZABETHAN 35 Peter Webster Ltd., England

| 10.54m/34'7 | 2.77m/9'1 | 1.78m/5'10 | 37.62m²/405sq.ft | 6 | £12,000 |

FAIRWIND F. A. Gebr Maas, Holland

| 10.59m/34'9 | 2.97m/9'9 | 1.75m/5'9 | 40.3m²/434sq.ft | 4/5 | o/a |

RAIDER Carl Ziegler Yacht Agency, England

| 10.64m/34'11 | — | 1.8m/5'11 | 36.5m²/393sq.ft | 6 | o/a |

BORDER MINSTRAL Eyemouth Boatbuilding Co., U.K.

| 10.67m/35'0 | — | 0.91m/3'0 | 29.7m²/320sq.ft | 4/6 | o/a |

FINNSAILER 35 Turun Veneveistämo, Finland
Ballena Marine, England

| 10.67m/35'0 | 3.15m/10'3 | 1.12m/3'8 | 33.4m²/360sq.ft | 7 | £15,800 |

HUSTLER 35 E. C. Landamore & Co. Ltd., England
Island Boat Sales, England

| 10.67m/35' | 3.22m/10'7 | 1.83m/6'0 | 44.8m²/482sq.ft | 6/7 | o/a |

MORGAN 35 Morgan Yacht Corp., U.S.A.
Peter Webster Ltd., England

| 10.67m/35'0 | 3.28m/10'9 | 1.3m/4'3 | 50.6m²/545sq.ft | 6 | $19,000 |

NAB 35 Reg Freeman (Yachts), England

| 10.67m/35'0 | 3.05m/10'0 | 1.37m/4'6 | 43.7m²/470sq.ft | 6 | £19,600 |

LOA	BEAM	DRAFT	SAIL AREA	BERTHS	PRICE

NORDIA 35 — Trewes International, England

| 10.67m/35'0 | — | 1.4m/4'7 | Various | — | o/a |

RASMUS 35 — XAX Corporation, U.S.A.

| 10.67m/35'0 | 3.15m/10'4 | 1.32m/4'4 | — | 6 | o/a |

S–35 — Spencer Boats, U.S.A.

| 10.67m/35'0 | 2.9m/9'6 | 1.6m/5'3 | 48.8m^2/525sq.ft | 6 | o/a |

SOVEREIGN 35 — J. W. & A. Uphams, England

| 10.67m/35'0 | 3.07m/10'1 | 1.52m/5'0 | Optional | 4/6 | £16,200 |

SPEY 35 — Jones Buckie Shipyard, Scotland

| 10.67m/35'0 | 3.43m/11'3 | 1.52m/5'0 | 41.3m^2/445sq.ft | 6 | o/a |

TRINTELLA 35 — Offshore Yachts, England

| 10.67m/35'0 | — | 1.4m/4'7 | 48m^2/517sq.ft | 7 | o/a |

WARRIOR Mk II — Swanwick Yacht Agency, England

| 10.67m/35'0 | 3.2m/10'6 | 1.52m/5'0 | 39.4m^2/424sq.ft | — | £14,200 |

WHITE QUEEN — J. Samuel White & Co., Scotland

| 10.67m/35'0 | 3.51m/11'6 | 1.07m/3'6 | 36.2m^2/390sq.ft | 6 | o/a |

CARIBBEAN 35 — Chris Craft Corp., U.S.A.
Carl Ziegler Yacht Agency, England

| 10.72m/35'2 | 3.35m/11'0 | 1.42m/4'8 | 53.6m^2/577sq.ft | 6 | £18,200 |

STRIDER 35 — Anstey Yachts, England

| 10.7m/35'2 | — | 1.83m/6'0 | 49.5m^2/533sq.ft | 6 | o/a |

LOA	BEAM	DRAFT	SAIL AREA	BERTHS	PRICE

CORONADO 35　　　　　Coronado Yachts, U.S.A.
Playvisa Coronado Yachts, England

| 10.74m/35'3 | 3.07m/10'1 | 1.68m/5'6 | 46.6m^2/502sq.ft | 6 | £15,750 |

GREAT DANE 35　　　　Klaus Baess, Denmark
Carl Ziegler Yacht Agency, England
Danyachts, U.S.A.

| 10.74m/35'3 | 3.28m/10'9 | 1.55m/5'1 | 55.7m^2/600sq.ft | 6 | £14,000 |

COLUMBINE — 1 Ton　　Camper & Nicholsons, England

| 10.77m/35'4 | 3.73m/12'3 | 1.93m/6'4 | 58.7m^2/632sq.ft | — | o/a |

DRAC 1 TONNER　　　　SARL, France

| 10.77m/35'4 | 3.30m/10'10 | 1.91m/6'3 | 96m^2/1033sq.ft | 6 | 230,000fr.f |

CRUSAIRE 36　　　　　Jules G. Felder, U.S.A.

| 10.82m/35'6 | 3.2m/10'6 | 1.58m/5'2 | 42.7m^2/460sq.ft | 6 | o/a |

CLIPPER 36　　　　　　Cheoy Lee Shipyard, Hong Kong
Lion Yachts, U.S.A.
Salterns Yacht Agency, England

| 10.87m/35'8 | 3.28m/10'9 | 1.6m/5'3 | 59m^2/635sq.ft | 6 | £17,250 |

STANDFAST 36　　　　Frans Maas BV, Holland
Chichester Yacht Agency, England

| 10.90m/35'9 | 3.70m/12'1½ | 2.05m/6'9 | 77m^2/829sq.ft | 6 | o/a |

OFFSHORE 36　　　　　Cheoy Lee, Hong Kong
Roland Reed, U.S.A.

| 10.92m/35'10 | 3.05m/10'0 | 1.42m/4'8 | 51.6m^2/555sq.ft | 6 | o/a |

	LOA	BEAM	DRAFT	SAIL AREA	BERTHS	PRICE

BOWMAN 36
Emsworth Marine Sales, England

LOA	BEAM	DRAFT	SAIL AREA	BERTHS	PRICE
10.97m/36'0	3.45m/11'4	1.68m/5'6	53.4m^2/575sq.ft	6/7	o/a

EASTERLY 36
Easterly Yachts, U.S.A.

| 10.97m/36'0 | 3.3m/10'10 | 1.6m/5'3 | 55m^2/592sq.ft | 6 | $24,200us |

EXCALIBUR
Tyler Boat Co., England

| 10.97m/36'0 | 3.05m/10'0 | 1.805m/5'11 | 55.1m^2/593sq.ft | 6 | o/a |

FINN CLIPPER
Offshore Yachts, England

| 10.97m/36'0 | — | 1.3m/4'3 | 30.2m^2/325sq.ft | 7 | o/a |

K-36 TRI

| 10.97m/36'0 | — | 0.61m/2'0 | 55.7m^2/600sq.ft | 6 | o/a |

PRINCESS 36
Allied Boat Co., U.S.A.

| 10.97m/36'0 | 3.35m/11'0 | 1.37m/4'6 | 56.1m^2/604sq.ft | 6 | $29,000us |

RANGER 36
Prout Marine, U.K.
Ocean Catamarans, U.S.A.

| 10.97m/36'0 | 4.57m/15'0 | 0.69m/2'3 | 53.7m^2/578sq.ft | 6/7 | o/a |

SNAPDRAGON 1100
Thames Marine, England

| 11.0m/36'0 | 3.50m/11'6 | 1.68m/5'6 | 60.6m^2/652sq.ft | 6/7 | £14,850 |

SWAN 36
Humell & Johnson, England

| 10.97m/36'0 | — | 1.83m/6'0 | 50m^2/538sq.ft | 7 | o/a |

SYMONS 36
Symons Sailing Inc., U.S.A.

| 10.97m/36'0 | 6.1m/20'0 | 0.79m/2'7 | 41.8m^2/450sq.ft | 8 | $32,850us |

LOA	BEAM	DRAFT	SAIL AREA	BERTHS	PRICE

HALBERDIER — A. H. Moody & Son, England

| 11m/36'1 | — | 1.52m/5'0 | various | 6 | o/a |

TASMAN CATAMARAN — O'Brien & Spencer, England

| 11m/36'1 | 5.48m/18'0 | 0.914m/3'0 | 64m^2/689sq.ft | 7/8 | £16,500 |

BREEON — East Coast Marine Co., England

| 11.02m/36'2 | 3.2m/10'6 | 1.45m/4'9 | 42.5m^2/458sq.ft | 7 | o/a |

CASCADE 36 — Yacht Constructors Inc., U.S.A.

| 11.02m/36'2 | 3.05m/10'0 | 1.68m/5'6 | 54.8m^2/590sq.ft | 6 | $3,650+ |

NICHOLSON 36 — Camper & Nicholsons, England / Camper & NIcholsons, U.S.A.

| 11.40m/36'3 | 3.00m/9'6 | 1.80m/5'11 | 62.1m^2/669sq.ft | 6 | £16,000 |

GULFSTAR 36 — Gulfstar Inc., U.S.A.

| 11.05m/36'3 | 3.73m/12'3 | — | 54.8m^2/590sq.ft | 6/7 | $29,500us |

PALMER JOHNSON 37 — 1 Ton — Palmer Johnson Inc., U.S.A.

| 11.1m/36'5 | — | — | 55.6m^2/598sq.ft | 8 | $42,500us |

SABINA — F. A. Gebr. Maas, Holland

| 11.1m/36'5 | 3.1m/10'2 | 1.8m/5'11 | 44.6m^2/480sq.ft | 7 | o/a |

ISLANDER 37 — Islander Yachts, U.S.A.

| 11.13m/36'6 | 3.3m/10'10 | 1.81m/5'11 | 48.3m^2/520sq.ft | 6 | $34,000us |

PEARSON 36 — Pearson Yachts, U.S.A.

| 11.15m/36'7 | 3.35m/11'0 | 1.83m/6'0 | 55.8m^2/601sq.ft | 7 | $29,700us |

LOA	BEAM	DRAFT	SAIL AREA	BERTHS	PRICE

GREAT DANE 37

Klauss Baess, Denmark
Danyachts, U.S.A.
Carl Ziegler Yacht Agency, England

11.2m/36'9	3.33m/10'11	1.68m/5'6	59m^2/635sq.ft	6	$43,100us

VICTORY 36

Tyler Boat Co., England

11.25m/36'11	3.20m/10'6	1.4m/4'7	57.6m^2/620sq.ft	6	£19,000+

BROWN 37' TRI

Border Marine, U.K.

11.28m/37'0	—	—	various	7	o/a

CHANCE 37

Wauguiez — Offsounding Yachts,
U.S.A.
Paceship Yachts, Canada

11.28m/37'0	3.2m/10'6	1.78m/5'10	73m^2/786sq.ft	7	o/a

IRWIN 37

Irwin Yacht & Marine Corp., U.S.A.

11.28m/37'0	3.51m/11'6	1.22m/4'0	52.1m^2/561sq.ft	6	$29,700us

MEADOWLARK

Buzzards Bay Boats, U.S.A.

11.28m/37'0	2.44m/8'0	0.48m/1'7	42.4m^2/456sq.ft	4/7	$24,000

TARTAN 37

Tartan Marine Co., U.S.A.

11.28m/37'0	3.2m/10'6	2.80m/9'4	57.4m^2/618sq.ft	6	$38,000us

OHLSON 38

Campbell/Sheehans Inc.
Alexander Robertson, Scotland

11.3m/37'1	3.12m/10'3	1.7m/5'7	51.9m^2/559sq.ft	7	$32,000

SEVEN SEAS

Fibocon BV, Holland

11.30m/37'1	3.50m/11'6	1.38m/4'6½	52.9m^2/569sq.ft	4	145,000 fl.

LOA	BEAM	DRAFT	SAIL AREA	BERTHS	PRICE

ALBERG 37 — 1 Ton Whitby Boat Works, Canada

| 11.33m/37'2 | 3.1m/10'2 | 1.68m/5'6 | 60.1m^2/647sq.ft | 7 | $30,500us |

FINNROSE 37 Turun Veneveistamo, Finland
Ballena Ltd., England
Continental Yachts, U.S.A.

| 11.35m/37'3 | 3.31m/10'11 | 1.6m/5'3 | 47.4m^2/510sq.ft | 6 | £20,000 |

HINCKLEY 38 Henry H. Hinckley & Co., U.S.A.

| 11.43m/37'6 | 3.2m/10'6 | 1.83m/6'0 | 57.4m^2/618sq.ft | 6 | $31,000us |

SPINDRIFT 37 International Marine Services, U.S.A.

| 11.43m/37'6 | 6.1m/20'0 | 0.51m/1'8 | 83.6m^2/900sq.ft | 6/10 | $32,000us |

PIET HEIN East Coast Yacht Agency, England

| 11.45m/37'7 | 3.3m/10'10 | 1.37m/4'6 | 48.3m^2/520sq.ft | 6 | o/a |

SANTANA 37 W. D. Schock & Co., U.S.A.

| 11.48m/37'8 | 3.55m/11'8 | 1.7m/5'7 | 58.3m^2/627sq.ft | 6 | $26,000us |

IRWIN 38 Irwin Yacht and Marine Corp., U.S.A.

| 11.51m/37'9 | 3.2m/10'6 | 1.75m/5'9 | 60.4m^2/649sq.ft | — | $26,333us |

SANDETTIE F. A. Gebr Maas, Holland

| 11.51m/37'9 | 3.99m/13'1 | 1.93m/6'4 | 67.6m^2/728sq.ft | 7 | o/a |

NORTH STAR 38 Northstar Yachts, Canada

| 11.53m/37'10 | 3.1m/10'2 | 1.83m/6'0 | 55.7m^2/600sq.ft | 6 | $31,000 |

LOA	BEAM	DRAFT	SAIL AREA	BERTHS	PRICE

NICHOLSON 38 — Camper & Nicholsons, England
Camper Nicholson, U.S.A.

11.56m/37'11	3.2m/10'6	1.58m/5'2	46m^2/495sq.ft	6	£23,700

INCHCAPE 38 — Eyemouth Boat Building Co., U.K.

11.58m/38'0	—	1.22m/4'0	35.8m^2/385sq.ft	4/7	o/a

P & H 38 — Porter & Haylett Ltd., England

11.58m/38'0	3.81m/12'6	1.45m/4'9	144.3m^2/1,553sq.ft	7/8	o/a

R–38 — Ryton Engineering Co., U.K.

11.58m/38'0	—	1.17m/3'10	55.7m^2/600sq.ft	6	o/a

SWAN 38 — Nautor, Finland
Dave Johnson, U.K.
Nautor Inc., U.S.A.

11.58m/38'0	3.53m/11'7	1.93m/6'4	59.1m^2/636sq.ft	—	£24,000

NORTH EAST 38 — Le Comte, Holland
Sparkman and Stephens, U.S.A.

11.66m/38'3	3.33m/10'11	1.62m/5'4	57.6m^2/620sq.ft	6/7	o/a

SIGMA 38 — Cheoy Lee, Hong Kong
Lion Yachts, U.S.A.

11.68m/38'4	3.12m/10'3	1.80m/5'11	60.5m^2/651sq.ft	6	o/a

VEGA — Szczecinska Stoczina Jacktowa, Poland
Turbonet Ltd., England

11.66m/38'3	2.90m/9'6	1.85m/6'1	55.4m^2/596sq.ft	6/7	o/a

LOA	BEAM	DRAFT	SAIL AREA	BERTHS	PRICE

CHANCE 33 – 2 Ton — Paceship Yachts, Canada

| 11.73m/38'6 | 3.2m/10'6 | 2.19m/7'2 | 70.1m²/755sq.ft | 6 | $38,000us |

EUROS — Amel, France

| 11.75m/38'6½ | 3.30m/10'10 | 1.50m/4'11 | 52m²/560sq.ft | 6 | 215,000fr.f |

BLOCK ISLAND 40 – 1 Ton — Metalmast Marine, U.S.A.

| 11.76m/38'7 | 3.56m/11'8 | 1.22m/4'0 | 57.8m²/622sq.ft | 7 | $43,000us |

COLUMBIA 39 — Columbia Yacht Corp., U.S.A.

| 11.76m/38'7 | 3.43m/11'3 | 1.83m/6'0 | 70m²/753sq.ft | 7 | o/a |

ENDURANCE 35 — Windward Boats Ltd., England

| 11.88m/39'0 | 3.35m/11'0 | 1.60m/5'3 | 63.5m²/683sq.ft | 4/6 | o/a |

ERICSON 39 — Ericson Yachts Inc., U.S.A. / Hamble Marine, U.K. / Nordmarine, Italy

| 11.9m/39'0 | 3.45m/11'4 | 1.81m/5'11 | 68.7m²/739sq.ft | 7 | £20,100 |

SALAR 40 — Essex Yacht Builders, England / Salterns Yacht Agency, England

| 11.89m/39'0 | 3.35m/11'0 | 1.68m/5'6 | 29.5m²/318sq.ft | 6/8 | £24,500 |

WHITBY 39 — Whitby Boat Works Ltd., Canada

| 11.89m/39'0 | 3.66m/12'0 | 1.45m/4'9 | 70m²/753sq.ft | 7 | $41,000us |

C & C 39 – 2 Ton — C & C Yachts Manufacturing, Canada / Anstey Yachts, England

| 11.96m/39'3 | 3.51m/11'6 | 1.91m/6'3 | 73.1m²787sq.ft | 7 | £25,000 |

LOA	BEAM	DRAFT	SAIL AREA	BERTHS	PRICE

PEARSON 39 Pearson Yachts, U.S.A.

| 11.96m/39'3 | 3.55m/11'8 | 1.42m/4'8 | 62.5m²/673sq.ft | 7 | $31,000us |

CAL 40 – 2 Ton Jensen Marine, U.S.A.

| 11.99m/39'4 | 3.35m/11'0 | 1.7m/5'7 | 65m²/700sq.ft | 8 | $45,000us |

SOLEXXON 39 CATAMARAN Solaris Marine, England

| 11.99m/39'4 | 5.33m/17'6 | 0.99m/3'3 | 83.6m²/900sq.ft | 8 | £21,500+ |

ALC 40 A. LeComte, Holland
A. LeComte Co., U.S.A.

| 12.04m/39'6 | 3.56m/11'8 | 1.75m/5'9 | 55.5m²/597sq.ft | 6/9 | o/a |

KRAKEN 40 International Marine Services, U.S.A.

| 12.04m/39'6 | 8.23m/27'0 | 0.53m/1'9 | 88.3m²/950sq.ft | 5/6 | $34,000us |

PALMER JOHNSON 40 Palmer Johnson Inc., U.S.A.

| 12.04m/39'6 | 3.3m/10'10 | 1.96m/6'5 | 65.6m²/706sq.ft | 8 | $52,500us |

ALLIED 39 Allied Boat Co., U.S.A.

| 12.14m/39'10 | 3.12m/10'3 | 1.78m/5'10 | 63m²/680sq.ft | 7 | o/a |

CHALLENGER 40 Challenger Yacht Corporation,
U.S.A.

| 12.17m/39'11 | 3.91m/12'10 | 1.83m/6'0 | 62.2m²/670sq.ft | 7 | $38,850us |

ALSO AVAILABLE 40'+

LOA	BEAM	DRAFT	SAIL AREA	BERTHS	PRICE
BROWN 40' TRI			Border Marine, U.K.		
12.19m/40'0	—	—	Various	8	o/a
CONTEST 40			Conyplex NV., Holland		
12.19m/40'0	3.43m/11'3	1.98m/6'6	$61m^2$/657sq.ft	6/8	$58,000us
DICKERSON 40			Dickerson Boatbuilders Inc., U.S.A.		
12.19m/40'0	3.66m/12'0	1.37m/4'6	$55.3m^2$/595sq.ft	6/8	$28,000us+
NANTUCKET 40			Buzzards Bay Boats, U.S.A.		
12.19m/40'0	3.43m/11'3	1.78m/5'10	$77m^2$/829sq.ft	6	$45,000us
NEWPORTER			Newport Shipyard, U.S.A.		
12.19m/40'0	3.96m/13'0	1.5m/4'11	$66.3m^2$/714sq.ft	6	o/a
PT 40			Plastrend, U.S.A.		
12.19m/40'0	3.35m/11'0	2.11m/6'11	$58.8m^2$/633sq.ft	8	$15,000us
SPEY 40			Jones Buckie Shipyard, Scotland		
12.192m/40'0	3.66m/12'0	1.524m/5'0	$46.45m^2$/500sq.ft	6/8	o/a
SPINDRIFT 40			International Marine Service, U.S.A.		
12.19m/40'0	6.40m/21'0	0.53m/1'9	$90.2m^2$/971sq.ft	8/10	$42,000us
MORGAN 40			Morgan Yacht Corporation, U.S.A. Peter Webster Ltd., England		
12.24m/40'2	3.43m/11'3	1.27m/4'2	$69.7m^2$/750sq.ft	6	$35000

LOA	BEAM	DRAFT	SAIL AREA	BERTHS	PRICE
VICTORY 40		Tyler Boat Co., England			
12.27m/40'3	3.51m/11'6	1.52m/5'0	70.7m^2/761sq.ft	6	£31,300
CORONADO 41		Coronada Yachts, U.S.A. Playvisa Coronado Yachts, England			
12.34m/40'6	3.43m/11'3	1.91m/6'3	59.3m^2/638sq.ft	8	$38,500us
H/96		Whisstocks Boatyard, England			
12,34m/40'6	—	1.52m/5'0	66.8m^2/719sq.ft	7	o/a
PASSAGE 41		Passage Marine Inc., U.S.A.			
12.34m/40'6	4.27m/14'0	1.45m/4'9	81.4m^2/876sq.ft	7	$57,500us
SUNCOAST RANGE		Jachtbouw Noord, Holland			
12.40m/40'8	3.85m/12'7½	1.40m/4'7	68.5m^2/737sq.ft	8	90,000 fl.
BERMUDA 40 Mk III		Henry R. Hinckley & Co., U.S.A.			
12.42m/40'9	3.58m/11'9	1.24m/4'1	72.1m^2/776sq.ft	6	$81,000+
OHLSON 41		Campbell/Sheehan Inc., U.S.A.			
12.42m/40'9	3.61m/11'10	1.85m/6'1	70.5m^2/759sq.ft	to spec.	o/a
RELIANT 41		Cheoy Lee, Hong Kong			
12.42m/40'9	3.28m/10'9	1.75m/5'9	69.7m^2/750sq.ft	6	o/a
APACHE 41		Sailcraft, England Symons Sailing Inc., U.S.A.			
12.45m/40'10	5.94m/19'6	0.91m/3'0	65.9m^2/710sq.ft	10/12	£30,000
YANKEE CLIPPER		Jack Kelly Yacht Sales, U.S.A.			
12.47m/40'11	3.71m/12'2	1.88m/6'2	72.5m^2/780sq.ft	7	$39,000us

LOA	BEAM	DRAFT	SAIL AREA	BERTHS	PRICE

DUFOUR 41
Michel Dufour, France
Michel Dufour SA., U.S.A.

12.5m/41'0	3.79m/12'5	1.75m/5'9	75.2m^2/810sq.ft	8	$64,000us+

KETTENBURG 41
Kettenburg Marine, U.S.A.

12.5m/41'0	3.15m/10'4	1.68m/5'6	58.2m^2/626sq.ft	6	o/a

MORGAN CUSTOM 41
Morgan Yacht Corporation, U.S.A.
Peter Webster Ltd., England

12.5m/41'0	3.4m/11'2	1.27m/4'2	71.8m^2/773sq.ft	6	o/a

NEWPORT 41 – S
Capital Yachts Inc., U.S.A.

12.5m/41'0	3.43m/11'3	1.91m/6'3	69.7m^2/750sq.ft	7	$32,000

OCEAN LADY 40
Beecham Marine, England

12.5m/41'0	4.01m/13'2	1.37m/4'6	65.4m^2/704sq.ft	5	o/a

S 30
AB Fisksätra varv, Sweden
Swedish Yacht Export AB, Sweden

12.50m/41'0	2.50m/8'2	1.47m/4'10	37.5m^2/404sq.ft	6	80,000 S.kr.

SORTILEGE
Michel Dufour, France
Michel Dufour, U.S.A.
Carl Ziegler Yacht Agency, England

12.5m/41'0	3.76m/12'4	2.03m/6'8	74m^2/796sq.ft	6/8	£32,800

HINCKLEY 41 COMPETITION   Henry Hinckley & Co., U.S.A.

12.55m/41'2	3.12m/10'3	1.88m/6'2	63.2m^2/680sq.ft	6	o/a

REBEL
Tyler Boat Co., England

12.55m/41'2	3.33m/10'11	2m/6'7	73.2m^2/788sq.ft	8	o/a

LOA	BEAM	DRAFT	SAIL AREA	BERTHS	PRICE

CUSTOM CRUISER   American Marine, U.S.A.

| 12.65m/41'6 | 3.86m/12'8 | 1.6m/5'3 | 7 combinations | 5/6 | o/a |

TREWS CLIPPER RANGE   Jachtwerf Jougert BV, Holland

| 12.65m/41'6 | 3.60m/11'10 | 1.55m/5'1 | 52.4m^2/564sq.ft | — | o/a |

XL - 2   Allied Boat Co., U.S.A.

| 12.65m/41'6 | 3.51m/11'6 | 1.27m/4'2 | 70.8m^2/762sq.ft | 7 | $50,500+ |

ROBB 42   Arthur Robb, England
Lion Yachts, U.S.A.

| 12.76m/41'10½ | 3.15m/10'4 | 2m/6'7 | 68.3m^2/735sq.ft | — | o/a |

ALBATROSS   Stebbings (Burnham), England

| 12.8m/42'0 | 3.61m/11'10 | 1.68m/5'6 | 72.2m^2/777sq.ft | 7 | o/a |

CASCADE 42   Yacht Constructors Inc., U.S.A.

| 12.8m/42'0 | 3.4m/11'2 | 1.83m/6'0 | 74.3m^2/800sq.ft | 8 | $4,950us |

CHESFORD 42   Chesford Marine, England

| 12.8m/42'0 | — | 1.75m/5'9 | 55.7m^2/600sq.ft | 6 | o/a |

COMANCHE 42   Chris Craft Corp., U.S.A.

| 12.8m/42'0 | 3.05m/10'0 | 1.98m/6'6 | 68.7m^2/740sq.ft | 7 | o/a |

MORGAN 42 Mk II   Morgan Yacht Corp., U.S.A.
Peter Webster Ltd., England

| 12.8m/42'0 | 3.51m/11'6 | 1.83m/6'0 | 73.2m^2/788sq.ft | 6 | $30,000us |

SYMONS 42   Symons Sailing Inc., U.S.A.

| 12.80m/42'0 | 6.76m/22'2 | 0.86m/2'10 | 57.1m^2/615sq.ft | 10 | $55,890us |

LOA	BEAM	DRAFT	SAIL AREA	BERTHS	PRICE

CHANCE 42/36 Chance Marine, U.S.A.
Scheepsbouw de Visser BV, Holland

| 12.90m/42'2 | 3.55m/11'7 | 2.36m/7'9 | 69.9m^2/752sq.ft | 8/9 | o/a |

S–42 Spencer Boats, U.S.A.

| 12.88m/42'3 | 3.45m/11'4 | 1.83m/6'0 | 75.1m^2/808sq.ft | 7 | o/a |

CLIPPER 42 Cheoy Lee, Hong Kong
Lion Yachts, U.S.A.
Salterns Yacht Agency, England

| 12.93m/42'5 | 3.68m/12'1 | 1.75m/5'9 | 86.2m^2/928sq.ft | 6 | £25,000 |

WESTSAIL 42 Westsail Corp., U.S.A.

| 13.05m/42'10 | 3.96m/13'0 | 1.73m/5'8 | 79m^2/850sq.ft | — | $52,000us |

CHALLENGER 42 MS Challenger Yacht Corp., U.S.A.

| 13.08m/42'11 | 3.96m/13'0 | 1.68m/5'6 | 52m^2/560sq.ft | 7 | $44,850us |

G43 Ryton Engineering, U.K.

| 13.11m/43'0 | — | 1.75m/5'9 | 74.3m^2/800sq.ft | 6/8 | o/a |

8 METER C/R Alex Robertson, Scotland

| 13.1m/43'0 | — | 1.9m/6'3 | 73.4m^2/790sq.ft | 7 | o/a |

PALMER JOHNSON 43 Palmer Johnson Inc., U.S.A.

| 13.11m/43'0 | 3.58m/11'9 | 2.03m/6'8 | 76.5m^2/824sq.ft | 8 | $75,500us |

SWAN 43 Dave Johnson, England
Nautor, Finland

| 13.11m/43'0 | — | 2.13m/7'0 | 97.1m^2/1,045sq.ft | 7 | £32,000 |

LOA	BEAM	DRAFT	SAIL AREA	BERTHS	PRICE

NICHOLSON 43   Camper & Nicholsons, England
Camper Nicholson, U.S.A.

| 13.18m/43'3 | 3.51m/11'6 | 2.06m/6'9 | 64.4m^2/693sq.ft | 7 | £28,600 |

PACIFIC   Walter F. Rayner Ltd., England

| 13.18m/43'3 | 3.81m/12'6 | 1.68m/5'6 | 67.2m^2/723sq.ft | 6 | o/a |

C & C CUSTOM 43   C & C Yachts Manufacturing, Canada
Anstey Yachts, England

| 13.21m/43'4 | 3.91m/12'10 | 2.13m/7'0 | 86.5m^2/931sq.ft | — | o/a |

OHLSON 44   Campbell/Sheehan, Inc., U.S.A.

| 13.26m/43'6 | 3.51m/11'6 | 1.98m/6'6 | 78.3m^2/843sq.ft | 7 | o/a |

OFFSHORE 44   Cheoy Lee, Hong Kong
Lion Yachts, U.S.A.

| 13.31m/43'8 | 3.96m/13'0 | — | 75.4m^2/812sq.ft | 6 | o/a |

COLUMBIA 43 Mk III   Columbia Yacht Corp., U.S.A.

| 13.34m/43'9 | 3.76m/12'4 | 2.13m/7'0 | 79.2m^2/852sq.ft | 8 | $39,995us |

S-44   Spencer Boats, U.S.A.

| 13.33m/43'9 | 3.51m/11'6 | 1.98m/6'6 | 79.6m^2/857sq.ft | 8 | o/a |

ISLANDER 44   Wayfarer Yacht Corp., U.S.A.

| 13.36m/43'10 | 3.35m/11'0 | 1.78m/5'10 | 71.9m^2/774sq.ft | 8 | $4,350 |

CAPE COD MERCER   Cape Cod Shipbuildings, U.S.A.

| 13.41m/44'0 | 3.58m/11'9 | 1.3m/4'3 | 82.2m^2/885sq.ft | 7 | $65,500us |

CARBINEER   A. H. Moody & Sons, England

| 13.41m/44'0 | — | 1.83m/6'0 | 81.3m^2/875sq.ft | 6/8 | o/a |

LOA	BEAM	DRAFT	SAIL AREA	BERTHS	PRICE

PALMER JOHNSON 44   Palmer Johnson Inc., U.S.A.

| 13.41m/44'0 | 3.96m/13'0 | 2.19m/7'2 | 81.3m^2/875sq.ft | 9 | $90,000us |

SWAN 44   Nautor, Finland
Dave Johnson, England

| 13.41m/44'0 | 3.83m/12'7 | 2.19m/7'2 | 106.9m^2/1,151sq.ft | 8/9 | £35,600 |

CAPE RACE   Interyacht, Germany

| 13.44m/44'1 | 4.32m/14'2 | 1.52m/5'0 | 74.2m^2/799sq.ft | 7 | o/a |

CHANCE 40   Chance Marine, U.S.A.

| 13.44m/44'1 | 3.76m/12'4 | 1.42m/4'8 | 85m^2/915sq.ft | 8 | o/a |

IRWIN 43   Irwin Yacht & Marine Corp., U.S.A.

| 13.64m/44'9 | 3.51m/11'6 | 1.98m/6'6 | 80.9m^2/871sq.ft | 6/7 | $43,000us |

OCEAN RANGER 45   G. Prout & Sons, England

| 13.72m/45'0 | — | 0.76m/2'6 | 65.2m^2/702sq.ft | 8 | o/a |

SOVEREL 45   Soverel Marine Inc., U.S.A.

| 13.72m/45'0 | 3.66m/12'0 | 4.27m/14'0 | 102.2m^2/1,100sq.ft | 8 | $75,000 |

COLUMBIA 45   Columbia Yacht Corp., U.S.A.

| 13.79m/45'3 | 3.76m/12'4 | 2.21m/7'3 | 64.5m^2/694sq.ft | 8 | $51,995us |

CORONADO 45   Coronado Yachts, U.S.A.
Playvisa Coronado Yachts, England

| 13.79m/45'3 | 3.76m/12'4 | 2.21m/7'3 | 75.2m^2/810sq.ft | 8 | $48,995us |

CAL CRUISING 46   Jensen Marine, U.S.A.

| 13.87m/45'6 | 3.81m/12'6 | 1.52m/5'0 | 65m^2/700sq.ft | 8 | o/a |

LOA	BEAM	DRAFT	SAIL AREA	BERTHS	PRICE

FASTNET 45
A. Le Comte Co. Inc., U.S.A.

13.89m/45'7	3.73m/12'3	2.06m/6'9	73.9m^2/795sq.ft	8	o/a

BUCCANEER
James D. Rosborough, Canada

13.92m/45'8	4.04m/13'3	1.81m/5'11	89.2m^2/960sq.ft	6/8	$54,500us

NOR'EASTER
James D. Rosborough, Canada
Port of Call Industries, U.S.A.

13.92m/45'8	3.86m/12'8	1.73m/5'8	95.7m^2/1,030sq.ft	6/8	$62,800us

DISTANT STAR
James D. Rosborough, Canada

13.92m/45'8	4.04m/13'3	1.85m/6'1 ·	148.6m^2/1,600sq.ft	6/8	$57,300us

CAPE PORPOISE
Cape Yachts Ltd., Hong Kong

13.94m/45'9	4.06m/13'4	1.68m/5'6	88.3m^2/950sq.ft	8	$33,000us

EP-46
Tillotson-Pearson Inc., U.S.A.

14.02m/46'0	3.91m/12'10	2.29m/7'6	92.9m^2/1,000sq.ft	7	o/a

FANTASIA
E. W. Etchells, U.S.A.

14.02m/46'0	3.66m/12'0	2.29m/7'6	87.9m^2/946sq.ft	5	o/a

FORTUNA 46
De Vries Leutsch, Holland

14.02m/46'0	4.72m/15'6	1.52m/5'0	Optional	7	£32,500

NAVAHO
Sail Craft Ltd., England
British Marine Industries, U.S.A.

14.02m/46'0	—	1.07m/3'6	69.7m^2/750sq.ft	12	o/a

CARBINEER 46
A. H. Moody & Sons, England

14.17m/46'6	3.71m/12'2	1.83m/6'0	79.1m^2/851sq.ft	6	£40,000+

LOA	BEAM	DRAFT	SAIL AREA	BERTHS	PRICE

TARTAN 48
Tartan Marine Co., U.S.A.

LOA	BEAM	DRAFT	SAIL AREA	BERTHS	PRICE
14.22m/46'8	4.27m/14'0	2.29m/7'6	91.2m²/982sq.ft	9	$80,000us

MENEMSHA 46
Buzzard Bay Boats, U.S.A.

| 14.25m/46'9 | 4.16m/13'8 | 1.50m/4'11 | 97.6m²/1,051sq.ft | 6 | $75,000us |

CAL 48
Jensen Marine, U.S.A.

| 14.55m/47'9 | 3.66m/12'0 | 1.98m/6'6 | 96.6m²/1,040sq.ft | 8 | $80,000us |

G-48
Ryton Engineering, U.K.

| 14.63m/48'0 | — | 1.75m/5'9 | 92.9m²/1,000sq.ft | 6/8 | o/a |

SOVEREL 48
Soverel Marine Inc., U.S.A.

| 14.63m/48'0 | 4.04m/13'3 | 1.22m/4'0 | 92.9m²/1,000sq.ft | 8 | $85,000us |

SWAN 48
Nautor, Finland
Dave Johnson, England
Nautor Inc., U.S.A.

| 14.63m/48'0 | 4.14m/13'7 | 2.36m/7'9 | 127.5m²/1,372sq.ft | 7/8 | £44,000 |

VANGUARD
Trewes International, England

| 14.63m/48'0 | 3.86m/12'8 | 1.75m/5'9 | 146m²/1,572sq.ft | 6/8 | o/a |

PALMER JOHNSON 48
Palmer Johnson Inc., U.S.A.

| 14.65m/48'1 | 4.14m/13'7 | 2.36m/7'9 | 98.4m²/1,059sq.ft | 9 | $124,000us |

C & C CUSTOM 48
C & C Yachts Manufacturing, Canada
Anstey Yachts, England

| 14.68m/48'2 | 4.16m/13'8 | 2.21m/7'3 | 103.2m²/1,111sq.ft | — | o/a |

HINCKLEY 48
Henry R. Hinckley & Co., U.S.A.

| 14.76m/48'5 | 3.96m/13'0 | 1.6m/5'3 | 96.6m²/1,040sq.ft | 8 | o/a |

LOA	BEAM	DRAFT	SAIL AREA	BERTHS	PRICE

ENDURANCE 40   Windward Boats Ltd., England

| 14.78m/48′6 | 3.78m/12′5 | 1.73m/5′9 | 185.8m^2/2,000sq.ft | 7 | £31,500 |

HINCKLEY 49   Henry Hinckley & Co., U.S.A.

| 14.78m/48′6 | 4.09m/13′5 | 1.66m/5′5 | 84.2m^2/906sq.ft | 4/8 | o/a |

CHALLENGER 48   Challenger Yacht Corp., U.S.A.

| 14.91m/48′11 | 4.67m/15′4 | 1.83m/6′0 | 96.6m^2/1,040sq.ft | 8 | $110,000us |

ST MALO   Port Hamble Ltd., England

| 15.01m/49′3 | 3.81m/12′6 | 1.83m/6′0 | 82.2m^2/885sq.ft | 6 | o/a |

SYMONS 49   Symons Sailing Inc., U.S.A.

| 15.01m/49′3 | 7.37m/24′2 | 1.07m/3′6 | 93.5m^2/1,006sq.ft | 10 | $70,000us |

C & C CUSTOM 50   C & C Yachts Manufacturing, Canada
Anstey Yachts, England

| 15.19m/49′10 | 4.42m/14′6 | 2.44m/8′0 | 106.9m^2/1,151sq.ft | — | o/a |

KENNER SKIPJACK 35   Kenner Sailing Yachts, U.S.A.

| 15.19m/49′10 | 3.61m/11′10 | 1.83m/6′0 | 67m^2/721sq.ft | 5 | o/a |

K-50 CAT   Derek Kelsall Limited, England

| 15.24m/50′0 | — | 0.76m/2′6 | 92.9m^2/1,000sq.ft | 12 | o/a |

OCEAN LADY 50   Beecham Marine, England

| 15.24m/50′0 | 4.27m/14′0 | 1.75m/5′9 | 107.6m^2/1,158sq.ft | 8/9 | o/a |

SEYCHELLE   SLM Boats, England

| 15.24m/50′0 | 4.27m/14′0 | 1.98m/6′6 | Optional | — | o/a |

LOA	BEAM	DRAFT	SAIL AREA	BERTHS	PRICE

BONAVENTURA-CLIPPER   Scheepsbouw de Visser bv, Holland

15.30m/50'2	4.00m/13'1½	1.70m/5'7	97m^2/1,044sq.ft	6/8	282,000 fl.

CHALLENGER 50   Challenger Yacht Corp., U.S.A.

15.34m/50'4	4.72m/15'6	1.98m/6'6	106.8m^2/1.150sq.ft	6+	$79,850us

OFFSHORE 50   Cheoy Lee, Hong Kong
Lion Yachts, U.S.A.
Salterns Yacht Agency, England

15.34m/50'4	4.01m/13'2	1.98m/6'6	84.4m^2/908sq.ft	6/9	£46,000

KETTENBURG 50   Kettenburg Marine, U.S.A.

15.47m/50'9	3.96m/13'0	2.08m/6'10	Various	8	o/a

OCEAN RACER 52   A. Le Comte Co., U.S.A.
Solent Yachts, England

15.8m/51'10	4.11m/13'6	2.13m/7'0	100.8m^2/1,085sq.ft	10	o/a

INCHCAPE 52   Eyemouth Boat Building Co.,
England

16m/52'6	—	1.83m/6'0	48.3m^2/520sq.ft	8/14	o/a

GALLANT 53   Southern Ocean Shipyard, England

16.15m/53'0	3.99m/13'1	2.23m/7'4	127.6m^2/1,373sq.ft	10	o/a

GULF STAR 53   Gulf Star Inc., U.S.A.

16.21m/53'2	4.57m/15'0	1.37m/4'6	103.6m^2/1,115sq.ft	6/8	$109,000us

PALMER JOHNSON 54   Palmer Johnson Inc., U.S.A.

16.46m/54'0	3.89m/12'9	1.6m/5'3	99.9m^2/1,075sq.ft	7	o/a

LOA	BEAM	DRAFT	SAIL AREA	BERTHS	PRICE

SWAN 55

Nautor, Finland
Dave Johnson, England
Nautor, U.S.A.

16.76m/55'0	4.34m/14'3	2.49m/8'2	152.4m^2/1,640sq.ft	10	£65,000+

PALMER JOHNSON 55   Palmer Johnson Inc., U.S.A.

16.86m/55'4	4.34m/14'3	2.46m/8'1	119m^2/1,281sq.ft	9	$149,000us

COLUMBIA 56 MS   Columbia Yachts, U.S.A.

16.94m/55'7	3.96m/13'0	2.44m/8'0	113.8m^2/1,225sq.ft	8	$150,000us

PRIVATEER 57/52   Trewes International, England

17.37m/57'0	—	1.68m/5'6	Optional	—	o/a

VENTURA

S. van de Meer, Holland
World Holidays Afloat, England

17.91m/58'9	4.65m/15'3	1.98m/6'6	130.1m^2/1,400sq.ft	8	o/a

BORDER KING   Eyemouth Boatbuilding Co., U.K.

18.29m/60'0	—	1.83m/6'0	Optional	10	o/a

C & C CUSTOM 61

C & C Yachts Manufacturing, Canada
Anstey Yachts, England

18.67m/61'3	4.6m/15'1	2.62m/8'7	158.5m^2/1,706sq.ft	—	o/a

SWAN 65

Nautor, Finland
Nautor, U.S.A.
Dave Johnson, England

19.51m/64'	4.95m/16'3	2.77m/9'1	210.9m^2/2,270sq.ft	11	£108,000

PRIVATEER 70/64   Trewes International, England

21,34m/70'0	—	2.13m/7'0	Optional	—	o/a

LOA	BEAM	DRAFT	SAIL AREA	BERTHS	PRICE

PALMER JOHNSON 65   Palmer Johnson Inc., U.S.A.

| 19.68m/64'7 | 4.98m/16'4 | 2.94m/9'8 | 159.1m^2/1,713sq.ft | 11 | $225,000us |

PRIVATEER 77/70   Trewes International, England

| 23.47m/77'0 | – | 2.13m/7'0 | 185.8m^2/2,000sq.ft | – | o/a |

PALMER JOHNSON 82   Palmer Johnson Inc., U.S.A.

| 24.99m/82'0 | – | – | 193.6m^2/2,084sq.ft | 10 | o/a |

BOATS NOT IN PRODUCTION
second-hand models normally available

NAME	LOA	MANUFACTURER
YANKEE SEAHORSE 24 ¼ TON	7.24m	Yankee Yachts, U.S.A.
CAL 2-24	7.32m	Jensen Marine, U.S.A.
CAL 24	7.32m	Jensen Marine, U.S.A.
GLADIATOR	7.32m	Golden West Yachts, U.S.A.
LAPWORTH 24	7.32m	
LARK	7.32m	Pearson Yachts, U.S.A.
SEAFARER 24	7.32m	Seafarer Fiberglass Yachts, Ltd.
CHANCE 24	7.34m	Paceship Yachts, Canada
YANKEE DOLPHIN	7.37m	Yankee Yachts, U.S.A.
CHALLENGER	7.42m	Columbia Yacht Corp., U.S.A.
MIRROR OFFSHORE	5.77m	Mirror Boats, England
BRISTOL 19	5.96m	Bristol Yacht Co., U.S.A.
HURLEY 20	6.1m	Hurley Marine, England
HIRLEY 22	6.71m	Hurley Marine, England
GULF COAST 22	6.71m	Gulf Coast Sailboats, U.S.A.
MUSTANG	6.71m	Plastrend, U.S.A.
ELECTRA	6.86m	Pearson Yachts, U.S.A,
CORONADO 23	6.88m	Coronado Yachts, U.S.A.
ERICSON 23	6.88m	Ericson Yachts, U.S.A.
SEAFARER 23	7.03m	Seafarer Fiberglass Yachts, U.S.A.
TEMPEST	7.06m	O'Day Co., U.S.A.
CUTLASS	7.19m	Richard D. Carlson, U.S.A.

NAME	LOA	MANUFACTURER
CORONADO 25	7.62m	Coronado Yachts, U.S.A.
VICTOIRE 25	7.67m	Yachtwerf Victoire, Holland
ARIEL	7.8m	Pearson Yachts, U.S.A.
COMMANDER	7.8m	Pearson Yachts, U.S.A.
SEAFARER 26	7.8m	Seafarer Fiberglass Yachts, U.S.A.
ERICSON 26	7.85m	Ericson Yachts, U.S.A.
EXCALIBUR 26	7.9m	William Crealock, U.S.A.
OUTLAW	7.92m	O'Day Co., U.S.A.
RAWSON 26	7.92m	Ron Rawson Inc., U.S.A.
CAP VERT	8m	Herbulot, France
HEWELL CADET	8.06m	Lion Yachts, U.S.A.
HURLEY 27	8.23m	Hurley Marine, England
TARTAN 27	8.23m	Tartan Marine Co., U.S.A.
IRWIN 27	8.25m	Irwin Yacht and Marine Corporation, U.S.A.
RENEGADE	8.28m	Pearson Yachts, U.S.A.
COLUMBIA 28	8.41m	Columbia Yacht Corp., U.S.A.
MORGAN 28	8.48m	Morgan Yacht Corporation, U.S.A.
CAL 28	8.53m	Jensen Marine, U.S.A.
HR 28	8.61m	George Hinterhoeller, U.S.A.
COLUMBIA 29	8.69m	Columbia Yacht Corporation, U.S.A.
TRITON	8.69m	Janet et Cie, France
SOVEREL 28	8.76m	Soverel Marine, U.S.A.
NORTH WIND	8.79m	Paceship Yachts, Canada
BRISTOL 29	8.99m	Bristol Yachts, U.S.A.

NAME	LOA	MANUFACTURER
CONTEST 29	8.94m	Conyplex, Holland
NORTH STAR 29	8.94m	North Star Yachts, U.S.A.
CONSTELLATION 30	9.04m	Graves Yacht Yards, U.S.A.
CAL 30	9.14m	Jensen Marine, U.S.A.
NIAGRA 30	9.14m	George Hinterhoeller, U.S.A.
CAL 2-30	9.2m	Jensen Marine, U.S.A.
NORTH COAST 30	9.22m	Richard D. Carlson, U.S.A.
REDWING 30	9.22m	C. &. C. Yachts, Canada
COLUMBIA 31	9.3m	Columbia Yacht Corporation, U.S.A.
MARINER 31	9.37m	Katoh/Clair Yachts, U.S.A.
C. & C. CORVETTE 31	9.52m	C. & C. Yachts, Canada
MARINER 32	9.68m	Katoh/Clair Yachts Inc., U.S.A.
MISTRESS	9.7m	Allied Boat Co., U.S.A.
CHEROKEE 32	9.75m	Chris-Craft Corporation, U.S.A.
BRISTOL 32	9.77m	Bristol Yacht Co., U.S.A.
COLUMBIA 5.5	9.88m	Columbia Yacht Corporation, U.S.A.
SABRE	9.88m	Columbia Yacht Corporation, U.S.A.
MORGAN 33 - ¾ ton	9.91m	Morgan Yacht Corporation, U.S.A.
VANGUARD	9.93m	Pearson Yachts, U.S.A.
SYMONS 33	9.95m	Symons Sailing Inc., U.S.A.
MANTUCKET 33	10.06m	Alan P. Gurney, U.S.A.
CAL 34	10.13m	Jensen Marine, U.S.A.
MEDALIST	10.13m	A le Comte Inc., U.S.A.
MISTRAL	10.21m	XAX Corporation U.S.A.

NAME	LOA	MANUFACTURER
BRISTOL 33	10.23m	Bristol Yachts, U.S.A.
COMPETITION 34	10.36m	Henry R. Hinckley Co., U.S.A.
MORGAN CUSTOM 34	10.36m	Morgan Yacht Corporation, U.S.A.
BRISTOL 34	10.44m	Bristol Yacht Co., U.S.A.
BRISTOL 35	10.56m	Bristol Yachts, U.S.A.
CORONADO 34	10.56m	Coronado Yachts, U.S.A.
ALBERG 35	10.59m	Whitby Boat Works, Canada
CAL 36	10.82m	Jensen Marine, U.S.A.
FRIGATE	10.87m	Belleville Marine, Canada
INVADER	10.87m	C. & C. Yachts, Canada
INTERNATIONAL 500	10.97m	Robert Henry, U.S.A.
PALMER JOHNSON 36	10.97m	Palmer Johnson Inc., U.S.A.
OHLSON 36	11.05m	Campbell/Sheehan Inc., U.S.A.
APACHE 37 Mk II	11.28m	Chris Craft, U.S.A.
BLACK WATCH	11.28m	Douglas and McLeod, U.S.A.
MORGAN 38	11.48m	Morgan Yacht Corporation, U.S.A.
INVICTA II	11.48m	Pearson Yachts, U.S.A.
SOVEREL 38	11.583m	Soverel Marine, U.S.A.
COLUMBIA 40	11.94m	Columbia Yacht Corporation, U.S.A.
BRISTOL 39	11.96m	Bristol Yachts, U.S.A.
C. & C. 40	12.09m	C. & C. Yachts Manufacturing Canada
CRUSADER	12.09m	Belleville Marine, Canada
CONCORDIA YAWL	12.14m	Concordia Co. Inc., U.S.A.
SYMONS 31	9.45m	Symons Sailing Inc., U.S.A.

NAME	LOA	MANUFACTURER
MARINER 40	12.29m	Katoh/Clair Yachts, U.S.A.
CONCORDIA 41	12.5m	Concordia Co. Inc., U.S.A.
RHODES 41	12.5m	Lion Yachts, U.S.A.
REDLINE 41 Mk II	12.62m	C. & C. Yachts, Canada
CARAVELLE 42	12.67m	John G. Alden, U.S.A.
CAL 43	13m	Jensen Marine, U.S.A.
PEARSON 43	13.03m	Pearson Yachts, U.S.A.
COUNTESS 44	13.56m	Pearson Yachts, U.S.A.
SAILMASTER 45	13.74m	Sparkman & Stephens, U.S.A.
MORGAN 45	13.92m	Morgan Yacht Corporation, U.S.A.
COLUMBIA 50	15.24m	Columbia Yacht Corporation U.S.A.
COLUMBIA 57	17.22m	Columbia Yacht Corporation U.S.A.

INDEX OF MANUFACTURERS

THE ANCHORAGE CO.,
Miller St., Warren, RI 02885, U.S.A.
ANDERSON MARINE,
136 South St., Lancing, Sussex, England
ANDERSON RIGDEN & PERKINS,
The Shipyard, Island Wall, Whitstable, Kent, England
ANGLIA YACHTS,
Broad Lane, Lottenham, Cambridgeshire, England
ANGLIA YACHTS,
Riverside Works, Mariner's Way, Cambridge, England
ANNAPOLIS BOAT RENTALS,
Annapolis, MD, U.S.A.
ANNAPOLIS SAILBOAT BUILDERS,
Generals Highway RFD1, Annapolis, MD 21401, U.S.A.
ANSTEY YACHTS,
Cobbs Quay, Denmark Rd., Poole, Dorset, England
APOLLO ASSOCIATION,
9 Buttercross Lane, Epping, Essex, England
AQUA BELL LTD.,
Brundall, Norwich, England
AQUABOATS LTD.,
261-263 Lymington Rd., Highcliffe on Sea, Christchurch, Hampshire, England
AQUAFIBRE INTERNATIONAL,
Rackheath, Norfolk, NOR 02Z, England
AQUARIUS NATIONAL ASSOCIATION,
4315 Le Jeune Rd., 202-204 Coral Gables, FL 33134, U.S.A.
ARDEN YACHTS LTD.,
27 East King St., Helensburgh, Dunbarton G84 7QQ, Scotland
ARENA CRAFT PRODUCTS INC.,
130 Buchanan Circle, Pacheco, California, U.S.A.
ARMA MARINE ENGINEERING CO.,
Waterside, The Shipyard, Brightlingsea, Essex, England
ARMA MARINE ENGINEERING CO. LTD.,
53 Whytecliffe Rd., Purley, Surrey, England
ARMSHIRE REINFORCED PLASTICS,
545 Ipswich Rd., Trading Estate, Slough, Buckinghamshire, England
ARROW ASSOCIATION,
120 Woodbine Ave., Wilmette, ILL 60091, U.S.A.
ARROW INFORMATION,
R. Wilson, 120 Midwest Rd., Scarborough, Ontario, Canada
ARROWGLASS BOAT & MFG. CORP.,
1371 Farmville Rd., Memphis, Tenn. 38122, U.S.A.
ARTEKNO,
SF 36220, Suorama Kangasala, Finland
ASSOCIATED YACHTS INC.,
119 Rowayton Ave., Rowayton, CT 06853, U.S.A.
ATLANTA MARINE,
Arnside Rd., Waterlooville, Hampshire, England
ATLANTIC ASSOCIATION,
Lawrence Heffron, 85 Main St., Southport, CT, U.S.A.
AUBIN,
110 Rue de la Basse Ile, 44400 Reze Les Nantes, France
AUSTRALIS ASSOCIATION,
R. Shiels, 26 Driftway Lane, Darien, CT 06820, U.S.A.
AWSON MARINE,
44 Ashley Rd., Boscombe, Bournemouth, Hampshire, England
KLAUS BAESS,
18 Kompagnistraede, Copenhagen K, Denmark

JOHN BAKER (KENTON FORGE) LTD.,
Kenton, Nr. Exeter, Devon, England
BAL MARINE,
30 The Hornet, Chichester, Sussex, England
BALLENA LTD.,
Castleton House, Hamble, Hampshire, England
BANSHEE INC.,
231 E Millbrae Ave., Millbrae, CA 94030, U.S.A.
BANSHEE NATIONAL ASSOCIATION,
Barry Bruch, 12186 Winton Way, Los Altos Hill, CA 94022, U.S.A.
BAREFOOT 12 ASSOCIATION,
R. Medve, 4241 Via Alondra, Palos Verdes Estates, CA 90274, U.S.A.
BARNEGAT BAY SNEAKBOX ASSOCIATION,
A. Chadwick, P. O. Box 312, Barnegat, NJ 08005, U.S.A.
BARNEGAT 17 NATIONAL ASSOCIATION,
D. Webster, Island Heights, NJ 08732, U.S.A.
BARON CRAFT,
Harvey Close, Crowther Industrial Estate, Washington New Town, Co. Durham
England
BARON CRAFT,
Unit 2, Runwood Rd., Charfleet Industrial Estate, Canvey Island, Essex, England
BARRON SAILBOAT DISTRIBUTORS,
25639 Ivanhoe, Detroit, MI 48239, U.S.A.
BARTON MARINE,
Riverside Estate, The Causeway, Staines, Middlesex, England
BASIN BOATCRAFT CO.,
Oakland, California, U.S.A.
BATFORDNEDLING SYD AB.,
Smotbatshammen 216, 12 Malmo, Sweden
BAYC,
1033 E Auburn Rd., Rochester, MI 48063, U.S.A.
BAYMASTER NATIONAL ASSOCIATION,
Bill Smith, 4321 Stillbroke, Houston, TX 77035, U.S.A.
BEBS MARINE LTD.,
Quay Works, Burnham on Crouch, Essex, England
BEETLE CAT ASSOCIATION,
C. E. Clapp, 15 Westminster St., Providence, RI 02903, U.S.A.
ALLAN BELL CATAMARANS,
Sea Wall, Whitstable, Kent, England
BELL WOODWORKING CO.,
199 Narborough Road South, Leicester, LE3 1LG, England
BIANCA YACHTS,
A/S Myrehøjvej, 31-33 DK 5700, Svendborg, Denmark
BIG APPLE ASSOCIATION,
G. Revett, Box 146, East Aurara, NY 14052, U.S.A.
BRUCE BINGHAM,
P.O. Box 1413, Santa Barbara, CA 93102, U.S.A.
B. LION ASSOCIATION,
R. Moore, A5 Devonshire East, English Village, North Wales, PA 19454, U.S.A.
BLOCK ISLAND ASSOCIATION,
Pane Rosenfeld, Box 471, Putnam, CT 06260, U.S.A.
BLUE CRAB ASSOCIATION,
Box 307, Glencester, VA 23061, U.S.A.
BLUE JAY ASSOCIATION,
11 East 44th St., New York, NY 10017, U.S.A.
BOB CRUISING CAT ASSOCIATION,
Flagstaff House, Muddeford, Hampshire, England

BOBBIN INTERNATIONAL ASSOCIATION,
M. Bennett, 49 North St., Wareham, Dorset, England
ARTHUR L. BOLTON,
125 Kelseytown Rd., Clinton, Conn. 06413, U.S.A.
BONITO ASSOCIATION,
44 Childsbridge Lane, Kemsing, Sevenoaks, Kent, England
BONITO NATIONAL ASSOCIATION,
R. Olsen, 26 Willis St., — Apt. #18, Framingham, MA, U.S.A.
BONWITCO,
38 Ebrington St., Kingsbridge, Devon, England
BORDER MARINE,
Sandstell Rd., Spittal, Berwick on Tweed, England
A/S BORRESENS BAADEBYGGERL,
Dragevej, 7100 Vejle, Denmark
BOSSOMS BOATYARD,
Medley, Oxford, England
BOSTON WHALER INC.,
1149 Higham St., Rockland, MA 02370, U.S.A.
BOSUN ASSOCIATION,
RN Club, Pembroke Rd., Portsmouth, Hampshire, England
BOURNE PLASTICS LTD.,
Harby Rd., Langar, Nottingham, England
BOWMAN BOATS LTD.,
Whiteways, 54 Beacon Rd., Chatham, Kent, England
BRAAE MARIN,
DK 6000, Kolding Standvaengt 12, Denmark
BRABOURNE MARINE LTD.,
115 Grays Inn Rd., London WC1, England
R.R.A. BRATT
North End Works, Millers Close, Dorchester, Dorset, England
EDWARD S. BREWER & ASSOCIATES,
Brooklin, ME 04616, U.S.A.
BRISTOL YACHTS,
Franklin St., Bristol, RI 02809, U.S.A.
BRITISH & EUROPEAN BOAT SALES,
Coronation Rd., Burnham-on-Crouch, Essex, England
BRITISH MOTH ASSOCIATION,
Broxhaven, Old Nazeing Rd., Broxbourne, Hertfordshire, England
BROADLAND MARINE,
Broadlands Boatyard, Caldicott Rd., Oulton Broad, Lowestoft, Suffolk, England
BROWNING MARINE DIVISION,
900 Chesaning St., St. Charles, MI 48655, U.S.A.
BRUCE BINGHAM,
P.O. Box 1413, Santa Barbara, CA 93102, U.S.A.
D. BRUCE CONNOLLY,
P.O. Box 1345, Waterbury, CT 06720, U.S.A.
BUCCANEER ASSOCIATION,
M.P. Scott, 24821 Five Mile Rd., Detroit, MI 48239, U.S.A.
BUCHAN BOAT WORKS,
2032, 43rd Ave. E., Seattle, WA 98102, U.S.A.
BUCKEYE NATIONAL ASSOCIATION,
W. Mynchenberg, 8467 Hallnorth Drive, Mentor, OH 44060, U.S.A.
BUCKLER BOAT CO.,
1 Bryanston Ave., Guildford, Surrey, England
BULLS' EYE ASSOCIATION,
George Warren Smith, P.O. Box 506, Pigeon Cove, MA 01966, U.S.A.
BUNYIP 20 ASSOCIATION,
B. Anderson, P. O. Box 1232, Thousand Oaks, CA 91360, U.S.A.

BURNE'S SHIPYARD,
Bosham, Sussex, England
BURR BROS. YACHT YARD,
Marion, Mass., U.S.A.
JOHN BUSHNELL (ENGINEERING) CO.,
The Boatyard, Station Rd., Wargrave, Berkshire, England
W.L. BUSSELL & CO.,
Hope Quay, Weymouth, Dorset, England
E.R. BUTLER & SONS,
25 Mugford St., Marblehead, MA 01945, U.S.A.
BUTLER MOULDINGS,
Victoria Rd., Gowerton, Glamorgan, SA4 3AH, Wales
BUZZARDS BAY BOATS,
Harbor Rd., Mattapoisett, MA 02739, U.S.A.
CACTUS ASSOCIATION,
c/o 4321 Stillbrooke, Houston, TX 77035, U.S.A.
CAL CAT ASSOCIATION,
c/o H. Sindle, Rte. 623, Gloucester, VA 23061, U.S.A.
CAMPBELL SHEEHAN INC.,
1415 Boston Post Rd., Larchmont, NY 10538, U.S.A.
CAMPER & NICHOLSONS LTD.,
The Green, Gosport, Hampshire, England
CAMPER & NICHOLSONS,
30/31 La Croisette, 06 Cannes, France
CAMPER & NICHOLSONS U.S.A.,
So Freeport, ME 04078, U.S.A.
CANADIAN BOAT MFG. CO.,
Rue des Erabies, Princeville, Quebec, Canada
CANADIAN SABOT ASSOCIATION,
c/o Mrs. Bickerstaff, P.O. Box 2446, Vancouver 3, BC, Canada
CANADIAN SAILCRAFT CO.,
8300 Yonge St., Willowdale, Ontario, Canada
CAPE COD KNOCKABOUT ASSOCIATION,
c/o Dr. Schaefer, Box 384, West Dennis, MA 02670, U.S.A.
CAPE COD MERCURY ASSOCIATION (NATIONAL),
c/o A. Runge, 901 Main St., Higham, MA, U.S.A.
CAPE COD SHIPBUILDING CO.,
Wareham, MA 02571, U.S.A.
CAPE DORY CO. INC.,
373 Crescent St., West Bridgewater, MA 02379, U.S.A.
CAPE YACHTS LTD.,
P.O. Box 6, Peng Chau, Hong Kong, BCC
CAPITAL YACHTS INC.,
25914 President Ave., Harbor City, CA 90710, U.S.A.
CAPRICE WORLD ASSOCIATION,
c/o Mrs. Tennyson, 67 Beandale Rd., Willowdale, Ontario, Canada
CAPRI CYCLONE ASSOCIATION,
8211 Lankershim Blvd., North Hollywood, CA 91605, U.S.A.
CAPRI SAILBOATS,
8211 Lankershim Blvd., North Hollywood, CA 91605, U.S.A.
CARDIFF BOATBUILDING CO.,
Roath Basin, Bute Dock, Cardiff, Glamorgan, Wales
CARDINAL ASSOCIATION,
c/o B. Smith, 4321 Stillbrooke, Houston, TX 77035, U.S.A.
RICHARD D. CARLSON,
North Coast Marine, Tennis Court Lane, Shelter Island, NY 11964, U.S.A.
CARTER OFFSHORE,
111 Coast Rd., West Mersea, Essex, England

CARTER OFFSHORE,
400 Nahant St., Nahant, MA 01808, U.S.A.
CASTLEMAIN MARINE LTD.,
8 South St., Chichester, Sussex, England
CATALINA YACHTS INC.,
8211 Lankershim Blvd., North Hollywood, CA 91605, U.S.A.
C & C YACHTS (EUROPEAN DIVISION),
19 King St., Emsworth, Hampshire, England
C & C YACHTS MFG. LTD.,
Box 970, 526 Regent St., Niagara-on-the-Lake, Ontario, Canada
CELEBRITY ASSOCIATION,
c/o J. Sark, 5736 Greene St., Philadelphia, PA 19144, U.S.A.
ALAN CHADWICK,
E. Brook St., Barnegat, NJ, U.S.A.
CHALLENGE ASSOCIATION,
St. Menas, 42 Swift Rd., Woolston, Southampton, SO2 9FN, England
CHALLENGER 15 ASSOCIATION,
c/o Leon F. Irish Co., 4300 Haggerty Rd., Walled Rd., MI 48088, U.S.A.
CHALLENGER YACHT CORP.,
1401 Dock St., Terminal Island, CA 90731, U.S.A.
CHANCE MARINE,
Box 483, 1634 Forest St., Wilmette, ILL 60091, U.S.A.
CHANTIER MALLARD,
La Rochelle, France
CHEETAH BOAT MFG.,
8091 Pacific Ave., Stanton, CA 90680, U.S.A.
CHEETAH CAT ASSOCIATION,
c/o L. Deschamps, 20 South Cherry Grove Ave., Annapolis, MD 21401, U.S.A.
CHESFORD MARINE,
Bridge Boat Yard, Frogmore Creek, Kingsbridge, Devon, England
CHESHIRE ASSOCIATION,
c/o B. Akers, 1986B Van Voorhis, Ft. Eustis, VA 23604, U.S.A.
DAVID CHEVERTON & PARTNERS LTD.,
West Medina Mills, Newport, Isle of Wight, England
CHIC ASSOCIATION,
c/o Peter D. van Dine & Co., P.O. Box 8, Annapolis, MD 21404, U.S.A.
CHICHESTER YACHT AGENCY,
10 North Pallant, Chichester, Sussex, England
CHRIS-CRAFT CORP.,
P.O. Box 860, Pompano Beach, FL 33061, U.S.A.
CHRYSLER O.D. SAILBOATS,
P.O. Box 2641, Detroit, MI 48231, U.S.A.
CIRCLE MARKETING,
Kelvin House, Totteridge Ave., High Wycombe, Buckinghamshire, England
CL 11 ASSOCIATION,
c/o M. Martens, 356 Henderson Ave., Burlington, Ontario, Canada
CL 16 ASSOCIATION,
C/o G. Dodd, 66 Broadway Ave., No. 105, Toronto 12, Ontario, Canada
J. G. CLARIDGE,
25 Woodside Ave., Lymington, Hampshire, England
C-LARK ASSOCIATION,
c/o D. Collins, 1725 Grand Ave., Medford, OR 97501, U.S.A.
CLARK BOAT CO.,
18817 East Valley Highway, Kent, WA 98031, U.S.A.
CLARKE SIMPSON YACHTS SALES,
999 Kingsway, Vancouver 10, BC, Canada
C & L BOATWORKS,
284 Fairall, Ajax, Ontario, Canada

CLEAREX PLASTICS LTD.,
Leisure Activities Division, Fench Houses, Houghton-le-Spring, Durham, England
CLIPPERCRAFT MARINE PRODUCTS,
Imperial Way, Watford, Hertfordshire, England
CLIPPER MARINE CORP.,
1919 E Occidental St., Santa Ana, CA 92704, U.S.A.
CLIPPER NATIONAL CLASS ASSOCIATION,
c/o C. Bogne, 121 Edwards St., Sausalito, CA 94965, U.S.A.
COASTAL RECREATION INC.,
940 W 17th St., Costa Mesa, CA 92627, U.S.A.
COAST CATAMARANS,
33012 Calle Perfecto, San Juan, Capistrano, CA 92675, U.S.A.
COBRAMOLD LTD.,
22nd St., Stanstead Airport, Essex, England
COLUMBIA 22 NATIONAL ASSOCIATION,
c/o J. Keith, 1711 Heather Ave., Tustin, CA 92680, U.S.A.
COLUMBIA YACHT CORP.,
275 McCormick Ave., Costa Mesa, CA 92626, U.S.A.
COMET CLASS ASSOCIATION,
230 W South St., Carlisle, PA 17013, U.S.A.
COMEXTRA,
15 Flambard Rd., Parkstone, Poole, Dorset, BH14 8SO, England
COMPOSITE TECHNOLOGY INC.,
1005 Blue Mound Rd., Fort Worth, TX 76131, U.S.A.
COMPTON PAGE LTD.,
White's Shipyard, Hazel Rd., Woolston, Southampton, Hampshire, England
CONCORDIA CO. INC.,
South Wharf, So. Dartmouth, MA 02748, U.S.A.
CONTENDER ASSOCIATION,
Al Santos, 965 Hutchinson Ave., Palo Alto, CA 94301, U.S.A.
CONYPLEX NV.,
Alkmaar, P.O. Box 17, Holland
COPLAND BOATS,
Belle Vue Rd., Ventnor, Isle of Wight, England
CORAIL MARINE,
23 Rue Sebastian Mercier, 75015 Paris, France
CORONADO 15 ASSOCIATION,
P.O. Box 1684, Whittier, CA 90603, U.S.A.
CORONADO YACHTS,
275 McCormick Ave., Costa Mesa, CA 92626, U.S.A.
COTTONTAIL ASSOCIATION,
c/o P. Donohue, 3 Colonial Court, Bay Shore, LI, NY, U.S.A.
COX MARINE LTD.,
The Shipyard Estate, Brightlingsea, Essex, England
CRAFTMAKERS LTD.,
Brownhill Bridge Mill, Dobcross, Oldham, Lancashire, England
RAYMOND CREEKMORE,
2440 Magna Ave., Coconut Grove, FL 33133, U.S.A.
CRESCENT SLOOP CLASS ASSOCIATION,
3417 Seminole Ave., Detroit, MI 48214, U.S.A.
NORMAN A. CROSS,
4326 Ashton St., San Diego, CA 92110, U.S.A.
CUB SCOW ASSOCIATION,
15906 Wayzata Blvd., Wayzata, MN 55391, U.S.A.
CUMBERLAND BOAT CO.,
Hesket Newmarket, Cumbria, England
CUSTOMFLEX INC.,
1817 Palmwood, Toledo, OH 43607, U.S.A.

CYGNUS NATIONAL ASSOCIATION,
c/o A. Macharen, 43 Collier St., Barrie, Ontario, Canada
DABCHICK INTERNATIONAL ASSOCIATION,
Jack Koper, 43 Byeway, Pinelands, Capetown, South Africa
DABCHICK INTERNATIONAL ASSOCIATION,
c/o D. Blue Jnr., P.O. Box 1090, Tulsa, OK 74101, U.S.A.
RICHARD DADSON,
114 Upper Brents, Faversham, Kent, England
DALEY YACHT & BOAT CO.,
Vicarage Lane, Hoo, Rochester, Kent, England
DANE-CRAFT,
31166 W 8 Mile Rd., Farnington, MI 48024, U.S.A.
DANYACHTS,
259 New Canaan Rd., Wilton, CT 06897, U.S.A.
DART MARINA LTD.,
Sandquay, Dartmouth, Devon, England
DAUNTLESS CO.,
Canvey Island, Essex, England
IVAN DAVIES,
623 Myra Way, San Francisco, California, U.S.A.
M.C. DAVIES,
113 High St., Cowes, Isle of Wight, England
DAY SAILER ASSOCIATION,
2801 Raleigh Lane, Cincinatti, OH 45215, U.S.A.
DEHLER BELGIUM,
119-127 Rue Ed. Faesstraat, B-1090 Brussels, Belgium
DEHLER BOOTSBAU,
D 5777 Freienohl/Ruhr, Im Langel, West Germany
DEHLER NEDERLAND,
E G van de Stadt BV, Zuiddijk 412, NL-Zaandam, Holland
F. DEKKER EN ZONEN,
Diemerzeedijk 3, Amsterdam Oost, Holland
DEMON ASSOCIATION,
c/o T. Wilke, 9840 Grewood, Overland Park, KS 66212, U.S.A.
DEVON CRAFT LTD.,
Shadycombe Creek, Salcombe, Devon, England
DICKERSON BOATBUILDERS INC.,
Trappe, MD 21673, U.S.A.
DILKS & CO.,
P.O. Box 341, Clarksville, AR 72830, U.S.A.
PETER V. VAN DINE & CO.,
P.O. Box 8, Annapolis, MD 21404, U.S.A.
THE DINGHY SHOP,
2905 SW 2nd Ave., Fort Lauderdale, FL 33315, U.S.A.
DISCOVERER ASSOCIATION,
c/o A. Garon, 3004 Bendix Lane, Bowie, MD 20715, U.S.A.
DOBSONS YACHT & BOATBUILDERS LTD.,
Shardlow Wharf, Shardlow, Nr. Derby, England
DOLPHIN SAILBOATS,
6105 W 34th St., Houston, TX 77018, U.S.A.
DOUGLASS & MCLEOD INC.,
P.O. Box 311, Painesville, OH 44077, U.S.A.
DOVEY HOLDINGS SOUTH WALES LTD.,
Cardiff, Wales
DOWN MARINE CO.,
163 Comber Rd., Dundonald, Belfast, Northern Ireland
MICHEL DUFOUR SA,
Zone Industrielle, 17 Perigny, La Rochelle, France

MICHEL DUFOUR U.S.A.,
15 Columbus Circle, New York, NY 10023, U.S.A.
J. DUNHILL ENTERPRISES,
48 Wellington St., Slough, Buckinghamshire, England
DUO ASSOCIATION,
P.O. Box 459, Stuyvesant St., New York, NY 10009, U.S.A.
DURABILT CORPORATION,
3081 Indiana Ave., Winston-Salem, North Carolina 27105, U.S.A.
DURRELLS BOAT AGENCY,
26 Durrels House, Warwick Gardens, W14 8QB, England
JACHTWERF VAN DUSSELDORP,
Nieuw Loosdrechtsedijk 204 B, Loosdrecht 1321, Holland
DUSTER ASSOCIATION,
c/o J. Kassar, P.O. Box 55, Riverton, NJ 08077, U.S.A.
DUTCH YACHTS IMPORTERS INC.,
4559 Oxfort 260, Montreal, Quebec, Canada
DYER DELTA ASSOCIATION,
c/o C. Street, 125 Governors Drive, Warwick, RI, U.S.A.
DYER DHOW 9' ASSOCIATION,
c/o J. Meade, Croton Lake Rd., Mt. Kisco, NY 10549, U.S.A.
DYER DHOW 12½ ASSOCIATION,
c/o W. Jones, 112 Congdon St., Providence, RI 02906, U.S.A.
DYER DINK 10 ASSOCIATION,
c/o J. Hansel, 191 Riverside Ave., Riverside, CT 06878, U.S.A.
EAST COAST MARINE CO.,
32 Sydney St., Brightlingsea, Essex, England
EAST COAST YACHT AGENCY (now INTERYACHT),
6 Quay St., Woodbridge, Suffolk, England
EASTERLY YACHTS,
P.O. Box 9104, 1729 Lake Ave., Metairie, LA 70005, U.S.A.
EDEY & DUFF INC.,
10 Harbor Rd., Mattapoisett, MA 02739, U.S.A.
RICHARD P. EDIE,
10 Westport Ave., Norwalk, Conn. 06851, U.S.A.
EIGHTEEN FOOT SKIFF ASSOCIATION,
c/o Mrs. Long, 30 The Gardens, Doddinghurst, Essex, CM15 0LU, England
ELEPHANT BOATYARD,
Old Bursledon, Hampshire, SO3 8DN, England
ROBIN ELSDALE LTD.,
3 Bridge St., Newhaven, Sussex, England
EL TORO INTERNATIONAL ASSOCIATION,
6211 La Salle Ave., Oakland, CA 94611, U.S.A.
EMSWORTH MARINE SALES,
The Yacht Harbour, Emsworth, Hampshire, England
ENGLAND'S SAILBOATS & YACHTING SERVICES,
Main Harbor, Barnette Reservoir, Box 12362 Jackson, MS 39211, U.S.A.
ENSIGN NATIONAL ASSOCIATION,
c/o Merle Hallett, Commodore, 320 Hallett Rd., Falmouth, Foreside, ME 04105,
U.S.A.
ENTERPRISE ASSOCIATION,
c/o D. McAllister, 145 Surf Place, Seal Beach, CA 90740, U.S.A.
ERICSON YACHTS INC.,
1931 Deere Ave., Santa Ana, CA 92705, U.S.A.
TERRY ERSKINE YACHTS,
11 Newport St., Stonehouse, Plymouth, Devon, England
ESB DINGHIES,
Maer Lane, Exmouth, Devon, England

ESSEX CO. LTD.,
P.O. Box 589, Camden, NJ 08101, U.S.A.
ESSEX YACHT BUILDERS,
Wallasea Bay, Rochford, Essex, SS4 2HG, U.S.A.
ESSOR NAVAL DU MIDI,
Balagvier, 83 La Seyne Sur Mer, France
ETCHELLS 22 NATIONAL ASSOCIATION,
c/o James Fulton, 720 The Crescent, Mamaroneck, NY 10543, U.S.A.
E.W. ETCHELLS,
P.O. Box 125, Old Greenwich, Connecticut 06870, U.S.A.
EUROPEAN RESEARCH & SUPPLY CORPORATION,
250 W 57th St., New York, U.S.A..
EUROYACHTS LTD.,
Scottish Boat Centre, Clyde Place, Glasgow, C.5, Scotland
P. EVANSON YACHT CO.,
Reserve Ave., Riverside, New Jersey 08075, U.S.A.
EYEMOUTH BOAT BUILDING CO.,
Harbour Rd., Eyemouth, Berwickshire, Scotland
FAIREY MARINE,
Hamble, Southampton, Hampshire, SO3 5ND, England
FAIRWAYS MARINE,
David Skellon Yachts, Hamble, Southampton, Hampshire, England
FALCON ASSOCIATION,
c/o M. Sazarin, 30 Laudry Ave., No. Attleboro, MA 02760, U.S.A.
FALMOUTH BOAT CONSTRUCTION,
Little Falmouth Yacht Yard, Falmouth, Cornwall, England
FASTNET MARINE,
Raheen Industrial Estate, Limerick and 136 South St., Lancing, Sussex, England
FEATHERWEIGHT MARINE,
10 Edgewood Ave., Glen Head, NY 11545, U.S.A.
FENNEC ASSOCIATION,
c/o Mrs. Gueydon, P.O. Box 459, Stuyvesant Station, New York, NY 10009,
U.S.A.
FENNEC DINGHIES,
17 Vale Close, Harpenden, Hertfordshire, England
FERGUSON BROS. (BRADWELL) LTD.,
Lock Hill, Heybridge, Maldon, Essex, England
FIBERFORM,
Div. of U.S. Industries Inc., Bldg. 20, Spokane Industrial Park, Spokane,
Washington 99216, U.S.A.
FIBOCON bv,
Kampen, Industrieweg 3, Holland
FIBROCELL LTD.,
Britannia Mill, Willow St., Oldham, Lancashire, England
FI-CRAFT,
Star Lane Industrial Estate, Great Wakering, England
FINN INTERNATIONAL ASSOCIATION,
c/o H. van Elst, Gravenzandestraat 6, Utrecht, Holland
FIREBALL INTERNATIONAL ASSOCIATION,
Alderfen, Neatishead, Norwich, NOR 37Z, England
FIREFLY ASSOCIATION,
c/o Sandy Bay YC, Rockport, MA, U.S.A.
505 NATIONAL ASSOCIATION,
c/o Victor Sheronas, 114 Forest Ave., Narberth, PA 19072, U.S.A.
505 INTERNATIONAL ASSOCIATION,
c/o Cmdr. Chandler, Seaside Way, St. Leonards on Sea, Sussex, England
FLIPPER ASSOCIATION,
c/o C. McCabe, 2596 Crestview Drive, Newport Beach, CA, U.S.A.

FLITE 12 ASSOCIATION,
c/o D. Bruce Connolly, P.O. Box 1345, Waterbury, CT 06720, U.S.A.
FLYING DUTCHMAN INTERNATIONAL ASSOCIATION,
c/o C. Gulcher, Graf W de Ondelaan 69, Naarden, Holland
FLYING DUTCHMAN NATIONAL ASSOCIATION,
c/o B. W. Wright, P.O. Box 3746, Baston Range, LA 70821, U.S.A.
FLYING FIFTEEN INTERNATIONAL ASSOCIATION,
c/o John Fleming, 86 Marlborough Ave., Glasgow W1, Scotland
FLYING FIFTEEN NATIONAL ASSOCIATION,
c/o Irving Rubin, 1609 Channing Way, Berkeley, CA 94703, U.S.A.
FLYING JUNIOR INTERNATIONAL ASSOCIATION,
c/o C. Gulcher, Graaf W de Ondelaan 69, Naarden, Holland
FLYING SCOT ASSOCIATION,
c/o Mrs. Doolittle, 531 Jenks Blvd., Kalamazoo, MI 49007, U.S.A.
FORMEX CORPORATION,
505 Belvedere, Elkhart, IN 46514, U.S.A.
FOSRITE PLASTICS LTD.,
Beam Station,Tetney, Nr. Grimsby, Lincolnshire, England
14' INTERNATIONAL ASSOCIATION,
26 Hillside Ave., Point Clare, Quebec, Canada
4.45 INTERNATIONAL ASSOCIATION,
39 Ave. de Clichy, Paris, France
420 INTERNATIONAL ASSOCIATION,
c/o H. Richter, 44 Inneidner Strasse, D-6 Frankfurt/Main, Germany
470 INTERNATIONAL ASSOCIATION,
22 Rue de Kater, 33 Bordeaux, Candevan, France
REG FREEMAN YACHTS,
Willments Shipyard, Woolston, Hampshire, England
FRERS EUROPE,
22 Marlborough Rd., Exeter, Devon, England
FRERS NORTH AMERICAN,
44 Saddle Ridge Rd., Wilton, CT 06897, U.S.A.
FRIENDSHIP MANUFACTURING CO.,
8820 SW 131 St., Miami, FL 33156, U.S.A.
JOHN FULFORD,
Ella Cottage, Wootten Bridge, Isle of Wight, England
G.D.B. MARINE,
Unit 31, Southampton Airport, Hampshire, England
GEARY 18 INTERNATIONAL YRA,
P.O. Box 3618, Santa Barbara, CA 93105, U.S.A.
PETER A. GEIS,
425 McKinsey Rd., Maryland 21146, U.S.A.
ANDREW GEMENY & SON,
5809 Annapolis Rd., Hyattsville, MD 20784, U.S.A.
GEMICO CORPORATION,
63 Atlantic Ave., Boston, MA 02110, U.S.A.
GEMINI ASSOCIATION,
c/o J. Young, 3 Plymouth Rd., Lexington, MA 02173, U.S.A.
GENERAL BOATS CORP.,
91 Deertrack Lane, Irvington on Hudson, NY 10533, U.S.A.
GEN-MAR INC.,
717 Valley Drive, Hermosa Beach, CA 90254, U.S.A.
GHOST 13 NATIONAL ASSOCIATION,
c/o R. Woods, 6952 Church Circus, Huntingdon Beach, CA 92648, U.S.A.
GIBERT MARINE SA.,
BP 32, 17230 Marans, France
GIB ASSOCIATION,
c/o N. Branden, 2905 SW 2nd Ave., Ft. Lauderdale, FL 33315, U.S.A.

LAURENT GILES & PARTNERS,
4 Quay Hill, Lymington, Hampshire, England
GLANDER BOATS INC.,
RRI Box 140, Tavernier, FL 33070, U.S.A.
GLASTRON ALPHA ASSOCIATION,
c/o R. Crist, P.O. Box 9477, Austin, TX 87857, U.S.A.
GLASTRON BOAT CO.,
P.O. Box 9447, Austin, TX 78757, U.S.A.
J.L. GMACH & CO. LTD.,
Ashford Works, 9 Ashford Rd., Fordingbridge, Hampshire, England
GOLDEN ARROW MARINE,
Estate Rd., Newhaven, Sussex, England
GOLDFISH ASSOCIATION,
c/o N. Fugat, 6926 Tokalon, Dallas, Texas, U.S.A.
GOSHAWK SHIPYARDS,
Bourne House, St. Mary Bourne, Hampshire, England
GOUTERON SA.,
Avenue des Salines, 44 La Baule, France
GP14 INTERNATIONAL ASSOCIATION,
c/o G. Mainwaring, Parkwood Manor Rd., Baldwins Gate, Newcastle, England
GRAMPIAN MARINE LTD.,
P.O. Box 69, Edenton, North Carolina 27932, U.S.A.
GRAMPIAN MARINE,
451 Woody Rd., Oakville, Ontario, Canada
GRANTA BOATS LTD.,
23 Great Whyte, Ramsey, Huntingdon, PE 17 1HG, England
GRAVES YACHT YARD,
89 Front St., Marblehead, MA 01945, U.S.A.
GREAT LAKES SPORTS MFG.,
5135 Richmond Rd., Cleveland, OH 44146, U.S.A.
GREAT PELICAN ASSOCIATION,
c/o M. Short, 203 Hawthorne Ave., Larkspur, CA 94939, U.S.A.
RAY GREENE & CO. INC.,
508 So. Byrne, Toledo, OH 43609, U.S.A.
G.R.P. ENGINEERING,
38a Magazine Lane, Wallasey, Cheshire, England
GRUMMAN BOATS,
Marathon, NY 13803, U.S.A.
LE GUEN & HEMIDY,
Z1 de Pommenanque, 50500 Careutan, France
GULF COAST SAILBOATS,
P.O. Box 12381, 6316 Long Dr., Houston, TX 77017, U.S.A.
GULFSTAR INC.,
6101 45th St. N, St. Petersburg, FL 33714, U.S.A.
HALMATIC,
Brookside Rd., Havant, Hampshire, England
JARED C. HALVERSON,
111 West End Ave., Shrewsbury, NJ 07701, U.S.A.
HAMBLE MARINE,
30 Holly Hill Lane, Sarisbury Green, Hampshire, England
HAMPTON O.D. ASSOCIATION,
c/o R. Thompson, RR-1 Box 312B, Lexington Park, MD 20653, U.S.A.
HAMPTON SHIPYARDS,
East Quoque, NY 11942, U.S.A.
HANNAY MARINE LTD.,
28 Merton Ave., London W4, England
HARKEN,
1251 East Wisconsin Ave., Pewaukee, Wisconsin 53072, U.S.A.

HARMONY BOATS LTD.,
Griffin Lane, Thorpe, Norwich, Norfolk, England
HARRIS & HEACOCK,
199 West Shore Rd., Great Neck, NY 11024, U.S.A.
HARTNELL BOAT BUILDERS LTD.,
Mayflower House, Armada Way, Plymouth, Devon, England
HARVEY CEDARS MARINA,
6318 Long Beach Blvd., Harvey Cedars, NJ 08008, U.S.A.
HARVIGLAS LTD.,
Alexandra St., Hyde, Cheshire, England
HAYDEN YACHTS,
39 Pratt St., Essex, Conn. 06426, U.S.A.
JACK A. HEHUS CO.,
821 Pepper St., Columbia, S. Carolina 29209, U.S.A.
HERON INTERNATIONAL ASSOCIATION,
c/o Chiltern Heath End, Flackwell Heath, High Wycombe, Buckinghamshire,
England
HERRSHOFF S. NATIONAL ASSOCIATION,
c/o M. Burggraf, 33 East Main St., Oyster Bay, NY 11771, U.S.A.
HEWSON MARINE,
Hawthorne Rd., So. Casco, ME 04077, U.S.A.
H.H. MARINE,
62 Murray Rd., Horndean, Hampshire, PO8 9JL, England
HIGHLANDER ASSOCIATION,
G. Bracken, 320 C Maple Rd., Valley Cottage, NY 10989, U.S.A.
HIGH PERFORMANCE SAILBOAT SALES AND MFG.,
4230 Glencoe Ave., Venice, CA 90201, U.S.A.
M.E. HILL,
3417 Seminole, Detroit, MI 48214, U.S.A.
D. HILLYARD,
The Shipyard, Littlehampton, Sussex, England
HENRY R. HINCKLEY & CO.,
Southwest Harbor, ME 04679, U.S.A.
HMS MARINE INC.,
904 W Hyde Park Blvd., Inglewood, CA 90302, U.S.A.
HOBIE CAT CLASS ASSOCIATION,
33012 Calle Perfecto, San Juan, Capistrano, CA 91675, U.S.A.
HOLIDAY CLASS ASSOCIATION,
Box 307, Gloucester, VA 23061, U.S.A.
HOLLAND BOAT COMPANY,
Postbus 79, Rivierdijk 597, Hardinxveld-Giessendam, Holland
HOLLAND YACHTS INC.,
303 Riverside Ave., Westport, CT 06880, U.S.A.
JACK HOLT LTD.,
The Embankment, Putney, London SW15, England
HONKER LANDSAILORS CORPORATION,
817 West 17th St., Suite 16, Costa Mesa, CA 92627, U.S.A.
HONNOR MARINE,
Seymour Wharf, Totnes, Devon, England
HORNET NATIONAL ASSOCIATION,
c/o B. Dingwall, 23 Aldenham Ave., Radlett, Hertfordshire, England
HOWELL EVERSON (BOATS) LTD.,
Retreat Boatyard, Topsham, Exeter, Devon, England
HUGHES BOAT WORKS,
Huron Park, Ontario, Canada
HUNGARIAN SHIPYARDS AND CRANE FACTORY,
Budapest XII, Vaci u 202, Hungary

HUNTER BOATS,
Sutton Wharf, Sutton Rd., Rochford, Essex, England
HURLEY MARINE,
Valley Rd., Plympton, Devon, England
HURLEY MARINE LTD.,
1839 Rt. 46, Parsippany, NJ 07054, U.S.A.
HUSTLER ASSOCIATION,
c/o C. Myserian, 33 Wing Rd., Lynnfield, MA 01940, U.S.A.
HYDRA ASSOCIATION,
50 Fleming Crescent, Leigh on Sea, Essex, England
HYDRO SWIFT CORPORATION,
3045 W 21 St., Salt Lake City, Utah, U.S.A.
ILES OF NORBURY,
139 Tennyson Rd., Norwood, London SE25, England
JOHN ILLINGWORTH & ASSOCIATES,
36 North St., Emsworth, Hampshire, England
ILYA,
P.O. Box 117, Nashotah, WI 53058, U.S.A.
IMPORTS CO. OF AMERICA,
85 St. John St., New Haven, Connetticut 06501, U.S.A.
IMS 16,
c/o B. Anderson, P.O. Box 1232, Thousand Oaks, CA 91360, U.S.A.
INDIAN CLASS ASSOCIATION,
895 Hope St., Bristol, RI 02809, U.S.A.
INTERDANE 404 ASSOCIATION,
c/o G. Trenter, 2985 Orchard Lake Rd., Keego Harbor, MI, U.S.A.
INTERMARINE,
Fairmile Wharf, Danes Hill, Gillingham, Kent, England
INTERMARINE LTD.,
P.O. Box 7323, Riverdale Station, Hampton, VA 23366, U.S.A.
INTERNATIONAL 21 ASSOCIATION,
Mentor Harbor YC, Mentor, OH 44060, U.S.A.
INTERNATIONAL 110 ASSOCIATION,
c/o A. Peloquin, 505 South Birney, Bay City, MI 48706, U.S.A.
INTERNATIONAL 210 ASSOCIATION,
c/o A. Harris, Jersey Lane, Manchester, MA 01944, U.S.A.
INTERNATIONAL AUSTRALIS ASSOCIATION,
P.O. Box 58, Alexandria 2015, Australia
INTERNATIONAL CADET ASSOCIATION,
37 Fleet Lane, Old Bailey, London EC4M 4YD, England
INTERNATIONAL CANOE FEDERATION,
c/o A. Neveling, Pintstvagen 30, Hagersten, Sweden
INTERNATIONAL CHERUB ASSOCIATION,
P.O. Box 2792, Auckland, New Zealand
INTERNATIONAL COUGAR ASSOCIATION,
2104 Hilda Rose Drive, #3, Silver Springs, MD 20902, U.S.A.
INTERNATIONAL DEVELOPMENT CLASS ASSOCIATION,
IYRU, 5 Buckingham Gate, London SW1, England
INTERNATIONAL DRAGON ASSOCIATION,
141 Garth Rd., Morden, Surrey, England
INTERNATIONAL LIGHTNING ASSOCIATION,
808 High St., Worthington, OH 43085, U.S.A.
INTERNATIONAL MARINE SERVICES,
P.O. Box 1136, Marina del Ray, CA 90291, U.S.A.
INTERNATIONAL MIRROR ASSOCIATION,
Quernmore, Cowbeech, Hailsham, Sussex, England
INTERNATIONAL O.D. INTERNATIONAL ASSOCIATION,
Eastern Yacht Club, Marblehead, MA 01945, U.S.A.

INTERNATIONAL SOLING ASSOCIATION,
18 Ostergade, DK 1100, Copenhagen K, Denmark
INTERNATIONAL THUNDERBIRD C.A.,
Box 199, Seattle, WA 98111, U.S.A.
INTERNATIONAL TORNADO ASSOCIATION,
11 Broad Walk, Orpington, Kent, England
INTERNATIONAL YNGLING ASSOCIATION,
Barge, Bringsvaerds Vaerft, Dvobak, Norway
INTERYACHT,
6 Quay St., Woodbridge, Suffolk, 1P12 1BY, England
INTERYACHT,
Kinkelstrasse 15, D-5 Cologne 41, Germany
LEON F. IRISH CO.,
4300 Haggarty Rd., Walled Lake, MI 48088, U.S.A.
ISLAND BOAT SALES,
23 Seaview Ave., West Mersea, Essex, England
ISLAND PLASTICS,
Edward St., Ryde, Isle of Wight, England
ISLANDER YACHTS,
777 W 17th St., Costa Mesa, CA 92627, U.S.A.
ISOTOPE ASSOCIATION,
c/o B. Akers, 1986B Van Voorhis Drive, Fort Eustis, VA 23604, U.S.A.
ITALY YACHTS LTD.,
Via del Partico Placidiano 105, 00054 Fiumicino, Rome, Italy
IW-VARVET,
AB S-440 90, Henam, Sweden
IYRU,
5 Buckingham Gate, London SW1, England
JANUS PLASTICS CO.,
10905 Inglewood Ave., Inglewood, CA 90304, U.S.A.
JAVELIN CLASS ASSOCIATION,
4119 Skyline Drive, Nashville, TN 37215, U.S.A.
J.B.M. ENGINEERING LTD.,
Roamer Marine, Ramsgate Rd., Sandwich, Kent, England
JEANNEAU CONSTRUCTIONS NAUTIQUES,
85500 Les Herbiers, France
JENSEN MARINE,
235 Fischer St., Costa Mesa, CA 92627, U.S.A.
JESTER YACHT CO.,
220 Cricklewood Broadway, London NW2, England
JET AMERICAN ASSOCIATION,
c/o C. King 354 S Highway, 17 Upper Sudale River, New Jersey, U.S.A.
JOEMARIN,
Oy Joensuu, Finland
DAVE JOHNSON,
Sally Point, Satchell Lane, Hamble, Hampshire, England
JOHNSON BOAT WORKS,
323 So Lake Ave., White Bear Lake, MI 55110, U.S.A.
JOHNSON & SHUTTLEWOOD,
The Marshes, Leigh-on-Sea, Essex, England
JOHNSON, SONS & JAGO LTD.,
Leigh Marshes, Leigh-on-Sea, Essex, England
JOLLYBOAT ASSOCIATION,
c/o R. C. Lynn, P.O. Box 6595, Richmond, VA 23230, U.S.A.
JOLLY BOAT DINGHY ASSOCIATION,
c/o N. Brandon, 2905 SW 2nd Ave., Fort Lauderdale, Florida, U.S.A.
JOLLY ROGER ASSOCIATION,
c/o B. Butler, Mackintosh Lane, Lincoln, MA 01773, U.S.A.

JOLLY YARE ASSOCIATION,
c/o Natalie Brandon, 2905 SW 2nd Ave., Fort Lauderdale, FL 33315, U.S.A.
JONES BUCKIE SHIPYARD LTD.,
Buckie, Banffshire, Scotland
JACHTWERF JONGERT bv,
Medemblik, Holland
P. JOUET & CO.,
Sartrouville, France
JUXTAMARE MARINE,
The Quay Works, Burnham, Essex, England
KADET CLASS,
Box 307, Gloucester, VA 23061, U.S.A.
JOHN KAISER ASSOCIATION,
Box 3982, Greenville, Delaware 19807, U.S.A.
KANGAROO ASSOCIATION,
c/o B. Anderson, P.O. Box 1232, Thousand Oaks, CA 91360, U.S.A.
KELLS CORP.,
109 Howe St., Fall River, MA 02724, U.S.A.
DEREK KELSALL,
Sandwich Marina, Sandwich, Kent, England
KEMROCK YACHTS,
Quayside Rd., Bitterne Manor, Southampton, Hampshire, SO9 3FE, England
JOHN KENNEDY,
P.O. Box 229, Marine del Ray, CA 90291, U.S.A.
KENNEDY INTERNATIONAL BOATS,
Drumsna, Carrick-on-Shannon, County Leitrim, Ireland
KESTREL ASSOCIATION,
c/o C Howard, 17 Parsonage Lane, Topsfield, MA 01983, U.S.A.
KETTENBURG MARINE,
2810 Carlton St., San Diego, CA 92106, U.S.A.
KIMBA KAT ASSOCIATION,
c/o F. Arnold, 20542 Vendall Drive, Lakewood, CA 90713, U.S.A.
KINCAID & CO.,
850 Broadway, Chula Vista, California, U.S.A.
KIRBY MARINE & INDUSTRIAL PLASTICS,
Roper Rd., Canterbury, Kent, England
KITE ASSOCIATION,
c/o N. Hargreaves, 8306 East Longden, San Gabriel, CA 91775, U.S.A.
KNICKERBOCKER NATIONAL ASSOCIATION,
c/o H. Greenburg, 4 Dunster Rd., Great Neck, NY 11021, U.S.A.
KNIGHT & PINK MARINE,
Castle St., Titchfield, Nr. Fareham, Hampshire, England
KNOXMORE BAGLEY,
Satchell Lane, Hamble, Hampshire, SO3 5HR, England
KOHINOOR ASSOCIATION,
c/o R. Wheat, 14 Roosevelt St., Corning, New York, U.S.A.
KONA 14 ASSOCIATION,
c/o L. Hernandaz, 1942 Pomona, Santa Ana, CA 92705, U.S.A.
KOOJIMAN EN DE VRIES JACHTBOUW bv,
Deilsedijk 62, Deil a/d Linge, Holland
KORALLE ASSOCIATION,
c/o B. Schabert, 2045 Oxford St., Sacramento, California, U.S.A.
KORALLE/EAST INC.,
141 English St., Hackinsack, New Jersey 07601, U.S.A.
KORALLE JUNIOR ASSOCIATION,
c/o J. Revette, 273 Park Dale Ave., East Aurora, NY 14052, U.S.A.
KORSAR ASSOCIATION,
c/o G. Outland, 2609 Bravado, No. B Rancho, Cordova, CA 95670, U.S.A.

TOM LACK CATAMARANS,
Flagstaff House, Mudeford, Christchurch, Hampshire, England
LANAVERRE,
Qui de la Salys 33, Bordeaux, France
E.C. LANDAMORE & CO.,
Elanco Works, Wroxham, Norfolk, England
LANGSTON MARINE,
Southmoor Lane, Havant, Hampshire, PO9 1JW, England
LARSHIP,
River Rd., Cos Cob (Greenwich), Conn. 06807, U.S.A.
LARSSON TRADE U.S.A. INC.,
50 E. 42nd St., New York, NY 10017, U.S.A.
LASER ASSOCIATION,
91 Hymns Blvd., Pointe Claire, Quebec, Canada
LATHAMS & SON (PARKSTONE),
Westons Point Boatyard, Turks Lane, Sandbanks Rd., Parkstone, Poole,
Dorset, England
LAVERS & CO.,
The Bight Boat Yard, Dartmouth, Devon, England
LEA CRAFT,
Industrial Estate, Cadmore Lane, Cheshunt, Hertfordshire, England
LE-COMTE HOLLAND NV,
A le Comte Co., P.O. Box 117, New Rochelle, NY 108002, U.S.A.
OLIVER LEE,
Newton House, Park Rd., Burnham-on-Crouch, Essex, England
CARL LEIGLER YACHT AGENCY,
44 Harrington Rd., London SW7, England
LENMAN INDUSTRIES INC.,
P.O. Box 689, 1010 SE 12th Court, Cape Coral, FL 33904, U.S.A.
LIDO 14 ASSOCIATION,
P.O. Box 1252, Newport Beach, CA 92660, U.S.A.
LINCOLN FIBERGLASS INC.,
Rt 62, Stow, MA 01775, U.S.A.
LINE CONTRACTS,
17 Willow Ridge, Turner's Hill, Sussex, England
LINGE YACHTS,
Stortingsgt, 14-Oslo 1, Norway
LION YACHTS,
Foot of South St., Stamford, Connecticut, U.S.A.
LION YACHTS,
Yacht Haven West, Foot of Washington Blvd., Stamford, CT 06902, U.S.A.
LOCKLEY MANUFACTURING INC.,
310 Grove St., New Castle, PA 16103, U.S.A.
LONE STAR 13,
c/o John Carson, P.O. Box 3061, Dallas, TX 75221, U.S.A.
LUDERS 16 ASSOCIATION,
230 E 17th St.,, Costa Mesa, CA 92627, U.S.A.
LUDERS 21 ASSOCIATION,
c/o P. Fuller, 7724 58th NE, Seattle, Washington 98115, U.S.A.
M-20 ASSOCIATION,
c/o W. Bentsen, Route 1, The Birches, Lake Geneva, WI 53147, U.S.A.
FRANS MAAS bv,
Postbus 13, Middenhavendam, Holland
MAC DINGHY ASSOCIATION,
P.O. Box 1951, Pittsburgh, PA 15230, U.S.A.
MacGREGOR YACHT CORP.,
1631 Placentia Ave., Costa Mesa, CA 92627, U.S.A.

MacWESTER MARINE CO.,
37 River Rd., Littlehampton, Sussex, England
MALIBU OUTRIGGER ASSOCIATION,
c/o V. Just, 21119 West Entrada Rd., Topanga, CA 90290, U.S.A.
MANOEL ISLAND YACHT YARD,
Gzira, Malta
MAN O'WAR ASSOCIATION,
c/o R. Pelkey, 6961 Mohican Lane, Westland, MI 48185, U.S.A.
MANX MARINE,
35 North Quay, Douglas, Isle of Man
MARBLEHEAD TRAINER ASSOCIATION,
c/o W. Butler, 25 Mugford St., Marblehead, MA, U.S.A.
MARINE CONSTRUCTION,
Willments Shipyard, Woolstron, Southampton, Hampshire, England
MARINE MARKETING,
133 Bush Rd., Cuxton, Rochester, Kent, England
MARINER 2 + 2 ASSOCIATION,
26 Radval Lane, Levittown, NY 11756, U.S.A.
MARINER'S BOATYARD,
Bosham, Sussex, England
MARINEWAYS LTD.,
25 St. Michaels Rd., Abergaveny, Monmouthshire, Wales
MARK ASSOCIATION,
c/o S. Parry, Coldthorn Barn, Coldthorn Lane, Hailsham, Sussex, England
MARSHALL TECHNICAL SERVICES,
26 North Rd., Bourne, Lincolnshire, England
MARTHA'S VINEYARD SHIPYARD,
Box 1236, Vineyard Haven, MA 02568, U.S.A.
MASTER MARINE,
Pleinmont Rd., Torteval, Guernsey
MAX-CRAFT,
Enefco House, The Quay, Poole, Dorset, England
MAXIM MARINE,
St. Johns Rd., Hedge End, Southampton, England
J.M. McCLINTOCK & CO.,
P.O. Box 335, Ingomar, PA 15127, U.S.A.
Wm. McCUTCHEON BOAT YARD,
New Rd., Wootton, Isle of Wight, England
McGRUER & CLARK,
Box 504, Owen Sound, Ontario, Canada
PETER McINTYRE LTD.,
Marine Rd., Port Bannatyne, Bute, England
McNAIR MARINE INC.,
Box 3775, Higganum, Connecticut 06441, U.S.A.
McNICHOLS BOAT SALES,
1617 East McNichols, Detroit, MI, U.S.A.
CPT. FRANK McNUTLY & SONS,
Victoria Rd., South Shields, Co. Durham, England
McVAY FIBREGLASS YACHTS,
Mahone Bay, Nova Scotia, Canada
J. G. MEAKES,
The Boat Centre, Marlow, Buckinghamshire, England
MEECHING BOATS,
Denton Island, Newhaven, Sussex, England
MELGES BOAT WORKS,
Zenda, WI 53195, U.S.A.
MELODY ASSOCIATION,
c/o B. Beatty, 1219 Yew St., San Mateo, California, U.S.A.

MERCURY NATIONAL ASSOCIATION,
c/o R. Johnson, 6 Merrill Way, Carmel Valley, CA 93924, U.S.A.
MERMAID BOATS,
19 Mareton Rd., Bosham, Sussex, England
MERMAID BOATS,
Hewarts Lane, Rose Green, Bognor Regis, Sussex, England
METALMAST MARINE,
P.O. Box 471, 55 Providence St., Putnam, CT 06260, U.S.A.
RICHARDS T. MILLER,
Box 392, Annapolis, MD, U.S.A.
MINISAIL WORLD ASSOCIATION,
226 Sheen Lane, London SW14, England
MIRAGE YACHTS LTD.,
20 Cartier Ave., Pointe Claire, Quebec, Canada
MIRROR 14 ASSOCIATION,
IPC Newspapers, 79 Camden Rd., London NW1, England
MIRROR 16 ASSOCIATION,
IPC Newspapers, 79 Camden Rd., London NW1, England
MIRROR 16 ASSOCIATION (USA),
c/o A. Siskind, 301 E 324th St., Wildwick, OH 44094, U.S.A.
MIRROR BOATS,
79 Camden Rd., London NW1 9NT, England
MITCHAM MARINE LTD.,
Denmark St., Diss, Norfolk, England
F.C. MITCHELL & SONS,
Turk's Lane, Sandbanks Rd., Parkstone, Poole, Dorset, England
MODULAR FLOTATION LTD.,
73 North St., Stranground, Peterborough, Northamptonshire, England
MONOCHORUM MANUFACTURERS,
Wixenford Farm, Colesdown Hill, Plymstock, Plymouth, Devon, England
VINCENT MONTE-SANO,
21 W 46th St., New York, U.S.A.
MONTGOMERY 6-8 ASSOCIATION,
c/o T. van Atta, 1808 Tam O'Shanter, Tucson, AZ 85710, U.S.A.
MONTGOMERY 7-11 ASSOCIATION,
c/o D. Blagg, 2209 N Laureen, Fresno, CA 93703, U.S.A.
MONTGOMERY 10 ASSOCIATION,
c/o R. Armstrong, 1668 Babcock A, Costa Mesa, CA 92627, U.S.A.
MONTGOMERY 12 ASSOCIATION,
c/o J. Montgomery, 302, 35th St., Newport Beach, CA 92660, U.S.A.
MONTGOMERY MARINE,
959 W 17th St., Costa Mesa, CA 92627, U.S.A.
A.H. MOODY & SON,
Swanick Shore Rd., Swanick, Southampton, England
R. MOORE & SONS LTD.,
Station Rd., Wroxham, Norfolk, NOR 60Z, England
MORGAN YACHT CORP.,
P.O. Box 11598, St. Petersburg, FL 33733, U.S.A.
MOTH INTERNATIONAL ASSOCIATION,
c/o Major Hibbert, The Salterns, Woodside, Lymington, Hampshire, England
MOTH NATIONAL ASSOCIATION,
c/o B. Krothe, 317 Ocean Ave., Ocean City, NJ 08226, U.S.A.
MOTIVATORS GRP PRODUCTS,
Smith's Quay, Hazel Rd., Woolston, Southampton, England
MOUETTE ASSOCIATION,
c/o J. Curtis, Route 1, Box 293, Trevor, Wisconsin, U.S.A.
MTA MARINE SALES,
5833 Shenandoah Ave., Los Angeles, CA 90056, U.S.A.

MULDER & RIJKE bv,
Ijmuiden, P.O. Box 48, Holland
D.A.D. MUNRO LTD.,
61 High St., Stone, Staffordshire, England
W. MYCHENBERG,
4983 Reed Rd., Columbus, OH 43221, U.S.A.
NAPLES SABOT ASSOCIATION,
5267 Castle Hills Drive, San Diego, CA 92109, U.S.A.
NARRASKETUCK ASSOCIATION,
In Bielenberg, 500 Everdell Ave., West Islip, NY 11795, U.S.A.
NASSAU DINGHY ASSOCIATION
c/o M. Brescher, 19192 Flag Drive, FL 33156, U.S.A.
NATIONAL DOLPHIN 17 ASSOCIATION,
P.O. Box 10881, Houston, TX 77018, U.S.A.
NATIONAL O.D. ASSOCIATION,
c/o T. Makielski, 52881 Ironwood Rd., So Bend, IN 46635, U.S.A.
NAUTICAL BOAT WORKS,
Glouchester, VA, U.S.A.
NAUTICA CORP.,
P.O. Box 26, Paramus, NJ, U.S.A.
NAUTOR,
Box 10, Pietarsaari, Finland
NAVY-HOLLAND,
Kantoor Lindelaan, 3 Bussum, Holland
THOMAS NELSON YACHT AGENCY,
18 London St., London EC3, England
NEWBRIDGE BOATS,
Church St. Bridport, Dorset, England
NEW ENGLAND SAILBOATS CO.,
2218 Ranway Rd., Monroeville, PA 15146, U.S.A.
NEWPORT 21 ASSOCIATION,
Box 307, Gloucester, VA 23061, U.S.A.
NEWPORT BOATS,
P.O. Box 307, Gloucester, VA 23061, U.S.A.
NEWPORTER SHIPYARD,
P.O. Box 281, Leesburg, NJ 08327, U.S.A.
NIPPER ASSOCIATION,
c/o J.J. Greene, 508 So Byrne, Toledo, OH 43609, U.S.A.
NORDEX BOATS,
P.O. Box T T Venice, FL 33595, U.S.A.
NORDMARINE,
Via G Frova 5, 20092 Cinisello, Milano, Italy
NORMAN CRUISERS LTD.,
Universal Works, Grains Rd., Nr. Oldham, Lancashire, England
JACHTBOUW NOORD NEDERLAND,
J.B. Hoogland, Staveren, Friesland, Holland
JACHTBOUW NOORD NEDERLAND,
Warns/Staveren, Kooyweg 10-12, Holland
NORTH AMERICAN ENGINEERING,
875 Florence St., London, Ontario N5W 2M6, Canada
NORTH AMERICAN FIBERGLASS MOULDING,
759 Hyde Park Rd., London 73, Ontario, Canada
NORTH AMERICAN FLYING TERN ASSOCIATION,
2AO C. Davey St., Bloomfield, NJ 07003, U.S.A.
NORTH AMERICAN YNGLING ASSOCIATION,
P.O. Box 90302, Milwaukee, WI 53202, U.S.A.
NORTHRUP ASSOCIATION,
2218 Ramsey Rd., Monroeville, PA 15146, U.S.A.

PACIFIC OCEAN YACHTS,
7 St. Denys Rd., Southampton, SO2 1GN, England
PALACE QUAY BOAT YARD,
Beaulieu, Hampshire, England
PALMER JOHNSON INC.,
61 Michigan St., Sturgeon Bay, WI 54235, U.S.A.
PAPER TIGER ASSOCIATION,
P.O. Box 229, Marina del Ray, CA 90291, U.S.A.
PAPER TIGER WORLD ASSOCIATION,
P.O. Box 1951, Auckland 1, New Zealand
G.W. PARKER & SON LTD.,
Station St., Boston, Lincolnshire, England
PARKER RIVER MARINE,
Rt 1A, Newbury, MA 01950, U.S.A.
PARKWAY MARINE LTD.,
Sandbanks Rd., Lilliput, Poole, Dorset, England
PARKWOOD MARINE SERVICES LTD.,
74/78 Park Rd., Whitchurch, Cardiff, Wales
PASSAGE MARINE INC.,
231 Commons Drive, Vienna, VA 22180, U.S.A.
PASSAGE MARINE,
Box 188, Gwynn, Virginia 23066, U.S.A.
PEANUT ASSOCIATION,
230 W Islip Rd., West Islip, NY 11795, U.S.A.
NORMAN PEARN LTD.,
Millpool Boatyard, Looe, Cornwall, England
PEARSON BROS. LTD.,
No. 1 Hanger Ford, Arundel, Sussex, England
PEARSON YACHTS,
West Shore Rd., Portsmouth, RI 02871, U.S.A.
PEGASUS INTERNATIONAL ASSOCIATION,
c/o P. Johnson, 20 Glebe Ave., Bedworth, Nuneaton, Warwickshire, England
PENGUIN ASSOCIATION,
c/o R. Black, 9 Juniper Rd., Rowayton, CT 06853, U.S.A.
PENNINGTON YACHTS,
11 Stern Lane, Industrial Estate, New Milton, Hampshire, England
PENRYN BOAT BUILDING CO. LTD.,
Ponshardyn, Penryn, Falmouth, Cornwall, England
PERFORMANCE SAILCRAFT CORPORATION,
91 Hymns Blvd., Pointe-Claire, Quebec, Canada
PERFORMANCE YACHTS,
Rock, Wadebridge, Cornwall, England
PETER'S BOATYARD,
Hamble, Hampshire, SO3 5NJ, England
PELLE PETTERSON (UK) LTD.,
18 Priory Close, Royston, Hertfordshire, England
JACHTBOUW PEUTEN,
Napoleonsweg 40, NL-Neer (L), Holland
PHILIP & SON LTD.,
Noss Shipyard, Dartmouth, Devon, England
PINTAIL ASSOCIATION,
c/o C. Licht, 26291 Pilsbury Drive, Farmington, MI 48024, U.S.A.
PIONEER ASSOCIATION,
c/o Mrs. Stevens, 8406 Wagon Wheel Rd., Alexandra, VA 22309, U.S.A.
PIPER INTERNATIONAL CLASS ASSOCIATION,
c/o Alex Robertson & Sons Ltd., Sandbank, Argyll, Scotland
PIPER NATIONAL CLASS ASSOCIATION,
1241 Jerome St., Garden Grove, CA 92641, U.S.A.

NORTH SEA CRAFT,
Hall Rd., Norwich, NOR 07C, England
NORTH STAR YACHTS,
Huron Park, Ontario, Canada
NORTHERN YACHT LTD.,
374 Fairall St., Ajax, Ontario, Canada
NOWAK & WILLIAMS CO.,
37 Gooding Ave., Bristol, RI 02809, U.S.A.
O'BRIEN & SPENCER LTD.,
Willment's Shipyard, Hazel Rd., Woolston, Southampton, Hampshire, England
OCQUETEAU GUY,
Chantier Naval, France
OCEAN CATAMARANS,
P.O. Box 486, Tamiami Station, Miami, FL 33144, U.S.A.
O'DAY,
848 Airport Rd., Fall River, MA 002720, U.S.A.
OD 11 ASSOCIATION,
c/o George O'Day, 33A Commercial Wharf, Boston, MA 02110, U.S.A.
OD 11 WORLD ASSOCIATION,
c/o A. Steinberg, P.O. Box 10077, Haifa, Israel
OK DINGHY INTERNATIONAL ASSOCIATION,
Craven House, West St., Farnham, Surrey, England
OK DINGHY U.S. ASSOCIATION,
2704 Coventry Rd., Columbus, OH 043221, U.S.A.
OFFSHORE YACHTS INTERNATIONAL,
Wroxham, Norfolk, England
OFFSHORE YACHTS INTERNATIONAL LTD.,
Mill Rd., Royston, Hertfordshire, England
OLD TOWN CANOE CO.,
Old Town, Maine, U.S.A.
OLD SALT SAILBOAT CENTRE,
7404 So University, Little Roack, Ark. 72205, U.S.A.
OLYMPIC YACHTS,
2615 Marcel St., Montreal 382, Quebec, Canada
OMEGA ASSOCIATION,
P.O. Box 254, Hermasa Beach, CA 90254, U.S.A.
ONE DESIGN YACHTS,
2955 Minerva Lake Rd., Columbus, OH 43229, U.S.A.
ONTARIO YACHTS,
243 Speers Rd., Oakville, Ontario, Canada
OPTIMIST CLUB,
Box 1031, Clearwater, FL 33517, U.S.A.
ORION ASSOCIATION,
c/o L. York, Maple Ave., Rutland, MA 01543, U.S.A.
OSPREY ASSOCIATION,
c/o B. Olliff, Rt 2, P. O. Box 14, Lark Park, GA 31636, U.S.A.
OSTERVILLE MARINE INC.,
Box 490, Osterville, MA 02655, U.S.A.
OUYANG BOAT WORKS LTD.,
1636 Charles St., Whitby, Ontario, Canada
OXFORD YACHTS SALES,
Oxford, MD 21654, U.S.A.
PACESHIP YACHTS,
Mahone Bay, Nova Scotia, Canada
PACIFIC 21 ASSOCIATION,
c/o L. Jenkins, 3 Altarinda Drive, Orinda, CA 94563, U.S.A.
PACIFIC CAT ASSOCITION,
c/o T. Mosher, 913 Chattanooga, Pacific Palicades, California, U.S.A.

PIRATE FISH ASSOCIATION,
45 Cedar Ave., Ext., Islip, NY 11751, U.S.A.
PIRATE FISH JNR. ASSOCIATION,
c/o W. Bower, 479 Smith Ave., Islip, NY 11751, U.S.A.
P.I. YACHTS,
Foss Quay, Millbrook, Plymouth, Devon, England
PLASTREND,
1005 Blue Mound Rd., Fort Worth, TX 76131, U.S.A.
PLAYVISA CORONADO YACHTS (UK) LTD.,
Quay St., Orford, Nr. Woodbridge, Suffolk, 1P1Z 2NO, England
PLYCRAFT,
Kenn Boat Yard, Clevedon, Somerset, BS21 6EW, England
MICHAEL POCOCK & PARTNERS,
Yarnell Craft, Ramley Rd., Lymington, Hants, England
POPULAR BOATS,
20 St. Johns Rd., Tunbridge Wells, Kent, England
SCHEEPSWERF PORSIUS,
Landsmeerderdijk 40, Kadoelen, Amsterdam 19, Holland
PORTER & HAYLETT LTD.,
Wroxham, Norfolk, England
PRINDLE 16 ASSOCIATION,
1009 S Hathaway St., Santa Ana, CA 92705, U.S.A.
R.J. PRIOR & SON LTD. (BURNHAM),
Quayside, Burnham-on-Crouch, Essex, England
PRIOR CRAFT LTD.,
St. Olaves, Norfolk, England
IAN PROCTOR,
Fenmead Brook Ave., Warsash, Southampton, England
PROUT MARINE,
The Point, Canvey Island, Essex, England
PUGET BOAT MFG.,
238 Central Building, Seattle, WA 98104, U.S.A.
PURBROOK ROSSITER,
Bridge St., Christchurch, Hampshire, BH23, 1DZ, England
RAINBOW CLASS ASSOCIATION,
Box 1895, Annapolis, MD 21404, U.S.A.
RANA BOATS U.K.,
East St., Ilminster, Somerset, England
RANGER FIBREGLASS BOAT MFG. CO.,
25802 Pacific Highway So., Kent, WA 98031, U.S.A.
RANGER YACHTS,
3090 Pullman St. Costa Mesa, CA 92627, U.S.A.
RASCAL ASSOCIATION,
c/o R. Greene, 508 So Byrne, Toledo, OH 43609, U.S.A.
RAWSON NATIONAL ASSOCIATION,
c/o Ron Rawson, 15014 NE 90th St., Redmond, WA 98052, U.S.A.
RON RAWSON INC.,
15014 NE 90th St., Redmond, WA 98052, U.S.A.
W.F. RAYNER LTD.,
23 Churchfield Rd., Parkstone, Poole, Dorset, England
R-BOAT NATIONAL ASSOCIATION,
c/o R. Wittiver. 3520 Lake Shore Drive, Chicago, ILL 60657, U.S.A.
RC MARINE DIVISION,
Causland & Browne Ltd., Piggery Wharf, Manor Farm Rd., Alperton, Wembley,
Middlesex, England
REBEL ASSOCIATION,
c/o L. Helpinstone, 209 E Goodwin Place, Mundellin, ILL 60060, U.S.A.

M.S. REDMAN,
Fenn Creek, South Woodham Ferrers, Chelmsford, Essex, CM3 5LX, England
REDWING ASSOCIATION,
c/o J. Fishley, Highwinds, 224 Fort Austin Ave., Plymouth PL6 5NY, England
REEDCRAFT LTD.,
The Quay, Reedham, Norfolk, England
RHODES 18 NATIONAL ASSOCIATION,
c/o Dr. Schinto, 61 Center Rd., Old Greenwich, CT, U.S.A.
RHODES 19 NATIONAL ASSOCIATION,
c/o I. Cohen, 1524 Henry Ave., Mamaroneck, NY 10543, U.S.A.
PAUL H.H. RHODES,
15 Hillway, Westcliffe on Sea, Essex, SS0 8QA, England
RHODES BANTAM ASSOCIATION,
4256 Ann Rose Court, Toledo, OH 43611, U.S.A.
RICHMOND MARINE,
48 The Green, Twickenham, Middlesex, England
GLEN RIDGE & CO.,
Yachthaven, Greenland Mills, Bradford on Avon, Wiltshire, England
RAY RIGDEN & PARTNERS LTD.,
The Dinghy Store, Sea Wall, Whitstable, Kent, England
M. RIMMER,
7 Norton Close, Chingford, London E4, England
RIVER DART SCHOOL OF SAILING, SEAMANSHIP & NAVIGATION,
Mill House, Mill Hill, Stoke, Gabriel, Totnes, Devon, England
RING MARINE CO.,
The Golden Hill Fort, Freshwater, Isle of Wight, England
ROAM YACHTWERF,
Ammerzoden, Wellesdam 39-41, Holland
ARTHUR ROBB,
20D New Cavendish St., London W1, England
ALEXANDER ROBERTSON & SONS LTD.,
Sandbank, Dunoon, Argyle, Scotland
A.V. ROBERTSON,
The Shipyard, Woodbridge, Suffolk, England
ROBIN ASSOCIATION,
c/o R. Lemman, 616A Old Lincoln Highway West, Irwin, PA, U.S.A.
ROCKWELL & NEWELL INC.,
12 E 41st St., New York, NY 10017, U.S.A.
J.C. ROGERS,
Waterloo Rd., Lymington, Hampshire, SO4 9EE, England
RONDAR BOATS,
12/16 Stem Lane, New Milton, Hampshire, BH25 5NN, England
ROOSTER ASSOCIATION,
Hawthorne Rd., Jamestown, RI 02835, U.S.A.
JAMES D. ROSBOROUGH,
P.O. Box 188, Armdale, Nova Scotia, Canada
ROTOMARINE LTD.,
30 The Hornet, Chichester, Sussex, England
WILLIAM RUSSELL & CO.,
292 South Compo Rd., Westport, CT, U.S.A.
RUSSELL MARINE LTD.,
Calvia Works, Prince Ave., Southend-on-Sea, Essex, SS0 0NE, England
RYDGEWAY MARINE LTD.,
Church Rd., Kessingland, Lowestoft, England
RYTON MARINE LTD.,
Stargate Works, Ryton-on-Tyne, Co. Durham, England
SAAMAN bv,
Dijkhvizenweg 98, Appingedam, Holland

SAILAWAY ASSOCIATION,
c/o R. Collons, 2 Crown Rd., Morden, Surrey, England
SAILCRAFT LTD.,
Waterside, Brightlingsea, Essex, England
SAILING CENTRE,
Rt. 5, Box 279 S, Fort Worth, Texas, U.S.A.
SAIL MANUFACTURING,
70 4th Ave., Union City, PA 16438, U.S.A.
SAILSKIFF SPORTS CRAFT LTD.,
52 Stokes Ave., Poole, Dorset, England
SALTERNS YACHT AGENCY LTD.,
Chichester Yacht Basin, Birdham, Chichester PO20 7EN, Sussex, England
SANDPIPER 15 ASSOCIATION,
c/o M. O'Brien, P.O. Box 421, Gloucester Point, VA 23062, U.S.A.
SANDPIPER MARINE LTD.,
Church End, Shirley, Southampton, Hampshire, England
SANDSHARK ASSOCIATION,
c/o H. Lane Wilson, Box 739, Gloucester, VA 23061, U.S.A.
A.J.S. SANDWICH,
Sandwich Marina, Sandwich, Kent, England
SAN FRANCISCO PELICAN ASSOCIATION,
c/o M. Short, 203 Hawthorne Ave., Larkspur, CA 94939, U.S.A.
SARL,
127 Boulevard des Orangers, 83 Saint Raphael, France
KELVIN SAVELL,
9819 Hawley Rd., El Cajon, CA 92021, U.S.A.
SCAMP ASSOCIATION,
5513 Ridge Park Rd., Edina, MN 55436, U.S.A.
W.D. SCHOCK CORP.,
3502 So. Greenville St., Santa Ana, CA 92704, U.S.A.
SCHWILL YACHTS INC.,
Factory St., Odessa, Ontario, Canada
SCORPION ASSOCIATION,
P.O. Box 5213, Charlotte, NC 28205, U.S.A.
THOMAS SCOTT,
901 Main St. Millville, NJ 08332, U.S.A.
SCOUT ASSOCIATION,
15906 Wayzata Building, Wayzata, MN 55391, U.S.A.
E SCOW ASSOCIATION,
c/o S. Merrick, 401 N St., Southwest, Washington DC 20024, U.S.A.
M SCOW ASSOCIATION,
P.O. Box 40, Williams Bay, WI 53191, U.S.A.
MC SCOW ASSOCIATION,
c/o T. Bischoff, P.O. Box 117, Nashotah, WI 53058, U.S.A.
W SCOW ASSOCIATION,
c/o C. Wagner, 928 Central Ave., Miamisburg, Ohio, U.S.A.
SEAFARER FIBREGLASS YACHTS,
760 Park Ave., Huntingdon, NY 11743, U.S.A.
SEAGULL ASSOCIATION,
c/o F. Gaines, P.O. Box 331, Waxahachie, Texas, U.S.A.
SEAMASTER LTD.,
20 Ongar Rd., Great Dunmow, Essex, OM6 1EU, England
SEASAFE BOATS LTD.,
Havyatt Manor, Havyatt, Glastonbury, Somerset, England
SEA SHARK ASSOCIATION,
c/o A. Greene, 140 Williamson Ave., East Rockaway, NY 11518, U.S.A.
SEAWARD YACHTS LTD.,
Faverham, Norfolk, England

SEAWIND SAILING ASSOCIATION,
P.O. Box 356, Red Bank, NJ 00701, U.S.A.
SENIOR MARINE LTD.,
Quayside Rd., Bitterne Manor, Southampton, England
SESAME ASSOCIATION,
c/o F.R. Arnold, 20542 Vendale Drive, Lakewood, CA 90713, U.S.A.
SHARK V ASSOCIATION,
59 Penhill Rd., Lancing, Sussex, England
12 sqm SHARPIE ASSOCIATION,
c/o T. Proctor, Honeysuckle Cottage, Burton End, Stanstead, Essex, England
SHAW CRAFT,
Stokes Rd., RD #3, Indian Mills, NJ 08088, U.S.A.
SHIELDS ONE DESIGN CLASS,
c/o G. Brazil Jnr., 6 Hazel Lane, Larchmont, NY 10538, U.S.A.
BILL SHIPSIDES (MARINE) LTD.,
The Boatyard, Gisburn Rd., Barrowford, Nelson, Lancashire, England
SIDNEY CO.,
4057 Lincoln Blvd., Marina del Ray, CA 90291, U.S.A.
SIGNET ASSOCIATION,
92 Peninsula Drive, Babylon, NY 11702, U.S.A.
SILVER STREAK ASSOCIATION,
c/o J. Highton, Waterloo Toft, Monks Beccles, Suffolk, England
SIMAC-PLAISANCE SOCIETE UMM,
53 rue des Ormes, 93 Romainville, France
SIMENDS BOATS,
529 Dennison Drive, Southbridge, MA 01550, U.S.A.
SKATE ASSOCIATION,
c/o R. Robb, Monument St., Concord, MA, U.S.A.
SKENE BOATS LTD.,
19 Caesar Ave., Ottawa, Ontario, Canada
K.R. SKENTLEBURY & SON LTD.,
Laira Bridge Boatyard, Plymouth, England
SKIPJACK ASSOCIATION,
Rt. 5, Box 279-S, Fort Worth, Texas 76126, U.S.A.
SKYLARK RACING ASSOCIATION,
110 E King St., Hillsborough, NC 27278, U.S.A.
SLIPPER ASSOCIATION,
c/o J. Greene, 508 S. Byrne, Toledo, OH 43609, U.S.A.
SLM BOATS,
Wouldham, Kent, England
SMALL CRAFT (BLOCKLEY) LTD.,
Blockley, Gloucestershire, England
SMALL CRAFT OF CANADA,
3839 Burnsland Rd., Calgary, Alberta, Canada
DAVID SMITHELLS YACHT SALES,
Birdham Pool, Chichester, Sussex, England
SMS YACHT BUILDERS,
178 Abbey Rd., Barking, Essex, England
SNARK PRODUCTS INC.,
Fort Lee, NJ 07024, U.S.A.
SNIPE ASSOCIATION (U.S.A.),
c/o Larry Lamb, Privateer Rd., Hixson, TX 37343, U.S.A.
SNUG HARBOUR BOAT WORKS,
101-121 Snug Harbour Rd., St. Petersburg 2, Florida, U.S.A.
SOLARIS MARINE LTD.,
5 Willments Shipyard, Hazel Rd., Woolston, Southampton, England
SOL CAT CATAMARANS,
2930 Grace Lance, Costa Mesa, CA 92626, U.S.A.

SOLO CANADIAN ASSOCIATION,
RR #1, Peachland, British Columbia, Canada
SOLO WORLD ASSOCIATION,
c/o D. Butler, 15 Cherrywood Court, Cambridge Rd., Teddington, Middlesex, England
SOUTH COAST FIBERGLASS PRODUCTS,
116A Rincon St., San Clemente, CA 92672, U.S.A.
SOUTH COAST SEACRAFT INC.,
P.O. Box 1674, Shreveport, LA 71165, U.S.A.
SOUTH DEVON BOATBUILDERS LTD.,
2 Iddlesleigh Terrace, Dawlish, Devon, England
SOUTH HANTS MARINE,
Winchester Rd., Chandlers Ford, Eastleigh, Hampshire, England
SOUTHERN BOATBUILDING CO.,
Willments Shipyard, Hazel Rd., Woolston, Southampton, SO2 7GB, England
SOUTHERN OCEAN SHIPYARD LTD.,
New Quay Rd., Poole, BH5 4AB, Dorset, England
SOUTHERN OCEAN SHIPYARD LTD.,
The Quay, Poole, Dorset, England
SOVEREL MARINE INC.,
2225 Idlewild Rd., N. Palm Beach, FL 33403, U.S.A.
SPAIR MARINE,
24 rue du Rocher, Paris 8, France
SPARKES MARINE,
Cranleigh, Lancing, Sussex, England
F.E. SPARKES MARINE LTD.,
The Shipyard, Littlehampton, Sussex, England
SPARKLER ASSOCIATION,
c/o E. Sieple, 1501 Carlos Ave., Clearwater, FL 33515, U.S.A.
SPAULDING 33 ASSOCIATION,
c/o I. Davies, 623 Myra Way, San Francisco, California, U.S.A.
S.P. MARINE,
12 Woodvale, Fareham, Hampshire, England
SPORT SKIFF INC.,
Cedar Hill Ave., Nyack, NY 10960, U.S.A.
SPROG ASSOCIATION,
11 Babbacombe Rd., Babbacombe, Torquay, Devon, England
SQUALL ASSOCIATION,
33 Martha's Lane, Chestnut Lane, MA, U.S.A.
SS ASSOCIATION,
c/o Mrs. Horton, Quoque St., Quoque, NY 11959, U.S.A.
STAMM BOAT CO.,
1264 Milwaukee St., Delafield, WI 53018, U.S.A.
STANGATE MARINE LTD.,
Wilhams Boatyard, Ropewalk, Littlehampton, Sussex, England
STANLEY PLASTICS,
P.O. Box 615, Willitis, CA 95490, U.S.A.
STARLIGHT MARINE LTD.,
Frankwell Quay, Welsh Bridge, Shrewsbury, England
STAR NATIONAL ASSOCIATION,
ISCYRA, 51 E 42nd St.; New York, NY 10017, U.S.A.
GEORGE STEAD YACHTS,
The Quay, Poole, Dorset, England
DONALD C. STEWART,
86 7th Ave., Huntingdon Sta., NY 11746, U.S.A.
JACHTBOUW STEYN bv,
Hoge Rijndijk 211, Zoeterwoude, Holland

G.V. STILLMAN, YACHT AGENCY,
The Quay, Hamble, Southampton, Hampshire, England
STINGRAY ASSOCIATION,
c/o F. Merchant, P.O. Box 3, Amsterdam, NY 12010, U.S.A.
J. STONE & SON.,
East Portlemouth, Salcombe, Devon, England
STONE MARINE STORE,
Southminster, Stone, Essex, England
CHARLES STREET,
125 Governors Drive, East Greenwich, RI 02818, U.S.A.
SUNFLOWER ASSOCIATION,
c/o A. Greene, 140 Williamson Ave., East Rockaway, NY 11518, U.S.A.
SUNSPORT ASSOCIATION,
c/o K. Loimand, 743 Kennedy Rd., Scarborough, Ontario, Canada
SUPER PORPOISE ASSOCIATION,
c/o E. Matteson, 10930 South Westnedge, Kalamazoo, MI 49081, U.S.A.
SURPRISE ASSOCIATION,
Box 307, Gloucester, VA 23061, U.S.A.
DUNCAN SUTPHEN INC.,
P.O. Box 83, Old Lyme, Conn. 06371, U.S.A.
SWALE LTD.,
43 High St., Bluetown, Sheerness, Kent, England
SWANICK YACHT AGENCY LTD.,
Cabin Boatyard, Burisedon, Huntingdonshire, England
SWEDISH YACHT EXPORT AB.,
Akaregatan 35, 603 60 Norrkoping, Sweden
SWEDISH YACHT EXPORT AB,
Postbox 186, S-59301,Vastervik, Sweden
SWEET 16 ASSOCIATION,
c/o Mrs. Kupersmith, 3800 Rogers Circle, Independence, MO 64050, U.S.A.
SYMONS SAILING INC.,
P.O.Box 415, 255 So. Ketcham Ave., Amityville, NY 11701, U.S.A.
TABUR MARINE LTD.,
66 Tilehurst Rd., Reading, Berkshire, England
TAHOE ASSOCIATION,
c/o R. Wing, 8428 Amigo Ave., Northridge, CA 91324, U.S.A.
TANZER INDUSTRIES,
P.O. Box 105, Rt. 2, Dorion (Montreal), Quebec, Canada
TARTAN MARINE CO.,
Box 27, 320 River St., Grand River, OH 44045, U.S.A,
J.J. TAYLOR & SONS,
2 Stadium Rd., Toronto 138, Ontario, Canada
TEDRUTH PLASTICS CORP.,
P.O. Box 607, Farningdale, NJ 07727, U.S.A.
ALLAN TEITGE BOAT BUILDERS,
4720 Cheyenne, Tacoma, WA 98407, U.S.A.
TEMPEST NATIONAL ASSOCIATION,
c/o W. Cox Jnr., 90 Nearwater Lane, Darben, CT 06820, U.S.A.
THAMES MARINE LTD.,
Churfleet, Canvey Island, Essex, England
THISTLE ASSOCIATION,
c/o Mrs. Abramson, 1303 Ridgewood Drive, Highland Park, IL 60035, U.S.A.
THUNDERBIRD PRODUCTS CORP.,
14100 Biscayne Blvd, North, Miami, FL 33100, U.S.A.
THUNDERCAT ASSOCIATION,
c/o D. Johnson, 12725 Forrest St., Tampa, Florida, U.S.A.
TIDEWATER BOATS INC.,
Annapolis Sailing Centre, Box 1669, Annapolis, MD 21404, U.S.A.

TIGER CAT ASSOCIATION,
c/o A. Gronkowski, P.O. Box 135, Rascommon, MI 48653, U.S.A.
TIGER CUB ASSOCIATION,
P.O. Box 1951, Auckland 1, New Zealand
TILLOTSON-PEARSON INC.,
P.O. Box 368, Warren, RI 02885, U.S.A.
TODD ENTERPRISES,
22 Pheasant Drive, Asherville, NC 28803, U.S.A.
TOWN CLASS ASSOCIATION,
c/o R. Forrest, Nahant, Massachussetts, U.S.A.
TRADEWIND YACHTS,
133 Fleet End Rd., Warsash, Southampton, Hampshire, England
TRADITION YACHTS,
66 Broad St., Stamford, CT 06901, U.S.A.
TRANSCAT MARINE,
Avon Works, Christchurch, Hampshire, England
TRANSPACIFIC MARINE CO.,
P.O. Box 26-65 Taipei, Taiwan
TREWES INTERNATIONAL bv,
S M vd Meer, Heiloo, Holland
TRIAD ASSOCIATION,
c/o J. Dobler, 801 South St., Manhattan Beach, CA 90266, U.S.A.
TRIUMPH 24 ASSOCIATION,
c/o L. Johnson, 1870B McFarland Ave., Saratoga, CA 95070, U.S.A.
TROWBRIDGE & SONS,
Durngate, Winchester, Hampshire, England
A.D. TRUMAN,
Old Maltings Boatyard, Oulton Broad, Lowestoft, Suffolk, England
ROBERT TUCKER DESIGNS,
58 Southbury Rd., Enfield, EN1 1YB, England
TURBORNET,
9 Chiltern St., London W1, England
TURUN VENEVEISTAMO,
20819 Turku 81, Finland
12-METER INTERNATIONAL ASSOCIATION,
I.Y.R.U., 5 Buckingham Gate, London SW1, England
22 SQUARE METER NATIONAL ASSOCIATION,
c/o Don Glasell, 331 Kedzie Evanston, IL 60202, U.S.A.
TYLER BOAT CO.,
13-14 Sovereign Way, Tonbridge, Kent, England
TYLERCRAFT INC.,
1439 Montauk Highway, Oakdale, NY 11769, U.S.A.
UDELL NATIONAL ASSOCIATION,
c/o Don Glasell, 331 Kadzie Evanston, IL 60202, U.S.A.
UIF LANDTBLOM YACHTAGENTUR,
Durnasvikens Marina, Saltsjobadsv Strandpromenaden, Fack 130 11,
Saltsico-Durnas, Sweden
UNIPLAISANCE COSTANTINI,
56470 La Trinite-sur-Mer, France
J.W. and A. UPHAM,
Brixham, Devon, England
U.S. ALBERCORE ASSOCIATION,
1319 28th St. NW, Washington DC 20007, U.S.A.
U.S. INTERNATIONAL 14 ASSOCIATION,
67 East St., Annapolis, MD 21401, U.S.A.
U.S. MARINER ASSOCIATION,
1548 Holiday Park Drive, Wantagh, NY 11793, U.S.A.

U.S. MIRROR ASSOCIATION,
15645 Normandy Ave., Cleveland, OH 44111, U.S.A.
U.S. MONOTYPE ASSOCIATION,
c/o H. Snyder, 6050 Haines Rd., St. Petersburg, Florida, U.S.A.
U.S. ONE DESIGN NATIONAL ASSOCIATION,
c/o J.B. Read Jnr., 4 Jefferson St., Marblehead, Massachussetts, U.S.A.
U.S. SOLING ASSOCIATION,
P.O. Box 185, Hartland, WI 53029, U.S.A.
E.G. van de STADT,
Scheepswerf NV, P.O. Box 113, Zaandam, Holland
VANDERSTADT & McGRUER,
Box 7, Owen Sound, Ontario, Canada
VARNE MARINE LTD.,
Charfleet Rd., Canvey Island, Essex, England
VELAMOTORE,
Piazza Maria Teresa 3, 10123-Torina, Italy
bv JACHTWERF VICTORIA,
Madame Curiestraat 3, Alkmaar/Oudorp, Holland
VICTORY NATIONAL ASSOCIATION,
c/o B. Klawuhm, 20800 Homestead Rd., 5B Cupertino, California, U.S.A.
VIKING OF AMERICA,
56 Chaucer St., Hartsdale, NY 10530, U.S.A.
VIKING 140 ASSOCIATION,
c/o L. Kivi, 4136 Ely Ave., Bronx, NY 10466, U.S.A.
VIKING 170 ASSOCIATION,
c/o C. King, 1222 Kensington Grosse Point, MI 48230, U.S.A.
VIKSUND BÅT,
A/s 5302, Strusshamm, Norway,
VIKSUND BOATS,
Low Risby, Roxby, Nr. Scunthorpe, Lincolnshire, England
VINEYARD NATIONAL ASSOCIATION,
c/o Lizette Mills, Smith College, Northampton, MA 01060, U.S.A.
VIPER ASSOCIATION,
c/o C. Greenham, 2215 Garden St. Panca City, OK 74601, U.S.A.
VITA DINGHY ASSOCIATION,
c/o J. Dobter, 801 8th St., Manhattan Beach, CA 90266, U.S.A.
JACHTWERF VOLENDAM,
Zeedijk 2, Volendam, Holland
WACANDA MARINE INC.,
Box 122, Colville, Washington 99114, U.S.A.
WALLABY ASSOCIATION,
c/o M. Anderson, P.O. Box 1232, 1232 Thousand Oaks, CA 91360, U.S.A.
CHARLES WARD (YACHT BUILDERS) LTD.,
Fakenham, Norfolk, England
WATERBUG ASSOCIATION,
c/o Mrs. Yost, 1002 Danworth Court, Kirkwood, MO 63122, U.S.A.
CHANTIER HENRI WAUQUIEZ,
179 Rue Vauban, 59420 Monvaux, France
WAYFARER ASSOCIATION,
c/o F. Berry, Alderfen, Neatishead, Norwich, Norfolk, NOR 372, England
WAYFARER ASSOCIATION,
c/o 14540 Berwick, Livonia, MI 48154, U.S.A.
WAYFARER YACHT CORP.,
1682 Placentia Ave., Costa Mesa, CA 92627, U.S.A.
WEATHERLY YACHTS LTD.,
46 Cloughey Rd., Portaferry, Co. Down, N. Ireland
DAN WEBB AND FESSEY,
Shipways, Maldon, Essex, England

PETER WEBSTER LTD.,
Ropewalk Boatyard, Lymington, Huntingdonshire, England
WELLS YACHTS,
50 Gregory St., Marblehead, Massachussetts, U.S.A.
WEST STOCKWITH YACHT SERVICE STATION,
Yacht Basin, West Stockwith, Doncaster, Yorkshire, England
WESTERLY MARINE CONSTRUCTION,
Aysgarth Rd., Waterlooville, Portsmouth PO7 7UF, Hampshire, England
WESTERLY MARINE CONSTRUCTION U.S.A.,
c/o Andrew Gemeny & Son, 5809 Annapolis Rd., Hyattsville, MD 20784, U.S.A.
WESTERN SAILCRAFT,
411 Mulvey Ave., Winnipeg 13, Manitoba, Canada
WESTFIELD ENGINEERING CO.,
Cabot Lane, Creekmoor, Poole, Dorset, England
WESTFIELD ENGINEERING CO. LTD.,
21 Carr Lane, Industrial Estate, Hoy Lakes, Cheshire, England
WESTON MARINE CENTRE,
Foulridge, Lancashire, England
WESTSAIL CORP.,
1626 Placentia Ave., Costa Mesa, CA 92627, U.S.A.
WESTWIND NATIONAL ASSOCIATION,
c/o 2218 Ramsey Rd., Monroeville, PA 15146, U.S.A.
JACHTWERF ANNE WEVER bv,
Ertveldweg 3, Orthen's Hertogenbosch, Holland
WHISTLER ASSOCIATION,
c/o T. Schroth, 15904 Longmeadow Drive, Dearborn, MI 48120, U.S.A.
WHITBY BOAT WORKS LTD.,
570 Finley Ave., Ajax, Ontario, Canada
WIANNO SENIOR KNOCKABOUT ASSOCIATION,
Stanley's Place, Hyannis, MA 02601, U.S.A.
WILDFIRE NATIONAL ASSOCIATION,
c/o Gemico Corporation, 63 Atlantic Ave., Boston, MA 02110, U.S.A.
WILGATE,
190 Coulsdon Rd., Caterham, Surrey, England
WINARD SABOT ASSOCIATION,
c/o P. Rettig, 23261 Erwin St., Woodland Hills, CA 91364, U.S.A.
WINDBOATS LTD.,
Wroxham, Norfolk, England
WINDERMERE AQUATIC LTD.,
Bowness Bay, Windermere, England
WINDJAMMER ASSOCIATION,
c/o F. Staggs, 465 Dumont Circus, Hampton, Virginia, U.S.A.
WINDMAILL ASSOCIATION,
c/o Mrs. Holler, 5399 York Lane South, Columbus, OH 43227, U.S.A.
WINDSURFER ASSOCIATION,
317 Beirut Ave., Pacific Palisades, CA 90272, U.S.A.
WINEGLASS ASSOCIATION,
c/o Mr. & Mrs. Whiting, Syam Nevak, Fawkham Rd., West Kingsdown, Sevenoaks,
Kent, TN15 6JS, England
WINEGLASS ASSOCIATION,
c/o R. Shaffer, 4550 Justine Utica, MI 48087, U.S.A.
WOOD PUSSY ASSOCIATION,
c/o D. Colyer, 52 Gillespie Ave., Fair Haven, New Jersey, U.S.A.
PAUL WRIGHT,
Buckenham Ferry Boatyard, Langley, Norwich, Norfolk, NOR 17W, England
WYCHE & COPPOCK,
Radford Mills, Norton St., Nottingham, NG7 3HP, England

X21 NATIONAL ASSOCIATION,
Box 381, Bedford, NY 10506, U.S.A.
YACHT CONSTRUCTORS INC.,
7030 NE 42nd Ave., Portland, OR 97218, U.S.A.
YANKEE YACHTS INC.,
2724 So. Grand Ave., Santa Ana, CA 92705, U.S.A.
YELLOW WHEELS (A.J. PADOLSKI & SON),
158 Ipswich Rd., Harford Bridges, Norwich, NOR 66D, England
Y-FLYER ASSOCIATION,
c/o G. Callahan, 900 Charles St., Trenton, OH 45067, U.S.A.
JACHTWERF ZAADNOORDIJK bv,
Leeuwarderstraativeg 121, Heerenveen, Holland
CARL ZEIGLER,
22 Quebec Street, London W1H 7DE, England
ZIP SLOOPS,
1580 NE 125th St., North Miami, FL 33161, U.S.A.
ZYGAL BOATS,
St. Peters St., Whitstable, Kent, England

INDEX OF BOAT NAMES

C

Cal 36	1185	Cascade 36	1163
Cal 39	1052	Cascade 42	1172
Cal 40	1168	Castle 48	1116
Cal 43	1186	Catalac 29	909
Cal 2–46	1104	Catalina 22	609
Cal 48	1177	Catalina 27	791, 792
Cal Cat	420	Catalina 27 ½ ton	791
Cal Cruising 46	1175	Catfish	1143
Calife	663	Cay	694
Callisto	1127	Cayat	422
Calypso	796	C & C 25	734
Campaigner	914	C & C 27	815
Canadian Sabot	148	C & C 30 ¾ ton	936
Cape	1157	C & C Corvette 31	1184
Cape 25	725	C & C 35	1159
Cape 30	914	C & C 39	1167
Cape 32	1152	C & C 40	1185
Cape Carib 33	992	C & C Redline 41 Mk II	1186
Cape Clipper 46	1105	C & C Custom 43	1174
Cape Cod Bluechip	886	C & C Custom 48	1177
Cape Cod Cat	505	C & C Custom 50	1178
Cape Cod Knockabout	148	C & C Custom 61	1180
Cape Cod Mercer	1174	'C' Class	112
Cape Cod Mercury	151	Celebrity	159
Cape Dory 10	153	Centaur, Westerly	769
Cape Dory 14	154	Centurion	982
Cape Dory 25	726	Challenge	32
Capelan	489	Challenger dinghy	152
Cape North 43	1095	Challenger cruiser	1182
Cape Porpoise 46	1176	Challenger 15	161
Cape Race	1176	Challenger 32	1154
Capitan 26	772	Challenger 35	1013
Capri 26/ Capri 30	774	Challenger 40	1168
Caprice	152	Challenger 42 ms	1173
Caprice Mk III	547	Challenger 48	1178
Capri Cyclone	155	Challenger 50	1179
Cap Vert	1183	Chance 24	1182
Caravel cruiser	723	Chance P29/25 ½ ton	859
Caravelle dinghy	156	Chance 30 – 30 ¾ ton	888
Caravelle 42	1186	Chance P32/28	986
Carbineer 46	1176	Chance 29 1 ton	1155
Carbineer	1174	Chance 37	1164
Cardinal	157	Chance 33 2 ton	1167
Carena 30 Ghoster	974	Chance 36	1089
Carinita	578	Chance 42/36	1173
Caribbean 35	1160	Chance 40	1176
Carter 30 ½ ton	882	Channel Rover	774
Carter 33	1154	Chappiquidick	738
Carter One Ton	1038	Char	158
Carter 39	1054	Charioteer	158
Carter 42	1090	Cheetah Cat	426
Cascade	868	Cherokee 32	1184

Cherokee 35	1068	Columbine	1161
Cherub	33	Colvic Craft 31	956
Chesapeake Bay Log Canoe	163	Colvic 23	649
Chesford 18 ms	527	Commanche 42	1172
Chesford 42	1172	Comet dinghy USA	170
Cheshire	427	Comet France	916
Chic	160	Commander	1182
Chickadee	160	Commander 31	949
Cheftain, Westerly	770	Commando	826
Chipmunk	165	Compass 31	964
Chorister	162	Competition 30	917
Chub	167	Competition 34	1185
Cinder	610	Compromis 720	1148
Cirrus, Westerly	626	Concordia 31	957
CL 11	162	Concordia Sloop Boat	168
CL 16	164	Concordia Yawl	1185
C Lark	169	Concordia 41	1186
Classic	548	Condor	113
Claymore 30	915	Conquest	557
Clipper dinghy England	32	Constellation 30	1184
Clipper dinghy USA	164	Contender	34
Clipper Mk 21	593	Contessa	711
Clipper 23	682	Contessa 26	746
Clipper Mk 26	752	Contessa 32	1152
Clipper 33	1155	Contessa 36	1028
Clipper 36	1161	Contest 25	716
Clipper 42	1173	Contest 27	818
Coast 13	166	Contest 29	1184
Cob	166	Contest 31	968
Cognac	704	Contest 31 HT	966
Colitalia 56	1125	Contest 33	1155
Columbi 27 ms	781	Contest 36	1026
Columbia 21	1143	Contest 38	1047
Columbia 22	168, 1147	Contest 40	1169
Columbia 23	653	Copperhead	171
Columbia 26 Mk II	748	Cornish Sea King	170
Columbia 28	1183	Coronado 15	173
Columbia 29	1183	Coronado 23	1182
Columbia 30 ¾ ton	890	Coronado 25	1182
Columbia 31	1184	Coronado 27	785
Columbia 5·5	1184	Coronado 28	838
Columbia 34 Mk II	1003	Coronado 30	891
Columbia 36	1034	Coronado 32 Mk II	980
Columbia 39	1167	Coronado 34	1185
Columbia 40	1185	Coronado 35	1161
Columbia 41 ms	1076	Coronado 41	1170
Columbia 43 Mk III	1174	Coronado 45	1175
Columbia 45	1175	Corribee 21 Mk II	597
Columbia 50	1186	Corsaire	536
Columbia 52	1120	Corvette 31, C & C	1184
Columbia 56 ms	1180	Costantini 30	942
Columbia 57	1186	Cottontail	172

Morgan 22	1147	Neptune cruiser	1153
Morgan 24	728	Neptunian Motor Sailor	1156
Morgan 25	1149	Newell Cadet	1183
Morgan 27	824	Newport 16	488
Morgan 28	1183	Newport 20	580
Morgan Out Island 28	846	Newport 21	1144
Morgan 30	894	Newport 21 − 2	600
Morgan 30/2	894	Newport 27 S ½ ton	802
Morgan 33	1184	Newport 28	842
Morgan Out Island 33	997	Newport 30 PH II	927
Morgan Custom 34	1185	Newport 41 − S	1171
Morgan 35	1159	Newporter	1169
Morgan 36 One Ton	1024	Niagra 30	1184
Morgan Out Island 36	1025	Nicholson 26	787
Morgan 38	1185	Nicholson 30	870
Morgan 40	1169	Nicholson 32 Mk X	984
Morgan Custom 41	1171	Nicholson 35	1020
Morgan Out Island 41	1085	Nicholson 36	1163
Morgan 42 Mk II	1172	Nicholson 38	1166
Morgan 45	1186	Nicholson 42	1088
Morgan Out Island 50	1186	Nicholson 43	1174
Morgan Custom 54	1122	Nicholson 45	1098
Mosquito trimaran	447	Nicholson 48	1112
Moth	75	Nicholson 55	1123
Mouette	286	Nimble	1063
MS 20	556	Nimrod, Westerly	524
Musard	284	Nipper England	294
Muscadet	599	Nipper USA	292
Musketeer	436	Nord 12	1144
Mustang	1182	Nordex Bat	292
Mutineer	287	Nordex Hawk	1144
Mystere	755	Nordfarer 33	1156
		Nordia 35	1160
N		Nor'Easter	1176
N - 30 Phase III	927	Norlin 34	1002
Nab 35	1159	Norlin 37	1035
Nadir	284	Norlin 41	1077
Naiad	289	Normandy	832
Nantucket 33	1184	33 Norseman	1157
Nantucket Clipper	977	North American 32	1153
Nantucket 40	1169	North Coast 30	1183
Naples Sabot	291	North East 38	1166
Narrasketuck	288	Northern ¼ ton	692
Nassau Dinghy	288	Northern 25	730
National Eighteen	76	Northern 29	872
National One Design	290	North Sea 24	960
National Twelve	72	North Star	700
Nautical 33	1156	North Star 22	634
Nauticat 33	1157	North Star 25	739
Navaho	1176	North Star 29	1184
Nelson 37	1043	North Star 500	732
Neptune dinghy	290	North Star 1000	895

Pearson 43	1186	Privateer UK	879
Pegasus	80	Privateer Canada	1107
Pelagian 33	1156	Privateer 57/52	1180
Pelican	304	Privateer 70/64	1180
Penguin	302	Privateer 77/70	1181
Pentland, Westerly	965	Project 2	550
Peregrine	305	Proton	516
Peter Duck	858	PT ¼	632
Petrel SB — 12	306	PT Mk II ¾ ton	929
P & H 38	1166	PT 40	1169
Phantom	83	PT 32 ¾ ton	976
Phantom 30	948	Puffer	315
Phialle	572	Puffin	316
Philip 43	1092	Puma 26	779
Philipa 27	804	Pursan	316
Phoenix	448		

Q

Piaf	307
Pi 25	904	Quick Cat	446

R

Picnic 17	515		
Piet Hein	1165		
Pike	294	R6	809
Pilot 6 ton	714	R30	920
Pilot 9 ton	928	R — 38	1166
Pintail dinghy	308	Radiant	1113
Pintail cruiser	816	Raider	1159
Pion ½ ton	896	Rainbow	1144
Pioneer dinghy England	1144	Rana Versatile	317
Pioneer dinghy USA	1144	Ranger	574
Pionier 10 metre	1153	Ranger	1150
Piper	309	Ranger II	319
Piper OD C Type	309	Ranger 12	321
Piranha 9	310	Ranger 14	318
Piranha 13	311	Ranger 16	323
Pirahna	502	Ranger 23	671
Pirate	313	Ranger 26	780
Pirate Fish	302	Ranger 27 cat	908
Pirate Fish Jnr.	302	Ranger 29	861
Pisces	82	Ranger 31 cat	1151
Playmate	312	Ranger 33	999
Plus	207	Ranger 36	1162
Polynesian Concept	1070	Ranger 1 ton	1041
Poole AB	312	Ranger canoe	318
Poole Sprat	1144	Rascal	320
Porpoise	314	Rasmus 35	1160
Pram	314	Raven	320
Prelude	558	Rawson 25	322
Prettycraft 9	1144	Rawson 26	1183
Prim'vent	587	Rawson 30	948
Princess 36	1162	R — Boat	322
Prindle 16	444	Rebcats Cougar Mk III	325
Prior 30	1151	Rebel USA	324
Privateer	561		

Sea — Cat	600	Seychelle	1178
Seacracker 8 ton	1154	Shako	874
Sea Devil	347	Shannon Cat	1149
Sea Dancer	1121	Shark multi	116
Sea Dog dinghy	346	Shark dinghy	116
Sea Dog cruiser	930	Shark cruiser	698
Seadrift	577	Shark V	1145
Seafarer Dinghy	348	Sharky	497
Seafarer	538	12 Sq M Sharpie	84
Seafarer 23	1183	She S 31 B	943
Seafarer 24K	1182	She 9 — 5 traveller	972
Seafarer Sail 'n Trail	701	She C32	987
Seafarer 26	1183	She D30	931
Seafarer 29	862	She D 35	1158
Seafarer 29K	862	She Joemarine	506
Seafarer 31 Mk I	967	Shearwater	632
Seafarer 31 Mk II	967	Shearwater Cat	117
Seafarer 34	1158	Shelduck	1145
Seafarer 38C	1046	Sheriff	575
Seafire	349	She S27 ¼ ton	764
Seafly	58	She Scandinavian	942
Seagull	351	Shetlander	1145
Sea Gull USA	350	Shetland Skiff	356
Seagull USA	350	Shields	356
Seagull	546	Shipmate Mk II	499
Sea Hawk	504	Shipmate Senior	499
Seahawk Range	786	Shooting Star	86
Seal dinghy	1145	Shrimp	358
Seal cruiser	621	Siani	1148
Sea Lark	352	Sidewinder	346
Seamaster Sailer 19	553	Sigma 38	1166
Seamaster Sailer 23	673	Signet	87
Seamew	638	Signet 20	566
Sea Moth II	450	Silex	1145
Sea Puppy	1145	Silhouette III	517
Searider 25	733	Silver Streak	84
Sea Scooter	352	Singoalla	1158
Sea Shanty	486	Siren	512
Sea Shanty 18	522	6 Metre	'358
Sea Skater Cat	451	Sizzler	118
Sea Snark	353	Skate	359
Sea Spray 15	453	Skeeter Cat	446
Sea Spray 18	454	Skipjack	361
Sea Sprite	1145	Skipper 12	360
Sea Swinger	354	Skipper 14	360
Seawind 30	950	Skipper 17/Mariner Mate	510
Selecta	940	Ski Sail	470
Seraph	830	Skunk	363
Serendipidty	848	Skylark	362
Sesame	355	SL — 140	365
Seven/Eleven	357	Slipper	362
Seven Seas ms	1164	Snapdragon	674

Snapdragon 21	601	Sprog	366
Snapdragon 26	767	Squall	366
Snapdragon 27	806	Squib	91
Snapdragon 600	564	S.S.	1145
Snapdragon 670	639	S & S 34	1157
Snapdragon 747	715	Standfast 36	1161
Snapdragon 890	870	Standfast 40	1074
Snapdragon 1100	1162	Star	92
Snipe	88	Starfish	371
Snowbird	364	Starflite	368
Snowgoose cat	1067	Stella	1149
Solaris 42	1137	Stingray	368
Sol Cat	119	Stone Horse	681
Solexxon 39 cat	1168	Stowaway 8	370
Soling	89	Stowaway 10	370
Solo	88	Strale	90
Sonata	1151	Strider 35	1160
Sortilege	1171	Sturgeon	642
South Coast 22	640	Sunbeam	372
South Coast One Design	757	Sun Cat	452
Southerly 28	825	Suncoast range	1170
Sovereign	1152	Sundance	565
Sovereign 32	1153	Sunfish	373
Sovereign 35	1160	Sunflower	374
Soverel 28	1183	Sunray 21	591
Soverel 30 Mk III	932	Sunspot	375
Soverel 37	1042	Sunspot 15 Mk II	493
Soverel 38	1185	Sunstar 5/57	540
Soverel 41	1086	Sunstar 18	540
Soverel 45	1175	Super Buc	904
Soverel 48	1177	Super Porpoise	376
Spanker 12.8	1093	Super Satellite	372
Sparkler	367	Super Scamper	377
Sparrow	479	Super Sovereign ketch	1017
Sparta	641	Super Swift	1145
Spartan	1148	Super Tiki	93
Spaulding 33	1157	Surfsailer	1145
Spey 35	1160	Surprise	379
Spey 40	1169	Sussex Cob	381
Spindrift	369	Swallow	94
Spindrift 37	1165	Swan 36	1162
Spindrift 40	1169	Swan 37	1037
Spindrift 45	1139	Swan 38	1166
Spindrift 51	1141	Swan 40	1057
Spinner Mk III	1149	Swan 41	1083
Spirit 24	709	Swan 43	1173
Spirit 28	846	Swan 44	1175
Splinter	603	Swan 48	1177
Sportyak I	364	Swan 55	1180
Sportyak II	364	Swan 65	1180
Sportyak III	364	Sweet 16	383
Sprite	1145	Swift	1145

Swift cat	120	Thistle	389
Swordfish	90	Tholense Schow	852
Symons 31	1185	Thrial	1145
Symons 33	1184	Thunderbird	390
Symons 36	1162	Thunderbird Pram	1145
Symons 42	1172	Thundercat	384
Symons 49	1178	Tiburon	521
System 30	936	Tiger Cub	452
		Tiger Cat	1145

T

		Tiger Westerly	736
T — 24	702	TMS Motor Sailer	572
T — 26	766	Toby Jug	617
T — 29	876	Tod 15	384
Tabasco	519	Tomahawk 25	743
Tabur Yak 2	378	Tom Boy	386
Tabur Yak 3	378	Tom Thumb	1145
Tahoe 10	1145	Topaz Mk II	523
Tailwind Hurley	1048	Topper	471
Talisman	532	Top Hat	737
Tango	95	Torch	1145
Tankard 19	550	Tornado catamaran	121
Tankard 23/710 Mk III	680	Tornado 31	1152
Tanzer 14	378	Town Class	386
Tanzer Overnighter	500	Toy	99
Tanzer 16	385	Trailer Sailer 14	484
Tanzer 22	652	Trailer Sailer 16	500
Tanzer 28 ½ ton	827	Trapper	850
Tarantelle 27	790	Treemter	1128
Tarpon	482	Trews Clipper range	1172
Tartan 26 ½ ton	768	Trewes Privateer range	1087
Tartan 27	1183	Triad	455
Tartan 30	932	Trident 24	703
Tartan 34	1158	Trifoil	457
Tartan 37	1164	Triform	1151
Tartan 41	1079	Trikini 13	459
Tartan 48	1177	Trikini 17	456
Tasman catamaran	1163	Trikini 'D'	456
Tavana 33	1156	Trimar 42	1138
Tavoy	1156	Trintel	830
TC 8	380	Trintella 35	1160
Tech II	387	Trintella I	866
Telstar trimaran	905	Trintella IIa	1154
Tempest	97	Trintella III	1021
Tempest USA cruiser	1182	Trintella IV	1075
Ten six	380	Trintella V	1115
Ten Sq. M. Canoe	96	Triton	1183
Tepco 12	1145	Triskel	875
Tequila Sport	688	Triumph 9'0	461
Tern USA	382	Triumph 24'0	458
Tern UK	480	Trotter	613
Tern	969	Tucker 23	1148
Thanet 14	382	Turnabout	391

Westerly Pentland	965	Wod	410
Westerly Renown	1154	Wood Pussey	413
Westerly Tiger	736	Wootton O.D.	1146
Westerly Warwick	1147	Wulfrun 9	1146
Westerly Windrush	1149	Wulfrun Cub	1146
Westsail 32	985		
Westsail 42	1173	**X**	
Westwalkcruiser	881		
West Wight C Type	487	X Boat	415
West Wight Potter	485	XL 2	1172
Westwind dinghy	402	X OD	103
Westwind cruiser	696	X 21	410
Weymouth Falcon	400		
Whistler	404	**Y**	
Whitby 39	1167		
Whitby 42	1091	Yankee 26 ¼ ton	771
White Lady 51	1119	Yankee 28 ½ ton	833
White Queen	1160	Yankee 30 Mk II	896
White Squaw	724	Yankee 30 Mk III	938
Wianno Senior Knockabout	404	Yankee 38 1 ton	1049
Wibo 930	933	Yankee Clipper	1170
Widgeon	405	Yankee Dolphin	1182
Wight Class	1152	Yankee Seahorse	1182
Wight II	1152	Y Boat	412
Wildfire	104	Yellow Wheel	412
Wildflower	406	Yeoman	414
Winard Sabot	402	Y Flyer	416
Windflite 14	407	Yngling 20'11	105
Windjammer	409	YW 7'9 Utility Pram	414
Windmill	411	YW Catamaran	460
Windsurfer	472	**Z**	
Wineglass	103		
Wing 25	730	Zef	106
Wing 30	950	Zenith	100
With Vito	406	Zephyr	417
With Vitress	408	Zip	418
With Vitting	408	Zulu	934